D1455047

CARL A. RUDISILL LIBRARY
LENOIR-RHYNE COLLEGE

THE OUTLINE OF HISTORY

BEING A PLAIN HISTORY OF
LIFE AND MANKIND BY

H. G. WELLS

REVISED AND BROUGHT UP TO THE END
OF THE SECOND WORLD WAR BY

RAYMOND POSTGATE

With Maps and Plans by

J. F. HORRABIN

VOLUME I

GARDEN CITY BOOKS
Garden City, New York

MANUFACTURED IN THE U. S. A.

SCHEME OF CONTENTS

VOLUME ONE

BOOK I

THE WORLD BEFORE MAN

BOOK III

THE FIRST CIVILIZATIONS

SCHEME OF THE OUTLINE

SCHEME OF THE OUTLINE

BOOK V

RISE AND COLLAPSE OF THE ROMAN EMPIRE

SCHEME OF THE OUTLINE

BOOK VI

CHRISTIANITY AND ISLAM

VOLUME TWO

BOOK VII

THE MONGOL EMPIRES OF THE LAND WAYS AND THE NEW EMPIRES OF THE SEA WAYS

PAGE

BOOK VIII

THE AGE OF THE GREAT POWERS

LIST OF MAPS AND ILLUSTRATIONS

LIST OF MAPS AND ILLUSTRATIONS

LIST OF MAPS AND ILLUSTRATIONS

LIST OF MAPS AND ILLUSTRATIONS

LIST OF MAPS AND ILLUSTRATIONS

THE OUTLINE OF HISTORY

THE STORY AND AIM OF THE OUTLINE OF HISTORY

§ 1. *How It Came to Be Written.* § 2. *The Method of Writing the* Outline. § 3. *Of Certain Omissions and Additions.* § 4. *Of Two Other Outlines that have arisen out of the Outline of History to Complete General Exposition of the Contemporary World.*

§ 1

THE *Outline of History* was first written in 1918–1919. It was published in illustrated parts, and it was carefully revised and printed again as a book in 1920. It was again revised very severely and rearranged for a reprint in 1923 (January); it was reissued in a revised and much more amply illustrated edition in 1925, and again in 1930 came a quite fresh edition, recast, rewritten in many places, and with much added new matter. This edition was further revised in 1939, and preparations were made during the first years of the second world war for yet another revision.

There were many reasons to move a writer to attempt a World History in 1918. It was the last, the weariest, most disillusioned year of the Great War. Everywhere there were unwonted privations; everywhere there was mourning. The tale of the dead and mutilated had mounted to many millions. Men felt they had come to a crisis in the world's affairs. They were too weary and heart-sick to consider complicated possibilities. They were not sure whether they were facing a disaster to civilization or the inauguration of a new phase of human association; they saw things with the simplicity of such flat alternatives, and they clung to hope. There was a copious discussion of possible new arrangements of world politics; of world treaties for the abolition of war, of leagues of nations, leagues of peoples. Everyone was "thinking internationally," or at least trying to do so. But there was a widespread realization that everywhere the essentials of the huge problems that had been thrust so suddenly and tragically upon the democracies of the world were insufficiently understood. "How had these things come about?" they asked, trying to probe behind the disputes about Sarajevo and the Belgian "scrap of paper" to the broader, remoter causes of things. What were the beginnings of this tragic feud across the Rhine? Why had it come to affect the whole world? Why was Japan, which half a century ago had been a romantic, picturesque country, a legend of flimsy art, a comic-opera land as remote almost as another planet, now patrolling the Mediterranean with great battleships? Why had the Tsardom vanished like a dream? What in truth was Turkey? Why was Constantinople so important in the world? What was an Empire? How had Empires begun? What had converted Germany from a diversity of little states into one aggressive will and power, and put the fear of German energy into half mankind?

Men and women tried to recall the narrow history teaching of their brief schooldays and found an uninspiring and partially forgotten list of national kings or presidents. They tried to read about these matters, and found an endless wilderness of books. They had been taught history, they found, in nationalist blinkers, ignoring every country but their own, and now they were turned out into a blaze. It was extraordinarily difficult for them to determine the relative values of the matters under discussion. Multitudes of people, all the intelligent people in the world, indeed—who were not already specially instructed—were seeking more or less consciously to "get the hang" of world affairs as a whole. They were, in fact, improvising "Outlines of History" in their minds for their own use.

The writer is not in any professional sense an historian, but he has been making out his own private Outline from the beginnings of his career. He has always been preoccupied with history as one whole and with the general forces that make history. It is the twist of his mind. Even when he was a science student he kept a notebook for historical reading. His first published story, *The Time Machine* (1894), was a fantastic speculation about the trend of human destiny; *When the Sleeper Awakes* was a picturesque exaggeration of the development of our civilization; *Anticipations* (1900) was an attempt to argue out some possible consequences of current processes. In quite a number of his books, in *The Research Magnificent* and *The Undying Fire* for example, little "outlines of history" are vignetted. And so this mental stir of the war time found him if not specially equipped, at least specially disposed, to take a comprehensive view of past and present things. For some time before he began this *Outline* he had been working upon the problems of after-war settlement and the project of a League of Nations; in the days, that is, before the late President Wilson took possession of that proposal. Such work necessarily involved participation in the disputes and organization of various propagandist unions and societies. The discussions in these associations brought out very vividly the vital importance in all political activities of a man's conception of the past. For, indeed, what are a man's political activities but the expression in action of his idea of the past? All the people who were interested in these league of nations projects were at sixes and sevens among themselves because they had the most vague, heterogeneous and untidy assumptions about what the world of men was, what it had been, and therefore of what it could be. In very many cases, there was extraordinarily exact special knowledge combined with the most crude and naïve assumptions about history in general.

It seemed more and more advisable to the writer to get together maps and notes, read rather more systematically than he had hitherto done, and clear up for himself a number of historical issues upon which he was still extremely vague. As soon as he had embarked upon this, it became evident to him that he might do much more useful work by developing his private memoranda upon the main shapes of history into a sort of general report and handbook for the use of men and women busier than himself or preoccupied with other things, than by wrangling more and more hopelessly over impossible constitutions for improbable world confederations. The more he entertained this project of writing a review of existing knowledge of man's place in space and time, the more difficult, attractive and unavoidable an undertaking it appeared to him.

To begin with he had contemplated a general review of European unity, a sort of summary of the rise and break-up of the Roman system, of the obstinate survival of the idea of the Empire in Europe, and of the various projects for the unification of Christendom that had been put forward at different times. But it was speedily evident that there was no real beginning of things in Rome or in Judea, and no possibility of confining the story to the western world. That much was only the latter act of a much greater drama. He found the story carrying him back on the one hand to the Aryan beginnings in the forests and plains of Europe and western Asia, and on the other to the earlier stages of civilization in Egypt, in Mesopotamia and the now submerged lands that seem once to have sustained a human population in the Mediterranean basin. He began to realize how severely European historians have minimized the share of the central uplands of Asia and of the Persian, the Indian and the Chinese cultures, in the drama of mankind. He began to see more and more plainly how living the remote past still is in our lives and institutions, and how little we can understand either the broad political or religious or social issues of to-day without some understanding of the earlier stages of human association. And that involved some understanding of human origins.

So the *Outline* spread and enlarged itself as he contemplated it. For a time he hesitated before the epic immensity of this broadening task. He asked himself whether this was not rather a work for an historian than for one whose chief writings hitherto had been either speculative essays or works of fiction. But there did not seem to be any historian available who was sufficiently superficial, shall we say—sufficiently wide and sufficiently shallow to cover the vast field of the project.

Historians are for the most part very scholarly men nowadays; they go in fear rather of small errors than of disconnectedness; they dread the certain ridicule of a wrong date more than the disputable attribution of a wrong value. It is right and proper that this should be so, and that in a hasty and headlong age a whole class of devoted men should maintain an exacting standard of fine precisions. But these high standards of detailed accuracy make it hopeless for us to go to the historians for what is required here. For them this would not be an attractive task but a distressing task. To them one must look for accumulated material, rather than for assembled and massed effects. They are, indeed, giving us now, in numerous volumes, by many hands, from many points of view and in a pleasing diversity of spirit and intention, great and noble compilations, of extreme value to students. But these magnificent performances are, for the everyday purposes of the ordinary citizen travelling about in life, as impressive and as useful for handy guidance as a many-volumed encyclopædia.

In America, indeed, there were to be found several useful small books on universal history, notably the Ancient and Modern History of Robinson and Breasted, and Hutton Webster's and

W. M. West's similar volumes, but these writers aim at the school and the college rather than at the general reader. *The Living Past* of F. S. Marvin again is an admirable essay on intellectual progress, but it gives little substantial fact. It would indeed have meant disaster to the academic reputation of any established historical authority to have admitted an intention of writing a complete Outline of History, and, even were that promise given, the general reader would still have had to wait many years for its performance. The standing of the present writer, however, who is by nature and choice as remote from academic respect as he is from a dukedom, enabled him to interest the public in history without any such sacrifice of dignity and distinction, such risks from hostile criticism, as a recognized authority would have had to incur. It was his happy privilege to offend inaccessibly; he is a literary Bedouin, whose home is the great outside, who knows no prouder title than his name, whose only conceivable honour is his own. This or that specialist might rage at his scandalous neglect of this or that precious item of that specialist's monopoly; it would not matter very much. He could go unblushingly to standard works and ordinarily accessible material; he was not even obliged to pretend to original discoveries or original points of view; his simpler undertaking was to collect, arrange, determine the proportion of the parts and phases of the great adventure of mankind, and write. He has added nothing to history. At least he hopes he has added nothing to history. He has merely made a digest of a great mass of material, some of it very new material, and he has done so in the character of a popular writer considering the needs of other ordinary citizens like himself.

Yet the subject is so splendid a one that no possible treatment, however unpretending, can rob it altogether of its sweeping greatness and dignity. If sometimes this *Outline* is laboured and pitifully insufficient, at others it seems almost to have planned and written itself. Its background is unfathomable mystery, the riddle of the stars, the measurelessness of space and time. There appears life struggling towards consciousness, gathering power, accumulating will, through millions of years and through countless billions of individual lives, until it reaches the tragic confusions and perplexities of the world of to-day, so full of fear and yet so full of promise and opportunity. We see man rising from lonely beginnings to this present dawn of world fellowship. We see all human institutions grow and change;

they are changing now more rapidly than they have ever done before. The display ends in a tremendous note of interrogation. The writer is just a guide who brings his reader at last to the present edge, the advancing edge of things, and stops and whispers beside him: "This is our inheritance."

It would be absurd to claim that this *Outline* is anything more than a current rendering of the opening vision of reality that the multitudinous activities of geologists, palæontologists, embryologists and every kind of naturalist, psychologists, ethnologists, archæologists, philologists and historical investigators, have unveiled during the last hundred years. History a century ago was mere bookishness. The bookish historian now accepts, reluctantly and ungraciously enough, his place as a mere contributor of doubtful documents to the broad ensemble.

On this huge prospect our *Outline* makes its report. To the best of the writer's ability this is how that vision looks to-day. But he writes within his own limitations and the limitations of his time. The *Outline* is a book of to-day—with no pretensions to immortality. It is the current account. This *Outline of History* of 1931 will in due course follow its earlier editions to the second-hand book-box and the dust-destructor. More gifted hands with fuller information and ampler means will presently write fresh Outlines in happier phrases. The *Outline of History* the writer would far prefer to his own would be the *Outline* of 2031; to read it and, perhaps with even more curiosity, to pore over its illustrations.

All of us, if by some miracle we could get that copy of the *Outline of History* for 2031, would, I suppose, turn first to the amazing illustrations of the last chapters and then to the accompanying text. What astonishing events! What unbelievable achievements! But, afterwards, this writer at least would go back to the early chapters to see how much of the story that is told here survived.

Probably the general shape of the early part would still be very much the same, but there would be hundreds of illuminating details now unknown and fascinating additional discoveries, of skulls, implements, buried cities and vestiges of lost and submerged peoples, as yet unsuspected. The stories of China and India would be much more exact and perhaps different in quality, and much more would be known of Central Asia, and perhaps of America before Columbus. Charlemagne and Cæsar would still be great figures in history, and some of our nearer giants,

Napoleon for example, might be found shrunken to comparative unimportance.

§ 2

The chief purpose of the present revision has been to make the *Outline* simpler and easier to read.

The writer has told how it grew out of notes and maps, and he will confess that now when he turns over the earlier editions, the first edition that was published in parts and the first book edition of 1920, he finds the flavour of notebooks altogether too strong. Much undigested and discordant matter was put into footnotes; there were far too many hesitating, ambiguous and guarded statements; the presentation was sometimes confused. The method he pursued led naturally to that. He called in to his aid four chief helpers, Sir Ray Lankester, Professor Gilbert Murray, Sir Harry Johnston and Mr. Ernest Barker, and he made them his advisers upon his reading and sources of information. In addition he secured the help and advice of various specially well-read men upon this or that point or region. Sir Denison Ross, Mr. Cranmer Byng and Mr. S. N. Fu, for example, were extremely helpful in regard to Central Asia and China. Dr. Charles Singer gave the most useful information upon classical science, Professor J. L. Myres was a valuable source for Mediterranean archæology, Mr. Philip Guedalla was his counsellor upon European politics in the eighteenth and early nineteenth centuries; and so forth and so on. Mr. J. F. Horrabin, with his genius for political and commercial geography, was not so much an illustrator as a collaborator. There were many others who gave their time and knowledge freely and generously; there are full lists of names in the previous editions; one hesitates between acknowledging one's obligations and implicating one's friends. Each chapter was first drafted by the author, multiple copies were made and sent out to all the possible helpers, who wrote, commented and slashed about upon them, as they thought proper. The author then sat down, chastened and instructed, amidst these mutilated and butchered duplicates, and wrote his chapter afresh. Finally proofs went out to all the chief helpers and to anyone else especially interested in the period dealt with.

In this way the correctness of names, dates and so forth was ensured. But though the writer upon all questions of fact followed with absolute fidelity the band of tutors he had evoked, he reserved to himself the fullest rights of private judgment upon matters of opinion. The result was the introduction of various lively controversies into the clustering footnotes and even into the text. For example, he fell foul of Professor Gilbert Murray in a comparison of the moral and intellectual quality of the common Athenian and of the Cockney, and though he conceded to his editor the completest intimacy with the former he maintained his right to judge the latter in his own fashion. There was also a page or so of disputation between the writer, Professor Murray and Mr. Barker, about the soundness of Mr. Gladstone's education. And various differences with Mr. Ernest Barker. To the writer the "greatness" of Napoleon I is a monstrous and altogether unsubstantial superstition. The facts, he thinks, speak for themselves, and they will be given in this *Outline* in their proper place and proportion. The man was of the quality of Mussolini and intellectually inferior to Napoleon III. But Mr. Barker was unable to accept this statement. "Put me down of the opposite opinion," he wrote, and so the footnote stood. Sir Harry Johnston's weakness—or rather his excessive strength—lay in the abnormal, though no doubt righteous, spelling of well-known historical names. He would have Solomon, Shelomoh, and Hebrews, Ibrim, which seemed likely to be difficult and confusing for the ordinary reader. That issue also flowered into footnotes.

These footnotes were as amusing to the writer and his friends as family jokes, and they were almost inevitable while the names of the four chief helpers stood with the writer's upon the title page, upholding and in a way guaranteeing it; but they were perplexing and tedious to most readers. Footnotes, references and qualifications are necessary things in a book written for the student, but in this *Outline* they were superfluous and even, the writer now confesses, a little pretentious. In this edition he releases his four chief helpers, with gratitude, from all further responsibility. Their names disappear from the title page. He drops his pilots. They have steered him past dangerous shoals, and along tortuous channels to his present freedom and confidence. And so helped and liberated he is able to simplify, clarify and give its fullest values to this great story their kindness made it possible for him to tell.

This is now the sixth complete reprinting of this work. The first publication in parts subjected it chapter by chapter to the scrutiny of over a hundred thousand readers. Many wrote offering comments, pointing out small errors, raising interesting points. All this correspondence was dealt with systematically and the first book edition benefited greatly in detail. That also went out to a great multitude of readers; in America alone over a quarter of a million copies were issued, and that again produced an abundant crop of emendations. That edition also evoked many able reviews and several critical pamphlets appeared. The second book edition in 1923, the third edition, that is, profited greatly by that second extensive examination. In addition to such revisions of detail the chapters of the third edition were rearranged. For some time the author had felt that his account of the Aryan culture came too early and minimized the share of the non-Aryan folk in the development of civilization. He altered the order of the earlier chapters so as to correct this effect. And also he inserted a fuller account of Lincoln and the American Civil War. This present edition has involved still further additions and revisions. It has been purged of footnotes and digressions and made more explicit, more fluent and more continuous than its predecessors. The disputes of the collaborators are no longer heard from behind the scenes. It has, the writer hopes, lost its last traces of the student's notebook and has become plainly and simply an *Outline of History*.

The reader of this book need be in no doubt about the facts, the names, the dates that are given here—after the test of these scrutinies and revisions. The book has been severely criticized, but never on the score of its general accuracy. Even so inveterate an antagonist of the writer as Mr. Belloc has conceded it that much merit. The objections made concern the relative prominence given to this part or that, to the influence of this culture or the importance of that. A certain type of classical scholar rages at the comparative neglect of Homer and the æsthetic side of Greek life, though the account of Greek science is full, and though the intellectual development of Greece is treated as a cardinal phase in human development. Another large body of opinion sees the world through Latin forms and is exasperated even by the simple statement of the comparative extent, duration and influence of, for instance, the Byzantine, Persian and Chinese systems. Rome is still aggressive in modern literature and criticism, and still seeks to minimize the non-Latin spaces in the picture. Dogmatic Freethinkers, again, consider the acceptance of Jesus as a real person insupportable; adherents of Islam cry out against the too familiar handling of their prophet. Communists are offended because the doctrines of Marx and Lenin are not made the basis of the entire story. Many people, with a rather materialistic theology in their minds, have been disagreeably impressed by the massed and accumulating evidences of man's animal descent. Even if that be true they think it highly demoralizing. Such criticisms were inevitable. There was no way of evading or satisfying these demands.

One realizes in the face of such attitudes and objections that nearly everyone has already a sort of implicit Outline of History in his mind, his working explanation of his world and of his place in the world, rejecting this view and assuming that, and more or less clear-mindedly he brings our version to the test of these half-buried acceptances. And naturally the writer, too, has his view, his bias. But the reader will never find a writer who has not that much personality. There never will be an Outline of History written that is not tendential. Here, as in every sort of descriptive and informative book, the reader has to bear in mind, just as a judge or a juryman has to bear in mind, the individual characteristics of the witness who is giving his account of what he saw. What is claimed here is that the witness does to the best of his ability tender a fair and honest general account from his point of view of the great spectacle of Time and Fate that has unfolded itself before him.

§ 3

In the criticism of the earlier editions of this *Outline,* the complaint was frequently repeated that the development of the arts, and particularly of music, was disregarded. The story of man's achievement of knowledge and social power was given at considerable length, but hardly anything was said of the appearance and extension of his conscious search for beauty. An attempt has now been made to meet these objections and several sections have been added to record how the artist, the poet and the imaginative writer appeared in human life. Yet the limitations upon any "history" of music or any other art are very narrow. One may note the appearance of new forms, new methods, new instruments, but the only way to the realization of imaginative arts is to hear it or see it or read it. It is no part of our plan to catalogue masters and masterpieces and help our readers to babble great names.

Additions have been made necessary by the progress of the excavator. It is hard nowadays for the writer to keep pace with the spade. Since the *Outline* was last revised there has been much vividly interesting work done in North India, Sumeria and all over Central Asia, and in China, *Sinanthropus*, most amazing of submen, has been unearthed. *Sinanthropus* is a complete reply to the clamour of the anti-Darwinians of half a century ago for the "missing link." Moreover it has been necessary to scrutinize the account of the Great War very closely and to rearrange and in part rewrite the post-war portion. That was much the weakest part of the preceding editions. The exciting hopes and stresses of the time were too close for restrained writing. There was a lack of proportion between this conclusion and the rest of the book; speeches by Mr. Lloyd George, the perfidies of the Irish struggle, lectures by obscure generals at the United Service Institution loomed portentous. Something of the pamphleteer, something of the partisan, came in. But now, seventeen years from the war and after a long excursion into a kindred but broadening and steadying field of thought, the writer believes himself able to get these last years into a truer perspective. This latter part has been severely pruned, and a fresh attempt to give a sounder analysis of the world-outlook has been made. It is not only in the political field that things have had to be thought out again. The nature of the financial and economic difficulties of the world has become much plainer now than it was before the crisis of 1929, and this again has necessitated very careful revision.

§ 4

The Outline of History proved an extremely successful book. The number of copies distributed in English and in translations is entering now upon the third million.

This extraordinary reception astonished both its publishers and its author. It revealed the existence of a new immense stratum of intelligent people in the modern community eager and ready to supply the deficiencies of school and college education. It was the world-wide need for such a general view of historical fact, far more than any literary merit of the *Outline*, which brought about this enormous sale.

The discovery of this great mass of enquiring minds, with all the political and social possibilities it revealed, was necessarily extremely stimulating to the writer of the *Outline* and his associates. They realized that here was a new element in the world's affairs: a great and as yet disorganized multitude capable of a modern ideology and needing only to be drawn together by a common system of knowledge and understandings, to become a dominating influence in the reconstruction in human affairs. It seemed almost ungrateful not to serve this receptive multitude to the utmost. It was not that those responsible for the *Outline* had any great conceit of themselves as leaders, but that the good fortune of that book had put them into a position of exceptional advantage to go on and complete the work of which the *Outline* was manifestly only a part. The responsibility of their opportunity far exceeded their powers. The *Outline* gave the framework of international ideas; it was a basis for political thought and activity, but it left certain other fields of universal human interest untouched. Nobody had such a chance of getting these gaps filled in a reasonably short space of time, if he could do it, as the writer of the *Outline*.

So there has now sprung from this beginning two other enterprises, which round off and complete a working statement of the general picture of our world needed by the modern citizen. The first of these is an outline of biological science, a statement of all that is currently known about the life in us and round us, our health, our mental activity, our origins, and the whole story of life's evolution since the beginning. This the writer has done in intimate collaboration with two able biologists, his son, G. P. Wells, and the grandson of his former professor, Professor Julian Huxley. They have made an up-to-date summary of all biological knowledge. For reasons that need not be gone into here, they have not called this work, *The Outline of Life,* but *The Science of Life.*

But still there was left a third main aspect of human existence, and that was the business existence, the work, anxiety, effort, pressure of everyday life. *The Outline of History* told a man of his origins and tradition, why war hung over him, and why he was under the law; *The Science of Life* told him of the nature of his bodily and mental life; the third outline to complete the exposition of his world had to be an outline of economics, of how and why man worked, why money has become essential to his well-being and his relations to his fellow creatures, and the general "go" of industry, wealth-winning and earning and spending. This again it was found better not to call an Outline, and after many changes of title it has been completed and is now published as *The Work, Wealth and Happiness of Mankind.* So the first statement from a modern standpoint of what man was and is and what he does is completed.

These works are offered to the world without arrogance and without compunction. They are no doubt faulty to a terrible extent, and in due course they will certainly be superseded by far better work upon the same lines. They are like the temporary sheds that precede a palace. Their substance will need condensation and simplification for school use into an elementary Account of Life for the young, and various portions of them may need expansion for the college student. But until they are so superseded these three works remain, in their pioneer and experimental fashion, a necessary bringing together of what a contemporary man or woman can know about the past, about self, and about the daily task.

H. G. W.

Wells never lived to make the changes that he intended. At intervals from the late 20's onwards he added sections to bring the *Outline* up to date; but they were episodic and had faults of which he was probably conscious. Certainly, there exists a copy which he had begun to correct, and in which everything after about 1930 is struck out in the "Table of Contents." All his detailed corrections have, of course, been incorporated in this edition; the most interesting of them are those that show a modification of his views upon the Russian revolution. Several of the more offensive adjectives had been removed.

In this edition I have found practically nothing of importance to alter up to the date where he had made his great crossing-out. Where I have had to change anything previously, it has always been because of an alteration in our knowledge, not because of an error. The planet Pluto has been discovered; the British King is no longer "Emperor of India"; and therefore some phrases have had to be modified. That is all; the monumentally solid quality of the body of the work has only been proved by time.

In later years I have naturally had to make more changes, but I have always endeavoured to remember, where doubt exists, that readers wish to hear the views of Wells, not those of Postgate; for that reason I have sometimes let stand judgments that would not be my own. I have also had to rewrite whole sections which Wells had merely sketched out. Those who are interested may note that much of section 7 and all of sections 9 and 12, of Chapter 39, are from my hand, and that the account of the second world war is wholly my own; all the rest is substantially H. G. Wells'.

R. W. P.

THE OUTLINE OF HISTORY

BOOK I

THE WORLD BEFORE MAN

I

THE EARTH IN SPACE AND TIME

§ 1. *The Great Expansion of Men's Ideas of Space and Time.* § 2. *The Earth in Space.* § 3. *How Long Has the Earth Endured?*

§ 1

AND first, before we begin the history of life, let us tell something of the stage upon which our drama is put and of the background against which it is played.

In the last few hundred years there has been an extraordinary enlargement of men's ideas about the visible universe in which they live. At the same time there has been perhaps a certain diminution in their individual self-importance. They have learnt that they are items in a whole far vaster, more enduring and more wonderful than their ancestors ever dreamed or suspected.

To the savage and primitive mind the earth seems to be the whole flat floor of the universe; the sky is a dome above it across which the sun and moon and stars pass and pass again, returning by some mysterious roundabout or subterranean route. The Babylonian and Chinese astronomers, after many centuries of star observation, still believed that the earth was flat. It was the Greek mind which first grasped clearly the spherical form of the world, but even so, it did not apprehend the universe as relatively very large. The globe of earth was the centre of being; the sun, the moon, the planets, the fixed stars, moved about it as their centre, in crystalline spheres. It was only in the fifteenth century that men's minds moved beyond this, and

Copernicus made his amazing guess that the sun was the centre and not the earth. It was only with the development of the telescope by Galileo in the opening of the seventeenth century that the views of Copernicus became widely accepted.

The development of the telescope marks, indeed, a new phase in human thought, a new vision of life. It is an extraordinary thing that the Greeks, with their lively and penetrating minds, never realized the possibilities of either microscope or telescope. They made no use of the lens. Yet they lived in a world in which glass had been known and had been made beautiful for hundreds of years; they had about them glass flasks and bottles, through which they must have caught glimpses of things distorted and enlarged. But science in Greece was pursued by philosophers in an aristocratic spirit, men who, with a few such exceptions as the ingenious Archimedes and Hiero, were too proud to learn from such mere artisans as jewellers and metal- and glass-workers.

Ignorance is the first penalty of pride. The philosopher had no mechanical skill and the artisan had no philosophical education, and it was left for another age, more than a thousand years later, to bring together glass and the astronomer. Since the time of Galileo astronomy and the telescope have advanced together, and a veil of ignorance and false assumptions has been rolled back from the deeps of space. The idea that the sun was the centre of the universe has followed the idea that the world was in that position. We know now that our sun cannot even be included among the greatest of the stars; it is merely one of the lesser lights.

The telescope has released the human imagination as no other implement has ever done. If there is any other apparatus worthy to be compared to its enlarging influence, it is the spectroscope, which was developed after the discoveries of Fraunhofer, the glass-worker, in 1814. Since man has lived on earth he has seen rainbows, but who could have told him that those bands of colour held in them a promise that one day he should be able to analyze the stars? But the spectroscope receives the rays from any luminous source, passes them through prisms, and breaks them up into rainbow-like bands. These bands reveal under examination transverse lines of brightness and darkness which vary with the heat and the chemical composition of the source of light and of any intervening vapour. So that men can now sit in observatories and learn the composition and take the temperature of stars incalculable billions of miles away.

The curtain that hid the unfathomable abyss of stellar distances has been drawn back only in the last three centuries. Still more recent is our realization of the immense duration of our universe in time. Among ancient peoples the Indian philosophers alone seem to have had any perception of the vast ages through which existence has passed. In the European world, until little more than a century and a half ago, men's ideas of the time things had lasted were astonishingly brief. In the *Universal History,* published by a syndicate of booksellers in London in 1779, it is stated that the world was created in 4004 B.C. and (with a pleasant exactitude) at the autumnal equinox, and that the making of man crowned the work of creation at Eden, upon the Euphrates, exactly two days' journey above Basra. The confidence of these statements arose from a too literal interpretation of the Bible narrative. Very few even of the sincerest believers in the inspiration of the Bible now accept them as matter-of-fact statements.

It is the science of geology and particularly the science of palæontology which has broken through this time barrier and opened beyond that little yesterday of scarcely six thousand years a million such yesterdays. Two main sets of facts, very frequently observed, were forcing themselves upon men's attention long before the eighteenth century. One was that in innumerable districts one saw exposed great thicknesses of stratified rocks that could only have been accumulated during long periods of time, and that in many cases these strata had been bent, contorted, and thrust about in a way that was inevitably suggestive of enormous forces operating through long periods of time. The other was the existence of fossils similar to, but not precisely like, the bones and skulls and other hard parts of existing species.

It was only in the eighteenth century that strata and fossils began to be studied systematically; it is only in the nineteenth that the recognition of the real scale and quality of these accumulations, the *Record of the Rocks,* became widespread. There was a great struggle to establish the authority of the Record against the prejudices of those to whom a strictly literal interpretation of the Bible was dear. Many men still living took an active part in that great emancipation of the human mind. Gradually the perspectives of mankind changed and elongated. Two hundred years ago the imagination of our race had a background of six thousand years. Now that curtain has risen also, and men look back to a past of scores and hundreds of millions of years.

§ 2

We will now summarize very compactly what is known of the material dimensions of our world. Our earth, it has been shown, is a spinning globe. Vast though it seems to us, it is a mere speck of matter in the greater vastness of space.

Space is, for the most part, emptiness. At great intervals in this emptiness there are flaring centres of heat and light, the "fixed stars." They are all moving about in space, notwithstanding that they are called fixed stars, but for a long time men did not realize their motion. They are so vast and at such tremendous distances that their motion is not perceived. Only in the course of many thousands of years is it appreciable. Scores of centuries ago the Egyptians made star-maps, and they show us that the shapes of the constellations have changed very considerably; many stars have moved measurably. Yet we still use the old convenient expression "fixed stars" to distinguish them from the planets. These fixed stars are so far off that, for all their immensity, they seem to be, even when we look at them through the most powerful telescopes, mere points of light, brighter or less bright. A few, however, when we turn a telescope upon them, are seen to be whirls and clouds of shining vapour which we call nebulæ. They are puffs and smears of luminous stuff, billions of miles in length. They are so far off that a movement of millions of miles would be imperceptible.

There are also, it has been realized quite recently, a number of "dark bodies" in space, and clouds of opaque matter—some of enormous size. We should still know nothing of their existence if it had not been that they blot out the luminous stars beyond them.

One star, however, is so near to us that it is like a great ball of flame. This one is the sun. The sun is itself in its nature like a fixed star, but it differs from the other stars in appearance because it is beyond comparison nearer than they are; and because it is nearer men have been able to learn something of its nature. Its mean distance from the earth is ninety-three million miles. It is a mass of flaming matter, having a diameter of 866,000 miles. Its bulk is a million and a quarter times the bulk of our earth. Many of the fixed stars are vastly greater.

These are difficult figures for the imagination. If a bullet fired from a Maxim gun at the sun kept its muzzle velocity unimpaired, it would take seven years to reach the sun. And yet we say the sun is quite close, measured by the scale of the stars. If the earth were a small ball, one inch in diameter, the sun would be a globe of nine feet diameter; it would fill a small bedroom. We know now that it is spinning round on its axis, but since it is an incandescent fluid, its polar regions do not travel with the same velocity as its equator, the surface of which rotates in about twenty-five days. The surface visible to us consists of clouds of incandescent metallic vapour. So hot is the sun's atmosphere that iron, nickel, copper, and tin are present in it in a gaseous state. At what lies below we can only guess.

About the sun at great distances circle not only our earth, but certain other kindred bodies called the planets. These shine in the sky because they reflect the light of the sun; they are near enough to us to note their movements quite easily. Night by night their positions change with regard to the fixed stars.

It is well to understand how empty of matter is space. If, as we have said, the sun were a globe nine feet across, our earth would, in proportion, be the size of a one-inch ball, and at a distance of 322 yards from the sun. This is over a sixth of a mile. It would mean 3½ minutes' smart walking from the ball to the nine-feet globe. The moon would be a speck the size of a small pea, thirty inches from the earth.

Nearer to the sun than the earth would be two other very similar specks, the planets Mercury and Venus, at a distance of a hundred and twenty-four and two hundred and thirty-two yards respectively. Beyond the earth would come the planets Mars, Jupiter, Saturn, Uranus, Neptune, and Pluto at distances from the sun of 488, 1,672, 3,067, 6,169, 9,666, and 13,300 yards respectively. From the sun to Neptune would be a two-hour walk. There would also be a certain number of very much smaller specks, flying about amongst these planets, more particularly a number called the asteroids circling between Mars and Jupiter, and occasionally a little puff of more or less luminous vapour and dust would drift into the system from the almost limitless emptiness beyond. Such a puff is what we call a comet. *All the rest of the space about us and around us and for unfathomable distances beyond is cold, lifeless, and void.* The nearest fixed star to us, *on this minute scale,* be it remembered—the earth as a one-inch ball, and the moon a little pea—would be over 40,000 miles away!

Most of the fixed stars we see would still be *on this scale* scores and hundreds of millions of miles off.

Let us now come back to the earth. The diameter of our world is a little under 8,000 miles. Its surface is rough, the more projecting parts of the roughness are mountains, and in the hollows of its surface there is a film of water, the oceans and seas. This film of water is about five miles thick at its deepest part—that is to say, the deepest oceans have a depth of five miles. This is very little in comparison with the bulk of the world.

About this sphere is a thin covering of air, the atmosphere. As we ascend in a balloon or go up a mountain the air is continually less dense, until it becomes too thin to support life. At a height of twenty miles there is scarcely any air at all. The highest point to which a bird can fly is about four miles up—the condor, it is said, can struggle up to that; but most small birds and insects which are carried up by aeroplanes or balloons drop off insensible at a much lower level; and the greatest height to which any mountaineer has ever climbed is about five miles. Men have flown in aeroplanes to a height of over seven miles, and balloons with men in them have reached very nearly seven miles, but at the cost of considerable physical suffering. Small experimental balloons, containing not men but recording instruments, have gone as high as twenty-three miles.

It is only in the upper few hundred feet of the crust of the earth, in the sea, and in the lower levels of the air below four miles that life is found. We do not know of any life at all except in these really very shallow films of air and water upon our planet. So far as we know, all the rest of space is as yet without life. Scientific men have discussed the possibility of life, or of some process of a similar kind, occurring upon such kindred bodies as the planets Venus and Mars. But they point merely to questionable possibilities.

§ 3

So much for the Earth in space. Let us now consider our subject from the point of view of time. Astronomers and geologists and those who study physics are now able to tell us something of the origin of the earth. They consider that, vast ages ago, the sun was a spinning, flaring mass of matter, not yet concentrated into a compact centre of heat and light, considerably larger than it is now, and spinning very much faster, and that as it whirled a series of fragments were detached from it by the near approach of some other body flying through space, and that those torn-off fragments became the planets. Our earth is one of these planets. The flaring mass that was the material of the earth broke into two masses as it spun; a larger, the earth itself, and a smaller, which is now the dead, still moon.

Astronomers give us convincing reasons for supposing that sun and earth and moon and all that system were then whirling about at a speed much greater than their speed to-day, and that at first our earth was a flaming thing upon which no life could live. They oblige us to believe that the sun, incandescent though it is, is now much cooler than it was, and that it spins more slowly now than it did, and that it continues to cool and slow down. And they also show that the rate at which the earth spins is diminishing and continues to diminish—that is to say, that our day is growing longer and longer, and that the heat at the centre of the earth wastes slowly. There was a time when the day was not a half and not a third of what it is to-day; when a blazing hot sun, much greater than it is now, must have moved visibly—had there been an eye to mark it—from its rise to its setting across the skies. There will be a time when the day will be as long as a year is now, and the cooling sun, shorn of its beams, will hang motionless in the heavens.

How long, some reader will ask, has the world endured? That is a question which has attracted much attention in the last few years. Gradually the earlier estimates, which varied very widely, have been brought towards agreement. Astronomers and mathematicians who base their computations on the rate of cooling of celestial bodies and in various processes of diffusion and atomic change give us 2,000 million years as the age of the earth as a body separate from the sun, and about 300 million years as the length of time since life appeared upon it in any abundance. The age of the sun as a star is now supposed to be somewhere in the nature of five million million years. The earth, says Sir James Jeans in his *Universe Around Us,* will in all probability go on for another million million years and then its equatorial temperature may be sinking to Arctic conditions. Since man has existed as a self-conscious social creature for only 30,000 years or less, this gives him illimitable opportunity for the attainment of knowledge and power. Long before he reaches that limit he may make himself master of time and space.

II

THE RECORD OF THE ROCKS

§ 1. *The First Living Things.* § 2. *Natural Selection and the Changes of Species.*

§ 1

WE DO not know certainly how life began upon the earth. Biologists have made many guesses and suggestions, and there seems to be a general agreement that life began in warm sunlit shallow water, possibly in pools and lagoons along the coasts of the first formed seas. It began perhaps as a slime, as a sort of sub-life that slowly and imperceptibly took on the distinctive qualities of life. Upon no part of earth at present are there the sort of conditions, chemical and physical, under which life can conceivably have begun. There is certainly no fresh beginning of life going on now. But out of inorganic matter it is possible to make slimes and films that faintly parody the structure, and even the spreading and growth, of living things. If the beginning of life was a natural unmiraculous process, then surely some day it will be possible for the man of science to imitate and repeat it. Until that can be done this question necessarily remains to a certain extent speculative. And if many biologists are convinced that life appeared under the requisite conditions as naturally and inevitably as ice appears when water under the normal pressure is cooled below the freezing-point, it is also the case that many other people of equal intelligence are of an opposite opinion. Here we cannot be expected to adjudicate upon the question.

The idea that life appeared on the earth as a natural and necessary chemical and physical process, without the intervention of any miraculous factor, seems to be very repugnant to many religious minds. But that repugnance is due, perhaps, rather to a confusion of thought in these minds than to any essential irreligiosity in the conception itself. They think of "life" as being in a way already "soul," they ascribe all sorts of moral qualities to it; they side with it against "dead matter." But it is difficult to see why a slug or a toadstool, a louse or a cancerous parasitic growth upon the bark of a tree, should be treated as though it and the processes of its existence were in some mysterious way "higher" than, for example, the beautifully marshalled elements in a crystalline group, or in a gem, or in a slab of patterned marble, or the lovely patternings of rippled water in the sunlight, or the undulations of wind-blown sand. Why should the maker of the universe take sides between the almost inanimate and the altogether inanimate?

The atmosphere was much denser in the days of life's beginning; usually great cloud masses obscured the sun, frequent storms darkened the heavens. The land of those days, upheaved by violent volcanic forces, was a barren land, without vegetation, without soil. Almost incessant rain-storms swept down upon it, and rivers and torrents carried great loads of sediment out to sea to become muds that hardened later into slates and shales, and sands that became sandstones.

The geologists have studied the whole accumulation of these sediments as it remains to-day, from those of the earliest ages to the most recent. Of course the oldest deposits are the most distorted and changed and worn, and in them there is now no certain trace to be found of life at all. Probably the earliest forms of life were small and soft, leaving no evidence of their existence behind them. It was only when some of these living things developed skeletons and shells of lime and such-like hard material that they left fossil vestiges after they died, and so put themselves on record for examination.

The literature of geology is very largely an account of the fossils that are found in the rocks and of the order in which layers after layers of rocks lie one on another. The very oldest rocks must have been formed before there was any sea at all, when the earth was too hot for a sea to exist, and when the water that is now sea was an atmosphere of steam mixed with the air. The higher levels of the atmosphere were dense with clouds, from which a hot rain fell towards the rocks below, to be converted again into steam long before it reached their incandescence. Below this steam atmosphere the molten world-stuff solidified as the first rocks. These first rocks must have solidified as a cake over glowing liquid material beneath, much as cooling lava does. They must have appeared first as crusts and clinkers. They must have been constantly remelted and recrystallized before any thickness of them became permanently solid. The name of Fundamental Gneiss is given to a great underlying system of crystalline rocks which probably formed age by age as this hot youth of the world drew to its close. The scenery of the world in the days when the Fundamental Gneiss was formed must have been more like the interior of an electric furnace than anything else to be found upon earth at the present time.

After long ages the steam in the atmosphere began also to condense and fall right down to earth, pouring at last over these warm primordial rocks in rivulets of hot water and gathering in depressions as pools and lakes and the first seas. Into those seas the streams that poured over the rocks brought with them dust and particles to form a sediment, and this sediment accumulated in layers, or, as geologists call them, *strata*, and formed the first Sedimentary rocks. Those earliest sedimentary rocks sank into depressions and were covered by others; they were bent, tilted up, and torn by great volcanic disturbances and by tidal strains that swept through the rocky crust of the earth. We find these first sedimentary rocks still coming to the surface of the land here and there, either not covered by later strata or exposed after vast ages of concealment by the wearing off of the rock that covered them later—there are great surfaces of them in Canada especially; they are cleft and bent, partially remelted, recrystallized, hardened and compressed, but recognizable for what they are. And they contain no single certain trace of life at all.

They are frequently called *Azoic* (lifeless) rocks. But since in some of these earliest sedimentary rocks a substance called graphite (black lead) occurs, and also red and black oxide of iron, and since it is asserted that these substances need the activity of living things for their production, which may or may not be the case, some geologists prefer to call these earliest sedimentary rocks *Archæozoic* (primordial life). They suppose that the first life was soft living matter that had no shells or skeletons or any such structure that could remain as a recognizable fossil after its death, and that its chemical influence caused the deposition of graphite and iron oxide. This is pure guessing, of course, and there is at least an equal probability that in the time of formation of the Azoic rocks life had not yet begun.

Overlying or overlapping these Azoic or Archæozoic rocks come others, manifestly also very ancient and worn, which do contain traces of life. These first remains are of the simplest description; they are the vestiges of simple plants called Algæ, or marks like the tracks made by worms in the sea mud. There are also the skeletons of the microscopic creatures called Radiolaria. This second series of rocks is called the *Proterozoic* (beginning of life) series, and marks a long age in the world's history.

Lying over and above the Proterozoic rocks is a third series, which is found to contain a considerable number and variety of traces of living things. First comes the evidence of a diversity of shell-fish, crabs and such-like crawling things, worms, seaweeds, and the like; then of a multitude of fishes and of the beginnings of land plants and land creatures. These rocks are called the *Palæozoic* (ancient life) rocks. They mark a vast era, during which life was slowly spreading, increasing, and developing in the seas of our world. Through long ages, through the earliest Palæozoic time, it was no more than a proliferation of such swimming and creeping things in the water. There were creatures called trilobites; these were crawling things like big sea woodlice, and they were probably related to the American king-crab of to-day. There were also sea-scorpions, the prefects of that early world. The individuals of certain species of these were nine feet long. These were the very highest sorts of life. There were abundant different sorts of an order of shell-fish called brachiopods. There were plant animals, rooted and joined together like plants, and loose weeds that waved in the waters.

It was not a display of life to excite our imaginations. There was nothing that ran or flew or even swam swiftly or skilfully. Except for the size of some of the creatures, it was not very different from, and rather less various than, the kind of life a student would gather from any summer-time ditch nowadays for microscopical examination.

Such was the life of the shallow seas through perhaps a score or a hundred million years or more in the early Palæozoic Period. The land during that time was apparently absolutely barren. We find no trace nor hint of land life. Everything that lived in those days lived under water for most or all of its life. For ages that stagger the imagination that was all that there was of life, and before that time the earth had spun hot and lifeless for millions of years.

Between the formation of these Lower Palæozoic rocks in which the sea-scorpion and trilobite ruled and our own time there have intervened almost immeasurable ages represented by layers and masses of sedimentary rocks. There are first the Upper Palæozoic rocks, and above these the geologists distinguish two great divisions. Next above the Palæozoic come the *Mesozoic* (middle life) rocks, a second vast system of fossil-bearing rocks, representing perhaps a hundred millions of swift years, and containing a wonderful array of fossil remains, bones of giant reptiles, and the like, which we will presently describe; and above these again are the *Cainozoic* (recent life) rocks, a third great volume in the history of life, an unfinished volume of which the sand and mud that were carried out to sea yesterday by the rivers of the world, to bury the bones and scales and bodies and tracks that will become at last fossils of the things of to-day, constitute the last written leaf.

The markings and fossils in the rocks, and the rocks themselves, are the first historical documents. The history of life that men have puzzled out and are still puzzling out from them is called the Record of the Rocks. But when we call these rocks and the fossils a record and a history, it must not be supposed that there is any sign of an orderly keeping of a record. It is merely that whatever happens leaves some trace, if only we are intelligent enough to detect the meaning of that trace. Nor are the rocks of the world in orderly layers one above the other convenient for men to read. They are not like the books and pages of a library. They are torn, disrupted, interrupted, flung about, defaced, like a carelessly arranged office after it has experienced in succession a bombardment, a hostile military occupation, looting, an earthquake, riots, and a fire. And so it is that for countless generations this Record of the Rocks lay unsuspected beneath the feet of men. Fossils were known to the Ionian Greeks in the sixth century B.C., they were discussed at Alexandria by Eratosthenes and others in the third century B.C., a discussion which is summarized in Strabo's *Geography* (? 20–10 B.C.). They were known to the Latin poet Ovid, but he did not understand their nature. He thought they were the first rude efforts of creative power. They were noted by Arabic writers in the tenth century. Leonardo da Vinci, who lived so recently as the opening of the sixteenth century (1452–1519), was one of the first Europeans to grasp the real significance of fossils, and, as we have said, it has been only within the last century and a half that man has begun the serious and sustained deciphering of these long-neglected early pages of his world's history.

§ 2

In the previous section we have had no clear definition of life. It may be well to put plainly certain general facts about this new thing which was creeping in the shallow waters and intertidal muds of the Early Palæozoic Period, and which is, perhaps, confined to our planet alone in all the immensity of space.

Life differs from all things whatever that are without life in certain general aspects. There are the most wonderful differences among living things to-day, but all living things past and present agree in possessing *a certain power of growth*, all living things *take nourishment*, all living things *move about* as they feed and grow, though the movement may be no more than the spread of roots through the soil, or of branches in the air. Moreover, living things reproduce; they give rise to other similar living things, either by growing and then dividing, or by means of seeds or spores or eggs or other ways of producing young. *Reproduction* is a characteristic of life.

No living thing goes on living for ever. There seems to be *a limit of growth* for every kind of living thing. Among very small and simple living things, such as that microscopic blob of living matter the *Amœba*, an individual may grow and then divide completely into two new individuals, which again may divide in their turn. Many other microscopic creatures live actively for a time, grow, and then become quiet and inactive, enclose themselves in an outer covering and break up wholly into a number of still smaller things, spores, which are released and scattered and again grow into the likeness of their parent. Among more complex creatures the reproduction is not usually such simple division, though division does occur even in the case of many creatures big enough to be visible to the unassisted eye. But the rule with almost all larger beings is that the individual grows up to a certain limit of size. Then, before it becomes unwieldy, its growth declines and stops. As it reaches its full size it *matures*, it begins to produce young, which are either born alive or hatched from eggs. But all of its body does not produce young. Only a special part does that. After the individual has lived and produced offspring for some time, it ages and dies. It does so by a sort of necessity. There is a practical limit to its life as well as to its growth. These things are as true of plants as they are of animals. And they are not true of things that do not live. Non-living things, such as crystals, grow, but they have no set limits of growth or size, they *do not move of their own accord* and there is *no stir within them.* Crystals once formed may last unchanged for millions of years. There is *no reproduction* for any non-living thing.

This growth and dying and reproduction of living things leads to some very wonderful consequences. The young which a living thing produces are, either directly or after some intermediate stages and changes (such as the change of a caterpillar into a butterfly), like the parent living thing. But they are never exactly like it or like each other. There is always a slight difference, which we speak of as *individuality.* A thousand butterflies this year may produce very many more next year; these latter will look to us almost exactly like their predecessors, but each one will have just that slight difference. It is hard for us to see individuality in butterflies, because we do not observe them very closely, but it is easy for us to see it in men. All the men and women in the world now are descended from the men and women of A.D. 1800, but not one of us now is exactly the same as one of that vanished generation. And what is true of men and butterflies is true of every sort of living thing, of plants as of animals. Every species changes all its individualities in each generation. That is as true of all the minute creatures that swarmed and reproduced and died in the Archæozoic and Proterozoic seas as it is of men to-day.

Every species of living things is continually dying, and being born again as a multitude of fresh individuals.

Consider then, what must happen to a new-born generation of living things of any species. Some of the individuals will be stronger or sturdier or better suited to succeed in life in some way than the rest, many individuals will be weaker or less suited. In particular single cases any sort of luck or accident may occur, but *on the whole* the better equipped individuals will live and grow up and reproduce themselves and the weaker will *as a rule* go under. The latter will be less able to get food, to fight their enemies and pull through. So that in each generation there is, as it were, a picking over of a species, a picking out of most of the weak or unsuitable and a preference for the strong and suitable. This process is called *Natural Selection* or the *Survival of the Fittest,* though *Survival of the Fitter* would be the more precise expression.

It follows therefore, from the fact that living things grow and breed and die, that every species, so long as the conditions under which it lives remain the same, becomes more and more perfectly fitted to those conditions in every generation.

But conditions do not remain the same and every species lives a little uneasily in its condition. Adaptation is always imperfect and sometimes it is very imperfect. And coming to the help of life in fitting itself to the exigencies of circumstance is the fact that ever and again appear novelties in structure, sudden marked differences called *mutations,* differences much greater than the ordinary individual difference. These mutations may be encumbrances in the struggle for life, or helps, or they may not affect an animal's chances at all. In the former case they are rejected by natural selection, in the second they are welcomed and encouraged, in the third they may spread throughout a species, unchallenged, features neither helpful nor harmful, a spontaneous change. We do not as yet know what causes mutations; we know only that life is continually experimenting in this way and that its experiments come to the sieve of natural selection for endorsement, indifference or elimination. Mutation itself seems to be an entirely haphazard process. A mutation may just hit the urgent need of the time, it may be a pointless irrelevance, or it may be an absurd variation. In the latter case it produces a "monster" which dies. In the former it spreads throughout the species. The manner of its spreading, elucidated by the Abbé Mendel, is too long a story to relate here. The reader will find it clearly explained in the *Science of Life*—now a companion work to this *Outline.* In the *Science of Life* he will find also a long and exhaustive account of contemporary evolutionary discussion and a far ampler history of the forms of life before man.

Let us, to take a simple instance, here consider the case of some little, furry, whity-brown animal living in a bitterly cold land which is usually under snow. Such individuals as have the thickest, whitest fur will be least hurt by the cold, less seen by their enemies, and less conspicuous as they seek their prey. Every mutation in that direction will be advantageous. The fur of this species will thicken and its whiteness increase with every generation, until there is no advantage in carrying any more fur.

Imagine now a change of climate that brings warmth into the land, sweeps away the snows, makes white creatures glaringly visible during the greater part of the year and thick fur an encumbrance. Then every individual with a touch of brown in its colouring and a thinner fur will find itself at an advantage, and very white and heavy fur will be a handicap. Every favourable mutation will be seized upon and welcomed by natural selection during the ages of stress. There will be a weeding out of the white in favour of the brown in each generation. If this change of climate comes about too quickly, and no favourable mutations chance along, the species may be exterminated; but if mutations appear of a helpful kind and have time to spread themselves widely, the species, although it may have a hard time, may yet be able to change itself and adapt itself generation by generation. This change and adaptation is called the *Modification of Species.*

Perhaps this change of climate does not occur all over the lands inhabited by the species; maybe it occurs only on one side of some great arm of the sea or some great mountain range or such-like divide, and not on the other. A warm ocean current like the Gulf Stream may be deflected, and flow so as to warm one side of the barrier, leaving the other still cold. Then on the cold side this species will still be going on to its utmost possible furriness and whiteness, and on the other side it will be modifying towards brownness and a thinner coat.

At the same time there will probably be other changes going on; a difference in the paws perhaps may be encouraged here and discouraged there, because one half of the species will be frequently scratching through snow for its food, while the other will be scampering over brown earth. Probably, also, the difference of climate will mean differences in the sort of food available, and that may favour differences in the teeth and the digestive organs. And there may be changes in the sweat and oil glands of the skin due to the changes in the fur, and these will affect the excretory organs and all the internal chemistry of the body. And so through all the structure of the creature. A time may come when the two separated varieties of this formerly single species may become so unlike each other through the accumulation of individual and mutational differences as to be recognizably different species. Such a splitting up of a species in the course of generations into two or more species is called the *Differentiation of Species.*

And it should be clear to the reader that, given these elemental facts of life, given growth and death and reproduction with individual variation and mutation in a world that changes, life *must* change in this way, modification and differentiation *must* occur, old species *must* disappear and new ones appear. We have chosen for our instance here a familiar sort of animal, but what is true of furry beasts in snow and ice is true of all life, and equally true of the soft jellies and simple beginnings that flowed and crawled for hundreds of millions of years between the tidal levels and in the shallow, warm waters of the Proterozoic seas. They were all varying and mutating and living in a world of change that encouraged many of their variations and mutations.

The early life of the early world, when the blazing sun rose and set in only a quarter of the time it now takes, when the warm seas poured in great tides over the sandy and muddy shores of the rocky lands and the air was full of clouds and steam, must have been modified and varied, and species must have developed, at a great pace. Life was probably as swift and short as the days and years; the generations, which natural selection picked over, followed one another in rapid succession.

Natural selection is a slower process with man than with any other creature. It takes twenty years or more before an ordinary western European grows up and reproduces. In the case of most animals the new generation is on trial in a year or less. With such simple and lowly beings, however, as first appeared in the primordial seas, growth and reproduction was probably a matter of a few brief hours or even of a few brief minutes. Modification and differentiation of species must accordingly have been extremely rapid, and life had already developed a great variety of widely contrasted forms before it began to leave traces in the rocks.

The Record of the Rocks does not begin, therefore, with any group of the closely related forms from which all subsequent and existing creatures are descended. It begins in the Sea, with nearly every main division of the animal kingdom already represented. Plants are already plants, and animals animals.

The brachiopods are already in their shells, consuming much the same sort of food that oysters and mussels do now; the great water-scorpions crawl among the seaweeds, the trilobites roll up into balls and unroll and scuttle away. In that ancient mud there was probably as rich a life of infusoria and the like as one finds in a drop of ditch-water to-day. In the ocean there was an abundance of minute and translucent, often phosphorescent, beings.

But the land above the high-tide line was still, so far as we can guess, a stony wilderness without a trace of life.

III

LIFE AND CLIMATE

§ 1. *Life and Water: Water Plants.* § 2. *The Earliest Land Animals.* § 3. *Why Life Must Change Continually.*

§ 1

WHEREVER the shore line ran there was life, and that life went on in and by and with water as its home, its medium, and its fundamental necessity.

The first jelly-like beginnings of life must have perished whenever they got out of the water, as jelly-fish dry up and perish on our beaches to-day. Drying up was the fatal thing for life in those days, against which at first it had no protection. But in a world of rain-pools and shallow seas and tides, any variation that enabled a living thing to hold out and keep its moisture during hours of low tide or drought met with every encouragement in the circumstances of the time. There must have been a constant risk of stranding. And, on the other hand, life had to keep rather near the shore and beaches in the shallows because it had need of air (dissolved, of course, in the water) and light.

No creature can breathe, no creature can digest its food, without water. We talk of breathing air, but what all living things really do is to breathe oxygen dissolved in water. The air we ourselves breathe must first be dissolved in the moisture in our lungs; and all our food must be liquefied before it can be assimilated. Water-living creatures which are always under water, wave the freely exposed gills by which they breathe in that water, and extract the air dissolved in it. But a creature that is to be exposed for any time out of the water must have its body and its breathing apparatus protected from drying up. Before the seaweeds could creep up out of the Early Palæozoic seas into the intertidal line of the beach, they had to develop a tougher outer skin to hold their moisture. Before the ancestor of the sea-

Note its general resemblance, except for size, to the microscopic summer ditch-water life of to-day.

scorpion could survive being left by the tide, it had to develop its casing and armour. The trilobites probably developed their tough covering and rolled up into balls far less as a protection against each other, and any other enemies they may have possessed, than as a precaution against drying. And when presently, as we ascend the Palæozoic rocks, the fish appear, first of all the backboned or vertebrated animals, it is evident that a number of them are already adapted, by the protection of their gills with gill covers, and by a sort of primitive lung swimming-bladder, to face the same risk of temporary stranding.

Now, the weeds and plants that were adapting themselves to intertidal conditions were also bringing themselves into a region of brighter light; and light is very necessary and precious to all plants. Any development of structure that would stiffen them and hold them up to the light, so that instead of crumpling and flopping when the waters receded they would stand up outspread, was a great advantage. And so we find them developing fibre and support, and the beginning of *woody fibre* in them. The early plants reproduced by soft spores, or half-animal "gametes," that were released in water, were distributed by water and could only germinate under water. The early plants were tied, and most lowly plants to-day are tied, by the conditions of their life-cycle, to water. But here again there was a great advantage to be got by the development of some protection of the spores from drought that would enable reproduction to occur without submergence. So soon as a species could do that, it could live and reproduce and spread above the high-water mark, bathed in light and out of reach of the beating and distress of the waves. The main classificatory divisions of the larger plants mark stages in the release of plant life from the necessity of submergence by the development of woody support and of a method of reproduction that is more and more defiant of drying up. The lower plants are still the prisoner attendants of water. The lower mosses must live in damp, and even the development of the spore of the ferns demands at certain stages extreme wetness. The highest plants have carried freedom from water so far that they can live and reproduce if only there is some moisture in the soil below them. They have solved their problem of living out of water altogether.

The essentials of that problem were worked out through the vast æons of the Proterozoic Age and the early Palæozoic Age by nature's method of experiment and trial. Then slowly, but in great abundance, a variety of new plants began to swarm away from the sea and over the lower lands, still keeping to swamp and lagoon and watercourse as they spread.

There was not, perhaps, the same distinction between sea plants and fresh-water plants that there is to-day. The sea was probably less salt than it is now.

§ 2

And after the plants came the animal life.

There is no sort of land animal in the world, as there is no sort of land plant, whose structure is not primarily that of a water-inhabiting being which has been adapted through the modification and differentiation of species to life out of the water. This adaptation is attained in various ways. In the case of the land-scorpion the gill-plates of the primitive sea-scorpion are sunken into the body so as to make the lung-books secure from rapid evaporation. The gills of crustaceans, such as the crabs, which run about in the air are protected by the gill-cover extensions of the back shell or carapace. The ancestors of the insects developed a system of air pouches and air tubes, the tracheal tubes, which carry the air all over the body before it is dissolved. In the case of the vertebrated land animals, the gills of the ancestral fish were first supplemented and then replaced by a bag-like growth from the throat, the primitive lung swimming-bladder.

To this day there survive certain mudfish which enable us to understand very clearly the method by which the vertebrated land animals worked their way out of the water. These creatures (the African lung-fish, for example) are found in tropical regions in which there is a rainy full season and a dry season during which the rivers become mere ditches of baked mud. During the rainy season these fish swim about and breathe by gills like any other

Australian Lung-fish breathing air (after Dean)

fish. As the waters of the river evaporate they bury themselves in the mud, their gills go out of action, and the creature keeps itself alive, until the waters return, by swallowing air, which passes into its swimming-bladder. The Australian lung-fish, when it is caught by the drying-up of the river in stagnant pools, and the water has become deaerated and foul, rises to the surface and gulps air. A newt in a pond does exactly the same thing. These creatures still remain at the transition stage, the stage at which the ancestors of the higher vertebrated animals were released from their restriction to an under-water life.

The amphibia (frogs, newts, tritons, etc.) still show in their life-history all the stages in the process of this liberation. They are still dependent on water for their reproduction; their eggs must be laid in sunlit water, and there they must develop. The young tadpole has branching external gills that wave in the water; then a gill-cover grows back over them and forms a gill chamber. Then, as the creature's legs appear and its tail is absorbed, it begins to use its lungs, and its gills dwindle and vanish. The tadpole can live under water continually. The adult frog can live all the rest of its days in the air, but it can be drowned if it is kept steadfastly below water.

When we ascend the scale of existence to the level of the reptile, however, we find an egg which is protected from evaporation by a tough egg case, and this egg produces young which breathe by lungs from the very moment of hatching. The reptile is on all fours with the seeding plant in its freedom from the necessity to pass any stage of its life-cycle in water. But it can be drowned if it is kept under water without intermission.

The later Palæozoic rocks of the northern hemisphere give us the materials for a series of pictures of this slow spreading of life over the land. Geographically it was an age of lagoons and shallow seas very favourable to this invasion. It is possible that as yet there were no seas as deep as the present oceans. The new plants, now that they had acquired the power to live the new aerial life, developed with an extraordinary richness and variety.

There were as yet no true flowering plants, no grasses nor trees that shed their leaves in winter; the first "flora" consisted of great tree-ferns, gigantic equisetums, cycad ferns, and kindred vegetation. Many of these plants took the form of huge-stemmed trees, of which great multitudes of trunks survive fossilized to this day. Some of these trees were over a hundred feet high, they belonged to orders and classes now vanished from the world. They stood with their stems in the water, in which no doubt there was a thick tangle of soft mosses and green slime and fungoid growths that left few plain vestiges behind them. The abundant pulped-up remains of these first swamp forests constitute the main coal-measures of the world to-day.

Amidst this luxuriant primitive vegetation crawled and glided and flew the first insects. They were rigid-winged, four-winged creatures, often very big, some of them having wings measuring a foot in length. There were numerous dragon-flies—one found in the Belgian coal-measures had a wing span of twenty-nine inches! There were also a great variety of flying cockroaches. Scorpions abounded, and a number of early spiders. The spinnerets of these spiders were absent or simple, so that they made no webs or very simple ones. Land snails appeared. So, too, did the first-known step of our own ancestry upon land, the amphibia. As we ascend the higher levels of the later Palæozoic record we find the process of air adaptation has gone as far as the appearance of true reptiles amidst the abundant and various amphibia.

The land life of the Upper Palæozoic Age was the life of an ever-green swamp forest without flowers or birds or the noises of modern insects. If a man could be transported back to those verdurous lagoons he would probably be terrified at the stillness. He would hear little but the ripple of water, the sound of wind in the leaves, or the crash of some falling tree. Everything would seem waiting and expectant. The trees and plants would look more like magnified mosses than any trees or plants he knew. There were no big land beasts at all; wallowing amphibia and primitive reptiles were the very highest creatures that life had so far produced. None of them had yet attained to very great dimensions. Whatever land lay away from the water or high above the water was still altogether barren and lifeless. But steadfastly, generation by generation, life was creeping away from the shallow sea-water of its beginning.

§ 3

The Record of the Rocks is like a great book that has been carelessly misused. All its pages are torn, worn, and defaced, and many are altogether missing. The outline of the story that we sketch here has been pieced together slowly and painfully in an investigation that is still incomplete and still in progress. The Carboniferous rocks, the "coal-measures," give us a vision of the first great expansion of life over the wet lowlands. Then come the torn pages of the Permian rocks (which count as the last of the Palæozoic) that preserve little of the land vestiges of their age. Only after a long interval of time does the history spread out generously again.

The Permian rocks record an age of harshness and desolation in the world's history. They mark the phase of transition from the Palæozoic age of fish and amphibia to the Mesozoic age of reptiles.

It must be borne in mind that great changes of climate have always been in progress, sometimes stimulating and sometimes checking life. Every species of living thing is always adapting itself more and more closely to its conditions, which are always changing. There is no finality in adaptation. There is a continuing urgency towards change.

We do, however, find certain creatures of a lowly type which early adapted themselves to widespread simple conditions so completely that they have never been greatly modified or exterminated or replaced. For example, there is a little shell-fish called *Lingula* fitted to an obscure sedentary life in warm seas. This genus has endured without conspicuous change throughout the entire geological record.

On the other hand, geologists show us collections of fossils in which one can trace modifications in only a few thousand years, as climate, food and enemies have changed.

About these changes of climate that are always in progress on the earth's surface some explanations are necessary here. They are not periodic changes; they are slow fluctuations between heat and cold. The reader must not think that because the sun and earth were once incandescent the climatic history of the world is a simple story of cooling down. The centre of the earth is certainly very hot to this day, but we feel nothing of that internal heat at the surface; the internal heat, except for volcanoes and hot springs, has not been perceptible at the surface since first the rocks grew solid. Even in the Azoic or Archæozoic Age there are traces in ice-worn rocks and the like of periods of intense cold. Such cold waves have always been going on everywhere, alternately with warmer conditions. And there have been periods of great wetness and periods of great dryness throughout the earth. They depend upon astronomical and terrestrial fluctuations of extreme complexity into which we will not enter here.

And, in accordance, we find from the Record in the Rocks that there have been long periods of expansion and multiplication when life flowed and abounded and varied, and harsh ages when there was a great weeding out and disappearance of species, genera, and classes, and the learning of stern lessons by all that survived.

It is probable that the warm spells have been long relatively to the cold ages. Our world to-day seems to be emerging with fluctuations from a prolonged phase of adversity and extreme conditions. Half a million years ahead it may be a winterless world with trees and vegetation even in the polar circles. At present we have no certainty in such a forecast, but as knowledge increases it may be possible that our race will make its plans thousands of years ahead to meet the coming changes.

DIAGRAM OF LIFE IN THE LATER PALAEOZOIC AGE

Life is creeping out of the water. An insect, like a dragon-fly, is shown. There were amphibia like gigantic newts and salamanders, and even primitive reptiles in these swamps.

IV

THE AGE OF REPTILES

§ 1. *The Age of Lowland Life.* § 2. *Dragons.* § 3. *The First Birds.* § 4. *An Age of Hardship and Death.* § 5. *The First Appearance of Fur and Feathers.*

§ 1

WE KNOW that for hundreds of thousands of years the wetness and warmth, the shallow lagoon conditions, that made possible the vast accumulations of vegetable matter which, compressed and mummified, are now coal, prevailed over most of the world. There were some cold intervals, it is true; but they did not last long enough to destroy the growths. Then that long age of luxuriant low-grade vegetation drew to its end, and for a time life on the earth seems to have undergone a period of world-wide bleakness. That is, so to speak, Part I in the history of life on this planet.

When the story resumes again after this arrest at the end of the Palæozoic Period, we find life entering upon a fresh phase of richness and expansion. Vegetation has made great advances in the art of living out of water. While the Palæozoic plants of the coal-measures probably grew with swamp water flowing over their roots, the Mesozoic flora from its very outset included palm-like cycads and low-ground conifers that were distinctly land plants growing on soil above the water level.

The lower levels of the Mesozoic land were no doubt covered by great fern brakes and shrubby bush and a kind of jungle growth of trees. But there existed as yet no grass, no turf or greensward, and no flowering plants at all, great or small. Probably the Mesozoic was not an age of very brightly coloured vegetation. It must have had a flora green in the wet season and brown and purple in the dry. Probably it was not nearly so beautiful as are the woods and thickets of to-day. There were no gay flowers, no bright autumn tints, before the fall of the leaf, because there was as yet no fall of the leaf. And beyond the lower levels the world was still barren, still unclothed, still exposed without any mitigation to the wear and tear of the wind and rain.

When one speaks of conifers in the Mesozoic the reader must not think of the pines and firs that clothe the high mountain slopes of our time. He must think of lowland evergreens. The mountains were still as bare and lifeless as ever. The only colour effects among the mountains were the colour effects of naked rock, such colours as make the landscape of Colorado so marvellous to-day.

Amidst this spreading vegetation of the lower plains the reptiles were increasing mightily in multitude and variety. They were now in many cases absolutely land animals. There are numerous anatomical points of distinction between a reptile and an amphibian; they held good between such reptiles and amphibians as prevailed in the carboniferous time of the Upper Palæozoic; but the fundamental difference between reptiles and amphibians which matters in this history is that the amphibian must go back to the water to lay its eggs, and that in the early stages of its life it must live in and under water. The reptile, on the other hand, has cut out all the tadpole stages from its life cycle, or, to be more exact, its tadpole stages are got through before the young leave the egg case. The reptile has come out of the water altogether. Some had gone back to it again, just as the hippopotamus and otter among mammals have gone back; but that is a further extension of the story, that is a detail and a complication, to which we cannot give much attention in this *Outline*.

In the Palæozoic Period, as we have said, life had not spread beyond the swampy river valleys and the borders of sea lagoons and the like; but in the Mesozoic life was growing ever more accustomed to the thinner medium of the air, was sweeping boldly up over the plains and towards the hill-sides. It is well for the student of human history and the human future to note that. If a disembodied intelligence with no knowledge of the future had come to earth and studied life during the Early Palæozoic Age, he might very reasonably have concluded that life was absolutely confined to the water, and that it could never spread over the land. It found a way. In the Later Palæozoic Period that visitant might have been equally sure that life could not go beyond the edge of a swamp. The Mesozoic Period would still have found him setting bounds to life far more limited than the bounds that are set to-day. And so to-day, though we mark how life and man are still limited to five miles of air and a depth of perhaps a mile or so of sea, we must not conclude from that present limitation that life, through man, may not presently spread out and up and down to a range of living as yet inconceivable.

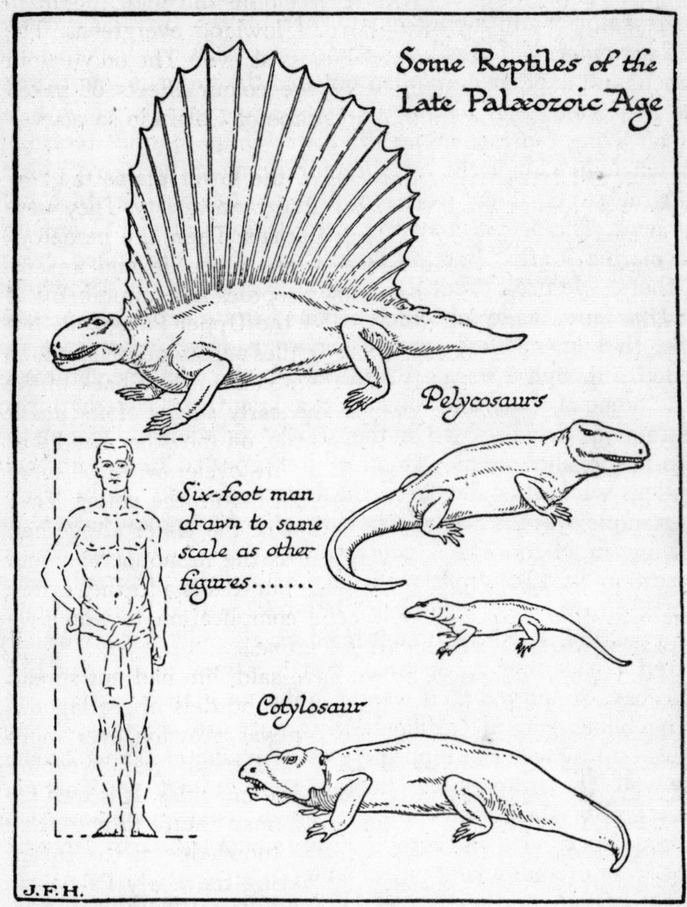

The earliest known reptiles were beasts with great bellies and not very powerful legs, very like their kindred amphibia, wallowing as the crocodile wallows to this day; but in the Mesozoic they soon began to stand up and go stoutly on all-fours, and several great sections of them began to balance themselves on tail and hind-legs, rather as the kangaroos do now, in order to release the fore-limbs for grasping food. The bones of one notable division of reptiles which retained a quadrupedal habit, a division of which many remains have been found in South African and Russian Early Mesozoic deposits, display a number of characters which approach those of the mammalian skeleton, and because of this resemblance to the mammals (beasts) this division is called the *Theriomorpha* (beastlike). Another division was the crocodile branch, and another developed towards the tortoises and turtles. The *Plesiosaurs* and *Ichthyosaurs* were two groups which have left no living representatives; they were huge reptiles returning to a whale-like life in the sea. *Pliosaurus*, one of the largest plesiosaurs, measured thirty feet from snout to tail tip—of which half was neck. The *Mosasaurs* were a third group of great porpoise-like marine lizards. But the largest and most diversified group of these Mesozoic reptiles was a varied group known as the *Dinosaurs*, many of which attained quite enormous proportions. In bigness these greater Dinosaurs have never been exceeded, although the sea can still show in the whales creatures as great. Some of these, and the largest among them, were herbivorous animals; they browsed on the rushy vegetation and among the ferns and bushes, or they stood up and grasped trees with their fore-legs while they devoured the foliage. Among the browsers, for example, was the *Diplodocus carnegii*, which measured eighty-four feet in length. The *Gigantosaurus*, disinterred by a German expedition in 1912 from rocks in East Africa, was still more colossal—it measured well over a hundred feet! Still larger bones are appearing. These great monsters had legs, and they are usually figured as standing up on them; but it is very doubtful if they could have supported their weight in this way out of water.

The bones end in cartilage: the joints are not very strong. Buoyed up by water or mud these monsters could have got along very well. The ordinary big Dinosaur has a bulky lower body and lower limbs, which were probably almost always submerged or floating. Neck, head and fore-limbs are much lighter in structure; these were probably kept out of water.

Another noteworthy type of Dinosaur was the *Triceratops*, a reptilian parallel of the hippopotamus, but with a rhinoceros-like horn. There were also a number of great flesh-eaters who preyed upon these herbivores. Of these, *Tyrannosaurus* seems almost the last word in "frightfulness" among living things. Some species of this genus measured forty feet from snout to tail. Apparently it carried this vast body kangaroo fashion on its tail and hind-

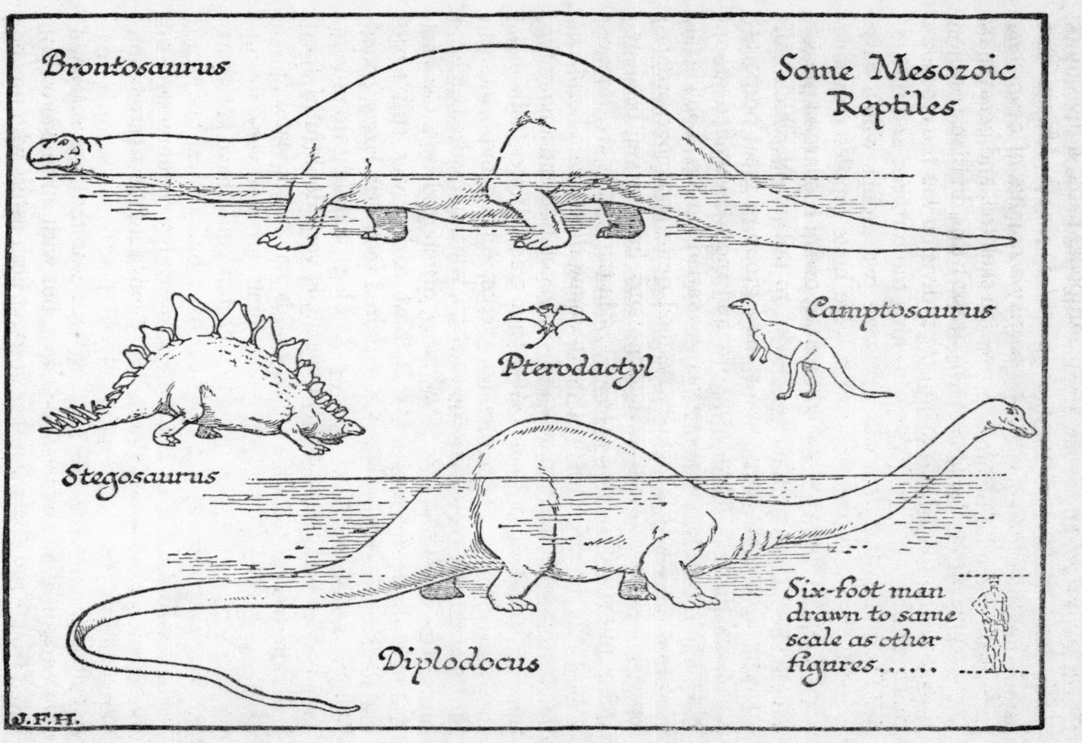
Some Mesozoic Reptiles
Brontosaurus
Camptosaurus
Pterodactyl
Stegosaurus
Diplodocus
Six-foot man drawn to same scale as other figures......
J.F.H.

legs. Probably it reared itself up. Some authorities even suppose that it leapt through the air. If so, it possessed muscles of a quite miraculous quality. A leaping elephant would be a far less astounding idea. Much more probably it waded half submerged in pursuit of the herbivorous marsh saurians. It may have fought out its kills in channels and sheets of water like the Norfolk Broads or the Everglades of Florida.

§ 2

One special development of the dinosaurian type of reptile was a light, hopping, climbing group of creatures which developed a bat-like web between the fourth finger and the side of the body which was used in gliding from tree to tree after the fashion of the flying squirrels. These bat-lizards were the *Pterodactyls*. They are often described as *flying* reptiles, and pictures are drawn of Mesozoic scenery in which they are seen soaring and swooping about. But their breastbone has no keel such as the breastbone of a bird has for the attachment of muscles strong enough for long-sustained flying. They must have flitted about like bats. They must have had a grotesque resemblance to heraldic dragons, and they played the part of bat-like birds in the Mesozoic jungles. But bird-like though they were, they were not birds nor ancestors of birds. The structure of their wings was altogether different from that of birds. The structure of their wings was that of a hand with one long finger and a web; the wing of a bird is like an arm with feathers projecting from its hind edge. And these Pterodactyls, so far as we know, had no feathers. The feather is a very specialized skin structure which was developed only once in the evolution of life.

§ 3

Far less prevalent at this time were certain other truly bird-like creatures, of which the earlier sorts also hopped and clambered and the later sorts skimmed and flew. These were at first—by all the standards of classification—Reptile. They developed into true birds as their reptilian scales became long and complicated fronds rather than scales, and so at last, by much spreading and splitting, feathers. Feathers are the distinctive covering of birds, and they give a power of resisting heat and cold far greater than that of any other integumentary covering except, perhaps, the thickest fur. At a very early stage this novel covering of feathers, this new heat-proof contrivance that life had chanced upon, enabled many species of birds to invade a province for which the pterodactyl was ill equipped. They took to sea fishing—if,

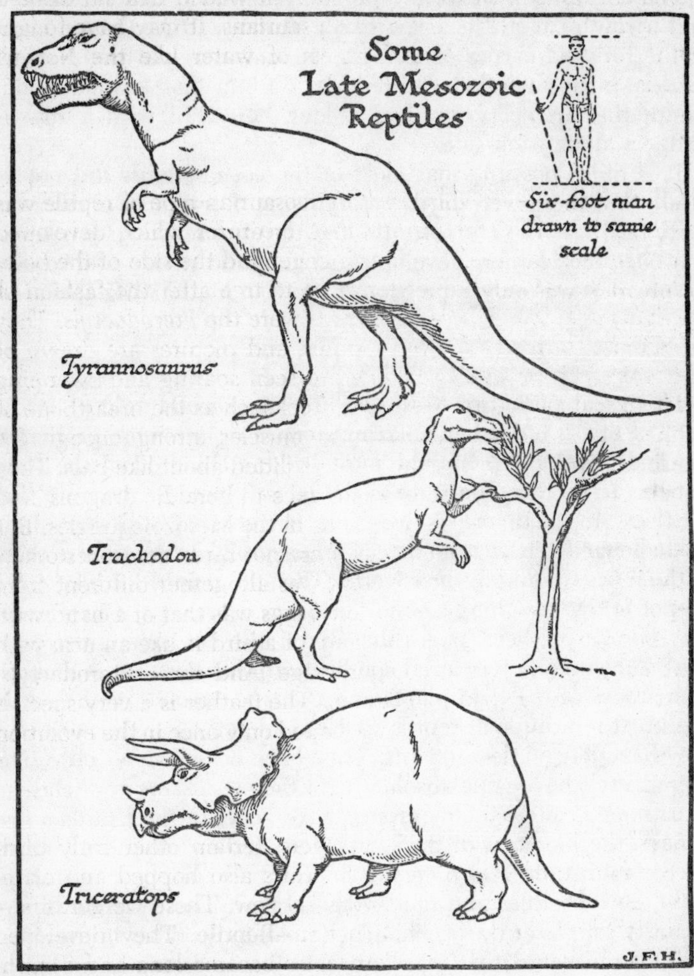

indeed, they did not begin with it—and spread to the north and south polewards beyond the temperature limits set to the true reptiles. The earliest birds seem to have been carnivorous divers and water-birds. To this day some of the most primitive bird forms are found among the sea-birds of the Arctic and Antarctic seas, and it is among these sea-birds that zoologists still find lingering traces of teeth which have otherwise vanished completely from the beak of the bird.

The earliest known bird (the *Archæopteryx*) had no beak; it had a row of teeth in a jaw like a reptile's. It had three claws at the forward corner of its wing. Its tail, too, was peculiar. All modern birds have their tail feathers set in a short compact bony rump; the *Archæopteryx* had a long bony tail with a row of feathers along each side.

It is quite possible that most of the earliest birds did not fly at all, that there were birds before flying. For example, one very early bird was the *Hesperornis,* and this had no wings whatever. But once the feathers developed, so light and strong, and so easy to spread, it was only a question of time before the wing appeared.

§ 4

This great period of Mesozoic life, this second volume of the book of life, is indeed an amazing story of reptilian life proliferating and developing. But the most striking thing of all the story remains to be told. Right up to the latest Mesozoic rocks we find all these reptilian orders we have enumerated still flourishing unchallenged. There is no hint of an enemy or competitor to them in the relics we find of their world. Then the record is broken. We do not know how long a time the break represents; many pages may be missing here, pages that may represent some great cataclysmal change of terrestrial conditions. When next we find abundant traces of the land plants and the land animals of the earth, this great multitude of reptile species had gone. For the most part they have left no descendants. They have been "wiped out." The pterodactyls have gone absolutely; of the plesiosaurs and ichthyosaurs none is alive; the mosasaurs have gone; of the lizards a few remain, the monitors of the Dutch East Indies being the largest; all the multitude and diversity of the dinosaurs have vanished. Only the crocodiles and the turtles and tortoises carry on in any quantity into later times. The place of all these types in the spectacle of the world that the Cainozoic fossils presently unfold to us is taken by other animals not closely related to the Mesozoic reptiles and certainly not descended from any of their ruling types. A new kind of life is in possession of the world.

This apparently abrupt ending-up of the reptiles is, beyond all question, the most striking revolution in the whole history of the earth before the coming of mankind. It is probably connected with the close of a vast period of equable warm conditions and the onset of a new austerer age, in which the winters were bitterer

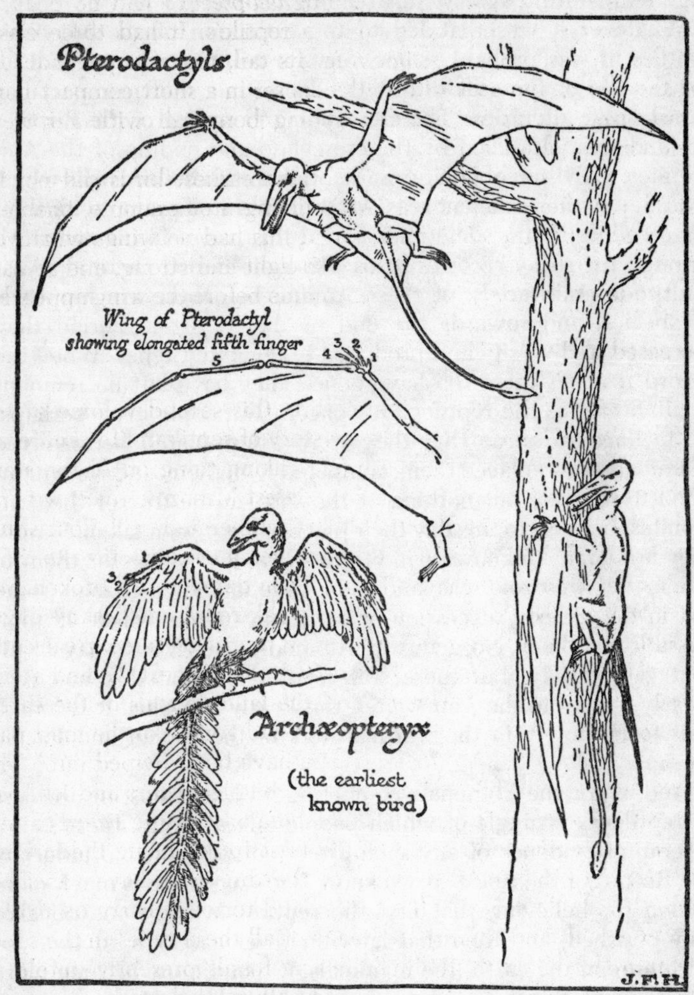

and the summers brief but hot. The Mesozoic life, animal and vegetable alike, was adapted to warm conditions and capable of little resistance to cold. The new life, on the other hand, was before all things capable of resisting great changes of temperature.

It was not only that the Reptiles as such had no fur nor feathers to equalize temperature conditions, but that the structure of the Reptilian heart is also not adapted to the maintenance of a high temperature against surrounding cold.

Whatever it was that led to the extinction of the Mesozoic reptiles, it was probably some very far-reaching change indeed, for the life of the seas did at the same time undergo a similar catastrophic alteration. The crescendo and ending of the Reptiles on land was paralleled by the crescendo and ending of the Ammonites, a division of creatures like squids with coiled shells which swarmed in those ancient seas. Most people are familiar with their huge coiling shells, sometimes two feet or more in diameter. All through the rocky record of this Mesozoic Period there is a vast multitude and variety of these Ammonites; there are hundreds of species, and towards the end of the Mesozoic Period they increased in diversity and produced exaggerated types. When the record resumes these too have gone. They have left no remnant at all. So far as the reptiles are concerned, people may, perhaps, be inclined to argue that they were exterminated because the Mammals that replaced them, competed with them, and were more fitted to survive; but nothing of the sort can be true of the Ammonites, because to this day their place has not been taken. Simply they are gone. Unknown conditions made it possible for them to live in the Mesozoic seas, and then some unknown change, some jolt in the orderly succession of days and seasons, made life impossible for them. No genus of Ammonite survives to-day of all that vast variety, but there still exists one isolated genus very closely related to the Ammonites, the Pearly Nautilus. It is found, it is to be noted, in the warm waters of the Indian and Pacific Oceans.

And as for the Mammals competing with and ousting the less fit reptiles, a struggle of which people talk at times, there is not a scrap of evidence of any such direct competition. To judge by the Record of the Rocks as we know it to-day, there is much more reason for believing that first the reptiles in some inexplicable way perished, and then that later on, after a very hard time for all life upon the earth, the mammals, as conditions became more genial again, developed and spread to fill the vacant world.

Nothing is known of the causes of this revolution in terrestrial conditions. In a previous section it has been said that if the pole of the earth were square to the plane of its orbit there would be no change of the seasons, Suppose now that in the earlier part of the world's history the earth's equator was not inclined or inclined very little to the orbit, then there would be just those equable conditions the fauna and flora of the Mesozoic Period

seem to indicate. Suppose, however, that some unknown cause tilted the axis of rotation to its present obliquity. At once all over the earth would come the alternation of summer and winter, heat and cold, and life would have to adapt itself afresh or die. The Reptiles perished for the most part, the Ammonites and a great variety of other creatures certainly perished, and only slowly was the abundance of life restored. But no one has ever been able to suggest a force that could suddenly twist our spinning world in that fashion. We do not know what jars and jolts the solar system may have suffered in the past. We are left guessing. Some huge dark projectile from outer space may have come hurtling through the planets and deflected or even struck our world and turned the whole course of evolution into a new direction.

Little projectiles of that sort are always striking us. They come flying into our atmosphere and catch fire with the heat of their rush through the air and burn—the shooting stars. Most of these meteors are burnt to nothing before they reach the ground, but many have reached and continue to reach the earth. Some in our museums are several yards in diameter.

Perhaps once one was big enough to produce a change such as we have supposed.

But this is a lapse into pure speculation. Let us return to our facts.

§ 5

Were there mammals in the Mesozoic Period?

No doubt there were, but they were small, obscure and rare, and palæontology has very little to tell about them. Patiently and steadily the geologists gather fresh evidence and reason out completer conclusions. At any time some new deposit may reveal fossils that will illuminate this question. Certainly either mammals, or the ancestors of the mammals, must have lived throughout the Mesozoic Period. In the very opening chapter of the Mesozoic volume of the Record there were those Theriomorphous Reptiles to which we have already alluded, and in the later Mesozoic a number of small jaw-bones are found, entirely mammalian in character.

But there is not a scrap, not a bone, to suggest that there lived any Mesozoic mammal which could look a dinosaur in the face. The Mesozoic mammals or mammal-like reptiles—for we do not know clearly which they were—seem to have been all obscure little beasts of the size of mice and rats, more like a downtrodden order of reptiles than a distinct class; probably they still laid eggs and were developing only slowly their distinctive covering of hair. They lived away from big waters, and perhaps in the desolate uplands, as marmots do now; probably they lived there beyond the pursuit of the carnivorous dinosaurs. Some, perhaps, went on all-fours, some chiefly went on their hind-legs and clambered with their fore-limbs. They became fossils only so occasionally that chance has not yet revealed a single complete skeleton in the whole long record of the Mesozoic rocks by which to check these guesses.

These little Theriomorphs, these ancestral mammals, developed hair. Hairs, like feathers, are long and elaborately specialized scales. Hair is, perhaps, the clue to the salvation of the early mammals. Leading lives upon the margin of existence, away from the marshes and the warmth, they developed an outer covering only second in its warmth-holding (or heat-resisting) powers to the down and feathers of the Arctic sea-birds. And so the mammals, like the birds, held out through the age of hardship between the Mesozoic and Cainozoic Ages, to which most of the true reptiles succumbed.

All the main characteristics of the flora and sea and land fauna that disappeared with the end of the Mesozoic Age were such as were adapted to an equable climate and to shallow and swampy regions. But, in the case of their Cainozoic successors, both hair and feathers gave a *power of resistance to variable temperatures* such as no reptile possessed, and with it they gave a range far greater than any animal had hitherto attained.

The range of life of the Lower Palæozoic Period was confined to warm water.

The range of life of the Upper Palæozoic Period was mainly confined to warm water or to warm swamps and wet ground.

The range of life of the Mesozoic Period as we know it was largely confined to water and fairly low-lying valley regions under equable conditions.

But in each of these periods there were types involuntarily extending the range of life beyond the prevailing limits; and when ages of extreme conditions prevailed, it was these marginal types which survived to inherit the depopulated world.

That, perhaps, is the most general statement we can make about the story of the geological record; it is a story of widening range. Classes, genera, and species of animals appear and disappear, but the range widens. It widens always. Life has never had so great a range as it has to-day. Life to-day, in the form of man, goes higher in the air than it has ever done before; man's geographical range is from pole to pole, he goes under the water in submarines, he sounds the cold, lifeless darkness of the deepest seas, he burrows into virgin levels of the rocks, and in thought and knowledge he pierces to the centre of the earth and reaches out to the uttermost star. Yet in all the relics of the Mesozoic time we find no certain memorials of his ancestry. His ancestors, like the ancestors of all the kindred mammals, must have been creatures so rare, so obscure, and so remote that they have left scarcely a trace amidst the abundant vestiges of the monsters that wallowed rejoicing in the steamy air and lush vegetation of the Mesozoic lagoons, or crawled or hopped or fluttered over the great river plains of that time.

V

THE AGE OF MAMMALS

§ 1. *A New Age of Life.* § 2. *Tradition Comes into the World.* § 3. *An Age of Brain Growth.* § 4. *The World Grows Hard Again.*

§ 1

THE third great division of the geological record sketched out in the beginning of chapter 2, the Cainozoic, opens with a world already physically very like the world we live in to-day. Probably the day was at first still perceptibly shorter, but the scenery had become very modern in its character. Climate was, of course, undergoing, age by age, its incessant and irregular variations; lands that are temperate to-day have passed, since the Cainozoic Age began, through phases of great warmth, intense cold, and extreme dryness; there may have been variations in the landscape, but, if it altered, it altered to nothing that cannot still be paralleled to-day in some part or other of the world.

In the place of the cycads, sequoias, and strange conifers of the Mesozoic, the plant names that now appear in the lists of fossils include birch, beech, holly, tulip trees, ivy, sweet gum, bread-fruit trees. Palms were now very important. Flowers had developed concurrently with bees and butterflies. We have come to the age of flowers. Flowering plants had already been in evidence in the later levels of the Mesozoic, that is, the American Cretaceous, but now they dominated the scene altogether and everywhere. Grass was becoming a great fact in the world. Certain grasses, too, had appeared in the later Mesozoic, but only with the Cainozoic Period came grass plains and turf spreading wide over a world that was once barren stone.

The period opened with a long phase of considerable warmth; then the world cooled. In the opening of this third part of the record, this Cainozoic Period, a gigantic crumpling of the earth's crust and an upheaval of mountain ranges was in progress. The Alps, the Andes, the Himalayas, are all Cainozoic mountain ranges; the background of an early Cainozoic scene to be typical should display an active volcano or so. It must have been an age of great earthquakes also.

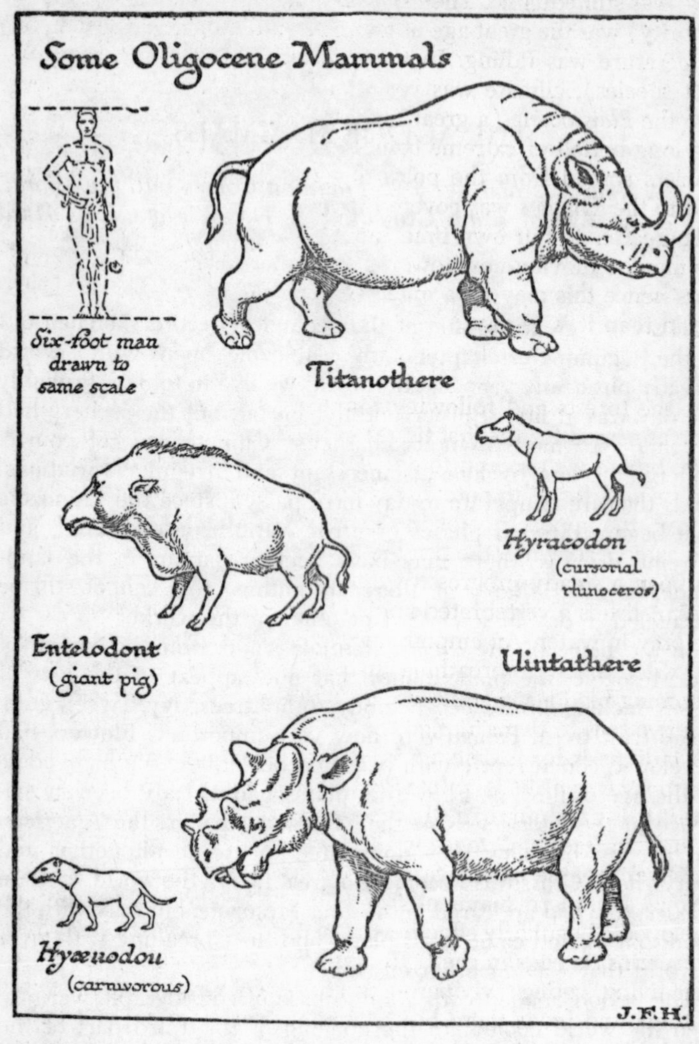

Geologists make certain main divisions of the Cainozoic Period, and it will be convenient to name them here and to indicate their climate. First comes the *Eocene* (which means "dawn of recent life"), an age of exceptional warmth in the world's history, subdivided into an older and newer Eocene; then the *Oligocene* (meaning "but little of recent life"), in which the climate was still equable. The *Miocene* (with living species still in a minority) was the great age of mountain building, and the general temperature was falling. In the *Pliocene* (more living than extinct species), climate was very much at its present phase; but with the *Pleistocene* (a great majority of living species) there set in a long period of extreme conditions—it was the Great Ice Age. Glaciers spread from the poles towards the equator, until England to the Thames was covered in ice.

Thereafter to our own time came a period of partial recovery. We may be moving now towards a warmer phase. Half a million years hence this may be a much sunnier and pleasanter world to live in than it is to-day.

§ 2

In the forests and following the grass over the Eocene plains there appeared for the first time a variety and abundance of mammals. Before we proceed to any description of these mammals, it may be well for us to note in general terms what a mammal is.

From the appearance of the vertebrated animals in the Lower Palæozoic Age, when the fish first swarmed out into the sea, there has been a steady progressive development of vertebrated creatures. A fish is a vertebrated animal that breathes by gills and can live only in water. An amphibian may be described as a fish that has added to its gill-breathing the power of breathing air with its swimming-bladder in adult life, and that has also developed limbs with five toes to them in place of the fins of a fish.

A tadpole is for a time a fish; it becomes a land creature as it develops. A reptile is a further stage in this detachment from water; it is an amphibian that is no longer amphibious; it passes through its tadpole stage—its fish stage, that is—in an egg. It can never breathe under water as a tadpole can do.

Now, a modern mammal is really a sort of reptile that has developed a peculiarly effective protective covering, hair; and that also retains its eggs in the body until they hatch so that it brings forth living young (viviparous); and even after birth it cares for them and feeds them by its mammæ for a longer or shorter period. Some reptiles, some vipers, for example, are viviparous, but none stands by its young as the real mammals do. Both the birds and the mammals, which escaped whatever destructive forces made an end of the Mesozoic reptiles, and which survived to dominate the Cainozoic world, have these two things in common—first, a far more effective protection against changes of temperature than any other variation of the reptile type ever produced, and, secondly, a peculiar care for their eggs to protect them from cold, the bird by incubation and the mammal by retention, and a disposition to look after the young for a certain period after hatching or birth. In comparison with the mammal, the ordinary reptile is altogether reckless of its offspring.

Hair was evidently the earliest distinction of the mammals from the rest of the reptiles. It is doubtful if the particular Theriodont reptiles who were developing hair in the early Mesozoic were viviparous. Two mammals survive to this day which not only do not suckle their young, but which lay eggs, the *Ornithorhynchus* and the *Echidna*, and in the Eocene there were a number of allied forms. These two creatures, although they do not suckle their young, secrete a nutritive fluid from glands scattered over the skin on the belly side. But the glands are not gathered into mammæ with nipples for suckling, as they are in other mammals. The stuff oozes out while the mother lies on her back, and the young browse upon her moist skin. They are the survivors of what was probably a much larger number and variety of small egg-laying hairy creatures, hairy reptiles, hoppers, climbers, and runners, which include the Mesozoic ancestors of all existing mammals up to and including man. At any time in some out-of-the-way deposit there may yet be a find of such "missing links."

We may put the essential facts about mammalian reproduction in another way. The *mammal is a family animal.* And the family habit involved the possibility of a new sort of continuity of experience in the world. Compare the completely closed-in life of an individual lizard with the life of even a quite lowly mammal of almost any kind. The former has no mental continuity with anything beyond itself; it is a little self-contained globe of experience that serves its purpose and ends; but the latter "picks up" from its mother, and "hands on" to its offspring.

All the mammals, except for the two genera we have named, had already before the lower Eocene Age arrived at this stage of pre-adult dependence and imitation. They were all more or less imitative in youth and capable of a certain modicum of education; they all, as a part of their development, received a certain amount of care and example and even direction from their mother. This is as true of the hyæna and rhinoceros as it is of the dog or man; the difference of educability is enormous, but the fact of protection and educability in the young stage is undeniable.

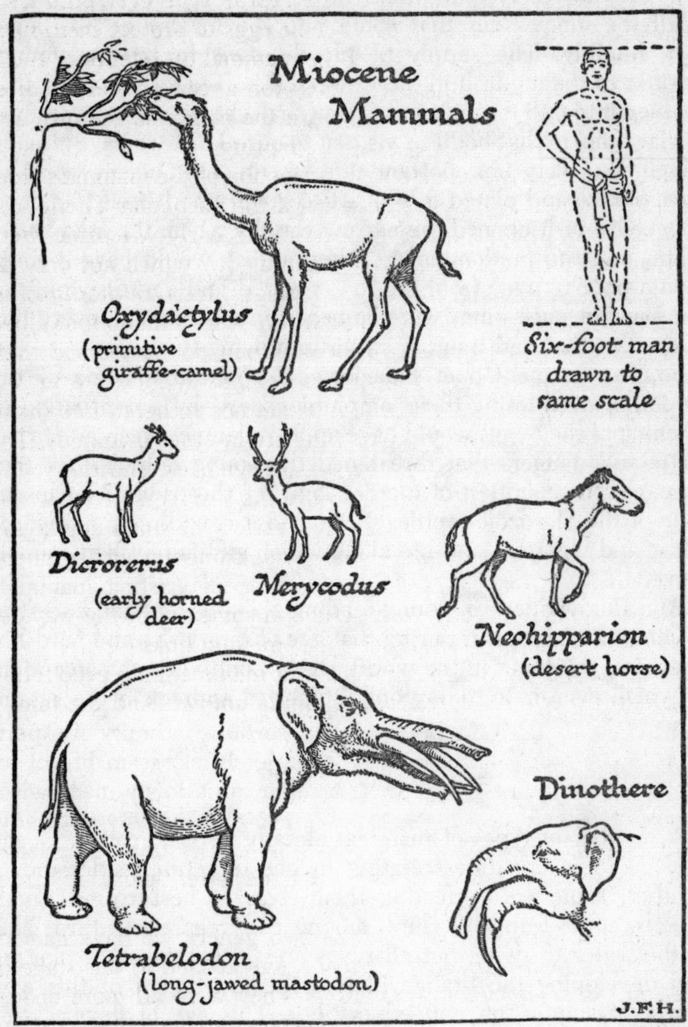

So far as the vertebrated animals go, these new mammals, with their viviparous, young-protecting disposition, and these new birds, with their incubating, young-protecting disposition, introduce at the opening of the Cainozoic Period a fresh thing into the expanding story of life, namely, social association, the addition to hard and inflexible instinct of *tradition*, and the nervous organization necessary to receive tradition.

All the innovations that come into the history of life begin very humbly. The supply of blood-vessels in the swimming-bladder of the mudfish in the Lower Palæozoic torrent-river, that enabled it to pull through a season of drought, would have seemed at that time, to that bodiless visitant to our planet we have already imagined, a very unimportant side fact in that ancient world of great sharks and plated fishes, sea-scorpions, and coral reefs and seaweed; but it opened the narrow way by which the land vertebrates arose to predominance. The mudfish would have seemed then a poor refugee from the too crowded and aggressive life of the sea. But once lungs were launched into the world, every line of descent that had lungs went on improving them.

So, too, in the Upper Palæozoic, the fact that some of the amphibia were losing their "amphibiousness" by a retardation of hatching of their eggs would have appeared a mere response to the distressful dangers that threatened the young tadpole. Yet that prepared the conquest of the dry land for the triumphant multitude of the Mesozoic reptiles. It opened a new direction towards a free and vigorous land-life along which all the reptilian animals moved.

And this viviparous, young-tending training that the ancestral mammalia underwent, during that age of inferiority and hardship for them, set going in the world a new continuity of perception, of which even man to-day only begins to appreciate the significance.

§ 3

A number of types of mammal already appear in the Eocene Period. Some are differentiating in one direction, and some in another; some are perfecting themselves as herbivorous quadrupeds, some leap and climb among the trees, some turn back to the water to swim, but all types are unconsciously exploiting and developing the brain which is the instrument of this new power of acquisition and educability. This age of flowers, this age of birds and mammals, the Cainozoic Age, might also be called the Age of the Growing Brain. In the Eocene rocks are found small early predecessors of the horse (Eohippus), tiny camels, pigs, early tapirs, early hedgehogs, monkeys and lemurs, opossums and carnivores. Now, all these were more or less ancestral to living forms, and all had brains relatively much smaller than their living representatives. There is, for instance, an early rhinoceros-like beast, *Titanotherium,* with a brain not one-tenth the size of that of the existing rhinoceros. The latter is by no means a perfect type of the attentive and submissive student, but even so it is ten times more observant and teachable than its predecessor. This sort of thing is true of all the orders and families that survive until to-day. All the Cainozoic mammals were doing this one thing in common under the urgency of a common necessity; they were all growing brain. It was a parallel advance. In the same order or family to-day, the brain is usually from six to ten times what it was in the Eocene ancestor.

The Eocene Period displayed a whole series of herbivorous brutes of which no representative survives to-day. Such were the *Uintatheres* and the *Titanotheres.* They were ousted by more specialized graminivorous forms as grass spread over the world. In pursuit of such beasts came great swarms of primitive dogs, some as big as bears, and the first cats, one in particular (*Smilodon*), a small fierce-looking creature with big knife-like canines, the first sabre-toothed tiger, which was to develop into greater things. American deposits in the Miocene display a great variety of camels: giraffe camels with long necks, gazelle camels, llamas, and true camels. North America, throughout most of the Cainozoic Period, appears to have been in open and easy continuation with Asia, and when at last the glaciers of the Great Ice Age, and then the Bering Strait, came to separate the two great continental regions, the last camels were left in the Old World and the llamas in the New World.

In the Eocene the first ancestors of the elephants appear in northern Africa as snouted creatures; the distinctive elephant's trunk dawned on the world in the Miocene and grew longer with the ages.

§ 4

Through millions of animal generations the spinning world circled about the sun; slowly its orbit, which may have been nearly circular during the equable days of the early Eocene, was drawn by the attraction of the circling outer planets into a more elliptical form. Its axis of rotation, which heeled over to the plane of its orbit, as the mast of a yacht under sail heels over towards the water, heeled over by imperceptible degrees a little more and a little more. And each year its summer point shifted a little farther from perihelion round its path.

These were small changes to happen to a one-inch ball, circling at a distance of 322 yards from a flaming sun nine feet across, in the course of a few million years. They were changes an immortal astronomer in Neptune, watching the earth from age to age, would have found almost imperceptible. But from the point of view of the abounding mammalian life of the Miocene they mattered profoundly. Age by age the winters grew, on the whole, colder and harder and longer relatively to the summers; age by age the summers grew briefer. On an average the winter snow lay a little later in the spring in each century, and the glaciers in the northern mountains gained an inch this year, receded half an inch next, came on again a few inches. . . .

The Record of the Rocks tells of the increasing chill. The Pliocene was a temperate time, and many of the warmth-loving plants and animals had gone from temperate latitudes. Then, rather less deliberately, some feet or some inches every year, the ice came on into the temperate regions of the earth.

An Arctic fauna—musk-ox, woolly mammoth, woolly rhinoceros, lemming—ushers in the Pleistocene. Over North America and Europe and Asia alike, the ice advanced. For thousands of years it advanced, and then for thousands of years it receded, to advance again. Europe down to the Baltic shores, Britain down to the Thames, North America down to New England, and more centrally as far south as Ohio, lay for ages under glaciers. Enormous volumes of water were withdrawn from the ocean and locked up in those stupendous ice caps so as to cause a world-wide change in the relative levels of land and sea. Vast areas were exposed that are now again sea bottom.

The world to-day is still coming slowly out of the last of a series of waves of cold. It is not growing warmer steadily. There have been and are fluctuations. Remains of bog-oaks, for example, which grew two or three thousand years ago, are found in Scotland at latitudes in which not even a stunted oak will grow at the present time. This uncertain change towards warmth may go on, or it may not. We do not know.

It is amidst the crescendo and diminuendo of frost and snow in the Glacial Age that we first recognize forms that are like the forms of men. The Age of Mammals culminated in ice and hardship and man.

BOOK II

THE MAKING OF MAN

VI

APES AND SUB-MEN AND MEN

§ 1. *The Origin of Man.* § 2. *First Traces of Man-like Creatures.* § 3. *The Heidelberg Sub-man.* § 4. *The Piltdown Sub-man.*

§ 1

THE origin of man and his relations to other animals has been the subject of great controversies during the last hundred years. The prevailing opinion among men of science is that man, like all other mammals, is descended from ancestors of a lowlier kind, that he and the large apes, the chimpanzee, the orang-outang and the gorilla, had once a common ancestor, and that this ancestor was evolved from yet lower forms, from some earlier type of mammal which was itself descended from a theriomorphous reptile, and this again from a series of amphibians, and these again from primitive fish. This genealogy is based on the comparison of man's anatomy with that of other vertebrated animals, and it is confirmed by the curious phases through which his body passes before birth. For he begins as if he were to be a fish, with gill-slits and a fish-like heart and kidney, he passes through phases that recall the amphibian and reptile, and then he recapitulates lower mammalian structures. He has for a time a tail. He does not begin human, even in his individual development; he struggles through to humanity. In a score of small things of no advantage to him, in the hair and the direction of the hair upon his limbs, for example, he recalls the ape.

Through millions and millions of lives, man has been shaped to such powers and hopes as he has to-day. He has come from a stir and movement in the waters to this, and he faces now, with a growing consciousness and will, his incalculable racial destinies. The writer follows this view of man's origins. It seems to him to be a quite firmly established one. But it is well to bear in mind that the animal ancestry of man is still passionately denied by many able and even learned people. The government of the state of Tennessee, for example, was so convinced to the contrary in the 1920's that it prohibited the teaching of this opinion in any of its schools and colleges. The family scandal is not, apparently, to be mentioned. And the authority of William Jennings Bryan (who followed his great prototype Jefferson in this matter) was weighed in the scale against the biological world in the trial at Dayton that ensued.

It is sometimes alleged that various religious bodies, and particularly the Roman Catholic Church, are opposed to this view of man's descent from animal ancestors, but this does not seem to be the case. The Roman Catholic Church is no more committed to the view that man was specially created than it is to the doctrine that the world is flat or that it is the centre about which the sun revolves. People once imagined that such were the doctrines of the Church, but all that has since been cleared up quite satisfactorily. Many individual believers dissent from the scientific opinion, because they feel it is more seemly to suppose that man has fallen rather than risen, but their objection does not commit their Church as a whole. The task of the historian is to deal not with what is seemly but with what is true. No considerable Christian body, indeed, now insists upon the exact and literal acceptance of the Bible narrative; to that the freedoms of great poetry are very properly conceded; and so long as the biologist does not insist upon an animal origin for the soul of man there is really no dispute between science and religion in this matter. It is not fair, however, to proceed to an account of man's descent without this preliminary intimation. The writer tells what he believes to be the truth, and it is not for him to state the arguments of opponents which do not appear to him to be valid and to which he could not do justice.

In the case of many of the great mammals it is possible to trace the descent of the existing species almost step by step from an Eocene ancestor. This is so with the elephants, for example, the camels and horses. The series in these instances are very complete. There are multitudes of specimens and close gradations. But it has to be admitted that the fossil remains of human ancestors are rare and imperfect and that broad gaps still remain to be filled in. In the days when the great English naturalist, Charles Darwin, first drew the attention of the world to this question with his *Descent of Man*, the known prehistoric remains of men were rare and unhelpful. Between the man and the great apes a great gulf seemed to be fixed, and the "missing link" became a by-word in popular discussion. It is only quite recently that vestiges have been found of creatures which seem to bridge that interval. The most striking of these are the Taungs skull, discovered in 1924, and subsequently described by Professor Dart of Johannesburg, and the wonderful series of skulls of a sub-human creature *Sinanthropus*, found still more recently at Peking. Both of these finds reveal creatures which were in many respects halfway between man and ape. The teeth, the brain-cases, the carriage of the head, and the slope of the forehead are more human than any ape's, and more simian than any recorded human being's.

It is frequently alleged that Darwin taught that man is descended from some man-like ape such as the chimpanzee, the orang-outang, or the gorilla, but that of course is as reasonable as saying that I am "descended" from some Hottentot or Esquimaux as young or younger than myself. Others, alive to this objection, say that man is descended from the common ancestor of the chimpanzee, the orang-outang, and the gorilla. Some "anthropologists" have even indulged in a speculation whether mankind may not have a double or treble origin; the negro being descended from a gorilla-like ancestor, the Chinese from a nearly orang-outang, and the "White" race from a champanzee-like ancestor, and so on. The chimpanzee by this brilliant theory is the European's lowly brother, with a better claim to dine and intermarry with the best "Nordic" families than the more distant negro or Chinaman. These are preposterous ideas, to be mentioned only to be dismissed. It was formerly assumed that the human ancestor was "probably arboreal," but the current idea among those who are qualified to form an opinion seems to be that he was a "ground ape," and that the existing apes have developed in the arboreal direction from a less arboreal origin.

If one puts the skeleton of a man and the skeleton of a gorilla side by side, their general resemblance is so great that it is easy to jump to the conclusion that the former is derived from such a type as the latter by a process of brain growth and general refinement. But if one examines closely into one or two differences the gap widens. Particular stress has recently been laid upon the tread of the foot. Man walks on his toes and his heel; his great toe is his chief lever in walking, as the reader may see for himself if he examines his own footprints on the bathroom floor and notes where the pressure falls as the footprints become fainter. His great toe is the king of his toes.

Among all the apes and monkeys, the only group that have their great toes developed on anything like the same fashion as man are some of the lemurs. The baboon walks on a flat foot and all his toes, using his middle toe as his chief throw off, much as the bear does. And the three great apes all walk on the outer side of the foot in a very different manner from the walking of man.

The great apes are forest dwellers; their walking is incidental; they have not the nimbleness of monkeys among trees but they are frequently and habitually off the ground. The gorilla is the heaviest and most terrestrial. When they are on the ground they often use their fore-limbs, running on their knuckles in a very unhuman fashion. Their arms are relatively much longer than man's. They have very distinctive methods of climbing; they swing by the arms much more than the monkeys do, and do not, like the latter, take off with a spring from the feet. They have no tails to help them. They have a specially developed climbing style of their own. But man walks so well and runs so swiftly as to suggest a very long ancestry upon the ground. Also, he does not climb well now; he climbs with caution and hesitation.

Conceivably, the precursor of the men and sub-men we shall presently describe was, at the opening of the Cainozoic Period, a running ape living chiefly on the ground, hiding among rocks rather than trees as the Gibraltar monkeys do. It could climb trees fairly well and hold things between its great toe and its second toe (as the Japanese can do this day), but it was already coming down to the ground again from a still remoter, a Mesozoic arboreal ancestry.

Moreover, it is to be noted that man does not swim naturally; he has to learn to swim, and that seems to point to a long-standing separation from rivers and lakes and the sea. It is quite understandable that such a creature would very rarely die in water in such circumstances as to leave bones to become fossilized.

It must always be borne in mind that among its many other imperfections that Geological Record necessarily contains abundant evidence only of water or marsh creatures or of creatures easily and frequently drowned. The same reasons that make any traces of the ancestors of the mammals rare and relatively unprocurable in the Mesozoic rocks probably make the signs of possible human ancestors rare and relatively unprocurable in the Cainozoic rocks. Such knowledge as we have of the earliest men, for example, is almost entirely obtained from a few caves into which they went and in which they have left their marks. Until the hard Pleistocene times they lived and died in the open or in the forest, and their bodies were consumed or decayed altogether.

Moreover, the ancestors of man, like the great apes of to-day, were probably never a very abundant race. They were not like wild horses and deer, for example, which can go in great herds and have been represented by hundreds and thousands if not millions of individuals in every generation. Plenty of these herbivora would always be getting drowned or pulled into the water by crocodiles or killed in the mud near a drinking-place. They fossilize easily, therefore. The great apes, on the contrary, go alone or in pairs with a young one or so; they range over wide areas in search of food, and drive away other competitors of their own species. They are solitary creatures needing each one a territory of its own. They need very special food. It is doubtful whether there are more than a few thousand and there may be only a few hundred gorillas in the world. Whole generations of them may pass away without a single one being fossilized. There is a mass of reasons for supposing that man's ancestor was a solitary ape of a similar type. He ranged alone or in small families over wide areas. Dozens of kindred species living under such conditions may have passed away completely and left scarcely a trace, and the chances that palæontologists will come upon that trace must be poor indeed.

It is well to bear in mind, also, that the Record of the Rocks has still to be thoroughly examined. It has been studied only for a few generations, and by only a few men in each generation. Practically only western Europe has been explored in this connection. There may be, there probably are, thousands of deposits still untouched containing fragments and vestiges of man and his progenitors. In Asia, in India or the East Indies, or in Africa, the most illuminating clues must be hidden. In America it seems less probable that anything sub-human will be found. But what we know to-day of early man may be the merest scrap of what will presently be known.

The apes and monkeys appear to have been differentiated already at the beginning of the Cainozoic Age, and there are a number of Oligocene and Miocene apes whose relations to one another and to their sub-human associates, to be presently described, have still to be made out. Among these we may mention

Dryopithecus of the Miocene Age, with a very human-looking jaw. There were numerous species of *Dryopithecus,* and it is not impossible that some one of them may have been in the direct line of human ancestry. In the Siwalik Hills of northern India remains of some very interesting apes have been found, of which *Sivapithecus* and *Palæopithecus* show some quasi-human traits. *Propliopithecus,* from the Oligocene of Egypt, must have been a very interesting creature. It was a little manly ape of the size of a small cat, and it may have been on the direct line of ancestry of the anthropoid apes of to-day. It was also very close to the ancestral human stem.

Probably all these animals, these near-men, used implements. Charles Darwin represents baboons as opening nuts by breaking them with stones, using stakes to prise up rocks in the hunt for insects, and striking blows with sticks and stones. The chimpanzee makes itself a sort of tree hut by intertwining branches. Stones apparently chipped for use have been found in strata of Oligocene Age at Boncelles in Belgium. Possibly the implement-using disposition was already present in the Mesozoic ancestors from which we appear to be descended.

§ 2

Among the earliest evidences of some creature more man-like than any living ape upon earth, are a number of flints and stones very roughly chipped and shaped so as to be held in the hand. These were probably used as hand-axes. These early implements ("Eoliths") are often so crude and simple that there was for a long time a controversy whether they were to be regarded as natural or artificial productions. Among the earlier pioneers of the latter view was Mr. Harrison, a grocer, of Ightham in Kent, one of those modest and devoted observers to whom British geology owes so much. At first his Eoliths were flouted and derided by archæologists, but to-day he has the scientific world with him in the recognition of the quasi-human origin of many of his specimens. With him we must honour Mr. W. J. Lewis Abbott, a jeweller, of St. Leonards, whose intimate knowledge of stone structure has been of the utmost value in these discussions; while the researches of Mr. J. Reid Moir in the Pliocene and Pleistocene deposits of East Anglia are most important in their bearings on the whole problem.

The date of the earliest of these Eoliths is put by geologists as Pliocene—that is to say, before the First Glacial Age. They occur also throughout the First Interglacial Period. We know of no bones or other remains in Europe or America of the quasi-

human beings of half a million years ago, who made and used these implements. A doubtful exception is a molar tooth found in gravels of the Upper Pliocene at Snake Creek, Nebraska, which is thought by some to have belonged to a creature to which the name *Hesperopithecus* (the Western Ape) has been given. It is much damaged, and may not have belonged to an anthropoid at all, but to some other fossil animal.

But at Trinil in Java, in strata which are said to correspond either to the later Pliocene or to the American and European First Ice Age, there have been found some scattered bones of a creature such as the makers of these early implements may have been. The top of a skull, some teeth, and a thigh-bone have been found. The skull shows a brain-case about half-way in size between that of the champanzee and man, but the thigh-bone is that of a creature as well adapted to standing and running as a man, and as free, therefore, to use its hands. The creature was not a man, nor was it an arboreal ape like the chimpanzee. It was a walking ape. It has been named by naturalists *Pithecanthropus erectus* (the walking ape-man).

POSSIBLE APPEARANCE OF THE SUB-MAN
Pithecanthropus

The face, jaws and teeth are mere guesswork (see text). The creature may have been much less human-looking than this.

Still more interesting is *Sinanthropus* from Pekin. Anatomically this is far more of a man than any ape. It was a sub-man. We have the remains now of numerous individuals. But there is no evidence at all that this particular sub-man knew of fire or made tools. It was exactly that "Missing Link" for which the opponents of Darwin had clamoured eighty years ago.

Of the makers of the European Eoliths we have yet no bones at all. We can only guess at their appearance.

While these early men or "sub-men" or "pseudo-men" of the Eoliths were running about Europe four or five hundred thousand years ago, there were mammoths, rhinoceroses, a huge hippopotamus, a giant beaver, and a bison and wild cattle in their world. There were also wild horses, and the sabre-toothed tiger still abounded. There are no traces of lions or true tigers at that time in Europe, but there were bears, otters, wolves and a wild boar. It may be that the early sub-man sometimes played jackal to the sabre-toothed tiger, and finished up the bodies on which the latter had gorged itself.

§ 3

The earliest member of the species *Homo* in the geological record is known only as a scrap of bone, a jaw-bone. This jaw-bone was found in a sandpit near Heidelberg, at a depth of eighty feet from the surface, and it is not the jaw-bone of a man as we understand man, but it is man-like in every respect, except that it has absolutely no trace of a chin; it is more massive than a man's, and its narrowness behind could not, it is thought, have given the tongue sufficient play for articulate speech. It is not an ape's jaw-bone; the teeth are human. The owner of this jaw-bone has been variously named *Homo Heidelbergensis* and *Palæonthropus Heidelbergensis*, according to the estimate formed of his humanity or sub-humanity by various authorities. He lived in a world not remotely unlike the world of the still earlier sub-man of the first implements; the deposits in which it was found show that there were elephants, horses, rhinoceroses, bison, a moose, and so forth with it in the world, but the sabre-toothed tiger was declining and the lion was spreading over Europe. The implements of this period (known as the Chellean Period) are a very considerable advance upon those of the Pliocene Age. They are well made but *very much bigger* than any truly human implements. The Heidelberg man may have had a very big body and large fore-limbs corresponding with the great size and massive character of the jaw. He may have been a hairy, strange-looking, inhuman creature.

§ 4

We must turn over the Record for, it may be, another 100,000 years for the next remains of anything human or sub-human. Then, in a deposit ascribed to the Third Interglacial Period, which may have begun 100,000 years ago and lasted 50,000 years, the smashed pieces of a whole skull turn up. The deposit is a gravel which may have been derived from the washing out of still earlier gravel strata, and this skull fragment may be in reality as old as the First Glacial Age. The bony remains discovered at Piltdown in Sussex display a creature still ascending only very gradually from the sub-human.

The first scraps of this skull were found in an excavation for road gravel in Sussex. Bit by bit other fragments of this skull were hunted out from the quarry heaps, until most of it could be pieced together. It is a thick skull, thicker than that of any living race of men, and it has a brain capacity intermediate between that of *Pithecanthropus* and man. This creature has been named *Eoanthropus*, the dawn-man. In the same gravel-pits were found teeth of rhinoceros, hippopotamus, and the leg-bone of a deer with marks upon it that may be cuts. A curious bat-shaped instrument of elephant bone has also been found.

There was, moreover, a jaw-bone among these scattered remains which was at first assumed, naturally enough, to belong to *Eoanthropus*, but which it was afterwards suggested was probably that of a chimpanzee. It is extraordinarily like that of a chimpanzee, but Sir Arthur Keith, one of the greatest authorities in these questions, assigns it, after an exhaustive analysis in his *Antiquity of Man* (Edition of 1925), to the skull with which it is found. It is, as a jaw-bone, far less human in character than the jaw of the much more ancient *Homo Heidelbergensis*, but the teeth are in some respects more like those of living men.

Sir Arthur Keith, swayed by the jaw-bone, does not think that *Eoanthropus*, in spite of its name, is a creature in the direct ancestry of man. Much less is it an intermediate form between the Heidelberg man and the Neanderthal man we shall presently describe. It was only related, he thinks, to the true ancestor of man as the orang is related to the chimpanzee. It was a member of a number of species of sub-human running apes of more than ape-like intelligence, and if it was not on the line royal it was at any rate a very close collateral.

After this glimpse of a skull, the Record for very many centuries gives nothing but flint implements, which improve steadily in quality. All the bones of the creatures that shaped them have gone, all the things of wood and skin their makers used; all is decayed and lost, and would have been forgotten if it were not for these stones. A very characteristic form is shaped like a sole, with one flat side stricken off at one blow and the other side worked. The archæologists, as the Record continues, are presently able to distinguish scrapers, borers, knives, darts, throwing-stones, and the like.

Progress is now more rapid; in a few centuries the shape of the hand-axe shows distinct and recognizable improvements.

And then comes quite a number of remains. The Fourth Glacial Age is rising towards its maximum. Man is taking to caves and leaving vestiges there; at Krapina in Croatia, at Neanderthal near Düsseldorf, at Spy, human remains have been found, skulls and bones of a creature that is certainly a man. Somewhere about 50,000 years ago, if not earlier, appeared *Homo Neanderthalensis* (also called *Homo antiquus* and *Homo primigenius*), a quite passable human being. His thumb was not quite equal in flexibility and usefulness to a human thumb, he stooped forward and could not hold his head erect as all living men do, he was chinless and perhaps incapable of speech, there were curious differences about the enamel, the pulp cavities, and the roots of his teeth from those of all living men, he was very thick-set, he was, indeed, not quite of the human species; but there is no dispute about his attribution to the genus *Homo*. He was certainly not descended from *Eoanthropus*, but his jaw-bone is so like the Heidelberg jaw-bone as to make it possible that the clumsier and heavier *Homo Heidelbergensis*, a thousand centuries before him, was of his blood and race.

VII

THE NEANDERTHAL MEN, AN EXTINCT RACE

(The Early Palaeolithic Age)

§ 1. *The world* 50,000 *Years Ago.* § 2. *The Daily Life of the Neanderthal Men.* § 3. *The Last Palæolithic Men.* § 4. *The Rhodesian Skull.*

§ 1

IN THE time of the Third Interglacial Period the outline of Europe and western Asia was very different from what it is to-day. Geologists are able to mark out the broad lines of the differences; we give a map of their conclusions. Vast areas to the west and north-west which are now under the Atlantic waters were then dry land; the Irish Sea and the North Sea were river valleys. Over these northern areas there spread and receded and spread again a great ice cap such as covers central Greenland to-day. This vast ice cap, which covered both polar regions of the earth, withdrew huge masses of water from the ocean, and the sea-level consequently fell, exposing great areas of land that are now submerged again. The Mediterranean area was probably a great valley below the general sea-level, containing two inland seas cut off from the general ocean. The climate of this Mediterranean basin was perhaps cold temperate, and the region of the Sahara to the south was not then a desert of baked rock and blown sand, but a well watered and fertile country. Between the ice sheets to the north and the Alps and Mediterranean valley to the south stretched a bleak wilderness whose climate changed from harshness to a mild kindliness, and then hardened again for the Fourth Glacial Age.

Across this wilderness, which is now the great plain of Europe, wandered a various fauna. At first there were hippopotami, rhinoceroses, mammoths, and elephants. The sabre-toothed tiger was diminishing towards extinction. Then, as the air chilled, the hippopotamus, and then other warmth-loving creatures, ceased to come so far north, and the sabre-toothed tiger disappeared altogether. The woolly mammoth, the woolly rhinoceros, the musk ox, the bison, the aurochs, and the reindeer became prevalent, and the temperate vegetation gave place to plants of a more arctic type. The glaciers spread southward to the maximum of the Fourth Glacial Age (about 50,000 years ago), and then receded again.

In the earlier phase, the Third Interglacial Period, a certain number of small family groups of men (*Homo Neanderthalensis*) and probably of sub-men (*Eoanthropus*) wandered over the land, leaving nothing but their flint implements to witness to their presence. There may have been other implement-making species of whom at present we have no more than a suspicion. They probably used a multitude and variety of wooden implements also; they had probably learnt much about the shapes of objects and the use of different shapes from wood, knowledge which they afterwards applied to stone; but none of this wooden material has survived; we can only speculate about its forms and uses.

As the weather hardened to its maximum of severity, the Neanderthal men—already, it would seem, acquainted with the use of fire—began to seek shelter under rock ledges and in caves, and so leave remains behind them. Hitherto they had been accustomed to squat in the open about the fire and near their water supply. But they were sufficiently intelligent to adapt themselves to the new and harder conditions.

As for the sub-men, they seem to have succumbed to the stresses of this Fourth Glacial Age altogether. The rudest implements presently disappear.

Not merely man was taking to the caves. This period also had a cave lion, a cave bear, and a cave hyæna. These creatures had to be driven out of the caves and kept out of the caves in which these early men wanted to squat and hide; and no doubt fire was an effective method of eviction and protection. Probably early men did not go deeply into the caves, because they had no means of lighting their recesses. They got in far enough to be out of the weather, and stored wood and food in odd corners. Perhaps they barricaded the cave mouths. Their only available light for going deeply into the caverns would be torches.

What did these Neanderthal men hunt? Their only possible weapons for killing such giant creatures as the mammoth or the cave bear, or even the reindeer, were spears of wood, wooden clubs, and those big pieces of flint they left behind them, the "Chellean" and "Mousterian" implements; and probably their usual quarry was smaller game. But they did certainly eat the flesh of the big beasts when they had a chance, and perhaps they followed them when sick or when wounded by combats, or took advantage of them when they were bogged or in trouble with ice or water. The Labrador Indians still kill the caribou with spears at awkward river crossings. At Dawlish, in Devon, an artificial trench has been found which is supposed to have been a Palæolithic trap for elephants. We know that the Neanderthalers partly ate their kill where it fell; but they brought back the big marrow-bones to the cave to crack and eat at leisure, because few ribs and vertebræ are found in the caves, but great quantities of cracked and split long bones. They used skins to wrap about them, and the women probably dressed the skins.

We know also that they were right-handed like modern men, because the left side of the brain (which serves the right side of the body) is bigger than the right. But while the back parts of the brain, which deal with sight and touch and the energy of the body, are well developed, the front parts, which are connected with thought and speech, are comparatively small. It was as big a brain as ours, but different. This species of *Homo* had certainly a very different mentality from ours; its individuals were not merely simpler and lower than we are, they were on another line. It may be they did not speak at all, or very sparingly. They had nothing that we should call a language.

§ 2

In Worthington Smith's *Man the Primeval Savage* there is a very vividly written description of early Palæolithic life, from which much of the following account is borrowed. In the original, Mr. Worthington Smith assumes a more extensive social life, a larger community, and a more definite division of labour among its members than is altogether justifiable in the face of such subsequent writings as J. J. Atkinson's memorable essay on Primal Law. For the little tribe Mr. Worthington Smith described, there has been substituted, therefore, a family group under the leadership of one Old Man, and the suggestions of Mr. Atkinson as to the behaviour of the Old Man have been worked into the sketch.

Mr. Worthington Smith describes a squatting-place near a

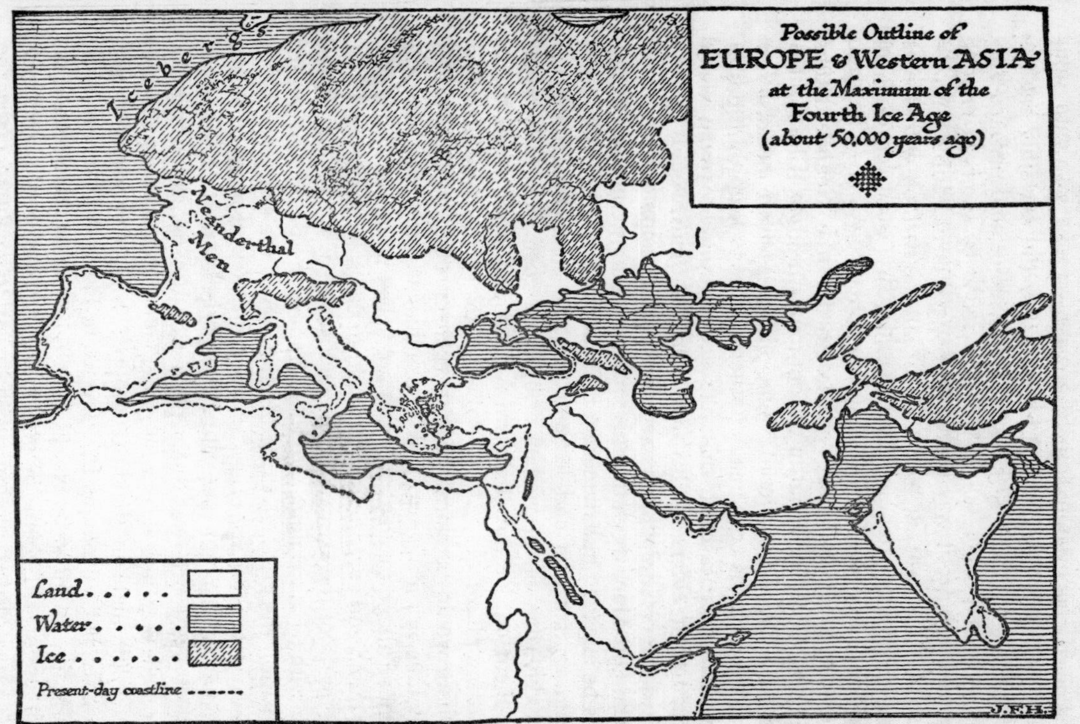

THIS MAP REPRESENTS THE PRESENT STATE OF OUR KNOWLEDGE OF THE GEOGRAPHY OF EUROPE AND WESTERN ASIA AT A PERIOD WHICH WE GUESS TO BE ABOUT 50,000 YEARS AGO, THE NEANDERTHALER AGE

stream, because primitive man, having no pots or other vessels, must needs have kept close to a water supply, and with some chalk cliffs adjacent from which flints could be got to work. The air was bleak, and the fire was of great importance, because fires once out were not easily relit in those days. When not required to blaze it was probably banked down with ashes. The most probable way in which fires were started was by hacking a bit of iron pyrites and flints amidst dry dead leaves; concretions of iron pyrites and flints are found together in England where the gault and chalk approach each other. The little group of people would be squatting about amidst a litter of fern, moss, and such-like dry material. Some of the women and children would need to be continually gathering fuel to keep up the fires. It would be a tradition that had grown up. The young would imitate their elders in this task. Perhaps there would be rude wind shelters of boughs on one side of the encampment.

The Old Man, the father and master of the group, would perhaps be engaged in hammering flints beside the fire. The children would imitate him and learn to use the sharpened fragments. Probably some of the women would hunt good flints; they would fish them out of the chalk with sticks and bring them to the squatting-place.

There would be skins about. It seems probable that at a very early time primitive men took to using skins. Probably they were wrapped about the children, and used to lie upon when the ground was damp and cold. A woman would perhaps be preparing a skin. The inside of the skin would be well scraped free of superfluous flesh with trimmed flints, and then strained and pulled and pegged out flat on the grass, and dried in the rays of the sun.

Away from the fire others of the man-pack prowled in search of food, but at night they all gathered closely round the fire and built it up, for it was their protection against the wandering bear and such-like beasts of prey. The Old Man was the only fully adult male in the little group. There were women, boys and girls, but so soon as the boys were big enough to rouse the Old Man's jealousy, he would fall foul of them and either drive them off or kill them. Some girls might perhaps go off with these exiles, or two or three of these youths might keep together for a time, wandering until they came upon some other group, from which they would try to steal a mate. Then they would probably fall out among themselves. Some day, when he was forty years old, perhaps, or even older, and his teeth were worn down and his energy abating, some younger male would stand up to the Old Man and kill him and reign in his stead. There was short shrift for the old at the squatting-place. So soon as they grew weak and bad-tempered, trouble and death came upon them.

What did they eat at the squatting-place?

"Primeval man is commonly described as a hunter of the great hairy mammoth, of the bear, and the lion, but it is in the highest degree improbable that the human savage ever hunted animals much larger than the hare, the rabbit, and the rat. Man was probably the hunted rather than the hunter.

While the waters were held up in the Polar Ice Caps, the sea-level was low enough to enable Palæolithic Man to reach Tasmania.

"The primeval savage was both herbivorous and carnivorous. He had for food hazel-nuts, beech-nuts, sweet chestnuts, earth-nuts, and acorns. He had crab-apples, wild pears, wild cherries, wild gooseberries, bullaces, sorbs, sloes, blackberries, yewberries, hips and haws, watercress, fungi, the larger and softer leaf-buds, nostoc (the vegetable substance called 'fallen stars' by countryfolk), the fleshy, juicy, asparagus like rhizomes or subterranean stems of the *Labiatæ* and like plants, as well as other delicacies of the vegetable kingdom. He had birds' eggs, young birds, and the honey and honeycomb of wild bees. He had newts, snails and frogs—the two latter delicacies are still highly esteemed in Normandy and Brittany. He had fish, dead and alive, and fresh-water mussels; he could easily catch fish with his hands, and paddle and dive for and trap them. By the seaside he would have fish, mollusca, and seaweed. He would have many of the larger birds and smaller mammals, which he could easily secure by throwing stones and sticks, or by setting simple snares. He would have the snake, the slow-worm, and the crayfish. He would have various grubs and insects, the large larvæ of beetles, and various caterpillars. The taste for caterpillars still survives in China, where they are sold in dried bundles in the markets. A chief and highly nourishing object of food would doubtlessly be bones smashed up into a stiff and gritty paste.

"A fact of great importance is this—primeval man would not be particular about having his flesh food over-fresh. He would constantly find it in a dead state, and, if semi-putrid, he would relish it none the less—the taste for high or half-putrid game still survives. If driven by hunger and hard pressed, he would perhaps sometimes eat his weaker companions or unhealthy children who happened to be feeble or unsightly or burthensome. The larger animals in a weak and dying state would no doubt be much sought for; when these were not forthcoming, dead and half-rotten examples would be made to suffice. An unpleasant odour would not be objected to; it is not objected to now in many continental hotels.

"The savages sat huddled close together round their fire, with fruits, bones, and half-putrid flesh. We can imagine the old man and his women twitching the skin of their shoulders, brows and muzzles as they were annoyed or bitten by flies or other insects. We can imagine the large human nostrils, indicative of keen scent, giving rapidly repeated sniffs at the foul meat before it was consumed; the bad odour of the meat and the various other disgusting odours belonging to a haunt of savages being not in the least disapproved.

"Man at that time was not a *degraded* animal, for he had never been higher; he was therefore an exalted animal, and, low as we esteem him now, he yet represented the highest stage of development of the animal kingdom of his time."

That is at least an acceptable sketch of a Neanderthal squatting-place. But before extinction overtook them, even the Neanderthalers learnt much and went far.

Whatever the old Palæolithic men did with their dead, there is reason to suppose that the later *Homo Neanderthalensis* buried some individuals at least with respect and ceremony. One of the best-known Neanderthal skeletons is that of a youth who may have been deliberately interred. He had been placed in a sleeping posture, head on the right forearm. The head and arm lay on a number of flint fragments carefully piled together "pillow fashion." A big hand-axe lay near his head, and around him were numerous charred and split ox bones, as though there had been a funeral feast.

This sort of men may have wandered, squatted about their fires, and died in Europe for a period extending over 100,000 years or more, if we assume, that is, that the Heidelberg jawbone belongs to a member of the species, a period so vast that all the subsequent history of our race becomes a thing of yesterday. Along its own line this species of men was accumulating a dim tradition, and working out its limited possibilities. Its thick skull imprisoned its brain, and to the end it was low-browed and brutish.

The opinion that the Neanderthal race (*Homo Neanderthalensis*) is an extinct species which did not interbreed with the true men (*Homo sapiens*) is held by Professor Osborn, but many writers do not share this view. Some prehistoric skulls are regarded by them as crosses between the Neanderthal and other types. Further, they write and speak of living "Neanderthalers" in contemporary populations. One observer has written in the past of such types in the west of Ireland; another has observed them in Greece. These so-called "living Neanderthalers" have neither the peculiarities of neck, thumb, nor teeth that distinguish the Neanderthal race of pre-men.

The cheek teeth of true men, for instance, have long fangs; the Neanderthaler's cheek tooth is *more complicated and specialized*, a long tooth with short fangs, and his canine teeth were *less* like dog-teeth than ours. Clearly he was on a different line of development. So far only western Europe has been properly explored for Palæolithic remains. Excepting one site, Krapina in Croatia, and the recently discovered Galilean skull, all we know of the Neanderthal species comes from that area. No doubt the ancestor of *Homo sapiens* (which species include the Tasmanians) was a very similar

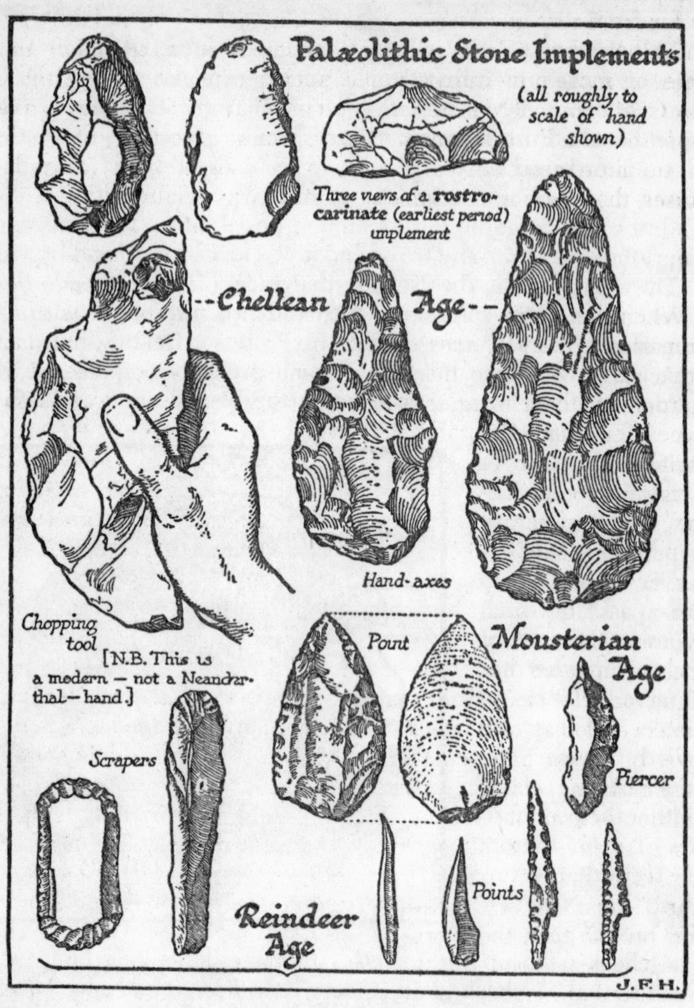

EARLY STONE IMPLEMENTS

The Mousterian Age Implements, and all above it, are those of the Neanderthal men or, possibly in the case of the rostro-carinates, of sub-men. The lower row (Reindeer Age) are the work of true men. The student should note the relatively *large size* of the prehuman implements.

and parallel creature to *Homo Neanderthalensis*. And we are not so far from that ancestor as to have eliminated not, indeed, "Neanderthal," but "Neanderthaloid" types. The existence of such types no more proves that the Neanderthal species, the makers of the Chellean and Mousterian implements, interbred with *Homo sapiens* in the European area than do monkey-faced people testify to an inter-breeding with monkeys; or people with faces like horses, that there is an equine strain in our population.

§ 3

When the Dutch discovered Tasmania, they found a detached human race not very greatly advanced beyond this Lower Palæolithic stage. But over most of the world the Lower Palæolithic culture had developed into a more complicated and higher life twenty or thirty thousand years ago. The Tasmanians were not racially Neanderthalers: their brain-cases, their neck-bones, their jaws and teeth, show that; they had no Neanderthal affinities; they were of the same species as ourselves. They represented a Neanderthaloid stage in the evolution of the true men. There can be hardly any doubt that throughout the hundreds of centuries during which the scattered little groups of Neanderthal men were all that represented men in Europe, real men of our own species, in some other part of the world, were working their way along parallel lines from much the same stage as the Neanderthalers ended at, and which the Tasmanians preserved to a higher level of power and achievement. The Tasmanians, living under unstimulating conditions, remote from any other human competition or example, lagged behind the rest of the human brotherhood. Yet even in this backward corner of the world early fossil remains, says Sir Arthur Keith, show that man has progressed. The Tasmanians of the early nineteenth century were less clumsy and brutish than their more ancient kinsmen.

§ 4

In the summer of 1921 a very interesting find was made in a cave on the Broken Hill property in South Africa. This was the skull, lacking the lower jaw, and also a number of bones of a new species of *Homo* intermediate between the Neanderthal Man and the True Men (*Homo sapiens*) of whom we shall presently tell. The skull was but little mineralized; its owner may

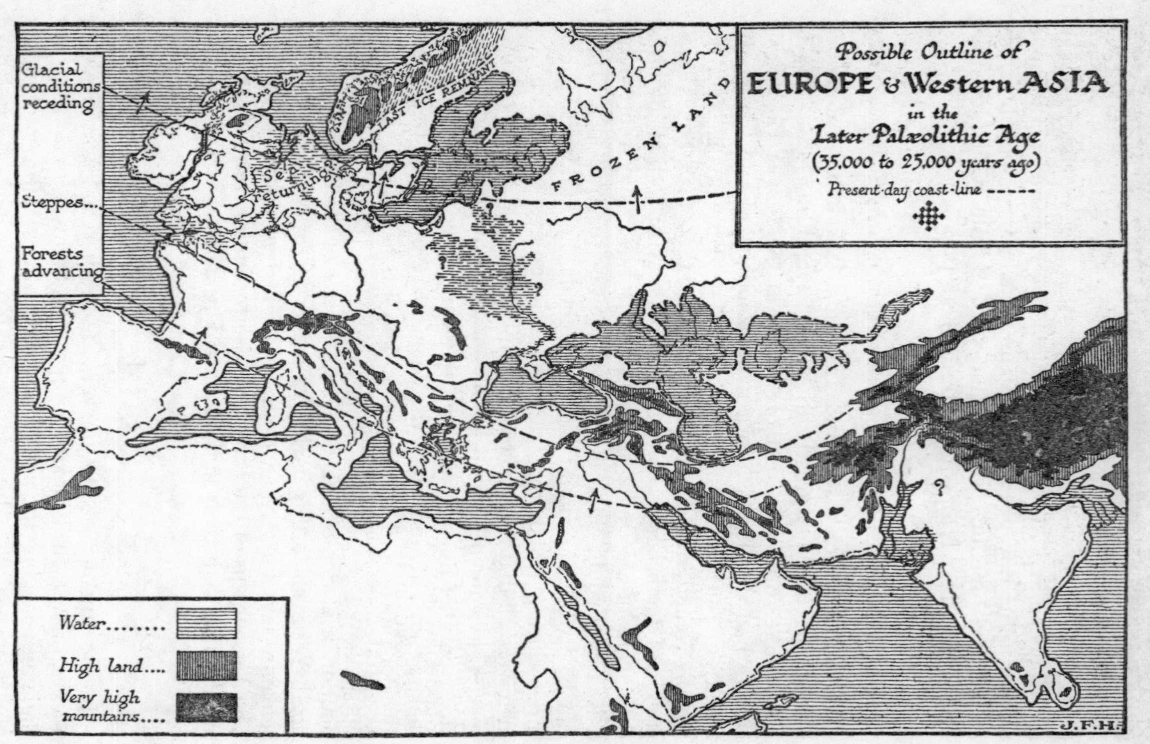
Possible Outline of
EUROPE & Western ASIA
in the
Later Palæolithic Age
(35,000 to 25,000 years ago)
Present-day coast-line
FROZEN LAND
LAST ICE REMNANT
Sea returning
Glacial conditions receding
Steppes
Forests advancing
Water
High land
Very high mountains
J.F.H.

have been alive but a few thousand years ago. The stratigraphy of this region remains vague. The Rhodesian man may have hunted the human apes of the Taungs type. This newly discovered creature (*Homo Rhodesiensis*), this Rhodesian Cave Man, while showing resemblances to Neanderthal man in certain features, had, so far as these remains show, none of the special characteristics of a Neanderthaler; its brain-case, neck, teeth and limbs were quite in the human line. (We know nothing of its hands.) But the size of the upper jaw and its articular surfaces indicate a lower jaw of more than Heidelberg massiveness, and there are ape-like brow ridges that rival the Neanderthaler's. The creature seems to have been an almost human being with an apish type of face. It may have survived to the human period, and have been contemporary with true men in South Africa. It may have been a terror to the children of the true men.

From several places in South Africa there come also remains of a true human race, the Boskop race, very ancient, but how ancient has not yet been determined. The Boskop men had skulls more like the living Bushmen than any other surviving people, but they were much thicker and very much larger, indeed they have a greater cubic content than modern European skulls. They were bigger, probably more intelligent Bushmen. They may be the earliest true men yet known to us. Skulls found at Wadjak in Java shortly before the discovery of *Pithecanthropus*, and probably of the Pleistocene Age, appear to bridge the gap between Rhodesian man and the Australian aborigines; while the Talgai skull found in Pleistocene deposits in Queensland represents an ancestral Australoid type, differing from the modern aboriginal chiefly in the greater size of the jaw.

VIII

THE LATER POSTGLACIAL PALÆOLITHIC MEN, THE FIRST TRUE MEN

(Later Palaeolithic Age)

§ 1. *The Coming of Men Like Ourselves.* § 2. *The Geography of the Palæolithic World.* § 3. *The Close of the Palæolithic Age.* § 4. *No Sub-men in America.*

§ 1

THE Neanderthal type of man prevailed in Europe at least for tens of thousands of years. For ages that make all history seem a thing of yesterday, these nearly human creatures prevailed. If the Heidelberg jaw was that of a Neanderthaler, and if there is no error in the estimate of the age of that jaw, then the Neanderthal race lasted out for more than 200,000 years! Finally, between 40,000 and 25,000 years ago, as the Fourth Glacial Age softened towards more temperate conditions, a different human type came upon the European scene, and it would seem, exterminated *Homo Neanderthalensis.*

This new type was probably developed in South Asia or Africa, or in lands now submerged in the Mediterranean basins, and as more remains are collected and evidence accumulates, men will learn more of their early stages. At present we can only guess where and how, through the slow ages, parallel with the Neanderthal cousin, these first *true men* arose out of some more apelike progenitor. For hundreds of centuries they were acquiring skill of hand and limb, and power and bulk of brain, in that still unknown environment. They were already far above the Neanderthal level of achievement and intelligence when first they come into our ken, and they had already split into two or more very distinctive races.

These newcomers did not migrate into Europe in the strict sense of the word, but rather, as century by century the climate ameliorated, they followed the food and plants to which they were accustomed, as these spread into the new realms that opened to them. The ice was receding, vegetation was increasing, big game of all sorts was becoming more abundant. Steppe-like conditions, conditions of pasture and shrub, were bringing with them vast herds of wild horse. Ethnologists (students of race) class these new human races in the same species as ourselves, and with all human races subsequent to them, under one common specific name of *Homo sapiens*. They had quite human brain-cases and hands. Their teeth and their necks were anatomically as ours are.

We know of two distinct sorts of skeletal remains in this period, the first of these known as the Cro-Magnon race, and the second the Grimaldi race; but the great bulk of the human traces and appliances we find are either without human bones or with insufficient bones for us to define their associated physical type. There may have been many more distinct races than these two. There may have been intermediate types. In the grotto of Cro-magnon it was that complete skeletons of one main type of these Newer Palæolithic men, these true men, were first found, and so it is that they are spoken of as Cro-Magnards.

These Cro-Magnards were a tall people with very broad faces, prominent noses, and, all things considered, astonishingly big brains. The brain capacity of the woman in the Cro-Magnon cave exceeded that of the average male to-day. Her head had been smashed by a heavy blow. There were also in the same cave with her the complete skeleton of an older man, nearly six feet high, the fragments of a child's skeleton and the skeletons of two young men. There were also flint implements and perforated sea-shells, used, no doubt, as ornaments. Such is one sample of the earliest true men. But at the Grimaldi cave near Mentone were discovered two skeletons also of the later Palæolithic Period but of a widely contrasted type, with negroid characteristics that point rather to the negroid type. They reach in type towards the Boskop race of South Africa of which we have already told. There can be no doubt that we have to deal in this period with at least two, and probably more, highly divergent races of true men. They may have overlapped in time, or Cro-Magnards may have followed the Grimaldi race, and either or both may have been contemporary with the late Neanderthal men. Various authorities have very strong opinions upon these points, but they are, at most, opinions.

The appearance of these truly human postglacial Palæolithic peoples was certainly an enormous leap forward in the history of mankind. Both of these main races had a human fore-brain, a human hand, an intelligence very like our own. They dispossessed *Homo Neanderthalensis* from his caverns and his stone quarries. And they agreed with modern ethnologists, it would seem, in regarding him as a different species. Unlike most savage conquerors, who take the women of the defeated side for their own and interbreed with them, it would seem that the true men would have nothing to do with the Neanderthal race, women or men. There is no trace of any intermixture between the races, in spite of the fact that the newcomers, being also flint users, were establishing themselves in the very same spots that their predecessors had occupied.

We know nothing of the appearance of the Neanderthal man, but this absence of intermixture seems to suggest an extreme hairiness, an ugliness, or a repulsive strangeness in his appearance over and above his low forehead, his beetle brows, his ape neck, and his inferior stature. Or he—and she—may have been too fierce to tame. Says Sir Harry Johnston, in a survey of the rise of modern man in his *Views and Reviews:* "The dim racial remembrance of such gorilla-like monsters, with cunning brains, shambling gait, hairy bodies, strong teeth, and possibly cannibalistic tendencies, may be the germ of the ogre in folklore. . . ."

These true men of the Palæolithic Age, who replaced the Neanderthalers, were coming into a milder climate, and although they used the caves and shelters of their predecessors, they lived largely in the open. They were hunting peoples, and some or all of them appear to have hunted the mammoth and the wild horse as well as the reindeer, bison, and aurochs. They ate much horse. At a great open-air camp at Solutré, where they seem to have had annual gatherings for many centuries, it is estimated that there are the bones of 100,000 horses, besides reindeer, mammoth, and bison bones. They probably followed herds of horses,

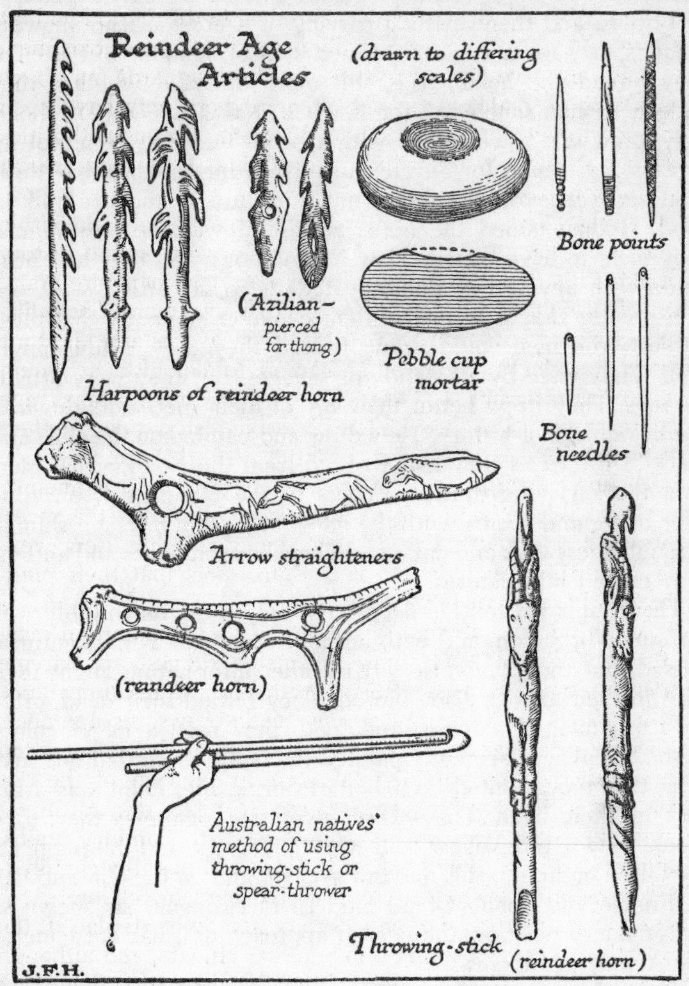

the little bearded ponies of that age, as these moved after pasture. They hung about on the flanks of the herd, and became very wise about its habits and dispositions. A large part of these men's lives must have been spent in watching animals.

Whether they tamed and domesticated the horse is still an open question. Perhaps they learnt to do so by degrees as the centuries passed. At any rate, we find late Palæolithic drawings of horses with marks about the heads that are strongly suggestive of bridles, and there exists a carving of a horse's head showing what is perhaps a rope of twisted skin or tendon. But even if they tamed the horse, it is still more doubtful whether they rode it or had much use for it when it was tamed. The horse they knew was a wild pony with a beard under its chin, not up to carrying a man for any distance. It is improbable that these men had yet learnt the rather unnatural use of animal's milk as food. If they tamed the horse at last, it was the only animal they seem to have tamed. They had no dogs, and they had little to do with any sort of domesticated sheep or cattle.

It greatly aids us to realize their common humanity that these earliest true men could draw. Indeed they drew astonishingly well. They were by all standards savages, but they were artistic savages. They drew better than any of their successors down to the beginnings of history. They drew and painted on the cliffs and walls of the caves they had wrested from the Neanderthal men. And the surviving drawings come to the ethnologist, puzzling over bones and scraps, with the effect of a plain message shining through guesswork and darkness. They drew on bones and antlers; they carved little figures.

These later Palæolithic people not only drew remarkably well for our information, and with an increasing skill as the centuries passed, but they have also left us other information about their lives in their graves. They buried. They buried their dead, often with ornaments, weapons, and food; they used a lot of colour in the burial, and evidently painted the body. From that one may infer that they painted their bodies during life. Paint was a big fact in their lives. They were inveterate painters; they used black, brown, red, yellow, and white pigments, and the pigments they used endure to this day in the caves and on the cliff surfaces of France and Spain. Of all modern races, none has shown so pictorial a disposition; the nearest approach to it has been among the American Indians.

These drawings and paintings of the later Palæolithic people went on through a long period of time, and present wide fluctuations in artistic merit. In its early stages the drawing is often primitive like the drawing of clever children; quadrupeds are usually drawn with one hind-leg and one fore-leg, as children draw them to this day; the legs on the other side were too much for the artists' technique. Possibly the first drawings began as children's drawings begin, out of idle scratchings. The savage scratched with a flint on a smooth rock surface, and was reminded of some line or gesture. But their solid carvings are at least

Painting in four colours (Cave of Altamira, Spain)

as old as their first pictures. The earlier drawings betray a complete incapacity to group animals.

As the centuries progressed more skilful artists appeared. The representations of beasts became at last astonishingly vivid and like. But even at the crest of their artistic time they still drew in profile as children do; perspective and the fore-shortening needed for back and front views were too much for them. The mammoth and the horse are among the commonest themes. In the caves of the north of Spain there are no drawings of men, only of animals; but in eastern Spain there are many paintings dating from the later divisions of this period in which human figures are displayed. Some of the people also made little ivory and soapstone statuettes, and among these are some very fat female figures. They are like Bushmen women. The human sculpture of the earlier times inclined to caricature, and generally such human figures as they represent are far below the animal studies in vigour and veracity.

Later on there was more grace and less coarseness in the human representations. One small ivory head discovered is that of a girl with an elaborate coiffure. These people at a later stage also scratched and engraved designs on ivory and bone. Some of the most interesting groups of figures are carved very curiously round bone, and especially round rods of deer bone, so that it is impossible to see the entire design all together. Figures have also been found modelled in clay, although no Palæolithic people made any use of pottery.

Many of the paintings are found in the depths of unlit caves. They are often difficult of access. The artists must have employed lamps to do their work, and shallow soapstone lamps in which fat could have been burnt have been found. Whether the seeing of these cavern paintings was in some way ceremonial or under what circumstances they were seen, we are now altogether at a loss to imagine. In the south and east of Spain, however, the drawings are not in caves, but upon overhung rock shelters in a good light.

Archæologists distinguish at present three chief stages in the history of these newer Palæolithic men, these true men, in Europe, and we must name these stages here. But it may be as well to note at the same time that it is a matter of the utmost difficulty to distinguish which of two deposits in different places is the older or newer. We may very well be dealing with the work of more or less contemporary and different races when we think we are dealing with successive ones. We are dealing, the reader must bear in mind, with little disconnected patches of material, a few score altogether.

The earliest stage usually distinguished by the experts is the *Aurignacian* (from the grotto of Aurignac); it is characterized by very well-made flint implements, and by a rapid development of art and more particularly of statuettes and wall paintings. The most esteemed of the painted caves is ascribed to the latter part of this the first of the three subdivisions of the newer Palæolithic. The second subdivision of this period is called the *Solutrian* (from Solutré), and is distinguished particularly by the quality and beauty of its stone implements; some of its razor-like blades are only equalled and not surpassed by the very best of the Neolithic work. They are of course unpolished, but the best specimens are as thin as steel blades and almost as sharp. Finally, it would seem, came the *Magdalenian* (from La Madeleine) stage, in which the horse and reindeer were dwindling in numbers and the red deer coming into Europe. The stone implements are smaller, and there is a great quantity of bone harpoons, spearheads, needles, and the like.

The hunters of the third and last stage of the later Palæolithic Age appear to have supplemented a diminishing food supply by fishing. The characteristic art of the period consists of deep reliefs done upon bone and line engraving upon bone. It is to this period that the designs drawn round bones belong, and it has been suggested that these designs upon round bones were used to print coloured designs upon leather. Some of the workmanship on bone was extraordinarily fine. Parkyn quotes from de Mortillet about the Reindeer Age (Magdalenian) bone needles, that they "are much superior to those of later, even historical, times, down to the Renaissance. The Romans, for example, never had needles comparable to those of the Magdalenian epoch."

It is quite impossible at present to guess at the relative lengths of these ages. We are not even positive about their relative relationship. Each lasted perhaps for four or five or more thousand years, more than double the time from the Christian era to our own day. Moreover, these divisions are based mainly upon the remains found in France and the north of Spain. As we go into the south of Spain and Italy and North Africa, their characteristics are no longer traceable. There was a different type of life to the south, different food and a different equipment.

At last it would seem that circumstances began to turn altogether against these hunting newer Palæolithic people who had flourished for so long in Europe. They disappeared. New kinds of men appeared from the south and east, replacing them. These latter seem to have brought in bow and arrows; they had domesticated animals and cultivated the soil. A new way of living, the Neolithic way of living, spread over the European area; and the life of the Reindeer Age and of the later Palæolithic men, after a reign vastly greater than the time between ourselves and the very earliest beginnings of recorded history, passed off the European stage.

There is, perhaps, a disposition on the part of some writers to exaggerate the intellectual and physical qualities of these later Palæolithic men and make a wonder of them. Collectively considered, these people had remarkable gifts, but a little reflection will show they had almost as remarkable deficiencies. The tremendous advance they display upon their Neanderthal predecessors and their special artistic gift must not blind us to their very obvious limitations. For all the quantity of their brains, the quality was narrow and special. They had vivid perceptions, an acute sense of animal form, they had the real artist's impulse to render; so far they were fully grown human beings. But that disposition to paint and draw is shown to-day by the Bushmen, by Californian Indians, and by Australian black fellows; it is not a mark of all-round high intellectual quality.

The cumulative effect of their drawings and paintings is very great, but we must not make the mistake of crowding all these achievements together in our minds as though they had suddenly flashed out upon the world in a brief interval of time, or as though they were all the achievements of one people. These races of Reindeer men were in undisturbed possession of Western Europe for a period at least ten times as long as the interval between ourselves and the beginning of the Christian era, and through all that immense time they were free to develop and vary their life to its utmost possibilities. They were in close contact with animals, but they never seemed to have got to terms with any animal unless it was the horse. They had no dogs. They had no properly domesticated animals at all. They watched and drew and killed and ate. They do not seem to have cooked their food. Perhaps they scorched and grilled it, but they could not have done much more, because they had no cooking implements.

Although they had clay available, and although there are several Palæolithic clay figures on record, they had no pottery. Although they had a great variety of flint and bone implements, they never rose to the possibilities of using timber for permanent shelters or such-like structures. They never made hafted axes, or the like that would enable them to deal with timber. There is a suggestion in some of the drawings of a fence of stakes in which a mammoth seems to be entangled. But here we may be dealing with superimposed scratchings. They had no buildings. It is not even certain that they had tents or huts. They may have had simple skin tents. Some of the drawings seem to suggest as much. It is doubtful if they knew of the bow. They left no good arrow-heads behind them. The doubt whether Palæolithic men of the Reindeer Age used the bow obviously does not apply to the Palæolithic men of the comparatively late Capsian culture. A careless reader might perhaps jump to the conclusion that the statement applies to *all* Palæolithic men. The earlier Palæolithic men, the Neanderthalers, were certainly without bows, and the Reindeer men probably knew nothing of archery. Certain of their implements are said to be "arrow-straighteners" by distinguished authorities, but that is about as much evidence as we have of arrows. They may have used sharpened sticks as arrows. They had no cultivation of grain or vegetables of any sort. Their women were probably squaws, smaller than the men; the earlier statuettes represent them as grossly fat, almost as the Bushmen women are often fat to-day. They are fatted for marriage, and so, perhaps, were these Stone Age squaws. They were smaller than the men because, no doubt, they began to bear children before they had grown to their fullest possibilities. Primitive woman was a subjected creature.

These later Palæolithic men clothed themselves, it would seem, in skins, if they clothed themselves at all. These skins they prepared with skill and elaboration, and towards the end of the age they used bone needles, no doubt to sew these pelts. One may guess pretty safely that they painted these skins, and it has even been supposed printed off designs upon them from bone cylinders. But their garments were mere wraps; there are no clasps or catches to be found. They do not seem to have used grass or suchlike fibre for textiles. Their statuettes are naked. They were, in fact, except for a fur wrap in cold weather, naked painted savages. In their women and their art they were like the Bushmen of South Africa; in their pursuit of the reindeer herd they were like the Indians of Labrador. Physically they were probably very like the Indians of Labrador.

These hunters lived on open steppes for two hundred centuries or so, ten times the length of the Christian era. They were, perhaps, overtaken by the growth of the European forests, as the climate became milder and damper. When the wild horse and the reindeer diminished in Europe, and a newer type of human culture, with a greater power over food supply, a greater tenacity of settlement, and probably a larger social organization, arose, the Reindeer men had to learn fresh ways of living or to disappear.

§ 2

It is very important to grasp the differences between the geography of the Reindeer age and the present time. It is a matter too often overlooked. Even so eminent a man as Dr. Fairfield Osborn is caught napping in this respect. He can write, for example, of the "invasion" of Spain by the Chellean and Mousterian cultures coming by way of North Africa from Egypt—as though then as now that was the only possible route. Professor Obermaier goes further. He speculates whether the Chellean culture reached Spain from Africa "on some primitive kind of raft!"

That raft was quite unnecessary. The approximate map of Europe and nearer Asia as it was about thirty thousand years ago (see p. 84) will show at a glance the absurdity of thus treating Spain as a permanently distinguishable piece of the world.

That, however, is a remark by the way; the broader issue is the manifestly *marginal* nature of all these Palæolithic peoples of Europe. We are not yet in possession of the main text of the human story. The life of the Reindeer men was a frontier life. They lived on bleak highlands to the north of the better lands of the world. To the south and west was the Mediterranean basin. There, hidden for ever perhaps under the blue waters, must be the remains of contemporaries of the Reindeer men who were probably much more advanced and sophisticated. These great valleys about the lakes of the Mediterranean bed and in the Red Sea triangle probably afforded admirable conditions for human development. The main stage of human history 20,000 years ago lay to the south-east of the Franco-Spanish area, the only area of the continent of Europe as yet at all adequately searched for vestiges of early man.

It is due largely to the labours of Professor Obermaier of Madrid that we begin to realize that while the Reindeer men prevailed in France and North Spain, the men who wandered over the greater part of the Spanish territory and North Africa were of a different culture, which he calls (after a place name in Tunis) the *Capsian* culture. The Capsian did not follow the Aurignacian, Solutrian and Magdalenian stages of France, but it was contemporary with it. It was different, and on the whole it suggests more advanced social conditions. It lacks, perhaps, the representative vigour of the northern art (which includes the wonderful painted Altamira caves), but on the other hand it has provided a considerable number of paintings of human beings engaged in various activities. They are for the most part painted on rock surfaces, and they resemble in character and treatment many ancient and modern rock paintings done by the

Bushmen of South Africa. Capsian paintings have also been found in Italy.

The life recorded by the Capsian paintings is an easier life under more agreeable climatic conditions than that of the Reindeer hunters to the north. Reindeer, bear and bison are not shown, and the chief animals are the ordinary deer and wild ox. Rhinoceros, wild ass and ibex also appear. Men carry bows and are naked, but most of the female figures are represented as clothed in skirts. Feather ornaments are frequent. One scene shows a boar hunt and another the smoking out of a hive of wild bees. There are also groupings that very probably represent ceremonial dances, and figures of men wearing masks representing animals over their heads and shoulders. When Professor Obermaier showed the author some of the tracings of these pictures in Madrid some years ago, he pointed out a curious disposition to distort the human figure, while representing animals without distortion very faithfully and recognizably. Always the human waist is elongated and much compressed, and often the legs are greatly inflated. This conventionality passes on in the later pictures into an almost diagrammatic treatment of human beings. The pictures cease to be pictures and become signs.

§ 3

It was about 12,000 or fewer years ago that, with the spread of forests and a great change of the fauna, the long prevalence of the hunting life in Europe drew to its end. Reindeer vanished. Changing conditions frequently bring with them new diseases. There may have been prehistoric pestilences. In France there seems to have been a gap before the new population appeared, but in the south of Europe the later Capsian culture passes by what Obermaier calls the Epipalæolithic stage into the Azilian (from the cave of the Mas d'Azil). The conventional painting of the Capsian folk is still more diagrammatic in the Azilian stage, and great numbers of pebbles are found painted with brush strokes that we now know to stand for standard types of man and beast. Various Australian tribes at the present time have very similar painted stones, which are called "soul stones," and are supposed to embody part or all of the soul or quality of a deceased ancestor.

These new people were a darkish, fine-featured people; they were the first comers of a race, the Mediterranean, dark-white or

Iberian race, which is still the prevailing race in southern Europe. Their communities extended northward with the spread of the

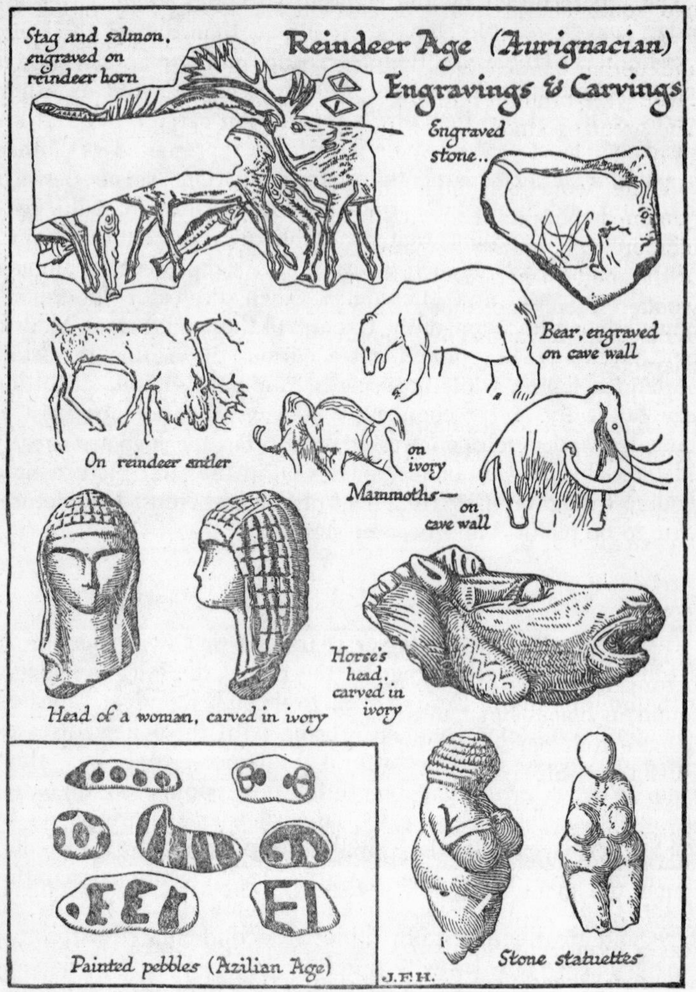

forests to replace the steppes, and the wane of the hunters, some 10,000 or 12,000 years ago.

The map of the world was assuming something like its present outlines, the landscape and the flora and fauna were taking on their existing characteristics. The prevailing animals in the spreading woods of Europe were the royal stag, the great ox, and the bison; the mammoth and the musk ox (Arctic forms) had gone. The great ox, or aurochs, is now extinct, but it survived in the German forests up to the time of the Roman Empire and perhaps much later. It was never domesticated. Domestic cattle were brought into Europe later and are of a different breed. The great ox stood eleven feet high at the shoulder, as high as an elephant.

There were still lions in the Balkan peninsula, and they remained there until about 1,000 or 1,200 B.C. The lions of Würtemberg and south Germany in those days were twice the size of the modern lion. South Russia and Central Asia were thickly wooded then, and there were elephants in Mesopotamia and Syria, and a fauna in Algeria that was tropical African in character.

Hitherto men in Europe had never gone farther north than the Baltic Sea or the British Isles, but now the Scandinavian peninsula and perhaps Great Russia were becoming possible regions for human occupation. There are no Palæolithic remains in Sweden or Norway. Man, when he entered these countries, was already at the Neolithic stage of social development.

§ 4

There is no really convincing evidence of man in America before the end of the Pleistocene. Eoliths are said to have been found in places but not abundantly. The same relaxation of the climate that permitted the retreat of the reindeer hunters into Russia and Siberia, as the Neolithic tribes advanced, may have allowed them to wander across the land that is now cut by Bering Strait, and so reach the American continent. They spread thence southward, age by age. When they reached South America, they found the giant sloth (the *Megatherium*), the glyptodon, and many other extinct creatures, still flourishing. The glyptodon was a monstrous South American armadillo, and it is said that a human skeleton has been found buried beneath its huge tortoise-like shell.

All the human remains in America are apparently of an Amer-Indian character. In America there does not seem to have been any preceding race of sub-men. We have already noted the one scrap of evidence to the contrary, a single doubtful tooth. Man was fully man when he entered America. The old world was the nursery of the sub-races of mankind. Somewhere between South Africa and the East Indies and the Mediterranean it was that these sub-races worked out their destinies, as lands rose and sank, and forests gave place to desert, and desert to forest. It may have been where now the Indian Ocean extends. Let it be repeated once more that the account of Palæolithic man is a partial account drawn from what is at present the only available material, the European material. The material for the main story is still inaccessible. The main story was going on while the Neanderthaler wandered over Europe, in some region as yet not defined and, it may be, submerged now beyond our exploration.

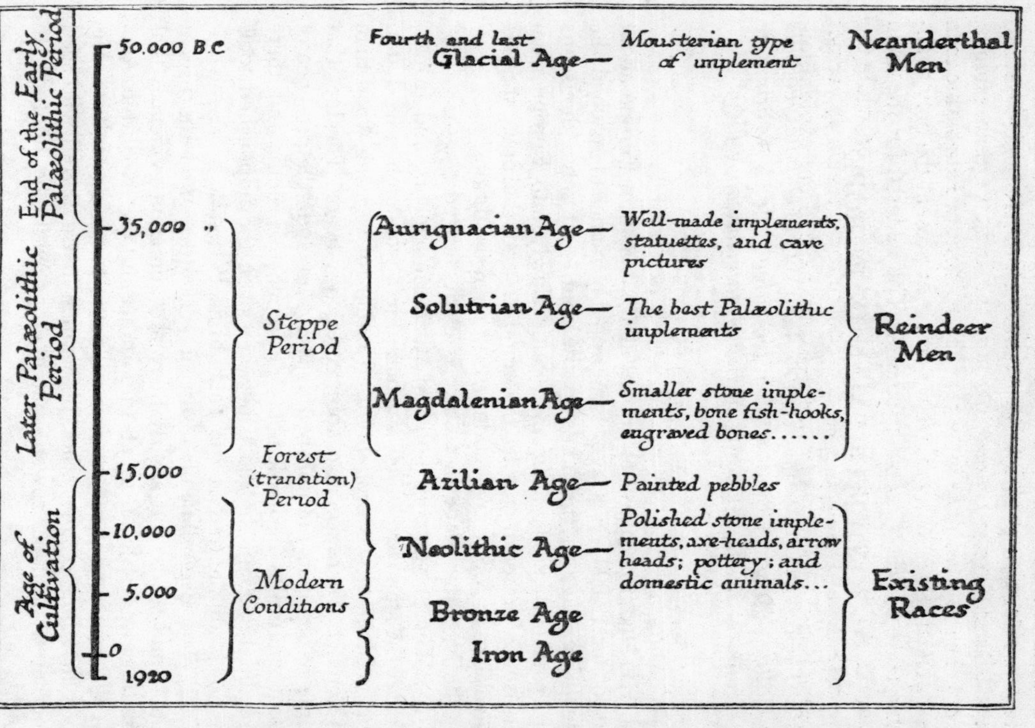

Time Diagram showing the estimated duration of the True Human Periods

IX

NEOLITHIC MAN IN EUROPE

§ 1. The Age of Cultivation Begins. § 2. Where Did the Neolithic Culture Arise? § 3. Everyday Neolithic Life. § 4. Primitive Trade. § 5. The Flooding of the Mediterranean Valley.

§ 1

THE Neolithic phase of human affairs began in Europe about 10,000 or 12,000 years ago. But probably men had reached the Neolithic stage in the lands to the south-east some thousands of years earlier. Neolithic men came slowly into Europe from the south or south-east as the reindeer and the open steppes gave way to forest and modern European conditions.

The Neolithic stage in culture is characterized by:

(1) The presence of polished stone implements, and in particular the stone *axe* which was bound to a wooden handle. Later, this implement was probably used rather for working wood than in conflict. There are also abundant arrow-heads. The fact that some implements are polished does not preclude the presence of great quantities of implements of unpolished stone. But there are differences in the make between even the unpolished tools of the Neolithic and of the Palæolithic Period.

(2) The beginning of a sort of agriculture, and the use of plants and seeds. But at first there are abundant evidences that hunting was still of great importance in the Neolithic Age. Neolithic man did not at first sit down to his agriculture. He took snatch crops; or, rather, his women first gathered wild seed and later, perhaps, sowed snatch crops while he hunted. He settled later.

(3) Pottery and proper cooking. The horse was no longer eaten.

(4) Domesticated animals. The dog appeared very early. The Neolithic man had domesticated cattle, sheep, goats, and

pigs. He was a huntsman turned herdsman of the herds he once hunted.

(5) Plaiting and weaving.

These Neolithic people probably "migrated" into Europe, in the same way that the Reindeer men had migrated before them; that is to say, generation by generation and century by century, as the climate changed, they spread after their accustomed food. They were not "nomads." Nomadism, like civilization, had still to be developed. Nomadism is just as recent and just as highly developed a condition as civilization.

At present we are quite unable to estimate how far the Neolithic people were new-comers and how far their arts were developed or acquired by the descendants of some of the hunters and fishers of the Later Palæolithic Age. Possibly the hunters of the reindeer receded, but the Capsian peoples partly developed, and partly learnt from more advanced people in the south and east, the new ways of living.

Whatever our conclusions in that matter, we may say with certainty there is no great break, no further sweeping away of one kind of man and replacement by another kind between the appearance of the Neolithic way of living and our own time. There are invasions, conquests, extensive emigrations and intermixtures, but the races as a whole still carry on and continue to adapt themselves to the areas into which they began to settle in the opening of the Neolithic Age. The Neolithic men of Europe were white men ancestral to the modern Europeans. They may have been of a darker complexion than many of their descendants; of that we cannot speak with certainty. But there is no real break in culture from their time onward until we reach the age of coal, steam, and power-driven machinery that began in the eighteenth century.

After a long time, gold, presumably the first known of the metals, appears among the bone ornaments with jet and amber. Irish prehistoric remains are particularly rich in gold. Perhaps 6,000 or 7,000 years ago, Neolithic people began to use copper in certain centres, making out of it implements of much the same pattern as their stone ones. They cast the copper in moulds made to the shape of the stone implements. Possibly they first found native copper and hammered it into shape. Native copper is still found to-day in Italy, Hungary, Cornwall, and many other places. But pure copper is inferior to flint as a material for implements; it will not keep an edge. Copper with a mixture of tin (up to one-tenth of tin) is much harder. Later—we will not venture upon figures—men had found out how to get copper from its ore. Perhaps, as Lord Avebury suggested, they discovered the secret of smelting by the chance putting of lumps of copper ore among the ordinary stones with which they built the fire pits they used for cooking.

In China, Cornwall, and elsewhere copper ore and tinstone occur in the same vein; in Hungary copper is associated with antimony; and so, it may be rather through dirtiness than skill, the ancient smelters hit upon the harder and better bronze, which is an alloy of copper and tin. Bronze is not only harder than copper, but the mixture of tin and copper is more fusable and easier to reduce. The so-called "pure copper" implements usually contain a small proportion of tin, and there are no tin implements known, nor very much evidence to show that early man knew of tin as a separate metal. A lump of tin has been found in the Swiss pile-dwelling deposits, and tin was known as a foreign import in Egypt under the XVIIIth Dynasty. There is (rare) Mycenæan tin, and there are (probably later, but not clearly dated) tin objects in the Caucasus. It is very difficult to distinguish tin from antimony. There is a good deal of Cyprus bronze which contains antimony; a good deal which seems to be tin *is* antimony—the ancients tried to get tin, but actually got antimony and thought it was tin. The plant of a prehistoric copper smelter has been found in Spain, and the material of bronze foundries in various localities. The method of smelting revealed by these finds carries out Lord Avebury's suggestion. In India, where zinc and copper ore occur together, brass (which is an alloy of the two metals) was similarly hit upon.

So slight was the change in fashions and methods produced by the appearance of bronze, that for a long time such bronze axes and so forth as were made were cast in moulds to the shape of the stone implements they were superseding.

Finally, perhaps as early as 3,000 years ago in Europe, and earlier in Asia Minor, men began to smelt iron. Iron had been known of long before that age, but it was meteoric iron. As most people know, meteoric stones are mainly lumps of iron and nickel. It was rare and used for jewellery or as magical stuff. Once smelting was known to men, there is no great marvel in the getting of iron. They smelted iron by blowing up a charcoal fire, and wrought it by heating and hammering. They produced it at first in comparatively small pieces; its appearance worked a gradual revolution in weapons and implements; but it did not suffice to change the general character of men's surroundings. Much the same daily life that was being led by the more settled Neolithic men 10,000 years ago was being led by peasants in out-of-the-way places all over Europe at the beginning of the eighteenth century.

People talk of the Stone Age, the Bronze Age, and the Iron Age in Europe, but it is misleading to put these ages as if they were of equal importance in history. Much truer is it to say that there were:

(1) An *Early Palæolithic Age,* of vast duration;

(2) A *Later Palæolithic Age,* that lasted not a tithe of the time; and

(3) The *Age of Cultivation,* the age of the white men in Europe, which began there 10,000 or at most 12,000 years ago, of which the Neolithic Period was the beginning, and which is still going on. Elliot Smith has suggested "Palæanthropic" for (1) and "Neoanthropic" for all that has followed.

§ 2

As we have said already, we do not know yet the region in which the ancestors of the brownish Neolithic peoples worked their way up from the Palæolithic stage of human development. Probably it was somewhere about south-western Asia, or in some region now submerged beneath the Mediterranean Sea or the Indian Ocean, that, while the Neanderthal men still lived their hard lives in the bleak climate of a glaciated Europe, the ancestors of the white men developed the rude arts of *their* Later Palæolithic Period. And through the hundred centuries or so while Reindeer men were living under comparatively unprogressive conditions upon the steppes of France, Germany, and Spain, the more favoured and progressive people to the south-east were mastering agriculture, learning to develop their appliances, taming the dog, domesticating cattle, and, as the climate to the north mitigated and the equatorial climate grew more tropical, spreading northward.

All these early chapters of the human story have yet to be disinterred. The material will probably be found in Asia Minor, Persia, Arabia, India, or North Africa, or it lies beneath the Mediterranean waters, or the Red Sea, or the Indian Ocean. Twelve thousand years ago, or thereabouts—we are still too early for anything but the roughest chronology—Neolithic peoples were scattered all over Europe, North Africa, and Asia. They were peoples at about the level of many of the Polynesian islanders of the last century, and they were the most advanced peoples in the world.

§ 3

It will be of interest here to give a brief account of the life of the European Neolithic people before the appearance of metals. We get our light upon that life from various sources. They scattered their refuse about, and in some places (e.g. on the Danish coast) it accumulated in great heaps, known as the kitchen-middens. They buried some of their people, but not the common herd, with great care and distinction, and made huge heaps of earth over their sepulchres; these heaps are the barrows which contribute a feature to the European, Indian, and American scenery in many districts to this day. In connection with these mounds, or independently of them, they set up great stones (megaliths), either singly or in groups, of which Stonehenge in Wiltshire and Carnac in Brittany are among the best-known examples. In various places their villages are still traceable.

One fruitful source of knowledge about Neolithic life comes from Switzerland, and was first revealed by the very dry winter of 1854, when the water level of one of the lakes, sinking to an unheard-of lowness, revealed the foundations of prehistoric pile-dwellings of the Neolithic and early Bronze Ages, built out over the water after the fashion of similar homes that exist to-day in Celebes and elsewhere. Not only were the timbers of those ancient platforms preserved, but a great multitude of wooden, bone, stone, and earthenware utensils and ornaments, remains of food and the like, were found in the peaty accumulations below them. Even pieces of net and garments have been recovered.

Similar lake dwellings existed in Scotland, Ireland, and elsewhere—there are well-known remains at Glastonbury in Somersetshire; in Ireland lake dwellings were inhabited from prehistoric times up to the days when O'Neil of Tyrone was fighting against the English before the plantation of Scotch colonists to replace the Irish in Ulster, in the reign of James I of England. These lake villages had considerable defensive value, and there was a sanitary advantage in living over flowing water.

Probably these Neolithic Swiss pile-dwellings did not shelter the largest communities that existed in those days. They were the homes of small patriarchal groups. Elsewhere upon fertile plains and in more open country there were probably already much larger assemblies of homes than in those mountain valleys.

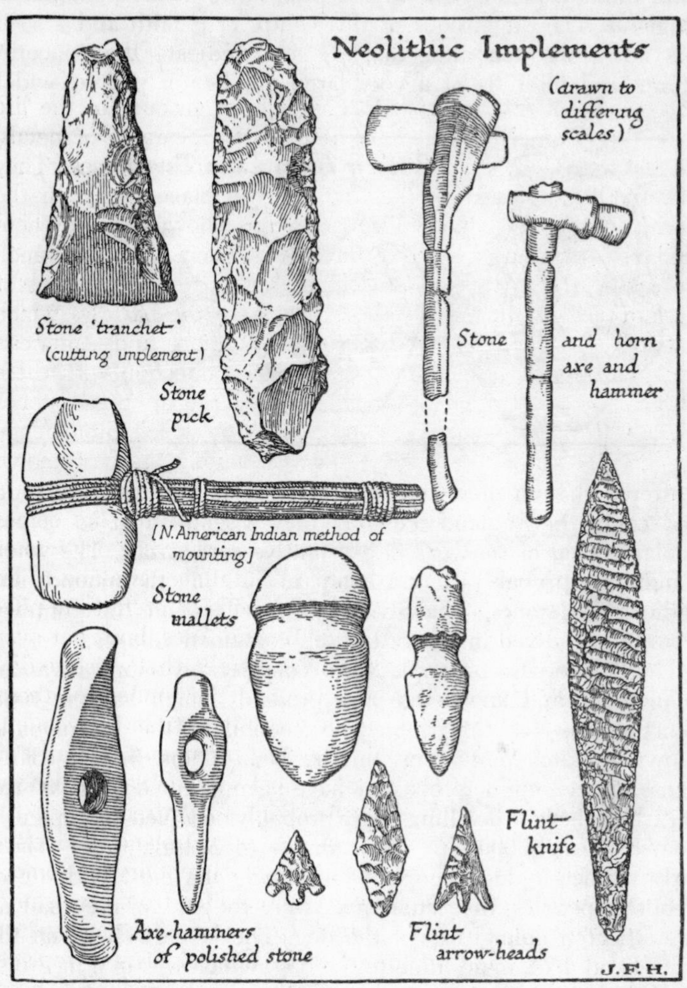

There are traces of such a large community of families in Wiltshire in England; for example, the remains of the stone circle of Avebury, near Silbury mound, were once the "finest megalithic ruin in Europe." It consisted of two circles of stones surrounded by a larger circle and a ditch, and covering altogether twenty-eight and a half acres. From it two avenues of stones, each a mile and a half long, ran west and south on either side of Silbury Hill. Silbury Hill is the largest prehistoric artificial mound in England. The dimensions of this centre of a faith and a social life now forgotten altogether by men indicate the concerted efforts and interests of a very large number of people, widely

scattered though they may have been over the west and south and centre of England. Possibly they assembled at some particular season of the year in a primitive sort of fair. The whole community probably "lent a hand" in building the mounds and hauling the stones. The Swiss pile-dwellers, on the contrary, seem to have lived in practically self-contained villages.

These lake-village people were considerably more advanced in methods and knowledge and probably much later in time, than the early Neolithic people who accumulated the shell mounds, known as kitchen-middens, on the Danish and Scotch coasts. These kitchen-midden folk may have been as early as 10,000 B.C. or earlier; the lake dwellings were probably occupied continuously from 5,000 or 4,000 B.C. down almost to historic times. Those early kitchen-midden people were among the most barbaric of Neolithic peoples, their stone axes were rough, and they had no domesticated animal except the dog. The lake-dwellers, on the other hand, had, in addition to the dog, which was of a medium-sized breed, oxen, goats, and sheep. Later on, as they were approaching the Bronze Age, they got swine. The remains of cattle and goats prevail in their debris, and, having regard to the climate and country about them, it seems probable that these beasts were sheltered in the buildings upon the piles in winter, and that fodder was stored for them. Probably the beasts lived in the same houses with the people, as the men and beasts do now in Swiss chalets.

The people in the houses possibly milked the cows and goats, and milk, perhaps, played as important a part in their economy as it does in that of the mountain Swiss of to-day. But of that we are not sure at present. Milk is not a natural food for adults; it must have seemed queer stuff to take at first; and it may have been only after much breeding that a continuous supply of milk was secured from cows and goats. Some people think that the use of milk, cheese, butter, and other milk products came later into human life when men became nomadic. The writer is, however, disposed to give the Neolithic men credit for having discovered milking. The milk, if they did use it (and, no doubt, in that case sour curdled milk also, but not well-made cheese and butter), they must have kept in earthenware pots, for they had pottery, though it was roughly hand-made pottery and not the shapely product of the potter's wheel.

They eked out this food supply by hunting. They killed and ate red deer and roe deer, bison and wild boar. And they ate the fox, a rather high-flavoured meat, and not what anyone would eat in a world of plenty. Oddly enough, they do not seem to have eaten the hare, although it was available as food. They are supposed to have avoided eating it, as some savages are said to avoid eating it to this day, because they feared that the flesh of so timid a creature might make them, by a sort of infection, cowardly.

Of their agricultural methods we know very little. No ploughs and no hoes have been found. They were of wood and have perished. Neolithic men cultivated and ate wheat, barley, and millet, but they knew nothing of oats or rye. Their grain they roasted, ground between stones, and stored in pots to be eaten when needed. And they made exceedingly solid and heavy bread, because round flat slabs of it have been got out of these deposits. Apparently they had no yeast. If they had no yeast, then they had no fermented drink.

One sort of barley that they had is the sort that was cultivated by the ancient Greeks, Romans, and Egyptians, and they also had an Egyptian variety of wheat, showing that their ancestors had brought or derived this cultivation from the south-east. The centre of diffusion of wheat was somewhere in the eastern Mediterranean region. A wild form is still found in the neighbourhood of Mt. Hermon. When the lake-dwellers sowed their little patches of wheat in Switzerland, they were already following the immemorial practice of mankind. The seed must have been brought age by age from that distant centre of diffusion. In the ancestral lands of the south-east men had already been sowing wheat perhaps for thousands of years. All Old World peoples who had entered upon the Neolithic stage grew and ate wheat, but the American Indians must have developed agriculture independently after their separation from the Old World populations. They never had wheat. Their cultivation was maize, Indian corn, a new-world grain. Those lake-dwellers also ate peas and crab-apples—the only apples that then existed in the world. Cultivation and selection had not yet produced the apple of to-day.

They dressed chiefly in skins, but they also made a rough cloth of flax. Fragments of that flaxen cloth have been discovered. Their nets were made of flax; they had as yet no knowledge of hemp and hempen rope. With the coming of bronze, their pins and ornaments increased in number. There is reason to believe they set great store upon their hair, wearing it in large shocks with pins of bone and afterwards of metal. To judge from the absence of realistic carvings or engravings or paintings, they either did not decorate their garments or decorated them with plaids, spots, interlacing designs, or similar conventional ornament. Before the coming of bronze there is no evidence of stools or tables; the Neolithic people probably squatted on their clay floors. There were no cats in these lake-dwellings; no mice or rats had yet adapted themselves to human dwellings; the cluck of the hen was not as yet added to the sounds of human life, nor the domestic egg to its diet.

Poultry and hens' eggs were late additions to the human cuisine, in spite of the large part they now play in our dietary. The hen is not mentioned in the Old Testament (but note the allusion to an egg, Job vi, 6), nor by Homer. Up to about 1,500 B.C. the only fowls in the world were jungle denizens in India and Burma. The crowing of jungle cocks is noted by Glasfurd, in his admirable accounts of tiger shooting, as the invariable preliminary of dawn in the Indian jungle. Probably poultry were first domesticated in Burma. They got to China, according to the records, only about 1,100 B.C. They reached Greece via Persia before the time of Socrates. In the New Testament, as compared with the Old, the crowing of the cock reproaches Peter for his desertion of the Master.

The chief tool and weapon of Neolithic man was his axe; his

next the bow and arrow. His arrow-heads were of flint, beautifully made, and he lashed them tightly to their shafts. Probably he prepared the ground for his sowing with a pole, or a pole upon which he had stuck a stag's horn. Fish he hooked or harpooned. These implements no doubt stood about in the interior of the house, from the walls of which hung his fowling-nets. On the floor, which was of clay or trodden cow-dung (after the fashion of hut floors in India to-day), stood pots and jars and woven baskets containing grain, milk, and such-like food. Some of the pots and pans hung by rope loops to the walls. At one end of the room, and helping to keep it warm in winter by their animal heat, stabled the beasts. The children took the cows and goats out to graze, and brought them in at night before the wolves and bears came prowling.

Since Neolithic man had the bow, he probably also had stringed instruments, for the rhythmic twanging of a bow-string seems almost inevitably to lead to that. He also had earthenware drums across which skins were stretched; perhaps, also, he made drums by stretching skins over hollow tree-stems. Bone whistles are known even from the Palæolithic time. One may guess that reed pipes were an early invention. We do not know when man began to sing, but evidently he was making music, and, since he had words, songs were no doubt being made. To begin with, perhaps, he just let his voice loose, as one may hear Italian peasants now behind their ploughs singing songs without words. After dark in the winter he sat in his house and talked and sang, and made implements by touch rather than sight. His lighting must have been poor, and chiefly firelight, but there was probably always some fire in the village, summer or winter. Fire was too troublesome to make for men to be willing to let it out readily. Sometimes a great disaster happened to those pile villages; the fire got free, and they were burnt out. The Swiss deposits contain evidence of such catastrophes.

All this we gather from the remains of the Swiss pile-dwellings, and such was the character of the human life that spread over Europe, coming with the forests from the south and from the east as the reindeer and the Reindeer men passed away. It is evident that we have here a way of life already separated by a great gap of thousands of years of invention from its original Palæolithic stage. The steps by which it rose from that condition we can only guess at. From being a hunter hovering upon the outskirts of flocks and herds of wild cattle and sheep, and from being a co-hunter with the dog, man by insensible degrees may have developed a sense of proprietorship in the beasts and struck up a friendship with his canine competitor. He learnt to turn the cattle when they wandered too far; he brought his better brain to bear to guide them to fresh pasture. He hemmed the beasts into valleys and enclosures where he could be sure to find them again. He fed them when they starved, and so slowly he tamed them. Perhaps his agriculture began with the storage of fodder. He reaped, no doubt, before he sowed. The Palæolithic ancestor away in that unknown land of origin to the south-east first supplemented the precarious meat supply of the hunter by eating roots and fruits and wild grains. It is doubtful if at any stage primitive man was wholly carnivorous.

Somewhen he began definitely to sow.

It is one of the most curious and fundamental facts in the growth of human society, as Sir J. G. Frazer has shown in his monumental *Golden Bough,* that the idea of sowing was inextricably entangled in the primitive Neolithic mind with the idea of a human sacrifice. It was an entanglement of the childish dreaming, myth-making primitive mind; no reasoned process will explain it. In the world of 10,000 years ago, whenever seedtime came round there was a human sacrifice. And it was not the sacrifice of any mean or outcast person; it was the sacrifice usually of a chosen youth or maiden, a youth most often, who was treated with profound respect and deference up to the moment of his immolation. He was often, as it were, a sacrificial god-king, and all the details of his killing had become a ritual directed by the old, knowing men and sanctioned by the accumulated usage of ages.

Wherever man has reached or passed the beginning of agriculture, this human sacrifice or some surviving trace of it appears.

§ 4

All these early beginnings must have taken place far back in time, and in regions of the world that have still to be effectively explored by the archæologist. Neolithic men were long past these beginnings; they were already close, a few thousand years, to the dawn of written tradition and the remembered history of mankind. Without any very great shock or break, bronze came at last into human life, giving a great advantage in warfare to those tribes who first obtained it. Written history had already begun before weapons of iron came into Europe to supersede bronze.

Already in those days a sort of primitive trade had sprung up. Bronze and bronze weapons, and such rare and hard stones as jade, gold because of its plastic and ornamental possibilities, amber because of its translucent beauty, and skins and flax-net and cloth, were being swapped and stolen and passed from hand to hand over great stretches of country. Salt also was probably being traded. On a meat dietary men can live without salt, but grain-consuming people need it just as herbivorous animals need it. Hopf says that bitter tribal wars have been carried on by the desert tribes of the Sudan in recent years for the possession of salt deposits in Fezzan. To begin with, barter, blackmail, tribute, and robbery by violence passed into each other by insensible degrees. Men got what they wanted by such means as they could.

§ 5

So far we have been telling of a history without events, a history of ages and periods and stages in development. But, before we conclude this portion of the human story, we must record what was probably an event of primary importance and at first, perhaps, of tragic importance to developing mankind, and that was the breaking in of the Atlantic waters to the great Mediterranean valley.

The reader must keep in mind that we are endeavouring to give him plain statements that he can take hold of comfortably. But both in the matter of our time charts and the maps we have given of pre-historic geography there is necessarily much speculative matter. We have dated the last Glacial Age and the appearance of the true men as about 50,000 or 35,000 years ago. Please bear that "about" in mind. The truth may be 60,000 or 20,000. But it is no good saying "a very long time" or "ages" ago, because then the reader will not know whether we mean centuries or millions of years. Figures are better than that. And similarly these maps we give represent not the truth, but something like the truth. The outline of the land was "some such outline." There were such seas and such land masses. But both Mr. Horrabin, who drew these maps, and the writer, who incited him to do so, have preferred to err on the timid side. We are not geologists enough to launch out into original research in these matters, and so we have stuck to the 40-fathom line and the recent deposits as our guides for our post-glacial map and for the map of 13,000 to 10,000 B.C. But in one matter we have gone beyond these guides. It is practically certain that at the end of the last Glacial Age the Mediterranean was a couple of land-locked sea basins, not connected—or only connected by a torrential overflow river. The eastern basin was the fresher; it was fed by the Nile, the "Adriatic" river, the "Red-Sea" river, and perhaps by a river that poured down amidst the mountains that are now the Greek Archipelago, from the very much bigger Sea of Central Asia that then existed. Almost certainly Neolithic men wandered over that now lost Mediterranean paradise.

The reasons for believing this are very good and plain. To this day the Mediterranean is a sea of evaporation. The rivers that flow into it do not make up for the evaporation from its surface. There is a constant current of water pouring into the Mediterranean from the Atlantic, and another current streaming in from the Bosphorus and Black Sea. For the Black Sea gets more water than it needs from the big rivers that flow into it; it is an overflowing sea, while the Mediterranean is a thirsty sea. From which it must be plain that when the Mediterranean was cut off both from the Atlantic Ocean and the Black Sea it must have been a shrinking sea with its waters sinking to a much lower level than those of the ocean outside. This is the case of the Caspian Sea to-day. Still more so is it the case with the Dead Sea.

But if this reasoning is sound, then where to-day roll the blue waters of the Mediterranean there must once have been great areas of land, and land with a very agreeable climate. This was probably the case during the last Glacial Age, and we do not know how near it was to our time when the change occurred that brought back the ocean waters into the Mediterranean basin. Certainly there must have been Azilian and Neolithic people going about in the valleys and forests of these regions that are now submerged. The Neolithic Dark Whites, the people of the Mediterranean race, may have gone far towards the beginnings of settlement and civilization in that lost Mediterranean valley.

Mr. W. B. Wright has made some very stimulating suggestions about this. He suggests that in the Mediterranean basin there were two lakes, "one a fresh-water lake, in the eastern depression, which drained into the other in the western depression. It is interesting to think what must have happened when the ocean level rose once more as a result of the dissipation of the ice-sheets, and its waters began to pour over into the Mediterranean area. The inflow, small at first, must have ultimately increased to enormous dimensions, as the channel was slowly lowered by erosion and the ocean level slowly rose. If there were any unconsolidated materials on the sill of the Strait, the result must have been a genuine debacle; and if we consider the length of time which even an enormous torrent would take to fill such a basin as that of the Mediterranean, we must conclude that this result was likely to have been attained in any case. Now, this

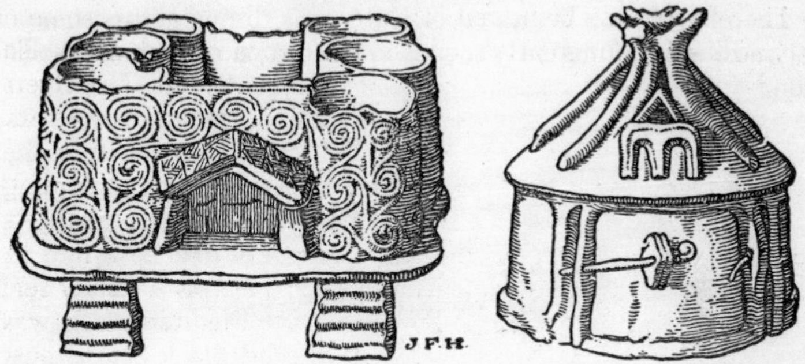

Hut urns. the first probably representing a lake-dwelling... After Lubbock.

may seem all the wildest speculation, but it is not entirely so, for if we examine a submarine contour map of the Straits of Gibraltar, we find there is an enormous valley running up from the Mediterranean deep, right through the Straits, and trenching some distance out on to the Atlantic shelf. This valley or gorge is probably the work of the inflowing waters of the ocean at the termination of the period of interior drainage."

This refilling of the Mediterranean, which by the rough chronology we are employing in this book may have happened somewhen between 15,000 and 10,000 B.C., must have been one of the greatest single events in the pre-history of our race. If the later date is the truer, then the crude beginnings of civilization, the first lake-dwellings and the first cultivation, were probably round that eastern Levantine lake, that fresh-water sea, into which there flowed not only the Nile, but the two great rivers that are now the Adriatic and the Red Sea.

Suddenly the ocean waters began to break through over the westward hills and to pour in upon these primitive peoples—the lake that had been their home and friend, became their enemy; its waters rose and never abated; their settlements were submerged; the waters pursued them in their flight. Day by day and year by year the waters spread up the valleys and drove mankind before them. Many must have been surrounded and caught by that continually rising salt flood. It knew no check; it came faster and faster; it rose over the tree-tops, over the hills, until it had filled the whole basin of the present Mediterranean and until it lapped the mountain cliffs of Arabia and Africa. Far away, long before the dawn of written history, this catastrophe occurred.

Thereby, it may be, a veil of water was drawn across some of the most fascinating early scenes in the drama of human association.

X

EARLY THOUGHT

§ 1. *Primitive Philosophy.* § 2. *The Old Man in Religion.* § 3. *Fear and Hope in Religion.* § 4. *Stars and Seasons.* § 5. *Story-telling and Myth-making.* § 6. *Complex Origins of Religion.*

§ 1

BEFORE we go on to tell how 6,000 or 7,000 years ago men began to gather into the first towns and to develop something more than the loose-knit tribes that had hitherto been their highest political association, something must be said about the things that were going on inside these brains of which we have traced the growth and development through a period of 500,000 years from the ape-man stage.

What was man thinking about himself and about the world in those remote days?

At first he thought very little about anything but immediate things. At first he was busy thinking such things as: "Here is a bear; what shall I do?" Or, "There is a squirrel; how can I get it?" Until language had developed to some extent there could have been little thinking beyond the range of actual experience, for language is the instrument of thought as book-keeping is the instrument of business. It records and fixes and enables thought to get on to more and more complex ideas. It is the hand of the mind to hold and keep.

Primordial man, before he could talk, probably saw very vividly, mimicked very cleverly, gestured, laughed, danced, and lived without much speculation about whence he came or why he lived. He feared the dark, no doubt, and thunderstorms, and big animals, and queer things and whatever he dreamt about, and no doubt he did things to propitiate what he feared or to change his luck and please the imaginary powers in rock and beast and river. He made no clear distinction between animate and inanimate things: if a stick hurt him, he kicked it; if the river foamed and flooded, he thought it was hostile. His thought was probably very much at the level of a bright little contemporary boy of four or five. He had the same subtle unreasonableness of transition and the same limitations. But since he had little or no speech he would do little to pass on the fancies that came to him, and develop any tradition or concerted acts about them.

The drawings even of Late Palæolithic man do not suggest that he paid any attention to sun or moon or stars or trees. He was preoccupied only with animals and men. Probably he took day and night, sun and stars, trees and mountains, as being in the nature of things—as a child takes its meal-times and its nursery staircase for granted. So far as we can judge, he drew no fantasies, no ghosts or anything of that sort. The Reindeer man's drawings are fearless familiar things, with no hint about them of any veneration. He may have felt that drawing a beast made it come; his drawings may have been magic drawings for luck in hunting, but they do not look like drawings for worship. There is scarcely anything that we can suppose to be a religious or mystical symbol at all in his productions.

No doubt he had a certain amount of what is called *fetishism* in his life; he did things we should now think unreasonable to produce desired ends—for that is all fetishism amounts to; it is only incorrect science based on guesswork or false analogy, and entirely different in its nature from religion. No doubt he was excited by his dreams, and his dreams mixed up at times in his mind with his waking impressions and puzzled him. Since he buried his dead, and since even the later Neanderthal men seem to have buried their dead, and apparently with food and weapons, it has been argued that he had a belief in a future life. But it is just as reasonable to suppose that early men buried their dead with food and weapons because they doubted if they were dead, which is not the same thing as believing them to have immortal spirits, and that their belief in their continuing vitality was reinforced by dreams of the departed. They may have ascribed a sort of were-wolf existence to the dead, and wished to propitiate them.

The Reindeer man, we feel, was too intelligent and too like ourselves not to have had some speech, but quite probably it was not very serviceable for anything beyond direct statement or matter-of-fact narration. He lived in a larger community than the Neanderthaler or his own Neanderthaloid ancestor or any great ape, but how large the tribe we do not know. Except when game is swarming, hunting communities must not keep together in large bodies or they will starve. The Indians who depend upon the caribou in Labrador must be living under circumstances rather like those of the Reindeer men. They scatter in small family groups, as the caribou scatter in search of food; but when the deer collect for the seasonal migration, the Indians also collect. That is the time for trade and feasts and marriage.

The simplest American Indian is 10,000 years more sophisticated than the Reindeer man, but probably that sort of gathering and dispersal was also the way of Reindeer men. At Solutré in France there are traces of a great camping and feasting place. There was no doubt an exchange of news there, but one may doubt if there was anything like an exchange of ideas. One sees no scope in such a life for theology or philosophy or superstition or speculation. Fears, yes; but unsystematic fears; fancies and freaks of the imagination, but personal and transitory freaks and fancies.

Perhaps there was a certain power of suggestion in these encounters. A fear really felt needs few words for its transmission; a value set upon something may be very simply conveyed.

In these questions of primitive thought and religion we must remember that the lowly and savage peoples of to-day probably throw very little light on the mental state of men before the days of fully developed language. Primordial man could have had little or no tradition before the development of speech. All savage and primitive peoples of to-day, on the contrary, are soaked in tradition—the tradition of thousands of generations. They may have weapons like their remote ancestors and methods like them, but what were slight and shallow impressions on the minds of their predecessors are now deep and intricate grooves worn throughout the intervening centuries generation by generation.

§ 2

Certain very fundamental things there may have been in men's minds long before the coming of speech. The mental life of the later Palæolithic man was close to our own, and like our own it was built on the foundations of that ancient more solitary, more animal, ape-like ancestor. The rapidly developing science of psycho-analysis is searching through our dreams, and our inadvertent moods and our childish ideas and what remains ascertainable of savage thought, for the foundation substance of that more primitive being who is our substratum, and it is rapidly building up an interpretation of our feelings upon that search. The great apes pair and rear their young. The young go in fear of the old male, and presently the young males rouse his jealousy and are killed or driven off. The females are the protected slaves of the old male. That is the general state of affairs with all slightly gregarious animals, and there is no reason to suppose that the sub-man differed in such respects.

The fear of the Old Man was the beginning of social wisdom. The young of the primitive squatting-place grew up under that fear. Objects associated with him were probably forbidden. Everyone was forbidden to touch his spear or to sit in his place, just as to-day little boys must not touch father's pipe or sit in his chair. He was probably the master of all the women. The youths of the little community had to remember that. Their mothers taught them to remember that. Their mothers instilled into them dread and respect and consideration for the Old Man.

The idea of *something forbidden,* the idea of things being, as it is called, *tabu,* not to be touched, not to be looked at, may thus have got well into the sub-human mind at a very early stage indeed. J. J. Atkinson, in his *Primal Law,* an ingenious analysis of these primitive tabus which are found among savage peoples all over the world, the tabus that separate brother and sister, the tabus that make a man run and hide from his step-mother, traces them to such a fundamental cause as this. Only by respecting this primal law, could the young male hope to escape the Old Man's wrath.

A disposition to propitiate the Old Man even after he was dead is also quite understandable. He must have been an actor in many a primordial nightmare. One was not sure that he *was* dead. He might only be asleep, or shamming. Long after an Old Man was dead, when there was nothing to represent him but a mound and a megalith, the women would continue to convey to their children how awful and wonderful he was. And being still a terror to his own little tribe, it was easy to go on to hoping that he would be a terror to other and hostile people. In his life he had fought for his tribe, even if he had bullied it. Why not when he was dead? One sees that the Old Man idea was an idea very natural to the primitive mind and capable of great developments. The fear of the Father passed by imperceptible degrees into the fear of the Tribal God.

And opposed to the Old Man, more human and kindlier, was

the Mother, who helped and sheltered and advised. It was she who trained her children to obey and fear him. She whispered in the corner and taught mysteries. The psycho-analysis of Freud and Jung has done much to help us to realize how great a part Father fear and Mother love still play in the adaptation of the human mind to social needs. Their exhaustive study of childish and youthful dreams and imaginations has done much to help in the reconstruction of the soul of primitive man. It was, as it were, the soul of a powerful child. He saw the universe in terms of the family Lord. His fear of, his abjection before, the Old Man mingled with his fear of the dangerous animals about him. Even in modern nurseries Dadda will sometimes become a bear. It was easy for the sublimated Old Man, the initial God, to put on an animal form.

The woman goddesses were kindlier and more subtle. They helped, they protected, they gratified, and consoled. Yet at the same time there was something about them less comprehensible than the direct brutality of the Old Man, a greater mystery. So that the Woman also had her vestiture of fear for primitive man. Goddesses were feared. They had to do with secret things.

§ 3

Another very fundamental idea probably arose in men's minds early out of the mysterious visitation of infectious diseases, and that was the idea of uncleanness and of being accurst. From that, too, there may have come an idea of avoiding particular places and persons, and persons in particular phases of health. Here was the root of another set of tabus.

Then man, from the very dawn of his mental life, may have had a feeling of the sinister about places and things. Animals, who dread traps, have that feeling. A tiger will abandon its usual jungle route at the sight of a few threads of cotton. Like most young animals, young human beings are easily made fearful of this or that by their nurses and seniors. Here is another set of ideas, ideas of repulsion and avoidance, that sprang up almost inevitably in men.

As soon as speech began to develop, it must have got to work upon such fundamental feelings and begun to systematize them, and keep them in mind. By talking together men would reinforce each other's fears, and establish a common tradition of tabus of things forbidden and of things unclean. With the idea of uncleanness would come ideas of cleansing and of removing a curse. The cleansing would be conducted through the advice and with the aid of wise old men or wise old women, and in such cleansing would lie the germ of the earliest priestcraft and witchcraft. To lift curses, to remove evils, to confirm and establish, one must needs do potent things. And was there anything more potent in existence than killing, the shedding of life-blood?

Speech from the first would be a powerful supplement to the merely imitative education and to the education of cuffs and blows conducted by a speechless parent. Mothers would tell their young and scold their young. As speech developed, men would find they had experiences and persuasions that gave them or seemed to give them power. They would make secrets of these things.

There is a double streak in the human mind, a streak of cunning secretiveness and a streak, perhaps of later origin, that makes us all anxious to tell and astonish and impress each other. Many people make secrets in order to have secrets to tell. These secrets of early man they would convey to younger, more impressionable people, more or less honestly and impressively in some process of initiation. Moreover, the pedagogic spirit overflows in the human mind; most people like "telling other people not to." Extensive arbitrary prohibitions for the boys, for the girls, for the women, also probably came very early into human history, and were congenial things to impose.

Sacrifice had a double origin. There must have been the disposition to propitiate the Old Man, and also that craving to do a powerful thing. Sacrifice has perhaps always been rather magic than propitiation. It dispelled, it confirmed, and because it did so then, when one came to think about it, one concluded that it must be pleasing to the spirit of the Old Man, grown into the Tribal God. But it was done because it was done and because it was a tremendous thing to do.

§ 4

Out of such ideas and a jumble of kindred ones grew the first quasi-religious elements in human life. With every development of speech it became possible to intensify and develop the tradition of tabus and restraints and ceremonies. There is not a savage or barbaric race to-day that is not held in a net of such tradition.

With the coming of primitive pasturage there would be a considerable broadening out of this sort of practice. Things hitherto unheeded would be found of importance in human affairs. Neolithic man was nomadic in a different spirit from the mere daylight drift after food of the primordial hunter. He was a herdsman upon whose mind a sense of direction and the lie of the land had been forced. He watched his flock by night as well as by day. The sun by day and presently the stars by night helped to guide his migrations; he began to find after many ages that the stars are steadier guides than the sun. He would begin to note particular stars and star groups; and to distinguish any individual thing was, for primitive man, to believe it individualized and personal. He would begin to think of outstanding stars as persons, very shining and dignified and trustworthy persons looking at him like bright eyes in the night. They came back night after night. They helped him even as the Tribal God helped him.

His primitive tillage strengthened his sense of the seasons. Particular stars ruled his heavens when seedtime was due. Up to a certain point, a mountain peak or what not, a bright star moved, night after night. It stopped there, and then night by night it receded. Surely this was a sign, a silent, marvellous warning to the wise. The beginnings of agriculture we must remember were in the subtropical zone, or even nearer the equator, where stars of the first magnitude shine with a splendour unknown in more temperate latitudes. The seasons there are not so plainly marked by snow and storm as in the north. It was difficult to be sure when the rains or the floods were due. But the stars did not lie.

And Neolithic man was counting, and falling under the spell of numbers. There are savage languages that have no word for any number above five. Some peoples cannot go above two. But Neolithic man in the lands of his origin in Asia and Africa even more than in Europe was already counting his accumulating possessions. He was beginning to use tallies, and wondering at the triangularity of three, and the squareness of four, and why some quantities like twelve were easy to divide in all sorts of ways, and others, like thirteen, impossible. Twelve became a noble, generous, and familiar number to him, and thirteen rather an outcast and disreputable one.

Probably man began reckoning time by the clock of the full and new moons. Moonlight is an important thing to herdsmen who no longer merely hunt their herds, but watch and guard them. Moonlight too was, perhaps, his time for love-making, as indeed it may have been for primordial man and the ground-ape ancestor before him. But from the phases of the moon, as his tillage increased, man's attitude would go on to the greater cycle of the seasons. Primordial man probably only drifted before the winter as the days grew cold. Neolithic man knew surely that the winter would come, and stored his fodder and presently his grain. He had to fix a seedtime, a propitious seedtime, or his sowing was a failure. The earliest recorded reckoning is by moons and by generations of men. With agriculture began the difficult task of squaring the lunar month with the solar year; a task which has left its scars on our calendar to-day. Easter shifts uneasily from year to year, to the great discomfort of holiday-makers; it is now inconveniently early and now late in the season, because of this ancient reference of time to the moon.

And when men began to move with set intention from place to place with their animal and other possessions, then they would begin to develop the idea of other places in which they were not, and to think of what might be in those other places. And in any valley where they lingered for a time, they would, remembering how they got there, ask, "How did this or that other thing get here?" They would begin to wonder what was beyond the mountains, and where the sun went when it set, and what was above the clouds.

§ 5

The capacity for telling things increased with their vocabulary. The simple individual fancies, the unsystematic fetish tricks and fundamental tabus of Palæolithic man began to be handed on and made into a more consistent system. Men began to tell stories about themselves, about the tribe, about its tabus and why they had to be, about the world and the why for the world. A tribal mind came into existence, a tradition. Palæolithic man was certainly more of a free individualist, more of an artist as well as more of a savage, than Neolithic man. Neolithic man was coming under prescription; he could be trained from his youth and told to do things and not to do things. He was not so free to form independent ideas of his own about things. He had thoughts given to him; he was under a new power of suggestion.

To have more words and to attend more to words is not simply to increase mental power; words themselves are powerful things and dangerous things. Palæolithic man's words, perhaps, were chiefly just names. He used them for what they were. But Neolithic man was thinking about these words, he was thinking about a number of things with a great deal of verbal confusion, and getting to some odd conclusions. In speech he had woven a net to bind his race together, but also a net to bind his feet. Man was binding himself into new and larger and more efficient combinations indeed, but at a price.

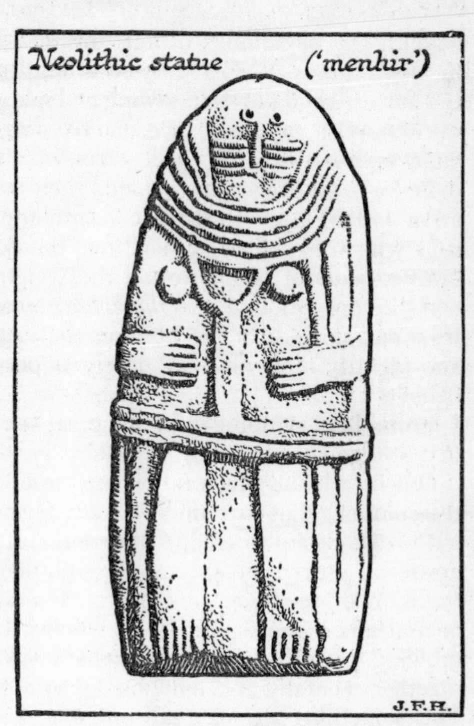

A Carved Statue ("Menhir") of the Neolithic Period—a contrast to the freedom and vigour of Palaeolithic Art

One of the most notable things about the Neolithic Age is the total absence of that free direct artistic impulse which was the supreme quality of later Palæolithic man. We find much industry, much skill, polished implements, pottery with conventional designs, co-operation upon all sorts of things, but no evidence of personal creativeness. Self-suppression is beginning for men. Man has entered upon the long and tortuous and difficult path towards a life for the common good, with all its sacrifice of personal impulse, which he is still treading to-day.

Certain things appear in the mythology of mankind again and again. Neolithic man was enormously impressed by serpents—and he no longer took the sun for granted. Nearly everywhere that Neolithic culture went, there went a disposition to associate the sun and the serpent in decoration and worship. This primitive serpent-worship spread ultimately far beyond the regions where the snake is of serious practical importance in human life. But when at last the centre of diffusion of the Neolithic way of living is determined, it will surely be a land in which snake and sunlight were the facts of primary importance.

§ 6

With the beginnings of agriculture a fresh set of ideas arose in men's minds. We have noted a long-established connection in the human mind between sowing and sacrifice. Sowing was becoming the most important of economic acts; it was natural to associate with it the most vivid of conceivable acts, the killing of a man. Sir J. G. Frazer has pursued the development of this association, linking up with it the conception of special sacrificial persons who were killed at seedtime, the conception of a specially purified class of people to kill these victims, the class of priests, and the conception of a *sacrament,* a ceremonial feast in which the tribe eat portions of the body of the victim in order to share in and identify themselves as closely as possible with the sacrificial benefits.

From this beginning grew the great seasonal sacrificial religions that still remain with us.

Out of all these factors, out of the Old Man tradition, out of the emotions that surround Women for men and Men for women, out of the desire to escape infection and uncleanness, out of the desire for power and success through magic, out of the sacrificial tradition of seedtime, and out of a number of like beliefs and mental experiments and misconceptions, a complex something was growing up in the lives of men which was beginning to bind them together mentally and emotionally in a common life and action. This something we may call *religion* (Lat. *religare,* to bind). It was not a simple or logical something, it was a tangle of ideas about commanding beings and spirits, about gods, about all sorts of "musts" and "must-nots." Like all other human interests, religion has grown. It must be clear from what has gone before that primitive man—much less his ancestral apes and his ancestral Mesozoic mammals—could have had no idea of God or Religion; only very slowly did his brain and his powers of comprehension become capable of such general conceptions. Religion is something that has grown up with and through human association. God has been and is still being discovered by man.

This book is not a theological book, and it is not for us to embark upon theological discussion; but it is a part, a necessary and central part, of the history of man to describe the dawn and development of his religious ideas and their influence upon his activities. All these factors we have noted must have contributed to this development, and various writers have laid most stress

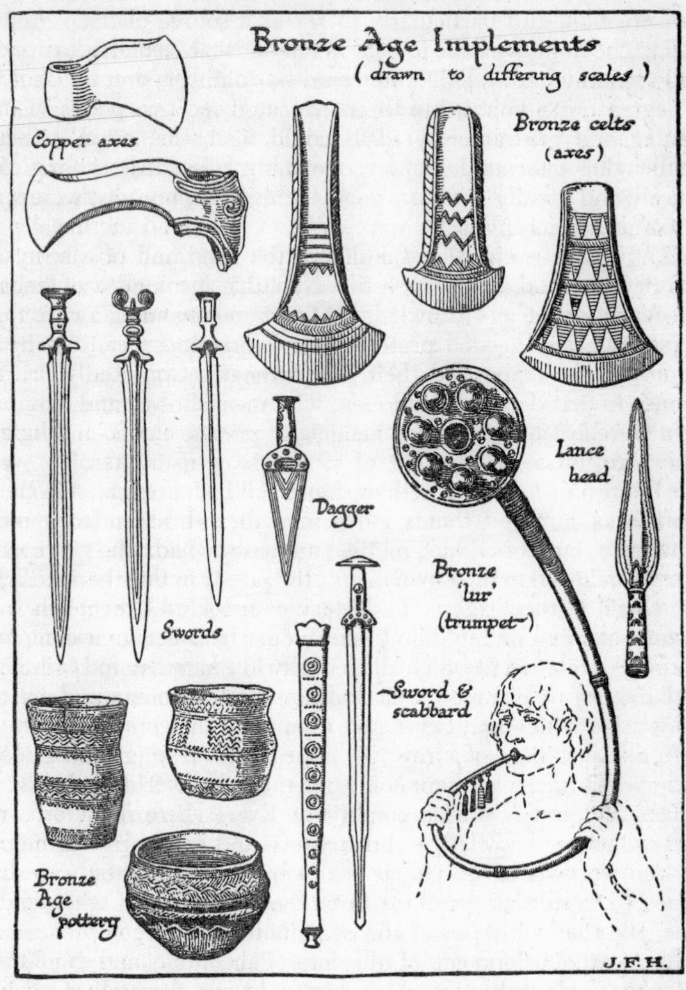

upon one or other of them. Sir J. G. Frazer has been the leading student of the derivation of sacraments from magic sacrifices. Grant Allen, following Herbert Spencer, in his *Evolution of the Idea of God,* laid stress chiefly on the posthumous worship of the

"Old Man." Sir E. B. Tylor (*Primitive Culture*) gave his attention mainly to the disposition of primitive man to ascribe a soul to every object, animate and inanimate. Mr. A. E. Crawley, in *The Tree of Life*, has called attention to other centres of impulse and emotion, and particularly to sex as a source of deep excitement. The thing we have to bear in mind is that Neolithic man was still mentally undeveloped, he could be confused, and illogical to a degree quite impossible to an educated modern person. Conflicting and contradictory ideas could lie in his mind without challenging one another; now one thing ruled his thoughts intensely and vividly and now another; his fears, his acts, were still disconnected as children's are.

Confusedly, under the stimulus of the need and possibility of co-operation and a combined life, Neolithic mankind was feeling out for guidance and knowledge. Men were becoming aware that personally they needed protection and direction, cleansing from impurity, power beyond their own strength. Confusedly, in response to that demand, bold men, wise men, shrewd and cunning men were arising to become magicians, priests, chiefs, and kings. They are not to be thought of as cheats or usurpers of power, nor the rest of mankind as their dupes. All men are mixed in their motives; a hundred things move men to seek ascendancy over other men, but not all such motives are base or bad. The magicians usually believed in their own magic, the priests in their ceremonies, the chiefs in their right. The history of mankind henceforth is a history of more or less blind endeavours to conceive a common purpose in relation to which all men may live happily, and to create and develop a common consciousness and a common stock of knowledge which may serve and illuminate that purpose.

In a vast variety of forms this appearance of kings and priests and magic men was happening all over the world under later Palæolithic and Neolithic conditions. Everywhere mankind was seeking where knowledge and mastery and magic power might reside; everywhere individual men were willing, honestly or dishonestly, to rule, to direct, or to be the magic beings who would reconcile the confusions of the community.

A queer development of the later Palæolithic and Neolithic Ages was self-mutilation. Men began to cut themselves about, to excise noses, ears, fingers, teeth and the like, and to attach all sorts of superstitious ideas to these acts. Many children today pass through a similar phase in their mental development. There is a phase in the life of most little girls when they are not to be left alone with a pair of scissors for fear that they will cut off their hair. No animal does anything of this sort. This, too, has left its trace in the rite of circumcision, upon the religions of Judaism and Islam.

	EUROPE	EGYPT	MESOPOTAMIA
18,000 B.C.	Steppe Period	Men entering upon Neolithic stage Agriculture beginning	
	Reindeer men going		
15,000	Forest (transition) Period		
13,000	Azilian		
10,000	Neolithic men spreading into Europe	Heliolithic culture developing	
8,000	First lake dwellings		Sumerian civilization dawns
			Bronze
6,000			Nippur & Eridu
5,000			First Sumerian writing
4,000		First Dynasty The Pyramids	
3000	Bronze		
2,000	Spreading of Aryan system of languages		Sargon I
1,000	Iron		Iron
320	Alexander the Great		
50	Julius Caesar		
A.D.			
1920	Christian Era		

J.F.H.

Time Diagram showing the general duration of the Neolithic Period in which Early Thought developed

In many ways the simplicity, directness, and detachment of a later Palæolithic rock-painter appeal more to modern adult sympathies than does the state of mind of these Neolithic men, full of the fear of some ancient Old Man who had developed into a Tribal God, obsessed by ideas of sacrificial propitiations, mutilations and magic murder. No doubt the reindeer hunter was a ruthless hunter and a combative and passionate creature, but he killed for reasons we can still understand; Neolithic man, under the sway of talk and a confused thought process, killed on theory, he killed for monstrous and now incredible ideas, he killed those he loved through fear and under direction. Those Neolithic men not only made human sacrifices at seedtime; there is every reason to suppose they sacrificed wives and slaves at the burial of their chieftains; they killed men, women, and children whenever they were under adversity and thought the gods were athirst. All these things were passed on into the Bronze Age. Hitherto a social consciousness had been asleep and not even dreaming in human history. Before it awakened it produced nightmares.

Away beyond the dawn of history, 3,000 or 4,000 years ago, one thinks of the Wiltshire uplands in the twilight of a midsummer day's morning. The torches pale in the growing light. One has a dim apprehension of a procession through the avenue of stone, of priests, perhaps fantastically dressed with skins and horns and horrible painted masks—not the robed and bearded dignitaries our artists represent the Druids to have been—of chiefs in skins adorned with necklaces of teeth and bearing spears and axes, their great heads of hair held up with pins of bone, of women in skins or flaxen robes, of a great peering crowd of shock-headed men and naked children. They have assembled from many distant places; the ground between the avenues and Silbury Hill is dotted with their encampments. A certain festive cheerfulness prevails. And amidst the throng march the appointed human victims, submissive, helpless, staring towards the distant smoking altar at which they are to die—that the harvests may be good and the tribe increase.

To that had life progressed 3,000 or 4,000 years ago from its starting-place in the slime of the tidal beaches.

XI

THE RACES OF MANKIND

§ 1. *Is Mankind Still Differentiating?* § 2. *The Main Races of Mankind.* § 3. *The Brunet Peoples.* § 4. *The So-called "Heliolithic" Culture.* § 5. *The American Indians.*

§ 1

IT IS necessary now to discuss plainly what is meant by a phrase, used often very carelessly, "The Races of Mankind."

It must be evident from what has already been explained that man, so widely spread and subjected therefore to great differences of climate, consuming very different food in different regions, attacked by different enemies, must always have been undergoing considerable local modification and differentiation. Man, like every other species of living thing, has constantly been tending to differentiate into several species; wherever a body of men has been cut off, in islands or oceans or by deserts or mountains, from the rest of humanity, it must have begun very soon to develop special characteristics, specially adapted to the local conditions. But, on the other hand, man is usually a wandering and enterprising animal, for whom there exist few insurmountable barriers. Men imitate men, fight and conquer them, interbreed, one people with another. Concurrently for thousands of years there have been two sets of forces at work, one tending to separate men into a multitude of local varieties, and another to remix and blend these varieties together before a separate species has been established.

These two sets of forces may have fluctuated in this relative effect in the past. Palæolithic man, for instance, may have been more of a wanderer, he may have drifted about over a much greater area, than later Neolithic man; he was less fixed to any sort of home or lair, he was tied by fewer possessions. Being a hunter, he was obliged to follow the migrations of his ordinary quarry. A few bad seasons may have shifted him hundreds of miles. He may therefore have mixed very widely and developed few varieties over the greater part of the world.

The appearance of agriculture tended to tie those communities of mankind that took it up the region in which it was most conveniently carried on, and so to favour differentiation. Mixing or differentiation is not dependent upon a higher or lower stage of civilization; many savage tribes wander now for hundreds of miles; many English villagers in the eighteenth century, on the other hand, had never been more than eight or ten miles from their villages, neither they nor their fathers nor grandfathers before them. Hunting peoples often have enormous range. The Labrador country, for instance, is inhabited by a few thousand Indians, who follow the one great herd of caribou as it wanders yearly north and then south again in pursuit of food. This mere handful of people covers a territory as large as France. Nomad peoples also range very widely. Some Kalmuck tribes are said to travel nearly a thousand miles between summer and winter pasture.

It carries out this suggestion, that Palæolithic man ranged widely and was distributed, thinly indeed but uniformly, throughout the world, that the Palæolithic remains we find are everywhere astonishingly uniform. To quote Sir John Evans, "The implements in distant lands are so identical in form and character with the British specimens that they might have been manufactured by the same hands. . . . On the banks of the Nile, many hundreds of feet above its present level, implements of the European types have been discovered; while in Somaliland, in an ancient river-valley at a great elevation above the sea, Mr. H. W. Seton-Karr has collected a large number of implements formed of flint and quartzite which, judging from their form and character, might have been dug out of the drift-deposits of the Somme and the Seine, the Thames or the ancient Solent."

Phases of spreading and intermixture have probably alternated with phases of settlement and specialization in the history of mankind. But up to a few hundred years ago it is probable that since the end of the Palæolithic Age at least mankind has on the whole been differentiating. The species has differentiated in that period into a very great number of varieties, many of which have been again blended with others, which have spread and undergone further differentiation or become extinct. Where ever there has been a strongly marked local difference of conditions and a check upon intermixture, there one is almost obliged to assume a variety of mankind must have appeared. Of such local varieties there must have been a great multitude.

In one remote corner of the world, Tasmania, a little cut-off population of people remained in the early Palæolithic stage until the discovery of that island by the Dutch in 1642. They are now, unhappily, extinct. The last Tasmanian died in 1876. They may have been cut off from the rest of mankind for 15,000 or 20,000 or 25,000 years.

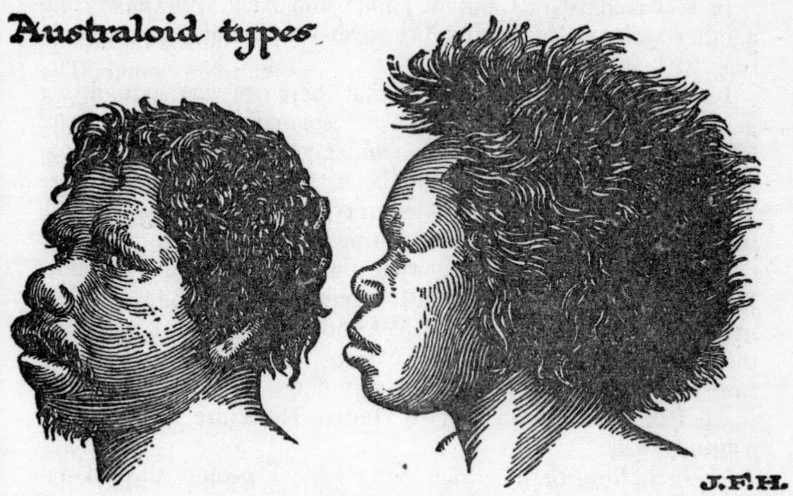

But among the numerous obstacles and interruptions to intermixture there have been certain main barriers, such as the Atlantic Ocean, the highlands and now vanished seas of Central Asia and the like, which have cut off great groups of varieties from other great groups of varieties over long periods of time. These separated groups of varieties developed very early certain broad resemblances and differences. Most of the varieties of men in eastern Asia and America, but not all, have now this in common—they have yellowish buff skins, straight black hair, and, often, high cheek-bones. Most of the native peoples of Africa south of the Sahara, but not all, have black or blackish skins, flat noses, thick lips, and frizzy hair. In north and western Europe a great number of peoples have fair hair, blue eyes, and ruddy complexions; and about the Mediterranean there is a prevalence of white-skinned peoples with dark eyes and black hair. These dark white people seem to be a central mass of people passing by almost insensible gradations northward, eastward and southward into the more specialized whites and yellows and the divergent blacks. The black hair of many of these dark whites is straight, but never so strong and waveless as the hair of the yellow peoples. It is straighter in the east than in the west. In southern India we find brownish and darker peoples with straight black hair, and these as we pass eastward give place to more distinctly yellow peoples.

In scattered islands and in Papua and New Guinea we find another series of black and brownish peoples of a more lowly type with frizzy hair.

But it must be borne in mind that these are very loose-fitting generalizations. Some of the areas and isolated pockets of mankind in the Asiatic area may have been under conditions more like those in the European area; some of the African areas are of a more Asiatic and less distinctively African type. We find a wavy-haired, fairish, hair-skinned race, the Ainu, in Japan. They are more like the Europeans in their facial type than the surrounding yellow Japanese. They may be a drifted patch of the whites or they may be a quite distinct people. We find primitive black people in the Andaman Islands far away from Australia and far away from Africa. There is a streak of very negroid blood traceable in south Persia and some parts of India. These are the "Asiatic" negroids.

There is little or no proof that all black people, the Australians, the Asiatic negroids and the negroes, derive from one origin, but only that they have lived for vast periods under similar conditions. Possibly the more ancient races of men were all dusky or black, and fairness is new. We must not assume that human beings in the eastern Asiatic area were all differentiating in one direction and all the human beings in Africa in another. There were great currents of tendency, it is true, but there were also backwaters, eddies, admixtures, readmixtures, and leakages from one main area to the other. A coloured map of the world to show the races would not present just four great areas of colour; it would have to be dabbed over with a multitude of tints and intermediate shades, simple here, mixed and overlapping there.

In the early Neolithic Period in Europe—it may be 10,000 or 12,000 years ago or so—*Homo sapiens* was differentiating all over the world, and he had already differentiated into a number of varieties, but he has never differentiated into different *species*.

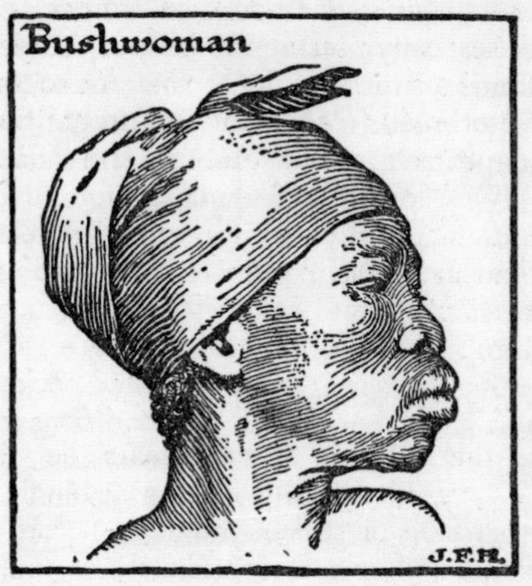
Bushwoman
J.F.H.

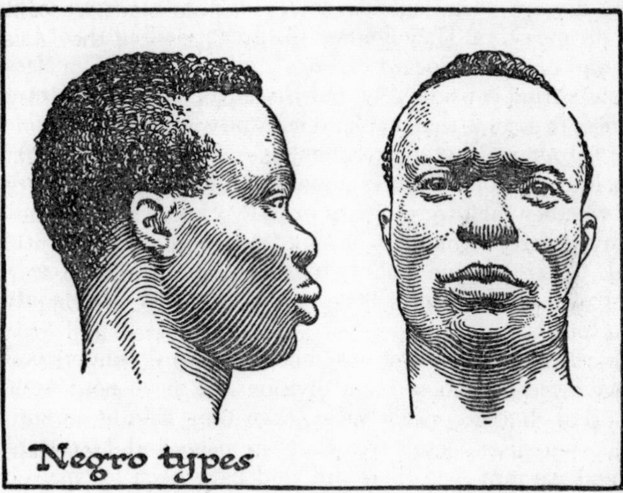
Negro types

The only other species of *Homo,* the Neanderthaler, was exterminated before history began. A "species," we must remember, in biological language is distinguished from a "variety" by the fact that varieties can interbreed, while species either do not do so or produce offspring which, like mules, are sterile. All mankind can interbreed freely, can learn to understand the same speech, can adapt itself to co-operation. And, in the present age, man is probably no longer undergoing differentiation at all. Readmixture is now a far stronger force than differentiation. Men mingle more and more. Mankind from the view of a biologist is an animal species in a state of arrested differentiation and possible readmixture.

§ 2

It is only in the last fifty or sixty years that the varieties of men came to be regarded in this light, as a tangle of differentiations recently arrested or still in progress. Before that time students of mankind, influenced, consciously or unconsciously, by the story of Noah and the Ark and his three sons, Shem, Ham, and Japheth, were inclined to classify men into three or four great races, and they were disposed to regard these races as having always been separate things, descended from originally separate ancestors. They ignored the great possibilities of blended races and of special local isolations and variations. The classification has varied considerably, but there has been rather too much readiness to assume that mankind *must* be completely divisible into three or four main groups. Ethnologists (students of race) have fallen into grievous disputes about a multitude of minor peoples, as to whether they were of this or that primary race, or "mixed," or strayed early forms, or what not. But all races are more or less mixed. There are, no doubt, four main groups, but each is a miscellany, and there are little groups that will not go into any of the four.

Subject to these reservations, when it is clearly understood that when we speak of these main divisions we mean not simple and pure races, but groups of races, then they have a certain convenience in discussion. Over the European and Mediterranean area and western Asia there are, and have been for many thousand years, white peoples usually called the CAUCASIANS, subdivided into two or three subdivisions, the northern blonds or Nordic race, an alleged intermediate race about which many authorities are doubtful, the so-called Alpine race, and the southern dark whites, the Mediterranean or Iberian race; over eastern Asia and America a second group of races prevails, the MONGOLIANS, generally with yellow skins, straight black hair, and sturdy bodies; over Africa the NEGROES, and in the region of Australia and New Guinea the black, primitive AUSTRALOIDS. These are convenient terms, provided the student bears in mind that they are not exactly defined terms. They represent only the common

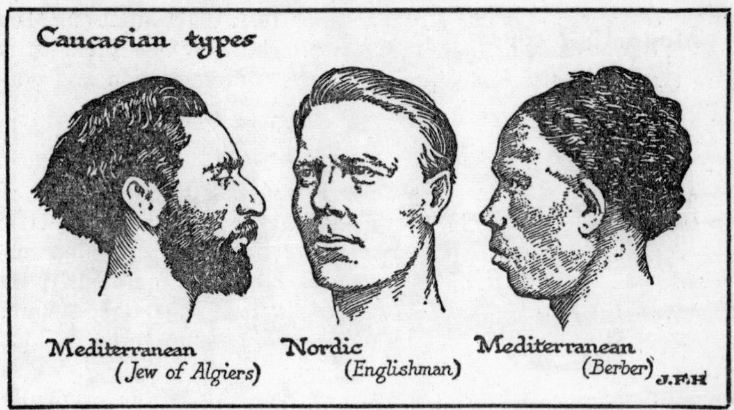

characteristics of certain main groups of races; they leave out a number of little peoples who belong properly to none of these diversions, and they disregard the perpetual mixing where the main groups overlap.

Whether the "Caucasian" race is to be divided into two or three main subdivisions depends upon the classificatory value to be attached to certain differences in the skeleton and particularly to the shape of the skull. The student in his further reading will meet with constant references to round-skulled (Brachycephalic) and long-skulled (Dolichocephalic) peoples. No skull looked at from above is completely round, but some skulls (the dolichocephalic) are much more oblong than others: when the width of a skull is four-fifths or more of its length from back to front, that skull is called brachycephalic; when the width is less than four-fifths of the length the skull is dolichocephalic.

While some ethnologists regard the difference between brachycephaly and dolichocephaly as a difference of quite primary importance, another school which the writer must confess has entirely captured his convictions dismisses this as a mere secondary distinction. It seems probable that the skull shapes of a people may under special circumstances vary in comparatively few generations.

The skull shape of the Lombards, says Sir F. Petrie, changed from dolichocephalic to brachycephalic in a few hundred years; and Boas claims to have shown that the skull shapes of immigrants to the United States alter in one generation. We do not

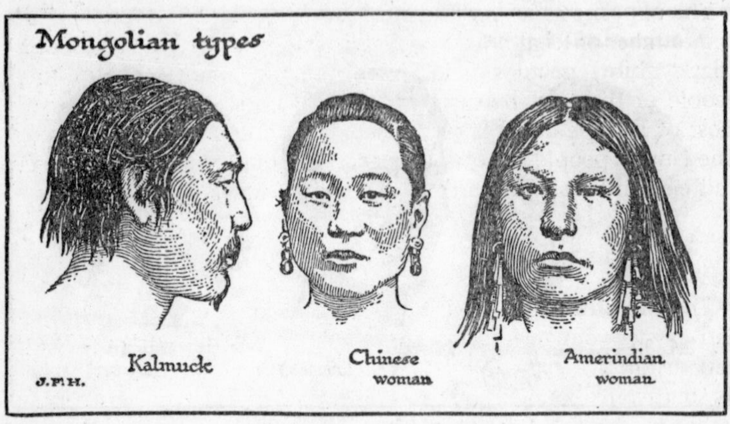

know what influences alter the shape of the skull, just as we do not know why people of British descent in the Darling region of Australia ("Cornstalks") grow exceptionally tall, or why in New England their jaw-bones seem to become slighter and their teeth in consequence rather crowded.

Even in Neolithic times dolichocephalic and brachycephalic skulls are found in the same group of remains and often buried together, and that is true of most peoples to-day. Some peoples, such as the mountain people of Central Europe, have more brachycephalic individuals per cent. than others; some, as the Scandinavians, are more prevalently dolichocephalic. In Neolithic Britain and in Scandinavia the earliest barrows (tomb mounds) are long grave-shaped barrows and the late ones round, and the skulls found in the former are usually dolichocephalic and in the latter most frequently brachycephalic. This points, perhaps, to a succession of races in western Europe in the Neolithic Period, but it may also point to changes of diet, habit or climate.

But it is this study of skull shapes which has led many ethnologists to divide the Caucasian race not, as it was divided by Huxley, into two, the northern *blonds* and the Mediterranean and North African *dark whites* or brunets, but into three. They split his blonds into two classes. They distinguish a northern European type, blond and dolichocephalic, the Nordic; a Mediterranean or Iberian race, the dark whites, which is dark-haired and dolichocephalic; and between these two they descry this third race, their brachycephalic race, the Alpine race.

The opposite school would treat the alleged Alpine race simply as a number of local brachycephalic varieties of Nordic or Iberian (dark white) peoples. The Iberian peoples were the Neolithic people of the long barrows and seem at first to have pervaded most of Europe and Western Asia. They dominate early history. The Nordic people appear later, coming from the forests and west and central coasts of North Europe and Asia.

§ 3

The Mediterranean or Iberian division of the Caucasian race had a wider range in early times, and was of a less specialized and distinctive type than the Nordic. It is very hard to define its southward boundaries from the Negro, or to mark off its early traces in central Asia from those of early Mongolians. Wilfrid Scawen Blunt says that Huxley "had long suspected a common origin of the Egyptians and the Dravidians of India, perhaps a long belt of brown-skinned men from India to Spain in very early days."

This "belt" of Huxley's, of dark-white and brown-skinned men, this race of brunet-brown folk, spread even farther than India; they reached to the shores of the Pacific, and they were everywhere the original possessors of the Neolithic culture and the beginners of what we call civilization. It is possible that these Brunet peoples are, so to speak, the *basic* peoples of our modern world. The Nordic and the Mongolian peoples may have been but north-western and north-eastern branches from this more fundamental stem. Or the Nordic race may have been a branch, while the Mongolian, like the Negro, may have been another equal and distinct stem with which the brunet-browns met and mingled in South China. Or the Nordic peoples also may have developed separately from a Palæolithic stage. Griffith Taylor seems to think that the Mongolian type developed from what he calls an "Aryan" type, which was the common basis of both

Mongolian and Nordic races. All these are open questions still, and may remain open for many years.

Mr. Horrabin and the writer have been at some pains to make a diagram that will summarize all this matter about human races, and we have contrived one that, so far as Europe, Asia, Australasia and North Africa goes, might almost be superimposed upon a map. We give (on p. 144) a genealogical stem showing the blood relationship between *Homo sapiens* and the chief subhuman species.

Then we have inserted a remark, so to speak, about the Cro-Magnon and Grimaldi types. It is based on certain differences, that may possibly have been exaggerated, among some Palæolithic skeletons in Europe. The Grimaldi bones had negroid traits. They suggested a race more like the more primitive Boskop race than the Red-Indian-like Cro-Magnon peoples. It is possible that two main races wandered over the same areas, one a proto-yellow-white race and the other a proto-negroid race. Accordingly the reader will note that the negroid and negro races are shown as first branching from the main stem, and then while the great body of humanity is represented by the dark-whites, two branches are shown of peoples going apart, the one towards the northern forests and the other towards the wind-blown sands of north-eastern Asia to develop the Nordic and Mongolian types respectively.

If the reader will glance again at the preceding paragraph, he will see that he may exercise a wide choice in varying the point at which either of these branches comes off from the main, the Brunet, stem. It is not suggested that either of these types, the Nordic or the Mongolian, except perhaps in the case of the Scandinavians and Esquimaux, have remained at all "pure." The branches turn back in our diagram to meet other branches and suggest racial admixture.

Moreover, our diagram is peppered with notes of interrogation, and, so seasoned, it probably comes much nearer the truth of racial relationships than any hard and exact classification of races can possibly do.

§ 4

At some period in human history (it is suggested in Elliot Smith's *Migrations of Early Culture*) there seems to have been a special type of Neolithic culture widely distributed in the world, which had a group of features so curious and so unlikely to have been independently developed in different regions of the earth as to compel us to believe that it was in effect one culture. It reached through all the regions inhabited by the brunet Mediterranean race, and beyond through India, Further India, up the Pacific coast of China, and it spread at last across the Pacific and to Mexico and Peru. It was a coastal culture.

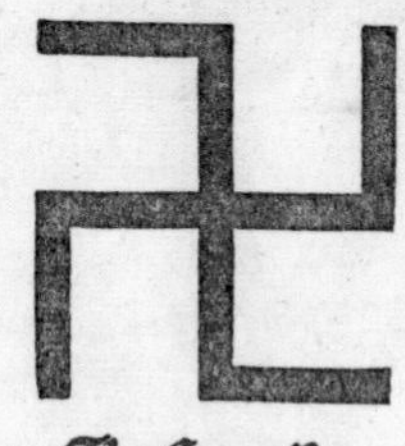
The Swastika

This peculiar development of the Neolithic culture, which Elliot Smith called the *heliolithic* ("Sun-stone") culture, included many or all of the following odd practices: (1) circumcision, (2) the queer custom of sending the *father* to bed when a child is born known as *couvade,* (3) the practice of massage, (4) the making of mummies, (5) megalithic monuments (*e. g.* Stonehenge), (6) artificial deformation of the heads of the young by bandages, (7) tattooing, (8) religious association of the sun and the serpent, and (9) the use of the symbol known as the swastika for good luck. This odd little symbol spins gaily round the world; it seems incredible that men would have invented and made a pet of it twice over.

Elliot Smith traces these associated practices in a sort of constellation all over this great Mediterranean-Indian Ocean-Pacific area. Where one occurs, most of the others occur. They link Brittany with Borneo and Peru. But this constellation of practices does not crop up in the primitive homes of Nordic or Mongolian peoples, nor does it extend southward much beyond equatorial Africa.

For thousands of years, from 15,000 to 1,000 B.C., such a heliolithic Neolithic culture and its brownish possessors may have been oozing round the globe through the warmer regions of the world, drifting by canoes often across wide stretches of sea. It was then the highest culture in the world; it sustained the longest, most highly developed communities. And its region of origin may have been, as Elliot Smith suggests, the Mediterranean and North-African region.

It migrated slowly age by age. It must have been spreading up the Pacific coast and across the island stepping-stones to America long after it had passed on into other developments in its areas of origin. Many of the peoples of the East Indies, Melanesia and Polynesia were still in this heliolithic stage of development when they were discovered by European navigators

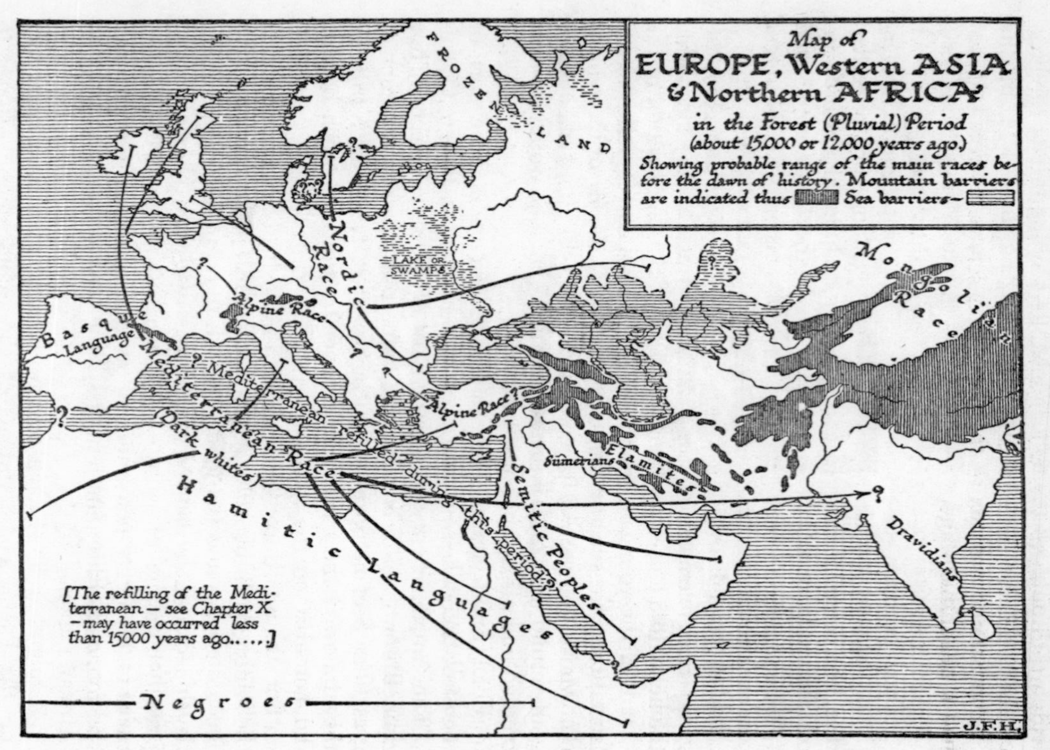
Map of
EUROPE, Western ASIA
& Northern AFRICA
in the Forest (Pluvial) Period
(about 15,000 or 12,000 years ago)
Showing probable range of the main races before the dawn of history. Mountain barriers are indicated thus Sea barriers—
FROZEN LAND
LAKE OR SWAMPS
Nordic Race
Alpine Race
Alpine Race?
Mongolian Race
Basque Language
Mediterranean refilled during this period?
Mediterranean Race
(Dark whites)
Sumerians
Elamites
Semitic Peoples
Dravidians
Hamitic Languages
[The refilling of the Mediterranean — see Chapter X — may have occurred less than 15000 years ago.....]
Negroes
J.F.H.

in the eighteenth century. The first civilizations in Egypt and the Euphrates-Tigris valley probably developed directly out of this widespread culture. We will discuss later whether the Chinese civilization had a different origin.

The Semitic nomads of the Arabian desert seem also to have had a heliolithic stage.

§ 5

The original American population belonged to the Mongolian race, and seems to have reached the American continent by way of Bering Strait at an early Neolithic stage of development. (There is still a coming and going of skin boats between the two continents.)

Later (though this is a matter for discussion among ethnologists) fresh elements of population and fresh cultural ideas at the heliolithic level may have reached America by sea.

If there were these later ingredients in the American population, then either they brought no wheat with them or it died out. Maize, the corn of the new world, is a different plant altogether from any known in the old world. But the religious life of the American peoples betrays the same entanglement of the idea of sowing with a human sacrifice that prevailed throughout the Neolithic Period in the old world.

The American tribes over the great part of the continent remained at a level of Neolithic barbarism. Over acres of seasonal grass they became nomadic, following the bison. In the far north they followed the caribou, the American reindeer. (The horse did not exist on the American continent in the human period until it was introduced by the Europeans.) In the tropical forests the American Indians became hunters of birds and small game. But in one or two fertile regions, as we shall note later, they developed a more elaborate social order, irrigated, erected important buildings of stone, which were adorned with elaborate carvings of highly conventionalized and often fantastic design, and founded cities and empires.

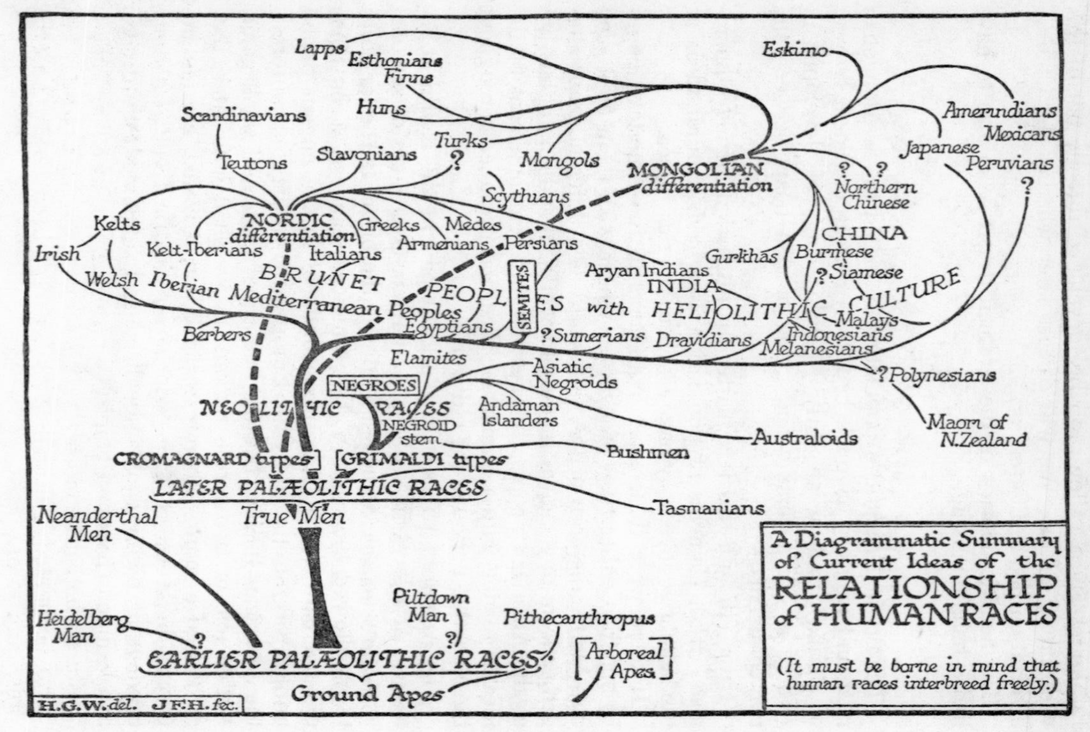
A Diagrammatic Summary of Current Ideas of the RELATIONSHIP of HUMAN RACES
(It must be borne in mind that human races interbreed freely.)
Lapps
Esthonians
Finns
Huns
Scandinavians
Teutons
Slavonians
Turks
?
Mongols
Eskimo
Amerindians
Mexicans
Japanese
Peruvians
?
MONGOLIAN differentiation
? ?
Northern Chinese
CHINA
Burmese
Gurkhas
? Siamese
Scythians
Kelts
Irish
NORDIC differentiation
Greeks
Medes
Kelt-Iberians
Italians
Armenians
Persians
Welsh
Iberian
BRUNET PEOPLES with HELIOLITHIC CULTURE
Mediterranean Peoples
SEMITES
Aryan Indians
INDIA
Malays
Indonesians
Melanesians
Egyptians
? Sumerians
Dravidians
Berbers
Elamites
Asiatic Negroids
? Polynesians
NEGROES
NEOLITHIC RACES
NEGROID stem
Andaman Islanders
Australoids
Maori of N.Zealand
Bushmen
CROMAGNARD types
GRIMALDI types
LATER PALÆOLITHIC RACES
Tasmanians
Neanderthal Men
True Men
Piltdown Man
?
Pithecanthropus
Heidelberg Man
?
EARLIER PALÆOLITHIC RACES
Arboreal Apes
Ground Apes
H.G.W. del. J.F.H. fec.

XII

THE LANGUAGES OF MANKIND

§ 1. *No One Primitive Language.* § 2. *The Aryan Languages.* § 3. *The Semitic Languages.* § 4. *The Hamitic Languages.* § 5. *The Ural-Altaic Languages.* § 6. *The Chinese Languages.* § 7. *Other Language Groups.* § 8. *A Possible Primitive Language Group.* § 9. *Some Isolated Languages.*

§ 1

IT IS improbable that there was ever such a thing as a common human language. We know nothing of the language of Palæolithic man; we do not even know whether Palæolithic man talked freely.

We know that Palæolithic man had a keen sense of form and attitude, because of his drawings; and it has been suggested that he communicated his ideas very largely by gesture. Probably such words as the earlier men used were mainly cries of alarm or passion or names for concrete things, and in many cases they were probably imitative sounds made by or associated with the things named. Sir Arthur Evans has suggested that in America sign-language arose before speech, because the sign-language is common to all Indians in North America, whereas the languages are different.

The first languages were probably small collections of interjections and nouns. Probably the nouns were said in different intonations to convey different meanings. If Palæolithic man had a word for "horse" or "bear," he probably showed by tone or gesture whether he meant "bear is coming," "bear is going," "bear is to be hunted," "dead bear," "bear has been here," "bear did this," and so on.

Only very slowly did the human mind develop methods of indicating action and relationship in a formal manner. Modern languages contain many thousands of words, but the earlier languages could have consisted only of a few hundred. It is said that even modern European peasants can get along with something less than a thousand words, and it is quite conceivable that so late as the Early Neolithic Period that was the limit of the available vocabulary. Probably men did not indulge in those days in conversation or description. For narrative purposes they danced and acted rather than told. They had no method of counting beyond a method of indicating two by a dual number, and some way of expressing many.

The growth of speech was at first a very slow process indeed, and grammatical forms and the expression of abstract ideas may have come very late in human history, perhaps only 400 or 500 generations ago.

§ 2

The students of languages (philologists) tell us that they are unable to trace with certainty any common features in all the languages of mankind. They find over great areas groups of languages which have similar root words and similar ways of expressing the same idea, but then they find in other areas languages which appear to be dissimilar down to their fundamental structure, which express action and relation by entirely dissimilar devices, and have an altogether different grammatical scheme.

One great group of languages now covers nearly all Europe and stretches out to India; it includes English, French, German, Spanish, Italian, Greek, Russian, Armenian, Persian, and various Indian tongues. It is called the Indo-European or ARYAN family. The same fundamental roots, the same grammatical ideas, are traceable through all this family. Compare, for example, English *father, mother,* German *vater, mutter,* Latin *pater, mater,* Greek *pater, meter,* French *père, mère,* Armenian *hair, mair,* Sanscrit *pitar, matar,* etc., etc. In a similar manner the Aryan languages ring the changes on a great number of fundamental words, *f* in the Germanic languages becoming *p* in Latin, and so on. They follow a law of variation called Grimm's Law. These languages are not different things, they are variations of one thing. The people who use these languages think in the same way.

At one time in the remote past, in the Neolithic Age, that is to say 8,000 years or more ago, there may have been one simple original speech from which all these Aryan languages have differentiated. Somewhere between Central Europe and Western

Asia there must have wandered a number of tribes sufficiently intermingled to develop and use one tongue. It is convenient here to call them the Aryan peoples. Sir H. H. Johnston has called them "Aryan Russians." They belonged mostly to the white group of races and to the blond and northern subdivision of the group—to the Nordic race, that is.

Here one must sound a note of warning. There was a time when the philologists were disposed to confuse languages and races, and to suppose that people who once all spoke the same tongue must be all of the same blood. That, however, is not the case, as the reader will understand if he will think of the negroes of the United States who now all speak English, or of the Irish who—except for purposes of political demonstration—no longer speak the old Erse language, or of the Cornish people who have lost their ancient Keltic speech. But what a common language does do, is to show that a common intercourse has existed, and the possibility of intermixture; and if it does not point to a common origin, it points at least to a common future.

But even this original Aryan language, which was a spoken speech perhaps 6,000 or 5,000 B.C., was by no means a *primordial* language or the language of a savage race. Its earliest speakers were at or past the Neolithic stage of civilization. It had grammatical forms and verbal devices of some complexity. The vanished methods of expression of the later Palæolithic peoples, of the Azilians, or of the early Neolithic kitchen-midden people for instance, were probably cruder than the most elementary form of Aryan.

Probably the Aryan group of languages became distinct in a wide region of which the Danube, Dnieper, Don and Volga were the main rivers, a region that extended eastward beyond the Ural Mountains north of the Caspian Sea. The area over which the Aryan speakers roamed probably did not for a long time reach to the Atlantic or to the south of the Black Sea beyond Asia Minor. There was no effectual separation of Europe from Asia then at the Bosporus. The Danube flowed eastward to a great sea that extended across the Volga region of south-eastern Russia right into Turkestan, and included the Black, Caspian, and Aral Seas, of to-day. Perhaps it sent out arms to the Arctic Ocean. It must have been a pretty effective barrier between the Aryan speakers and the people in north-eastern Asia.

South of this sea stretched a continuous shore from the Balkans to Afghanistan. North-west of it a region of swamps and lagoons reached to the Baltic.

§ 3

Next to Aryan, philologists distinguish another group of languages which seem to have been made quite separately from the Aryan languages, the Semitic. Hebrew and Arabic are kindred, but they seem to have even a different set of root words from the Aryan tongues; they express their ideas of relationship in a different way; the fundamental ideas of their grammars are different. They were in all probability made by human communities quite out of touch with the original Aryans, separately and independently.

Hebrew, Arabic, Abyssinian, ancient Assyrian, ancient Phœnician, and a number of associated tongues are put together as being derived from this second primary language, which is called the Semitic.

In the very beginnings of recorded history—that is, by 4,000 B.C. and earlier—we find Aryan-speaking peoples and Semitic-speaking peoples carrying on the liveliest intercourse of war and trade around and about the eastern end of the Mediterranean, but the fundamental differences of the primary Aryan and primary Semitic languages oblige us to believe that in Neolithic times, before the historical period there must for thousands of years have been an almost complete separation of the Aryan-speaking and the Semitic-speaking peoples.

The latter seem to have lived either in south Arabia or in north-east Africa. In the early Neolithic Age the original Semitic speakers and the original Aryan speakers were probably living so to speak, in different worlds.

§ 4

Philologists speak with less unanimity of a third group of languages, the Hamitic, which some declare to be distinct from, and others allied to, the Semitic. The weight of opinion inclines now towards the idea of some primordial connection of these two groups.

The Hamitic group is certainly a much wider and more various language group than the Semitic or the Aryan, and the Semitic tongues are more of a family, have more of a common likeness than the Aryan. The Semitic languages may have arisen as some specialized proto-Hamitic group, just as the birds arose from one special group of reptiles, and the Aryan also from another proto-Hamitic group, as the mammals did from another group of reptiles. It is a very tempting speculation, but one for which there is really no basis of justifying fact, to suppose that the rude primordial ancestor group of the Aryan tongues branched off from the proto-Hamitic speech forms at some still earlier date than the separation and specialization of Semitic.

The Hamitic speakers to-day, like the Semitic speakers, are mainly of the Mediterranean race. Among the Hamitic languages are the ancient Egyptian and Coptic, the Berber languages (of the mountain people of North Africa, the Masked Tuaregs, and other such peoples), and what are called the Ethiopic group of African languages in eastern Africa, including the speech of the Gallas and the Somalis. These Hamitic languages may have radiated from a centre on the African coast of the Mediterranean, and they may have extended over the then existing land connections very widely into western Europe.

All these three great groups of languages, the Aryan, Semitic, and Hamitic, it may be noted, have one feature in common which they do not share with any other language, and that is grammatical gender; but whether that has much weight as evidence of a remote common origin of Aryan, Semitic and Hamitic is a question for the philologist rather than for the general student. It does not affect the clear evidence of a very long and very ancient prehistoric separation of the speakers of these three diverse groups of tongues.

The Semitic and Nordic "races" have a much more distinctive physiognomy; they seem, like their characteristic languages, to be more marked and specialized than the broader, more fundamental Hamitic-speaking peoples.

§ 5

Across to the north-east of the Aryan and Semitic areas there must once have spread a further distinct language system which is now represented by a group of languages known as the TURANIAN, or URAL-ALTAIC group. This includes the Lappish of Lapland and the Samoyed speech of Siberia, the Finnish language, Magyar, Turkish or Tartar, Manchu and Mongol; it has not as a group been so exhaustively studied by European philologists, and there is insufficient evidence yet whether it does or does not include the Korean and Japanese languages. H. B. Hulbert has issued a comparative grammar of Korean and certain of the Dravidian languages of India to demonstrate the close affinity he finds between them.

§ 6

A fifth region of language formation was south-eastern Asia, where there still prevails a group of languages consisting of monosyllables without any inflections, in which the tone used in uttering a word determines its meaning. This may be called the Chinese or MONOSYLLABIC group, and it includes Chinese, Burmese, Siamese and Tibetan.

The difference between any of these Chinese tongues and the more western languages is profound. In the Pekinese form of Chinese there are only about 420 primary monosyllables, and consequently each of these has to do duty for a great number of things, and the different meanings are indicated either by the context or by saying the word in a distinctive tone.

The relations of these words to each other are expressed by quite different methods from the Aryan methods. Chinese grammar is a thing different in nature from English grammar; it is a separate and different invention. Many writers declare there is no Chinese grammar at all, and that is true if we mean by grammar anything in the European sense of inflections and concords. Consequently, any such thing as a literal translation from Chinese into English is an impossibility. The very method of the thought is different. Their philosophy remains still largely a sealed book to the European on this account, and vice versa, because of the different nature of the expressions.

We may give an illustration of this profound difference in method. The four Chinese characters indicating "Affairs, query, imperative, old," placed in that order, for example, represent "Why walk in the ancient ways?" The Chinaman thus gives the bare cores of his meaning; the Englishman gets to the same sense by a bold metaphor. He may be talking of conservatism in cooking or in bookbinding, but he will say: "Why walk in the ancient ways?"

Mr. Arthur Waley, in the interesting essay on Chinese thought and poetry which precedes his book, *170 Chinese Poems* (Constable, 1918), makes it clear how in these fields Chinese thought is kept practical and restricted by the limitations upon metaphor that are imposed by the contracted structure of Chinese.

§ 7

In addition to these families of languages, the following other great language groups are distinguished by the philologist. All the American-Indian languages, which vary widely among themselves, are separable from any Old World group. Here we may lump them together not so much as a family as a miscellany.

There is one great group of languages in Africa, from a little way north of the equator to its southern extremity, the BANTU, and in addition a complex of other languages across the centre of the continent about which we will not trouble here.

There are also two probably separate groups, the DRAVIDIAN in South India, and the MALAYO-POLYNESIAN stretched over Polynesia and also now including Indian tongues.

Now, it seems reasonable to conclude from these fundamental differences that about the time when men were beginning to form rather larger communities than the family tribe, when they were beginning to tell each other long stories and argue and exchange ideas, human beings were distributed about the world in a number of areas which communicated very little with each other. They were separated by oceans, seas, dense forests, deserts or mountains from one another. There may have been in that remote time, it may be 10,000 years ago or more, Aryan, Semitic, Hamitic, Turanian, American and Chinese-speaking tribes and families, wandering over their several areas of hunting, pasture and occasional cultivation, all at very much the same stage of culture, and each developing its linguistic instrument in its own way. Probably each of these original tribes was not more numerous altogether than the Indians in North-west Territories to-day. Systematic agriculture was barely beginning then, and until agriculture made a denser population possible all the human beings in the world may have numbered only a few score thousand. It is a point that few people grasp, that until the Later Palæolithic Age man was an extremely rare animal. If agriculture was becoming at all important in human life, and if at that time population was anywhere denser, it was probably in the Mediterranean region, and possibly in areas now submerged.

In addition to these Neolithic tribes there must have been various still more primitive forest folks in Africa and in India. These could only have numbered a few thousand. They were probably as rare as, or rarer than, the gorilla is now. Central Africa, from the Upper Nile, was then a vast forest, impenetrable to ordinary human life, a forest of which the Congo forests of to-day are the last shrunken remains.

Possibly the spread of men of a race higher than primitive Australoids into the East Indies and the development of the languages of the Malayo-Polynesian type came later in time than the origination of these other language groups. The Polynesian seems to be a late eastward extension of the Brunet peoples, probably with an infiltration of Nordic blood.

The language divisions of the philologist do tally, it is manifest, in a broad sort of way with the main race classes of the ethnologist, and they carry out the same idea of a very small and thinly distributed human population and of age-long separations between the great divisions of mankind. In the Glacial Age, ice, or at least a climate too severe for the free spreading of peoples, extended from the north pole into Central Europe and across Russia and Siberia to the great tablelands of Central Asia. After the last Glacial Age, this cold north mitigated its severities very slowly, and was for long without any other population than the wandering hunters who spread eastward and across Bering Strait. North and Central Europe and Asia did not become sufficiently temperate for agriculture until quite recent times—times, that is, within the limit of 12,000 or possibly even 10,000 years ago—and a dense forest period intervened between the age of the hunter and the agricultural clearings.

This forest period was also a very wet period. It has been called the Pluvial or Lacustrine Age, the rain or pond period. It has to be remembered that the outlines of the land of the world have changed greatly even in the last hundred centuries. Nothing is so frequently overlooked by the students of pre-historic man as geographical change.

Across European Russia, from the Baltic to the Caspian Sea, as the ice receded there certainly spread much water and many impassable swamps; the Caspian Sea and the Sea of Aral and parts of the Desert of Turkestan are the vestiges of a great extent of sea that reached far up to the Volga valley and sent an arm westward to join the Black Sea. Mountain barriers much higher than they are now, and the arm of the sea that is now the region of the Indus, completed the separation of the early Nordic races from the Mongolians and the Dravidians, and made the broad racial differentiation of those groups possible.

Again, the blown-sand Desert of Sahara—it is not a dried-up, sea, but a wind desert, once fertile and rich in life, becoming more and more dry and sandy—cut the Mediterranean race off from the sparse primitive Negro population of the central forest region of Africa.

The Persian Gulf extended very far to the north of its present head, and combined with the Syrian desert, to cut off the Semitic peoples from the eastern areas; while on the other hand the south of Arabia, much more fertile than it is to-day, may have reached across what is now the Gulf of Aden towards Abyssinia and Somaliland. The Mediterranean and Red Sea during the Pluvial Age may even have been fertile valleys containing a string of fresh-water lakes. The Himalayas and the higher and vaster massif of Central Asia and the northward extension of the Bay of Bengal up to the present Ganges valley divided off the Dravidians from the Mongolians, the canoe was the chief link between Dravidian and Southern Mongol, and the Gobi system of seas and lakes which presently became the Gobi desert, and the great system of mountain chains which follow one another across Asia from the centre to the north-east, split the Mongolian races into the Chinese and the Ural-Altaic language groups.

Bering Strait, when this came into existence, before or after the Pluvial Period, isolated the Amer-Indians.

We are not suggesting here, be it noted, that these ancient separations were absolute separations, but that they were effectual enough at least to prevent any great intermixture of blood or any great intermixture of speech in those days of man's social beginnings. There was, nevertheless, some amount of meeting and exchange even then, some drift of knowledge that spread the crude patterns and use of various implements, and the seeds of a primitive agriculture about the world. Presently canoes and then ships appeared to increase this agricultural and trade propaganda.

§ 8

The fundamental tongues of these nine main language groups we have noted were not by any means all the human speech beginnings of the Neolithic Age. They are the latest languages, the survivors, which have ousted their more primitive predecessors. There may have been other, and possibly many other, ineffective centres of speech which were afterwards overrun by the speakers of still surviving tongues, and of elementary languages which faded out. We find strange little patches of speech still in the world which do not seem to be connected with any other language about them.

Sometimes, however, an exhaustive inquiry seems to affiliate these disconnected patches, seems to open out to us tantalizing glimpses of some simpler, wider and more fundamental and universal form of human speech. One language group that has been keenly discussed is the Basque group of dialects. The Basques live now on the north and south slopes of the Pyrenees; they number perhaps 600,000 altogether in Europe, and to this day they are a very sturdy and independent-spirited people. Their language, as it exists to-day, is a fully developed one. But it is developed upon lines absolutely different from those of the Aryan languages about it.

Basque newspapers have been published in the Argentine and in the United States to supply groups of prosperous emigrants. The earliest "French" settlers in Canada were Basque, and Basque names are frequent among the French Canadians to this day. Ancient remains point to a much wider distribution of the Basque speech and people over Spain.

For a long time this Basque language was a profound perplexity to scholars, and its structural character led to the suggestion that it might be related to some Amer-Indian tongue. A. H. Keane, in *Man Past and Present,* assembles reasons for linking it—though remotely—with the Berber language of North Africa, and through the Berber with the general body of Hamitic languages; but this relationship is questioned by other philologists. They find Basque more akin to certain similarly stranded vestiges of speech found in the Caucasian Mountains, and they are disposed to regard it as a last surviving member, much changed and specialized, of a once very widely extended group of pre-Hamitic languages, otherwise extinct, spoken chiefly by peoples of that brunet Mediterranean race which once occupied most of western and southern Europe and western Asia. They think it may have been very closely related to the Dravidian of India and the languages of the peoples with the heliolithic culture who spread eastward through the East Indies to Polynesia and beyond.

It is quite possible that over western and southern Europe language groups extended eight or ten thousand years ago that have completely vanished before Aryan tongues. Later on we shall note, in passing, the possibility of three lost language groups represented by (1) Ancient Cretan, Lydian, and the like (though these may have belonged, says Sir Harry H. Johnston, to the "Basque

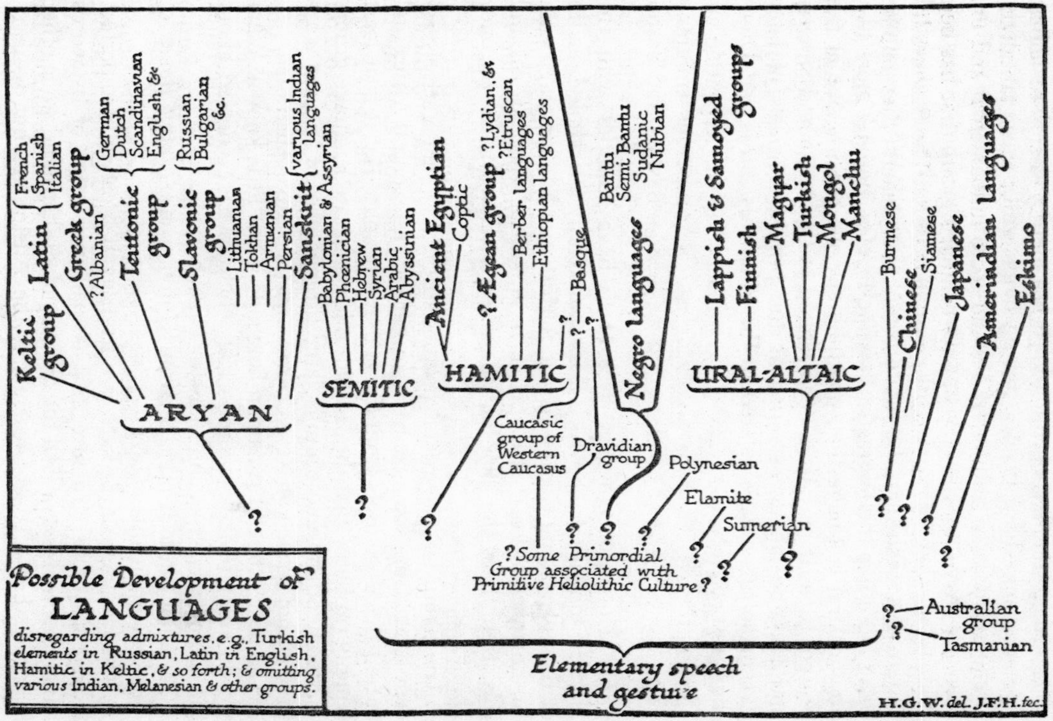

Possible Development of

LANGUAGES

disregarding admixtures, e.g., Turkish elements in Russian, Latin in English, Hamitic in Keltic, & so forth; & omitting various Indian, Melanesian & other groups.

ARYAN ?
Keltic group
Latin { French, Spanish, Italian
Greek group
?Albanian
Teutonic group { German, Dutch, Scandinavian, English, &c
Slavonic group { Russian, Bulgarian &c.
Lithuanian
Tokhan
Armenian
Persian
Sanskrit { various Indian languages

SEMITIC ?
Babylonian & Assyrian
Phoenician
Hebrew
Syrian
Arabic
Abyssinian

HAMITIC ?
Ancient Egyptian
Coptic
? Ægean group ?Lydian, &c ?Etruscan
Berber languages
Ethiopian languages

Caucasic group of Western Caucasus
? Basque ?
Dravidian group ?
Negro languages
Bantu
Semi Bantu
Sudanic
Nubian
Polynesian ?
Elamite ?
Sumerian ?
? Some Primordial Group associated with Primitive Heliolithic Culture ?

URAL-ALTAIC ?
Lappish & Samoyed groups
Finnish
Magyar
Turkish
Mongol
Manchu

Burmese ?
Chinese
Siamese ?
Japanese ?
Amerindian languages ?
Eskimo ?

?—Australian group
?—Tasmanian

Elementary speech and gesture

H.G.W. del. J.F.H. fec.

Caucasian-Dravidian [!] group"), (2) Sumerian, and (3) Elamite.

The suggestion has been made—it is a mere guess—that ancient Sumerian may have been a linking language between the early Basque-Caucasian and early Mongolian groups. If this is true, then we have in this "Basque-Caucasian-Dravidian-Sumerian-proto-Mongolian" group a still more ancient and more ancestral system of speech than the fundamental Hamitic. We have something more like the linguistic "missing-link," something more like an ancestral language than anything else we can imagine at the present time. It may have been related to the Aryan and Semitic and Hamitic languages much as the primitive lizards of later Palæozoic times were related to the Mammals, Birds and Dinosaurs respectively.

§ 9

The Hottentot language is said to have affinities with the Hamitic tongues, from which it is separated by the whole breadth of Bantu-speaking Central Africa. A Hottentot-like language with Bushman affinities is still spoken in equatorial East Africa, and this strengthens the idea that the whole of East Africa was once Hamitic-speaking.

The Bantu languages and peoples spread, in comparatively recent times, from some centre of origin in West Central Africa and cut off the Hottentots from the Hamitic peoples. But it is at least equally probable that the Hottentot is a separate language group.

Among other remote and isolated little patches of languages are the Papuan speech of New Guinea and the native Australian.

The now extinct Tasmanian language is but little known. What we do know of it is in support of what we have guessed about the comparative speechlessness of Palæolithic man.

We may quote a passage from Hutchinson's *Living Races of Mankind* upon this matter:—

"The language of the natives is irretrievably lost, only imperfect indications of its structure and a small proportion of its words having been preserved. In the absence of sibilants and some other features, their dialects resembled the Australian, but were of ruder, of less developed structure, and so imperfect that, according to Joseph Milligan, our best authority on the subject, they observed no settled order or arrangement of words in the construction of their sentences, but conveyed in a supplementary fashion by tone, manner, and gesture those modifications of meaning which we express by mood, tense, number, etc.

"Abstract terms were rare; for every variety of gum-tree or wattle-tree there was a name, but no word for 'tree' in general, nor for qualities such as hard, soft, warm, cold, long, short, round, etc. Anything hard was 'like a stone,' anything round 'like the moon,' and so on, usually suiting the action to the word and confirming by some sign the meaning to be understood."

BOOK III

THE FIRST CIVILIZATIONS

XIII

THE EARLY EMPIRES

§ 1

WE WILL now resume and expand what has been said already in the preceding chapters about the coming of agriculture. Its onset marks a profound change in human conditions. It developed slowly and with much variation in human life during several thousand years between, at earliest, twenty thousand years ago, and, at latest, eight thousand years ago.

Before that time man was a comparatively rare animal. He was a wandering, implement-using beast of prey, a savage. He lived in small communities; his speech was probably still largely undeveloped. His only possessions were portable possessions. His whole life was spent in a food hunt, and he alternated between long stretches of hunger and spells of plenty and repletion. He followed animals as they followed their food and the seasons. He was free and needy and his life was incessantly dangerous.

Then began this business of deliberate food-growing and of food preservation. He began to herd the beasts he had hunted and to heed where he found the seeds and roots and fruits that supplemented his meat. His hunter's prowlings were restricted by the grazing of his half-domesticated cattle and by his expectation of crops where he had sown. His implements multiplied. By eight thousand years ago man had become in some regions an extremely numerous animal. No ape or other kindred animal had ever been numerous before him. He had made houses and acquired possessions; in the place of a mere food hunt he had settled down to regular periodic work to get food. He stored food. Labour had begun for him. From meals that were happy finds and adventures, he had achieved meal-times. He had ceased to be a haphazard animal and he had become an economic animal.

He is the only mammal that has become an economic animal. There has never been any other economic mammal. Beavers build and store, the squirrel hoards, and dogs bury their bones, but we must go to the ants and bees before we come to other living creatures that associate in communities and work regularly to prepare and store and share out food and shelter.

Before settlement there was exertion, anxiety and need in human life, but there was no systematic labour. Work there was in the life of the later Palæolithic men, but it was occasional and usually interesting work. Implements had to be made from time to time, but probably they were made by those who had to use them. Skins had to be scraped. Food had to be hunted for. Someone had to look after the fire; it was a serious nuisance to have it go out, and it is supposed by some authorities that special people were appointed for that responsibility, and that the vestal virgins with their sacred fire were a survival of the primitive fire-minders. But in the hunting stage of mankind there was no steady, regular toil of the sort that we refer to as labour.

Most of the troublesome work that had to be done was probably put upon the women. Primitive man had no chivalry. When the little human group shifted its ground the women and girls carried such gear as there was, while the men went unencumbered with the weapons, ready for any eventuality. The care of the children fell entirely on the women.

It has been suggested that women began agriculture. This is highly probable. The collection of seed and vegetable foodstuffs fell on them, while the men were away hunting. It was the women who may have observed that grain grew at the old camping-places, who may have first consciously scattered grain as an offering to some local god with the idea of its being returned later a hundredfold. The earliest stage of agriculture was a snatch crop. Men, still largely pastoral, may have sowed and returned later to reap. It may be that the close association of human sacrifice with sowing may be dated from the days of such snatch crops left to grow and ripen: a man may have been slaughtered and left behind to watch over the crop.

The earliest agriculture was almost certainly a patch agriculture, a cultivation of little garden patches by hand—probably by women's hands. It was an accessory food supply. Probably it only became more important under very exceptional conditions.

It is easy to imagine that men noticed very early the advantage of sowing upon periodically flooded lands. They cast their bread upon the water and found that it was returned to them very abundantly. Elliot Smith thinks that systematic agriculture as a staple undertaking rather than a side activity began in Egypt, and certainly no country is so obviously adapted to teach men the art of sowing in due season. At first, perhaps, the systematic sowing was done in flooded lands. It was a pretty easy step from that to assisted floods, that is to say to irrigation.

Cultivation is not civilization. The growing of wheat had spread to the Atlantic and to the Pacific coast with the distribution of the Neolithic culture by, perhaps, 15,000 or 10,000 B.C., before the beginnings of civilization. Civilization is something more than the occasional seasonal growing of wheat. It is the settlement of men upon an area continuously cultivated and possessed, who live in buildings continuously inhabited, with a common rule and a common city or citadel.

The first condition necessary to a real settling down of Neolithic men, as distinguished from a mere temporary settlement among abundant food, was of course a trustworthy all-the-year-round supply of water, fodder for their animals, food for themselves, and building materials for their homes. There had to be everything they could need at any season, and no want that would tempt them to wander further. This was a possible state of affairs, no doubt, in many European and Asiatic valleys; and in many such valleys, as in the case of the Swiss lake-dwellings, men settled from a very early date indeed; but nowhere, of any countries now known to us, were these favourable conditions found upon such a scale, and nowhere did they hold good so surely year in and year out as in Egypt and in the country between the upper waters of the Euphrates and Tigris and the Persian Gulf.

Here was a constant water supply under enduring sunlight; trustworthy harvests year by year; in Mesopotamia wheat yielded, says Herodotus, two hundredfold to the sower; Pliny says that it was cut twice and afterwards yielded good fodder for sheep; there were abundant palms and many sorts of fruits; and as for building material, in Egypt there was clay and easily worked stone, and in Mesopotamia a clay that becomes a brick in the sunshine.

In such countries men would cease to wander, and settle down almost unawares; they would multiply and discover themselves

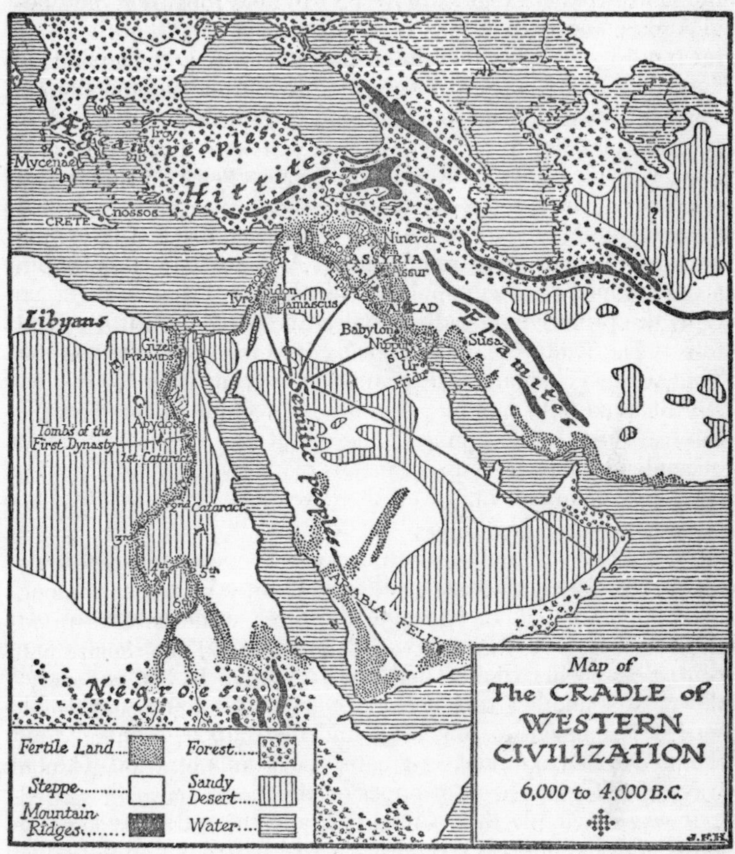

numerous, and by their numbers safe from any casual assailant. They multiplied, producing a denser human population than the earth had ever known before; their houses became more substantial, wild beasts were exterminated over great areas, the security of life increased so that ordinary men went about in the towns and fields without encumbering themselves with weapons, and among themselves, at least, they became peaceful peoples. Men took root as man had never taken root before.

Mesopotamia and Egypt were the most favourable countries for the first permanent settling-down of man. We give a map here of these countries as they were about six or seven thousand years ago. The Red Sea valleys and the valleys of the eastern Mediterranean were already flooded by that time, but the coasts of Arabia, and particularly the south-west corner of Arabia, were far more fertile than they have since become, and the Red Sea flowed by an open channel into the Mediterranean, and the Persian Gulf extended much further northward than it does at the present time.

Now, while in the great river valleys men were taking root and multiplying, in the less fertile and more seasonal lands outside these favoured areas, in the forests of Europe, the Arabian deserts and the seasonal pastures of Central Asia, there was developing a thinner, more active population of peoples of a quite divergent type, the primitive nomadic peoples. In contrast with the settled folk, the agriculturists, these nomads lived freely and dangerously. They were in comparison lean and hungry men. Their herding was still blended with hunting; they fought constantly for their pastures against hostile families. The discoveries in the elaboration of implements and the use of metals made by the settled peoples spread to them and improved their weapons. They followed the settled folk from Neolithic phase to Bronze phase. They became more warlike with better arms, and more capable of rapid movements with the improvement of their transport.

One must not think of a nomadic stage as a predecessor of a settled stage in human affairs. To begin with, man was a slow drifter, following food. Then one sort of men began to settle down, and another sort became more distinctly nomadic. The settled sort began to rely more and more upon grain for food; the nomad began to make a greater use of milk for food. The two ways of life specialized in opposite directions.

It was inevitable that nomad folk and the settled folk should clash, and that nomads should seem hard barbarians to the settled peoples, and the settled peoples soft and effeminate and very good plunder to the nomad peoples. Along the fringes of the developing civilizations there must have been a constant raiding and bickering between hardy nomad tribes and mountain tribes, and the more numerous and less warlike peoples in the towns and villages.

For the most part this was a mere raiding of the borders. The settled folk had the weight of numbers on their side; the herdsmen might raid and loot, but they could not stay. That kind of mutual friction might go on for many generations. But ever and again we find some leader or some tribe, amidst the disorder of free and independent nomads, powerful enough to force a sort of unity upon its kindred tribes, and then woe betide the nearest civilization. Down pour the united nomads on the unwarlike, unarmed plains, and there ensues a war of conquest. Instead of carrying off the booty, the conquerors settle down on the conquered land, which becomes all booty for them; the villagers and townsmen are reduced to servitude and tribute-paying, they become hewers of wood and drawers of water, and the leaders of the nomads become kings and princes, masters and aristocrats. They, too, settle down, they learn many of the arts and refinements of the conquered, they cease to be lean and hungry, but for many generations they retain traces of their old nomadic habits, they hunt and indulge in open-air sports, they drive and race chariots, they regard work, especially agricultural work, as the lot of an inferior race and class.

This in a thousand variations has been one of the main stories in history for the last seventy centuries or more. In the first history that we can clearly decipher we find already in all the civilized regions a distinction between a non-working ruler class and the working mass of the population. And we find, too, that after some generations the aristocrat, having settled down, begins to respect the arts and refinements and law-abidingness of settlement, and to lose something of his original hardihood. He intermarries, he patches up a sort of toleration between conqueror and conquered; he exchanges religious ideas and learns the lessons upon which soil and climate insist. He becomes a part of the civilization he has captured. And as he does so, events gather toward a fresh invasion by the free adventurers of the outer world.

We will now give a bald statement of the names and successions of the early civilizations in Western Asia (§§ 2A, 2B, 2C, 2D, and 2E) and the parallel development in Egypt (§ 3). Perhaps we ought to give the Egyptian beginning first. There is a fine controversy between those who would put Western Asia before Egypt in the order of time and those to whom Egypt is the birthplace of all civilization. It is a controversy from which the present writer abstains. It will then be convenient to glance at the contemporary state of affairs in India, China, and America. Necessarily this will be a recital of names, but we will give as few as possible, and the reader who brings little or no previous knowledge to this portion will find all that follows much clearer if he gives these sections a reasonably close attention and compares with the map on p. 161 and the diagram at the end of Book III, p. 251.

§ 2A

The alternation of settlement, nomadic conquest, refinement, fresh conquest, refinement, which is characteristic of this phase of human history, is particularly to be noted in the region of the Euphrates and Tigris, which lay open in every direction to great

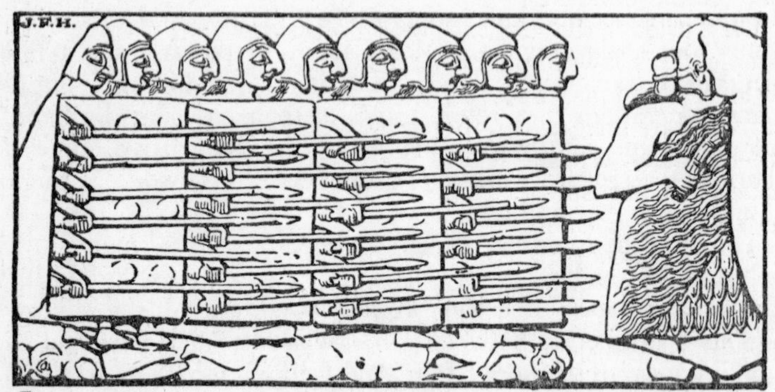

A very early Sumerian stone carving showing Sumerian warriors in phalanx

areas which are not arid enough to be complete deserts, but which were not fertile enough to support civilized populations. Perhaps the earliest people to form real cities in this part of the world, or, indeed, in any part of the world, were a people called the Sumerians. They were probably brunets of Iberian or Dravidian affinities. They used a kind of writing which they scratched upon clay, and their language has been deciphered. It was a language more like the unclassified Caucasic language groups than any others that now exist. These languages may be connected with Basque and may represent what was once a widespread primitive language group extending from Spain and Western Europe to Eastern India, and reaching southwards to Central Africa.

Excavations conducted at Eridu by Captain R. Campbell Thompson during the first world war revealed an early Neolithic agricultural stage, before the invention of writing or the use of bronze, beneath the earliest Sumerian foundations. The crops of the pre-Sumerians were cut by sickles of earthenware.

The Sumerians shaved their heads and wore simple tunic-like

garments of wool. They settled first on the lower courses of the great river and not very far from the Persian Gulf, which in those days ran up for a hundred and thirty miles and more beyond its present head. Sayce, in *Babylonian and Assyrian Life*, estimates that in 6,500 B.C. Eridu was on the sea-coast. The Sumerians fertilized their fields by letting water run through irrigation trenches, and they gradually became very skilful hydraulic engineers; they had cattle, asses, sheep, and goats, but no horses; their collections of mud huts grew into towns, and their religion raised up tower-like temple buildings.

Clay, dried in the sun, was a very great factor in the lives of these people. This lower country of the Euphrates-Tigris valleys had little or no stone. They built of brick, they made pottery and earthenware images, and they drew and presently wrote upon thin tile-like cakes of clay. They do not seem to have had paper or to have used parchment. Their books and memoranda, even their letters, were potsherds.

At Nippur they built a great tower of brick to their chief god, El-lil (Enlil), the memory of which is supposed to be preserved in the story of the Tower of Babel. They seem to have been divided up into city states, which warred among themselves and maintained for many centuries their military capacity. Their soldiers carried long spears and shields, and fought in close formation. Sumerians conquered Sumerians. Sumer remained unconquered by any stranger race for a very long period of time indeed. They developed their civilization, their writing, and their shipping, through a period that may be twice as long as the whole period from the Christian era to the present time. Then slowly they gave way before the Semitic peoples.

The first of all known empires was that founded by the high priest of the god of the Sumerian city of Erech. It reached, says an inscription at Nippur, from the Lower (Persian Gulf) to the Upper (Mediterranean or Red?) Sea. Among the mud-heaps of the Euphrates-Tigris valley the record of that vast period of history, that first half of the Age of Cultivation, is buried. There flourished the first temples and the first priest-rulers that we know of among mankind.

Traces of Sumerian trade, and perhaps of Sumerian settlement, have been found in North-west India, but it is still uncertain whether the Sumerians reached India overland or by the sea. Probably it was by sea. They may have been quite nearly related in race and culture to the peoples then inhabiting the Ganges valley.

§ 2B

Upon the western edge of this country appeared nomadic tribes of Semitic-speaking peoples who traded, raided, and fought with the Sumerians for many generations. Then arose at last a great leader among these Semites, Sargon (2,750 B.C.), who united them, and not only conquered the Sumerians, but extended his rule from beyond the Persian Gulf on the east to the Mediterranean on the west. His own people were called the Akkadians and his empire is called the Sumerian Akkadian empire. It endured for over two hundred years.

From the time of Sargon I until the fourth and third centuries B.C., a period of over two thousand years, the Semitic peoples were in the ascendant throughout all the near east. But though the Semites conquered and gave a king to the Sumerian cities, it was the Sumerian civilization which prevailed over the simpler Semitic culture. The newcomers learnt the Sumerian writing (the "cuneiform" writing) and the Sumerian language; they set up no Semitic writing of their own. The Sumerian language became for these barbarians the language of knowledge and power, as Latin was the language of knowledge and power among the barbaric peoples of the Middle Ages in Europe. This Sumerian learning had a very great vitality. It was destined to survive through a long series of conquests and changes that now began in the valley of the two rivers.

§ 2C

As the people of the Sumerian Akkadian empire lost their political and military vigour, fresh inundations of a warlike people, the Elamites, began from the east, while from the west came the Semitic Amorites, pinching the Sumerian Akkadian empire between them. The Elamites were of unknown language and race, "neither Sumerians nor Semites," says Sayce. Their central city was Susa. Their archæology is still largely an unworked mine. They are believed by some, says Sir H. H. Johnston, to have been negroid in type. There is a strong negroid strain in the modern people of Elam. The Amorites, on the other hand, were of the same stock as Abraham and the later Hebrews. The Amorites settled in what was at first a small up-river town, named Babylon;

and after a hundred years of warfare became masters of all Mesopotamia under a great king, Hammurabi (2,100 B.C.), who founded the first Babylonian empire.

Again came peace and security and a decline in aggressive prowess, and in another hundred years fresh nomads were invading Babylonia, bringing with them the horse and the war chariot, and setting up their own king in Babylon. These were the Kassites.

§ 2D

Higher up the Tigris, above the clay lands and with easy supplies of workable stone, a Semitic people, the Assyrians, while the Sumerians were still unconquered by the Semites, were settling about a number of cities of which Assur and Nineveh were the chief. Their peculiar physiognomy, the long nose and thick lips, was very like that of the commoner type of Polish Jew to-day. They wore great beards and ringleted long hair, tall caps and long robes. They were constantly engaged in mutual raiding with the Hittites to the west; they were conquered by Sargon I, and became free again; a certain Tushratta, King of Mitanni, to the northwest, captured and held their capital, Nineveh, for a time; they intrigued with Egypt against Babylon and were in the pay of Egypt; they developed the military art to a very high pitch, and became mighty raiders and exacters of tribute; and at last, adopting the horse and the war chariot, they settled accounts for a time with the Hittites, and then, under Tiglath Pileser I, conquered Babylon for themselves (about 1,100 B.C.). But their hold on the lower, older, and more civilized land was not secure, and Nineveh, the Semitic stone city, as distinguished from Babylon, the Semitic brick city, remained their capital. For many centuries power swayed between Nineveh and Babylon, and sometimes it was an Assyrian and sometimes a Babylonian who claimed to be "king of the world."

For four centuries Assyria was restrained from expansion towards Egypt by a fresh northward thrust and settlement of another group of Semitic peoples, the Arameans, whose chief city was Damascus, and whose descendants are the Syrians of to-day. (There is, we may note, no connection whatever between the words Assyrian and Syrian. It is an accidental similarity.) Across these Syrians the Assyrian kings fought for power and expansion south-westward. In 745 B.C. arose another Tiglath Pileser, Tiglath

Pileser III, the Tiglath Pileser of the Bible (II Kings xv, 29, and xvi, 7 *et seq.*). He not only directed the transfer of the Israelites to Media (the "Lost Ten Tribes" whose ultimate fate has exercised so many curious minds), but he conquered and ruled Babylon, so founding what historians know as the New Assyrian Empire. His son, Shalmaneser IV (II Kings xvii, 3), died during the siege of Samaria and was succeeded by a usurper, who, no doubt to flatter Babylonian susceptibilities, took the ancient Akkadian Sumerian name of Sargon —Sargon II. He seems to have armed the Assyrian forces for the first time with iron weapons. It was probably Sargon II who actually carried out the deportation of the Ten Tribes that Tiglath Pileser III had ordered.

Assyrian warrior
(Bas-relief from the palace of Sargon II

Such shiftings-about of population became a very distinctive part of the political methods of the Assyrian new empire. Whole nations who were difficult to control in their native country would be shifted *en masse* to unaccustomed regions and amidst strange neighbours, where their only hope of survival would lie in obedience to the supreme power.

Sargon's son, Sennacherib, led the Assyrian hosts to the borders of Egypt. There Sennacherib's army was smitten by a pestilence, a disaster described in the nineteenth chapter of the Second Book of Kings:—

"And it came to pass that night, that the angel of the Lord went out, and smote in the camp of the Assyrians an hundred fourscore and five thousand: and when they arose early in the morning, behold, they were all dead corpses. So Sennacherib king of Assyria departed, and went and returned, and dwelt at Nineveh."

To be murdered by his sons.

Sennacherib's grandson, Assurbanipal (called by the Greeks Sardanapalus), did succeed in conquering and for a time holding Lower Egypt.

§ 2E

The Assyrian Empire lasted only a hundred and fifty years after Sargon II. Fresh nomadic Semites coming from the south-east, the Chaldeans, assisted by two Aryan-speaking peoples from the north, the Medes and Persians, combined against it, and took Nineveh in 606 B.C. This is the first appearance of the Aryan-speaking peoples in this history. They drift down out of the northern and north-western plains and forests, a hardy war-like group of tribes. Some pass south-eastward into India, taking with them a dialect of Aryan that developed into Sanscrit; others turn back upon the old civilizations. Hitherto the nomadic conquerors of the agricultural lands have been Elamites and Semites; now it is the Aryans who for half a dozen centuries take on the conquering rôle. The Elamites fade out of history.

The Chaldean Empire, with its capital at Babylon (Second Babylonian Empire), lasted under Nebuchadnezzar the Great (Nebuchadnezzar II) and his successors until 538 B.C., when it collapsed before the attack of Cyrus, the founder of the Persian power. . . .

So the story goes on. In 330 B.C., as we shall tell later in some detail, a Greek conqueror, Alexander the Great, is looking on the murdered body of the last of the Persian rulers.

The story of the Tigris and Euphrates civilizations, of which thus far we have given only the bare outline, is a story of conquest following after conquest, and each conquest replaces old rulers and ruling classes by new: races like the Sumerian and the Elamite are swallowed up, their languages vanish, they interbreed and are lost; the Assyrian melts away into Chaldean and Syrian, the Hittites lose distinction, the Semites who swallowed up the Sumerians give place to rulers of these new Aryan tribes from the north. Medes and Persians appear in the place of the Elamites and the (Aryan) Persian language dominates the empire until the Aryan Greek ousts it from official life.

Meanwhile the plough does its work year by year, the harvests are gathered, the builders build as they are told, the tradesmen work and acquire fresh devices; the knowledge of writing spreads; novel things, the horse and wheeled vehicles and iron, are introduced and become part of the permanent inheritance of mankind;

the volume of trade upon sea and desert increases, men's ideas widen and knowledge grows. There are set-backs, massacres, pestilence; but the story is, on the whole, one of enlargement. For four thousand years this new thing, civilization, which had set its root into the soil of the two rivers, grew as a tree grows; now losing a limb, now stripped by a storm, but always growing and resuming its growth. It changed its dominant race; it changed its language, but it remained essentially the same development. After four thousand years the warriors and conquerors were still going to and fro over this growing thing they did not understand, but men had by that time (330 B.C.) got iron, horses, writing and computation, money, a far greater variety of foods and textiles, a far wider knowledge of their world than the old Sumerians.

The time that elapsed between the empire of Sargon I and the conquest of Babylon by Alexander the Great was as long, be it noted, at the least estimate, as the time from Alexander the Great to the present day. And before the time of Sargon I men had been settled in the Sumerian land, living in towns, worshipping in temples, following an orderly agricultural life in an organized community, for at least as long again. "Eridu, Lagash, Ur, Isin, Larsa, have already an immemorial past when first they appear in history."

One of the most difficult things for both the writer and student of history is to sustain the sense of these time-intervals and prevent these ages becoming shortened by perspective in his imagination. Half the duration of human civilization and the keys to all its chief institutions are to be found *before* Sargon I. Moreover, the reader cannot too often compare the scale of the dates in these latter fuller pages of man's history with the succession of countless generations to which the time diagrams already given bear witness. The time diagram given at the end of Book III, p. 251, indicates the broad intervals in this succession of the first empires in Asia.

§ 3

Parallel with the ancient beginnings of civilization in Sumeria, a similar process was going on in Egypt. It is still a matter of dispute which was the more ancient of these two beginnings or how far they had a common origin or derived one from the other.

The story of the Nile valley from the dawn of its traceable history until the time of Alexander the Great is not very dissimilar from that of Babylonia; but while Babylonia lay open on every side to invasion, Egypt was protected by desert to the west and by desert and sea to the east, while to the south she had only negro peoples. Consequently her history is less broken by the invasions of strange races than is the history of Assyria and Babylon, and until towards the eighth century B.C., when she fell under an Ethiopian dynasty, whenever a conqueror did come into her story, he came in from Asia by way of the Isthmus of Suez.

The Stone Age remains in Egypt are of very uncertain date; there are Palæolithic and then Neolithic remains. It is not certain whether the Neolithic pastoral people who left those remains were the direct ancestors of the later Egyptians. In many respects they differed entirely from their successors. They buried their dead, but before they buried them they cut up the bodies and apparently ate portions of the flesh. They seem to have done this out of a feeling of reverence for the departed; the dead were "eaten with honour," according to the phrase of Sir Flinders Petrie. It may have been that the survivors hoped to retain thereby some vestige of the strength and virtue that had died. Traces of similar savage customs have been found in the long barrows that were scattered over Western Europe before the spreading of the Aryan peoples, and they have pervaded negro Africa, where they are only dying out at the present time.

About 5,000 B.C., or earlier, the traces of these primitive peoples cease, and the true Egyptians appear on the scene. The former people were hut builders and at a comparatively low stage of Neolithic culture; the latter were already a civilized Neolithic people—they used brick and wood buildings instead of their predecessors' hovels, and they were working stone. Very soon they passed into the Bronze Age. They possessed a system of picture-writing almost as developed as the contemporary writing of the Sumerians, but quite different in character. Possibly there was an irruption from Southern Arabia by way of Aden of a fresh people, who came into Upper Egypt and descended slowly towards the delta of the Nile. Dr. Wallis Budge writes of them as "conquerors from the East." But their gods and their ways, like their picture-writing, were very different indeed from the Sumerian. One of the earliest known figures of a deity is that of a hippopotamus goddess, and so very distinctively African.

The clay of the Nile is not so fine and plastic as the Sumerian clay, and the Egyptians made no use of it for writing. But they early resorted to strips of the papyrus reed fastened together, from whose name is derived our word "paper." Assyrian writing was done with a style or stamp fashioned to make a wedge-shaped impression; Egyptian with a brush. To that we owe the far greater expressiveness of the latter.

The broad outline of the history of Egypt is simpler than the history of Mesopotamia. It has long been the custom to divide the rulers of Egypt into a succession of Dynasties, and in speaking of the periods of Egyptian history it is usual to speak of the first, fourth, fourteenth, and so on, Dynasty. The Egyptians were ultimately conquered by the Persians after their establishment in Babylon; and when finally Egypt fell to Alexander the Great, in 332 B.C., it was Dynasty XXXI that came to an end.

In that long history of over 4,000 years—a much longer period than that between the career of Alexander the Great and the present day—certain broad phases of development may be noted here. There was a phase known as the "old kingdom," which began with the consolidation of the Northern and Southern Kingdoms by Menes, and culminated in the IVth Dynasty; this dynasty marks a period of wealth and splendour, and its monarchs were obsessed by such a passion for making monuments for themselves as no men have ever before or since had a chance to display and gratify. It was Cheops (3,733 B.C., Wallis Budge) and Chephren and Mycerinus of this IVth Dynasty who raised the vast piles of the great and the second and the third pyramids at Gizeh. The Great Pyramid is 450 feet high and its sides are 700 feet long. It is calculated (says Wallis Budge) to weigh 4,883,000 tons. All this stone was lugged into place chiefly by human muscle. These unmeaning sepulchral piles of an almost incredible vastness, erected in an age when engineering science had scarcely begun, exhausted the resource of Egypt through three long reigns, and left her wasted as if by a war.

The story of Egypt from the IVth to the XVth Dynasty is a story of conflicts between alternative capitals and competing religions, of separations into several kingdoms and reunions. It is, so to speak, an internal history. This is often called the Feudal Period. Here we can name only one of that long series of Pharaohs, Pepi II, who reigned ninety years, the longest reign in history, and left a great abundance of inscriptions and buildings. At last there happened to Egypt what happened so frequently to the civilizations of Mesopotamia. Egypt was conquered by nomadic Semites, who founded a "shepherd" dynasty, the Hyksos (XVIth), which was finally expelled by native Egyptians. This invasion probably happened while that first Babylonian Empire which Hammurabi founded was flourishing, but the exact correspondences of dates between early Egypt and Babylonia are still very doubtful. Only after a long period of servitude did a popular uprising expel these foreigners again. Hatred of the foreigners had unified the spirit of Egypt.

RACIAL TYPES. . . . FROM EGYPTIAN TOMB-PAINTINGS.
(AFTER CHAMPOLLION.)

After this war of liberation (*circa,* 1,600 B.C.) there followed a period of great prosperity in Egypt, the New Empire. Egypt became a great and united military state, and pushed her expeditions at last as far as the Euphrates, and so the age-long struggle between the Egyptian and Babylonian-Assyrian power began. Hitherto these two great systems had seemed too remote for war, but now man's powers of communication had reached a point when armies could march from one great river system to the other.

For a time Egypt was the ascendant power in this conflict. Thothmes III and Amenophis III (XVIIIth Dynasty) ruled from Ethiopia to the Euphrates in the fifteenth century B.C. For various reasons these two kings stand out with unusual distinctness in the Egyptian record. They were great builders, and left many monuments and inscriptions. Amenophis III founded Luxor, and added greatly to Karnak. At Tell-el-Amarna a mass of letters has been found, the royal correspondence with Babylonian and Hittite and other monarchs, including that Tushratta who took Nineveh, throwing a flood of light upon the political and social affairs of this particular age. Of Amenophis IV we shall have more to tell later, but of one, the most extraordinary and able of Egyptian monarchs, Queen Hatasu, we have no space to tell. She is represented upon her monuments in masculine garb, and with a long beard as a symbol of wisdom.

Thereafter there was a brief Syrian conquest of Egypt, a series of changing dynasties, among which we may note the XIXth, which included Rameses II, a great builder of temples, who reigned sixty-seven years (about 1,317 to 1,250 B.C.), and who is supposed by some to have been the Pharaoh of Moses, and the XXIInd, which included Shishak, who plundered Solomon's temple (*circa* 930 B.C.). An Ethiopian conqueror from the Upper Nile founded the XXVth Dynasty, a foreign dynasty, which went down (670 B.C.) before the new Assyria Empire created by Tiglath Pileser III, Sargon II, and Sennacherib, of which we have already made mention. For the first time Babylonia lorded it over the Nile.

The days of any Egyptian predominance over foreign nations were drawing to an end. For a time under Psammetichus I of the XXVIth Dynasty (664–600 B.C.) native rule was restored, and Necho II recovered for a time the old Egyptian possessions in Syria up to the Euphrates while the Medes and Chaldeans were attacking Nineveh. From those gains Necho II, after the fall of Nineveh and the Assyrians, was routed out again by Nebuchadnezzar II, the great Chaldean king, the Nebuchadnezzar of the Bible. The Jews, as we shall note later, who had been the allies of Necho II, were taken into captivity by Nebuchadnezzar to Babylon.

When, in the sixth century B.C., Chaldea fell to the Persians, Egypt followed suit. A rebellion later made Egypt independent once more for sixty years. In 332 B.C. she welcomed Alexander the Great as her conqueror, to be ruled thereafter by foreigners, first by Greeks, then by Romans, then in succession by Arabs, Turks, and British, until the quasi-independence of the present day. Such briefly is the history of Egypt from its beginnings; a history first of isolation and then of increasing entanglement with the affairs of other nations, as increasing facilities of communication drew the peoples of the world into closer and closer interaction.

§ 4

The history we need to tell here of India is simpler even than this brief record of Egypt. The Dravidian peoples in the Ganges valley developed upon parallel lines to the Sumerian and Egyptian societies. Seals bearing a close resemblance to those of Sumer have been found in North India. But it is doubtful if the early Indian communities ever got to so high a stage of social development as Sumer and early Egypt attained; they have left few monuments and they never achieved any form of writing. In those ancient times there do not seem to have been any Semitic conquests in India.

Somewhere about the time of Hammurabi or later, a branch of the nomadic Aryan-speaking people, who then occupied North Persia and Afghanistan, pushed down the north-west passes into India. They were closely related to the ancestors of the Medes and Persians. They conquered their way until they prevailed over all the darker populations of North India, and spread their rule or influence over the whole peninsula. They never achieved any unity in India; their history is a history of warring kings and republics.

The Persian Empire, in the days of its expansion after the capture of Babylon, pushed its boundaries beyond the Indus, and later Alexander the Great marched as far as the border of the desert that separates the Punjab from the Ganges valley. But with this bare statement we will for a time leave the history of India.

§ 5

Meanwhile, as this triple system of White Man civilizations developed in India and in the lands about the meeting-places of Asia, Africa, and Europe, another and quite distinct civilization was developing and spreading out from the then fertile but now dry and desolate valley of the Tarim and from the slopes of the Kuen-lun mountains in two directions down the course of the Hwang-ho, and later into the valley of the Yang-tse-kiang. We know little as yet of the archæology of China. Stone implements have been found in various parts of the country, and we know something of the culture of the Stone Age in this part of the world from excavations in Honan and Manchuria. The people appear to have been not unlike the present inhabitants of Northern China. They lived in villages and had domesticated the pig. They used axes and rectangular knives of stone, and arrow-heads of slate, bone, and mussel-shell; they were acquainted with spinning and made pottery, some of it of much the same type as is made to-day. Apart from this scanty evidence, our ideas at present of this early civilization are derived from the still very imperfectly explored Chinese literature. It has evidently been from the first and throughout a Mongolian civilization. Until after the time of Alexander the Great there are few traces of any Aryan or Semitic, much less of Hamitic influence. All such influences were still in another world, separated by mountains, deserts, and wild nomadic tribes until that time. The Chinese seem to have made their civilization spontaneously and unassisted. Some recent writers suppose, indeed, a connection with ancient Sumer, and the occurrence of a peculiar type of painted pottery in the excavations in Honan, similar to pottery found on a few early sites in Central and Western Asia and in Eastern Europe, suggests the possibility of a remote cultural contact. Of course both China and Sumer arose on the basis of the almost world-wide early Neolithic culture, but the Tarim valley and the lower Euphrates are separated by such vast obstacles of mountain and desert as to forbid the idea of any migration or interchange of peoples who had once settled down.

Perhaps the movement from the north met another movement of culture coming from the south. Though the civilization of China is wholly Mongolian, it does not follow that its northern roots are its only ones. If it grew first in the Tarim valley, then, unlike all other civilizations (including the Mexican and Peruvian), it did not grow out of the heliolithic culture. We Europeans know very little as yet of the ethnology and pre-history of Southern China. There the Chinese mingle with such kindred peoples as the Siamese and Burmese, and seem to bridge over towards the darker Dravidian peoples and towards the Malays.

It is quite clear from the Chinese records that there were

southern as well as northern beginnings of a civilization, and that the Chinese civilization that comes into history 2,000 years B.C. is the result of a long process of conflicts, minglings, and interchanges between a southern and a northern culture, of which the southern may have been the earlier and more highly developed. The southern Chinese perhaps played the rôle towards the northern Chinese that the Hamites or Sumerians played to the Aryan and Semitic peoples in the west, or that the settled Dravidians played towards the Aryans in India. They may have been the first agriculturists and the first temple-builders. But so little is known as yet of this attractive chapter in pre-history that we cannot dwell upon it further here.

The chief foreigners mentioned in the early annals of China were a Ural-Altaic people on the north-east frontier, the Huns, against whom certain of the earlier emperors made war.

Chinese history is still very little known to European students, and our accounts of the early records are particularly unsatisfactory. About 2,700 to 2,400 B.C. reigned five emperors, who seem to have been almost incredibly exemplary beings.

There followed upon these first five emperors a series of dynasties, of which the accounts became more and more exact and convincing as they become more recent. China has to tell a long history of border warfare and of graver struggles between the settled and nomad peoples. To begin with, China, like Sumer and like Egypt, was a land of city states. The government was at first a government of numerous kings; they became loosely feudal under an emperor, as the Egyptians did; and then later, as with the Egyptians, came a centralizing empire. Shang (1,750 to 1,125 B.C.) and Chow (1,125 to 250 B.C.) are named as being the two great dynasties of the feudal period. Bronze vessels of these earlier dynasties, beautiful, splendid, and with a distinctive style of their own, still exist, and there can be no doubt of the existence of a high state of culture even before the days of Shang.

It is perhaps a sense of symmetry that made the later historians of Egypt and China talk of the earlier phases of their national history as being under dynasties comparable to the dynasties of the later empires, and of such early "Emperors" as Menes (in Egypt) or the First Five Emperors (in China). The early dynasties exercised far less centralized powers than the later ones. Such unity as China possessed under the Shang Dynasty was a religious rather than an effective political union. The "Son of Heaven" offered sacrifices for all the Chinese. There was a common script, a common civilization, and a common enemy in the Huns of the north-western borders.

The last of the Shang Dynasty was a cruel and foolish monarch who burnt himself alive (1,125 B.C.) in his palace after a decisive defeat by Wu Wang, the founder of the Chow Dynasty. Wu Wang seems to have been helped by the south-western tribes as well as by a popular revolt.

For a time China remained loosely united under the Chow emperors, as loosely united as was Christendom under the popes in the Middle Ages; the Chow emperors had become the traditional high priests of the land in the place of the Shang Dynasty and claimed a sort of overlordship in Chinese affairs, but gradually the loose ties of usage and sentiment that held the empire together lost their hold upon men's minds. Hunnish peoples to the north and west took on the Chinese civilization without acquiring a sense of its unity. Feudal princes began to regard themselves as independent.

In *China and the League of Nations,* Mr. Liang Chi-Chao, one of the Chinese representatives at the Paris Conference of 1919, states that between the eighth and fourth centuries B.C. "there were in the Hwang-ho and Yang-tse valleys no less than five or six thousand small states with about a dozen states dominating over them." The land was subjected to perpetual warfare ("Age of Confusion"). In the sixth century B.C. the great powers in conflict were Ts'i and Ts'in, which were northern Hwang-ho states, and Ch'u, which was a vigorous power in the Yang-tse valley. A confederation against Ch'u laid the foundation for a league that kept the peace for a hundred years; the league subdued and incorporated Ch'u and made a general treaty of disarmament. It became the foundation of a new pacific empire.

The knowledge of iron entered China at some unknown date, but iron weapons began to be commonly used only about 500 B.C. —that is to say, two or three hundred years or more after their use had become customary in Assyria, Egypt, and Europe. Iron was probably introduced from the north into China by the Huns.

The last rulers of the Chow Dynasty were ousted by the kings of Ts'in; the latter seized upon the sacred sacrificial bronze tripods, and so were able to take over the imperial duty of offering sacrifices to Heaven. In this manner was the Ts'in Dynasty established. It ruled with far more vigour and effect than any previous family.

The reign of Shi-Hwang-ti (meaning "first universal emperor")

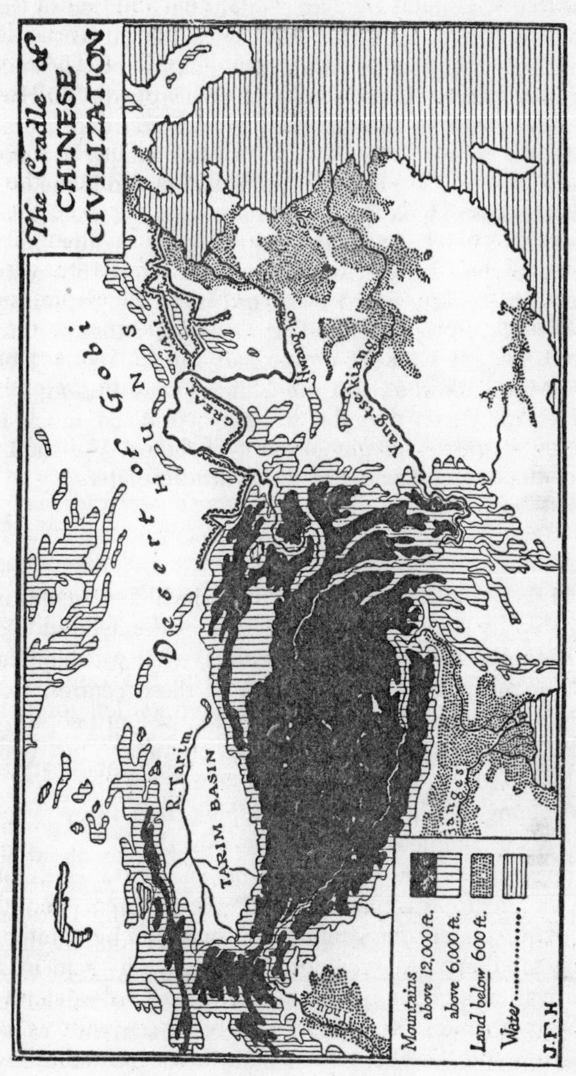
The Cradle of
CHINESE
CIVILIZATION
Desert of Gobi
HUNS
GREAT WALL
Hwang-ho
Yang-tse-Kiang
R. Tarim
TARIM BASIN
Ganges
Indus
Mountains
above 12,000 ft.
above 6,000 ft.
Land below 600 ft.
Water
J.F.H.

of this dynasty is usually taken to mark the end of feudal and divided China. He seems to have played the unifying rôle in the east that Alexander the Great might have played in the west, but he lived longer, and the unity he made (or restored) was comparatively permanent, while the empire of Alexander the Great fell to pieces, as we shall tell, at his death. Shi-Hwang-ti, among other feats in the direction of common effort, organized the building of the Great Wall of China against the Huns. A civil war followed close upon his reign, and ended in the establishment of the Han Dynasty.

Under this Han Dynasty the empire grew greatly beyond its original two river valleys, the Huns were effectively restrained, and the Chinese penetrated westward until they began to learn at last of civilized races and civilizations other than their own.

By 100 B.C. the Chinese power had spread across Tibet and into Western Turkestan, and the Chinese were trading by camel caravans with Persia and the western world. So much for the present must suffice for our account of China. We shall return to the distinctive characters of its civilization later.

§ 6

And in these thousands of years during which man was making his way step by step from the barbarism of the heliolithic culture to civilization at these old-world centres, what was happening in the rest of the world? To the north of these centres, from the Rhine to the Pacific, the Nordic and Mongolian peoples, as we have told, were also learning the use of metals; but while the civilizations were settling down these men of the great plains were becoming migratory and developing from a slow wandering life towards a complete seasonal nomadism.

To the south of the civilized zone, in central and southern Africa, the negro was making a slower progress, and that, it would seem, under the stimulus of invasion by whiter tribes from the Mediterranean regions, bringing with them in succession cultivation and the use of metals. These tribes came to the black by two routes: across the Sahara to the west as Berbers and Tuaregs and the like, to mix with the negro and create such quasi-white races as the Fulas; and also by way of the Nile, where the Baganda (= Gandafolk) of Uganda, for example, may possibly include some element of a remote white origin. The African forests were denser then, and spread eastward and northward from the Upper Nile.

The islands of the East Indies, three thousand years ago, were probably still only inhabited here and there by stranded patches of Palæolithic Australoids, who had wandered thither in those immemorial ages when there was a nearly complete land bridge by way of the East Indies to Australia. The islands of Oceania were uninhabited. The spreading of the heliolithic peoples by sea-going canoes into the islands of the Pacific came much later in the history of man, at earliest a thousand years B.C. Still later did they reach Madagascar. The beauty of New Zealand also was as yet wasted so far as mankind was concerned; its highest living creatures were a great ostrich-like bird, the moa, now extinct, and the little kiwi, which has feathers like coarse hair and the merest rudiments of wings.

In North America a group of Mongoloid tribes were now cut off altogether from the old world. They were spreading slowly southward, hunting the innumerable bison of the plains. They had still to learn for themselves the secrets of a separate agriculture based on maize, and in South America to tame the llama to their service, and to build up in Mexico and Yucatan and Peru three separate civilizations of a very curious and distinctive type.

When men reached the southern extremity of America, the *Megatherium,* the giant sloth, and the *Glyptodon,* the giant armadillo, were still living. . . .

These American primitive civilizations may ultimately prove of very great help to our understanding of human development, because they seem to have preserved, right up to the time of their extinction by the European discoverers at the end of the fifteenth century A.D., ideas and methods that passed out of old-world experience five or six thousand years B.C. They never got to the use of iron; their metallurgy was of the simplest kind, and their chief metals, copper and gold, they found native. Their stonework, pottery, and weaving, however, were at a very high level, and they were extremely skilful dyers. Like the long superseded primitive civilizations of the old world, these communities displayed a close association of human sacrifice with the processes of seed-time and harvest, but while in the old world these primary social ideas were mitigated and overlaid by many others, in America they were developed to an extraordinary degree of intensity. The serpent was the predominant symbol in religious decoration. These American civilizations seem to have been essentially priest-ridden countries; their war chiefs and peace leaders were under a rigorous rule of law and interpreted omen.

Their priests carried astronomical science to a high level of accuracy. They knew their year far better than did the Babylonians. The Yucatan civilization developed a kind of writing, the Maya writing, of the most elaborate character. So far as we have been able to decipher it, it was used for keeping the exact and complicated calendars upon which the priests expended their intellectual energy. The art of the Maya civilization was particularly well developed. Some of the simpler sculpture of Peru is suggestive of Sumerian work, but the Maya stuff is like nothing the old world has ever produced, and it rises to very great executive beauty. The nearest resemblances, and they are not very near, are to be found in some South Indian carvings. It astonishes by its great plastic power and its perfection of design, but it perplexes by a grotesqueness, a sort of insane intricacy and conventionality. Many Maya inscriptions resemble a certain sort of elaborate drawing made by lunatics in European asylums more than they do any other old-world production. It is as if the Maya mind had developed along a different line from that followed by the old-world mind, had acquired a different twist to its ideas, was not, indeed, by old-world standards a strictly rational mind at all.

This linking of these aberrant American civilizations to the idea of a general mental aberration finds support in their obsession by the thought of shedding human blood. The Aztec (Mexican) civilization ran blood; it offered thousands of human victims yearly. The cutting open of living victims, the tearing out of the still beating heart, was an act that dominated the minds and lives of these strange priesthoods. The public life, the seasonal festivities, all turned on this fantastically horrible fixed idea.

The Maya writing was not only carven on stone but painted and written upon skins. These manuscripts are painted brightly, and have an odd resemblance to the cheap coloured papers which are sold to children in America and Europe to-day. There is the same repetition of figures with variations, as if a story was being told. In Peru the beginnings of writing were superseded by a curious and complicated method of keeping records by means of knots tied upon strings and various colours and shapes. It is said that even laws and orders could be conveyed by this code. These string bundles were called *quipus,* but though *quipus* are still to be found in collections, the art of reading them is altogether lost. The Chinese histories, Mr. L. Y. Chen informs us, state that a similar method of record by knots was used in China before the invention of writing there. The Peruvians also got to making maps and the use of counting-frames.

When the Spaniards came to America, the Mexicans knew nothing of the Peruvians nor the Peruvians of the Mexicans. Whatever links had ever existed were lost and forgotten. The Mexicans had never heard of the potato, which was a principal article of Peruvian diet. In 5,000 B.C. the Sumerians and Egyptians probably knew as little of one another. America had in fact lagged 6,000 years behind the old world.

§ 7

Here, perhaps, is the place to notice the unsubstantial legend of the Lost Atlantis. Quite a large number of people are persuaded that there is evidence of a great civilized state that existed three thousand years ago or so in the Atlantic beyond the Straits of Gibraltar. It was a large country, a "continent." There was the garden of the Hesperides. Their belief is sustained by numerous allusions in Greek and later literature to such a vanished land. The story is of the quality that makes things acceptable to cinematograph producers and audiences. It has no support at all in geographical, geological, or archæological fact.

At a remote period in geological time there is good reason for supposing that there was land where now the Atlantic waters roll, but there is no evidence for and much against any westward extension of Europe or Asia since the Miocene period. But civilization is a matter of at most the last twenty thousand years and probably only of the last ten, and man has been man only since the Pleistocene. The human remains we find in Spain and North Africa give no indication of any higher state of culture to the west, and in the earlier Greek literature, in Homer and Hesiod, there is a total ignorance of the existence even of Spain, much less of the Atlantic Ocean.

Mr. Reginald Fessenden has made a very careful study of these Atlantis stories, and he has come to the conclusion that they refer not to a lost land in the Atlantic but to what is an altogether more probable thing, a once much more important civilization in the region of the Caucasus. We do know that waters have spread and receded over the south of Russia and over Central Asia within the human period so that what are deserts were once seas, and where now there is hardly herbage enough to sustain life there were once dense forests. We have every reason for believing that considerable finds of early civilizations may be made in that part of the world. The coast of the Black Sea may have been flooded out in some catastrophic manner at some date before the southward movement of the Aryan peoples. There may have been sudden submergences. A rise of only fifty feet in the sea-level would join the Black Sea to the Caspian now. A cycle of wet cold years which would check surface evaporation from these waters might almost achieve that. At the present time we are all so well equipped with maps, and have such definite geographical ideas, that it is difficult for us to imagine the geographic vagueness of even the best-informed people in the second millennium B.C. Wonder stories about a lost country to which one once went by sea through the Dardanelles, might easily get changed, as the Greek and Phœnician traders opened up the western end of the Mediterranean, into wonder stories about the same legendary land transplanted now to beyond the new-found straits. Georgia is undoubtedly a country of great archæological possibilities, and if anything of primary value in the relationships of the early civilizations remains to be discovered it will possibly be found in the region between the Black Sea and Western Turkestan. A remarkable number of Greek fables and legends concentrate on Georgia; it was the land of the Golden Fleece, the goal of the Argonauts, and there Prometheus was chained with the vulture gnawing at his vitals. No less an authority than Sir Flinders Petrie gives countenance to the idea that there was some very early connection between Colchis (the country to the south of the Caucasus) and prehistoric Egypt. Herodotus remarked upon a series of resemblances between the Colchians and the Egyptians.

XIV

SEA PEOPLES AND TRADING PEOPLES

§ 1. *The Earliest Ships and Sailors.* § 2. *The Ægean Cities before History.* § 3. *The First Voyages of Exploration.* § 4. *Early Traders.* § 5. *Early Travellers.*

§ 1

THE first boats were made very early indeed in the Neolithic stage of culture by riverside and lakeside peoples. They were no more than trees and floating wood, used to assist the imperfect natural swimming powers of men. Then came the hollowing out of the trees, and then, with the development of tools and a primitive carpentry, the building of boats. Men in Egypt and Mesopotamia also, developed a primitive type of basketwork boat caulked with bitumen. Such was the "ark of bulrushes" in which Moses was hidden by his mother.

A kindred sort of vessel grew up by the use of skins and hides expanded upon a wicker framework. To this day cowhide wicker boats (coracles) are used upon the west coast of Ireland, where there are plenty of cattle and a poverty of big trees. They are also still used on the Euphrates, and on the Towy in South Wales. In Alaska, also, boats of this ancient type are found, and men will cross in them from America to Siberia. Inflated skins may have preceded the coracle, and are still used on the Euphrates and Upper Ganges. In the valleys of the great rivers boats must early have become an important means of communication; and it seems natural to suppose that it was from the mouths of the great rivers that man, already in a reasonably seaworthy vessel, first ventured out upon what must have seemed to him then the trackless and homeless sea.

No doubt he ventured at first as a fisherman, having learnt the elements of seacraft in creeks and lagoons. Men may have navigated boats upon the Levantine lake before the refilling of the Mediterranean by the Atlantic waters. The canoe was an integral part of the heliolithic culture, it drifted with that culture upon the warm waters of the earth from the Mediterranean to (at last) America. There were not only canoes, but Sumerian boats and ships, upon the Euphrates and Tigris, when these rivers in 7,000 B.C. fell by separate mouths into the Persian Gulf.

The Sumerian city Eridu, which stood at the head of the Persian Gulf (from which it is now separated by a hundred and thirty miles of alluvium), had ships upon the sea then. We also find evidence of a fully developed sea life six thousand years ago at the eastern end of the Mediterranean, and possibly at that time there were already canoes on the seas among the islands of the nearer East Indies. There are pre-dynastic Neolithic Egyptian representations of Nile ships of a fair size, capable of carrying elephants.

Very soon the seafaring men must have realized the peculiar freedom and opportunities the ship gave them. They could get away to islands; no chief nor king could pursue a boat or ship with any certainty; every captain was a king. The seamen would find it easy to make nests upon islands and in strong positions on the mainland. There they could harbour, there they could carry on a certain agriculture and fishery; but their specialty and their main business was, of course, the expedition across the sea. That was not usually a trading expedition; it was much more frequently a piratical raid. From what we know of mankind, we are bound to conclude that the first sailors plundered when they could, and traded when they had to.

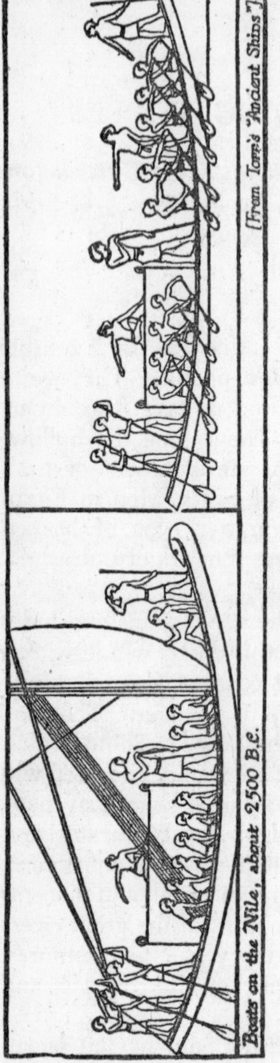

Boats on the Nile, about 2500 B.C. [From Torr's "Ancient Ships"]

Because it developed in the comparatively warm and tranquil waters of the eastern Mediterranean, the Red Sea, the Persian Gulf, and the western horn of the Indian Ocean, the shipping of the ancient world retained throughout certain characteristics that make it differ very widely from the ocean-going sailing shipping, with its vast spread of canvas, of the last four hundred years. "The Mediterranean," says Mr. Torr, "is a sea where a vessel with sails may lay becalmed for days together, while a vessel with oars would easily be traversing the smooth waters, with coasts and islands everywhere at hand to give her shelter in case of storm. In that sea, therefore, oars became the characteristic instruments of navigation, and the arrangement of oars the chief problem in shipbuilding. And while Mediterranean nations dominated Western Europe, vessels of the southern type were built upon the northern coasts, though there was wind enough for sails and too much for oars. . . .

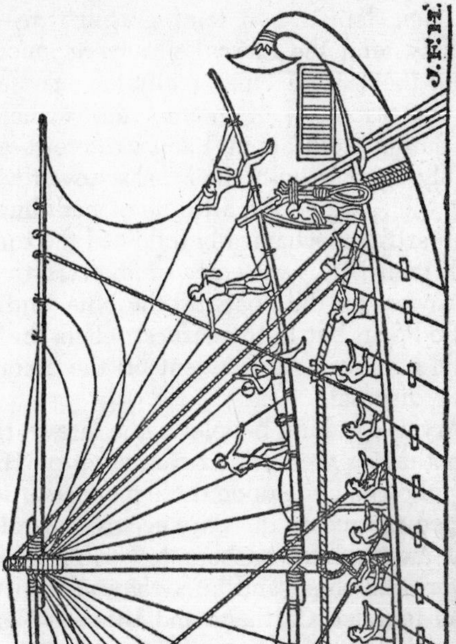

Egyptian ship on the Red Sea, about 1250 B.C. [*From Torr's "Ancient Ships."*]

Mr. Langton Cole calls attention to the rope *truss* in this illustration, stiffening the beam of the ship. No other such use of the truss is known until the days of modern engineering.

"The art of rowing can first be discerned upon the Nile. Boats with oars are represented in the earliest pictorial monuments of

Egypt; and although some crews are paddling with their faces towards the bow, others are rowing with their faces towards the stern. The paddling is certainly the older practice, for the hieroglyph *chen* depicts two arms grasping an oar in the attitude of paddling, and the hieroglyphs were invented in the earliest ages. And that practice may really have ceased before 2,500 B.C., despite the testimony of monuments of that date; for in monuments dating from about 1,250 B.C. crews are represented unmistakably rowing with their faces towards the stern and yet grasping their oars in the attitude of paddling, so that even then Egyptian artists mechanically followed the turn of the hieroglyph to which their hands were accustomed. In these reliefs there are twenty rowers on the boats on the Nile, and thirty on the ships on the Red Sea; but in the earliest reliefs the number varies considerably, and seems dependent on the amount of space at the sculptor's disposal."

The Aryan-speaking peoples came late to the sea. The earliest ships on the sea were either Sumerian or Hamitic; the Semitic peoples followed close upon these pioneers. Along the eastern end of the Mediterranean, the Phœnicians, a Semitic people, set up a string of independent harbour towns, of which Acre, Tyre, and Sidon were the chief; and later they pushed their voyages westward and founded Carthage and Utica in North Africa. Possibly Phœnician keels were already in the Mediterranean by 2,000 B.C. Both Tyre and Sidon were originally on islands, and so easily defensible against a land raid.

But before we go on to the marine exploits of this great seagoing race, we must note a very remarkable and curious nest of early sea people whose remains have been discovered in Crete.

§ 2

These early Cretans were of a race akin to the Iberians of Spain and Western Europe and the dark whites of Asia Minor and North Africa, and their language is unknown. This race lived not only in Crete, but in Cyprus, Greece, Asia Minor, Sicily, and South Italy. It was a civilized people for long ages before the fair Nordic Greeks spread southward through Macedonia. At Cnossos, in Crete, there have been found the most astonishing ruins and remains, and Cnossos, therefore, is apt to overshadow the rest of these settlements in people's imaginations, but it is well to bear in mind that though Cnossos was no doubt a chief city of this Ægean civilization, these "Ægeans" had in the fullness of their sway many cities and a wide range.

At Cnossos there are Neolithic remains as old or older than any of the pre-dynastic remains of Egypt. The Bronze Age began in Crete as soon as it did in Egypt, and there have been vases found by Sir Flinders Petrie in Egypt and referred by him to the Ist Dynasty, which he declares to be importations from Crete. Stone vases, amulets, and impressions of seals found in Crete point to relations with the Nile valley even before the historic dynasties. Stone vessels have been found of forms characteristic of the IVth (pyramid-building) Dynasty, and there can be no doubt that there was a vigorous trade between Crete and Egypt in the time of the XIIth Dynasty. This continued until about 1,000 B.C. It is clear that this island civilization arising upon the soil of Crete is at least as old as the Egyptian, and that it was already launched upon the sea as early as 4,000 B.C., before either Semite or Aryan had made a figure upon the stage of history.

The great days of Crete were not so early as this. It was only about 2,500 B.C. that the island appears to have been unified under one ruler. Then began an age of peace and prosperity unexampled in the history of the ancient world. Secure from invasion, living in a delightful climate, trading with every civilized community in the world, the Cretans were free to develop all the arts and amenities of life.

This Cnossos was not so much a town as the vast palace of the king and his people. It was not even fortified. The kings, it would seem, were called Minos always, as the kings of Egypt were all called Pharaoh; the king of Cnossos figures in the early legends of the Greeks as King Minos, who lived in the Labyrinth and kept there a horrible monster, half man, half bull, the Minotaur, to feed which he levied a tribute of youths and maidens from the Athenians. These stories are a part of Greek literature, and have always been known, but it is only in the last few decades that the excavations at Cnossos have revealed how close these legends were to the reality. The Cretan Labyrinth was a building as stately, complex, and luxurious as any in the ancient world. We find waterpipes, bathrooms, and the like conveniences, such as have hitherto been regarded as the latest refinements of modern life.

The pottery, the textile manufactures, the sculpture and painting of these people, their gem and ivory work, their metal and inlaid work, are as admirable as any that mankind has produced.

They were much given to festivals and shows, and, in particular, they were addicted to bull-fights and gymnastic entertainments. Their female costume became astonishingly "Victorian" in style; their women wore corsets and flounced dresses. They had a system of writing which has not yet been deciphered.

It is the custom nowadays to make a sort of wonder of these achievements of the Cretans, as though they were a people of incredible artistic ability living in the dawn of civilization. But their great time was long past that dawn; as late as 2,000 B.C. It took them many centuries to reach their best in art and skill, and their art and luxury are by no means so great a wonder if we reflect that for 3,000 years they were immune from invasion, that for a thousand years they were at peace. Century after century their artisans could perfect their skill, and their men and women refine upon refinement. Whenever men of almost any race have been comparatively safe in this fashion for such a length of time, they have developed much artistic beauty. Given the opportunity, all races are artistic. Greek legend has it that it was in Crete that Dædalus attempted to make the first flying machine. Dædalus (= cunning artificer) was a sort of personified summary of mechanical skill. It is curious to speculate what germ of fact lies behind him and those waxen wings that, according to the legend, melted and plunged his son Icarus into the sea. It is quite possible that Icarus was the first glider.

There came at last a change in the condition of the lives of these Cretans, for other peoples, the Greeks and the Phœnicians, were also coming out with powerful fleets upon the seas. We do not know what led to the disaster nor who inflicted it; but somewhere about 1,400 B.C. Cnossos was sacked and burnt, and, though the Cretan life struggled on there rather lamely for another four centuries, there came at last a final blow about 1,000 B.C. (that is to say, in the days of the Assyrian ascendancy in the East). The palace at Cnossos was destroyed, and never rebuilt nor reinhabited. Possibly this was done by the ships of those newcomers into the Mediterranean, the barbaric Greeks, a group of Aryan-speaking tribes from the north, who may have wiped out Cnossos as they wiped out the city of Troy. The legend of Theseus tells of such a raid. He entered the labyrinth (which may have been the Cnossos Palace) by the aid of Ariadne, the daughter of Minos, and slew the Minotaur.

The *Iliad* makes it clear that destruction came upon Troy because the Trojans stole Greek women. Modern writers, with modern ideas in their heads, have tried to make out that the Greeks assailed Troy in order to secure a trade-route to Colchis or some such fine-spun commercial advantage. If so, the authors of the *Iliad* hid the motives of their characters very skilfully. It would be about as reasonable to say that the Homeric Greeks went to war with the Trojans in order to be well ahead with a station on the Berlin to Bagdad railway. The Homeric Greeks were a healthy barbaric Aryan people, with very poor ideas about

ÆGEAN CIVILIZATION

trade and "trade-routes"; they went to war with the Trojans because they were thoroughly annoyed about this stealing of women. It is fairly clear from the Minos legend and from the evidence of the Cnossos remains, that the Cretans kidnapped or stole youths and maidens to be slaves, bull-fighters, athletes, and perhaps sacrifices. They traded fairly with the Egyptians, but it may be they did not realize the gathering strength of the Greek barbarians; they "traded" violently with them, and so brought sword and flame upon themselves.

Another people earlier upon the sea than the Greeks were the Phœnicians. They were great seamen because they were great traders. Their colony of Carthage (founded before 800 B.C. by Tyre) became at last greater than any of the older Phœnician cities, but already before 1,500 B.C. both Sidon and Tyre had settlements upon the African coast.

Carthage was comparatively inaccessible to the Assyrian and Babylonian hosts, and, profiting greatly by the long siege of Tyre by Nebuchadnezzar II, became the greatest maritime power the world had hitherto seen. She claimed the Western Mediterranean as her own, and seized every ship she could catch west of Sardinia. Roman writers accuse her of great cruelties. She fought the Greeks for Sicily, and later (in the second century B.C.) she fought the Romans. Alexander the Great formed plans for her conquest; but he died, as we shall tell later, before he could carry them out.

§ 3

At her zenith Carthage probably had the hitherto unheard-of population of a million. This population was largely industrial, and her woven goods were universally famous. As well as a coasting trade, she had a considerable land trade with Central Africa.

There were, we may note here, no domesticated camels in Africa until after the Persian conquest of Egypt, and the camel as a beast of transport was seemingly not introduced into North Africa till the Arab invasions of the seventh century A.D. This must have greatly restricted the desert routes. But the Sahara desert of 3,000 or 2,000 years ago was less perched and sterile than it is to-day. From rock engravings we may deduce the theory that the desert was crossed from oasis to oasis by riding oxen and by ox-carts; perhaps, also, on horses and asses.

Carthage, thus placed between the hinterlands of Africa and the sea, sold negro slaves, ivory, metals, precious stones and the like, to all the Mediterranean people; she worked Spanish copper mines, and her ships went out into the Atlantic and coasted along Portugal and France northward as far as the Cassiterides (the Scilly Isles, or Cornwall, in England) to get tin.

About 520 B.C. a certain Hanno made a voyage that is still one of the most notable in the world. This Hanno—if we may trust the *Periplus of Hanno,* the Greek translation of his account which still survives—followed the African coast southwards from the Straits of Gibraltar as far as the confines of Liberia. He had sixty big ships, and his main task was to found or reinforce certain Carthaginian stations upon the Moroccan coast. Then he pushed southward. He founded a settlement in the Rio de Oro and sailed on past the Senegal River. The voyagers passed on for seven days beyond the Gambia, and landed at last upon some island. This they left in a panic, because, although the day was silent with the silence of the tropical forest, at nights they heard the sound of flutes, drums and gongs, and the sky was red with the blaze of the bush fires. The coast country for the rest of the voyage was one blaze of fire, from the burning of the bush. Streams of fire ran down the hills, and at length a blaze arose so loftily that it touched the skies. Three days further brought them to an island containing a lake (? Sherbro Island). In this lake was another island (? Macaulay Island), and on this were wild, hairy men and women, "whom the interpreters called gorilla."

The Carthaginians, having caught some of the females of these "gorillas"—they were probably chimpanzees—turned back and eventually deposited the skins of their captives—who had proved impossibly violent guests to entertain on board ship—in the Temple of Juno.

A still more wonderful Phœnician sea voyage, long doubted, but now supported by some archæological evidence, is related by Herodotus, who declares that the Pharaoh Necho of the XXVIth Dynasty commissioned some Phœnicians to attempt the circumnavigation of Africa, and that starting from the Gulf of Suez southward they did finally come back through the Mediterranean to the Nile delta. They took nearly three years to complete their voyage. Each year they landed, and sowed and harvested a crop of wheat before going on.

§ 4

The great trading cities of the Phœnicians are the most striking of the early manifestations of the peculiar and characteristic gift of the Semitic peoples to mankind, trade and exchange. While the Semitic Phœnician peoples were spreading themselves upon the seas, another kindred Semitic people, the Arameans, whose occupation of Damascus we have already noted, were developing the caravan routes of the Arabian and Persian deserts, and becoming the chief trading people of Western Asia. There was also an early sea trade out of the Red Sea and Persian Gulf southward. Recently, ancient Bushmen rock paintings have been found in South Africa, very similar in style and treatment to the paintings of Palæolithic men in the east of Spain, and in these paintings white men with what may be Assyrian head-dresses are shown.

The Semitic peoples, earlier civilized than the Aryan, have always shown, and still show to-day, a far greater sense of quality and quantity in marketable goods than the latter; it is to their need of account-keeping that the development of alphabetical writing is to be ascribed, and it is to them that most of the great advances in computation are due. Our modern numerals are Arabic; our arithmetic and algebra are essentially Semitic sciences.

The Semitic peoples, we may point out here, are to this day *counting peoples* strong in their sense of equivalents and reparation. The moral teaching of the Hebrews was saturated by such ideas. "With what measure ye mete, the same shall be meted unto you." Other races and peoples have imagined diverse and fitful and marvellous gods, but it was the trading Semites who first began to think of God as a Righteous Dealer, Whose promises were kept, Who failed not the humblest creditor, and called to account every spurious act.

The trade that was going on in the ancient world before the sixth or seventh century B.C. was almost entirely a barter trade. There was little or no credit or coined money. The early empires got along without coin altogether. The ordinary standard of value with the early Aryans, and probably with all communities before they settled down, was cattle, as it still is with the Zulus and Kaffirs to-day. In the *Iliad*, the respective values of two shields are stated in head of cattle, and the Roman word for money, *pecunia*, is derived from *pecus*, cattle. Cattle as money had this advantage: it did not need to be carried from one owner to another; and if it needed attention and food, at any rate it bred. But it was inconvenient for ship or caravan transit. Many other substances have at various times been found convenient as a standard; tobacco was once legal tender in the colonial days in North America, and in West Africa fines are paid and bargains made in bottles of trade gin. The early Asiatic trade included metals; and weighed lumps of metal, since they were in general demand and were convenient for hoarding and storage, costing nothing for fodder and needing small house room, soon asserted their superiority over cattle and sheep.

Iron, which seems to have been first reduced from its ores by the Hittites, was, to begin with, a rare and much-desired substance. It is stated by Aristotle to have supplied the first currency. Iron bars of fixed weight were used for coin in Britain, says Cæsar in his *De Bello Gallico*. In the collection of letters found at Tell-el-Amarna, addressed to and from Amenophis III (already mentioned) and his successor Amenophis IV, one from a Hittite king promises iron as an extremely valuable gift. Gold, then as now, was the most precious and therefore most portable of all metallic value standards. In early Egypt silver was almost as rare as gold until after the XVIIIth Dynasty. Later the general standard of value in the Eastern world became silver, measured by weight. It established something like its modern relationship in value to gold, and has always since retained it.

To begin with, metals were handed about in ingots and weighed at each transaction. Then they were stamped to indicate their fineness and guarantee their purity. The earliest coinage of the west coast of Asia Minor was in electrum, a mixture of gold and silver, and there is an interesting controversy as to whether the first issues were stamped by cities, temples, or private bankers. The first recorded coins were minted about 600 B.C. in Lydia, a gold-producing country in the west of Asia Minor. The first known gold coins were minted in Lydia by Crœsus, whose name has become a proverb for wealth; he was conquered, as we shall tell later, by that same Cyrus the Persian who took Babylon in 539 B.C.

But very probably coined money had been used in Babylonia before that time. The "sealed shekel," a stamped piece of silver, came very near to being a coin. The Servants of the Temple of the Moon God of Ur (about 2,000 B.C.) when sent on a journey carried letters of credit written on clay tablets enabling them to get supplies at the towns through which they passed.

The promise to pay so much silver or gold on "leather" (=parchment) with the seal of some established firm is probably as old or older than coinage. The Carthaginians used such "leather money."

We know very little of the way in which small traffic was conducted in the ancient world. Common people, who in those ancient times were in dependent positions, seem to have had no money at all; they did their business by barter. Early Egyptian paintings show this going on.

Small change was in existence before the time of Alexander. The Athenians had a range of exceedingly small silver coins, running almost down to the size of a pinhead, which were generally carried in the mouth; a character in Aristophanes was suddenly assaulted, and swallowed his change in consequence.

§ 5

When one realizes the absence of small money or of any conveniently portable means of exchange in the pre-Alexandrian world, one perceives how impossible was private travel in those days. The first "inns"—no doubt a sort of caravanserai—are commonly said to have come into existence in Lydia in the third or fourth century B.C. That, however, is too late a date. They are certainly older than that. There is good evidence of them at least as early as the sixth century. Æschylus twice mentions inns. His word is "all-receiver," or "all-receiving house." Private travellers may have been fairly common in the Greek world, including its colonies, by that time. But private travel was a comparatively new thing. The early historians Hecatæus and Herodotus travelled widely.

"I suspect," says Professor Gilbert Murray, "that this sort of travel 'for Historie' or 'for discovery' was rather a Greek invention. Solon is supposed to have practised it; and even Lycurgus." . . .

The earliest travellers were traders travelling in a caravan or in a shipload, and carrying their goods and their moneys and shekels of metal or gems or bales of fine stuff with them, or else they were government officials travelling with letters of introduction and a proper retinue. Possibly there were a few mendicants, and, in some restricted regions, religious pilgrims. In Egypt there was a good deal of travel under fairly safe conditions up and down the Nile. There were excursions down river to the ancient pyramids in the days of Amenophis III. The "tripper" first appeared there.

That earlier world before 600 B.C. was one in which a lonely "stranger" was a rare and suspected and endangered being. He might suffer horrible cruelties, for there was little law to protect such as he. Few individuals strayed, therefore. One lived and died attached and tied to some patriarchal tribe if one was a nomad, or to some great household if one was civilized, or to one of the big temple establishments which we will presently discuss. Or one was a herded slave.

One knew nothing, except for a few monstrous legends, of the rest of the world in which one lived. We know more to-day, indeed, of the world of 600 B.C. than any single living being knew at that time. We map it out, see it as a whole in relation to past and future. We begin to learn precisely what was going on at the same time in Egypt and Spain and Media and India and China. We can share in imagination not only the wonder of Hanno's sailors, but of the men who lit the warning beacons on the shore. We know that those "mountains flaming to the sky," of which the *Periplus* speaks, were only the customary burnings of the dry grass at that season of the year. Year by year, more and more rapidly, our common knowledge increases. In the years to come men will understand still more of those lives in the past, until, perhaps, they will understand them altogether.

XV

WRITING

§ 1. *Picture Writing.* § 2. *Syllable Writing.* § 3. *Alphabet Writing.* § 4. *The Place of Writing in Human Life.*

§ 1

IN THE preceding chapters we have sketched in broad outline the development of the chief human communities from the primitive beginnings of the earliest civilizations to the great historical kingdoms and empires in the sixth century B.C. We must now study a little more closely the general process of social change, the growth of human ideas, and the elaboration of human relationships that were going on during these ages between 10,000 B.C. and 500 B.C. What we have done so far is to draw the map and name the chief kings and empires, to define the relations in time and space of the empires of Babylonia, Assyria, Egypt, India, and China; we come now to the real business of history, which is to get down below these outer forms to the thoughts and lives of individual men.

By far the most important thing that was going on during those fifty or sixty centuries of social development was the invention of writing and its gradual progress to importance in human affairs. It was a new instrument for the human mind, an enormous enlargement of its range of action, a new means of continuity. We have seen how in later Palæolithic and early Neolithic times the elaboration of articulate speech gave men a mental handhold for consecutive thought, and a vast enlargement of their powers of co-operation. For a time this new acquirement seems to have overshadowed their earlier achievement of drawing, and possibly it checked the use of gesture. But drawing presently appeared again, for record, for signs, for the joy of drawing. Before real writing came picture-writing, such as is still practised by the Amerindians, the Bushmen, and savage and barbaric peoples in all parts of the world. It is essentially a drawing of things and acts, helped out by heraldic indications of proper names, and by strokes and dots to represent days and distances and such-like quantitative ideas.

Quite kindred to such picture-writing is the pictograph that one finds still in use to-day in international railway time-tables upon the continent of Europe, where a little black sign of a cup indicates a stand-up buffet for light refreshments; a crossed knife and fork, a restaurant; a little steamboat, a transfer to a steamboat; and a postilion's horn, a diligence. Similar signs are used in the well-known Michelin guides for automobilists in Europe to show a

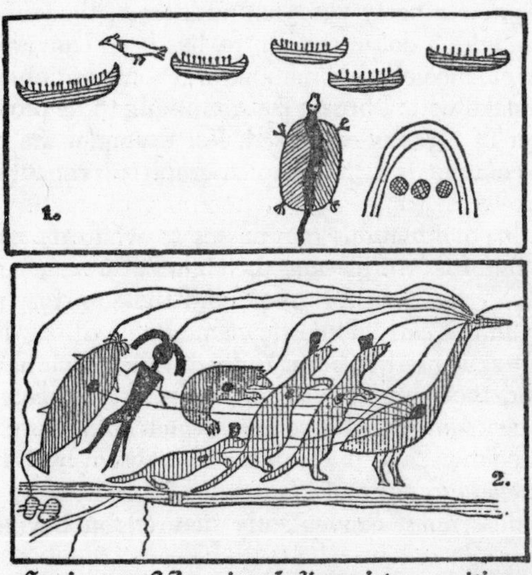

Specimens of American Indian picture-writing (after Schoolcraft.)

No. 1, painted on a rock on the shore of Lake Superior, records an expedition across the lake, in which five canoes took part. The upright strokes in each indicate the number of the crew, and the bird represents a chief, "The Kingfisher." The three circles (suns) under the arch (of heaven) indicate that the voyage lasted three days, and the tortoise, a symbol of land, denotes a safe arrival.

No. 2, is a petition sent to the United States Congress by a group of Indian tribes, asking for fishing rights in certain small lakes. The tribes are represented by their totems: martens, bears, manfish, and catfish, led by the crane. Lines running from the heart and eye of each animal to the heart and eye of the crane denote that they are all of one mind; and a line runs from the eye of the crane to the lakes, shown in the crude little "map" in the lower left-hand corner.

post-office (envelope) or a telephone (telephone receiver). The quality of hotels is shown by an inn with one, two, three, or four gables, and so forth. Similarly, the roads of Europe are marked with wayside signs, representing a gate to indicate a level crossing ahead, a sinuous bend for a dangerous curve, and the like. From such pictographic signs to the first element of Chinese writing is not a very long stretch.

In Chinese writing there are still traceable a number of pictographs. Most are now difficult to recognize. A mouth was originally written as a mouth-shaped hole, and is now, for convenience of brushwork, squared; a child, originally a recognizable little mannikin, is now a hasty wriggle and a cross; the sun, originally a large circle with a dot in the centre, has been converted, for the sake of convenience of combination, into a crossed oblong, which is easier to make with a brush. By combining these pictographs, a second order of ideas is expressed. For example, the pictograph for mouth combined with the pictograph of vapour expressed "words."

From such combinations one passes to what are called *ideograms*: the sign for "words" and the sign for "tongue" combine to make "speech"; the sign for "roof" and the sign for "pig" make "home"—for in the early domestic economy of China the pig was as important as it used to be in Ireland. But, as we have already noted earlier, the Chinese language consists of a comparatively few elementary monosyllabic sounds, which are all used in a great variety of meanings, and the Chinese soon discovered that a number of these *pictographs* and *ideographs* could be used also to express other ideas, not so conveniently pictured, but having the same sound.

Characters so used are called *phonograms*. For example, the sound *fang* meant not only "boat," but "a place," "spinning," "fragrant," "inquire," and several other meanings according to the context. But while a boat is easy to draw, most of the other meanings are undrawable. How can one draw "fragant" or "inquire"? The Chinese, therefore, took the same sign for all these meanings of "fang," but added to each of them another distinctive sign, the *determinative*, to show what sort of *fang* was intended. A "place" was indicated by the same sign as for "boat" (*fang*) and the determinative sign for "earth"; "spinning" by the sign for *fang* and the sign for "silk"; "inquire" by the sign for *fang* and the sign for "words," and so on.

One may perhaps make this development of pictographs, ideograms, and phonograms a little clearer by taking an analogous case in English. Suppose we were making up a sort of picture-writing in English, then it would be very natural to use a square with a slanting line to suggest a lid, for the word and thing *box*. That would be a pictograph. But now suppose we had a round sign for money, and suppose we put this sign inside the box sign, that would do for "cash-box" or "treasury." That would be an ideogram. But the word "box" is used for other things than boxes. There is the box shrub which gives us boxwood. It would be hard to draw a recognizable box-tree distinct from other trees, but it is quite easy to put our sign "box" and add our sign for shrub as a determinative to determine that it is that sort of box and not a common box that we want to express. And then there is "box," the verb, meaning to fight with fists. Here, again, we need a determinative; we might add the two crossed swords, a sign which is used very often upon maps to denote a battle. A box at a theatre needs yet another determinative, and so we go on, through a long series of phonograms.

Now, it is manifest that here in the Chinese writing is a very peculiar and complex system of sign-writing. A very great number of characters have to be learnt and the mind habituated to their use. The power it possesses to carry ideas and discussion is still ungauged by western standards, but we may doubt whether with this instrument it will ever be possible to establish such a wide common mentality as the simpler and swifter alphabets of the western civilizations permit. In China it created a special reading-class, the mandarins, who were also the ruling and official class. Their necessary concentration upon words and classical forms, rather than upon ideas and realities, seems, in spite of her comparative peacefulness and the very high individual intellectual quality of her people, to have greatly hampered the social and economic development of China. Probably it is the complexity of her speech and writing, more than any other imaginable cause, that has made China to-day politically, socially, and individually a vast pool of industrious, unenterprising population rather than the foremost power in the whole world.

§ 2

But while the Chinese mind thus made for itself an instrument which is probably too elaborate in structure, too laborious in use, and too inflexible in its form to meet the modern need for simple, swift, exact, and lucid communications, the growing civilizations of the West were working out the problem of a written record upon rather different and, on the whole, more advantageous lines. They did not seek to improve their script to make it swift and easy, but circumstances conspired to make it so.

The Sumerian picture-writing, which had to be done upon clay, and with little styles which made curved marks with difficulty and inaccurately, rapidly degenerated, by a conventionalized dabbing down of wedge-shaped marks (cuneiform=wedge-shaped), into almost unrecognizable hints of the shapes intended. It helped the Sumerians greatly to learn to write, that they had to draw so badly. They got very soon to the Chinese pictographs, ideographs, and phonograms, and beyond them.

Most people know a sort of puzzle called a rebus. It is a way of representing words by pictures, not of the things the words represent, but by the pictures of other things having a similar sound. For example, two gates and a head is a rebus for Gateshead; a little streamlet (beck), a crowned monarch, and a ham, Beckingham. The Sumerian language was a language well adapted to this sort of representation. It was apparently a language of often quite vast polysyllables, made up of very distinct inalterable syllables; and many of the syllables taken separately were the names of concrete things. So that this cuneiform writing developed very readily into a syllabic way of writing, in which each sign conveys a syllable just as each act in a charade conveys a syllable.

When presently the Semites conquered Sumeria, they adapted the syllabic system to their own speech, and so this writing became entirely a sign-for-a-sound writing. It was so used by the Assyrians and by the Chaldeans. But it was not a letter-writing, it was a syllable-writing. This cuneiform script prevailed for long ages over Assyria, Babylonia, and the Near East generally; its survival is evident in several of the letters of our alphabet to-day.

§ 3

But, meanwhile, in Egypt and upon the Mediterranean coast yet another system of writing grew up. Its beginnings are probably to be found in the priestly picture-writing (hieroglyphics) of the Egyptians, which, also, in the usual way became partly a sound-sign system. As we see it on the Egyptian monuments, the hieroglyphic writing consists of decorative but stiff and elaborate forms, but for such purpose as letter-writing and the keeping of recipes and the like, the Egyptian priests used a much simplified and flowing form of these characters, the *hieratic script.*

Side by side with this hieratic script rose another, derived partly from the hieroglyphics, a script now lost to us, which was taken over by various non-Egyptian peoples in the Mediterranean, the Phœnicians, Libyans, Lydians, Cretans, and Celt-Iberians, and used for business purposes. A number of letters were borrowed from the later cuneiform. In the hands of foreigners this mixed writing was, so to speak, cut off from its roots; it lost all but a few traces of its early pictorial character. It ceased to be pictographic or ideographic; it became simply a pure sound-sign system, an *alphabet.*

There were a number of such alphabets in the Mediterranean, differing widely from each other. It may be noted that the Phœnician alphabet (and perhaps others) omitted vowels. Possibly they pronounced their consonants very hard and had rather indeterminate vowels, as is said to be still the case with tribes of South Arabia. Quite probably, too, the Phœnicians used their alphabet at first not so much for writing as for single initial letters in their business accounts and tallies.

One of these Mediterranean alphabets reached the Greeks, long after the time of the *Iliad,* who presently set to work to make it express the clear and beautiful sounds of their own highly developed Aryan speech. It consisted at first of consonants, and the Greeks added the vowels. They began to write for record, to help and fix their bardic tradition. And so written literature began, a rivulet that has become a flood.

§ 4

Thus it was by a series of very natural steps that writing grew out of drawing. At first and for long ages it was the interest and the secret of only a few people in a special class, a mere accessory to the record of pictures. But there were certain very manifest advantages, quite apart from increased expressiveness, to be gained by making writing a little less plain than straightforward pictures, and inconventionalizing and codifying it. One of these was that so messages might be sent understandable by the sender and receiver but not plain to the uninitiated. Another was that so one might put down various matters and help one's memory and the memory of one's friends without giving away too much to the common herd. Among some of the earliest Egyptian writings, for example, are medical recipes and magic formulæ.

Accounts, letters, recipes, name-lists, itineraries: these were the earliest of written documents. Then, as the art of writing and reading spread, came that odd desire, that pathetic desire so common among human beings, to astonish some strange and remote person by writing down something striking, some secret one knew, some strange thought, or even one's name, so that long after one had gone one's way it might strike upon the sight and mind of another reader. Even in Sumeria men scratched on walls, and all that remains to us of the ancient world, its rocks, its buildings, is plastered thickly with the names and the boasting of those foremost among human advertisers, its kings. Perhaps half the early inscriptions in that ancient world are of this nature—if, that is, we group with the name-writing and boasting the epitaphs, which were probably in many cases pre-arranged by the deceased.

For long the desire for crude self-assertion of the name-scrawling sort and the love of secret understandings kept writing within a narrow scope; but that other, more truly social desire in men, the desire to *tell,* was also at work. The profounder possibilities of a vast extension and definition and settlement of knowledge and tradition, grew apparent only after long ages. But it will be interesting at this point and in this connection to recapitulate certain elemental facts about life, upon which we laid stress in our earlier chapters, because they illuminate not only the huge value of writing in man's history, but also the rôle it is likely to play in his future.

1. Life had at first, it must be remembered, only a discontinuous repetition of consciousness, as the old died and the young were born.

Such a creature as a reptile has in its brain a capacity for experience, but when the individual dies its experience dies with it. Most of its motives are purely instinctive, and all the mental life that it has is the result of heredity (birth inheritance).

2. But ordinary mammals have added to pure instinct *tradition,* a tradition of experience imparted by the imitated example of the mother, and in the case of such mentally developed animals as dogs, cats, or apes, by a sort of mute precept also. For example, the mother cat chastises her young for misbehaviour. So do mother apes and baboons.

3. Primitive man added to his powers of transmitting experi-

ence, representative art and speech. Pictorial and sculptured record and *verbal tradition* began.

Verbal tradition was developed to its highest possibility by the bards. They did much to make language what it is to-day.

4. With the invention of writing, which developed out of pictorial record, human tradition was able to become fuller and much more exact. Verbal tradition, which had hitherto changed from age to age, began to be fixed. Men separated by hundreds of miles could now communicate their thoughts. An increasing number of human beings began to share a common written knowledge and a common sense of a past and a future. Human thinking became a larger operation in which hundreds of minds in different places and in different ages could react upon one another; it became a process constantly more continuous and sustained.

5. For hundreds of generations the full power of writing was not revealed to the world, because for a long time the idea of multiplying writings by taking prints of a first copy did not become effective. The only way of multiplying writings was by making one copy at a time, and this made books costly and rare. The tendency to keep things secret, to make a cult and mystery of them, and so to gain an advantage over the generality of men, has always been very strong in men's minds. It is only nowadays that the great masses of mankind are learning to read, and reaching out towards the treasures of knowledge and thought already stored in books.

Nevertheless, from the first writings onward a new sort of tradition, an enduring and immortal tradition, began in the minds of men. Life, through mankind, grew thereafter more and more distinctly conscious of itself and its world. It is a thin streak of intellectual growth we trace in history, at first in a world of tumultuous ignorance and forgetfulness; it is like a mere line of light coming through the chink of an opening door into a darkened room; but slowly it widens, it grows. At last came a time in the history of Europe when the door, at the push of the printer, began to open more rapidly. Knowledge flared up, and as it flared it ceased to be the privilege of a favoured minority. For us now that door swings wider, and the light behind grows brighter.

Misty it is still, glowing through clouds of dust and reek. The door is not half open. Our world to-day is only in the beginning of knowledge.

XVI

GODS AND STARS, PRIESTS AND KINGS

§ 1. *The Priest Comes into History.* § 2. *Priests and the Stars.* § 3. *Priests and the Dawn of Learning.* § 4. *King against Priest.* § 5. *How Bel-Marduk Struggled against the Kings.* § 6. *The God-Kings of Egypt.* § 7. *Shi Hwang-ti Destroys the Books.*

§ 1

WHEN we drew our attention to these new accumulations of human beings that were beginning in Egypt and Mesopotamia, we find that one of the most conspicuous objects in all these cities is a temple or a group of temples. In some cases there arises beside it in these regions a royal palace, but as often the temple towers over the palace. This presence of the temple is equally true of the Phœnician cities and of the Greek and Roman as they arise. The palace of Cnossos, with its signs of comfort and pleasure-seeking, and the kindred cities of the Ægean peoples, include religious shrines, but in Crete there are also temples standing apart from the palatial city-households. All over the ancient civilized world we find them; wherever primitive civilization set its foot in Africa, Europe, or western Asia, a temple arose; and where the civilization is most ancient, in Egypt and in Sumer, there the temple is most in evidence. When Hanno reached what he thought was the most westerly point of Africa, he set up a temple to Hercules.

The beginnings of civilization and the appearance of temples are simultaneous in history. The two things belong together. The beginning of cities is the temple stage of history. The city community arose around the altar of the seed-time blood sacrifice.

In all these temples there was a shrine; dominating the shrine there was commonly a great figure, usually of some monstrous half-animal form, before which stood an altar for sacrifices. In the Greek and Roman temples of a later stage, however, the image was generally that of a divinity in human form. This figure was either regarded as the god, or as the image or symbol of the god, for whose worship the temple existed. And connected with the temple there were a number and often a considerable number, of priests or priestesses, and temple servants, generally wearing a distinctive costume and forming an important part of the city population. They belonged to no household; they made up a new kind of household of their own. They were a caste and a class apart, attracting intelligent recruits from the general population.

J.F.H. from photos. by
Britis School at Athens.

Faience figure from Cnossos..... A-votary of the Snake Goddess.....

The primary duty of this priesthood was concerned with the worship of and the sacrifices to the god of the temple. And these things were done, not at any time, but at particular times and seasons. The seed-time sacrifice was first and foremost of these. There had come into the life of man with his herding and agriculture a sense of a difference between the parts of the year and of a difference between day and day. The temple, by its festivals, kept count. The temple in the ancient city was like the clock and calendar upon a writing-desk.

But it was a centre of other functions than its primary one of seasonal sacrifice and calendar observation. It was in the early temples that the records and tallies of events were kept and that writing began. And knowledge was there. The people went to the temple not only *en masse* for festivals, but individually for help. The early priests were also doctors and magicians. In the earliest temples we already find those little offerings for some private and particular end, which are still made in the chapels of Catholic churches of to-day, *ex votos,* little models of hearts relieved and limbs restored, acknowledgment of prayers answered and accepted vows. In the Temple of the Moon God at Ur, four thousand years ago, when that centre of the worship of the god had become an important landowner, we find business methods and industrialism already in being. Strict accounts were kept of the payments in kind of those who farmed the lands, and receipts were given, of which there were duplicates. The women devotees and slaves worked in the temple factories, spinning and weaving the wool brought in as tribute, and receiving rations according to their work, which was carefully recorded.

It is clear that here we have that comparatively unimportant element in the life of the early hunters, the medicine-man, the shrine-keeper and luck-bringer, developed, with the development of the community and as a part of the development of the community from barbarism to civilized settlement and from casual living to methodical work, into something of very much greater importance. And it is equally evident that those primitive fears of (and hopes of help from) strange beings, the desire to propitiate unknown forces, the primitive desire for cleansing and the primitive craving for power and knowledge, which we discussed in our chapter on "Early Thought," have all contributed to elaborate this new social fact of the temple.

The temple was accumulated by complex necessities, it grew from many roots and needs, and the god or goddess that dominated the temple was the creation of many imaginations and made up of all sorts of impulses, ideas, and half-ideas. Here there was a god in which one sort of idea predominated, and there another. It is necessary to lay some stress upon this confusion and variety of origin in gods, because there is a very abundant literature now in existence upon religious origins, in which a number of writers insist, some on this leading idea and some on that—we have noted several in our chapter on "Early Thought"—as though it were the only idea. Professor Max Müller in his time, for example, harped perpetually on the idea of sun stories and sun worship. He would have had us think that early man never had lusts or fears, cravings for power, nightmares or fantasies, but that he meditated perpetually on the beneficent source of light and life in the sky. Now, dawn and sunset are very moving facts in the daily life, but they are only two among many.

Early men, three or four hundred generations ago, had brains very like our own. The fancies of our childhood and youth are perhaps the best clue we have to the ground-stuff of early religion, and anyone who can recall those early mental experiences will understand very easily the vagueness, the monstrosity, and the incoherent variety of the first gods. There were sun gods, no doubt, early in the history of temples, but there were also hippopotamus gods and hawk gods; there were cow deities, there were monstrous male and female gods, there were gods of terror and gods of an adorable quaintness, there were gods who were nothing but lumps of meteoric stone that had fallen amazingly out of the sky, and gods who were mere natural stones that had chanced to have a queer and impressive shape.

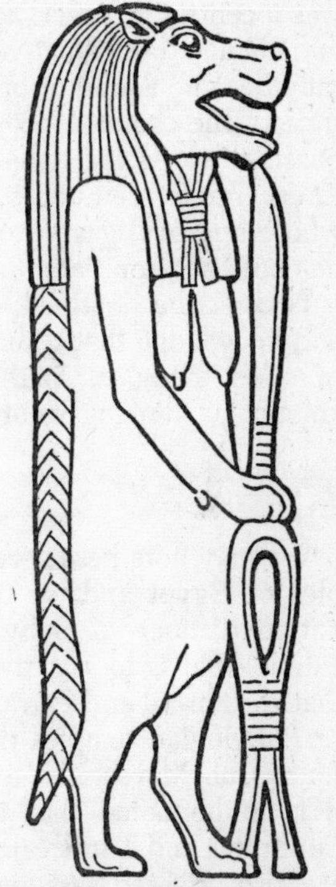

Early figure of the Egyptian hippopotamus goddess

Some gods, like Marduk of Babylon and the Baal (=the Lord) of the Phœnicians, Canaanites, and the like, were quite probably at bottom just legendary wonder beings, such as little boys will invent for themselves to-day. The settled peoples, it is said, as soon as they thought of a god, invented a wife for him; most of the Egyptian and Babylonian gods were married. But the gods of the nomadic Semites had not this marrying disposition. Children were less eagerly sought by the inhabitants of the food-grudging steppes.

Even more natural than to provide a wife for a god is to give him a house to live in, to which offerings can be brought. Of this house the knowing man, the magician, would naturally become the custodian. A certain seclusion, a certain aloofness, would add greatly to the prestige of the god. The steps by which the early temple and the early priesthood developed so soon as an agricultural population settled and increased are all quite natural and understandable, up to the stage of the long temple with the image, shrine and altar at one end and the long nave in which the worshippers stood.

And this temple, because it had records and secrets, because it was a centre of power, advice, and instruction, because it sought and attracted imaginative and clever people for its service, naturally became a kind of brain in the growing community. The attitude of the common people who tilled the fields and herded the beasts towards the temple would remain simple and credulous. There, rarely seen and so imaginatively enhanced, lived the god whose approval gave prosperity, whose anger meant misfortune; he could be propitiated by little presents and the help of his servants could be obtained. He was wonderful, and of such power and knowledge that it did not do to be disrespectful to him even in one's thoughts. Within the priesthood, however, a certain amount of thinking went on at a rather higher level than that.

§ 2

We may note here a very interesting fact about the chief temples of Egypt and, so far as we know—because the ruins are not so distinct—of Babylonia, and that is that they were "oriented"—that is to say, that the same sort of temple was built so that the shrine and entrance always faced in the same direction. In Babylonian temples this was most often due east, facing the sunrise on March 21st and September 21st, the equinoxes; and it is to be noted that it was at the spring equinox that the Euphrates and Tigris came down in flood. The Pyramids of Gizeh are also oriented east and west, and the Sphinx faces due east; but very many of the Egyptian temples to the south of the delta of the Nile do not point due east, but to the point where the sun rises at the longest day—and in Egypt the inundation comes close to that date. Others, however, pointed nearly northward, and the others again pointed to the rising of the Star Sirius or to the rising-point of other conspicuous stars.

The fact of orientation links up with the fact that there early arose a close association between various gods and the sun and various fixed stars. Whatever the mass of people outside were thinking, the priests of the temples were beginning to link the movements of those heavenly bodies with the power in the shrine.

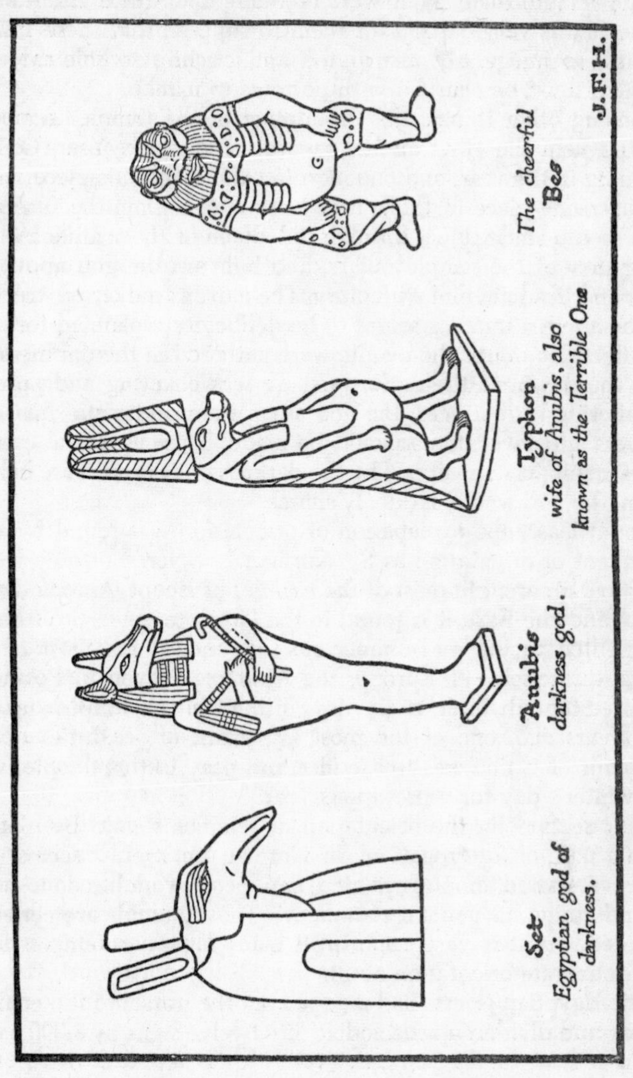
Set
Egyptian god of darkness.
Anubis
darkness god.
Typhon
wife of Anubis, also known as the Terrible One
The cheerful
Bes
J.F.H.

They were thinking about the gods they served and thinking new meanings into them. They were brooding upon the mystery of the stars. It was very natural for them to suppose that these shining bodies, so irregularly distributed and circling so solemnly and silently, must be charged with portents to mankind.

Among other things, this orientation of the temples served to fix and help the great annual festival of the New Year. On one morning in the year, and one morning alone, in a temple oriented to the rising-place of the sun at Midsummer Day, the sun's first rays would smite down through the gloom of the temple and the long alley of the temple pillars, and light up the god above the altar and irradiate him with glory. The narrow, darkened structure of the ancient temples seems to be deliberately planned for such an effect. No doubt the people were gathered in the darkness before the dawn; in the darkness there was chanting and perhaps an offering of sacrifices; the god alone stood mute and invisible. Prayers and invocations would be made. Then upon the eyes of the worshippers, sensitized by the darkness, as the sun rose behind them, the god would suddenly shine.

So, at least, one explanation of orientation was found by such a student of orientation as Sir Norman Lockyer. Not only is orientation apparent in most of the temples of Egypt, Assyria, Babylonia, and the East, it is found in the Greek temples; Stonehenge is oriented to the midsummer sunrise, and so are most of the megalithic circles of Europe; the Altar of Heaven in Peking is oriented to midwinter. In the days of the Chinese Empire, up to a few years ago, one of the most important of all duties of the Emperor of China was to sacrifice and pray in this temple upon midwinter's day for a propitious year.

This section on the orientation of temples should be marked with a note of interrogation. Sir Norman Lockyer, it seems, was too eager to find temples oriented, and recent work has done much to undermine his general statements. The Pyramids are certainly oriented, but it is very doubtful if many Egyptian temples have any deliberate orientation at all.

The Egyptian priests had mapped out the stars into the constellations and divided up the zodiac into twelve signs by 3,000 B.C.

§ 3

This clear evidence of astronomical inquiry and of a development of astronomical ideas is the most obvious, but only the most

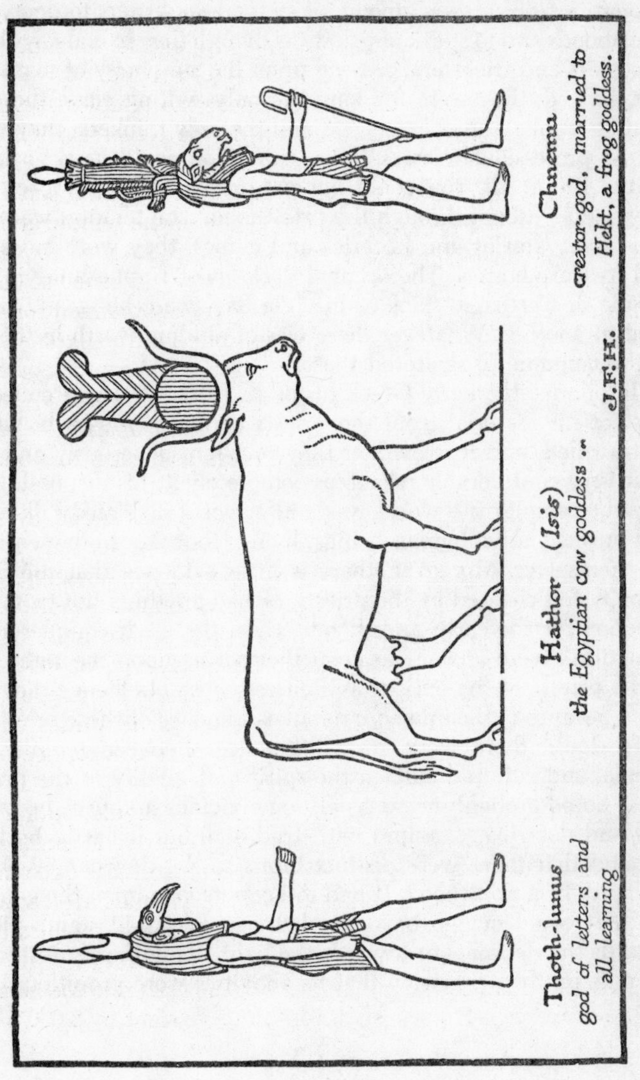
Thoth-lunus
god of letters and
all learning
Hathor (Isis)
the Egyptian cow goddess ..
Chnemu
creator-god, married to
Hekt, a frog goddess.
J.F.H.

obvious evidence of the very considerable intellectual activities that went on within the temple precincts in ancient times. There is a curious disposition among many modern writers to deprecate priesthoods and to speak of priests as though they had always been impostors and tricksters, preying upon the simplicity of mankind. But, indeed, they were for long the only writing class, the only reading public, the only learned and the only thinkers; they were all the professional classes of the time. You could have no intellectual life at all, you could not get access to literature or any knowledge, except through the priesthood. The temples were not only observatories and libraries and clinics, they were museums and treasure-houses. The original *Periplus* of Hanno hung in one temple in Carthage, skins of his "gorillas" were hung and treasured in another. Whatever there was of abiding worth in the life of the community sheltered there.

Herodotus, the early Greek historian (485–425 B.C.), collected most of his material from the priests of the countries in which he travelled, and it is evident they met him generously and put their very considerable resources completely at his disposal. Outside the temples the world was still a world of blankly illiterate and unspeculative human beings, living from day to day entirely for themselves. Moreover, there is little evidence that the commonalty felt cheated by the priests, or had anything but trust and affection for the early priesthoods. Even the great conquerors of later times were anxious to keep themselves upon the right side of the priests of the nations and cities whose obedience they desired, because of the immense popular influence of these priests.

No doubt there were great differences between temple and temple, and cult and cult, in the spirit and quality of the priesthood. Some probably were cruel, some vicious and greedy, many dull and doctrinaire, stupid with tradition, but it has to be kept in mind that there were distinct limits to the degeneracy or inefficiency of a priesthood. It had to keep its grip upon the general mind. It could not go beyond what people would stand—either towards the darkness or towards the light. Its authority rested, in the end, on the persuasion that its activities were propitious.

§ 4

The earliest civilized governments were thus priestly governments. It was not kings and captains who first set men to the plough and a settled life. It was the ideas of the gods and plenty, working with the acquiescence of common men. The early rulers of Sumer we know were all priests, kings only because they were chief priests. And priestly government had its own weaknesses as well as its peculiar deep-rooted strength. The power of a priesthood is a power over their own people alone. It is a subjugation through mysterious fears and hopes. The priesthood can gather its people together for war, but its traditionalism and all its methods unfit it for military control. Against the enemy without, a priest-led people is feeble.

Moreover, a priest is a man vowed, trained, and consecrated, a man belonging to a special corps, and necessarily with an intense *esprit de corps.* He has given up his life to his temple and his god. This is a very excellent thing for the internal vigour of his own priesthood, his own temple. He lives and dies for the honour of his particular god. But in the next town or village is another temple with another god. It is his constant preoccupation to keep his people from that god. Religious cults and priesthoods are sectarian by nature; they will convert, they will overcome, but they will never coalesce. Our first perceptions of events in Sumer, in the dim uncertain light before history began, is of priests and gods in conflict; until the Sumerians were conquered by the Semites they were never united. And the same incurable conflict of priesthoods scars all the temple ruins of Egypt. It was impossible that it could have been otherwise, having regard to the elements out of which religion arose.

In all the old world this state of affairs in which the priest was entirely dominant had passed away twenty-five centuries ago, but in America a primitive sacrificial priesthood was still to be found ruling an entire civilization as late as a thousand years ago. This was in Central America and in Yucatan. In Mexico the priestly people were under a monarchy very much on the lines of the Babylonian monarchy, the temple and the palace were side by side, so to speak; and in Peru there was a divine monarch like the Pharaoh. But in the now vanished Maya civilization which has left such wonderful ruins in the forest jungles of South Mexico and the Isthmus states, the priestly caste sustained a bloody and pedantic predominance. Everywhere else in the world priesthoods passed their zenith in due season and made room for other powers beside them, but the Maya priesthood became at last an extreme development, a last exaggerated caricature of the priestly system. They elaborated and complicated their calendar until it became a maze of concealed observations, and they carried the ritual of sacrifice to the very highest degree of sensuous excitement. Their sculpture, very skilful and elaborate sculpture, is a record of strange frustrations, with a touch of delirium in its decoration.

It was out of the two main weaknesses of all priesthoods—namely, the incapacity for efficient military leadership and their inevitable jealousy of all other religious cults—that the power of secular kingship arose. The foreign enemy either prevailed and set up a king over the people, or the priesthoods, who would not give way to each other, set up a common fighting captain, who retained more or less power in peace time. This secular king developed a group of officials about him and began, in relation to military organization, to take a share in the administration of the people's affairs. So, growing out of priestcraft and beside the priest, the king, the protagonist of the priest, appears upon the stage of human history, and a very large amount of the subsequent experiences of mankind is only to be understood as an elaboration, complication, and distortion of the struggle, unconscious or deliberate, between these two systems of human control, the temple and the palace.

It was in the original centres of civilization that this antagonism was most completely developed. The barbaric Aryan peoples, who became ultimately the masters of all the ancient civilizations of the Orient and of the western world, may never have passed through a phase of temple rule on their way to civilization; they came to civilization late; they found that drama already half-played. They took over the ideas of both temple and kingship, when those ideas were already elaborately developed, from the more civilized Hamitic or Semitic peoples they conquered.

The greater importance of the gods and the priests in the earlier history of the Mesopotamian civilization is very apparent, but gradually the palace won its way until it was at last in a position to struggle definitely for the supreme power. At first, in the story, the palace is ignorant and friendless in the face of the temple; the priests alone read, the priests alone know, the people are afraid of them. But in the dissensions of the various cults comes the opportunity of the palace. From other cities, from among captives, from defeated or suppressed religious cults, the palace gets men who also can read and who can do magic things. It can pit the stranger Moses against the native magicians. The court also becomes a centre of writing and record; the king thinks for himself and becomes politic. Traders and foreigners drift to the court, and if the king has not the full records and the finished scholarship of the priests, he has a wider and fresher first-hand knowledge of many things, he is closer to reality.

The priest comes into the temple when he is very young; he passes many years as a neophyte; the path of learning the clumsy

An Assyrian King & his Chief Minister

letters of primitive times is slow and toilsome; he becomes erudite and prejudiced rather than a man of the world. Some of the more active-minded young priests may even cast envious eyes at the king's service. There are many complications and variations in this ages-long drama of the struggle going on beneath the outward conflicts of priest and king, between the made man and the born man, between learning and originality, between established knowledge and settled usage on the one hand, and creative will and imagination on the other.

It is not always, as we shall find later, the priest who is the conservative and unimaginative antagonist. Sometimes a king struggles against narrow and obstructive priesthoods; sometimes priesthoods uphold the standards of civilization against savage, egotistical, or reactionary kings.

One or two outstanding facts and incidents of the early stages of this fundamental struggle in political affairs are all that we can note here between 4,000 B.C. and the days of Alexander.

§ 5

In the early days of Sumer and Akkadia the city-kings were priests and medicine-men rather than kings, and it was only when foreign conquerors sought to establish their hold in relation to existing institutions that the distinction of priest and king became definite. But the god of the priests remained as the real overlord of the land and of priest and king alike. He was the universal landlord; the wealth and authority of his temples and establishments outshone those of the king. Especially was this the case within the city walls. Hammurabi, the founder of the first Babylonian empire, is one of the earlier monarchs whom we find taking a firm grip upon the affairs of the community. He does it with the utmost politeness to the gods. In an inscription recording his irrigation work in Sumer and Akkadia, he begins: "When Anu and Bel entrusted me with the rule of Sumer and Akkad——." We possess a code of laws made by this same Hammurabi—it is the earliest known code of law—and at the head of this code we see the figure of Hammurabi receiving the law from its nominal promulgator, the god Shamash.

Of an earlier date than this figure of Hammurabi is the recently excavated stele from Ur which shows the Moon God directing King Ur-Engur to build him a temple and assisting him in the operations. The king is the servant.

An act of great political importance in the conquest of any city was the carrying off of its god to become a subordinate in the temple of its conqueror. This was far more important than the subjugation of king by king. Merodach, the Babylonian Jupiter, was carried off by the Elamites, and Babylon did not feel independent until its return.

But sometimes a conqueror was afraid of the god he had conquered. In the collection of letters addressed to Amenophis III and IV at Tell-el-Amarna in Egypt, to which allusion has already been made, is one from a certain king, Tushratta, King of Mitanni, who has conquered Assyria and taken the statue of the goddess Ishtar. Apparently he has sent this statue into Egypt, partly to acknowledge the overlordship of Amenophis, but partly because he fears her anger. (Winckler.) In the Bible is related (I Sam. v, 1) how the Ark of the Covenant of the God of the Hebrews was carried off by the Philistines, as a token of conquest into the temple of the fish-god Dagon at Ashdod, and how Dagon fell down and was broken, and how the people of Ashdod were smitten with disease. In the latter story particularly, the gods and priests fill the scene: there is no king in evidence at all.

Right through the history of the Babylonian and Assyrian empires no monarch seems to have felt his tenure of power secure in Babylon until he had "taken the hand of Bel"—that is to say, that he had been adopted by the priesthood of "Bel" as the god's son and representative. As our knowledge of Assyrian and Babylonian history grows clearer, it becomes plainer that the politics of that world, the revolutions, usurpations, changes of dynasty, intrigues with foreign powers, turned largely upon issues between the great wealthy priesthoods and the growing but still inadequate power of the monarchy. The king relied on his army, and this was usually a mercenary army of foreigners, speedily mutinous if there was no pay or plunder, and easily bribed. We have already noted the name of Sennacherib, the son of Sargon II, among the monarchs of the Assyrian Empire. Sennacherib was involved in a violent quarrel with the priesthood of Babylon; he never "took the hand of Bel"; and finally struck at that power by destroying altogether the holy part of the city of Babylon (691 B.C.) and removing the statue of Bel-Marduk to Assyria. He was assassinated by one of his sons, and his successor, Esar-haddon (his son, but not the son who was his assassin), found it expedient to restore Bel-Marduk and rebuild his temple, and make his peace with the god.

Assurbanipal (Greek, Sardanapalus), the son of this Esar-haddon, is a particularly interesting figure from this point of view of the relationship of priesthood and king. His father's reconcilation with the priests of Bel-Marduk went so far that Sardanapalus was given a Babylonian instead of a military Assyrian education. He became a great collector of the clay documents of the past, and his library, which has been unearthed, is now the most precious source of historical material in the world. But for all his learning he kept his grip on the Assyrian army; he made a temporary conquest of Egypt; suppressed a rebellion in Babylon, and carried out a number of successful expeditions. He was almost the last of the Assyrian monarchs. The Aryan tribes, who knew more of war than of priestcraft, and particularly the Scythians, the Medes and Persians, had long been pressing upon Assyria from the north and north-east. The Medes and Persians formed an alliance with the nomadic Semitic Chaldeans of the south for the joint undoing of Assyria. Nineveh, the Assyrian capital, fell to these Aryans in 606 B.C.

Sixty-seven years after the taking of Nineveh by the Aryans, which left Babylonia to the Semitic Chaldeans, the last monarch of the Chaldean Empire (the Second Babylonian Empire), Nabonidus, the father of Belshazzar, was overthrown by Cyrus, the Persian. This Nabonidus, again, was a highly educated monarch, who brought far too much intelligence and imagination and not enough of the short-range wisdom of this world to affairs of state. He conducted antiquarian researches, and to his researches it is that we owe the date of 3,750 B.C. assigned to Sargon I and still accepted by many authorities. He was proud of this determination, and left inscriptions to record it. It is clear he was a religious innovator; he built and rearranged temples and attempted to centralize religion in Babylon by bringing a number of local gods to the temple of Bel-Marduk. No doubt he realized the weakness and disunion of his empire due to these conflicting cults, and had some conception of unification in his mind.

Events were marching too rapidly for any such development. His innovation had manifestly raised the suspicion and hostility of the priesthood of Bel. They sided with the Persians. "The soldiers of Cyrus entered Babylon without fighting." Nabonidus was taken prisoner, and Persian sentinels were set at the gates of the temple of Bel, "where the services continued without intermission."

Cyrus did, in fact, set up the Persian Empire in Babylon with the blessing of Bel-Marduk. He gratified the conservative instincts of the priests by packing off the local gods back to their ancestral temples. He also restored the Jews to Jerusalem. These were merely matters of immediate policy to him. But in bringing in the irreligious Aryans, the ancient priesthood was paying too highly for the continuation of its temple services. It would have been wiser to have dealt with the innovations of Nabonidus, that earnest heretic, to have listened to his ideas, and to have met the needs of a changing world. Cyrus entered Babylon 539 B.C.; by 521 B.C. Babylon was in insurrection again, and in 520 B.C. another Persian monarch, Darius, was pulling down her walls. Within two hundred years the life had altogether gone out of those venerable rituals of Bel-Marduk, and the temple of Bel-Marduk was being used by builders as a quarry.

§ 6

The story of priest and king in Egypt is similar to, but by no means parallel with, that of Babylonia. The kings of Sumer and Assyria were priests who had become kings; they were secularized priests. The Pharaoh of Egypt does not appear to have followed precisely that line. Already in the very oldest records the Pharaoh has a power and an importance exceeding that of any priest. He is, in fact, a god, and more than either priest or king.

CHEPHREN

We do not know how he got to that position. No monarch of Sumer or Babylonia or Assyria could have induced his people to do for him what the great pyramid-building Pharaohs of the IVth Dynasty made their people do in those vast erections. The earlier Pharaohs were not improbably regarded as incarnations of the dominant god. The falcon god Horus sits behind the head of the great statue of Chephren. So late a monarch as Rameses III (XXth Dynasty) is represented upon his sarcophagus (now at

Cambridge) bearing the distinctive symbols of the three great gods of the Egyptian system. He carries the two sceptres of Osiris, the god of Day and Resurrection; upon his head are the horns of the cow goddess Hathor, and also the sun ball and feathers of Ammon Ra. He is not merely wearing the symbols of these gods as a devout Babylonian might wear the symbols of Bel-Marduk; he *is* these three gods in one.

The student will find much more in Sir J. G. Frazer's *Golden Bough* about the ancient use of human beings as well as statues to represent gods. Here we have merely to point to an apparent dif-

Relief on the cover of the sarcophagus (at Cambridge). After Sharpe.

INSCRIPTION (ROUND THE EDGES OF COVER) AS FAR AS DECIPHERABLE:

"Osiris, King of Upper and Lower Egypt, lord of the two countries . . . son of the Sun, beloved of the gods, lord of diadems, Rameses, prince of Heliopolis, triumphant! Thou art in the condition of a god, thou shalt arise as Usr, there is no enemy to thee, I give to thee triumph among them. . . ." BUDGE, *Catalogue, Egyptian Collection, Fitzwilliam Museum, Cambridge.*

ference of idea between the Asiatic and African monarchies in this respect.

We find also a number of sculptures and paintings to enforce the idea that the Pharaohs were the actual sons of gods. The divine fathering and birth of Amenophis III, for instance (of the XVIIIth Dynasty), is displayed in extraordinary detail in a series of sculptures at Luxor. Moreover, it was held that the Pharaohs, being of so divine a strain, could not marry common clay, and consequently they were accustomed to marry blood relations within the degrees of consanguinity now prohibited, even marrying their sisters.

The struggle between palace and temple came into Egyptian history, therefore, at a different angle from that at which it came into Babylonia. Nevertheless, it came in. Professor Maspero (in his *New Light on Ancient Egypt*) gives a very interesting account of the struggle of Amenophis IV with the priesthoods, and particularly with priests of the great god, Ammon Ra, Lord of Karnak.

The mother of Amenophis IV was not of the race of Pharaoh; it would seem that his father, Amenophis III, made a love match with a subject, a beautiful Syrian named Tii, and Professor Maspero finds in the possible opposition to and annoyance of this queen by the priests of Ammon Ra the beginnings of the quarrel. She may, he thinks, have inspired her son with a fanatical hatred of Ammon Ra. But Amenophis IV may have had a wider view. Like the Babylonian Nabonidus, who lived a thousand years later, he may have had in mind the problem of moral unity in his empire. We have already noted that Amenophis III ruled from Ethiopia to the Euphrates, and that the store of letters to himself and his son found at Tell-el-Amarna show a wide range of interest and influence. At any rate, Amenophis IV set himself to close all the Egyptian and Syrian temples, to put an end to all sectarian worship throughout his dominions, and to establish everywhere the worship of one god, Aton, the solar disk. He left his capital, Thebes, which was even more the city of Ammon Ra than later Babylon was the city of Bel-Marduk, and set up his capital at Tell-el-Amarna; he altered his name from "Amenophis," which consecrated him to Ammon (Amen), to "Akhnaton," the Sun's Glory; and he held his own against all the priesthoods of his empire for eighteen years and died a Pharaoh.

Opinions upon Amenophis IV, or Akhnaton, differ very widely. There are those who regard him as the creature of his mother's hatred of Ammon and the uxorious spouse of a beautiful wife. Certainly he loved his wife very passionately; he showed her great honour—Egypt honoured women, and was ruled at different times by several queens—and he was sculptured in one instance with his wife seated upon his knees, and in another in the act of kissing

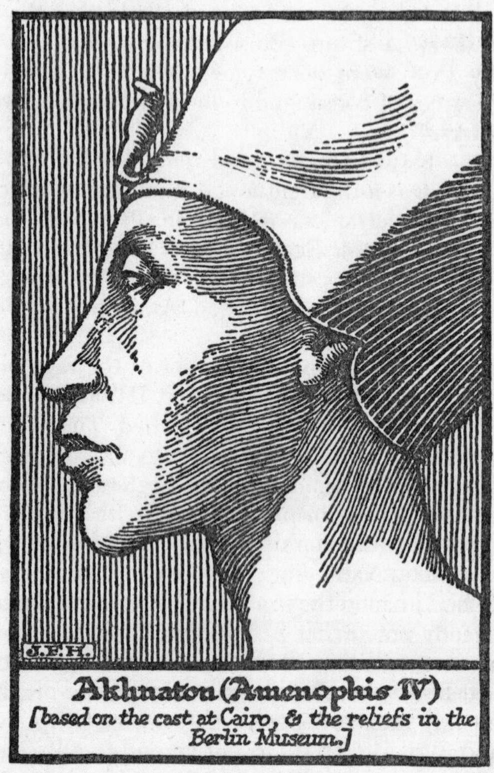

Akhnaton (Amenophis IV)
[based on the cast at Cairo, & the reliefs in the Berlin Museum.]

her in a chariot; but men who live under the sway of their womenkind do not sustain great empires in the face of the bitter hostility of the most influential organized bodies in their realm. Others write of him as a "gloomy fanatic." Matrimonial bliss is rare in the cases of gloomy fanatics. It is much more reasonable to regard him as the Pharaoh who refused to be a god. It is not simply his religious policy and his frank display of natural affection that seem to mark a strong and very original personality. His æsthetic ideas were his own. He refused to have his portrait conventionalized into the customary smooth beauty of the Pharaoh god, and his face looks out at us across an interval of thirty-three centuries, a man amidst ranks of divine insipidities.

A reign of eighteen years was not long enough for the revolution he contemplated, and his son-in-law who succeeded him went back to Thebes and made his peace with Ammon Ra. He was one of the last three monarchs of the XVIIIth Dynasty, a trio which included the Pharaoh Tut-ankh-amen about whom so much fuss has been made in recent years. He was an inconspicuous youth who was married to Akhnaton's daughter and heiress, and he seems to have been entirely in the hands of the priests of Ammon. Either he died young or he was put out of the way. But it happens that his tomb was almost the only tomb of a Pharaoh that was not subsequently broken into and plundered. It survived intact until our own time. Then it was opened and explored, with a journalistic uproar quite out of proportion to its historical importance. The XVIIIth Dynasty ended soon after the passing of Tut-ankh-amen, and the XIXth, founded by Haremhab, became one of the most brilliant and glorious of all the Egyptian Dynasties.

To the very end of the story the divinity of kings haunted the Egyptian mind, and infected the thoughts of other races. When Alexander the Great reached Babylon, the prestige of Bel-Marduk was already far gone in decay, but in Egypt Ammon Ra was still god enough to make a snob of the conquering Grecian. The priests of Ammon Ra, about the time of the XVIIIth or XIXth Dynasty (*circa* 1,400 B.C.), had set up in an oasis of the desert a temple and oracle. Here was an image of the god which could speak, move its head, and accept or reject scrolls of inquiry. This oracle was still flourishing in 332 B.C. The young master of the world, it is related, made a special journey to visit it; he came into the sanctuary, and the image advanced out of the darkness at the back to meet him.

There was an impressive exchange of salutations. Some such formula as this must have been used (says Professor Maspero):

"Come, son of my loins, who loves me so that I give thee the royalty of Ra and the royalty of Horus! I give thee valiance, I give thee to hold all countries and all religions under thy feet; I give thee to strike all the peoples united together with thy arm!"

So it was that the priests of Egypt conquered their conqueror, and an Aryan monarch first became a god.

§ 7

The struggle of the priest and king in China cannot be discussed here at any length. It was different again, as in Egypt it was different from Babylonia, but we find the same effort on the part of the ruler to break up tradition because it divides up the people. The Chinese Emperor, the "Son of Heaven," was himself a high priest, and his chief duty was sacrificial; in the more disorderly phases of Chinese history he ceases to rule and continues only to sacrifice. This survived down to recent times. It is only a few years ago that the custom fell into disuse by which it was the duty of the emperor to begin the ploughing of the soil with his own hand every spring. The literary class was detached from the priestly class at an early date. It became a bureaucratic body serving the local kings and rulers. That is a fundamental difference between the history of China and any Western history.

While Alexander was overrunning Western Asia, China, under the last priest-emperors of the Chow Dynasty, was sinking into a state of great disorder. Each province clung to its separate nationality and traditions, and the Huns spread from province to province. The King of T'sin (who lived about eighty years after Alexander the Great), impressed by the mischief tradition was doing in the land, resolved to destroy the entire Chinese literature, and his son, Shi Hwang-ti, the "first universal Emperor," made a strenuous attempt to seek out and destroy the existing classics. They vanished while he ruled, and he ruled without tradition, and welded China into a unity that endured for some centuries; but when he had passed, the hidden books crept out again.

China remained united, though not under his descendants. After a civil war a fresh dynasty, the Han Dynasty (206 B.C.), came into power. The first Han monarch did not sustain the campaign of Shi Hwang-ti against the *literati*, and his successor made his peace with them and restored the text of the classics.

XVII

SERFS, SLAVES, SOCIAL CLASSES, AND FREE INDIVIDUALS

§ 1. *The Common Man in Ancient Times.* § 2. *The Earliest Slaves.* § 3. *The First "Independent" Persons.* § 4. *Social Classes Three Thousand Years Ago.* § 5. *Classes Hardening into Castes.* § 6. *Caste in India.* § 7. *The System of the Mandarins.* § 8. *A Summary of Ten Thousand Years.* § 9. *Plastic and Pictorial Art in the Ancient World.* § 10. *Literature, Drama and Music in the Ancient World.*

§ 1

WE HAVE been sketching in the last four chapters the growth of civilized states out of the primitive Neolithic agriculture that began somewhere in or about the Eastern Mediterranean perhaps 15,000 years ago. It was at first horticulture rather than agriculture; it was done with the hoe before the plough, and at first it was quite supplementary to the hunting and the sheep, goat and cattle tending that made the "living" of the family tribe.

We have traced the broad outlines of the development in regions of exceptional fruitfulness of the first settled village communities into more populous towns and cities, and the growth of the village shrine and the village medicine-man into the city temple and the city priesthood. We have noticed the beginnings of organized war, first as a bickering between villages, and then as a more disciplined struggle between the priest-king and god of one city and those of another. Our story has passed on with a gathering rapidity from the first indications of conquest and empire in Sumer, 5,000 or 6,000 B.C., to the spectacle of great empires growing up, with roads and armies, with inscriptions and written documents, with educated priesthoods and kings and rulers sustained by a tradition already ancient. We have seen Egypt following the same course. We have traced in broad outline the appearance and conflicts and replacements of these empires of the great rivers. We have directed attention, in particular, to the evidences of still wider political ideas betrayed in the actions and utterances of such men as Nabonidus and Amenophis IV. It has been an outline of the accumulations of human experience for ten or fifteen thousand years, a vast space of time in comparison with all subsequent history, but a brief period when we measure it against the succession of endless generations that intervenes between us and the first flint-using human creatures of the Pleistocene dawn. But for these last four chapters we have been writing almost entirely not about mankind generally, but only about the men who thought, the men who could draw and read and write, the men who were altering their world. Beneath their activities what was the life of the mute multitude?

The life of the common man was, of course, affected and changed by these things, just as the lives of the domestic animals and the face of the cultivated country were changed; but for the most part it was a change suffered, and not a change in which the common man upon the land had any voice or will. Reading and writing were not yet for the likes of him. He went on cultivating his patch, loving his wife and children, beating his dog and tending his beasts, grumbling at hard times, fearing the increasing magic of the priests and the growing power of the gods, desiring little more except to be left alone by the powers above him.

So he was in 10,000 B.C.; so he was, unchanged in nature and outlook, in the time of Alexander the Great; so over the greater part of the world he remains to-day. He got rather better tools, better seeds, better methods, a slightly sounder shelter, he bartered his produce in a more organized market as civilization progressed. But a certain freedom and a certain equality passed out of human life when men ceased to wander. Men paid in liberty and they paid in toil, for safety, shelter, and regular meals. By imperceptible degrees the common man found the patch he cultivated was not his own; it belonged to the god; and he had to pay a fraction of his produce to the god. Or the god had given it to the king, who exacted his rent and tax. Or the king had given it to an official, who was the lord of the common man. And sometimes the god or the king or the noble had work to be done, and then the common man had to leave his patch and work for his master.

How far the patch he cultivated was his own was never very

clear to him. In ancient Assyria the land seems to have been held as a sort of freehold, and the occupier paid taxes; in Babylonia the land was the god's, and he permitted the cultivator to work thereon. In Egypt the temples or Pharaoh-the-god or the nobles under Pharaoh were the owners and rent receivers. But the cultivator was not a slave; he was a peasant, and only bound to the land in so far that there was nothing else for him to do but cultivate, and nowhere else for him to go. He lived in a village or town, and went out to his work. The village, to begin with, was often merely a big household of related people under a patriarch headman, the early town a group of householders under its elders.

There was a process of enslavement as civilization grew; the headmen and leaderly men grew in power and authority, and the common man did not keep pace with them; he fell by imperceptible degrees into a tradition of dependence and subordination.

On the whole, the common men were fairly content to live under lord or king or god and obey their bidding. It was safer. It was easier. All animals—and man is no exception—begin life as dependents. Most men never shake themselves loose from the desire for leading and protection. Most men accept such conditions as they are born to, without further question.

In Breasted's *Religion and Thought in Ancient Egypt,* he gives various stories and passages to show that before 2,000 B.C. there was social discontent, but it was a naïve unrevolutionary discontent. There are complaints that men are treacherous and that judges are unjust. Rich men are capricious and exacting and do not pity and help the poor. There are quarrels about the scale of payment, and strikes against bad food and harsh conditions. But there is no question of the right of Pharaoh to rule nor of the righteousness of riches. There is no challenge to the social order; never do the complaints materialize in action.

§ 2

The earlier wars did not involve remote or prolonged campaigns, and they were waged by levies of the common people. But war brought in a new source of possessions, plunder, and a new social factor, the captive. In the earlier, nomadic times, the captive man was kept only to be tortured or sacrificed to the victorious god; the captive women and children were assimilated into the tribe. Nomads have little use for slaves. But later many captives were spared to be slaves because they had exceptional gifts or peculiar arts. It would be the kings and captains who would take these slaves at first—and it would speedily become apparent to them that these men were much more their own than were the peasant cultivators and common men of their own race. The slave could be commanded to do all sorts of things for his master that the quasi-free common man would not do so willingly because of his attachment to his own patch of cultivation. The slave could be used for mass labour, for making embankments or working mines.

From a very early period the artificer was often a household slave. The manufacture of trade goods, pottery, textiles, metal ware, and so forth, such as went on vigorously in the household city of the Minos of Cnossos, was probably a slave industry

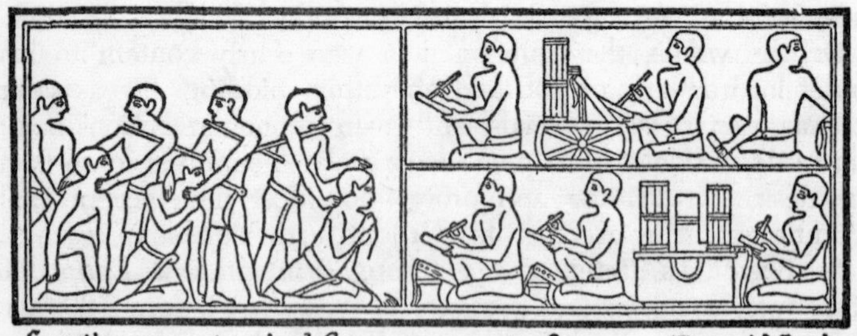

Egyptian peasants seized for non-payment of taxes ... (Pyramid Age)

from the beginning. Sayce, in his *Babylonians and Assyrians,* quotes Babylonian agreements for the teaching of trades to slaves, and dealing with the exploitation of slave products. Slaves produced slave children, enslavement in discharge of debts added to the slave population; it is probable that as the cities grew larger, a larger part of the new population consisted of these slave artificers and slave servants in the large households. They were by no means abject slaves; in later Babylon their lives and property were protected by elaborate laws. Nor were they all war captives. Parents might sell their children into slavery, and brothers their orphan sisters. Free men who had no means of livelihood would even sell themselves into slavery. And slavery was the fate of the insolvent debtor. Craft apprenticeship, again, was a sort of fixed-term slavery.

Out of the slave population, by a converse process, arose the freed-man and freed-woman, who worked for wages and had still more definite individual rights. Since in Babylon slaves could themselves own property, many slaves saved up and bought their freedom. Probably the town slave was often better off and practically as free as the cultivator of the soil, and as the rural population increased, its sons and daughters came to mix with and swell the growing ranks of artificers, some bond, some free.

As the extent and complexity of government increased, the number of households multiplied. Under the king's household grew up the households of his great ministers and officials, under the temple grew up the personal households of temple functionaries; it is not difficult to realize how houses and patches of land would become more and more distinctly the property of the occupiers, and more and more definitely alienated from the original owner-god. The earlier empires in Egypt and China both passed into a feudal stage, in which families, originally official, became for a time independent noble families. In the later stages of Babylonian civilization we find an increasing propertied class of people appearing in the social structure, neither slaves nor peasants nor priests nor officials, but widows and descendants of such people, or successful traders and the like, and all *masterless* folk.

Traders came in from the outside. Babylon was full of Aramean traders, who had great establishments, with slaves, freedmen, employees of all sorts. (Their bookkeeping was a serious undertaking in a civilization without paper. It involved storing a great multitude of earthenware tablets in huge earthenware jars.) Upon this gathering mixture of more or less free and detached people would live other people, traders, merchants, small dealers, catering for their needs. Sayce gives the particulars of an agreement for the setting up and stocking of a tavern and beerhouse, for example. The passer-by, the man who happened to be about, had come into existence.

The least kindly aspect of slavery has always been gang slavery. If it did not figure very largely in the ancient cities, it was very much in evidence elsewhere. The king was, to begin with, the chief *entrepreneur*. He made the canals and organized the irrigation (*e.g.* Hammurabi's enterprises noted in the previous chapter). He exploited mines. He seems (at Cnossos, *e.g.*) to have organized manufactures for export. The Pharaohs of the Ist Dynasty were already working the copper and turquoise mines in the peninsula of Sinai. For many such purposes gangs of natives were cheaper and far more controllable than levies of the king's own people.

From an early period, too, captives have tugged the oars of the galleys, though Torr (*Ancient Ships*) notes that up to the age of Pericles (450 B.C.) the free Athenians were not above this task. And the monarch also found slaves convenient for his military expeditions. They were uprooted men; they did not fret to go home, because they had no homes to go to. The Pharaohs hunted slaves in Nubia, in order to have black troops for their Syrian expeditions. Closely allied to such slaves were the mercenary barbaric troops the monarchs caught into their service, not by positive compulsion, but by the bribes of food and plunder and under the pressure of need. As the old civilization developed, these mercenary armies replaced the national levies of the old order more and more, and servile gang labour became a more and more important and significant factor in the economic system.

Brawl among boatmen... (From tomb of Ptah-hetep — —Pyramid Age).

From mines and canal and wall-building, the servile gang spread into cultivation. Nobles and temples adopted the gang-slave system for their estates. Plantation gangs began to oust the patch cultivation of the labourer serf in the case of some staple products.

§ 3

So we trace the development of the simple social structure of the early Sumerian cities to the multitude of individuals varying in race, tradition, education, and function, varying in wealth, freedom, authority, and usefulness, in the great cities of the last thousand years B.C. The most notable thing of all is the gradual increase amidst this heterogeneous multitude of what we may call *free individuals,* detached persons who are neither priests, nor kings, nor officials, nor serfs, nor slaves, who are under no great pressure to work, who have time to read and inquire. They appear side by side with the development of social security and private property.

The methods of reckoning developed. The operations of the Arameans and such-like Semitic trading people led to the organization of credit and monetary security. In the earlier days almost the only property, except a few movables, consisted of rights in land and in houses; later, one could deposit and lend securities, could go away and return to find one's property faithfully held and secure. Towards the middle of the period of the Persian Empire there lived one free individual, Herodotus, who has a great interest for us because he was among the first writers of critical and intelligent history, as distinguished from a mere priestly or court chronicle. It is worth while to glance here very briefly at the circumstances of his life. Later on we shall quote from the history he wrote.

We have already noted the conquest of Babylonia by the Aryan Persians under Cyrus in 539 B.C. We have noted, further that the Persian Empire spread into Egypt, where its hold was precarious; and it extended also over Asia Minor. Herodotus was born about 484 B.C. in a Greek city of Asia Minor, Halicarnassus, which was under the overlordship of the Persians, and directly under the rule of a political boss or tyrant. There is no sign that he was obliged either to work for a living or spend very much time in the administration of his property. We do not know the particulars of his affairs, but it is clear that in this minor Greek city, under foreign rule, he was able to obtain and read and study manuscripts of nearly everything that had been written in the Greek language before his time.

He travelled, so far as one can gather, with freedom and comfort about the Greek archipelagos; he stayed wherever he wanted to stay, and he seems to have found tolerable accommodation; he went to Babylon and to Susa, the new capital the Persians had set up in Babylonia to the east of the Tigris; he toured along the coast of the Black Sea, and accumulated a considerable amount of knowledge about the Scythians, the Aryan people who were then distributed over South Russia; he went to the south of Italy, explored the antiquities of Tyre, coasted Palestine, landed at Gaza, and made a long stay in Egypt. He went about Egypt looking at temples and monuments and gathering information. We know not only from him, but from other evidence, that in those days the older temples and the pyramids (which were already nearly three thousand years old) were visited by strings of tourists, a special sort of priests acting as guides. The inscriptions the sightseers scribbled upon the walls remain to this day, and many of them have been deciphered and published.

As his knowledge accumulated, he conceived the idea of writing a great history of the attempts of Persia to subdue Greece. But in order to introduce that history he composed an account of the past of Greece, Persia, Assyria, Babylonia, Egypt, Scythia, and of the geography and peoples of those countries. He then set himself, it is said, to make his history known among his friends in Halicarnassus by reciting it to them, but they failed to appreciate it; and he then betook himself to Athens, the most flourishing of all Greek cities at that time. There his work was received with applause. We find him in the centre of a brilliant circle of intelligent and active-minded people, and the city authorities voted him a reward of ten talents (a sum of money equivalent to £2,400) in recognition of his literary achievement.

But we will not complete the biography of this most interesting man, nor will we enter into any criticism of his garrulous, marvel-telling, and most entertaining history. It is a book to which all intelligent readers come sooner or later, abounding as it does in illuminating errors and Boswellian charm. We give these particulars here simply to show that in the fifth century B.C. a new factor was becoming evident in human affairs. Reading and writing had already escaped from the temple precincts and the ranks of the court scribes. Record was no longer confined to court and temple. A new sort of people, these people of leisure and independent means, were asking questions, exchanging knowledge and views, and developing ideas. So beneath the march of armies and the policies of monarchs, and above the common lives of illiterate and incurious men, we note the beginnings of what is becoming at last nowadays a dominant power in human affairs, the *free intelligence of mankind.*

Of that free intelligence we shall have more to say when, in a subsequent chapter, we tell of the Greeks in the city states of the Archipelago and Asia Minor.

§ 4

We may summarize the discussion of the last two chapters here by making a list of the chief elements in this complicated accumulation of human beings which made up the later Babylonian and Egyptian civilization of from two thousand five hundred to three thousand years ago. These elements grew up and became distinct from one another in the great river valleys of the world in the course of five or six thousand years. They developed mental dispositions and traditions and attitudes of thought one to another. The civilization in which we live to-day is simply carrying on and still further developing and working out and rearranging these relationships. This is the world from which we inherit. It is only by the attentive study of their origins that we can detach ourselves from the prejudices and immediate ideas of the particular class to which we may belong, and begin to understand the social and political questions of our own time.

(1) First, then, came the priesthood, *the temple system*, which was the nucleus and the guiding intelligence about which the primitive civilizations grew. It was still in these later days a great power in the world, the chief repository of knowledge and tradition, an influence over the lives of everyone, and a binding force to hold the community together. But it was no longer all-powerful, because its nature made it conservative and inadaptable. It no longer monopolized knowledge nor initiated fresh ideas. Learning had already leaked out to other less pledged and controlled people, who thought for themselves. About the temple system were grouped its priests and priestesses, its scribes, its physicians, its magicians, its lay brethren, treasurers, managers, directors, and the like. It owned great properties and often hoarded huge treasures.

(2) Over against the priesthood, and originally arising out of it, was the *court system*, headed by a king or a "king of kings," who was in later Assyria and Babylonia a sort of captain and lay controller of affairs, and in Egypt a god-man who had released himself from the control of his priests. About the monarch were accumulated his scribes, counsellors, record keepers, agents, captains, and guards. Many of his officials, particularly his provincial officials, had great subordinate establishments, and were constantly tending to become independent. The nobility of the old river valley civilization arose out of the court system. It was, therefore, a different thing in its origin from the nobility of the early Aryans, which was a republican nobility of elders and leading men.

(3) At the base of the social pyramid was the large and most necessary class in the community, *the tillers of the soil.* Their

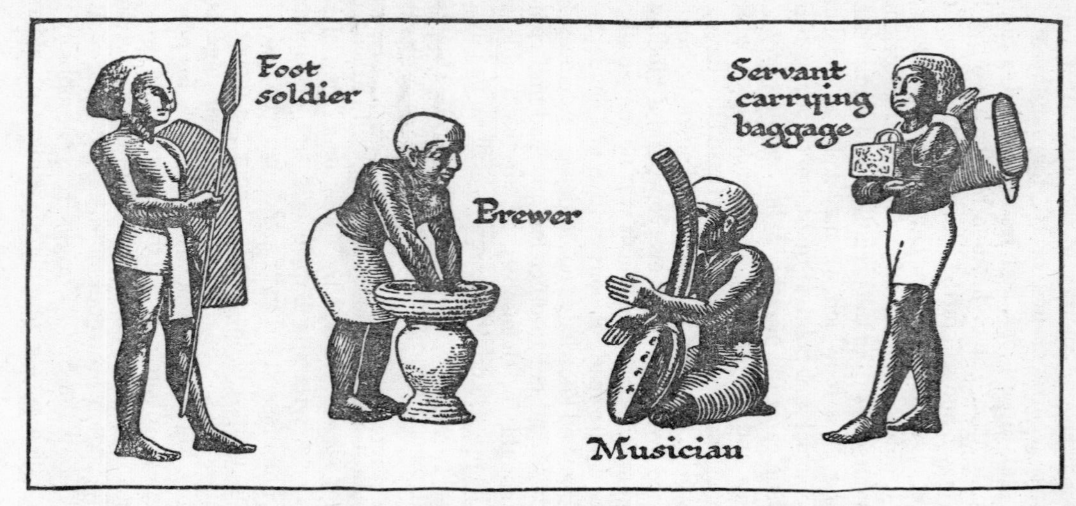

STATUETTES FROM MIDDLE-CLASS EGYPTIAN TOMBS SHOWING LOW-CLASS SOCIAL TYPES IN THE ANCIENT COMMUNITIES

status varied from age to age and in different lands; they were free peasants paying taxes, or serfs of the god, or serfs or tenants of king or noble, or of a private owner, paying him a rent; in most cases tax or rent was paid in produce. In the states of the river valleys they were high cultivators, cultivating comparatively small holdings; they lived together for safety in villages, and had a common interest in maintaining their irrigation channels and a sense of community in their village life. The cultivation of the soil is an exacting occupation; the seasons and the harvest sunsets will not wait for men; children can be utilized at an early age, and so the cultivator class is generally a poorly educated, close-toiling class, superstitious by reason of ignorance and the uncertainty of the seasons, ill-informed and easily put upon. It is capable at times of great passive resistance, but it has no purpose in its round but crops and crops, to keep out of debt and hoard against bad times. So it has remained to our own days over the greater part of Europe and Asia.

(4) Differing widely in origin and quality from the tillers of the soil was *the artisan class.* At first, this was probably in part a town-slave class, in part it consisted of peasants who had specialized upon a craft. But in developing an art and mystery of its own, a technique that had to be learnt before it could be practised, each sort of craft probably developed a certain independence and a certain sense of community of its own. The artisans were able to get together and discuss their affairs more readily than the toilers on the land, and they were able to form guilds to restrict output, maintain rates of pay, and protect their common interest.

(5) As the power of the Babylonian rulers spread out beyond the original areas of good husbandry into grazing regions and less fertile districts, a class of *herdsmen* came into existence. In the case of Babylonia these were nomadic Semites, the Bedouin, like the Bedouin of to-day. They probably grazed their flocks over great areas much as the sheep ranchers of California do. They were paid and esteemed much more highly than the husbandmen.

(6) The first *merchants* in the world were shipowners, like the people of Tyre and Cnossos, or nomads who carried and traded goods as they wandered between one area of primitive civilization and another. In the Babylonian and Assyrian world the traders were predominantly the Semitic Arameans, the ancestors of the modern Syrians. They became a distinct factor in the life of the community; they formed great households of their own. Usury developed largely in the last thousand years B.C. It had been prac-

tised even in Sumerian times. Traders needed accommodation; cultivators wished to anticipate their crops. Sayce gives an account of the Babylonian banking-house of Egibi, which lasted through several generations and outlived the Chaldean Empire.

(7) A class of *small retailers,* one must suppose, came into existence with the complication of society during the later days of the first empires, but it was not probably of any great importance.

(8) A growing class of *independent property owners.*

(9) As the amenities of life increased, there grew up in the court, temples, and prosperous private houses a class of *domestic servants,* slaves or freed slaves, or young peasants taken into the household.

(10) *Gang workers.*—These were prisoners of war or debt slaves, or impressed or deported men.

(11) *Mercenary soldiers.*—These also were often captives or impressed men. Sometimes they were enlisted from friendly foreign populations in which the military spirit still prevailed.

(12) *Seamen.*

In modern political and economic discussions we are apt to talk rather glibly of "labour." Much has been made of the *solidarity of labour* and its sense of community. It is well to note that in these first civilizations, what we speak of as "labour" is represented by five distinct classes dissimilar in origin, traditions, and outlook—namely, classes 3, 4, 5, 9, 10, and the oar-tugging part of 12. The "solidarity of labour" is, we shall find when we come to study the mechanical revolution of the nineteenth century A.D., a new idea and a new possibility in human affairs.

§ 5

Let us, before leaving this discussion of the social classes that were developing in these first civilizations, devote a little attention to their fixity. How far did they stand aloof from each other, and how far did they intermingle? So far as the classes we have counted as 9, 10, 11 and 12 go, the servants, the gang labourers and slaves, the gang soldiers, and, to a lesser extent, the sailors, or at any rate the galley rowers among the sailors, they were largely recruited classes, they did not readily and easily form homes, they were not distinctively breeding classes; they were probably replenished generation after generation by captives, by the failures of other classes, and especially from the failures of the class of small retailers, and by persuasion and impressment from among the cultivators. But so far as the sailors go, we have to distinguish between the mere rower and the navigating and ship-owning seamen of such ports as Tyre and Sidon. The shipowners pass, no doubt, by insensible gradations into the mercantile class, but the navigators must have made a peculiar community in the great seaports, having homes there and handing on the secrets of seacraft to their sons.

The eighth class we have distinguished was certainly a precarious class, continually increased by the accession of the heirs and dependents, the widows and retired members of the wealthy and powerful, and continually diminished by the deaths or speculative losses of these people and the dispersal of their properties. The priests and priestesses too, so far as all this world west of India went, were not a very reproductive class; many priesthoods were celibate, and that class, too, may also be counted as a recruited class. Nor are servants, as a rule, reproductive. They live in the households of other people; they do not have households and rear large families of their own. This leaves us as the really vital classes of the ancient civilized community:

(*a*) The royal and aristocratic class, officials, military officers, and the like;

(*b*) The mercantile class;

(*c*) The town artisans;

(*d*) The cultivators of the soil; and

(*e*) The herdsmen.

Each of these classes reared its own children in its own fashion, and so naturally kept itself more or less continuously distinct from the others. General education was not organized in those ancient states, education was mainly a household matter (as it is still in many parts of India to-day), and so it was natural and necessary for the sons to follow in the footsteps of their father and to marry women accustomed to their own sort of household. Except during times of great political disturbance, therefore, there would be a natural and continuous separation of classes; which would not, however, prevent exceptional individuals from intermarrying or passing from one class to another. Poor aristocrats would marry rich members of the mercantile class; ambitious herdsmen, artisans, or sailors would become rich merchants. So far as one can gather, that was the general state of affairs in both Egypt and Babylonia. The idea was formerly entertained that in Egypt there was a fixity of classes, but this appears to be a misconception due to a misreading of Herodotus. The only exclusive class in Egypt which did not intermarry was the semi-divine royal family.

At various points in the social system there were probably developments of exclusiveness, an actual barring out of interlopers. Artisans of particular crafts possessing secrets, for example, have among all races and in all ages tended to develop guild organizations restricting the practice of their craft and the marriage of members outside their guild. Conquering people have also, and especially when there were marked physical differences of race, been disposed to keep themselves aloof from the conquered peoples, and have developed an aristocratic exclusiveness. Such organizations of restriction upon free intercourse have come and gone in great variety in the history of all long-standing civilizations. The natural boundaries of function were always there, but sometimes they have been drawn sharply and laid stress upon, and sometimes they have been made little of. There has been a general tendency among the Aryan peoples to distinguish noble (patrician) from common (plebeian) families; the traces of it are evident throughout the literature and life of Europe to-day, and it has received a picturesque enforcement in the "science" of heraldry. This tradition is still active even in democratic America. Germany, the most methodical of European countries, had in the Middle Ages a very clear conception of the fixity of such distinctions. Below the princes (who themselves constituted an exclusive class which did not marry beneath itself) there were the:

(*a*) Knights—the military and official caste, with heraldic coats-of-arms;

(*b* and *c*) The Bürgerstand—the merchants, shipping people, and artisans; and

(*d*) The Bauernstand—the cultivating serfs or peasants.

Mediæval Germany went as far as any of the Western heirs of the first great civilizations towards a fixation of classes. The idea is far less congenial both to the English-speaking people and to the French and Italians, who, by a sort of instinct, favour a free movement from class to class. Such exclusive ideas began at first among, and were promoted chiefly by, the upper classes, but it is a natural response and a natural Nemesis to such ideas that the mass of the excluded should presently range themselves in antagonism to their superiors. It was in Germany, as we shall see in the concluding chapters of this story, that the conception of a natural and necessary conflict, "the class war," between the miscellaneous multitudes of the disinherited ("the class-conscious proletariat" of the Marxist) and the rulers and merchants first arose. It was an idea more acceptable to the German mind than to the British or French.

But before we come to that conflict, we must traverse a long history of many centuries.

§ 6

If now we turn eastward from this main development of civilization in the world between Central Asia and the Atlantic to the social development of India in the 2,000 years next before the Christian era, we find certain broad and very interesting differences. The first of these is that we find such a fixity of classes in process of establishment as no other part of the world can present. This fixity of classes is known to Europeans as the institution of *caste* (from *casta,* a word of Portuguese origin; the Indian word is *varna,* colour). Its origins are still in complete obscurity, but it was certainly well rooted in the Ganges valley before the days of Alexander the Great. It is a complicated horizontal division of the social structure into classes or castes, the members of which may neither eat nor intermarry with persons of a lower caste under penalty of becoming outcasts, and who may also "lose caste" for various ceremonial negligences and defilements. By losing caste a man does not sink to a lower caste; he becomes outcast.

The various subdivisions of caste are very complex; many are practically trade organizations. Each caste has its local organization which maintains discipline, distributes various charities, looks after its own poor, protects the common interests of its members, and examines the credentials of newcomers from other districts. (There is little to check the pretensions of a travelling Hindu to be of a higher caste than is legitimately his.) Originally, the four main castes seem to have been:

The Brahmins—the priests and teachers;

The Kshatriyas—the warriors;

The Vaisyas—herdsmen, money-lenders, merchants, and landowners;

The Sudras;

And, outside the castes, the Pariahs.

But these primary divisions have long been complicated by subdivision into a multitude of minor castes, all exclusive, each holding its members to one definite way of living and one group of associates. In Bengal the Kshatriyas and Vaisyas have largely disappeared. . . . But this is too intricate a question for us to deal with here in any detail.

Next to this extraordinary fission and complication of the social body we have to note that the Brahmins, the priests and teachers of the Indian world, unlike so many Western priesthoods, are a marrying, reproductive and exclusive class, taking no recruits from any other social stratum.

Whatever may have been the original incentive to this extensive fixation of class in India, there can be little doubt of the rôle played by the Brahmins as the custodians of tradition and the only teachers of the people in sustaining it. By some it is supposed that the first three of the four original castes, known also as the "twice-born," were the descendants of the Vedic Aryan conquerors of India, who established these hard-and-fast separations to prevent racial mixing with the conquered Sudras and Pariahs. The Sudras are represented as a previous wave of northern conquerors, and the Pariahs are the original Dravidian inhabitants of India. But these speculations are not universally accepted, and it is, perhaps, rather the case that the uniform conditions of life in the Ganges valley throughout long centuries served to stereotype a difference of classes that have never had the same steadfastness of definition under the more various and variable conditions of the greater world to the West.

However caste arose, there can be no doubt of its extraordinary hold upon the Indian mind. In the sixth century B.C. arose Gautama, the great teacher of Buddhism, proclaiming, "As the four streams that flow into the Ganges lose their names as soon as they mingle their waters in the holy river, so all who believe in Buddha cease to be Brahmins, Kshatriyas, Vaisyas, and Sudras." His teaching prevailed in India for some centuries; it spread over China, Tibet, Japan, Burma, Ceylon, Turkestan, Manchuria; it is to-day the religion of a large fraction of the human race, but it was finally defeated and driven out of Indian life by the vitality and persistence of the Brahmins and of their caste ideas.

§ 7

In China we find a social system travelling along yet another, and only a very roughly parallel line to that followed by the Indian and Western civilizations. The Chinese civilization even more than the Hindu is organized for peace, and the warrior plays a small part on its social scheme. As in the Indian civilization, the leading class is an intellectual one; less priestly than the Brahmin and more official. But unlike the Brahmins, the mandarins, who are the literate men of China, are not a caste: one is not a mandarin by birth, but by education; mandarins are drawn by education and examination from all classes of the community, and the son of a mandarin has no prescriptive right to succeed his father. As a consequence of these differences, while the Brahmins of India are, as a class, ignorant even of their own sacred books, mentally slack, and full of a pretentious assurance, the Chinese mandarin has the energy that comes from hard mental work. But since his education so far has been almost entirely a scholarly study of the classical Chinese literature, his influence has been entirely conservative. Before the days of Alexander the Great, China had already formed itself and set its feet in the way in which it was still walking in the year A.D. 1900. Invaders and dynasties have come and gone, but the routine of life of the yellow civilization has remained unchanged.

The traditional Chinese social system recognized four main classes below the priest-emperor.

(*a*) The literary class, which was equivalent partly to the officials of the Western world and partly to its teachers and clerics. In the time of Confucius its education included archery and horsemanship. Rites and music, history and mathematics, completed the "Six Accomplishments."

(*b*) The cultivators of the land.

(*c*) The artisans.

(*d*) The mercantile class.

But since from the earliest times it has been the Chinese way to divide the landed possessions of a man among all his sons, there has never been in Chinese history any class of great landowners renting their land to tenants, such as most other countries have displayed. The Chinese land has always been cut up into small holdings, which are chiefly freeholds and cultivated intensively. There are landlords in China who own one or a few farms and rent them to tenants, but there are no great, permanent estates. When a patch of land, by repeated division, is too small to sustain a man, it is sold to some prospering neighbour, and the former owner drifts to one of the great towns of China to join the mass of wage-earning workers there. In China, for many centuries, there have been these masses of town population with scarcely any property at all, men neither serfs nor slaves, but held to their daily work by their utter impecuniousness. From such masses it is that the soldiers needed by the Chinese Government are recruited, and also such gang labour as has been needed for the making of canals, the building of walls and the like has been drawn. The war captive and the slave class play a smaller part in Chinese history than in any more westerly record of these ages before the Christian era.

One fact, we may note, is common to all these three stories of developing social structure, and that is the immense power exercised by the educated class in the early stages before the crown or the commonalty began to read and, consequently, to think for itself. In India, by reason of their exclusiveness, the Brahmins, the educated class, retain their influence to this day; over the masses of China, along entirely different lines and because of the complexities of the written language, the mandarinate has prevailed. The diversity of race and tradition in the more various and eventful world of the West has delayed, and perhaps arrested for ever, any parallel organization of the specially intellectual elements of society into a class ascendancy. In the Western world, as we have already noted, education early "slopped over," and soaked away out of the control of any special class: it escaped from the limitation of castes and priesthoods and traditions into the general life of the community. Writing and reading had been simplified down to a point when it was no longer possible to make a cult and mystery of them. It may be due to the peculiar elaboration and difficulty of the Chinese characters, rather than to any racial difference, that the same thing did not happen to a like extent in China.

§ 8

In these last six chapters we have traced in outline the whole process by which, in the course of 10,000 or 12,000 years—that is to say, in something between 300 and 400 generations—man ceased to be a rare, hungry, prowling, rather unsocial animal, thinly distributed about the warmer parts of the earth, and became an abundant social creature swarming densely over the more favourable regions of the old world. Toil began, enslavement—and security. In that period mankind passed from the stage of early Neolithic husbandry, in which the primitive skin-clad family tribe reaped and stored in their rude mud huts the wild-growing fodder and grain-bearing grasses with sickles of stone, to the days of the fourth century B.C., when all round the shores of the Mediterranean and up the Nile, and across Asia to India, and again over the great alluvial areas of China, spread the fields of human cultivation and busy cities, great temples, and the coming and going of human commerce. Galleys and lateen-sailed ships entered and left crowded harbours, and made their careful way from headland to headland and from headland to island, keeping always close to the land. Phœnician shipping under Egyptian owners was penetrating to the East Indies and perhaps even further into the Pacific. We have Bushmen rock paintings in South Africa showing white men with headdresses of a type worn for a time in Assyria and known also in North Europe, but unknown as indigenous in Africa. Across the deserts of Africa and Arabia and through Turkestan toiled the caravans with their remote trade; silk was already coming from China, ivory from Central Africa, and tin from Britain to the centres of this new life in the world. Damascus was already making Damask, and "Damascening" steel. Men had learnt to weave fine linen and delicate fabrics of coloured wool; they could bleach and dye; they had iron as well as copper, bronze, silver, and gold; they had made the most beautiful pottery and porcelain; there was hardly a variety of precious stone in the world that they had not found and cut and polished; they could read and write; divert the courses of rivers, pile pyramids, and make walls a thousand miles long. The hundred centuries or so in which all this had been achieved may seem a long time in comparison with the threescore and ten years of a single human life, but it is utterly inconsiderable in comparison with the stretches of geological time. Measuring backward from these Alexandrian cities to the days of the first stone implements, the *rostro-carinate* implements of the Pliocene Age, gives us an extent of time fully a hundred times as long.

We have tried in this account, and with the help of maps and figures and time charts, to give a just idea of the order and shape of these eventful centuries of man's development. Our business is with that outline. We have named but a few names of individuals; though henceforth the personal names must increase in number. But the content of this Outline that we have drawn here in a few diagrams and charts cannot but touch the imagination. If only we could look closelier, we should see through all these sixty centuries a procession of lives more and more akin in their fashion to our own. We have shown how the painted Palæolithic savage gave place to the Neolithic cultivator, a type of man still to be found in the backward places of the world. We have given an illustration of Sumerian soldiers copied from a carved stone that was set up long before the days when the Semitic Sargon I conquered the land. Day by day some busy brownish man carved those figures, and, no doubt, whistled as he carved. In those days the plain of the Egyptian delta was crowded with gangs of swarthy workmen unloading the stone that had come down the Nile to add a fresh course to the current pyramid. One might paint a thousand scenes from those ages: of some hawker merchant in Egypt spreading his stock of Babylonish garments before the eyes of some pretty, rich lady; of a miscellaneous crowd swarming between the pylons to some temple festival at Thebes; of an excited, dark-eyed audience of Cretans, like the Spaniards of to-day, watching a bull-fight, with the bull-fighters in trousers and tightly girded, exactly like any contemporary bull-fighter; of children learning their cuneiform signs (at Nippur the clay exercise tiles of a school have been found); of a woman with a sick husband at home slipping into some great temple in Carthage to make a vow for his recovery.

Or perhaps it is a wild Greek, skin-clad and armed with a bronze axe, standing motionless on some Illyrian mountain-crest, struck with amazement at his first vision of a many-oared Cretan galley crawling like a great insect across the amethystine mirror of the Adriatic Sea. He went home to tell his folk a strange story of a monster. Briareus with his hundred arms. Of millions of such stitches in each of these 200 generations is the fabric of this history woven. But unless they mark the presence of a primary seam or join, we cannot pause now to examine any of these stitches.

§ 9

Let us, however, before we go on to the thousand-year struggle and interaction of Aryan and Semite in the Western world that constitutes the main substance of the next three books of this Outline, give two brief sections to record the appearance of a conscious search for beauty in men's lives. In two books we have told how man arose from the condition of a wandering rare animal to the multitudinous, toilsome, but secured and more abundant life of civilization. For a fortunate minority civilization meant great releases of energy; for all it meant a certain freedom from urgent feat and necessity. And the released energy flowed into a prolongation of "play" into the adult life and into a conscious search for delights. Man ceased to be wholly occupied in the search for food and shelter. He lifted his eyes to beauty. Even the Neanderthaler animal was not wholly a beast. It collected shells and curious stones and such-like odd things and wore them, it would seem, for pleasure and adornment.

In the later Palæolithic time there was, as we have noted already, a considerable outbreak of drawing and carving. These things were done for pleasure. No doubt they also had a magic significance; that was inevitable. There is an incurable tendency in the human mind to overload things with personal significance. To this day people feel that jewels or ornaments are lucky or unlucky, and no doubt Palæolithic man thought that his drawings of animals had a propitious effect on the game. But some of his statuettes were manifestly burlesque. Much stress has been laid on the fact that a great proportion of the Palæolithic paintings and drawings that have survived are in dark caves and obscure corners. But these may be only a small remnant of the decoration with which early man covered the trees and rocks of his time. The exposed would have been destroyed naturally in a few years.

Later Palæolithic man drew and carved; he danced, as his drawings testify, and dancing seems to imply rhythmic shoutings and beatings. Here are the first factors of fine art and music. The shelter that he built and the huts and holes of early Neolithic man were, however, sternly utilitarian; it was only as civilization dawned and a considerable accumulation of population was achieved, that the shrine and the head-man's hut began to be something more than mere shelters, and conscious architecture began. Insensibly men came to feel that a building might have dignity and mystery, might impress by its grace and beauty.

Perhaps the most considerable building effort Stone Age man ever made were the barrows in which great men were interred. Always there was a central chamber of big piled stones and then earth or mud brick. The great pyramids of Egypt, those vast graceless bulks, are essentially huge barrows of stone. Silbury Hill in England is an earth pyramid. These accumulations were oriented with great care; the Egyptian pyramids indicate considerable mechanical skill as well as a stupendous mass effort; but one can scarcely speak of architecture in connection with these piles.

The architects of the Mesopotamian region and those of the Nile valley began with very little knowledge of each other's activities and had little or no influence upon each other. Their first forms were in each case determined by the peculiarities of sun-dried mud bricks and timber. The Sumerian, however, had little stone available; the Egyptian, on the other hand, had abundant and various stone close at hand, easily quarried and easily got to the Nile. Sun-dried bricks are compressible; they necessitate a broadening-out of the walls at the base, and both the Sumerian-Babylonian and the Egyptian buildings have that sloping of the outer wall that gives them their distinctive air of dignified permanence. The inner passages were narrow because of the yet unmastered difficulties of carrying a roof. In Sumeria, the important buildings developed into the "ziggurat" form, which continued to be characteristic of this region. A ziggurat is a staged, many-storied building; each story is narrower than the one below and has a terrace about it with staircases. The softer brick is faced with tiles and harder burnt brick. The remains we now excavate in these regions are only the stumps of the original buildings which often towered to seven or eight stories. Pillars were rarely or never used in the earlier Mesopotamian architecture—there was no suitable material—and the chambers seem generally to have been vaulted not with arches but with each course of bricks on the massive wall coming in a little more than the one below. There are, however, massive brick pillars in Sumerian buildings at Ur and at Kish. Decorative effects were got with buttresses and brick panels. Stucco and terra-cotta play a large part in the ornamental work. Stone appears in caved slabs and for such like special uses. It is only when we reach Assyrian architecture that we come into a stone region and the buildings begin to be faced with stone masonry and freely adorned with stone. It is only when communications have developed with Egypt, in the second millennium B.C., that the stone pillar appears in the Euphrates-Tigris region.

The Egyptian architecture never produced many-storied piles of the ziggurat type. Except the pyramids, obelisks and pylons, Egyptian architecture kept broad and low. The stone appears first as a substitute for wood, stone lintels and beams replace wooden ones and imitate their shapes. Wooden supports give place to rounded pillars of stone. Upon which pillars the forms of men and animals are presently painted or carved in relief. One early temple, the temple of the Sphinx, near to and contemporary with the pyramids, is largely carved out of the living rock. It has no columns. Columns and colonnades appear about the time of the XIIth Dynasty.

The great days of the Egyptian style were in the time of the XVIIIth Dynasty. To that period we owe the huge assembly of temple buildings at Thebes. The XIXth Dynasty was also a great dynasty of builders.

Sculpture and painting were at first entirely accessory to the master art of architecture in both centres of civilization. Sculpture began as relief and as the carved pylon; painting filled the panel and covered the blank wall. To the dry Egyptian climate we owe the preservation of great spaces of wonderfully painted surface, representing a thousand aspects of everyday Egyptian life and revealing much of the thought and imagination of these people. The records of Assyria and Babylon are sparing in comparison.

The Ægean architecture has a distinctive quality of its own, but on the whole it is closer to the Egyptian than to the Babylonian in spirit. Pillars are used early, and the buildings have a labyrinthine arrangement quite different from either Egyptian or Babylonian ground plans. Fresco painting and mosaic were carried to a very high level.

While these three great arts developed there was also in all these civilizations an enormous output of cuts and engraved gems, goldsmith's work and other metal work, small statuettes, models and such-like toys and ornaments, seats, beds, thrones, and graceful furnishings. Wood and ivory carving were beautifully done. Crete was particularly productive of beautiful gold work and of pottery. The Cretan vases were traded all over the ancient Orient.

§ 10

Imaginative literature and music do not seem to have been so highly developed in the ancient civilizations as the arts that appeal to the eye. Tale-telling has been an important living thing in human life since speech began, and the most important elements of prose literature, a sense of phrase, invention, character study, are to be found wherever two or three women of any race gossip together. Dreams, very often monstrous and embodying the reactions against the necessary suppressions of primitive society, supplied a fantastic element in the early tale. Tales have always eked themselves out by dramatic gestures and interludes except among the very coldest and most restrained people, and from an early age the memory of great events, the procedure of great occasions, was sustained by periodic narrative dances, in which speech and chant, imitation, rhythmic movement and instrumental sound were inextricably interwoven.

These things were in human life before civilization; and the familiar forms of story and sketch and homely dance went on no doubt among the common folk of the ancient civilizations when the periodic commemorations were exalted to become the ceremonial of the temples. But though the priests took up various systems of legends, the Creation story for example, and expanded many of the primitive fables into a complex mythology, they do not seem to have cast them into moulds of beautiful language. The spectacle was the thing. Neither in Egypt nor in Babylonia was there any serious development of the drama as such. The peasants had their show perhaps, but no one else heeded it. The possible dramatic developments of the Ægean peoples we do not yet understand sufficiently to discuss. Perhaps they had no drama. They had exhibitions of a crueller, intenser interest. The bull-fight was their common entertainment. The probably kindred Etruscans, like the pre-European American civilizations, entertained themselves by butchering slaves and making captives fight for life before them.

The writer is unable to discover any record at all of professional story-tellers, or story-chanters in the life of these old civilizations, even in the village life. If there were no professional memorizers, then until the art of writing had developed there could be little expansion of literary art. People would have flashes of happy expression, but they would not be preserved to grow into a literary method and tradition. The earliest Egyptian writings seem to be charms and other recipes, moral aphorisms, bare records. The people of both Egypt and Sumer probably took themselves for granted to an amazing extent, and after childhood indulged very rarely in wonder or dreams of adventure. They were simple, practical peoples. Even about death the Egyptians were astoundingly practical. They furnished forth the dead with care and comfort. The greatest Egyptian tale was the story, told with a hundred variations, of the journey of the departed soul to Osiris; it was a simple, moral, unmetaphysical Baedeker of the other world, the Book of the Dead.

The Jews were yet to develop their book, the first book of power in the world, the Bible, which, as I shall tell, effected a synthesis of many of the shattered elements of the old Semitic world. The Aryans were reciting in their woodlands, but they had not yet learnt to write down the tales and hymns of their singers.

In all the ancient world music never became detached and an art in itself; it was always ancillary to chant or dance. Ancient music had rhythm, had melody, but it had no harmonies. It was

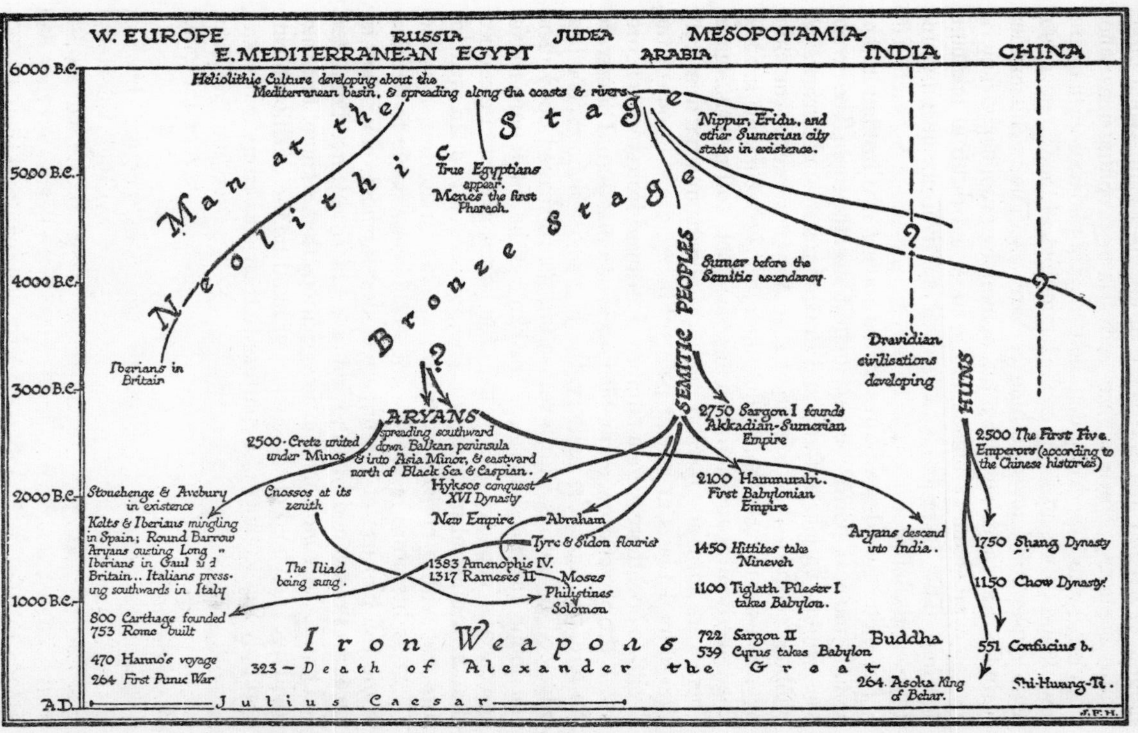

W. EUROPE
E. MEDITERRANEAN
RUSSIA
EGYPT
JUDEA
ARABIA
MESOPOTAMIA
INDIA
CHINA
6000 B.C.
5000 B.C.
4000 B.C.
3000 B.C.
2000 B.C.
1000 B.C.
A.D.
Heliolithic Culture developing about the Mediterranean basin, & spreading along the coasts & rivers
Man at the Neolithic Stage
Bronze Stage
Nippur, Eridu, and other Sumerian city states in existence.
True Egyptians appear. Menes the first Pharaoh.
Sumer before the Semitic ascendancy
Iberians in Britain
SEMITIC PEOPLES
Dravidian civilisations developing
HUNS
ARYANS spreading southward down Balkan peninsula & into Asia Minor, & eastward north of Black Sea & Caspian.
2750 Sargon I founds Akkadian-Sumerian Empire
2500 The First Five Emperors (according to the Chinese histories)
2500 · Crete united under Minos
2100 Hammurabi. First Babylonian Empire
Stonehenge & Avebury in existence
Cnossos at its zenith
Hyksos conquest XVI Dynasty
New Empire
Abraham
Aryans descend into India.
Kelts & Iberians mingling in Spain; Round Barrow Aryans ousting Long " Iberians in Gaul and Britain.. Italians pressing southwards in Italy
Tyre & Sidon flourish
1450 Hittites take Nineveh
1750 Shang Dynasty
The Iliad being sung.
1383 Amenophis IV.
1317 Rameses II
Moses
Philistines
Solomon
1100 Tiglath Pileser I takes Babylon.
1150 Chow Dynasty
800 Carthage founded
753 Rome built
Iron Weapons
722 Sargon II
539 Cyrus takes Babylon
Buddha
551 Confucius b.
470 Hanno's voyage
264 First Punic War
323 – Death of Alexander the Great
264. Asoka King of Behar.
Shi-Huang-Ti.
Julius Caesar
J.F.H.

shouted or banged or blown more or less in unison. Women and youths sang an octave higher than the men. Stamping, hand-clapping, primitive drumming helped. This is true also of the Jewish and Greek music up to the beginnings of the Christian era. Arab music still knows nothing of harmony. The music consists of rhythmical cadences with a rather monotonous melody. Voices, strings, cymbals go in unison to the incessant throb of the tambourines. This is probably a perfect survival of the music of Egypt and Babylon.

The pictures and sculptures of the ancient civilizations representing musical performances suggest exactly that. The drum is shown in a variety of forms and the timbrel or tambourine. The cymbals clashed—they are shown in Assyrian reliefs—and the Egyptian sistrum gave a jangling undertow of melodious sounds. There were flutes and double flutes, flageolets and mouth organs. There were horns and metal trumpets, simple trumpets that merely uttered loud blasts at salient points. Finally, growing out of the Neolithic bow there were a number of stringed instruments across which the player drew either his fingers or a plectrum. These were the lyre, the harp, the psaltery, the lute and dulcimer. The lute enhanced its strings with a resonating gourd-shaped body. The mandoline has this shape also. The banjo is the lute's vulgar little descendant. The harp was perhaps the largest and best developed of ancient musical instruments. The dulcimer was a stringed instrument with a horizontal frame.

Just as literature in the ancient world was unable to develop to the full because of the imperfect development of writing, so music was restrained by the want of a practicable notation. Men had much the same ears and imaginations then as now, but they could not keep hold of the subject or hand on their achievements to supply fresh points of departure to their successors.

BOOK IV

JUDEA, GREECE, AND INDIA

XVIII

THE HEBREW SCRIPTURES AND THE PROPHETS

§ 1. *The Place of the Israelites in History.* § 2. *Saul, David, and Solomon.* § 3. *The Jews a People of Mixed Origin.* § 4. *The Importance of the Hebrew Prophets.*

§ 1

WE ARE now in a position to place in their proper relationship to this general outline of human history the Israelites and the most remarkable collection of ancient documents in the world, that collection which is known to all Christian peoples as the Old Testament. We find in these documents the most interesting and valuable lights upon the development of civilization, and the clearest indications of a new spirit that was coming into human affairs during the struggles of Egypt and Assyria for predominance in the world of men.

All the books that constitute the Old Testament were certainly in existence, and in very much their present form, at latest by the year 100 B.C. Most of them were probably recognized as sacred writings in the time of Alexander the Great (330 B.C.). They were the sacred literature of a people, the Jews, who, except for a small remnant of common people, had recently been deported to Babylonia from their own country in 587 B.C. by Nebuchadnezzar II, the Chaldean. They had returned to their city, Jerusalem, and had rebuilt their temple there under the auspices of Cyrus, that Persian conqueror who, we have already noted, in 539 B.C. overthrew Nabonidus, the last of the Chaldean rulers in Babylon. The Babylonian Captivity had lasted about fifty years, and many authorities are of opinion that there was a considerable admixture during that period both of race and ideas with the Babylonians.

The position of the land of Judea and of Jerusalem, its capital, is a peculiar one. The country is a band-shaped strip between the Mediterranean to the west and the desert beyond the Jordan to the east; through it lies the natural high road between the Hittites, Syria, Assyria, and Babylonia to the north and Egypt to the south. It was a country predestined, therefore, to a stormy history. Across it Egypt, and whatever power was ascendant in the north, fought for empire; against its people they fought for a trade route. It had itself not the area, the agricultural possibilities, nor the mineral wealth to be important. The story of its people that these scriptures have preserved runs like a commentary to the greater history of the two systems of civilization to the north and south and of the sea peoples to the west.

These scriptures consist of a number of different elements. The first five books, the *Pentateuch,* were early regarded with peculiar respect. They begin in the form of a universal history with a double account of the Creation of the world and mankind, of the early life of the race, and of a great Flood by which, except for certain favoured individuals, mankind was destroyed. This Flood story is very widely distributed in ancient tradition; it may be a memory of that flooding of the Mediterranean valley which occurred in the Neolithic age of mankind. Or it may recall some great catastrophe in Georgia and the Caspian region. Excavations have revealed Babylonian versions of both the Creation story and the Flood story of prior date to the restoration of the Jews, and it is therefore argued by Biblical critics that these opening chapters were acquired by the Jews during their captivity. They constitute the first ten chapters of Genesis.

There follows a history of the fathers and founders of the Hebrew nation, Abraham, Isaac, and Jacob. They are presented as patriarchal Bedouin chiefs, living the life of nomadic shepherds in the country between Babylonia and Egypt. The existing Biblical account is said by the critics to be made up out of several pre-existing versions; but whatever its origins, the story, as we have it to-day, is full of colour and vitality. What is called Palestine to-day was at that time the land of Canaan, inhabited by a Semitic people called the Canaanites, closely related to the Phœnicians who founded Tyre and Sidon, and to the Amorites who took Babylon and, under Hammurabi, founded the first Babylonian Empire.

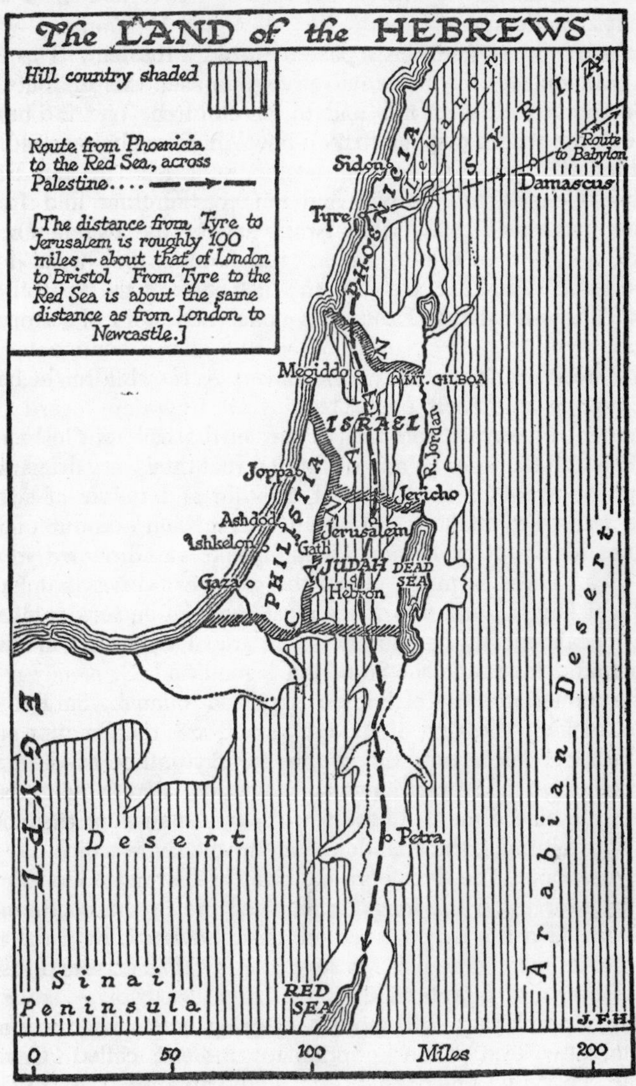
The LAND of the HEBREWS
Hill country shaded
Route from Phoenicia to the Red Sea, across Palestine....
[The distance from Tyre to Jerusalem is roughly 100 miles—about that of London to Bristol From Tyre to the Red Sea is about the same distance as from London to Newcastle.]
SYRIA
Lebanon
PHOENICIA
Route to Babylon
Sidon
Damascus
Tyre
CANAAN
Megiddo
MT. GILBOA
ISRAEL
R. Jordan
Joppa
Jericho
Ashdod
Ashkelon
Gath
Jerusalem
PHILISTIA
JUDAH
DEAD SEA
Gaza
Hebron
EGYPT
Desert
Petra
Arabian Desert
Sinai Peninsula
RED SEA
J.F.H.
0
50
100
Miles
200

The Canaanites were a settled folk in the days—which were perhaps contemporary with the days of Hammurabi—when Abraham's flocks and herds passed through the land. The God of Abraham, says the Bible narrative, promised this smiling land of prosperous cities to him and to his children. To the book of Genesis the reader must go to read how Abraham, being childless, doubted this promise, and of the births of Ishmael and Isaac. And in Genesis, too, he will find the lives of Isaac and Jacob, whose name was changed to Israel, and of the twelve sons of Israel; and how in the days of a great famine, they went down into Egypt. With that, Genesis, the first book of the Pentateuch, ends. The next book, Exodus, is concerned with the story of Moses.

The story of the settlement and slavery of the children of Israel in Egypt is a difficult one. There is an Egyptian record of a settlement of certain Semitic peoples in the land of Goshen by the Pharaoh Rameses II, and it is stated that they were drawn into Egypt by want of food. But of the life and career of Moses there is no Egyptian record at all; there is no account of any plagues of Egypt or of any Pharaoh who was drowned in the Red Sea. There is much about the story of Moses that has a mythical flavour, and one of the most remarkable incidents in it, his concealment by his mother in an ark of bulrushes, has also been found in an ancient Sumerian legend.

The Sumerian story of Sargon I runs as follows: "Sargon, the powerful king the king of Akkadia am I; my mother was poor, my father I knew not; the brother of my father lived in the mountains. . . . My mother, who was poor, secretly gave birth to me; she placed me in a *basket of reeds*, she shut up the mouth of it with bitumen, she abandoned me to the river, which did not overwhelm me. The river bore me away and brought me to Akki the irrigator. Akki the irrigator received me in the goodness of his heart. Akki the irrigator reared me to boyhood. Akki the irrigator made me a gardener. My service as a gardener was pleasing unto Ishtar and I became king."

This is perplexing. Still more perplexing is the discovery of a clay tablet written by the Egyptian governors of a city in Canaan to the Pharaoh Amenophis IV, who came in the XVIIIth Dynasty before Rameses II, apparently mentioning the Hebrews by name and declaring that they are overrunning Canaan. Manifestly, if the Hebrews were conquering Canaan in the time of the XVIIIth Dynasty, they could not have been made captive and oppressed, before they conquered Canaan, by Rameses II of the XIXth Dynasty. But it is quite understandable that the Exodus story, written long after the events it narrates, may have concentrated and simplified, and perhaps personified, and symbolized, what was really a long and complicated history of tribal invasions. One Hebrew tribe may have drifted down into Egypt and become enslaved, while the others were already attacking the outlying Canaanite cities. It is even possible that the land of the captivity was not Egypt (Hebrew, Misraim), but Misrim in the north of Arabia, on the other side of the Red Sea. These questions are discussed fully and acutely in the *Encyclopœdia Biblica* (articles *Moses* and *Exodus*), to which the curious reader must be referred.

Two other books of the Pentateuch, Deuteronomy and Leviticus, are concerned with the Law and the priestly rules. The book of Numbers takes up the wanderings of the Israelites in the desert and their invasion of Canaan.

Whatever the precise particulars of the Hebrew invasion of Canaan may be, there can be no doubt that the country they invaded had changed very greatly since the days of the legendary promise, made centuries before, to Abraham. Then it seems to have been largely a Semitic land, with many prosperous trading cities. But great waves of strange peoples had washed along this coast. We have already told how the dark Iberian or Mediterranean peoples of Italy and Greece, the peoples of that Ægean civilization which culminated at Cnossos, were being assailed by the southward movement of Aryan-speaking races, such as the Italians and Greeks, and how Cnossos was sacked about 1,400 B.C., and destroyed altogether about 1,000 B.C. It is now evident that the people of these Ægean seaports were crossing the sea in search of securer land rests. They invaded the Egyptian delta and the African coast to the west, they formed alliances with the Hittites and other Aryan or Aryanized races.

This happened after the time of Rameses II, in the time of Rameses III. Egyptian monuments record great sea fights, and also a march of these people along the coast of Palestine towards Egypt. Their transport was in the ox-carts characteristic of the Aryan tribes, and it is clear that these Cretans were acting in alliance with some early Aryan invaders. No connected narrative of these conflicts that went on between 1,300 B.C. and 1,000 B.C. has yet been made out, but it is evident from the Bible narrative that when the Hebrews under Joshua pursued their slow subjugation of the promised land, they came against a new people, the Philistines, who were settling along the coast in a series of cities of which Gaza, Gath, Ashdod, Ashkelon and Ekron became the chief, who were really, like the Hebrews, newcomers, and probably chiefly these Cretans from the sea and from the north. The invasion, therefore, that began as an attack upon the Canaanites speedily became a long and not very successful struggle for the coveted and promised land with these much more formidable newcomers, the Philistines.

It cannot be said that the promised land was ever completely in the grasp of the Hebrews. Following after the Pentateuch in the Bible come the books of Joshua, Judges, Ruth (a digression), Samuel I and II, and Kings I and II, with Chronicles repeating with variation much of the matter of Samuel II and Kings; there is a growing flavour of reality in most of this later history, and in these books we find the Philistines steadfastly in possession of the fertile lowlands of the south, and the Canaanites and Phœnicians holding out against the Israelites in the north. The first triumphs of Joshua are not repeated. The book of Judges is a melancholy catalogue of failures. The people lose heart. They desert the worship of their own god Jehovah, and worship Baal and Ashtaroth (= Bell and Ishtar). They mix their race with the Philistines, with the Hittites, and so forth, and become, as they have always subsequently been, a racially mixed people. Under a series of wise men and heroes they wage a generally unsuccessful and never very united warfare against their enemies. In succession they are conquered by the Moabites, the Canaanites, the Midianites, and the Philistines. The story of these conflicts, of Gideon and of Samson and the other heroes who now and then cast a gleam of hope upon the distresses of Israel, is told in the book of Judges. In the first book of Samuel is told the story of their great disaster at Ebenezer in the days when Eli was judge.

This was a real pitched battle in which the Israelites lost 30,000 (!) men. They had previously suffered a reverse and lost 4,000 men, and then they brought out their most sacred symbol, the Ark of the Covenant of God.

"And when the ark of the covenant of the Lord came into the camp, all Israel shouted with a great shout, so that the earth rang again. And when the Philistines heard the noise of the shout, they said, 'What meaneth the noise of this great shout in the camp of the Hebrews?' And they understood that the ark of the Lord was come into the camp. And the Philistines were afraid, for they said, 'God is come into the camp.' And they said, 'Woe unto us! for there hath not been such a thing heretofore. Woe unto us! who shall deliver us out of the hand of these mighty Gods? these are the Gods that smote the Egyptians with all the plagues in the wilderness. Be strong, and quit yourselves like men, O ye Philistines, that ye be not servants unto the Hebrews, as they have been to you: quit yourselves like men, and fight.'"

And the Philistines fought, and fought heroically. "Israel was smitten, and they fled every man into his tent: and there was a very great slaughter, for there fell of Israel thirty thousand footmen. And the ark of God was taken; and the two sons of Eli, Hophni and Phinehas, were slain.

"And there ran a man of Benjamin out of the army, and came to Shiloh the same day, with his clothes rent, and with earth upon his head. And when he came, lo, Eli sat upon a seat by the wayside watching: for his heart trembled for the ark of God. And when the man came into the city, and told it, all the city cried out. And when Eli heard the noise of the crying, he said, 'What meaneth the noise of this tumult?' And the man came in hastily, and told Eli. Now Eli was ninety and eight years old; and his eyes were dim that he could not see. And the man said unto Eli, 'I am he that came out of the army, and I fled to-day out of the army.' And he said, 'What is there done, my son?' And the messenger answered and said, 'Israel is fled before the Philistines, and there hath been also a great slaughter among the people, and thy two sons also, Hophni and Phinehas, are dead, and the ark of God is taken.' And it came to pass, when he made mention of the ark of God, that Eli fell from off the seat backward, by the side of the gate, and his neck brake, and he died: for he was an old man, and heavy. And he had judged Israel forty years.

"And his daughter-in-law, Phinehas' wife, was with child, near to be delivered: and when she heard the tidings that the ark of God was taken, and that her father-in-law and her husband were dead, she bowed herself and travailed: for her pains came upon her. And about the time of her death the women that stood by her said unto her, 'Fear not, for thou hast born a son.' But she answered not, neither did she regard it. And she named the child I-chabod ('Where is the glory?'), saying, 'The glory is departed from Israel': because the ark of God was taken, and because of her father-in-law and her husband." (I Sam., chap. iv.)

The successor of Eli and the last of the judges was Samuel, and at the end of his rule came an event in the history of Israel which paralleled and was suggested by the experience of the greater nations around. A king arose. We are told in vivid language the plain issue between the more ancient rule of priestcraft and the newer fashion in human affairs. It is impossible to avoid a second quotation. How clearly the deep resentment of the priest shows in the Lord's speech to Samuel!

"Then all the elders of Israel gathered themselves together, and came to Samuel unto Ramah, and said unto him: 'Behold, thou art old, and thy sons walk not in thy ways: now make us a king to judge us like all the nations.'

"But the thing displeased Samuel, when they said, 'Give us a king to judge us.' And Samuel prayed unto the Lord. And the Lord said unto Samuel, 'Hearken unto the voice of the people in all that they say unto thee: for they have not rejected thee, but they have rejected me, that I should not reign over them. According to all the works which they have done since the day that I brought them up out of Egypt even unto this day, wherewith they have forsaken me, and served other gods; so do they also unto thee. Now, therefore, hearken unto their voice; howbeit yet protest solemnly unto them, and shew them the manner of the king that shall reign over them.'

"And Samuel told all the words of the Lord unto the people that asked of him a king. And he said, 'This will be the manner of the king that shall reign over you: He will take your sons, and appoint them for himself, for his chariots, and to be his horsemen; and some shall run before his chariots. And he will appoint him captains over thousands, and captains over fifties; and will set them to ear his ground, and to reap his harvest, and to make his instruments of war, and instruments of his chariots. And he will take your daughters to be confectionaries, and to be cooks, and to be bakers. And he will take your fields, and your vineyards, and your oliveyards, even the best of them, and give them to his servants. And he will take the tenth of your seed, and of your vineyards, and give to his officers, and to his servants. And he will take your menservants, and your maidservants, and your goodliest young men, and your asses, and put them to his work. He will take the tenth of your sheep: and ye shall be his servants. And ye shall cry out in that day because of your king which ye shall have chosen you; and the Lord will not hear you in that day.'

"Nevertheless, the people refused to obey the voice of Samuel; and they said, 'Nay; but we will have a king over us; that we also may be like all the nations; and that our king may judge us, and go out before us, and fight our battles.' " (I Sam., chap. viii.)

§ 2

But the nature and position of their land was against the Hebrews, and their first king Saul was no more successful than the judges. The long intrigues of the adventurer David against Saul are told in the rest of the first book of Samuel, and the end of Saul was utter defeat upon Mount Gilboa. His army was overwhelmed by the prowess of the Philistine archers.

"And it came to pass on the morrow, when the Philistines came to strip the slain, that they found Saul and his three sons fallen in Mount Gilboa. And they cut off his head, and stripped off his armour, and sent into the land of the Philistines round about, to publish it in the house of their idols, and among the people. And they put his armour in the house of Ashtaroth; and they fastened his body to the wall of Beth-shan." (I Sam., chap. xxxi.)

David (990 B.C. roughly) was more politic and successful than his predecessor, and he seems to have placed himself under the protection of Hiram, King of Tyre. This Phœnician alliance sustained him, and was the essential element in the greatness of his son Solomon. His story, with its constant assassinations and executions, reads rather like the history of some savage chief than of a civilized monarch. It is told with great vividness in the second book of Samuel.

The first book of King's begins with the reign of King Solomon (960 B.C. roughly). The most interesting thing in that story, from the point of view of the general historian, is the relationship of Solomon to the national religion and the priesthood, and his dealings with the tabernacle, the priest Zadok, and the prophet Nathan.

The opening of Solomon's reign is as bloody as his father's. The last recorded speech of David arranges for the murder of Shimei; his last recorded word is "blood." "But his hoar head bring thou down to the grave with blood," he says, pointing out that though old Shimei is protected by a vow David had made to the Lord so long as David lives, there is nothing to bind Solomon in that matter. Solomon proceeds to murder his brother, who has sought the throne but quailed and made submission. He then deals freely with his brother's party. The weak hold of religion upon the racially and mentally confused Hebrews at that time is shown by the ease with which he replaces the hostile chief priest by his own adherent Zadok, and still more strikingly by the murder of Joab by Benaiah, Solomon's chief ruffian, in the tabernacle, while the victim is claiming sanctuary and holding to the very horns of Jehovah's altar. Then Solomon sets to work, in what was for that time a thoroughly modern spirit, to recast the religion of his people. He continues the alliance with Hiram, King of Tyre, who uses Solomon's kingdom as a high-road by which to reach and build shipping upon the Red Sea, and a hitherto unheard-of wealth accumulates in Jerusalem as a result of this partnership.

Gang labour appears in Israel; Solomon sends relays of men to cut cedarwood in Lebanon under Hiram, and organizes a service of porters through the land. (There is much in all this to remind the reader of the relations of some Central African chief to a European trading concern.) Solomon then builds a palace for himself, and a temple not nearly as big for Jehovah. Hitherto the Ark of the Covenant, the divine symbol of these ancient Hebrews, had abode in a large tent, which had been shifted from one high place to another, and sacrifices had been offered to the God of Israel upon a number of different high places. Now the ark is brought into the golden splendours of the inner chamber of a temple of cedar-sheathed stone, and put between two great winged figures of gilded olivewood, and sacrifices are henceforth to be made only upon the altar before it.

This centralizing innovation will remind the reader of both Akhnaton and Nabonidus. Such things as this are done successfully only when the prestige and tradition and learning of the priestly order has sunken to a very low level.

"And he appointed, according to the order of David his father, the courses of the priests to their service, and the Levites to their charges, to praise and minister before the priests, as the duty of every day required; the porters also by their courses at every gate; for so had David the man of God commanded. And they departed not from the commandment of the king unto the priests and Levites concerning any matter, or concerning the treasures."

Neither Solomon's establishment of the worship of Jehovah in Jerusalem upon this new footing nor his vision of and conversation with his God at the opening of his reign stood in the way of his developing a sort of theological flirtatiousness in his declining years. He married widely, if only for reasons of state and splendour, and he entertained his numerous wives by sacrificing to their national deities, to the Sidonian goddess Ashtaroth (Ishtar), to Chemosh (a Moabitish god), to Moloch, and so forth. The Bible account of Solomon does, in fact, show us a king as unstable and in no way more religious than any other, a people superstitious and as mentally confused as the people of the surrounding world.

A point of considerable interest in the story of Solomon, because it marks a phase in Egyptian affairs, is his marriage to a daughter of Pharaoh. This must have been one of the Pharaohs of the XXIst Dynasty. In the great days of Amenophis III, as the Tell-el-Amarna letters witness. Pharaoh could condescend to receive a Babylonian princess into his harem, but he refused absolutely to grant so divine a creature as an Egyptian princess in marriage to the Babylonian monarch. It points to the steady decline of Egyptian prestige that now, three centuries later, such a petty monarch as Solomon could wed on equal terms with an Egyptian princess. There was, however, a revival with the next Egyptian dynasty (XXII); and the Pharaoh Shishak, the founder, taking advantage of the cleavage between Israel and Judah, which had been developing through the reigns of both David and Solomon, took Jerusalem and looted the all-too-brief splendours both of the new temple and of the king's house.

Shishak seems also to have subjugated Philistia. From this time onward it is to be noted that Philistines fade in importance. They had already lost their Cretan language and adopted that of the Semites they had conquered, and although their cities remain more or less independent, they merge gradually into the general Semitic life of Palestine.

There is evidence that the original rude but convincing narrative of Solomon's rule, of his various murders, of his association with Hiram, of his palace and temple building, and the extravagances that weakened his kingdom and finally tore it in twain, has been subjected to extensive interpolations and expansions by a later writer, anxious to exaggerate his prosperity and glorify his wisdom. This is not the place to deal with the criticism of Bible origins, but it is a matter of ordinary common sense rather than of scholarship to note the manifest reality and veracity of the main substance of the account of David and Solomon, an account explaining sometimes and justifying sometimes, but nevertheless relating facts, even the harshest facts, as only a contemporary or almost contemporary writer, convinced that they cannot be concealed, would relate them, and then to remark the sudden lapse into adulation when the inserted passages occur.

It is a striking tribute to the power of the written assertion over realities in men's minds, that this Bible narrative has imposed, not only upon the Christian, but upon the Moslem world, the belief that King Solomon was not only one of the most magnificent but one of the wisest of men. Yet the first book of Kings tells in detail his utmost splendours, and beside the beauty and wonder of the buildings and organizations of such a great monarch as Thothmes III or Rameses II or half a dozen other Pharaohs, or of Sargon II or Sardanapalus or Nebuchadnezzar the Great, they are trivial. His temple measured internally was twenty cubits broad, about 35 feet—that is, the breadth of a small villa residence —and sixty cubits, say 100 feet, long. Estimates of the cubit vary. The greatest is 44 inches. This would extend the width to seventy odd feet and the length to 200 feet. And as for his wisdom and statecraft, one need go no farther than the Bible to see that Solomon was a mere helper in the wide-reaching schemes of the trader-king Hiram, and his kingdom a pawn between Phœnicia and Egypt. His importance was due largely to the temporary enfeeblement of Egypt, which encouraged the ambition of the Phœnician and made it necessary to propitiate the holder of the key to an alternate trade route to the East. To his own people Solomon was a wasteful and oppressive monarch, and already before his death his kingdom was splitting visibly to all men.

With the reign of King Solomon the brief glory of the Hebrews ends; the northern and richer section of his kingdom, long oppressed by taxation to sustain his splendours, breaks off from Jerusalem to become the separate kingdom of Israel, and this split ruptures that linking connection between Tyre and Sidon and the Red Sea by which Solomon's gleam of wealth was possible. There is no more wealth in Hebrew history. Jerusalem remains the capital of one tribe, the tribe of Judah, the capital of a land of barren hills, cut off by Philistia from the sea and surrounded by enemies.

The tale of wars, of religious conflicts, of usurpations, assassinations, and of fratricidal murders to secure the throne goes on for three centuries. It is a tale frankly barbaric. Israel wars with Judah and the neighbouring states; forms alliances first with one and then with the other. The power of Aramean Syria burns like a baleful star over the affairs of the Hebrews, and then there rises behind it the great and growing power of the last Assyrian empire. For three centuries the life of the Hebrews was like the life of a man who insists upon living in the middle of a busy thoroughfare, and is consequently being run over constantly by omnibuses and motor-lorries.

"Pul" (apparently the same person as Tiglath Pileser III) is, according to the Bible narrative, the first Assyrian monarch to appear above the Hebrew horizon, and Menahem buys him off with a thousand talents of silver (738 B.C.). But the power of Assyria is heading straight for the now aged and decadent land of Egypt, and the line of attack lies through Judea; Tiglath Pileser III returns and Shalmaneser follows in his steps, the King of Israel intrigues for help with Egypt, that "broken reed," and in 721 B.C., as we have already noted, his kingdom is swept off into captivity and utterly lost to history. The same fate hung over Judah, but for a little while it was averted. The fate of Sennacherib's army in the reign of King Hezekiah (701 B.C.), and how he was murdered by his sons (II Kings xix, 37), we have already mentioned. The subsequent subjugation of Egypt by Assyria finds no mention in Holy Writ, but it is clear that before the reign of Sennacherib, King Hezekiah had carried on a diplomatic correspondence with Babylon (700 B.C.), which was in revolt against Sargon II of Assyria. There followed the conquest of Egypt by Esarhaddon, and then for a time Assyria was occupied with her own troubles; the Scythians and Medes and Persians were pressing her on the north, and Babylon was in insurrection. As we have already noted, Egypt, relieved for a time from Assyrian pressure, entered upon a phase of revival, first under Psammetichus and then under Necho II.

Again the little country in between made mistakes in its alliances. But on neither side was there safety. Josiah opposed Necho, and was slain at the battle of Megiddo (608 B.C.). The king of Judah became an Egyptian tributary. Then when Necho, after pushing as far as the Euphrates, fell before Nebuchadnezzar II, Judah fell with him (604 B.C.). Nebuchadnezzar, after a trial of three puppet kings, carried off the greater part of the people into captivity in Babylon (586 B.C.), and the rest, after a rising and a massacre of Babylonian officials, took refuge from the vengeance of Chaldea in Egypt.

"And all the vessels of the house of God, great and small, and the treasures of the house of the Lord, and the treasures of the king, and of his princes; all these he brought to Babylon. And they burnt the house of God and brake down the wall of Jerusalem, and burnt all the palaces thereof with fire, and destroyed all the goodly vessels thereof. And them that had escaped from the sword carried he away to Babylon; where they were servants to him and his sons until the reign of the kingdom of Persia." (II Chron., xxxvi, 18, 19, 20.)

So the four centuries of Hebrew kingship come to an end. From first to last it was a mere incident in the larger and greater history of Egypt, Syria, Assyria, and Phœnicia. But out of it there were now to arise moral and intellectual consequences of primary importance to all mankind.

§ 3

The Jews who returned, after an interval of more than two generations, to Jerusalem from Babylonia in the time of Cyrus were a very different people from the warring Baal worshippers and Jehovah worshippers, the sacrificers in the high places and sacrificers at Jerusalem of the kingdoms of Israel and Judah. The plain fact of the Bible narrative is that the Jews went to Babylon barbarians and came back civilized. They went a confused and divided multitude, with no national self-consciousness; they came back with an intense and exclusive national spirit. They went with no common literature generally known to them, for it was only about forty years before the captivity that King Josiah is said to have discovered "a book of the law" in the temple (II Kings xxii), and besides that, there is not a hint in the record of any reading of books; and they returned with most of their material for the Old Testament. It is manifest that, relieved of their bickering and murderous kings, restrained from politics and in the intellectually stimulating atmosphere of that Babylonian world, the Jewish mind made a great step forward during the captivity.

It was an age of historical inquiry and learning in Babylonia. The Babylonian influences that had made Sardanapalus collect a great library of ancient writings in Nineveh were still at work. We have already told how Nabonidus was so preoccupied with antiquarian research as to neglect the defence of his kingdom against Cyrus. Everything, therefore, contributed to set the exiled Jews inquiring into their own history, and they found an inspiring leader in the prophet Ezekiel. From such hidden and forgotten records as they had with them, genealogies, contemporary histories of David, Solomon, and their other kings, legends and traditions, they made out and amplified their own story, and told it to Babylon and themselves. The story of the Creation and the Flood, much of the story of Moses, much of Samson, were probably incorporated from Babylonian sources. One version of the Creation story and one of the Eden story, though originally from Babylon, seem to have been known to the Hebrews before the exile. When the Jews returned to Jerusalem, only the Pentateuch had been put together into one book, but the grouping of the rest of the historical books was bound to follow.

The rest of their literature remained for some centuries as separate books, to which a very variable amount of respect was paid. Some of the later books are frankly post-captivity compositions. Over all this literature were thrown certain leading ideas. There was an idea, which even these books themselves gainsay in detail, that all the people were pure-blooded children of Abraham; there was next an idea of a promise made by Jehovah to Abraham that he would exalt the Jewish race above all other races; and thirdly, there was the belief first of all that Jehovah was the greatest and most powerful of tribal gods, and then that he was a god above all other gods, and at last that he was the only true god. The Jews became convinced at last, as a people, that they were the chosen people of the one God of all the earth.

And arising very naturally out of these three ideas, was a fourth, the idea of a coming leader, a saviour, a Messiah who would realize the long-postponed promises of Jehovah.

This welding together of the Jews into one tradition-cemented people in the course of the "seventy years," is the first instance in history of the new power of the written word in human affairs. It was a mental consolidation that did much more than unite the people who returned to Jerusalem. This idea of belonging to a chosen race predestined to pre-eminence was a very attractive one. It possessed also those Jews who remained in Babylonia. Its literature reached the Jews now established in Egypt. It affected the mixed people who had been placed in Samaria, the old capital of the kings of Israel when the ten tribes were deported to Media. It inspired a great number of Babylonians and the like to claim Abraham as their father, and thrust their company upon the returning Jews. Ammonites and Moabites became adherents. The book of Nehemiah is full of the distress occasioned by this invasion of the privileges of the chosen. The Jews were already a people dispersed in many lands and cities, when their minds and hopes were unified and they became an exclusive people. But at first their exclusiveness is merely to preserve soundness of doctrine and worship, warned by such lamentable lapses as those of

King Solomon. To genuine proselytes of whatever race, Judaism long held out welcoming arms.

To Phœnicians after the fall of Tyre and Carthage, conversion to Judaism must have been particularly easy and attractive. Their language was closely akin to Hebrew. It is possible that the great majority of African and Spanish Jews are really of Phœnician origin. There were also great Arabian accessions. In South Russia, as we shall note later, there were even Mongolian Jews.

§ 4

The historical books from Genesis to Nehemiah, upon which the idea of the promise to the chosen people had been imposed later, were no doubt the backbone of Jewish mental unity, but they by no means complete the Hebrew literature from which finally the Bible was made up. Of such books as Job, said to be an imitation of Greek tragedy, the Song of Solomon, the Psalms, Proverbs, and others, there is no space to write in this *Outline*, but it is necessary to deal with the books known as "the Prophets" with some fullness. For those books are almost the earliest and certainly the best evidence of the appearance of a new kind of leading in human affairs.

These prophets are not a new class in the community; they are of the most various origins—Ezekiel was of the priestly caste and of priestly sympathies, and Amos was a shepherd; but they have this in common, that they bring into life a religious force outside the sacrifices and formalities of priesthood and temple. The earlier prophets seem most like the earlier priests, they are oracular, they give advice and foretell events; it is possible that at first, in the days when there were many high places in the land and religious ideas were comparatively unsettled, there was no great distinction between priest and prophet.

The prophets danced, it would seem, somewhat after the Dervish fashion, and uttered oracles. Generally they wore a distinctive mantle of rough goatskin. They kept up the nomadic tradition as against the "new ways" of the settlement. But after the building of the temple and the organization of the priesthood the prophetic type remains over and outside the formal religious scheme. They were probably always more or less of an annoyance to the priests. They became informal advisers upon public affairs, denouncers of sin and strange practices, "self-constituted," as we should say, having no sanction but an inner light. "Now the word of the Lord came unto"—so and so; that is the formula.

In the latter and most troubled days of the kingdom of Judah, as Egypt, North Arabia, Assyria, and then Babylonia closed like a vice upon the land, these prophets became very significant and powerful. Their appeal was to anxious and fearful minds, and at first their exhortation was chiefly towards repentance, the pulling down of this or that high place, the restoration of worship in Jerusalem, or the like. But through some of the prophecies there runs already a note like the note of what we call nowadays a "social reformer." The rich are "grinding the faces of the poor"; the luxurious are consuming the children's bread; influential and wealthy people imitate the splendours and vices of foreigners, and sacrifice the common people to these new fashions; and this is hateful to Jehovah, who will certainly punish the land.

But with the broadening of ideas that came with the Captivity, the tenor of prophecy broadens and changes. The jealous pettiness that disfigures the earlier tribal ideas of God gives place to a new idea of a god of universal righteousness. It is clear that the increasing influence of prophets was not confined to the Jewish people; it was something that was going on in those days all over the Semitic world. The breaking down of nations and kingdoms to form the great and changing empires of that age, the smashing up of cults and priesthoods, the mutual discrediting of temple by temple in their rivalries and disputes—all these influences were releasing men's minds to a freer and wider religious outlook. The temples had accumulated great stores of golden vessels and lost their hold upon the imaginations of men.

It is difficult to estimate whether, amidst these constant wars, life had become more uncertain and unhappy than it had ever been before, but there can be no doubt that men had become more conscious of its miseries and insecurities. Except for the weak and the women, there remained little comfort or assurance in the sacrifices, ritual, and formal devotions of the temples. Such was the world to which the later prophets of Israel began to talk of the One God, and of a Promise that some day the world should come to peace and unity and happiness. This great God that men were now discovering lived in a temple "not made with hands, eternal in the heavens." There can be little doubt of a great body of such thought and utterance in Babylonia, Egypt, and throughout the Semitic east. The prophetic books of the Bible can be but specimens of the prophesyings of that time.

We have already drawn attention to the gradual escape of writing and knowledge from their original limitation to the priesthood and the temple precincts, from the shell in which they were first developed and cherished. We have taken Herodotus as an interesting specimen of what we have called the free intelligence of mankind. Now here we are dealing with a similar overflow of moral ideas into the general community. The Hebrew prophets and the steady expansion of their ideas towards one God in all the world, is a parallel development of the free conscience of mankind. From this time onward there runs through human thought, now weakly and obscurely, now gathering power, the idea of one rule in the world, and of a promise and possibility of an active and splendid peace and happiness in human affairs. From being a temple religion of the old type, the Jewish religion becomes, to a large extent, a prophetic and creative religion of a new type. Prophet succeeds prophet.

Later on, as we shall tell, there was born a prophet of unprecedented power, Jesus, whose followers founded the great universal religion of Christianity. Still later Muhammad, another prophet, appears in Arabia and founds Islam. In spite of very distinctive features of their own, these two teachers do in a manner arise out of, and in succession to, these Jewish prophets. It is not the place of the historian to discuss the truth and falsity of religion, but it is his business to record the appearance of great constructive ideas. Two thousand four hundred years ago, and six or seven or eight thousand years after the walls of the first Sumerian cities arose, the ideas of the moral unity of mankind and of a world peace had come into the world.

XIX

THE ARYAN-SPEAKING PEOPLES IN PREHISTORIC TIMES

§ 1. *The Spreading of the Aryan-Speakers.* § 2. *About the Original Life of the Aryans.* § 3. *The Aryan Family.*

§ 1

WE HAVE spoken of the Aryan language as probably arising in the region of the Danube and South Russia and spreading from that region of origin. We say "probably," because it is by no means certainly proved that that was the centre; there have been vast discussions upon this point and wide divergences of opinion. We give the prevalent view. It was originally the language of a group of peoples of the Nordic race. As it spread widely, Aryan began to differentiate into a number of subordinate languages. To the west and south it encountered the Basque language, which prevailed in Spain, and also possibly various other Mediterranean languages.

Before the expansion of the Aryans from their lands of origin southward and westward, the Iberian race was distributed over Great Britain, Ireland, France, Spain, North Africa, South Italy and in a more civilized state, Greece and Asia Minor. It was closely related to the Egyptian. To judge by its European vestiges it was a rather small human type, generally with an oval face and a long head. It buried its chiefs and important people in megalithic chambers—i.e., made of big stones—covered over by great mounds of earth; and these mounds of earth, being much longer than they are broad, are spoken of as the long barrows. These people sheltered at times in caves, and also buried some of their dead therein; and from the traces of charred, broken, and cut human bones, including the bones of children, it is inferred that they were cannibals.

These short dark Iberian tribes (and the Basques also if they were a different race) were thrust back westward, and conquered and enslaved by slowly advancing waves of the taller and fairer Aryan-speaking peoples coming southward and westward through Central Europe, who are spoken of as the Kelts. Only the Basque resisted the conquering Aryan speech. Gradually these Keltic-speakers made their way to the Atlantic, and all that now remains of the Iberians is mixed into the Keltic population. How far the Keltic invasion affected the Irish population is a matter of debate at the present time; in that island the Kelts may have been a mere caste of conquerors who imposed their language on a larger subject population. The same may be true of Spain. It is even doubtful if the north of England is more Nordic than pre-Keltic in blood. There is a sort of short dark Welshman, and certain types of Irishmen, who are Iberians by race. The modern Portuguese are also largely of Iberian blood.

The Kelts spoke a language, Keltic, of which it has been said that it combined an Aryan vocabulary with a Berber (or Iberian) grammar, which was in its turn to differentiate into the language of Gaul, Welsh, Breton, Scotch and Irish Gaelic, and other tongues. The Kelts buried the ashes of their chiefs and important people in round barrows. While these Nordic Kelts were spreading westward, other Nordic Aryan peoples were pressing down upon the dark white Mediterranean race in the Italian and Greek peninsulas, and developing the Latin and Greek groups of tongues. Certain other Aryan tribes were drifting towards the Baltic and across into Scandinavia, speaking varieties of Aryan which became ancient Norse—the parent of Swedish, Danish, Norwegian, and Icelandic—Gothic, and Low and High German.

While the primitive Aryan speech was thus spreading and breaking up into daughter languages to the west, it was also spreading and breaking up to the east. North of the Carpathians and the Black Sea, Aryan-speaking tribes were using a distinctive dialect called Slavonian, from which came Russian, Serbian, Polish, Czech, and other tongues; other variations of Aryan distributed over Asia Minor and Persia were also being individualized as Armenian and Indo-Iranian, the parent of Sanscrit and Persian. In this book we have used the word Aryan for all this family of languages, but the term Indo-European is sometimes used for the entire family, and "Aryan" itself restricted in a narrower sense to the Indo-Iranian speech. This Indo-Iranian speech was destined to split later into a number of languages, including Persian and Sanscrit, the latter being the language of certain tribes of

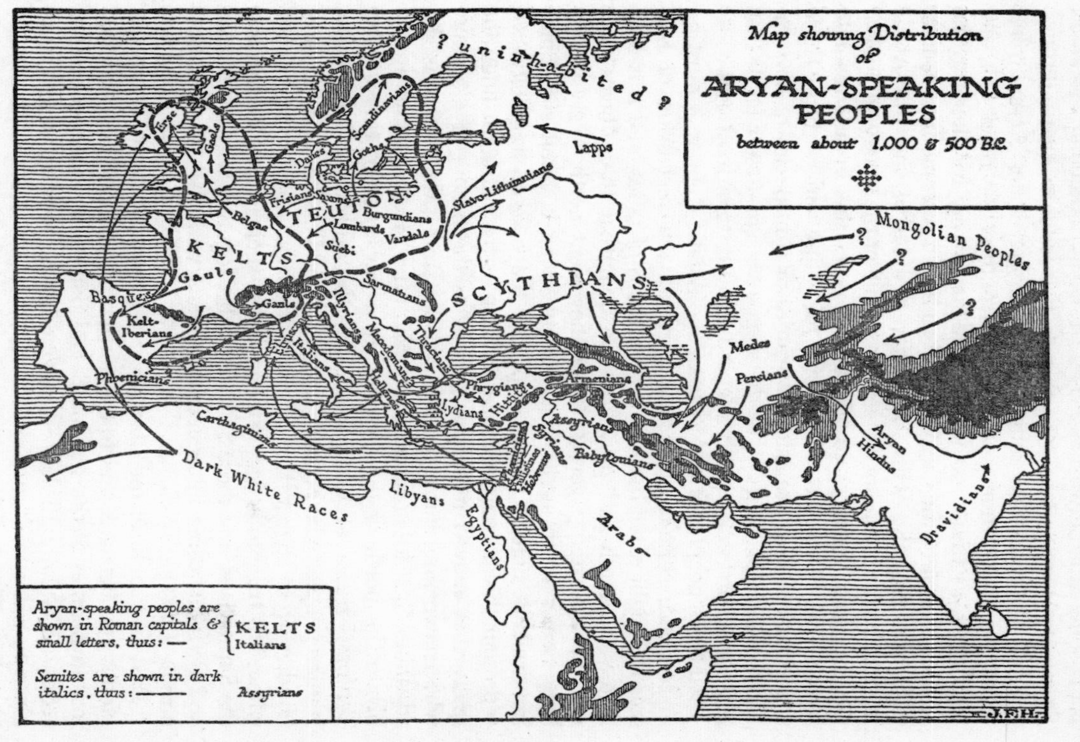
Map showing Distribution of
ARYAN-SPEAKING PEOPLES
between about 1,000 & 500 B.C.
? uninhabited ?
Lapps
Mongolian Peoples
Erse
Gaels
Danes
Goths
Scandinavians
Frisians
Saxons
TEUTONS
Burgundians
Lombards
Vandals
Suebi
Belgae
KELTS
Gauls
Slavo-Lithuanians
SCYTHIANS
Sarmatians
Basques
Kelt-Iberians
Illyrians
Macedonians
Thracians
Italians
Hellenes
Phrygians
Hittites
Lydians
Armenians
Assyrians
Syrians
Babylonians
Medes
Persians
Aryan Hindus
Dravidians
Phoenicians
Carthaginians
Dark White Races
Libyans
Egyptians
Hebrews
Philistines
Arabs
Aryan-speaking peoples are shown in Roman capitals & small letters, thus:— KELTS Italians
Semites are shown in dark italics, thus:— Assyrians
J.F.H.

fair-complexioned Aryan speakers who pushed eastward into India some time between 3,000 and 1,000 B.C. and conquered dark Dravidian peoples who were then in possession of that land.

From their original range of wandering, other Aryan tribes spread to the north as well as to the south of the Black Sea, and ultimately, as these seas shrank and made way for them, to the north and east of the Caspian, and so began to come into conflict with and mix also with Mongolian peoples of the Ural-Altaic linguistic group, the horse-keeping people of the grassy steppes of Central Asia. From these Mongolian races the Aryans seem to have acquired the use of the horse for riding and warfare. There were three or four prehistoric varieties or sub-species of horse in Europe and Asia, but it was the steppe or semi-desert lands that first gave horses of a build adapted to other than food uses.

All these peoples of the Russian and Asiatic steppes, it must be understood, shifted their ground rapidly; a succession of bad seasons might drive them many hundreds of miles, and it is only in a very rough and provisional manner that their "beats" can now be indicated. Every summer they went north, every winter they swung south again. This annual swing covered sometimes hundreds of miles. On our maps, for the sake of simplicity, we represent the shifting of nomadic peoples by a straight line; but really they moved in annual swings, as the broom of a servant who is sweeping out a passage swishes from side to side as she advances. Spreading round the north of the Black Sea, and probably to the north of the Caspian from the range of the original Teutonic tribes of Central and North-Central Europe to the Iranian peoples who became the Medes and Persians and (Aryan) Hindus, were the grazing lands of a confusion of tribes, about whom it is truer to be vague than precise, such as the Cimmerians, the Sarmatians, and those Scythians who, together with the Medes and Persians, came into effective contact with the Assyrian Empire by 1,000 B.C. or earlier.

East and south of the Black Sea, between the Danube and the Medes and Persians, and to the north of the Semitic and Mediterranean peoples of the sea coasts and peninsulas, ranged another series of equally ill-defined Aryan tribes, moving easily from place to place and intermixing freely—to the great confusion of historians. They seem, for instance, to have broken up and assimilated the Hittite civilization, which was probably pre-Aryan in its origin. These latter Aryans were, perhaps, not so far advanced along the nomadic line as the Scythians of the great plains.

§ 2

What sort of life did these prehistoric Aryans lead, these Nordic Aryans who were the chief ancestors of most Europeans and most white Americans and European colonists of to-day, as well as of the Persians and high-caste Hindus? They may also have been the ancestors of the Armenians, but these were more probably a non-Aryan, it may be a Hittite, people who learnt an Aryan speech.

In answering that question, we have a new source of knowledge, in addition to the dug-up remains and vestiges upon which we have had to rely in the case of the predecessors of the Aryans. We have language. By a careful study of the Aryan languages it has been found possible to deduce a number of conclusions about the life of these peoples 5,000 or 4,000 years ago.

All these languages have a common resemblance; each, as we have already explained, rings the changes upon a number of common roots. When we find the same root word running through all or most of these tongues, it seems reasonable to conclude that the thing that root word signifies must have been known to the common ancestors. Of course, if they have *exactly the same word* in their languages, this may not be the case; it may be the new name of a new thing or of a new idea that has spread over the world quite recently. "Gas," for instance, is a word that was made by Van Helmont, a Dutch chemist, about 1625, and has spread into most civilized tongues; and "tobacco" again is an American-Indian word which followed the introduction of smoking almost everywhere. But if the same word turns up in a number of languages, and *if it follows the characteristic modifications of each language*, we may feel sure that it has been in that language, and a part of that language, since the beginning, suffering the same changes with the rest of it. We know, for example, that the words for wagon and wheel run in this fashion through the Aryan tongues, and so we are able to conclude that the primitive Aryans, the more purely Nordic Aryans had wagons, though it would seem from the absence of any common roots for spokes, rim, or axle that their wheels were not wheelwright's wheels with spokes, but made of the trunks of trees shaped out with an axe between the ends.

These primitive wagons were drawn by oxen. The early Aryans did not ride or drive horses; they had very little to do with horses. The Neolithic Mongols were a horse-people, but the Neolithic Aryans were a cow-people. They ate beef, not horse; and after many ages they began this use of draught cattle. They reckoned wealth by cows. They wandered, following pasture, and "trekking" their goods, as the South African Boers do, in ox-wagons, though of course their wagons were much clumsier than any to be found in the world to-day. They probably ranged over very wide areas. They were migratory, but not in the strict sense of the word "nomadic"; they moved in a slower, clumsier fashion than did the later, more specialized nomadic peoples. They were forest and parkland people without horses. They were developing a migratory life out of the more settled "forest clearing" life of the earlier Neolithic period. Changes of climate which were replacing forest by pasture, and the accidental burning of forests by fire, may have assisted this development.

We have already described the sort of home the primitive Aryan occupied and his household life, so far as the remains of the Swiss pile-dwellings enable us to describe these things. Mostly his houses were of too flimsy a sort, probably of wattle and mud, to have survived, and possibly he left them and trekked on for very slight reasons. The Aryan peoples burnt their dead, a custom they still preserve in India, but their predecessors, the long-barrow people, the Iberians, buried their dead lying on the side in a sitting position. In some ancient Aryan burial mounds (round barrows) the urns containing the ashes of the departed are shaped like houses, and these represent rounded huts with thatched roofs.

The grazing of the primitive Aryan was far more important to him than his agriculture. At first he cultivated with a rough wooden hoe; then, after he had found out the use of cattle for draught purposes, he began real ploughing with oxen, using at first a suitably bent tree bough as his plough. His first cultivation before that came about must have been rather in the form of garden patches near the house buildings than of fields. Most of the land his tribe occupied was common land on which the cattle grazed together.

He never used stone for building house walls until upon the very verge of history. He used stone for hearths (*e.g.*, at Glastonbury), and sometimes stone sub-structures. He did, however, make a sort of stone house in the centre of the great mounds in which he buried the ashes of his illustrious dead. He may have learnt this custom from his Iberian neighbours and predecessors. It was these dark whites of the megalithic culture, and not the primitive Aryans, who were responsible for such temples as Stonehenge in Wiltshire or Carnac in Brittany.

These Aryans were congregated not in cities but in districts of pasturage, as clans and tribal communities. They formed loose leagues of mutual help under chosen leaders, they had centres where they could come, together with their cattle, in times of danger, and they made camps with walls of earth and palisades, many of which are still to be traced in the history-worn contours of the European scenery. The leaders under whom men fought in war were often the same men as the sacrificial purifiers who were their early priests.

The knowledge of bronze spread late in Europe. The Nordic European had been making his slow advances age by age for 7,000 or 8,000 years before the metals came. By that time his social life had developed so that there were men of various occupations and men and women of different ranks in the community. There were men who worked wood and leather, potters and carvers. The women span and wove and embroidered. There were chiefs and families that were distinguished as leaderly and noble.

The Aryan tribesman varied the monotony of his herding and wandering; he consecrated undertakings and celebrated triumphs, held funeral assemblies, and distinguished the traditional seasons of the year, by *feasts*. His meats we have already glanced at; he was an eager user of intoxicating drinks. He made these of honey, of barley, and, as the Aryan-speaking tribes spread southward, of the grape. And he got merry and drunken. Whether he first used yeast to make his bread light or to ferment his drink we do not know.

At his feasts there were individuals with a gift for "playing the fool," who did so no doubt to win the laughter of their friends, but there was also another sort of men, of great importance in their time and still more important to the historian, certain singers of songs and stories, the bards or rhapsodists. These *bards* existed among all the Aryan-speaking peoples; they were a consequence of and a further factor in that development of spoken language which was the chief of all the human advances made in Neolithic times. They chanted or recited stories of the past, or stories of the living chief and his people; they told other stories that they invented; they memorized jokes and catches. They found and seized upon and improved the rhythms, rhymes, alliterations, and such-like possibilities latent in language; they probably did much to elaborate and fix grammatical forms. They were perhaps the first great artists of the ear, as the later Aurignacian rock painters were the first great artists of the eye and hand. No doubt they used much gesture; probably they learnt appropriate gestures when they learnt their songs; but the order and sweetness and power of language was their primary concern.

These bards mark a new step forward in the power and range of the human mind. They sustained and developed in men's minds a sense of a greater something than themselves, the tribe, and of a life that extended back into the past. They not only recalled old hatreds and battles, they recalled old alliances and a common inheritance. The feats of dead heroes lived again. The Aryans began to live in thought before they were born and after they were dead.

Like most human beings, this bardic tradition grew first slowly and then more rapidly. By the time bronze was coming into Europe there was not an Aryan people that had not a profession and training of bards. In their hands language became as beautiful as it is ever likely to be. These bards were living books, man-histories, guardians and makers of a new and more powerful tradition in human life. Every Aryan people had its long poetical records thus handed down, its sagas (Teutonic), its epics (Greek), its vedantic narrative poems (Old Sanscrit). The earliest Aryan people were essentially a people of the voice. The recitation seems to have predominated even in those ceremonial and dramatic dances and that "dressing up" which among most human races have also served for the transmission of tradition.

At that time there was no writing, and when first the art of writing crept into Europe, as we shall tell later, it must have seemed far too slow, clumsy, and lifeless a method of record for men to trouble very much about writing down these glowing and beautiful treasures of the memory. Writing was at first kept for accounts and matters of fact. The bards and rhapsodists flourished for long after the introduction of writing. They survived, indeed, in Europe as the minstrels into the Middle Ages.

Unhappily their tradition had not the fixity of a written record. They amended and reconstructed, they had their fashions and their phases of negligence. Accordingly we have now only the very much altered and revised vestiges of that spoken literature of prehistoric times. One of the most interesting and informing of these prehistoric compositions of the Aryans survives in the Greek *Iliad.* An early form of *Iliad* was probably recited by 1,000 B.C., but it was not written down until perhaps 700 or 600 B.C. Many men must have had to do with it as authors and improvers, but later Greek tradition attributed it to a blind bard named Homer, to whom also is ascribed the *Odyssey,* a composition of a very different spirit and outlook. It is possible that many of the Aryan bards were blind men. According to Professor J. L. Myres, the bards were blinded to prevent their straying from the tribe. Mr. L. Lloyd has seen in Rhodesia the musician of a troupe of native dancers who had been blinded by his chief for this very reason. The Slavs called all bards *sliepac,* which was also their word for blind man.

The original recited version of the *Iliad* was older than that of the *Odyssey.* "The *Iliad* as a complete poem is older than the *Odyssey,*" says Professor Gilbert Murray, "though the material of the *Odyssey,* being largely undatable folk-lore, is older than any of the historical material in the *Iliad.*" Both epics were probably written over and rewritten at a later date, in much the same manner that Lord Tennyson, the poet laureate of Queen Victoria, in his *Idylls of the King,* wrote over the *Morte d'Arthur* (which was itself a writing over by Sir Thomas Malory, *circ.* 1450, of pre-existing legends), making the speeches and sentiments and the characters more in accordance with those of his own time. But the events of the *Iliad* and the *Odyssey,* the way of living they describe, the spirit of the acts recorded, belong to the closing centuries of the prehistoric age. These sagas, epics, and vedas do supply, in addition to archæology and philology, a third source of information about those vanished times. Here, for example, is the concluding passage of the *Iliad,* describing very exactly the making of a prehistoric barrow. (We have taken here Chapman's rhymed translation, correcting certain words with the help of the prose version of Lang, Leaf, and Myers.)

". . . Thus oxen, mules, in waggons straight they put,
Went forth, and an unmeasur'd pile of sylvan matter cut;
Nine days employ'd in carriage, but when the tenth morn shin'd
On wretched mortals, then they brought the bravest of his kind
Forth to be burned. Troy swam in tears. Upon the pile's most height
They laid the body, and gave fire. All day it burn'd, all night.
But when th' elev'nth morn let on earth her rosy fingers shine,
The people flocked about the pile, and first with gleaming wine
Quench'd all the flames. His brothers then, and friends, the snowy bones
Gather'd into an urn of gold, still pouring out their moans.
Then wrapt they in soft purple veils the rich urn, digg'd a pit,
Grav'd it, built up the grave with stones, and quickly piled on it
A barrow. . . .
. . . The barrow heap'd once, all the town
In Jove-nurs'd Priam's court partook a sumptuous fun'ral feast,
And so horse-taming Hector's rites gave up his soul to rest."

Combat between Menelaus & Hector (in the Iliad)

From a platter ascribed to the end of the seventh century in the British Museum. This is probably the earliest known vase bearing a Greek inscription. Greek writing was just beginning. Note the Swastika.

There remains also an old English saga, *Beowulf*, made long before the English had crossed from Germany into England, which winds up with a similar burial. The preparation of a pyre is first described. It is hung round with shields and coats of mail. The body is brought and the pyre fired, and then for ten days the warriors built a mighty mound to be seen afar by the traveller on sea or land.

Beowulf, which is at least a thousand years later than the *Iliad*, is also interesting because one of the main adventures in it is the looting of the treasures of a barrow already ancient in those days.

§ 3

The Greek epics reveal the early Greeks with no knowledge of iron, without writing, and before any Greek-founded cities existed in the land into which they had evidently come quite recently as conquerors. They were spreading southward from the Aryan region of origin. They seem to have been a fair people, newcomers in Greece, newcomers to a land that had been held hitherto by the Mediterranean or Iberian peoples.

Let us, at the risk of a slight repetition, be perfectly clear upon one point. The *Iliad* does not give us the primitive Neolithic life of that Aryan region of origin; it gives us that life already well on the move towards a new state of affairs. Between 15,000 and

6,000 B.C. the Neolithic way of living had spread with the forests and abundant vegetation of the Pluvial Period, over the greater part of the old world, from the Niger to the Hwang-ho and from Ireland to the south of India. Now, as the climate of great portions of the earth was swinging towards drier and more open conditions again, the earlier simpler Neolithic life was developing along two divergent directions. One was leading to a more wandering life, towards at last a constantly migratory life between summer and winter pasture, which is called NOMADISM; the other, in certain sunlit river valleys, was towards a water-treasuring life of irrigation, in which men gathered into the first towns and made the first CIVILIZATION.

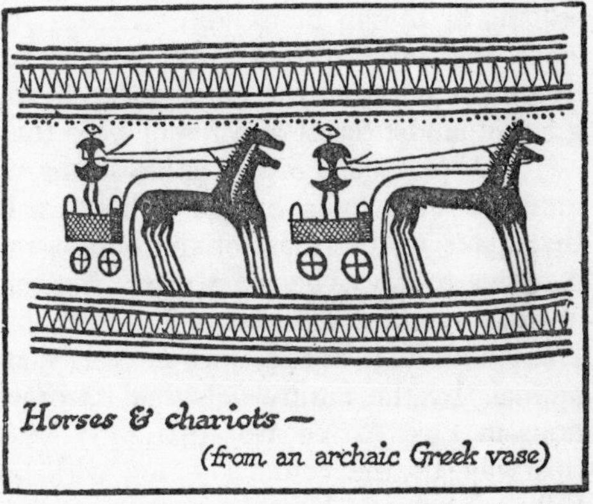

Horses & chariots—
(from an archaic Greek vase)

We have already described the first civilizations and their liability to recurrent conquests by nomadic peoples. We have already noted that for many thousands of years there has been an almost rhythmic recurrence of conquests of the civilizations by the nomads. Here, we have to note that the Greeks, as the *Iliad* presents them, are neither simple Neolithic nomads, innocent of civilization, nor are they civilized men. They are nomads in an excited state, because they have just come upon civilization, and regard it as an opportunity for war and loot.

These early Greeks of the *Iliad* are sturdy fighters, but without discipline—their battles are a confusion of single combats. They have horses, but no cavalry; they use the horse, which is a comparatively recent addition to Aryan resources, to drag a rude fighting chariot into battle. The horse is still novel enough to be something of a terror in itself. For ordinary draught purposes, as in the quotation from the *Iliad* we have just made, oxen were employed.

The only priests of these Aryans are the keepers of shrines and sacred places. There are chiefs, who are heads of families and who also perform sacrifices, but there does not seem to be much mystery or sacramental feeling in their religion. When the Greeks go to war, these heads and elders meet in council and appoint a king, whose powers are very loosely defined. There are no laws, but only customs; and no exact standards to conduct.

The social life of the early Greeks centred about the households of these leading men. There were, no doubt, huts for herds and the like, and outlying farm buildings; but the hall of the chief was a comprehensive centre, to which everyone went to feast, to hear the bards, to take part in games and exercises. The primitive craftsmen were gathered there. About it were cowsheds and stabling and such-like offices. Unimportant people slept about anywhere as retainers did in the mediæval castles and as people still do in Indian households. Except for quite personal possessions, there was still an air of patriarchal communism about the tribe. The tribe, or the chief as the head of the tribe, owned the grazing lands; forest and rivers were the wild.

The Aryan social organization seems, and indeed all early communities seem, to have been without the little separate households that make up the mass of the population in Western Europe or America to-day. The tribe was a big family; the nation a group of tribal families; a household often contained hundreds of people. Human society began, just as herds and droves begin among animals by the family delaying its breaking up. Nowadays the lions in East Africa are apparently becoming social animals in this way, by the young keeping with the mother after they are fully grown, and hunting in a group. Hitherto the lion has been much more of a solitary beast. If men and women do not cling to their families nowadays as much as they did, it is because the state and the community supply now safety and help and facilities that were once only possible in the family group.

In the Hindu community of to-day these great households of the earlier stages of human society are still to be found. Mr. Bhupendranath Basu has recently described a typical Hindu household. It is an Aryan household refined and made gentle by thousands of years of civilization, but its social structure is the same as that of the households of which the Aryan epics tell.

"The joint family system," he said, "has descended to us from time immemorial, the Aryan patriarchal system of old still holding sway in India. The structure, though ancient, remains full of life. The joint family is a co-operative corporation, in which men and women have a well-defined place. At the head of the corporation is the senior member of the family, generally the eldest male member, but in his absence the senior female member often assumes control." (Cp. Penelope in the *Odyssey*.)

"All able-bodied members must contribute their labour and earnings, whether of personal skill or agriculture and trade, to the common stock; weaker members, widows, orphans, and destitute relations, all must be maintained and supported; sons, nephews, brothers, cousins, all must be treated equally, for any undue preference is apt to break up the family. We have no word for cousins—they are either brothers or sisters, and we do not know what are cousins two degrees removed. The children of a first cousin are your nephews and nieces, just the same as the children of your brothers and sisters. A man can no more marry a cousin, however removed, than he can marry his own sister, except in certain parts of Madras, where a man may marry his maternal uncle's daughter. The family affections, the family ties, are always very strong, and therefore the maintenance of an equal standard among so many members is not so difficult as it may appear at first sight. Moreover, life is very simple. Until recently shoes were not in general use at home, but sandals without any leather fastenings. I have known of a well-to-do middle-class family of several brothers and cousins who had two or three pairs of leather shoes between them, these shoes being only used when they had occasion to go out, and the same practice is still followed in the case of the more expensive garments, like shawls, which last for generations, and with their age are treated with loving care, as having been used by ancestors of revered memory.

"The joint family remains together sometimes for several generations, until it becomes too unwieldy, when it breaks up into smaller families, and you thus see whole villages peopled by members of the same clan. I have said that the family is a co-operative society, and it may be likened to a small state, and is kept in its place by strong discipline based on love and obedience. You see nearly every day the younger members coming to the head of the family and taking the dust of his feet as a token of benediction; whenever they go on an enterprise, they take his leave and carry his blessing. . . . There are many bonds which bind the family together—the bonds of sympathy, of common pleasures, of common sorrows; when a death occurs, all the members go into mourning; when there is a birth or a wedding, the whole family rejoices. Then above all is the family deity, some image of Vishnu, the preserver; his place is in a separate room, generally known as the room of God, or in well-to-do families in a temple attached to the house, where the family performs its daily worship. There is a sense of personal attachment between this image of the deity and the family, for the image generally comes down from past generations, often miraculously acquired by a pious ancestor at some remote time. . . . With the household gods is intimately associated the family priest. . . . The Hindu priest is a part of the family life of his flock, between whom and himself the tie has existed for many generations. The priest is not generally a man of much learning; he knows, however, the traditions of his faith. . . . He is not a very heavy burden, for he is satisfied with little—a few handfuls of rice, a few home-grown bananas or vegetables, a little unrefined sugar made in the village, and sometimes a few pieces of copper, are all that is needed. . . .

"A picture of our family life would be incomplete without the household servants. A female servant is known as the 'jhi,' or daughter, in Bengal—she is like the daughter of the house; she calls the master and the mistress father and mother, and the young men and women of the family brothers and sisters. She participates in the life of the family; she goes to the holy places along with her mistress, for she could not go alone, and generally she spends her life with the family of her adoption; her children are looked after by the family. The treatment of men servants is very similar. These servants, men and women, are generally people of the humbler castes, but a sense of personal attachment grows up between them and the members of the family, and as they get on in years they are affectionately called by the younger members elder brothers, uncles, aunts, etc. . . .

"In a well-to-do house there is always a resident teacher, who instructs the children of the family as well as other boys of the village; there is no expensive school building, but room is found in some veranda or shed in the courtyard for the children and their teacher, and into this school low-caste boys are freely admitted. These indigenous schools were not of a very high order, but they supplied an agency of instruction for the masses which was probably not available in many other countries. . . .

"With Hindu life is bound up its traditional duty of hospitality. It is the duty of a householder to offer a meal to any stranger who may come before midday and ask for one; the mistress of the house does not sit down to her meal until every member is fed, and, as sometimes her food is all that is left, she does not take her meal until well after midday lest a hungry stranger should come and claim one." . . .

We have been tempted to quote Mr. Basu at some length, because here we do get to something like a living understanding of the type of household which has prevailed in human communities since Neolithic days, which still prevails to-day in India, China, and the Far East, but which in the West is rapidly giving ground before a state and municipal organization of education and a large-scale industrialism within which an amount of individual detachment and freedom is possible, such as these great households never knew. . . .

But let us return now to the history preserved for us in the Aryan epics.

The Sanscrit epics tell a very similar story to that underlying the *Iliad,* the story of a fair, beef-eating people—only later did they become vegetarians—coming down from Persia into the plain of North India and conquering their way slowly towards the Indus. From the Indus they spread over India, but as they spread they acquired much from the dark Dravidians they conquered, and they seem to have lost their bardic tradition. The ancient verses, says Mr. Basu, were transmitted chiefly in the households by the women. . . .

The oral literature of the Keltic peoples who pressed westward has not been preserved so completely as that of the Greeks or Indians; it was written down many centuries later, and so, like the barbaric, primitive English *Beowulf,* has lost any clear evidence of a period of migration into the lands of an antecedent people. If the pre-Aryans figure in it at all, it is as the fairy folk of the Irish stories.

Ireland, most cut off of all the Keltic-speaking communities, retained to the latest date its primitive life; and the *Táin,* the Irish *Iliad,* describes a cattle-keeping life in which war chariots are still used, and war dogs also, and the heads of the slain are carried off slung round the horses' necks. The *Táin* is the story of a cattle raid. Here, too, the same social order appears as in the *Iliad;* the chiefs sit and feast in great halls, they build halls for themselves, there is singing and story-telling by the bards, and drinking and intoxication. Priests are not very much in evidence, but there is a sort of medicine man who deals in spells and prophecy.

XX

THE GREEKS AND THE PERSIANS

§ 1

THE Greeks appear in the dim light before the dawn of history (say 1,500 B.C.) as one of the wandering imperfectly nomadic Aryan peoples who were gradually extending the range of their pasturage southward into the Balkan peninsula and coming into conflict and mixing with that preceding Ægean civilization of which Cnossos was the crown.

In the Homeric poems these Greek tribes speak one common language, and a common tradition upheld by the epic poems keeps them together in a loose unity; they call their various tribes by a common name, *Hellenes.* They probably came in successive waves. Three main variations of the ancient Greek speech are distinguished; the Ionic, the Æolic, and the Doric. There was a great variety of dialects. The Ionians seem to have preceded the other Greeks and to have mixed very intimately with the civilized peoples they overwhelmed. Racially the people of such cities as Athens and Miletus may have been less Nordic than Mediterranean. The Doric apparently constituted the last, most powerful and least civilized wave of the migration. These Hellenic tribes conquered and largely destroyed the Ægean civilization that had preceded their arrival; upon its ashes they built up a civilization of their own. They took to the sea and crossed by way of the islands to Asia Minor; and, sailing through the Dardanelles and Bosphorus, spread their settlements along the south, and presently along the north borders of the Black Sea. They spread also over the south of Italy, which was called at last Magna Græcia, and round the northern coast of the Mediterranean. They founded the town of Marseilles on the site of an earlier Phœnician colony. They began settlements in Sicily in rivalry with the Carthaginians as early as 735 B.C.

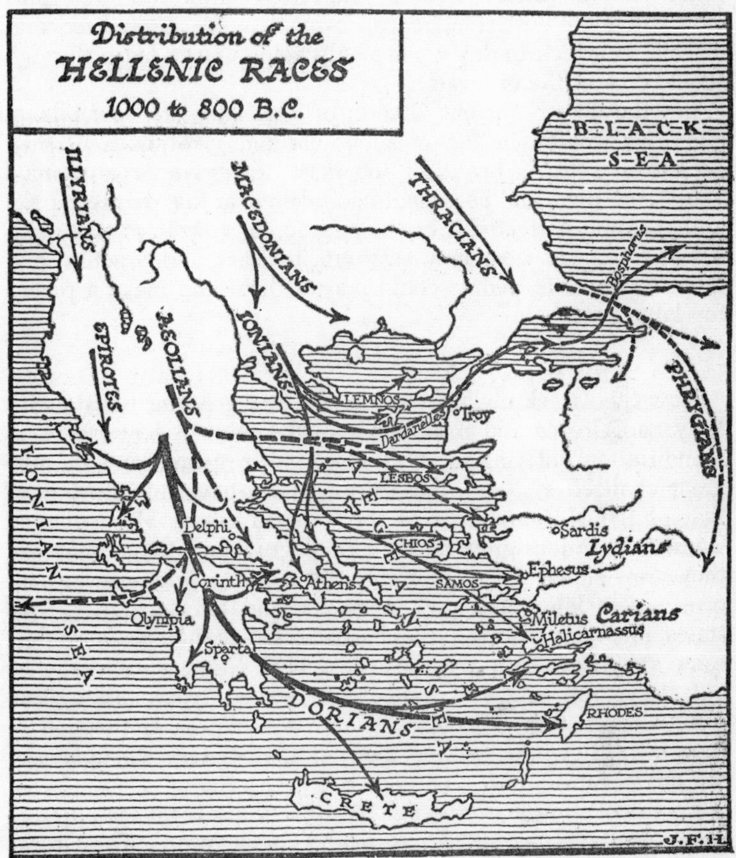

In the rear of the Greeks proper came the kindred Macedonians and Thracians; on their left wing the Phrygians crossed by the Bosphorus into Asia Minor.

We find all this distribution of the Greeks affected before the beginnings of written history. By the seventh century B.C.—that is to say, by the time of the Babylonian captivity of the Jews—

the landmarks of the ancient world of the pre-Hellenic civilization in Europe have been obliterated. Tiryns and Cnossos are unimportant sites; Mycenæ and Troy survive in legend; the great cities of this new Greek world are Athens, Sparta (the capital of Lacedemon), Corinth, Thebes, Samos, Miletus. The world our grandfathers called "Ancient Greece" had arisen on the forgotten ruins of a still more Ancient Greece, in many ways as civilized and artistic, of which to-day we are only beginning to learn through the labours of the excavator.

But the newer Ancient Greece, of which we are now telling, still lives vividly in the imaginations and institutions of men because it spoke a beautiful and most expressive Aryan tongue akin to our own, and because it had taken over the Mediterranean alphabet and perfected it by the addition of vowels, so that reading and writing were now easy arts to learn and practise, and great numbers of people could master them and make a record for later ages.

§ 2

Now this Greek civilization that we find growing up in South Italy and Greece and Asia Minor in the seventh century B.C. is a civilization differing in many important respects from the two great civilized systems whose growths we have already traced, that of the Nile and that of the Two Rivers of Mesopotamia. These civilizations grew through long ages where they are found; they grew slowly about a temple life out of a primitive agriculture; priest kings and god kings consolidated such early city states into empires. But the barbaric Greek herdsmen raiders came southward into a world whose civilization was already an old story. Shipping and agriculture, walled cities and writing were already there. The Greeks did not grow a civilization of their own; they wrecked one, and put another together upon and out of the ruins.

To this we must ascribe the fact that there is no temple-state stage, no stage of priest kings, in the Greek record. The Greeks got at once to the city organization that in the east had grown round the temple. They took over the association of temple and city; the idea was ready-made for them. What impressed them most about the city was probably its wall. It is doubtful if they took to city life and citizenship straight away. At first they lived in open villages outside the ruins of the cities they had destroyed, but there stood the model for them, a continual suggestion. They thought first of a city as a safe place in a time of strife, and of the temple uncritically as a proper feature of the city. They came into this inheritance of a previous civilization with the ideas and traditions of the woodlands still strong in their minds. The heroic social system of the *Iliad* took possession of the land, and adapted itself to the new conditions. As history goes on the Greeks became more religious and superstitious as the faiths of the conquered welled up from below.

We have already said that the social structure of the primitive Aryans was a two-class system of nobles and commoners, the classes not very sharply marked off from each other and led in warfare by a king who was simply the head of one of the noble families, *primus inter pares,* a leader among his equals. With the conquest of the aboriginal population, and with the building of towns, there was added to this simple social arrangement of two classes a lower stratum of farm-workers and skilled and unskilled workers, who were for the most part slaves. But all the Greek communities were not of this "conquest" type. Some were "refugee" cities representing smashed communities and in these the aboriginal substratum would be missing.

An early Greek sea-fight. From a painted vase, about 550 B.C.

J.F.H.

In many of the former cases the survivors of the earlier population formed a subject class, slaves of the state as a whole, as, for instance, the Helots in Sparta. The nobles and commoners became landlords and gentlemen farmers; it was they who directed the shipbuilding and engaged in trade. But some of the poorer free citizens followed mechanic arts, and, as we have already noted, would even pull an oar in a galley for pay. Such priests as there were in this Greek world were either the guardians of shrines and temples or sacrificial functionaries; Aristotle, in his *Politics*, makes them a mere subdivision of his official class. The citizen served as warrior in youth, ruler in his maturity, priest in his old age. The priestly *class*, in comparison with the equivalent class in Egypt and Babylonia, was small and insignificant.

The gods of the Greeks proper, the gods of the heroic Greeks, were, as we have already noted, glorified human beings, and they were treated without very much fear or awe; but beneath these gods of the conquering freemen lurked other gods of the subjugated peoples, who found their furtive followers among slaves and women. The original Aryan gods were not expected to work miracles or control men's lives. But Greece, like most of the Eastern world in the thousand years B.C., was much addicted to consulting *oracles* or soothsayers. Delphi was particularly famous for its oracle. "When the Oldest Men in the tribe could not tell you the right thing to do," says Gilbert Murray, "you went to the blessed dead. All oracles were at the tombs of Heroes. They told you what was 'Themis,' what was the right thing to do, or, as religious people would put it now, what was the Will of the God."

The priests and priestesses of these temples were not united into one class, nor did they exercise any power as a class. It was the nobles and free commoners, two classes which, in some cases, merged into one common body of citizens, who constituted the Greek state. In many cases, especially in great city states, the population of slaves and unenfranchised strangers greatly outnumbered the citizens. But for them the state existed only by courtesy; it existed legally for the select body of citizens alone. It might or might not tolerate the outsider and the slave, but they had no legal voice in their treatment—any more than if it had been a despotism.

This is a social structure differing widely from that of the Eastern monarchies. The exclusive importance of the Greek citizen reminds one a little of the exclusive importance of the children of Israel in the later Jewish state, but there is no equivalent on the Greek side to the prophets and priests, nor to the idea of an overruling Jehovah.

Another contrast between the Greek states and any of the human communities to which we have hitherto given attention is their continuous and incurable division. The civilizations of Egypt, Sumer, China, and no doubt North India, all began in a number of independent city states, each one a city with a few miles of dependent agricultural villages and cultivation around it, but out of this phase they passed by a process of coalescence into kingdoms and empires. But to the very end of their independent history the Greeks did not coalesce. Commonly, this is ascribed to the geographical conditions under which they lived. Greece is a country cut up into a multitude of valleys by mountain masses and arms of the sea that render intercommunication difficult; so difficult that few cities were able to hold many of the others in subjection for any length of time. Moreover, many Greek cities were on islands and scattered along remote coasts. To the end the largest city states of Greece remained smaller than many English counties; and some had an area of only a few square miles. Athens, one of the largest of the Greek cities, at the climax of its power had a population of perhaps a third of a million. Few other Greek cities exceeded 50,000. Of this number, half or more were slaves and strangers, and two-thirds of the free body women and children.

§ 3

The government of these city states varied very widely in its nature. As they settled down after their conquests the Greeks retained for a time the rule of their kings, but these kingdoms drifted back more and more to the rule of the aristocratic class. In Sparta (Lacedemon) kings were still distinguished in the sixth century B.C. The Lacedemonians had a curious system of a double kingship; two kings, drawn from different royal families, ruled together.

But most of the Greek city states had become aristocratic republics long before the sixth century. There is, however, a tendency towards slackness and inefficiency in most families that rule by hereditary right; sooner or later they decline; and as the Greeks got out upon the seas and set up colonies and commerce extended, new rich families arose to jostle the old and bring new personalities into power. These *nouveaux riches* became members of an expanded ruling class, a mode of government known as oligarchy—in opposition to aristocracy—though, strictly, the term oligarchy (= government by the few) should include hereditary aristocracy as a special case.

In many cities persons of exceptional energy, taking advantage of some social conflict or class grievance, secured a more or less irregular power in the state. This combination of personality and opportunity has occurred in the United States of America, for example, where men exercising various kinds of informal power are called *bosses*. In Greece they were called *tyrants*. But the tyrant was rather more than a boss; he was recognized as a monarch, and claimed the authority of a monarch. The modern boss, on the other hand, shelters behind legal forms which he has "got hold of" and uses for his own ends. Tyrants were distinguished from kings, who claimed some sort of right, some family priority, for example, to rule. They were supported, perhaps, by the poorer class with a grievance; Peisistratus, for example, who was tyrant of Athens, with two intervals of exile, between 560 and 527 B.C., was supported by the poverty-stricken Athenian hillmen. Sometimes, as in Greek Sicily, the tyrant stood for the rich against the poor. When, later on, the Persians began to subjugate the Greek cities of Asia Minor, they set up pro-Persian tyrants.

Aristotle, the great philosophical teacher, who was born under the hereditary Macedonian monarchy, and who was for some years tutor to the king's son, distinguishes in his *Politics* between kings who ruled by an admitted and inherent right, such as the king of Macedonia, whom he served, and tyrants who ruled without the consent of the governed. As a matter of fact, it is hard to conceive of a tyrant ruling without the consent of many, and the active participation of a substantial number of his subjects; and the devotion and unselfishness of your "true kings" has been known to rouse resentment and questioning. Aristotle was also able to say that while the king ruled for the good of the state, the tyrant ruled for his own good. Upon this point, as in his ability to regard slavery as a natural thing and to consider women unfit for freedom and political rights, Aristotle was in harmony with the trend of events about him.

A third form of government that prevailed increasingly in Greece in the sixth, fifth, and fourth centuries B.C. was known as *democracy*. As the modern world nowadays is constantly talking of democracy, and as the modern idea of democracy is something widely different from the democracy of the Greek city states, it will be well to be very explicit upon the meaning of democracy in Greece. Democracy then was government by the commonalty, the Demos; it was government by the whole body of the citizens, by the many as distinguished from the few. But let the modern reader mark the word "citizen." The slave was excluded, the freedman was excluded, the stranger; even the Greek born in the city, whose father had come eight or ten miles from the city beyond the headland, was excluded. The earlier democracies (but not all) demanded a property qualification from the citizen, and property in those days was land; this was subsequently relaxed, but the modern reader will grasp that here was something very different from modern democracy. At the end of the fifth century B.C. this property qualification had been abolished in Athens, for example; but Pericles, a great Athenian statesman of whom we shall have more to tell later, had established a law (451 B.C.) restricting citizenship to those who could establish Athenian descent on both sides. Thus, in the Greek democracies quite as much as in the oligarchies, the citizens formed a *close corporation,* ruling sometimes, as in the case of Athens in its great days, a big population of slaves and "outlanders."

Rowers in an Athenian warship, about 400 B.C. (Fragment of relief found on the Acropolis)

A modern politician used to the idea, the entirely new and different idea, that democracy in its perfected form means that every adult man and woman shall have a voice in the government, would, if suddenly spirited back to the extremist Greek democracy, regard it as a kind of oligarchy. The only real difference between a Greek "oligarchy" and a Greek democracy was that in the former the poorer and less important citizens had no voice in the government, and in the latter every citizen had.

Aristotle, in his *Politics,* betrays very clearly the practical outcome of this difference. Taxation sat lightly on the rich in the oligarchies; the democracies, on the other hand, taxed the rich, and generally paid the impecunious citizen a maintenance allowance and special fees. In Athens fees were paid to citizens even for attending the general assembly. But the generality of people outside the happy order of citizens worked and did what they were told; and if one desired the protection of the law, one sought a citizen to plead for one. For only the citizen had any standing in the law courts. The modern idea, that anyone in the state should be a citizen, would have shocked the privileged democrats of Athens profoundly.

One obvious result of this monopolization of the state by the class of citizens was that the patriotism of these privileged people took an intense and narrow form. They would form alliances but never coalesce with other city states. That would have obliterated every advantage by which they lived. The narrow geographical limits of these Greek states added to the intensity of their feeling. A man's love for his country was reinforced by his love for his native town, his religion, and his home; for these were all one. Of course the slaves did not share in these feelings, and in the oligarchic states very often the excluded class got over its dislike of foreigners in its greater dislike of the class at home which oppressed it. But in the main, patriotism in the Greek was a personal passion of an inspiring and dangerous intensity. Like rejected love, it was apt to turn into something very like hatred. The Greek exile resembled the French or Russian *émigré* in being ready to treat his beloved country pretty roughly in order to save her from the devils in human form who had taken possession of her and turned *him* out.

In the fifth century B.C. Athens formed a system of relationships with a number of other Greek city states which is often spoken of by historians as the Athenian Empire. But all the other city states retained their own governments. One "new fact" added by the Athenian Empire was the complete and effective suppression of piracy; another was the institution of a sort of international law. The law, indeed, was Athenian law; but actions could now be brought and justice administered between citizens of the different states of the League which, of course, had not been possible before.

The Athenian Empire had really developed out of a league of

mutual defence against Persia; its seat had originally been in the island of Delos, and the allies had contributed to a common treasure at Delos; the treasure of Delos was carried off to Athens because it was exposed to a possible Persian raid. Then one city after another offered a monetary contribution instead of military service, with the result that in the end Athens was doing almost all the work and receiving almost all the money. She was supported by one or two of the larger islands. The "League" in this way became gradually an "Empire," but the citizens of the allied states remained, except where there were special treaties of intermarriage and the like, practically foreigners to one another. And it was chiefly the poorer citizens of Athens who sustained this empire by their most vigorous and incessant personal service. Every citizen was liable to military service at home or abroad between the ages of eighteen and sixty, sometimes on purely Athenian affairs and sometimes in defence of the cities of the Empire whose citizens had bought themselves off. There was probably no single man over twenty-five in the Athenian Assembly who had not served in several campaigns in different parts of the Mediterranean or Black Sea, and who did not expect to serve again. Modern imperialism is denounced by its opponents as the exploitation of the world by the rich; Athenian imperialism was the exploitation of the world by the poorer citizens of Athens.

Another difference from modern conditions, due to the small size of the Greek city states, was that in a democracy every citizen had the right to attend and speak and vote in the popular assembly. For most cities this meant a gathering of only a few hundred people; the greatest had no more than some thousands of citizens. Nothing of this sort is possible in a modern "democracy" with, perhaps, seven million voters. The modern "citizen's" voice in public affairs is limited to the right to vote for one or other of the party candidates put before him. He, or she, is then supposed to have "assented" to the resultant government. Aristotle, who would have enjoyed the electoral methods of our modern democracies keenly, points out very subtly how the outlying farmer class of citizens in a democracy can be virtually disenfranchised by calling the popular assembly too frequently for their regular attendance. In the later Greek democracies (fifth century) the appointment of public officials, except in the case of officers requiring very special knowledge, was by casting lots. This was supposed to protect the general corporation of privileged citizens from the continued predominance of rich, influential, and conspicuously able men.

Some democracies (Athens and Miletus, *e.g.*) had an institution called the ostracism—from *ostrakon,* a tile; the voter wrote a name on a tile or shell—by which in times of crisis and conflict the decision was made whether some citizens should go into exile for ten years. This may strike a modern reader as an envious institution, but that was not its essential quality. It was, says Gilbert Murray, a way of arriving at a decision in a case when political feeling was so divided as to threaten a deadlock. There were in the Greek democracies parties and party leaders, but no regular government in office and no regular opposition. There was no way, therefore, of carrying out a policy, although it might be the popular policy, if a strong leader or a strong group stood out against it. But by the ostracism the least popular or the least trusted of the chief leaders in the divided community was made to retire for a period without loss of honour or property.

This institution of the ostracism has immortalized one obscure and rather illiterate member of the democracy of Athens. A certain Aristides had gained a great reputation in the law courts for his righteous dealing. He fell into a dispute with Themistocles upon a question of naval policy; Aristides was for the army, Themistocles was a "strong navy" man, and a deadlock was threatened. There was resort to an ostracism to decide between them. Plutarch relates that as Aristides walked through the streets while the voting was in progress, he was accosted by a strange citizen from the agricultural environs unaccustomed to the art of writing, and requested to write his own name on the proffered potsherd.

"But why?" he asked. "Has Aristides ever injured you?"

"No," said the citizen. "No. Never have I set eyes on him. But, oh! I am so *bored* by hearing him called Aristides the Just."

Whereupon, says Plutarch, without further parley Aristides wrote as the man desired. . . .

When one understands the true meaning of these Greek constitutions, and in particular the limitation of all power, whether in the democracies or the oligarchies, to a locally privileged class, one realizes how impossible was any effective union of the hundreds of Greek cities scattered about the Mediterranean region, or even of any effective co-operation between them for a common end. Each city was in the hands of a few or a few hundred men, to whom its separateness meant everything that was worth having in life. Only conquest from the outside could unite the Greeks, and until Greece was conquered they had no political unity. When at last they were conquered, they were conquered so completely that their unity ceased to be of any importance even to themselves; it was a unity of subjugation.

Yet there was always a certain tradition of unity between all the Greeks, based on a common language and script, on the common possession of the heroic epics, and on the continuous intercourse that the maritime position of the states made possible. And, in addition, there were certain religious bonds of a unifying kind. Certain shrines—the shrines of the god Apollo in the island of Delos and at Delphi, for example—were sustained not by single states, but by leagues of states or Amphictyonies (=League of neighbours), which in such instances as the Delphic amphictyony became very wide-reaching unions. The league protected the shrine and the safety of pilgrims, kept up the roads leading thereunto, secured peace at the time of special festivals, upheld certain rules to mitigate the usages of war among its members, and—the Delian league especially—suppressed piracy. A still more important link of Hellenic union was the Olympian games that were held every four years at Olympia. Foot races, boxing, wrestling, javelin throwing, quoit throwing, jumping, and chariot and horse racing were the chief sports, and a record of victors and distinguished visitors was kept. From the year 776 B.C. onward these games were held regularly for over a thousand years, and they did much to maintain that sense of a common Greek life (pan-Hellenic) transcending the narrow politics of the city states. 776 B.C. is the Year of the First Olympiad, a valuable starting-point in Greek chronology.

Such links of sentiment and association were of little avail against the intense "separatism" of the Greek political institutions. From the *History of Herodotus* the student will be able to gather a sense of the intensity and persistence of the feuds that kept the Greek world in a state of chronic warfare. In the old days (say, to the sixth century B.C.) fairly large families prevailed in Greece, and something of the old Aryan household system, with its strong clan feeling and its capacity for maintaining an enduring feud, still remained. The history of Athens circles for many years about the feud of two great families, the Alcmæonidæ and the Peisistratidæ; the latter equally an aristocratic family, but founding its power on the support of the poorer class of the populace and the exploitation of their grievances. Later on, in the sixth and fifth centuries, a limitation of births and a shrinkage of families to two or three members—a process Aristotle notes without perceiving its cause—led to the disappearance of the old aristocratic clans, and the later wars were due rather to trade disputes and grievances caused and stirred up by individual adventurers than to family vendettas.

It is easy to understand, in view of this intense separatism of the Greeks, how readily the Ionians of Asia and of the islands fell first under the domination of the kingdom of Lydia, and then under that of the Persians when Cyrus overthrew Crœsus, the king of Lydia. They rebelled only to be reconquered. Then came the turn of European Greece. It is a matter of astonishment, the Greeks themselves were astonished, to find that Greece itself did not fall under the dominion of the Persians, those barbaric Aryan masters of the ancient civilizations of Western Asia. But before we tell of this struggle we must give some attention to these Asiatics against whom the Greeks were pitted; and particularly to these Medes and Persians who, by 538 B.C., were already in possession of the ancient civilizations of Assyria, Babylonia, and about to subjugate Egypt.

§ 4

We have had occasion to mention the kingdom of Lydia, and it may be well to give a short note here upon the Lydians before proceeding with our story. The original population of the larger part of Asia Minor may perhaps have been akin to the original population of Greece and Crete. If so, it was of "Mediterranean" race. Or it may have been another branch of those still more generalized and fundamental darkish people from whom arose the Mediterranean race to the west and the Dravidians to the east. Remains of the same sort of art that distinguishes Cnossos and Mycenæ are to be found scattered over Asia Minor. But just as the Nordic Greeks poured southward into Greece to conquer and mix with the aborigines, so did other and kindred Nordic tribes pour over the Bosphorus into Asia Minor. Over some areas these Aryan peoples prevailed altogether, and became the bulk of the inhabitants and retained their Aryan speech. Such were the Phrygians, a people whose language was almost as close to that of the Greeks as the Macedonian. But over other areas the Aryans did not so prevail. In Lydia the original race and their language held their own. The Lydians were a non-Aryan people speaking a non-Aryan speech, of which at the present time only a few words are known. Their capital city was Sardis.

Their religion was also non-Aryan. They worshipped a Great Mother goddess. The Phrygians also, though retaining their Greek-like language, became infected with mysterious religion, and much of the mystical religion was secret ceremonial that pervaded Athens at a later date was Phrygian (when not Thracian) in origin.

At first the Lydians held the western sea-coast of Asia Minor, but they were driven back from it by the establishment of Ionian Greeks coming by the sea and founding cities. Later on, however, these Ionian Greek cities were brought into subjection by the Lydian kings.

The history of this country of Lydia is still not clearly known, and were it known it would scarcely be of sufficient importance to be related in this historical outline, but in the eighth century B.C. one monarch, named Gyges, became noteworthy. The country under his rule was subjected to another Aryan invasion; certain nomadic tribes called the Cimmerians came pouring across Asia Minor, and they were driven back with difficulty by Gyges and his son and grandson. Sardis was twice taken and burnt by these barbarians. And it is on record that Gyges paid tribute to Sardanapalus, which serves to link him up with our general ideas of the history of Assyria, Israel, and Egypt. Later, Gyges rebelled against Assyria, and sent troops to help Psammetichus I to liberate Egypt from its brief servitude to the Assyrians.

It was Alyattes, the grandson of Gyges, who made Lydia into a considerable power. He reigned for seven years, and he reduced most of the Ionian cities of Asia Minor to subjection. The country became the centre of a great trade between Asia and Europe; it had always been productive and rich in gold, and now the Lydian monarch was reputed the richest in Asia. There was a great coming and going between the Black and Mediterranean Seas, and between the East and West. Lydia was reputed to be the first country in the world to produce coined money and to provide the convenience of inns for travellers and traders. The Lydian dynasty seems to have been a trading dynasty of the type of Minos in Crete, with a banking and financial development. . . . So much we may note of Lydia by way of preface to the next section.

§ 5

Now, while one series of Aryan-speaking invaders had developed along the lines we have described in Greece, Magna Græcia, and around the shores of the Black Sea, another series of Aryan-speaking peoples, whose originally Nordic blood was perhaps already mixed with a Mongolian element, were settling and spreading to the north and east of the Assyrian and Babylonian empires.

We have already spoken of the arc-like dispersion of the Nordic Aryan peoples to the north of the Black and Caspian Seas; it was probably by this route that the Indo-Persian Aryan-speaking races gradually came down into what is now the Persian country, and spread, on the one hand, eastward to India (? 2,000 to 1,000 B.C.), and, on the other, increased and multiplied in the Persian uplands until they were strong enough to assail first Assyria (650 B.C.) and then Babylon (538 B.C.).

There is much that is not yet clear about the changes of climate that have been going on in Europe and Asia during the last 10,000 years. The ice of the last glacial age receded gradually and gave way to a long period of steppe or prairie-like conditions over the great plain of Europe. About 12,000 or 10,000 years ago, as it is reckoned now, this state of affairs was giving place to forest conditions. We have already noted how, as a consequence of these changes, the Solutrean horse hunters gave place to Magdalenian fishers and forest deer hunters; and these, again, to the Neolithic herdsmen and agriculturists. For some thousands of years the European climate seems to have been warmer than it is to-day. A great sea spread from the coast of the Balkan peninsula far into Central Asia and extended northward into Central Russia, and the shrinkage of that sea and the consequent hardening of the climate of South Russia and Central Asia were going on contemporaneously with the development of the first civilizations in the river valleys. Many facts seem to point to a more genial climate in Europe and Western Asia, and still more strongly to a greater luxuriance of plant and vegetable life, 4,000 to 3,000 years ago, than we find today. There were forests then in South Russia and in the country which is now Western Turkestan, where now steppes and deserts prevail. On the other hand, between 1,500 and 2,000 years ago the Aral-Caspian region was probably drier and those seas smaller than they are at the present time.

We may note in this connection that Thothmes III (say, the fifteenth century B.C.), in his expedition beyond the Euphrates, hunted a herd of 120 elephants in that region. Again, an Ægean dagger from Mycenæ, dating about 2,000 B.C., shows a lion-hunt in progress. The hunters carry big shields and spears, and stand in rows one behind the other. The first man spears the lion, and when the wounded beast leaps at him drops flat under the protection of his big shield, leaving the next man to repeat his stroke, and so on, until the lion is speared to death. This method of

Map showing the relation of the MEDIAN and Second BABYLONIAN (Chaldæan) EMPIRES in the reign of Nebuchadnezzar the Great

hunting is practised by the Masai to-day, and could only have been worked out by a people in a land where lions were abundant. But abundant lions imply abundant game, and that again means abundant vegetation. About 2,000 B.C. the hardening of the climate in the central parts of the Old World, to which we have already referred, was turning the faces of the nomadic Aryan peoples southward towards the fields and forests of the more settled and civilized nations.

Lions we may note lingered in the Balkan peninsula till about the fourth century B.C., if not later. Elephants had perhaps disappeared from Western Asia by the eighth century B.C. The lion (much bigger than the existing form) stayed on in Southern Germany till the Neolithic period. The panther inhabited Greece, Southern Italy, and Southern Spain till the beginning of the historical period (say 1,000 B.C.).

One of the few existing representations of the Ancient Scythians. *From a Greek Electrum Vase.*

The Aryan peoples come down from the East Caspian regions into history about the time that Mycenæ and Troy and Cnossos are falling to the Greeks. It is difficult to disentangle the different tribes and races that appear under a multitude of names in the records and inscriptions that record their first appearance, but, fortunately, these distinctions are not needed in an elementary outline such as this present history. A people called the Cimmerians appear in the districts of Lakes Urumiya and Van, and shortly after Aryans have spread from Armenia to Elam. In the ninth century B.C., a people called the Medes, very closely related to the Persians to the east of them, appear in the Assyrian inscriptions. Tiglath Pileser III and Sargon II, names already familiar in this story, profess to have made them pay tribute. They are spoken of in the inscriptions as the "dangerous Medes." They are as yet a tribal people, not united under one king.

About the seventh century B.C., Elam and the Elamites, whose capital was Susa, a people which possessed a tradition and civilization at least as old as the Sumerian, suddenly vanish from history. We do not know what happened. They seem to have been overrun and the population absorbed by the conquerors. Susa is in the hands of the Persians.

A fourth people, related to these Aryan tribes, who appear at this time in the narrative of Herodotus, are the "Scythians." For a while the monarchs of Assyria play off these various kindred peoples, the Cimmerians, the Medes, the Persians, and the Scythians, against each other. Assyrian princesses (a daughter of Esarhaddon, *e.g.*) are married to Scythian chiefs. Nebuchadnezzar the Great, on the other hand, marries a daughter of Cyaxares, who has become king of all the Medes. The Aryan Scythians are for the Semitic Assyrians; the Aryan Medes for the Semitic Babylonians. It was this Cyaxares who took Nineveh, the Assyrian capital, in 606 B.C., and so released Babylon from the Assyrian yoke, to establish, under Chaldean rule, the Second Babylonian Empire. The Scythian allies of Assyria drop out of the story after this. They go on living their own life away to the north without much interference with the peoples to the south. A glance at the map of this period shows how, for two-thirds of a century, the Second Babylonian Empire lay like a lamb within the embrace of the Median lion.

Into the internal struggles of the Medes and Persians, that ended at last in the accession of Cyrus "the Persian" to the throne of Cyaxares in 550 B.C., we will not enter. In that year Cyrus was ruling over an empire that reached from the boundaries of Lydia to Persia and perhaps to India. Nabonidus, the last of the Babylonian rulers, was, as we have already told, digging up old records and building temples in Babylonia.

§ 6

But one monarch in the world was alive to the threat of the new power that lay in the hands of Cyrus. This was Crœsus, the Lydian king. His son had been killed in a very tragic manner, which Herodotus relates, but which we will not describe here. Says Herodotus:

"For two years, then, Crœsus remained quiet in great mourning, because he was deprived of his son; but after this period of time, the overthrowing of the rule of the son of Cyaxares by Cyrus, and the growing greatness of the Persians, caused Crœsus to cease from his mourning, and led him to a care of cutting short the power of the Persians if by any means he might, while yet it was in growth and before they should have become great."

He then made trial of the various oracles:

"To the Lydians who were to carry these gifts to the temples Crœsus gave charge that they should ask the Oracles this question: whether Crœsus should march against the Persians, and, if so, whether he should join with himself any army of men as his friends. And when the Lydians had arrived at the places to which they had been sent and had dedicated the votive offerings, they inquired of the Oracles, and said: 'Crœsus, king of the Lydians and of other nations, considering that these are the only true Oracles among men, presents to you gifts such as your revelations deserve, and asks you again now whether he shall march against the Persians, and, if so, whether he shall join with himself any army of men as allies.' They inquired thus, and the answers of both the Oracles agreed in one, declaring to Crœsus that if he should march against the Persians he should destroy a great empire. . . . So when the answers were brought back and Crœsus heard them, he was delighted with the Oracles, and expecting that he would certainly destroy the kingdom of Cyrus, he sent again to Pytho, and presented to the men of Delphi, having ascertained the number of them, two staters of gold for each man: and in return for this the Delphians gave to Crœsus and to the Lydians precedence in consulting the Oracle and freedom from all payments, and the right to front seats at the games, with this privilege also for all time, that any one of them who wished should be allowed to become a citizen of Delphi."

So Crœsus made a defensive alliance both with the Lacedemonians and the Egyptians. "And," Herodotus continues, "while Crœsus was preparing to march against the Persians, one of the Lydians, who even before this time was thought to be a wise man, but in consequence of this opinion got a very great name for wisdom among the Lydians, advised Crœsus as follows: 'O King, thou art preparing to march against men who wear breeches of leather, and the rest of their clothing is of leather also; and they eat food not such as they desire, but such as they can obtain, dwelling in a land which is rugged; and, moreover, they make no use of wine but drink water; and no figs have they for dessert, nor any other good thing. On the one hand, if thou shalt overcome them, what wilt thou take away from them, seeing they have nothing? and, on the other hand, if thou shalt be overcome, consider how many good things thou wilt lose; for once having tasted our good things, they will cling to them fast, and it will not be possible to drive them away. I, for my own part, feel gratitude to the gods that they do not put it into the minds of the Persians to march against the Lydians.' Thus he spoke, not persuading Crœsus; for it is true indeed that the Persians before they subdued the Lydians had no luxury nor any good thing."

Crœsus and Cyrus fought an indecisive battle at Pteria, from which Crœsus retreated. Cyrus followed him up, and he gave battle outside his capital town of Sardis. The chief strength of the Lydians lay in their cavalry; they were excellent, if undisciplined, horsemen, and fought with long spears.

"Cyrus, when he saw the Lydians being arrayed for battle, fearing their horsemen, did on the suggestion of Harpagos, a Mede, as follows: All the camels which were in the train of his army carrying provisions and baggage he gathered together, and he took off their burdens and set men upon them provided with the equipment of cavalry; and, having thus furnished them, forth he appointed them to go in front of the rest of the army towards the horsemen of Crœsus; and after the camel-troop he ordered the infantry to follow; and behind the infantry he placed his whole force of cavalry. Then, when all his men had been placed in their several positions, he charged them to spare none of the other Lydians, slaying all who might come in their way, but Crœsus himself they were not to slay, not even if he should make resistance when he was being captured. Such was his charge: and he set the camels opposite the horsemen for this reason—because the horse has a fear of the camel and cannot endure either to see his form or to scent his smell: for this reason then the trick had been devised, in order that the cavalry of Crœsus might be useless, that very force wherewith the Lydian king was expecting most to shine. And as they were coming together to the battle, so soon as the horses scented the camels and saw them, they turned away back, and the hopes of Crœsus were at once brought to nought."

In fourteen days Sardis was stormed and Crœsus taken prisoner. . . .

"So the Persians having taken him brought him into the presence of Cyrus; and he piled up a great pyre and caused Crœsus to go up upon it bound in fetters, and along with him twice seven sons of Lydians, whether it was that he meant to dedicate this offering as first-fruits of his victory to some god, or whether he desired to fulfil a vow, or else had heard that Crœsus was a god-fearing man, and so caused him to go up on the pyre because he wished to know if any one of the divine powers would save him, so that he should not be burnt alive. He, they say, did this; but to Crœsus as he stood upon the pyre there came, although he was in such evil case, a memory of the saying of Solon, how he had said with divine inspiration that no one of the living might be called happy. And when this thought came into his mind, they say that he sighed deeply and groaned aloud, having been for long silent, and three times he uttered the name of Solon. Hearing this, Cyrus bade the interpreters ask Crœsus who was this person on whom he called; and they came near and asked. And Crœsus for a time, it is said, kept silence when he was asked this, but afterwards, being pressed, he said: 'One whom more than much wealth I should have desired to have speech with all monarchs.' Then, since his words were of doubtful import, they asked again of that which he said; and as they were urgent with him and gave him no peace, he told how once Solon, an Athenian, had come and having inspected all his wealth had made light of it, with such and such words; and how all had turned out for him according as Solon had said, not speaking at all especially with a view to Crœsus himself, but with a view to the whole human race, and especially those who seem to themselves to be happy men. And while Crœsus related these things, already the pyre was lighted and the edges of it round about were burning. Then they say that Cyrus, hearing from the interpreters what Crœsus had said, changed his purpose and considered that he himself also was but a man, and that he was delivering another man, who had been not inferior to himself in felicity, alive to the fire; and, moreover, he feared the requital, and reflected that there was nothing of that which men possessed which was secure; therefore, they say, he ordered them to extinguish as quickly as possible the fire that was burning, and to bring about Crœsus and those who were with him from the pyre; and they, using endeavours, were not able now to get the mastery of the flames. Then it is related by the Lydians that Crœsus, having learned how Cyrus had changed his mind, and seeing that everyone was trying to put out the fire, but that they were no longer able to check it, cried aloud, entreating Apollo that if any gift had ever been given by him which was acceptable to the god, he would come to his aid and rescue him from the evil which was now upon him. So he with tears entreated the god, and suddenly, they say, after clear sky and calm weather, clouds gathered and a storm burst, and it rained with a very violent shower, and the pyre was extinguished.

"Then Cyrus, having perceived that Crœsus was a lover of the gods and a good man, caused him to be brought down from the pyre and asked him as follows: 'Crœsus, tell me who of all men was it who persuaded thee to march upon my land and so to become an enemy to me instead of a friend?' And he said: 'O king, I did this to thy felicity and to my own misfortune, and the causer of this was the god of the Hellenes, who incited me to march with my army. For no one is so senseless as to choose of his own will war rather than peace, since in peace the sons bury their fathers, but in war the fathers bury their sons. But it was pleasing, I suppose, to the divine powers that these things should come to pass thus.'"

But Herodotus is too alluring a companion for one who would write an Outline of History; and the rest of the life of Crœsus, and how he gave wise counsels to Cyrus, must be read in his ampler page.

When Lydia was subdued, Cyrus turned his attention to Nabonidus in Babylon. He defeated the Babylonian army, under Belshazzar, outside Babylon, and then laid siege to the town. He entered the town (538 B.C.), probably, as we have already suggested, with the connivance of the priests of Bel.

§ 7

Cyrus was succeeded by his son Cambyses, who took an army into Egypt (525 B.C.). There was a battle in the delta, in which Greek mercenaries fought on both sides. Herodotus declares that he saw the bones of the slain still lying on the field fifty or sixty years later, and comments on the comparative thinness of the Persian skulls. Herodotus never relaxed from anti-Persian propaganda. After this battle Cambyses took Memphis and most of Egypt.

In Egypt, we are told, Cambyses went mad. He took great liberties with the Egyptian temples, and remained at Memphis "opening ancient tombs and examining the dead bodies." He had already murdered both Crœsus, ex-king of Lydia, and his own brother Smerdis before coming to Egypt, and he died in Syria, on the way back to Susa, of an accidental wound, leaving no heirs to succeed him. He was presently succeeded by Darius the Mede (521 B.C.), the son of Hystaspes, one of the chief councillors of Cyrus.

The empire of Darius I was larger than any one of the preceding empires whose growth we have traced. It included all Asia Minor and Syria, that is to say the ancient Lydian and Hittite empires, all the old Assyrian and Babylonian empires, Egypt, the Caucasus and Caspian regions, Media, Persia, and it extended, perhaps, into India to the Indus. The nomadic Arabians, alone of all the peoples of what is nowadays called the Near East, did not pay tribute to the satraps (provincial governors) of Darius. The organization of this great empire seems to have been on a much higher level of efficiency than any of its precursors. Great arterial roads joined province to province, and there was a system of royal posts; at stated intervals post-horses stood always ready to carry the government messenger, or the traveller if he had a government permit, on to the next stage of his journey. The Hittites seem to have had paved high roads running across their country much earlier than this, but this is the first organization of posts we know of. Apart from the imperial right-of-way and the payment of tribute, the local governments possessed a very considerable amount of local freedom. They were restrained from internecine conflict, which was all to their own good. And at first the Creek cities of the mainland of Asia paid the tribute and shared in this Persian Peace.

Darius was first incited to attack the Greeks in Europe by a homesick Greek physician at his court, who wanted at any cost to be back in Greece. Darius had already made plans for an expedition into Europe, aiming not at Greece, but to the northward of Greece, across the Bosphorus and Danube. He wanted to strike at South Russia, which he believed to be the home country of the Scythian nomads who threatened him on his northern and north-eastern frontiers. But he lent an attentive ear to the tempter, and sent agents into Greece.

This great expedition of Darius opens out our view in this history. It lifts a curtain upon the Balkan country behind Greece about which we have said nothing hitherto; it carries us to and over the Danube. The nucleus of his army marched from Susa, gathering up contingents as they made their way to the Bosphorus. Here Greek allies (Ionian Greeks from Asia) had made a bridge of boats, and the army crossed over while the Greek allies sailed on in their ships to the Danube, and, two days' sail up from its mouth, landed to make another floating bridge. Meanwhile, Darius and his host advanced along the coast of what is now Bulgaria, but which was then called Thrace. They crossed the Danube, and prepared to give battle to the Scythian army and take the cities of the Scythians.

But the Scythians had no cities, and they evaded a battle, and the war degenerated into a tedious and hopeless pursuit of more mobile enemies. Wells were stopped up and pastures destroyed by the nomads. The Scythian horsemen hung upon the skirts of the great army, which consisted mostly of foot soldiers, picking off stragglers and preventing foraging; and they did their best to persuade the Ionian Greeks, who had made and were guarding the bridge across the Danube, to break up the bridge, and so ensure the destruction of Darius. So long as Darius continued to advance, however, the loyalty of his Greek allies remained unshaken.

But privation, fatigue, and sickness hindered and crippled the Persian army; Darius lost many stragglers and consumed his supplies, and at last the melancholy conviction dawned upon him that a retreat across the Danube was necessary to save him from complete exhaustion and defeat.

In order to get a start in his retreat he sacrificed his sick and wounded. He had these men informed that he was about to attack the Scythians at nightfall, and under this pretence stole out of the camp with the pick of his troops and made off southward, leaving the camp fires burning and the usual noises and movements of the camp behind him. Next day the men left in the camp realized the trick their monarch had played upon them, and surrendered themselves to the mercy of the Scythians; but Darius had got his start, and was able to reach the bridge of boats before his pursuers came upon him. They were more mobile than his troops, but they missed their quarry in the darkness. At the river the retreating Persians "were brought to an extremity of fear," for they found the bridge partially broken down and its northern end destroyed.

At this point a voice echoes down the centuries to us. We see a group of dismayed Persians standing about the Great King upon the bank of the streaming river; we see the masses of halted troops, hungry and war-worn; a trail of battered transport stretches away towards the horizon, upon which at any time the advance guards of the pursuers may appear. There is not much noise in spite of the multitude, but rather an inquiring silence. Standing out like a pier from the further side of the great stream are the remains of the bridge of boats, an enigma. . . . We cannot discern whether there are men over there or not. The

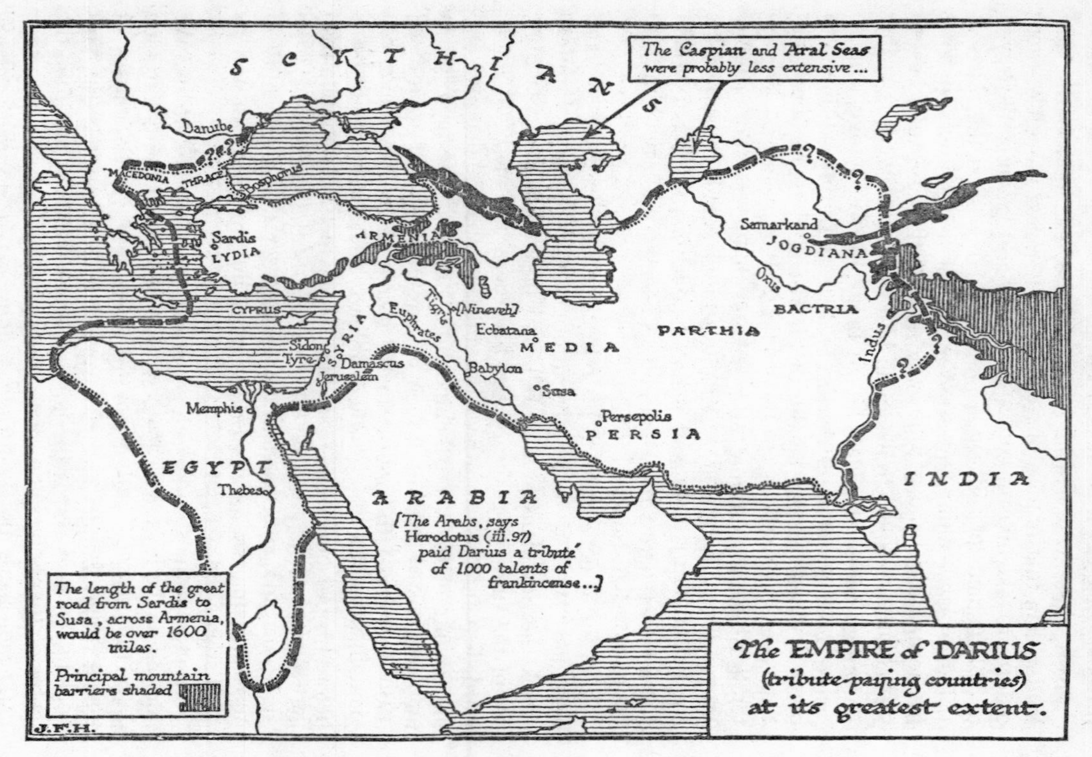
SCYTHIANS
The Caspian and Aral Seas were probably less extensive ...
Danube
MACEDONIA
THRACE
Bosphorus
Sardis
LYDIA
ARMENIA
CYPRUS
SYRIA
Sidon
Tyre
Damascus
Jerusalem
Memphis
EGYPT
Thebes
Euphrates
Tigris
(Nineveh)
Ecbatana
MEDIA
Babylon
Susa
Persepolis
PERSIA
PARTHIA
Samarkand
SOGDIANA
Oxus
BACTRIA
Indus
INDIA
ARABIA
[The Arabs, says Herodotus (iii.97) paid Darius a tribute of 1,000 talents of frankincense...]
The length of the great road from Sardis to Susa, across Armenia, would be over 1600 miles.
Principal mountain barriers shaded
J.F.H.
The EMPIRE of DARIUS
(tribute-paying countries)
at its greatest extent.

shipping of the Ionian Greeks seems still to be drawn up on the further shore, but it is all very far away.

"Now there was with Darius an Egyptian who had a voice louder than that of any other man on earth, and this man Darius ordered to take his stand upon the bank of the Ister (Danube) and to call Histiæus of Miletus."

This worthy—a day is to come, as we shall presently tell, when his decapitated head will be sent to Darius at Susa—appears approaching slowly across the waters in a boat.

There is a parley, and we gather that it is "all right."

The explanation Histiæus has to make is a complicated one. Some Scythians have been and have gone again. Scouts, perhaps, these were. It would seem there had been a discussion between the Scythians and the Greeks. The Scythians wanted the bridge broken down; they would then, they said, undertake to finish up the Persian army and make an end of Darius and his empire, and the Ionian Greeks of Asia could then free their cities again. Miltiades, the Athenian, was for accepting this proposal. But Histiæus had been more subtle. He would prefer, he said, to see the Persians completely destroyed before definitely abandoning their cause. Would the Scythians go back and destroy the Persians to make sure of them while the Greeks on their part destroyed the bridge? Anyhow, whichever side the Greeks took finally, it was clear to him that it would be wise to destroy the northern end of the bridge, because otherwise the Scythians might rush it. Indeed, even as they parleyed the Greeks set to work to demolish the end that linked them to the Scythians as quickly as possible. The Scythians rode off in search of the Persians, and so left the Greeks safe in either event. If Darius escaped, they could be on his side; if he were destroyed, there was nothing of which the Scythians could complain.

Histiæus did not put it quite in that fashion to Darius. He had at least kept the shipping and most of the bridge. He represented himself as the loyal friend of Persia, and Darius was not disposed to be too critical. The Ionian ships came over. With a sense of immense relief the remnant of the wasted Persians were presently looking back at the steely flood of the Danube streaming wide between themselves and their pursuers. . . .

The pleasure and interest had gone out of the European expedition for Darius. He returned to Susa, leaving an army in Thrace, under a trusted general Megabazus. This Megabazus set himself to the subjugation of Thrace, and among other states which submitted reluctantly to Darius was a kingdom which thus comes into our history for the first time, the kingdom of Macedonia, a country inhabited by a people so closely allied to the Greeks that one of its princes had already been allowed to compete and take a prize in the Olympian games.

Darius was disposed to reward Histiæus by allowing him to build a city for himself in Thrace, but Megabazus had a different opinion of the trustworthiness of Histiæus, and prevailed upon the king to take him to Susa, and, under the title of councillor, to keep him a prisoner there. Histiæus was at first flattered by this court position, and then realized its true meaning. The Persian court bored him, and he grew homesick for Miletus. He set himself to make mischief, and was able to stir up a revolt against the Persians among the Ionian Greeks on the mainland. The twistings and turnings of the story, which included the burning of Sardis by the Ionians and the defeat of a Greek fleet at the battle of Ladé (495 B.C.), are too complicated to follow here. It is a dark and intricate story of treacheries, cruelties, and hate, in which the death of the wily Histiæus shines almost cheerfully. The Persian governor of Sardis, through which town he was being taken on his way back to Susa as a prisoner, having much the same opinion of him as Megabazus had, and knowing his ability to humbug Darius, killed him there and then, and sent on the head only to his master.

Cyprus and the Greek islands were dragged into this contest that Histiæus had stirred up, and at last Athens. Darius realized the error he had made in turning to the right and not to the left when he had crossed the Bosphorus, and he now set himself to the conquest of all Greece. He began with the islands.

Tyre and Sidon, those great Semitic trading cities, were subject to Persia, and ships of the Phœnician and of the Ionian Greeks provided the Persians with a fleet by means of which one Greek island after another was subjugated.

§ 8

The first attack upon Greece proper was made in 490 B.C. It was a sea attack upon Athens, with a force long and carefully prepared for the task, the fleet being provided with specially built transports for the conveyance of horses. This expedition made a landing near Marathon in Attica. The Persians were guided into Marathon by a renegade Greek, Hippias, the son of Peisistratus who had been tyrant of Athens. If Athens fell, then Hippias was to be its tyrant, under the protection of the Persians. Meanwhile, so urgent was the sense of a crisis in the affairs of Hellas, that a man, a herald and runner, went from Athens to Sparta, forgetful

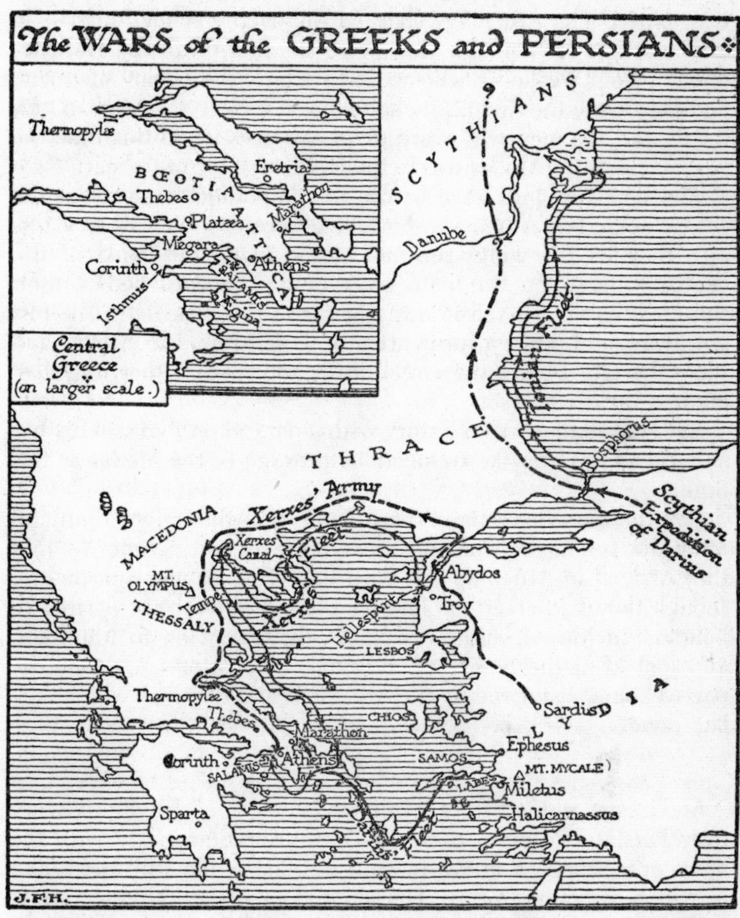

of all feuds, to say: "Lacedemonians, the Athenians make request of you to come to their help, and not to allow a city most anciently established among the Hellenes to fall into slavery by the means of Barbarians; for even now Eretria has been enslaved and Hellas has become the weaker by a city of renown."

This man, Pheidippides, did the distance from Athens to Sparta, nearly a hundred miles as the crow flies, and much more if we allow for the contours and the windings of the way, in something under eight-and-forty hours.

But before the Spartans could arrive on the scene the battle was joined. The Athenians charged the enemy. They fought—"in a memorable fashion: for they were the first of all the Hellenes about whom we know who went to attack the enemy at a run, and they were the first also who endured to face the Median garments and the men who wore them, whereas up to this time the very name of the Medes was to the Hellenes a terror to hear."

The Persian wings gave before this impetuous attack, but the centre held. The Athenians, however, were cool as well as vigorous; they let the wings run and closed in on the flanks of the centre, whereupon the main body of the Persians fled to their ships. Seven vessels fell into the hands of the Athenians; the rest got away, and, after a futile attempt to sail round to Athens and seize the city before the Greek army returned thither, the fleet made a retreat to Asia.

Let Herodotus close the story with a paragraph that still further enlightens us upon the tremendous prestige of the Medes at this time:

"Of the Lacedemonians there came to Athens two thousand after the full moon, making great haste to be in time, so that they arrived in Attica on the third day after leaving Sparta; and though they had come too late for the battle, yet they desired to behold the Medes; and accordingly they went on to Marathon and looked at the bodies of the slain; then afterwards they departed home, commending the Athenians and the work which they had done."

§ 9

So Greece, unified for a while by fear, gained her first victory over Persia. The news came to Darius simultaneously with the news of a rebellion in Egypt, and he died while still undecided in which direction to turn. His son and successor, Xerxes, turned first to Egypt and set up a Persian satrap there; then for four years he prepared a second attack upon Greece. Says Herodotus, who was, one must remember, a patriotic Greek, approaching now to the climax of his History:

"For what nation did Xerxes not lead out of Asia against Hellas? and what water was not exhausted, being drunk by his host, except only the great rivers? For some supplied ships, and others were appointed to serve in the land army; to some it was appointed to furnish cavalry, and to others vessels to carry horses, while they served in the expedition themselves also; others were ordered to furnish ships of war for the bridges, and others again ships with provisions."

Xerxes passed into Europe, not as Darius did at the half-mile crossing of the Bosphorus, but at the Hellespont (=the Dardanelles). In his account of the assembling of the great army, and its march from Sardis to the Hellespont, the poet in Herodotus takes possession of the historian. The great host passes in splendour by Troy, and Xerxes, who although a Persian and a Barbarian, seems to have had the advantages of a classical education, turns aside, says our historian, to visit the citadel of Priam. The Hellespont was bridged at Abydos, and upon a hill was set a marble throne from which Xerxes surveyed the whole array of his forces.

"And seeing all the Hellespont covered over with the ships and all the shores and the plains of Abydos full of men, then Xerxes pronounced himself a happy man, and after that he fell to weeping. Artabanus, his uncle, therefore perceiving him—the same who at first boldly declared his opinion advising Xerxes not to march against Hellas—this man, I say, having observed that Xerxes wept, asked as follows: 'O king, how far different from one another are the things which thou hast done now and a short while before now! for, having pronounced thyself a happy man, thou art now shedding tears.' He said: 'Yea, for after I had reckoned up, it came into my mind to feel pity at the thought how brief was the whole life of man, seeing that of these multitudes not one will be alive when a hundred years have gone by.'"

This may not be exact history, but it is great poetry. It is as splendid as anything in *The Dynasts*.

The Persian fleet, coasting from headland to headland, accompanied this land multitude during its march southward; but a violent storm did the fleet great damage and 400 ships were lost, including much corn transport. At first the united Hellenes marched out to meet the invaders at the Vale of Tempe near Mount Olympus, but afterwards retreated through Thessaly, and chose at last to await the advancing Persians at a place called Thermopylæ, where at that time—2,400 years have altered these things greatly—there was a great cliff on the landward side and the sea to the east, with a track scarcely wide enough for a chariot between. The great advantage to the Greeks of this position at

Thermopylæ was that it prevented the use of either cavalry or chariots, and narrowed the battle front so as to minimize their numerical inequality. And there the Persians joined battle with them one summer day in the year 480 B.C.

Monument of Athenian foot soldier, found near Marathon.

For three days the Greeks held this great army, and did them much damage with small loss to themselves, and then on the third day a detachment of Persians appeared upon the rear of the Greeks, having learnt of a way over the mountains from a peasant. There were hasty discussions among the Greeks; some were for withdrawing, some for holding out. The leader of the whole force, Leonidas, was for staying; and with him he would keep, he said, 300 Spartans. The rest of the Greek army could, meanwhile, make good its retreat to the next defensible pass. The Thespian contingent of 700, however, refused to fall back. They preferred to stay and die with the Spartans. Also a contingent of 400 Thebans remained. As Thebes afterwards joined the Persians, there is a story that these Thebans were detained by force against their will, which seems on military as well as historical grounds improbable. These 1,400 stayed, and were, after a conflict of heroic quality, slain to a man. Two Spartans happened to be away, sick with ophthalmia. When they heard the news, one was too ill to move; the other made his helot guide him to the battle, and there struck blindly until he was killed. The survivor, Aristodemus, was taken away with the retreating troops, and returned to Sparta, where he was not actually punished for his conduct, but was known as Tresas, "the man who retreated." It was enough to distinguish him from all other Spartans, and he got himself killed at the battle of Platæa, a year later, performing prodigies of reckless courage. . . . For a whole day this little band had held the pass, assailed in front and rear by the entire force of the Persians. They had covered the retreat of the main Greek army, they had inflicted great losses on the invaders and they had raised the prestige of the Greek warrior over that of Mede higher even than the victory of Marathon had done.

The Persian cavalry and transport filtered slowly through the narrow passage of Thermopylæ, and marched on towards Athens, while a series of naval encounters went on at sea. The Hellenic fleet retreated before the advance of the Persian shipping, which suffered seriously through its comparative ignorance of the intricate coasts and of the tricks of the local weather. Weight of numbers carried the Persian army forward to Athens; now that Thermopylæ was lost, there was no line of defence nearer than the Isthmus of Corinth, and this meant the abandonment of all the intervening territory, including Athens. The population had either to fly or submit to the Persians. Thebes with all Bœotia submitted, and was pressed into the Persian army, except one town, Platæa, whose inhabitants fled to Athens. The turn of Athens came next, and great efforts were made to persuade her to make terms; but, instead, the whole population determined to abandon everything and take to the shipping. The women and non-combatants were carried to Salamis and various adjacent islands. Only a few people too old to move and a few dissentients remained in the town, which was occupied by the Persians and burnt. The sacred objects, statues, etc., which were burnt at this time, were afterwards buried in the Acropolis by the returning Athenians, and have been dug up in our own day with the marks of burning visible upon them. Xerxes sent off a mounted messenger to Susa with the news, and he invited the sons of Peisistratus, whom he had brought back with him, to enter upon their inheritance and sacrifice after the Athenian manner upon the Acropolis.

Meanwhile, the Hellenic confederate fleet had come round to Salamis, and in the council of war there were bitter differences of opinion. Corinth and the states behind the Isthmus wanted the fleet to fall back to that position, abandoning the cities of Megara and Ægina. Themistocles insisted with all his force on fighting in the narrows of Salamis. The majority was steadily in favour of retreat, when there suddenly arrived the news that retreat was cut off. The Persians had sailed round Salamis and held the sea on the other side. This news was brought by that Aristides the Just of whose ostracism we have already told; his sanity and eloquence did much to help Themistocles to hearten the hesitating commanders. These two men had formerly been bitter antagonists; but, with a generosity rare in those days, they forgot their differences before the common danger. At dawn the Greek ships pulled out to battle.

The fleet before them was a fleet more composite and less united than their own. But it was about three times as great. On one wing were the Phœnicians, on the other Ionian Greeks from Asia and the Islands. Some of the latter fought stoutly; others remembered that they too were Greeks. The Greek ships, on the other hand, were mostly manned by freemen fighting for their homes. Throughout the early hours the battle raged confusedly. Then it became evident to Xerxes, watching the combat, that his fleet was attempting flight. The flight became disaster.

Xerxes had taken his seat to watch the battle. He saw his galleys rammed by the sharp prows of other galleys; his fighting-men shot down; his ships boarded. Much of the sea-fighting in those days was done by ramming; the big galleys bore down their opponents by superior weight of impact, or sheared off their oars and so destroyed their manœuvring power and left them helpless. Presently Xerxes saw that some of his broken ships were surrendering. In the water he could see the heads of Greeks swimming to land; but "of the Barbarians the greater number perished in the sea, not knowing how to swim." The clumsy attempt of the hard-pressed first line of the Persian fleet to put about led to indescribable confusion. Some were rammed by the rear ships of their own side. This ancient shipping was poor, unseaworthy stuff by any modern standards. The west wind was blowing and many of the broken ships of Xerxes were now drifting away out of his sight to be wrecked on the coast beyond. Others were being towed towards Salamis by the Greeks. Others, less injured and still in fighting trim, were making for the beaches close beneath him that would bring them under the protection of his army. Scattered over the further sea, beyond the headlands, remote and vague, were ships in flight and Greek ships in pursuit. Slowly, incident by incident, the disaster had unfolded under his eyes. We can imagine something of the coming and going of messengers, the issuing of futile orders, the changes of plan, throughout the day.

In the morning Xerxes had come out provided with tables to mark the most successful of his commanders for reward. In the gold of the sunset he beheld the sea power of Persia utterly scattered, sunken and destroyed, and the Greek fleet over against Salamis unbroken and triumphant, ordering its ranks, as if still incredulous of victory.

Soldiers of the Persian body-guard (From frieze in the audience hall of Darius at Susa.)

The Persian army remained as if in indecision for some days close to the scene of this sea fight, and then began to retreat to Thessaly, where it was proposed to winter and resume the campaign. But Xerxes, like Darius I before him, had conceived a disgust for European campaigns. He was afraid of the destruction of the bridge of boats. With part of the army he went on to the Hellespont, leaving the main force in Thessaly under a general, Mardonius. Of his own retreat the historian relates:

"Whithersoever they came on the march and to whatever nation, they seized the crops of that people and used them for provisions;

and if they found no crops, then they took the grass which was growing up from the earth, and stripped off the bark from the trees and plucked down the leaves and devoured them; alike of the cultivated trees and of those growing wild; and they left nothing behind them: thus they did by reason of famine. Then plague too seized upon the army, and dysentery, which destroyed them by the way, and some of them also who were sick the king left behind, laying charge upon the cities where at the time he chanced to be in his march, to take care of them and support them; of these he left some in Thessaly, and some at Siris in Paionia, and some in Macedonia. . . . When, passing on from Thrace, they came to the passage, they crossed over the Hellespont in haste to Abydos by means of the ships, for they did not find the floating bridges still stretched across, but broken up by a storm. While staying there for a time they had distributed to them an allowance of food more abundant than they had had by the way, and from satisfying their hunger without restraint and also from the changes of water there died many of those in the army who had remained safe till then. The rest arrived with Xerxes at Sardis."

§ 10

The rest of the Persian army remained in Thessaly under the command of Mardonius, and for a year he maintained an aggressive campaign against the Greeks. Finally, he was defeated and killed in a pitched battle at Platæa (479 B.C.), and on the same day the Persian fleet and a land army met with joint disaster under the shadow of Mount Mycale on the Asiatic mainland, between Ephesus and Miletus. The Persian ships, being in fear of the Greeks, had been drawn up on shore and a wall built about them; but the Greeks disembarked and stormed this enclosure. They then sailed to the Hellespont to destroy what was left of the bridge of boats, so that later the Persian fugitives, retreating from Platæa, had to cross by shipping at the Bosphorus, and did so with difficulty.

Encouraged by these disasters of the imperial power, says Herodotus, the Ionian cities in Asia began for a second time to revolt against the Persians.

With this the ninth book of the *History of Herodotus* comes to an end. He was born about 484 B.C., so that at the time of the battle of Platæa he was a child of five years old. Much of the substance of his story was gathered by him from actors in, and eye-witnesses of, the great events he relates. The war still dragged on for a long time; the Greeks supported a rebellion against Persian rule in Egypt, and tried unsuccessfully to take Cyprus; it did not end until about 449 B.C. Then the Greek coasts of Asia Minor and the Greek cities in the Black Sea remained generally free, but Cyprus and Egypt continued under Persian rule. Herodotus, who had been born a Persian subject in the Ionian city of Halicarnassus, was five-and-thirty years old by that time, and he must have

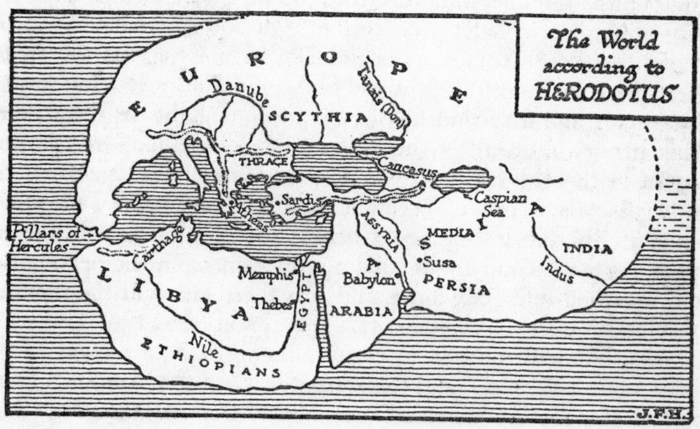

taken an early opportunity after this peace of visiting Babylon and Persia. He probably went to Athens, with his History ready to recite, about 438 B.C.

The idea of a great union of Greece for aggression against Persia was not altogether strange to Herodotus. Some of his readers suspect him of writing to enforce it. It was certainly in the air at that time. He describes Aristagoras, the son-in-law of Histiæus, as showing the Spartans "a tablet of bronze on which was engraved a map of the whole earth with all the seas and rivers." He makes Aristagoras say: "These Barbarians are not valiant in fight. You, on the other hand, have now attained to the utmost skill in war. They fight with bows and arrows and a short spear; they go into battle wearing trousers and having caps on their heads. You have perfected your weapons and discipline. They are easily to be conquered. Not all the other nations of the world have what they possess; gold, silver, bronze, embroidered garments, beasts and slaves; *all this you might have for yourselves, if you so desired.*"

It was a hundred years before these suggestions bore fruit.

Xerxes was murdered in his palace about 465 B.C., and thereafter Persia made no further attempts at conquest in Europe. We have no such knowledge of the things that were happening in the empire of the Great King as we have of the occurrences in the little states of Central Greece. Greece had suddenly begun to produce literature, and put itself upon record as no other nation had ever done hitherto. After 479 B.C. (Platæa) the spirit seems to have gone out of the government of the Medes and Persians. The empire of the Great King enters upon a period of decay. An Artaxerxes, a second Xerxes, a second Darius, pass across the stage; there are rebellions in Egypt and Syria; the Medes rebel; a second Artaxerxes and a second Cyrus, his brother, fight for the throne. This history is even as the history of Babylonia, Assyria, and Egypt in the older times. It is autocracy reverting to its normal state of palace crime, blood-stained magnificence, and moral squalor. But the last-named struggle produced a Greek masterpiece, for this second Cyrus collected an army of Greek mercenaries and marched into Babylonia, and was there killed at the moment of victory over Artaxerxes II. Thereupon the Ten Thousand Greeks, left with no one to employ them, made a retreat to the coast again (401 B.C.), and this retreat was immortalized in a book, one of the first of personal war books, the *Anabasis*, by their leader Xenophon.

Murders, revolts, chastisements, disasters, cunning alliances, and base betrayals, and no Herodotus to record them. Such is the texture of Persian history. An Artaxerxes III, covered with blood, flourishes dimly for a time. "Artaxerxes III is said to have been murdered by Bagoas, who places Arses, the youngest of the king's sons, on the throne, only to slay him in turn when he seemed to be contemplating independent action."

So it goes on. Athens, prospering for a time after the Persian repulse, was smitten by the plague, in which Pericles, its greatest ruler, died (429 B.C.). But, as a noteworthy fact amidst these confusions, the Ten Thousand of Xenophon were scattering now among the Greek cities, repeating from their own experience the declaration of Aristogoras that the Persian empire was a rich confusion which it would be very easy for resolute men to conquer.

XXI

GREEK THOUGHT, LITERATURE AND ART

§ 1. *The Athens of Pericles.* § 2. *Socrates.* § 3. *Plato and the Academy.* § 4. *Aristotle and the Lyceum.* § 5. *Philosophy becomes Unworldly.* § 6. *The Quality and Limitations of Greek Thought.* § 7. *The First Great Imaginative Literature.* § 8. *Greek Art.*

§ 1

GREEK history for the next forty years after Platæa and Mycale is a story of comparative peace and tranquillity. There were wars, but they were not intense wars. For a little while in Athens, for a section of the prosperous, there was leisure and opportunity. And by a combination of accidents and through the character of a small group of people, this leisure and opportunity produced the most memorable results.

The achievement of a method of writing that could render the sounds and subtleties of spoken language had now made literature possible, and much beautiful literature was produced; the plastic arts flourished, and the foundations of modern science already laid by the earlier philosophers of the Ionian Greek cities were consolidated. Then, after an interlude of fifty odd years, the long-smouldering hostility between Athens and Sparta broke out into a fierce and exhausting war, which sapped at last the vitality of this creative movement.

This war is known in history as the Peloponnesian War; it went on for nearly thirty years, and wasted all the power of Greece. At first Athens was in the ascendant, then Sparta. Then arose Thebes, a city not fifty miles from Athens, to overshadow Sparta. Once more Athens flared into importance as the head of a confederation. It is a story of narrow rivalries and inexplicable hatreds, that would have vanished long ago out of the memories of men were it not that it is recorded and reflected in a great literature.

Through all this time Persia appears and reappears as the ally first of this league and then of that. About the middle of the fourth century B.C., Greece becomes aware of a new influence in its affairs, that of Philip, King of Macedonia. Macedonia does, indeed, arise in the background of this incurably divided Greece, as the Medes and Persians arose behind the Chaldean Empire. A time comes when the Greek mind turns round, so to speak, from its disputes, and stares in one united dismay at the Macedonian.

Planless and murderous squabbles are still planless and murderous squabbles even though Thucydides tells the story, even though the great beginnings of a new civilization are wrecked by their disorders; and in this general outline we can give no space at all to the particulars of these internecine feuds, to the fights and flights that sent first this Greek city and then that up to the sky in flames. Upon a one-foot globe Greece becomes a speck almost too small to recognize; and in a short history of mankind, all this century and more of dissension between the days of Salamis and Platæa and the rise of King Philip, shrinks to a little, almost inaudible clash of disputation, to a mere note upon the swift passing of opportunity for nations as for men.

But what does not shrink into significance, because it has entered into the intellectual process of all subsequent nations, because it is inseparably a part of our mental foundation, is the literature that Greece produced during such patches and gleams of tranquillity and security as these times afforded her.

Says Professor Gilbert Murray:

"Their outer political history, indeed, like that of all other nations, is filled with war and diplomacy, with cruelty and deceit. It is the inner history, the history of thought and feeling and character, that is so grand. They had some difficulties to contend with, which are now almost out of our path. They had practically no experience, but were doing everything for the first time; they were utterly weak in material resources, and their emotions, their '*desires and fears and rages,*' were probably wilder and fiercer than ours. Yet they produced the Athens of Pericles and of Plato."

This remarkable culmination of the long-gathering creative power of the Greek mind, which for three-and-twenty centuries has been to men of intelligence a guiding and inspiring beacon out of the past, flared up after the battles of Marathon and Salamis had made Athens free and fearless and, without any great excesses of power, predominant in her world. It was the work of a quite small group of men. A number of her citizens lived for the better part of a generation under conditions which, in all ages, have disposed men to produce good and beautiful work: they were secure, they were free, and they had pride; and they were without that temptation of apparent and unchallenged power which disposes all of us to inflict wrongs upon our fellow-men. When political life narrowed down again to the waste and crimes of a fratricidal war with Sparta, there was so broad and well-fed a flame of intellectual activity burning that it lasted through all the windy distresses of this war and beyond the brief lifetime of Alexander the Great, for a period altogether of more than a hundred years after the wars began.

Flushed with victory and the sense of freedom fairly won, the people of Athens did for a time rise towards nobility. Under the guidance of a great demagogue, Pericles, the chief official of the Athenian general assembly, and a politician-statesman rather of the calibre of Gladstone or Lincoln in modern history, they were set to the task of rebuilding their city and expanding their commerce. For a time they were capable of following a generous leader generously, and Fate gave them a generous leader. In Pericles there was mingled in the strangest fashion political ability with a real living passion for deep and high and beautiful things. He kept in power for over thirty years. He was a man of extraordinary vigour and liberality of mind. He stamped these qualities upon his time. As Winckler has remarked, the Athenian democracy had for a time "the face of Pericles." He was sustained by what was probably a very great and noble friendship. There was a woman of unusual education, Aspasia, from Miletus, whom he could not marry because of the law that restricted the citizenship of Athens to the home-born, but who was in effect his wife. She played a large part in gathering about him men of unusual gifts. All the great writers of the time knew her, and several have praised her wisdom. Plutarch, it is true, accuses her of instigating a troublesome and dangerous but finally successful war against Samos, but, as he himself shows later, this was necessitated by the naval hostility of the Samians, which threatened the overseas trade of Athens, upon which all the prosperity of the republic depended.

Men's ambitions are apt to reflect the standards of their intimates. Pericles was content, at any rate, to serve as a leader in Athens rather than to dominate as a tyrant. Alliances were formed under his guidance, new colonies and trading stations were established from Italy to the Black Sea; and the treasures of the league at Delos were brought to Athens. Convinced of his security from

Persia, Pericles spent the war hoard of the allies upon the beautification of his city. This was an unrighteous thing to do by our modern standards, but it was not a base or greedy thing to do. Athens had accomplished the work of the Delian League, and is not the labourer worthy of his hire? This sequestration made a time of exceptional opportunity for architects and artists. The Parthenon of Athens, whose ruins are still a thing of beauty, was but the crown set upon the clustering glories of the Athens Pericles rebuilt. Such sculptures as those of Phidias, Myron, and Polyclitus that still survive, witness to the artistic quality of the time.

The reader must bear in mind that illuminating remark of Winckler's, which says that this renascent Athens bore for a time the face of Pericles. It was the peculiar genius of this man and of his atmosphere that let loose the genius of men about him, and attracted men of great intellectual vigour to Athens. Athens wore his face for a time as one wears a mask, and then became restless and desired to put him aside. There was very little that was great and generous about the common Athenian. We have told of the spirit of one sample voter for the ostracism of Aristides, and Lloyd (in his *Age of Pericles*) declares that the Athenians would not suffer the name of Miltiades to be mentioned in connection with the battle of Marathon. The sturdy self-respect of the common voters revolted presently against the beautiful buildings rising about them; against the favours shown to such sculptors as Phidias over popular worthies in the same line of business; against the donations made to a mere foreigner like Herodotus of Halicarnassus; against the insulting preference of Pericles for the company and conversation of a Milesian woman. The public life of Pericles was conspicuously orderly, and that presently set the man in the street thinking that his private life must be very corrupt. One gathers that Pericles was "superior" in his demeanour; he betrayed at times a contempt for the citizens he served.

"Pericles acquired not only an elevation of sentiment, and a loftiness and purity of style far removed from the low expression of the vulgar, but likewise a gravity of countenance which relaxed not into laughter, a firm and even tone of voice, an easy deportment, and a decency of dress which no vehemence of speaking ever put into disorder. These things, and others of a like nature, excited admiration in all that saw him. Such was his conduct, when a vile and abandoned fellow loaded him a whole day with reproaches and abuse; he bore it with patience and silence, and continued in public for the despatch of some urgent affairs. In the evening he walked softly home, this impudent wretch following, and insulting him all the way with the most scurrilous language. And as it was dark when he came to his own door, he ordered one of his servants to take a torch and light the man home. The poet Ion, however, says he was proud and supercilious in conversation, and that there was a great deal of vanity and contempt of others mixed with his dignity of manner. . . . He appeared not in the streets except when he went to the forum or the senate house. He declined the invitations of his friends, and all social entertainments and recreations; insomuch that in the whole time of his administration, which was a considerable length he never went to sup with any of his friends but once, which was at the marriage of his nephew Euryptolemus, and he stayed there only until the ceremony of libation was ended. He considered that the freedom of entertainments takes away all distinction of office, and that dignity is but little consistent with familiarity. . . ."

There was as yet no gutter journalism to tell the world of the vileness of the conspicuous and successful; but the common man, a little out of conceit with himself, found much consolation in the art of comedy, which flourished exceedingly. The writers of comedy satisfied that almost universal craving for the depreciation of those whose apparent excellence offends our self-love. They threw dirt steadily and industriously at Pericles and his friends. Pericles was portrayed in a helmet; a helmet; became him, and it is to be feared he knew as much. This led to much joy and mirth over the pleasant suggestion of a frightfully distorted head, an onion head. The "goings on" of Aspasia were of course a fruitful vineyard for the inventions of the street. . . .

Dreaming souls, weary of the vulgarities of our time, have desired to be transferred to the sublime Age of Pericles. But, plumped down into that Athens, they would have found themselves in very much the atmosphere of the lower sort of contemporary music-hall, very much in the vein of our popular newspapers; the same hot blast of braying libel, foul imputation, greedy "patriotism," and general baseness would have blown upon them, the "modern note" would have pursued them. As the memories of Platæa and Salamis faded and the new buildings grew familiar, Pericles and the pride of Athens became more and more offensive to the homely humour of the crowd. He was never ostracized—his prestige with the quieter citizens saved him from that; but he was attacked with increasing boldness and steadfastness. He lived and died a poor man; he was perhaps the most honest of demagogues; but this did not save him from an abortive prosecution for peculation. Defeated in that, his enemies resorted to a more devious method; they began to lop away his friends.

Religious intolerance and moral accusations are the natural weapons of the envious against the leaders of men. His friend Damon was ostracized. Phidias was attacked for impiety. On the shield of the great statue of the goddess Athene, Phidias had dared to put, among the combatants in a fight between Greeks and Amazons portraits of Pericles and himself. Phidias died in prison. Anaxagoras, a stranger welcomed to Athens by Pericles—when there were plenty of honest fellows already there quite willing to satisfy any reasonable curiosities—was saying the strangest things about the sun and stars, and hinting not obscurely that there were no gods but only one animating spirit (*nous*) in the world. The comedy writers suddenly found they had deep religious feelings that could be profoundly and even dangerously shocked, and Anaxagoras fled the threat of a prosecution. Then came the turn of Aspasia. Athens seemed bent upon deporting her, and Pericles was torn between the woman who was the soul of his life and the ungracious city he had saved, defended, and made more beautiful and unforgettable than any other city in history. He stood up to defend Aspasia; he was seized by a storm of very human emotion, and as he spoke he wept. His tears saved Aspasia for a time.

Athene of the Parthenon.

The Athenians were content to humiliate Pericles, but he had served them so long that they were indisposed to do without him. He had been their leader now for a third of a century.

In 431 B.C. came the war with Sparta. Plutarch accuses Pericles of bringing it on because he felt his popularity waned so fast that a war was needed to make him indispensable.

"And as he himself was become obnoxious to the people upon Phidias' account, and was afraid of being called in question for it, he urged on the war, which as yet was uncertain, and blew up that flame which till then was stifled and suppressed. By this means he hoped to obviate the accusations that threatened him, and to mitigate the rage of envy, because such was his dignity and power, that in all important affairs, and in every great danger, the republic could place its confidence in him alone."

But the war was a slow and dangerous war, and the Athenian people were impatient. A certain Cleon arose, ambitious to oust Pericles from his leadership. There was a great clamour for a swift ending of the war. Cleon set out to be "the man who won the war." The popular poets got to work in this fashion:

> "Thou king of satyrs . . . why boast thy prowess,
> Yet shudder at the sound of sharpened swords;
> Spite of the flaming Cleon?"

An expedition under the leadership of Pericles was unsuccessful, and Cleon seized the opportunity for a prosecution. Pericles was suspended from his command and fined. The story goes that his eldest son—this was not the son of Aspasia, but of a former wife—turned against him, and pursued him with vile and incredible accusations. This young man was carried off by the plague. Then the sister of Pericles died, and then his last legitimate son. When, after the fashion of the time, he put the funeral garlands on the boy, he wept aloud. Presently, he himself took the contagion and died (429 B.C.).

The salient facts of this brief summary will serve to show how discordant Pericles was with much of the life of his city. This intellectual and artistic outbreak in Athens was no doubt favoured by the conditions of the time, but it was also due in part to the appearance of some very unusual men. It was not a general movement; it was the movement of a small group of people exceptionally placed and gifted.

§ 2

Another leading figure in this Athenian movement, a figure still more out of harmony with the life around him, and quite as much an original source and stimulant of the enduring greatness of his age, was a man called Socrates, the son of a stone mason. He was born about sixteen years later than Herodotus, and he was beginning to be heard of about the time when Pericles died. He himself wrote nothing, but it was his custom to talk in public places. There was in those days a great searching for wisdom going on; there was a various multitude of teachers called sophists who reasoned upon truth, beauty, and right living, and instructed the developing curiosities and imaginations of youth. This was so because there were no great priestly schools in Greece. And into these discussions this man came, a clumsy and slovenly figure, barefooted, gathering about him a band of admirers and disciples.

His method was profoundly sceptical; he believed that the only possible virtue was true knowledge; he would tolerate no belief, no hope that could not pass the ultimate acid test. For himself this means virtue, but for many of his weaker followers it meant the loss of beliefs and moral habits that would have restrained their impulses. These weaklings became self-excusing, self-indulging scoundrels. Among his young associates were Plato, who afterwards immortalized his method in a series of philosophical dialogues, and founded the philosophical school of the Academy, which lasted nine hundred years; Xenophon, of the Ten Thousand, who described his death; and Isocrates, one of the wisest of Greek political thinkers: but there were also Critias, who, when Athens was utterly defeated by Sparta, was leader among the Thirty Tyrants appointed by the Spartans to keep the crushed city under and destroy its educational organization; Charmides, who was killed beside Critias when the Thirty were overthrown; and Alcibiades, a brilliant and complex traitor, who did much to lead Athens into the disastrous expedition against Syracuse which destroyed her strength, who betrayed her to the Spartans, and who was at last assassinated while on his way to the Persian court to contrive mischief against Greece. These latter pupils were not the only young men of promise whose vulgar faith and patriotism Socrates destroyed, to leave nothing in its place. His most inveterate enemy was a certain Anytus, whose son, a devoted disciple of Socrates, had become a hopeless drunkard. Through Anytus it was that Socrates was at last prosecuted for "corrupting" the youth of Athens, and condemned to death by drinking a poisonous draught made from hemlock (399 B.C.).

His death is described with great beauty in the dialogue of Plato called by the name of *Phœdo*.

§ 3

Plato was born 427 B.C., and he lived for eighty years.

In mental temperament Plato was of an altogether different type from Socrates. He was a most artistic and delicate writer, and Socrates could write nothing consecutive. He cared for beautiful things, and Socrates despised them. He was supremely concerned with the ordering of public affairs and the scheming of happier human relationships, while Socrates, heedless of heat and cold and the opinion of his fellow-creatures, concentrated his mind upon a serene disillusionment. Life, said Socrates, was deception; only the Soul lived. Plato had a very great affection for this rugged old teacher, he found his method of the utmost value in distentangling and clearing up opinions, and he made him the central figure of his immortal dialogues; but his own thoughts and disposition turned him altogether away from the sceptical attitude. In many of the dialogues the voice is the voice of Socrates, but the thought is the thought of Plato.

Plato was living in a time of doubt and questioning about all human relationships. In the great days of Pericles, before 450 B.C., there seems to have been a complete satisfaction in Athens with social and political institutions. Then there seemed no reason for questioning. Men felt free; the community prospered; one suffered chiefly from jealousy. The *History of Herodotus* displays little or no dissatisfaction with Athenian political institutions.

But Plato, who was born about the time Herodotus died, and who grew up in the atmosphere of a disastrous war and great social distress and confusion, was from the first face to face with human discord and the misfit of human institutions. To that challenge his mind responded. One of his earlier works and his latest are bold and penetrating discussions of the possible betterment of social relations. Socrates had taught him to take nothing for granted, not even the common relations of husband and wife or parent and child. His *Republic*, the first of all Utopian books, is a young man's dream of a city in which human life is arranged according to a novel and a better plan; his last, unfinished work, the *Laws*, is a discussion of the regulation of another such Utopia. There is much in Plato at which we cannot even glance here, but it is a landmark in this history; it is a new thing in the development of mankind, this appearance of the idea of wilfully and completely recasting human conditions. So far mankind has been living by traditions under the fear of the gods. Here is a man who says boldly to our race, and as if it were a quite reasonable and natural thing to say, "Take hold of your lives. Most of these things that distress you, you can avoid; most of these things that dominate you, you can overthrow. You can do as you will with them."

One other thing besides the conflicts of the time perhaps stimulated the mind of Plato in this direction. In the days of Pericles Athens had founded many settlements overseas, and the setting up of these settlements had familiarized men with the idea that a community need not grow, it could also be made.

Closely associated with Plato was a younger man, who later also maintained a school in Athens and lived to an even greater age. This was Isocrates. He was what we should call a publicist, a writer rather than an orator, and his peculiar work was to develop the idea of Herodotus, the idea of a unification of Greece against the Persian Empire, as a remedy for the baseness and confusion of her politics and the waste and destruction of her internecine wars. His political horizon was in some respects broader than Plato's, and in his later years he looked towards monarchy, and particularly towards the Macedonian monarchy of Philip, as a more unifying and broadening method of government than city democracy. The same drift to monarchist ideas had occurred in the case of that Xenophon, whose *Anabasis* we have already mentioned. In his old age Xenophon wrote the *Cyropœdia,* a "vindication both theoretically and practically of absolute monarchy as shown in the organization of the Persian Empire."

§ 4

Plato taught in the Academy. To him in his old age came a certain good-looking youngster from Stagria in Macedonia. Aristotle, who was the son of the Macedonian king's physician, and a man with a very different type of mind from that of the great Athenian. He was naturally sceptical of the imaginative will, and with a great respect for and comprehension of established fact. Later on, after Plato was dead, he set up a school at the Lyceum in Athens and taught, criticizing Plato and Socrates with a certain hardness. When he taught, the shadow of Alexander the Great lay across the freedom of Greece, and he favoured slavery and constitutional kings. He had previously been the tutor of Alexander for several years at the court of Philip of Macedon.

Intelligent men were losing heart in those days, their faith in the power of men to make their own conditions of life was fading. There were no more Utopias. The rush of events was manifestly too powerful for such organized effort as was then practicable between men of fine intelligence. It was possible to think of recasting human society when human society was a little city of a few thousand citizens, but what was happening about them was something cataclysmal; it was the political recasting of the whole known world, of the affairs of what even then must have amounted to something between fifty and a hundred million people. It was recasting upon a scale no human mind was yet equipped to grasp. It drove thought back upon the idea of a vast and implacable Fate. It made men snatch at whatever looked stable and unifying. Monarchy, for instance, for all its manifest vices, was a conceivable government for millions; it had, to a certain extent, *worked;* it imposed a ruling will where it would seem that a collective will was impossible. This change of the general intellectual mood harmonized with Aristotle's natural respect for existing fact. If, on the one hand, it made him approve of monarchy and slavery and the subjection of women as reasonable institutions, on the other hand it made him eager to understand fact and to get some orderly knowledge of these realities of nature and human nature that were now so manifestly triumphant over the creative dreams of the preceding generation.

He is terribly sane and luminous, and terribly wanting in self-sacrificial enthusiasm. He questions Plato when Plato would exile poets from his Utopia, for poetry is a power; he directs his energy along a line diametrically opposed to Socrates' depreciation of Anaxagoras. He anticipated Bacon and the modern scientific movement in his realization of the importance of ordered knowledge. He set himself to the task of gathering together and setting down knowledge. He was first natural historian. Other men before him had speculated about the nature of things, but he, with every young man he could win over to the task, set himself to classify and compare things. Plato says in effect: "Let us take hold of life and remodel it"; this soberer successor: "Let us first know more of life and meanwhile serve and use the king." It was not so much a contradiction as an immense qualification of the master.

The peculiar relation of Aristotle to Alexander the Great enabled him to procure means for his work such as were not available again for scientific inquiry for long ages. He could command hundreds of talents (a talent = about £240) for his expenses. At one time he had at his disposal a thousand men scattered throughout Asia and Greece, collecting matter for his natural history. They were, of course, very untrained observers, collectors of stories rather than observers; but nothing of the kind had ever been attempted, had even been thought of, so far as we know, before his time. Political as well as natural science began. The students of the Lyceum under his direction made an analysis of 158 political constitutions. . . .

This was the first gleam of organized scientific inquiry in the world. The early death of Alexander, and the breaking up of his empire almost before it had begun, put an end to endowments on this scale for 2,000 years. Only in Egypt at the Alexandria Museum did any scientific research continue, and that only for a few generations. Of that we will presently tell. Fifty years after Aristotle's death the Lyceum had already dwindled to insignificance.

§ 5

The general drift of thought in the concluding years of the fourth century B.C. was not with Aristotle, nor towards the laborious and necessary accumulation of ordered knowledge. It is possible that without his endowments from the king he would have made but a small figure in intellectual history. Through them he was able to give his splendid intelligence substance and effect. The ordinary man prefers easy ways so long as they may be followed, and is almost wilfully heedless whether they end at last in a cul-de-sac. Finding the stream of events too powerful to control at once, the generality of philosophical teachers drifted in those days from the scheming of model cities and the planning of new ways of living into the elaboration of beautiful and consoling systems of evasion.

Perhaps that is putting things coarsely and unjustly. But let Professor Gilbert Murray speak upon this matter:

"The cynics cared only for virtue and the relation of the soul to God; the world and its learning and its honours were as dross to them. The Stoics and Epicureans, so far apart at first sight, were very similar in their ultimate aim. What they really cared about was ethics—the practical question how a man should order his life. Both, indeed, gave themselves to some science—the Epicureans to physics, the Stoics to logic and rhetoric—but only as a means to an end. The Stoic tried to win men's hearts and convictions by sheer subtlety of abstract argument and dazzling sublimity of thought and expression. The Epicurean was determined to make Humanity go its way without cringing to capricious gods and without sacrificing Free-Will. He condensed his gospel into four maxims: 'God is not to be feared; Death cannot be felt; the Good can be won; all that we dread can be borne and conquered.'"

And meanwhile the stream of events flowed on, with a reciprocal indifference to philosophy.

§ 6

If the Greek classics are to be read with any benefit by modern men, they must be read as the work of men like ourselves. Regard must be had to their traditions, their opportunities, and their limitations. There is a disposition to exaggeration in all human admiration; most of our classical texts are very much mangled, and all were originally the work of human beings in difficulties, living in a time of such darkness and narrowness of outlook as makes our own age by comparison a period of dazzling illumination. What we shall lose in reverence by this familiar treatment, we shall gain in sympathy for that group of troubled, uncertain, and very modern minds. The Athenian writers were, indeed, the first of modern men. They were discussing questions that we still discuss; they began to struggle with the great problems that confront us to-day. Their writings are our dawn.

Jung, in his *Psychology of the Unconscious*, is very good on the differences between ancient (pre-Athenian) thought and modern thought. The former he calls Undirected Thinking, the latter Directed Thinking. The former was a thinking in images, akin to dreaming; the latter a thinking in words. Science is an organization of directed thinking. The Antique spirit (before the Greek thinkers, i.e.) created not science but mythology. The ancient human world was a world of subjective fantasies like the world of children and uneducated young people to-day, and like the world of savages and dreams. Infantile thought and dreams are a re-echo of prehistoric and savage methods of thinking. Myths, says Jung, are the mass dreams of peoples, and dreams the myths of individuals. We have already directed the reader's attention to the resemblance of the early gods of civilization to the fantasies of children. The work of hard and disciplined thinking by means of carefully analyzed words and statements, which was begun by the Greek thinkers and resumed by the scholastic philosophers in the middle ages, was a necessary preliminary to the development of modern science.

The Greek philosophers began an inquiry, and they arrived at no solutions. We cannot pretend to-day that we have arrived at solutions to most of the questions they asked. The mind of the Hebrews, as we have already shown, awoke suddenly to the endless miseries and disorders of life, saw that these miseries and disorders were largely due to the lawless acts of men, and concluded that salvation could come only through subduing ourselves to the service of the one God who rules heaven and earth. The Greek, rising to the same perception, was not prepared with the same idea of a patriarchal deity; he lived in a world in which there was not God but the gods; if perhaps he felt that the gods themselves were limited, then he thought of Fate behind them, cold and impersonal. So he put his problem in the form of an inquiry as to what was right living, without any definite correlation of the right-living man with the will of God. . . .

To us, looking at the matter from a standpoint purely historical, the common problem can now be presented in a form that, for the purposes of history, covers both the Hebrew and Greek way of putting it. We have seen our kind rising out of the unconsciousness of animals to a continuing racial self-consciousness, realizing the unhappiness of its wild diversity of aims, realizing the inevitable tragedy of individual self-seeking, and feeling its way blindly towards some linking and subordinating idea to save it from the pains and accidents of mere individuality. The gods, the god-king, the idea of the tribe, the idea of the city; here are ideas that have claimed and held for a time the devotion of men, ideas in which they have a little lost their individual selfishness and escaped to the realization of a more enduring life. Yet, as our wars and disasters prove, none of these greater ideas has yet been great enough. The gods have failed to protect, the tribe has proved itself vile and cruel, the city ostracized one's best and truest friends, the god-king made a beast of himself. . . .

As we read over the speculative literature of this great period of the Greeks, we realize three barriers set about the Greek mind, from which it rarely escaped, but from which we now perhaps are beginning to escape.

The first of these limitations was the obsession of the Greek mind by the idea of the city as the ultimate state. In a world in which empire had followed empire, each greater than its predecessor, in a world through which men and ideas drove ever more loosely and freely, in a world visibly unifying even then, the Greeks, because of their peculiar physical and political circumstances, were still dreaming impossibly of a compact little city state, impervious to outer influences, valiantly secure against the whole world. Plato's estimate of the number of citizens in a perfect state varied between 1000 (the *Republic*) and 5,040 (the *Laws*). Said Aristotle in his *Politics:* "For the proper administration of justice and for the distribution of authority it is necessary that the citizens be acquainted with each other's characters, so that, where this cannot be, much mischief ensues, both in the use of authority and in the administration of justice; for it is not just to decide arbitrarily, as must be the case with excessive population." The sort of parish-state thus sketched out was to go to war and hold its own against other cities of the same size. And this was not a couple of generations after the hosts of Xerxes had crossed the Hellespont!

Perhaps these Greeks thought the day of world empires had passed for ever; whereas it was only beginning. At the utmost their minds reached out to alliances and leagues. There must have been men at the court of Artaxerxes thinking far away beyond these little ideas of the rocky creek, the island, and the mountain-encircled valley. But the need for unification against the greater powers that moved outside the Greek-speaking world the Greek mind disregarded wilfully. These outsiders were barbarians, not to be needlessly thought about; they were barred out now from Greece forever. One took Persian money; everybody took Persian money; what did it matter? Or one enlisted for a time in their armies (as Xenophon did) and hoped for his luck with a rich prisoner. Athens took sides in Egyptian affairs, and carried on minor wars with Persia, but there was no conception of a common policy or a common future for Greece. . . .

Until at last a voice in Athens began to shout "Macedonia!" to clamour like a watch-dog, "Macedonia!" This was the voice of the orator and demagogue, Demosthenes, hurling warnings and threats and denunciations at King Philip of Macedon, who had learnt his politics not only from Plato and Aristotle, but also from Isocrates and Xenophon, and from Babylon and Susa, and who was preparing quietly, ably, and steadfastly to dominate all Greece, and through Greece to conquer the known world. . . .

There was a second thing that cramped the Greek mind, the institution of domestic slavery. Slavery was implicit in Greek life; men could conceive of neither comfort nor dignity without it. But slavery shuts off one's sympathy not only from a class of one's fellow subjects; it puts the slave-owner into a class and organization against all stranger men. One is of an elect tribe. Plato, carried by his clear reason and the noble sanity of the spirit beyond the things of the present, would have abolished slavery; much popular feeling and the New Comedy were against it; the Stoics and Epicureans, many of whom were slaves, condemned it as unnatural, but finding it too strong to upset, decided that it did not affect the soul and might be ignored. With the wise there was no bound or free. To the matter-of-fact Aristotle, and probably to most practical men, its abolition was inconceivable. So they declared that there were in the world men "naturally slaves." . . .

Finally, the thought of the Greeks was hampered by a want of knowledge that is almost inconceivable to us to-day. They had no knowledge of the past of mankind at all; at best they had a few shrewd guesses. They had no knowledge of geography beyond the range of the Mediterranean basin and the frontiers of Persia. We know far more to-day of what was going on in Susa, Persepolis, Babylon, and Memphis in the time of Pericles than he did. Their astronomical ideas were still in the state of rudimentary speculations. Anaxagoras, greatly daring, thought the sun and moon were vast globes, so vast that the sun was probably "as big as all the Peloponnesus." Their ideas in physics and chemistry were the results of profound cogitation; it is wonderful that they did guess at atomic structure.

One has to remember their extraordinary poverty in the matter of experimental apparatus. They had coloured glass for ornament, but no clear glass; no accurate means of measuring the minor intervals of time, no really efficient numerical notation, no very accurate scales, no rudiments of telescope or microscope. A modern scientific man dumped down in the Athens of Pericles would have found the utmost difficulty in demonstrating the elements of his knowledge, however crudely, to the men he would have found there. He would have had to rig up the simplest apparatus under every disadvantage, while Socrates pointed out the absurdity of seeking Truth with pieces of wood and string and metal such as small boys use for fishing. A snobbish aloofness between the philosopher and the artisan kept the former away from any apparatus. No Greek gentleman would have tinkered with glass or metals. And our professor of science would also have been in constant danger of a prosecution for impiety. The democracy of Athens would have tolerated Darwin as little as the democracy of Tennessee.

Our world to-day draws upon relatively immense accumulations of knowledge of fact. In the age of Pericles scarcely the first stone of our comparatively tremendous cairn of things recorded and proved had been put in place. When we reflect upon this difference, then it ceases to be remarkable that the Greeks, with all their aptitude for political speculation, were blind to the insecurities of their civilization from without and from within, to the necessity for effective unification, to the swift rush of events that was to end for long ages these brief freedoms of the human mind.

It is not in the results it achieved, but in the attempts it made, that the true value for us of this group of Greek talkers and writers lies. It is not that they answered questions, but that they dared to ask them. Never before had man challenged his world and the way of life to which he found his birth had brought him. Never had he said before that he could alter his conditions. Tradition and a seeming necessity had held him to life as he had found it grown up about his tribe since time immemorial. Hitherto he had taken the world as children still take the homes and habits in which they have been reared.

So in the fifth and fourth centuries B.C. we perceive, most plainly in Judea and in Athens, but by no means confined to those centres, the beginnings of a moral and an intellectual process in mankind, an appeal to righteousness and an appeal to the truth from the passions and confusions and immediate appearances of existence. It is like the dawn of the sense of responsibility in a youth, who suddenly discovers that life is neither easy nor aimless. Mankind is growing up. The rest of history for three-and-twenty centuries is threaded with the spreading out and development and interaction and the clearer and more effective statement of these main leading ideas. Slowly, more and more, men apprehended the reality of human brotherhood, the needlessness of wars and cruelties and oppression, the possibilities of a common purpose for the whole of our kind. In every generation thereafter there is the evidence of men seeking for that better order to which they feel our world must come.

But everywhere and wherever in any man the great constructive ideas have taken hold, the hot greeds, the jealousies, the suspicions and impatience that are in the nature of every one of us, war against the struggle towards greater and broader purposes. The last twenty-three centuries of history are like the efforts of some impulsive, hasty immortal to think clearly and live rightly. Blunder follows blunder; promising beginnings end in grotesque disappointments; streams of living water are poisoned by the cup that conveys them to the thirsty lips of mankind. But the hope of men rises again at last after every disaster. . . .

§ 7

We have already remarked in this *Outline* that the development of literature had to wait upon the development of a method of writing sufficiently subtle to convey turns of expression and beauties of sound. Before that time written literature could convey only meaning. The early Aryan peoples had, as we have told already, a memorized metrical literature before they had writing; they had minstrel songs, stories and histories and moral precepts, preserved by a special social class, the bards. These traditional possessions only became fixed when they were written. The two chief Greek epics, the *Iliad* and the *Odyssey* appear to have been set down in writing about 700 B.C., and they are both in Ionian Greek. It is said that Peisistratus first had the Homeric poems collected. There were a number of different versions of these epics; the existing text was only established in the second century B.C. There were other epics, continuations and amplifications of the *Iliad* and *Odyssey,* and separate adventure stories, that now have almost completely perished.

It was generally held by the Greeks that the *Iliad* and the *Odyssey* were the work of a single poet, Homer, who was born in seven different cities and at various dates between 1,100 and 800 B.C. Of one fact only is tradition certain, and that is that he was blind. These two epics were held in such love and veneration by the Greeks that it was not until the second century B.C. that anyone observed the fact, obvious even in a translation, that these two great works are as entirely different in spirit, tone and quality as the sound of a trumpet from the sound of a flute. But as Homer could be born so widely and with such sustained perseverance, it adds but little to his marvellousness that he had two brains and two voices. These are matters for the classical scholar. It is the classical scholar alone who can appreciate these works at their full value. They are, he assures us, of a splendour, beauty, wisdom and melody that no translation can convey. No translation does convey anything to justify the ecstasies of the learned about these primary masterpieces of European literature. Into the work of every translator creeps a certain tediousness, a certain puerility. Even the indescribably delightful melodies of the Greek language recited by its enthusiastic advocates to the uncultivated doubter prove to be more than a little suggestive of the noises caused by indifferent plumbing in a defective hot-water system. None the less, these epics contain much beauty and interest, they are suffused with a delightful boyishness, there are flashes of the intensest feeling and the most vivid observation, and it is a pity that the ridiculous extravagances of scholastic admirers, who speak of them as supreme and unapproachable and so forth, have brought upon them the awe-stricken neglect of the general reader.

Side by side with the name of Homer stands that of Hesiod. Hesiod was more probably a real person. The date of his birth is known within two centuries, the ninth and the seventh B.C. His epics, the *Works and Days* and the *Theogony*, preserve, the one, much of the life and labours of the Bœotian farmer, and the other the current traditions about the origins and relationships of the Greek gods.

Epic poetry was in Greece the foundation of all other poetry; for several centuries no other was cultivated. This was the essential Aryan poetry. Then appeared certain other types. There was elegiac poetry, soft and tender, sung to the music of the Lydian flute, and lyric poetry sung to the seven-stringed lyre. On these forms it is impossible to enlarge here. It is idle also to give the names of poets without some indication of the nature and quality of their poems. The names of Pindar and Simonides can have meaning only for those who can give the necessary time to what still remains accessible of their work. But we may note here that one of the greatest of the early love-poets of Greece was a woman, Sappho, of Lesbos.

The written drama as well as the written poetry began in the Grecian world. Drama arose as part of the periodic celebration of Dionysus, the wine god. Originally the celebration was a song in chorus telling of the doings of the god. Then a leader, the *corypheus,* would stand out and recite alone, and the chorus would respond. Æschylus (born 525 B.C.) introduced a second actor who stood out and answered the first. Finally, with Sophocles (born 495 B.C.) came a third actor; the dialogue and acting were developed and the chorus became subordinate to the dramatic action. Hitherto the drama had been performed upon wooden platforms. Now in the sixth century theatres began to be built. That much an Outline of History may record, and also that within a period of a century came the greatest days of the Greek drama. The names of Æschylus, Sophocles, and Euripides (born 480 B.C.) are the culminating names of Greek tragedy, but here they can only be unmeaning names to the reader who will not seek out their work either in the original or in reputable translations and who will not try to see performances of their plays.

Concurrently with the development of tragedy, the graver side of the worship of Dionysus, a more derisive and entertaining form arose, comedy. From the first, comedy was more flexible than tragedy; sometimes it burlesqued tragedy, but at times it became frankly sketches of manners and of entertaining aspects of life. Aristophanes in the fifth century B.C. created a delightful mixture of fancy and political satire. Menander a hundred years later was the outstanding master of the comedy of manners. Greek tragedy was a temporary and formal thing, it was evolved and worked out to its highest possibilities in little more than a century, but comedy is an essential need of human societies. There has been mocking, imitation, comedy, wherever two or three human beings gathered together, since human associations began. The stream of written comedy has never really ceased in the world since first dialogue could be written. Only as the art of reading spread through the community did the written tale begin to rival comedy in its popularity. There were collections of "good stories," and so forth, in Greece, but the development of fiction as a great art awaited a wide reading public and the rapid multiplication of books. Unhappily the greater number of both the tragedies and comedies of Greece have vanished from the world again.

Prose literature appeared first as history and serious discussion. Of Herodotus we have told already, and we have quoted from his work. That comes earlier in the book, but the reader will note that the "Father of History" visited Athens in the time of Pericles, and when he wrote, Athenian tragedy was already past its climax. Thucydides, still later, told the story of the Peloponnesian War. Xenophon and his *Anabasis* also we have noted. Another important portion of the Greek literature that still remains to us are the orations written down of various great speakers. Finally there are to be noted the austere prose statements and arguments of the scientific literature as it was written by Aristotle, and its artistic dramatization in the discussions of the dialogues of Plato.

So briefly we note here the forms of the first great literature in the world. It is all we can do in the space at our disposal. The reader of English who would go on to a fuller account will find it, with a number of skilfully interwoven quotations, in *Greeks and Barbarians* by J. A. K. Thomson. But the only way of achieving a real grasp of any literature whatever is the attentive reading of particular books and writers.

§ 8

Before the discovery of the pre-Greek art of the Ægean peoples and the realization of the vast artistic production of the early empires, the modern world, between the Renaissance and the end of the nineteenth century, had a disproportionate esteem for the achievements of Greek plastic art. It stood out alone in men's imaginations as though it had leapt out of nothingness into being, as though all that went before it was clumsiness and all that came after vulgarization and decay. It produced ecstasies in the cultivated that fill us now more with wonder than sympathy.

We know now that while the literary and intellectual initiatives of Greece mark a distinct new phase in human experience, the plastic art of Greece is no more than a continuation of the civilizations that had gone before. The goldwork, the jewellery, the seals, the statuettes and vases and so forth of Greek manufacture in this great period approach, but do not excel those of the preceding Ægean people nor those of the XVIIIth Dynasty in Egypt. The architecture has a grace and perfection of its own. Its dominant feature is the colonnade, serene and noble with the stout Doric capital, or graceful with the Ionic, or florid with the Corinthian. The Corinthian column and its ramifications became in Roman times the universal weed of architecture, and still sprouts wherever the bank branch or the hotel-de-luxe is to be found.

It is the Greek sculpture, however, that stands out as the distinctive excellence of the period. Formal at first, it reached between the days of Peisistratus and Pericles an unprecedented freedom and naturalness. In the time of Akhnaton Egyptian sculpture made a sudden turn towards ease and realism, but nothing then achieved can compare to the freedoms of the Greek release. We are told that most of the Greek sculpture was tinted in colours. That peculiar austere white beauty, ennobled by the touch of death and completion, that now dominates our sensibilities when we are confronted by the best remains of Greek work, was no part of the artist's intention. The temples, too, in their ruin have a moonlight magic, an unearthly excellence, that was surely wanting in their garish youth.

Of Greek painting we know very little. Masterpieces are mentioned, but they have perished. We can only judge by what may be the degenerating continuation of the tradition in the days of

Imperial Rome. In Pompeii and Herculaneum the painting is gay, skilful and interesting, and beyond comparison more natural and confident than any Egyptian or Babylonian work.

The music of the time was subsidiary to the song and without harmony. Sir W. H. Hadow speaks of the "ugliness of such specimens of Greek music as have been preserved and deciphered."

XXII

THE CAREER OF ALEXANDER THE GREAT

§ 1. *Philip of Macedonia.* § 2. *The Murder of King Philip.* § 3. *Alexander's First Conquests.* § 4. *The Wanderings of Alexander.* § 5. *Was Alexander Indeed Great?* § 6. *The Successors of Alexander.* § 7. *Pergamum a Refuge of Culture.* § 8. *Alexander as a Portent of World Unity.*

§ 1

THE true hero of the story of Alexander is not so much Alexander as his father Philip. The author of a piece does not shine in the limelight as the actor does, and it was Philip who planned much of the greatness that his son achieved, who laid the foundations and forged the tools, who had indeed already begun the Persian expedition at the time of his death. Philip, beyond doubting, was one of the greatest monarchs the world has ever seen; he was a man of the utmost intelligence and ability, and his range of ideas was vastly beyond the scope of his time. He made Aristotle his friend; he must have discussed with him those schemes for the organization of real knowledge which the philosopher was to realize later through Alexander's endowments. Philip, so far as we can judge, seems to have been Aristotle's "Prince"; to him Aristotle turned as men turn only to those whom they admire and trust. To Philip also Isocrates appealed as the great leader who should unify and ennoble the chaotic public life of Greece.

In many books it is stated that Philip was a man of incredible cynicism and of uncontrolled lusts. It is true that at feasts, like all the Macedonians of his time, he was a hard drinker and sometimes drunken—it was probably considered unamiable not to drink excessively at feasts; but of the other accusations there is no real proof, and for evidence we have only the railings of such antagonists as Demosthenes, the Athenian demagogue and orator, a man of reckless rhetoric. The quotation of a phrase or so will serve to show to what the patriotic anger of Demosthenes could bring him. In one of the *Philippics*, as his denunciations of Philip are called, he gives vent in this style:

"Philip—a man who not only is no Greek, and no way akin to the Greeks, but is not even a barbarian from a respectable country—no, a pestilent fellow of Macedon, a country from which we never get even a decent slave." And so on and so on. We know, as a matter of fact, that the Macedonians were an Aryan people very closely akin to the Greeks, and that Philip was probably the best-educated man of his time. This was the spirit in which the adverse accounts of Philip were written.

PHILIP OF MACEDON

When Philip became king of Macedonia in 359 B.C., his country was a little country without either a seaport or any considerable city. It had a peasant population, Greek almost in language, and ready to be Greek in sympathies, but more purely Nordic in blood than any people to the south of it. Philip made this little barbaric state into a great one; he created the most efficient military organization the world had so far seen, and he had brought most of Greece into one confederacy under his leadership at the time of his death. And his extraordinary quality, his power of thinking out beyond the current ideas of his time, is shown not so much in those matters as in the care with which he had his son trained to carry on the policy he had created. He is one of the few monarchs in history who cared for his successor. Alexander was, as few other monarchs have ever been, a king specially educated for empire. Aristotle was but one of the several able tutors his father chose for him. Philip confided his policy to him, and entrusted him with commands and authority by the time he was sixteen. He commanded the cavalry at Chæronea under his father's eye. He was nursed into power—generously and unsuspiciously.

To anyone who reads his life with care it is evident that Alexander started with an equipment of training and ideas of unprecedented value. As he got beyond the wisdom of his upbringing he began to blunder and misbehave—sometimes with a dreadful folly. The defects of his character had triumphed over his upbringing long before he died.

Philip was a king after the old pattern, a leader-king, first among his peers, of the ancient Nordic Aryan type. The army he found in Macedonia consisted of a general foot levy and a noble equestrian order called the "companions." The people were farmers and hunters and somewhat drunken in their habits, but ready for discipline and good fighting stuff. And if the people were homely, the government was intelligent and alert. For some generations the Court language had been Attic (=Athenian) Greek, and the Court had been sufficiently civilized to shelter and entertain such great figures as Euripides, who died there in 406 B.C., and Zeuxis the artist. Moreover, Philip, before his accession, had spent some years as a hostage in Greece. He had had as good an education as Greece could give at that time. He was, therefore, quite familiar with what we may call the idea of Isocrates—the idea of a great union of the Greek states in Europe to dominate the Eastern world; and he knew, too, how incapable was the Athenian democracy, because of its constitution and tradition, of taking the opportunity that lay before it. For it was an opportunity that would have to be shared. To the Athenians or the Spartans it would mean letting in a "lot of foreigners" to the advantages of citizenship. It would mean lowering themselves to the level of equality and fellowship with Macedonians—a people from whom "*we*" do not get "even a decent slave."

There was no way to secure unanimity among the Greeks for the contemplated enterprise except by some revolutionary political action. It was no love of peace that kept the Greeks from such an adventure; it was their political divisions. The resources of the several states were exhausted in a series of internecine wars—wars arising out of the merest excuses and fanned by oratorical wind. The ploughing of certain sacred lands near Delphi by the Phocians was, for example, the pretext for a sanguinary Sacred War.

Philip's first years of kingship were devoted to the discipline of his army. Hitherto most of the main battle fighting in the world had been done by footmen in formation. In the very ancient Sumerian battle-pieces we see spearmen in close order forming the main battle, just as they did in the Zulu armies of the nineteenth century; the Greek troops of Philip's time were still fighting in that same style; the Theban phalanx was a mass of infantry holding spears, the hinder ranks thrusting their longer spears between the front-line men. Such a formation went through anything less disciplined that opposed it. Mounted archers could, of course, inflict considerable losses on such a mass of men, and accordingly, as the horse came into warfare, horsemen appeared on either side as an accessory to this main battle. The reader must remember that the horse did not come into very effective use in Western war until the rise of the Assyrians, and then at first only as a chariot horse. The chariots drove full tilt at the infantry mass and tried to break it. Unless its discipline was very solid they succeeded. The Homeric fighting is chariot fighting. It is not until the last thousand years B.C. that we begin to find mounted soldiers, as distinct from charioteers, playing a part in warfare. At first they appear to have fought in a scattered fashion, each man doing his personal feats. So the Lydians fought against Cyrus. It was Philip who seems to have created charging cavalry. He ordered his "companions" to drill for a massed charge. And also he strengthened his phalanx by giving the rear men longer spears than had been used hitherto, and so deepening its mass. The Macedonian phalanx was merely a more solid version of the Theban phalanx. None of these massed infantry formations was flexible enough to stand a flank or rear attack. They had very slight manœuvring power. Both Philip's and his son's victories followed, therefore, with variations, one general scheme of co-operation between these two arms. The phalanx advanced in the centre and held the enemy's main body; on one wing or the other the cavalry charges swept away the enemy cavalry, and then swooped round upon the flank and rear of the enemy phalanx, the front of which the Macedonian phalanx was already smiting. The enemy main battle then broke and was massacred. As Alexander's military experience grew, he also added a use of catapults in the field, big stone-throwing affairs, to break up the enemy infantry. Before his time catapults had been used in sieges, but never in battles. He invented "artillery preparation."

With the weapon of his new army in his hand, Philip first turned his attention to the north of Macedonia. He carried expeditions into Illyria and as far as the Danube; he also spread his power along the coast as far as the Hellespont. He secured possession of a port, Amphipolis, and certain gold mines adjacent. After several Thracian expeditions he turned southward in good earnest. He took up the cause of the Delphic amphictyony against

those sacrilegious Phocians and so appeared as the champion of Hellenic religion.

There was a strong party of Greeks, it must be understood, a Pan-Hellenic party, in favour of the Greek leadership of Philip. The chief writer of this Pan-Hellenic movement was Isocrates. Athens, on the other hand, was the head and front of the opposition to Philip, and Athens was in open sympathy with Persia, even sending emissaries to the Great King to warn him of the danger to him of a united Greece. The comings and goings of twelve years cannot be related here. In 338 B.C. the long struggle between division and Pan-Hellenism came to a decisive issue, and at the battle of Chæronea Philip inflicted a crushing defeat upon Athens and her allies. He gave Athens peace upon astonishingly generous terms; he displayed himself steadfastly resolved to propitiate and favour that implacable city; and in 338 B.C. a congress of Greek states recognized him as captain-general for the war against Persia.

He was now a man of forty-seven. It seemed as though the world lay at his feet. He had made his little country into the leading state in a great Græco-Macedonian confederacy. That unification was to be the prelude to a still greater one, the unification of the Western world with the Persian Empire into one world state of all known peoples. Who can doubt he had that dream? The writings of Isocrates convince us that he had it. Who can deny that he might have realized it? He had a reasonable hope of living for perhaps another quarter-century of activity. In 336 B.C. his advance guard crossed into Asia. . . .

But he never followed with his main force. He was assassinated.

§ 2

It is necessary now to tell something of the domestic life of King Philip. The lives of both Philip and his son were pervaded by the personality of a restless and evil woman, Olympias, the mother of Alexander.

She was the daughter of the king of Epirus, a country to the west of Macedonia, and, like Macedonia, a semi-Greek land. She met Philip, or was thrown in his way, at some religious gathering in Samothrace. Plutarch declares the marriage was a love-match, and there seems to be at least this much in the charges against Philip that, like many energetic and imaginative men, he was prone to impatient love impulses. He married her when he was already a king, and Alexander was born to him three years later.

It was not long before Olympias and Philip were bitterly estranged. She was jealous of him, but there was another and graver source of trouble in her passion for religious mysteries. We have already noted that beneath the fine and restrained Nordic religion of the Greeks the land abounded with religious cults of a darker and more ancient kind, aboriginal cults with secret initiations, orgiastic celebrations, and often with cruel and obscene rites. These religions of the shadows, these practices of the women and peasants and slaves, gave Greece her Orphic, Dionysiac, and Demeter cults; they have lurked in the tradition of Europe down almost to our own times. The witchcraft of the Middle Ages, with its resort to the blood of babes, scraps of executed criminals, incantations and magic circles, seems to have been little else than the lingering vestiges of these solemnities of the dark whites. In these matters Olympias was an expert and an enthusiast, and Plutarch mentions that she achieved considerable celebrity by a use of tame serpents in these pious exercises. The snakes invaded her domestic apartments, and history is not clear whether Philip found in them matter for exasperation or religious awe. These occupations of his wife must have been a serious inconvenience to Philip, for the Macedonian people were still in that sturdy stage of social development in which neither enthusiastic religiosity nor uncontrollable wives are admired.

Macedonian warrior.

Bas-relief from Pella.

The evidence of a bitter hostility between mother and father peeps out in many little things in the histories. She was evidently jealous of Philip's conquests; she hated his fame. There are many signs that Olympias did her best to set her son against his father and attach him wholly to herself. A story survives (in Plutarch's *Life*) that "whenever news was brought of Philip's victories, the capture of a city or the winning of some great battle, he never seemed greatly rejoiced to hear it; on the contrary, he used to say to his playfellows: 'Father will get everything in advance, boys; he won't leave any great task for me to share with you.'" . . .

It is not a natural thing for a boy to envy his father in this fashion without some inspiration. That sentence sounds like an echo.

We have already pointed out how manifest it is that Philip planned the succession of Alexander, and how eager he was to thrust fame and power into the boy's hands. He was thinking of the political structure he was building—but the mother was thinking of the glory and pride of that wonderful lady Olympias.

She masked her hatred of her husband under the cloak of a mother's solicitude for her son's future. When in 337 B.C. Philip, after the fashion of kings in those days, married a second wife who was a native Macedonian, Cleopatra, "of whom he was passionately enamoured," Olympias made much trouble.

Plutarch tells of a pitiful scene that occurred at Philip's marriage to Cleopatra. There was much drinking of wine at the banquet, and Attalus, the father of the bride, being "intoxicated with liquor," betrayed the general hostility to Olympias and Epirus by saying he hoped there would be a child by the marriage to give them a truly Macedonian heir. Whereupon Alexander, taut for such an insult, cried out, "What then am I?" and hurled his cup at Attalus. Philip, enraged, stood up and, says Plutarch, drew his sword, only to stumble and fall. Alexander, blind with rage and jealousy, taunted and insulted his father.

"Macedonians," he said, "see there the general who would go from Europe to Asia! Why, he cannot get from one table to another!"

How that scene lives still, the sprawled, the flushed faces, the angry voice of the boy! Next day Alexander departed with his mother—and Philip did nothing to restrain them. Olympias went home to Epirus; Alexander departed to Illyria. Thence Philip persuaded him to return.

Fresh trouble arose. Alexander had a brother of weak intellect, Aridæus, whom the Persian governor of Caria sought as a son-in-law. "Alexander's friends and his mother now infused notions into him again, though perfectly groundless, that by so noble a match, and the support consequent upon it, Philip designed the crown for Aridæus. Alexander, in the uneasiness these suspicions gave him, sent one Thessalus, a player, into Caria, to desire the grandee to pass by Aridæus, who was of spurious birth and deficient in point of understanding, and to take the lawful heir to the crown into his alliance. Pixodarus was infinitely more pleased with this proposal. But Philip no sooner had intelligence of it, than he went to Alexander's apartment, taking along with him Philotas, the son of Parmenio, one of his most intimate friends and companions, and, in his presence, reproached him with his degeneracy and meanness of spirit, in thinking of being son-in-law to a man of Caria, one of the slaves of a barbarian king. At the same time he wrote to the Corinthians, insisting that they should send Thessalus to him in chains. Harpal and Niarchus, Phrygius and Ptolemy, some of the other companions of the prince, he banished. But Alexander afterwards recalled them, and treated them with great distinction."

There is something very touching in this story of the father pleading with the son he manifestly loved, and baffled by the web of mean suggestion which had been spun about the boy's imagination.

It was at the marriage of his daughter to her uncle, the king of Epirus and the brother of Olympias, that Philip was stabbed. He was walking in a procession into the theatre, unarmed, in a white robe, and he was cut down by one of his body-guard. The murderer had a horse waiting, and would have got away, but the foot of his horse caught in a wild vine, and he was thrown from the saddle by the stumble, and slain by his pursuers. . . .

So at the age of twenty Alexander was at the end of his anxiety about the succession, and established king in Macedonia.

Olympias then reappeared in Macedonia, a woman proudly vindicated. It is said that she insisted upon paying the same funeral honours to the memory of the murderer as to Philip.

In Greece there were great rejoicings over this auspicious event, and Demosthenes, when he had the news, although it was but seven days after the death of his own daughter, went into the public assembly at Athens in gay attire wearing a chaplet.

Whatever Olympias may have done about her husband's assassin, history does not doubt about her treatment of her supplanter, Cleopatra. So soon as Alexander was out of the way (and a revolt of the hillmen in the north called at once for his attention), Cleopatra's newly-born child was killed in its mother's arms, and Cleopatra—no doubt after a little taunting—was then strangled. These excesses of womanly feeling are said to have shocked Alexander, but they did not prevent him from leaving his mother in a position of considerable authority in Macedonia. She wrote letters to him upon religious and political questions, and he showed a dutiful disposition in sending her always a large share of the plunder he made.

§ 3

These stories have to be told because history cannot be understood without them. Here was the great world of men between India and the Adriatic ready for union, ready as it had never been before for a unifying control. Here was the wide order of the Persian empire with its roads, its posts, its general peace and prosperity, ripe for the fertilizing influence of the Greek mind. And these stories display the quality of the human beings to whom those great opportunities came. Here was this Philip who was a very great and noble man, and yet he was drunken, he could keep no order in his household. Here was Alexander, in many ways gifted above any man of his time, and he was vain, suspicious, and passionate, with a mind set awry by his mother.

We are beginning to understand something of what the world might be, something of what our race might become, were it not for our still raw humanity. It is barely a matter of seventy generations between ourselves and Alexander; and between ourselves and the savage hunters our ancestors, who charred their food in the embers or ate it raw, intervene some four or five hundred generations. There is not much scope for the modification of a species of four or five hundred generations. Make men and women only sufficiently jealous or fearful or drunken or angry, and the hot red eyes of the cavemen will glare out at us to-day. We have writing and teaching, science and power; we have tamed the beasts and schooled the lightning; but we are still only shambling towards the light. We have tamed and bred the beasts, but we have still to tame and breed ourselves.

From the very beginning of his reign the deeds of Alexander showed how well he had assimilated his father's plans, and how great were his own abilities. A map of the known world is needed to show the course of his life. At first, after receiving assurances from Greece that he was to be captain-general of the Grecian forces, he marched through Thrace to the Danube; he crossed the river and burnt a village, the second great monarch to raid the Scythian country beyond the Danube; then recrossed it and marched westward, and so came down by Illyria. By that time the city of Thebes was in rebellion, and his next blow was at Greece. Thebes—unsupported, of course, by Athens—was taken and looted; it was treated with extravagant violence; all its buildings, except the temple and the house of the poet Pindar, were razed, and thirty thousand people sold into slavery. Greece was stunned, and Alexander was free to go on with the Persian campaign.

This destruction of Thebes betrayed a streak of violence in the new master of human destinies. It was too heavy a blow to have dealt. It was a barbaric thing to do. If the spirit of rebellion was killed, so also was the spirit of help. The Greek states remained inert thereafter, neither troublesome nor helpful. They would not support Alexander with their shipping, a thing which was to prove a very grave embarrassment to him.

There is a story told by Plutarch about this Theban massacre, as if it redounded to the credit of Alexander, but indeed it shows only how his saner and his crazy sides were in conflict. It tells of a Macedonian officer and a Theban lady. This officer was among the looters, and he entered this woman's house, inflicted unspeakable insults and injuries upon her, and at last demanded whether she had gold or silver hidden. She told him all her treasures had been put into the well, conducted him thither, and, as he stooped to peer down pushed him suddenly in and killed him by throwing great stones upon him. Some allied soldiers came upon this scene and took her forthwith to Alexander for judgment.

She defied him. Already the extravagant impulse that had ordered the massacre was upon the wane, and he not only spared her but had her family and property and freedom restored to her. This Plutarch makes out to be a generosity, but the issue is more complicated than that. It was Alexander who was outraging and plundering and enslaving all Thebes. That poor crumpled Macedonian brute in the well had been doing only what he had been told he had full liberty to do. Is a commander first to give cruel orders, and then to forgive and reward those who slay his instruments? This gleam of remorse at the instance of one woman, who was not perhaps wanting in tragic dignity and beauty, is a poor set-off to the murder of a great city.

Mixed with the craziness of Olympias in Alexander were the sanity of Philip and the teachings of Aristotle. This Theban business certainly troubled the mind of Alexander. Whenever afterwards he encountered Thebans, he tried to show them special favour. Thebes, to his credit, haunted him.

Yet the memory of Thebes did not save three other great cities from similar brain storms; Tyre he destroyed, and Gaza, and a city in India, in the storming of which he was knocked down in fair fight and wounded; and of the latter place not a soul, not a child, was spared. He must have been badly frightened to have taken so evil a revenge.

At the outset of the war the Persians had this supreme advantage, they were practically masters of the sea. The ships of the Athenians and their allies sulked unhelpfully. Alexander, to get at Asia, had to go round by the Hellespont; and if he pushed far into the Persian empire, he ran the risk of being cut off completely from his base. His first task, therefore, was to cripple the enemy at sea, and this he could only do by marching along the coast of

Asia Minor and capturing port after port until the Persian sea-bases were destroyed. If the Persians had avoided battle and hung upon his lengthening line of communications they could probably have destroyed him, but this they did not do. A Persian army not very much greater than his own gave battle on the banks of the Granicus (334 B.C.) and was destroyed. This left him free to take Sardis, Ephesus, Miletus, and, after a fierce struggle, Halicarnassus. Meanwhile the Persian fleet was on his right and between him and Greece, threatening much but accomplishing nothing.

In 333 B.C., pursuing this attack upon the sea bases, he marched along the coast as far as the head of the gulf now called the Gulf of Alexandretta. A huge Persian army, under the great king Darius III, was inland of his line of march, separated from the coast by mountains, and Alexander went right beyond this enemy force before he or the Persians realized their proximity. Scouting was evidently very badly done by Greek and Persian alike. The Persian army was a vast, ill-organized assembly of soldiers, transport, camp followers, and so forth. Darius, for instance, was accompanied by his harem, and there was a great multitude of harem slaves, musicians, dancers, and cooks. Many of the leading officers had brought their families to witness the hunting down of the Macedonian invaders. The troops had been levied from every province in the empire; they had no tradition or principle of combined action. Seized by the idea of cutting off Alexander from Greece, Darius moved this multitude over the mountains to the sea; he had the luck to get through the passes without opposition, and he encamped on the plain of Issus between the mountains and the shore. And there Alexander, who had turned back to fight, struck him. The cavalry charge and the phalanx smashed this great brittle host as a stone smashes a bottle. It was routed. Darius escaped from his war chariot—that out-of-date instrument—and fled on horseback, leaving even his harem in the hands of Alexander.

All the accounts of Alexander after this battle show him at his best. He was restrained and magnanimous. He treated the Persian princesses with the utmost civility. And he kept his head; he held steadfastly to his plan. He let Darius escape, unpursued, into Syria, and he continued his march upon the naval bases of the Persians—that is to say, upon the Phœnician ports of Tyre and Sidon.

Sidon surrendered to him; Tyre resisted.

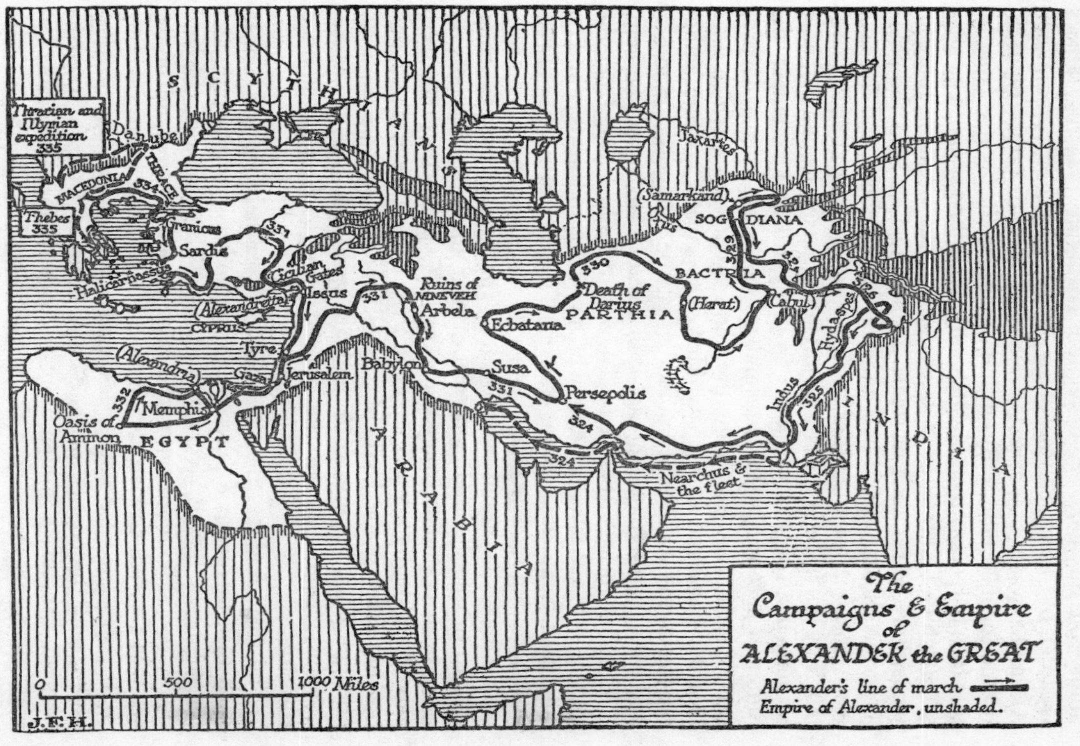

The Campaigns & Empire of ALEXANDER the GREAT
Alexander's line of march
Empire of Alexander, unshaded.
0
500
1000 Miles
J.F.H.
SCYTHIANS
Thracian and Illyrian expedition 335
Danube
Thebes 335
MACEDONIA
334
THRACE
Granicus
Sardis
Halicarnassus
333
Cilician Gates
Issus
(Alexandretta)
CYPRUS
Tyre
(Alexandria)
Gaza
Jerusalem
332
Memphis
Oasis of Ammon
EGYPT
331
Ruins of NINEVEH
Arbela
Babylon
Susa
Persepolis
Ecbatana
Death of Darius
330
PARTHIA
(Herat)
BACTRIA
(Samarkand)
SOGDIANA
Jaxartes
329
327
(Cabul)
326
Hydaspes
Indus
325
INDIA
324
Nearchus & the fleet
ARABIA

Here, if anywhere, we have the evidence of great military ability on the part of Alexander. His army was his father's creation, but Philip had never shone in the siege of cities. When Alexander was a boy of sixteen, he had seen his father repulsed by the fortified city of Byzantium upon the Bosphorus. Now he was face to face with an inviolate city which had stood siege after siege, which had resisted Nebuchadnezzar the Great for fourteen years. For the standing of sieges Semitic peoples hold the palm. Tyre was then an island half a mile from the shore, and her fleet was unbeaten. On the other hand, Alexander had already learnt much by the siege of the citadel of Halicarnassus; he had gathered to himself a corps of engineers from Cyprus and Phœnicia, the Sidonian fleet was with him, and presently the king of Cyprus came over to him with a hundred and twenty ships, which gave him the command of the sea. Moreover, great Carthage, either relying on the strength of the mother city or being disloyal to her, and being furthermore entangled in a war in Sicily, sent no help.

The first measure of Alexander was to build a pier from the mainland to the island, a dam which remains to this day; and on this, as it came close to the walls of Tyre, he set up his towers and battering-rams. Against the walls he also moored ships in which towers and rams were erected. The Tyrians used fire-ships against this flotilla, and made sorties from their two harbours. In a big surprise raid that they made on the Cyprian ships they were caught and badly mauled; many of their ships were rammed, and one big galley of five banks of oars and one of four were captured outright. Finally a breach in the walls was made, and the Macedonians, clambering up the debris from their ships, stormed the city.

The siege had lasted seven months. Gaza held out for two. In each case there was a massacre, the plundering of the city, and the selling of the survivors into slavery. Then towards the end of 332 B.C. Alexander entered Egypt, and the command of the sea was assured. Greece, which all this while had been wavering in its policy, decided now at last that it was on the side of Alexander, and the council of the Greek states at Corinth voted its "captain-general" a golden crown of victory. From this time onward the Greeks were with the Macedonians.

The Egyptians also were with the Macedonians. But they had been for Alexander from the beginning. They had lived under Persian rule for nearly two hundred years, and the coming of Alexander meant for them only a change of masters; on the whole, a change for the better. The country surrendered without a blow. Alexander treated its religious feelings with extreme respect. He unwrapped no mummies as Cambyses had done; he took no liberties with Apis, the sacred bull of Memphis. Here, in great temples and upon a vast scale, Alexander found the evidences of a religiosity, mysterious and irrational, to remind him of the secrets and mysteries that had entertained his mother and impressed his childhood. During his four months in Egypt he flirted with religious emotions.

He was still a very young man, we must remember, divided against himself. The strong sanity he inherited from his father had made him a great soldier; the teaching of Aristotle had given him something of the scientific outlook upon the world. He had destroyed Tyre; in Egypt, at one of the mouths of the Nile, he now founded a new city, Alexandria, to replace that ancient centre of trade. To the north of Tyre, near Issus, he founded a second port, Alexandretta. Both of these cities flourish to this day, and for a time Alexandria was perhaps the greatest city in the world. The sites, therefore, must have been wisely chosen. But also Alexander had the unstable emotional imaginativeness of his mother, and side by side with such creative work he indulged in religious adventures. The gods of Egypt took possession of his mind. He travelled four hundred miles to the remote oasis of the Oracle of Ammon. He wanted to settle certain doubts about his true parentage. His mother had inflamed his mind by hints and vague speeches of some deep mystery about his parentage. Was so ordinary a human being as Philip of Macedon really his father?

For nearly four hundred years Egypt had been a country politically contemptible, overrun now by Ethiopians, now by Assyrians, now by Babylonians, now by Persians. As the indignities of the present became more and more disagreeable to contemplate, the past and the other world became more splendid to Egyptian eyes. It is from the festering humiliations of peoples that arrogant religious propagandas spring. To the triumphant the downtrodden can say, "It is naught in the sight of the true gods." So the son of Philip of Macedon, the master-general of Greece was made to feel a small person amidst the gigantic temples. And he had an abnormal share of youth's normal ambition to impress everybody. How gratifying, then, for him to discover presently that he was no mere successful mortal, not one of these modern vulgar Greekish folk, but ancient and divine, the son of a god, the Pharaoh god, son of Ammon Ra!

Already in a previous chapter we have given a description of that encounter in the desert temple.

Not altogether was the young man convinced. He had his moments of conviction; he had his saner phases when the thing was almost a jest. In the presence of Macedonians and Greeks he doubted if he was divine. When it thundered loudly, the ribald Aristarchus could ask him: "Won't *you* do something of the sort, O Son of Zeus?" But the crazy notion was, nevertheless, present henceforth in his brain, ready to be inflamed by wine or flattery.

Next spring (331 B.C.) he returned to Tyre, and marched thence round towards Assyria, leaving the Syrian desert on his right. Near the ruins of forgotten Nineveh he found a great Persian army, that had been gathering since the battle of Issus, awaiting him. It was another huge medley of contingents, and it relied for its chief force upon that now antiquated weapon, the war chariot. Of these Darius had a force of two hundred, and each chariot had scythes attached to its wheels and to the pole and body of the chariot. There seem to have been four horses to each chariot, and it will be obvious that if one of those horses was wounded by javelin or arrow, that chariot was held up. The outer horses acted chiefly as buffers for the inner wheel horses; they were hitched to the chariot by a single outside trace which could be easily cut away, but the loss of one of the wheel horses completely incapacitated the whole affair. Against broken footmen or a crowd of individualist fighters such vehicles might be formidable; but Darius began the battle by flinging them against the cavalry and light infantry. Few reached their objective and those that did were readily disposed of. There was some manœuvring for position. The well-drilled Macedonians moved obliquely across the Persian front, keeping good order; the Persians, following this movement to the flank, opened gaps in their array. Then suddenly the disciplined Macedonian cavalry charged at one of these torn places and smote the centre of the Persian host. The infantry followed close upon their charge. The centre and left of the Persians crumpled up. For a while the light cavalry on the Persian right gained ground against Alexander's left, only to be cut to pieces by the cavalry from Thessaly, which by this time had become almost as good as its Macedonian model. The Persian forces ceased to resemble an army. They dissolved into a vast multitude of fugitives streaming under great dust-clouds and without a single rally across the hot plain towards Arbela. Through the dust and the flying crowd rode the victors, slaying and slaying until darkness stayed the slaughter. Darius led the retreat.

Such was the battle of Arbela. It was fought on October the 1st, 331 B.C. We know its date so exactly because it is recorded that, eleven days before it began, the soothsayers on both sides had been greatly exercised by an eclipse of the moon.

Darius fled to the north into the country of the Medes. Alexander marched on to Babylon.

The ancient city of Hammurabi (who had reigned seventeen hundred years before) and of Nebuchadnezzar the Great and of Nabonidus was still, unlike Nineveh, a prosperous and important centre. Like the Egyptians, the Babylonians were not greatly concerned at a change of rule to Macedonian from Persian. The temple of Bel-Marduk was in ruins, a quarry for building material, but the tradition of the Chaldean priests still lingered, and Alexander promised to restore the building.

Thence he marched on to Susa, once the chief city of the vanished and forgotton Elamites, and now the Persian capital.

He went on to Persepolis, where, as the climax of a drunken carouse, he burnt down the great palace of the king of kings. This he afterwards declared was the revenge of Greece for the burning of Athens by Xerxes.

§ 4

And now begins a new phase in the story of Alexander. For the next seven years he wandered with an army chiefly of Macedonians in the north and east of what was then the known world. At first it was a pursuit of Darius. Afterwards it became—? Was it a systematic survey of a world he meant to consolidate into one great order, or was it a wild-goose chase? His own soldiers, his own intimates, thought the latter, and at last stayed his career beyond the Indus. On the map it looks very like a wild-goose chase; it seems to aim at nothing in particular and to get nowhere.

The pursuit of Darius III soon came to a pitiful end. After the battle of Arbela his own generals seem to have revolted against his weakness and incompetence; they made him a prisoner, and took him with them in spite of his desire to throw himself upon the generosity of his conqueror. Bessus, the satrap of Bactria they made their leader. There was at last a hot and exciting chase of the flying caravan which conveyed the captive king of kings. At dawn, after an all-night pursuit, it was sighted far ahead. The flight became a headlong bolt. Baggage, women, everything was abandoned by Bessus and his captains; and one other impediment also they left behind. By the side of a pool of water far away from the road a Macedonian trooper presently found a deserted mule-cart with its mules still in the traces. In this cart lay Darius, stabbed in a score of places and bleeding to death. He had refused to go on with Bessus, refused to mount the horse that was brought to him. So his captains had run him through with their spears and left him. He asked his captors for water. What else he may have said we do not know. The historians have seen fit to fabricate a quite impossible last dying speech for him. Probably he said very little. . . .

When, a little after sunrise, Alexander came up, Darius was already dead. . . .

To the historian of the world the wanderings of Alexander have an interest of their own quite apart from the light they throw upon his character. Just as the campaign of Darius I lifted the curtain behind Greece and Macedonia, and showed us something of the silent background to the north of the audible and recorded history of the early civilizations, so now Alexander's campaigns take us into regions about which there had hitherto been no trustworthy record made.

We discover they were not desert regions, but full of a gathering life of their own.

He marched to the shores of the Caspian, thence he travelled eastward across what is now called Western Turkestan. He founded a city that is now known as Herat; whence he went northward by Cabul and by what is now Samarkand, right up into the mountains of Central Turkestan. He returned southward, and came down into India by the Khyber Pass. He fought a great battle on the Upper Indus against a very tall and chivalrous king, Porus, in which the Macedonian infantry encountered an array of elephants and defeated them. Possibly he would have pushed eastward across the deserts to the Ganges valley, but his troops refused to go further. Possibly, had they not done so, then or later he would have gone on until he vanished eastward out of history. But he was forced to turn about. He built a fleet and descended to the mouth of the Indus. There he divided his forces. The main army he took along the desolate coast back to the Persian Gulf, and on the way it suffered dreadfully and lost many men through thirst. The fleet followed him by sea, and rejoined him at the entrance to the Persian Gulf. In the course of this six-year tour he fought battles, received the submission of many strange peoples, and founded cities. He saw the dead body of Darius in June, 330 B.C.; he returned to Susa in 324 B.C. He found the empire in disorder: the provincial satraps raising armies of their own, Bactria and Media in insurrection, and Olympias making government impossible in Macedonia. Harpalus, the royal treasurer, had bolted with all that was portable of the royal treasure, and was making his way, bribing as he went, towards Greece. Some of the Harpalus money is said to have reached Demosthenes.

But before we deal with the closing chapter of the story of Alexander, let us say a word or so about these northern regions into which he wandered. It is evident that from the Danube region right across South Russia, right across the country to the north of the Caspian, right across the country to the east of the Caspian, as far as the mountain masses of the Pamir Plateau and eastward into the Tarim basin of Eastern Turkestan, there spread then a series of similar barbaric tribes and peoples all at about the same stage of culture, and for the most part Aryan in their language and possibly Nordic in their race. They had few cities, mostly they were nomadic; at times they settled temporarily to cultivate the land. They were certainly already mingling in Central Asia with Mongolian tribes, but the Mongolian tribes were not then prevalent there.

An immense process of drying up and elevation has been going on in these parts of the world during the last ten thousand years. Ten thousand years ago there was probably a continuous water barrier between the basin of the Obi and the Aral-Caspian sea. As this had dried up and the marshy land had become steppe-like country, Nordic nomads from the west and Mongolian nomads from the east had met and mixed, and the riding horse had come back into the western world. It is evident this great stretch of country was becoming a region of accumulation for these barbaric peoples. They were very loosely attached to the lands they occupied. They lived in tents and wagons rather than in houses. A brief cycle of plentiful and healthy years, or a cessation of tribal warfare under some strong ruler, would lead to considerable increases of population; then two or three hard years would suffice to send the tribes wandering again in search of food.

From before the dawn of recorded history this region of human accumulation between the Danube and China had been, as it were, intermittently *raining* out tribes southward and westward. It was like a cloud-bank behind the settled landscape that accumulated and then precipitated invaders. We have noted how the Keltic peoples drizzled westward, how the Italians, the Greeks and their Epirote, Macedonian, and Phrygian kindred came south. We have noted too the Cimmerian drive from the east, like a sudden driving shower of barbarians across Asia Minor, the southward coming of the Scythians and Medes and Persians, and the Aryan descent into India. About a century before Alexander there had been a fresh Aryan invasion of Italy by a Keltic people, the Gauls, who had settled in the valley of the Po. Those various races came down out of their northern obscurity into the light of history; and meanwhile beyond that light the reservoir accumulated for fresh discharges. Alexander's march in Central Asia brings now into our history names that are fresh to us; the Parthians a race of mounted bowmen who were destined to play an important rôle in history a century or so later, and the Bactrians, who lived in the sandy native land of the camel. Everywhere he seems to have met Aryan-speaking peoples. The Mongolian barbarians to the north-eastward were still unsuspected; no one imagined there was yet another great cloud-bank of population beyond the Scythians and their kind, in the north of China, that was presently also to begin a drift westward and southward, mixing as it came with the Nordic Scythians and every other people of kindred habits that it encountered. As yet only China knew of the Huns; there were no Turks in Western Turkestan or anywhere else then, no Tartars in the world.

This glimpse of the state of affairs in Turkestan in the fourth century B.C. is one of the most interesting aspects of the wanderings of Alexander; another is his raid through the Punjab. From the point of view of the teller of the human story it is provocative that he did not go on into the Ganges country, and that consequently we have no independent accounts by Greek writers of the life in ancient Bengal. But there is a considerable literature in various Indian languages, dealing with Indian history and social life, that still needs to be made accessible to European readers.

§ 5

Alexander had been in undisputed possession of the Persian Empire for six years. He was now thirty-one. In those six years he had created very little. He had retained most of the organization of the Persian provinces, appointing fresh satraps or retaining the former ones; the roads, the ports, the organization of the empire were still as Cyrus, his greater predecessor, had left them; in Egypt he had merely replaced old provincial governors by new ones; in India he had defeated Porus, and then left him in power much as he had found him, except that Porus was now called a satrap by the Greeks. Alexander had, it is true, planned out a number of towns, and some of them were to grow into great towns; seventeen Alexandrias he founded altogether; their names have undergone various changes – *e.g.* Candahar (Iskender) and Secunderabad; but he had destroyed Tyre, and with Tyre the security of the sea routes which had hitherto been the chief westward outlet for Mesopotamia. Historians say that he Hellenized the East. But Babylonia and Egypt swarmed with Greeks before his time; he was not the cause, he was a part of the Hellenization. For a time the whole world, from the Adriatic to the Indus, was under one ruler; so far he had realized the dreams of Isocrates and Philip his father. But how far was he making this a permanent and enduring union? How far as yet was it anything more than a dazzling but transitory flourish of his own magnificent self?

Alexander the Great
(silver coin of Lysimachus, 321-281 B.C.)

He was making no great roads, setting up no sure sea communications. It is idle to accuse him of leaving education alone, because the idea that empires must be cemented by education was still foreign to human thought. But he was forming no group of statesmen about him; he was thinking of no successor; he was creating no tradition—nothing more than a personal legend. The idea that the world would have to go on after Alexander, engaged in any other employment than the discussion of his magnificence, seems to have been outside his mental range. He was still young, it is true; but well before Philip was one-and-thirty he had been thinking of the education of Alexander.

Was Alexander a statesman at all?

Some students of his career assure us that he was; that now at Susa he planned a mighty world empire, seeing it not simply as a Macedonian conquest of the world, but as a melting together of racial traditions. He did one thing, at any rate, that gives colour to this idea; he held a great marriage feast, in which he and ninety of his generals and friends were married to Persian brides. He himself married a daughter of Darius, though already he possessed an Asiatic wife in Roxana, the daughter of the king of Samarkand. This wholesale wedding was made a very splendid festival, and at the same time all of his Macedonian soldiers, to the number of several thousands, who had married Asiatic brides, were given wedding gifts. This has been called the Marriage of Europe and Asia; the two continents were to be joined, wrote Plutarch, "in lawful wedlock and by community of offspring." And next he began to train recruits from Persia and the north, Parthians, Bactrians, and the like, in the distinctive disciplines of the phalanx and the cavalry. Was that also to assimilate Europe and Asia, or was it to make himself independent of his Macedonians? They thought the latter, at any rate, and mutinied, and it was with some difficulty that he brought them to a penitent mood and induced them to take part in a common feast with the Persians. The historians have made a long and eloquent speech for him on this occasion, but the gist of it was that he bade his Macedonians begone, and gave no sign of how he proposed they should get home out of Persia. After three days of dismay they submitted to him and begged his forgiveness.

Here is the matter for a very pretty discussion. Was Alexander really planning a racial fusion or had he just fallen in love with the pomp and divinity of an Oriental monarch, and wished to get rid of these Europeans to whom he was only a king-leader? The writers of his own time, and those who lived near to his time, lean very much to the latter alternative. They insist upon his immense vanity. They relate how he began to wear the robes and tiara of a Persian monarch. "At first only before the barbarians and privately, but afterwards he came to wear it in public when he sat for the dispatch of business." And presently he demanded Oriental prostrations from his friends.

One thing seems to support the suggestion of great personal vanity in Alexander. His portrait was painted and sculptured frequently, and always he is represented as a beautiful youth, with wonderful locks flowing backward from a broad forehead. Previously most men had worn beards. But Alexander, enamoured of his youthful loveliness, would not part with it; he remained a sham boy at thirty-two; he shaved his face, and so set a fashion in Greece and Italy that lasted many centuries.

The stories of violence and vanity in his closing years cluster thick upon his memory. He listened to tittle-tattle about Philotas, the son of Parmenio, one of his most trusted and faithful generals. Philotas, it was said, had boasted to some woman he was making love to that Alexander was a mere boy; that, but for such men as his father and himself, there would have been no conquest of Persia, and the like. Such assertions had a certain element of truth in them. The woman was brought to Alexander, who listened to her treacheries. Presently Philotas was accused of conspiracy, and, upon very insufficient evidence, tortured and executed. Then Alexander thought of Parmenio, whose other two sons had died for him in battle. He sent swift messengers to assassinate the old man before he could hear of his son's death! Now, Parmenio had been one of the most trusted of Philip's generals; it was Parmenio who had led the Macedonian armies into Asia before the murder of Philip. There can be little doubt of the substantial truth of this story, nor about the execution of Callisthenes, the nephew of Aristotle, who refused Alexander divine honours, and "went about with as much pride as if he had demolished a tyranny, while the young men followed him as the only freeman among thousands." Mixed with such incidents we have the very illuminating story of the drunken quarrel in which he killed Clitus. The monarch and his company had been drinking hard, and the drink had made the talk loud and free. There was much flattery of the "young god," much detraction of Philip, at which Alexander had smiled with satisfaction. This drunken self-complacency was more than the Macedonians could stand; it roused Clitus, his foster-brother, to a frenzy. Clitus reproached Alexander with his Median costume, and praised Philip; there was a loud quarrel, and, to end it, Clitus was hustled out of the room by his friends. He was, however, in the obstinate phase of drunkenness, and he returned by another entrance. He was heard outside quoting Euripides "in a bold and disrespectful tone":

> "Are these your customs? Is it thus that Greece
> Rewards her combatants? Shall one man claim
> The trophies won by thousands?"

Whereupon Alexander snatched a spear from one of his guards and ran Clitus through the body as he lifted the curtain to come in. . . .

One is forced to believe that this was the real atmosphere of the young conqueror's life. Then the story of his frantic and cruel display of grief for Hephæstion can scarcely be all invention. If it is true, or in any part true, it displays a mind ill-balanced and altogether wrapped up in personal things, to whom empire was no more than opportunity for egoistic display, and all the resources of the world stuff for freaks of that sort of "generosity" which robs a thousand people to extort the admiration of one astounded recipient.

Hephæstion, being ill, was put upon a strict diet, but in the absence of his physician at the theatre he ate a roasted fowl and drank a flagon of iced wine, in consequence of which he died. Thereupon Alexander decided upon a display of grief. It was the grief of a lunatic. He had the physician crucified! He ordered every horse and mule in Persia to be shorn, and pulled down the battlements of the neighbouring cities. He prohibited all music in his camp for a long time, and, having taken certain villages of the Cusæans, he caused all the adults to be massacred as a sacrifice to the manes of Hephæstion. Finally, he set aside no less than ten thousand talents for a tomb. For those days this was an enormous sum of money. None of which things did any real honour to Hephæstion, but they served to demonstrate to an awe-stricken world what a tremendous thing the sorrow of Alexander could be.

This last story and many such stories may be lies or distortions or exaggerations. But they have a vein in common. After a bout of hard drinking in Babylon a sudden fever came upon Alexander (323 B.C.), and he sickened and died. He was still only thirty-three years of age. Forthwith the world empire he had snatched at and held in his hands, as a child might snatch at and hold a precious vase, fell to the ground and was shattered to pieces.

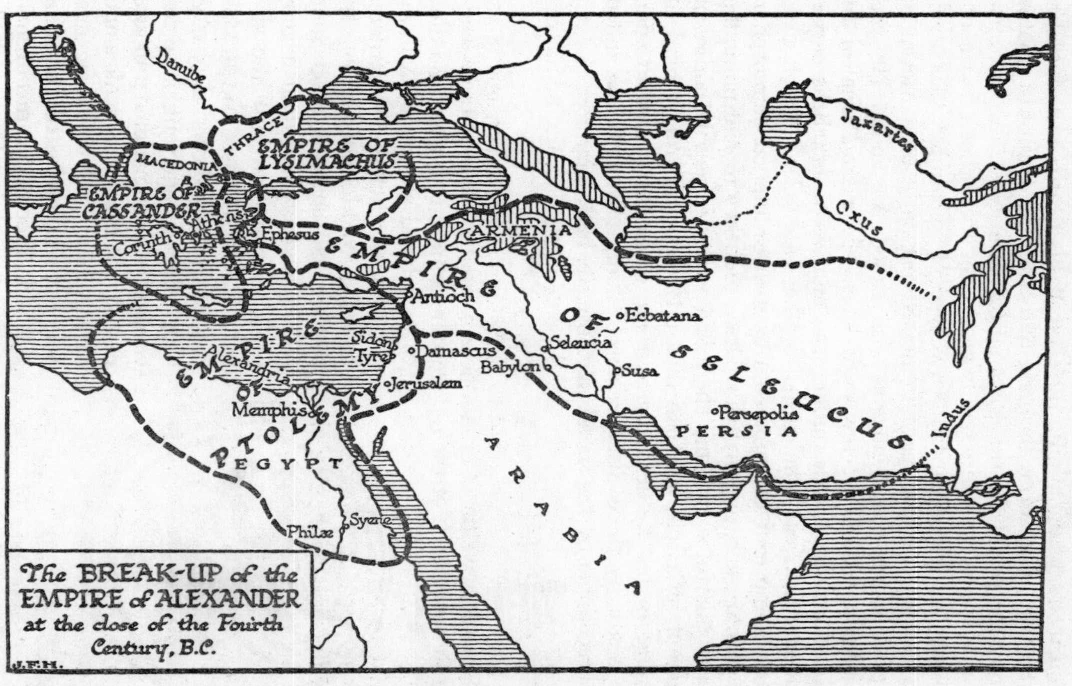

The BREAK-UP of the EMPIRE of ALEXANDER at the close of the Fourth Century, B.C.

Whatever appearance of a worldwide order may have gleamed upon men's imaginations, vanished at his death. The story becomes the story of a barbaric autocracy in confusion. Everywhere the provincial rulers set up for themselves. In the course of a few years the entire family of Alexander had been destroyed. Roxana, his barbarian wife, was prompt to murder, as a rival, the daughter of Darius. She herself presently bore Alexander a posthumous son, who was also called Alexander. He was murdered, with her, a few years later (311 B.C.). Hercules, the only other son of Alexander, was murdered also. So too was Aridæus, the weak-minded half-brother (see § 2). Plutarch gives a last glimpse of Olympias during a brief interval of power in Macedonia, accusing first this person and then that of poisoning her wonderful son. Many she killed in her fury. The bodies of some of his circle who had died after his death she caused to be dug up, but we do not know if any fresh light was shed upon his death by these disinterments. Finally Olympias was killed in Macedonia by the friends of those she had slain.

§ 6

From this welter of crime there presently emerged three leading figures. Much of the old Persian empire, as far as the Indus eastward and almost to Lydia in the west, was held by one general Seleucus, who founded a dynasty, the Seleucid Dynasty; Macedonia fell to another Macedonian general, Antigonus; a third Macedonian, Ptolemy secured Egypt, and, making Alexandria his chief city, established a sufficient naval ascendancy to keep also Cyprus and most of the coast of Phœnicia and Asia Minor. The Ptolemaic and Seleucid empires lasted for a considerable time; the forms of government in Asia Minor and the Balkans were more unstable. Two maps will help the reader to a sense of the kaleidoscopic nature of the political boundaries of the third century B.C. Antigonus was defeated and killed at the battle of Ipsus (301), leaving Lysimachus, the governor of

Tetradrachm with head of Seleucus I.

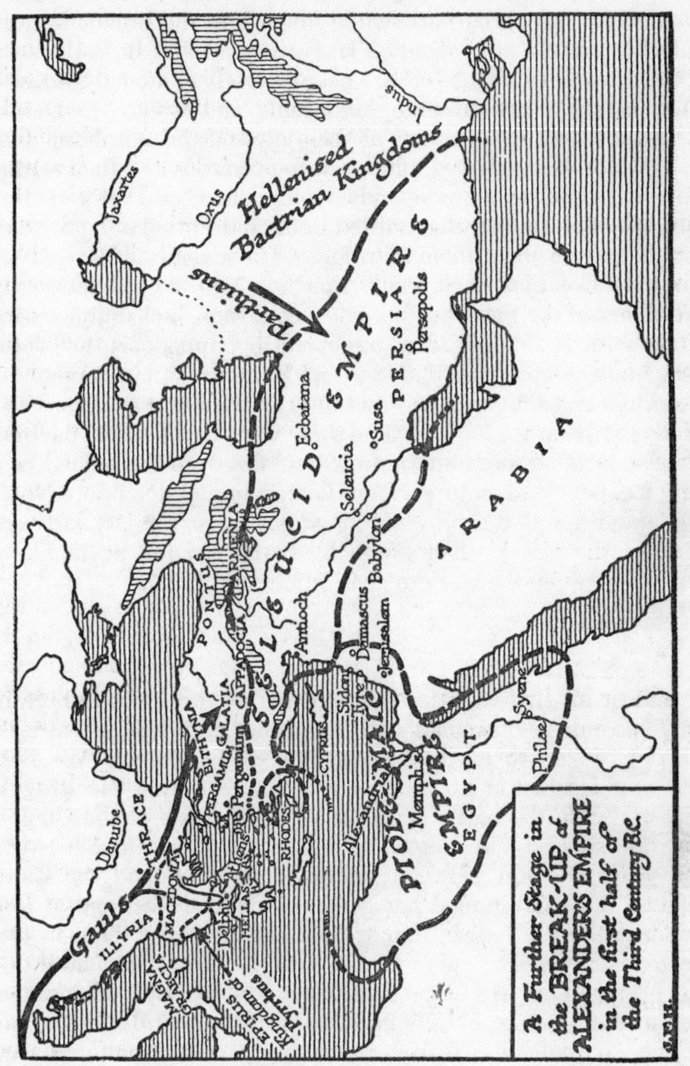

A Further Stage in the BREAK-UP of ALEXANDER'S EMPIRE in the first half of the Third Century B.C.

Thrace, and Cassander, of Macedonia and Greece, as equally transitory successors. Minor governors carved out smaller states. Meanwhile the barbarians swung down into the broken-up and enfeebled world of civilization from the west and from the east. From the west came the Gauls, a people closely related to the Kelts. They raided down through Macedonia and Greece to Delphi (279 B.C.), and two sections of them crossed the Bosphorus into Asia Minor, being first employed as mercenaries and then setting up for themselves as independent plunderers; and after raiding almost to the Taurus, they settled in the old Phrygian land, holding the people about them to tribute. (These Gauls of Phrygia became the Galatians of St. Paul's Epistle.) Armenia and the southern shores of the Black Sea became a confusion of changing rulers. Kings with Hellenistic ideas appeared in Cappadocia, in Pontus (the south shore of the Black Sea), in Bithynia, and in Pergamum. From the east the Scythians and the Parthians and Bactrians also drove southward. . . . For a time there were Greek-ruled Bactrian states becoming more and more Orientalized; in the second century B.C. Greek adventurers from Bactria raided down into North India and founded short-lived kingdoms there, the last eastward fling of the Greek; then gradually barbarism fell again like a curtain between the western civilizations and India.

§ 7

Amidst all these shattered fragments of the burst bubble of Hellenic empire one small state stands out and demands at least a brief section to itself, the kingdom of Pergamum. We hear first of this town as an independent centre during the struggle that ended in the battle of Ipsus. While the tide of the Gaulish invasion swirled and foamed to and fro in Asia Minor between the years 277 and 241, Pergamum for a time paid the Gauls tribute, but she retained her general independence, and at last, under Attalus I, refused her tribute and defeated them in two decisive battles. For more than a century thereafter (until 133 B.C.) Pergamum remained free, and was perhaps during that period the most highly civilized state in the world. On the hill of the Acropolis was reared a rich group of buildings, palaces, temples, a museum, and a library, rivals of those of Alexandria of which we shall presently tell, and almost the first in the world. Under the princes of Pergamum, Greek art blossomed afresh, and the reliefs of the altar of the temple of Zeus and the statues of the fighting and dying Gauls which were made there, are among the artistic treasures of mankind.

In a little while, as we shall tell later, the influence of a new power began to be felt in the Eastern Mediterranean, the power of the Roman republic, friendly to Greece and to Greek civilization; and in this power the Hellenic communities of Pergamum and Rhodes found a natural and useful ally and supporter against the Galatians and against the Orientalized Selucid empire. We shall relate how at last the Roman power came into Asia, how it defeated the Seleucid empire at the battle of Magnesia (190 B.C.), and drove it out of Asia Minor and beyond the Taurus Mountains, and how finally in 133 B.C. Attalus III, the last King of Pergamum, bowing to his sense of an inevitable destiny, made the Roman republic the heir to his kingdom, which became then the Roman province of "Asia."

§ 8

Nearly all historians are disposed to regard the career of Alexander the Great as marking an epoch in human affairs. It drew together all the known world, excepting only the Western Mediterranean, into one drama. But the opinions men have formed of Alexander himself vary enormously. They fall, most of them, into two main schools. One type of scholar is fascinated by the youth and splendour of this young man. These Alexander worshippers seem disposed to take him at his own valuation, to condone every crime and folly either as the mere ebullience of a rich nature or as the bitter necessity to some gigantic scheme, and to regard his life as framed upon a design, a scheme of statesmanship, such as all the wider knowledge and wider ideas of these later times barely suffice to bring into the scope of our understanding. On the other hand, there are those who see him only as a wrecker of the slowly maturing possibilities of a free and tranquil Hellenized world.

Before we ascribe to Alexander or to his father Philip schemes of world policy such as a twentieth-century historian-philosopher might approve, we shall do well to consider very carefully the utmost range of knowledge and thought that was possible in those days. The world of Plato, Isocrates, and Aristotle had practically no historical perspective at all; there had not been such a thing as history in the world, history, that is, as distinguished from mere priestly chronicles, until the last couple of centuries. Even highly educated men had the most circumscribed ideas of geography and foreign countries. For most men the world was still flat and limitless. The only systematic political philosophy was based on the experiences of minute city states, and took no thought of empires. Nobody knew anything of the origins of civilization. No one had speculated upon economics before that time. No one had worked out the reaction of one social class upon another. We are too apt to consider the career of Alexander as the crown of some process that had long been afoot; as the climax of a crescendo. In a sense, no doubt, it was that; but much more true is it that it was not so much an end as a beginning; it was the first revelation to the human imagination of the oneness of human affairs. The utmost reach of the thought of Greece before his time was of a Persian empire Hellenized, a predominance in the world of Macedonians and Greeks. But before Alexander was dead, and much more after he was dead and there had been time to think him over, the conception of a world law and organization was a practicable and assimilable idea for the minds of men.

For some generations Alexander the Great was for mankind the symbol and embodiment of world order and world dominion. He became a fabulous being. His head, adorned with the divine symbols of the demi-god Hercules or the god Ammon Ra, appears on the coins of such among his successors as could claim to be his heirs. Then the idea of world dominion was taken up by another great people, a people who for some centuries exhibited considerable political genius, the Romans; and the figure of another conspicuous adventurer, Cæsar, eclipsed for the western half of the old world the figure of Alexander.

So by the beginning of the third century B.C. we find already arisen in the western civilization of the old world three of the great structural ideas that rule the mind of contemporary mankind. We have already traced the escape of writing and knowledge from the secrets and mysteries and initiations of the old-world priesthoods, and the development of the idea of a universal knowledge, of a universally understandable and communicable history and philosophy. We have taken the figures of Herodotus and Aristotle as typical exponents of this first great idea, the idea *of science*—using the word science in its widest and properest sense, to include history and signify a clear vision of man in relation to the things about him. We have traced also the generalization of religion among the Babylonians, Jews, and other

Semitic peoples, from the dark worship in temples and consecrated places of some local or tribal god to the open service of *one universal God of Righteousness,* whose temple is the whole world. And now we have traced also the first germination of the idea of *a world policy.* The rest of the history of mankind is very largely the history of those three ideas of science, of a universal righteousness, and of a human commonweal, spreading out from the minds of the rare and exceptional persons and peoples in which they first originated, into the general consciousness of the race, and giving first a new colour, then a new spirit, and then a new direction to human affairs.

XXIII

SCIENCE AND RELIGION AT ALEXANDRIA

§ 1. *The Science of Alexandria.* § 2. *Philosophy of Alexandria.* § 3. *Alexandria as a Factory of Religions.* § 4. *Alexandria and India.*

§ 1

ONE of the most prosperous fragments of the brief world-empire of Alexander the Great was Egypt, which fell to the share of the Ptolemy whom we have already noted as being one of those associates of Alexander whom King Philip had banished. The country was at a secure distance from plundering Gaul or Parthian, and the destruction of Tyre and the Phœnician navy and the creation of Alexandria gave Egypt a temporary naval ascendancy in the Eastern Mediterranean. Alexandria grew to proportions that rivalled Carthage; eastward she had an overseas trade through the Red Sea with Arabia and India; and westward her traffic competed with the Carthaginian. Her commercial importance was destined to last for many centuries; it was to grow, indeed, to its greatest proportions under the Roman emperors.

In the Macedonian and Greek governors of the Ptolemies, the Egyptians found a government more sympathetic and tolerable than any they had ever known since they ceased to be a self-governing empire. Indeed, it is rather that Egypt conquered and annexed the Ptolemies politically than that the Macedonians ruled Egypt.

There was a return to Egyptian political ideas, rather than any attempt to Hellenize the government of the country. Ptolemy became Pharaoh, the god-king, and his administration continued the ancient tradition of Pepi, Thothmes, Rameses, and Necho. Alexandria, however, for her town affairs, and subject to the divine overlordship of Pharaoh, had a constitution of the Greek city type. And the language of the court and administration was Attic Greek. Greek became so much the general language of educated people in Egypt that the Jewish community there found it necessary to translate their Bible into the Greek language, many men of their own people being no longer able to understand Hebrew. Attic Greek for some centuries before and after Christ was the language of all educated men from the Adriatic to the Persian Gulf.

Of all Alexander's group of young men, Ptolemy seems to have done most to carry out those ideas of a systematic organization of knowledge with which Aristotle had, no doubt, familiarized the court of Philip of Macedon. Ptolemy was a man of very extraordinary intellectual gifts, at once creative and modest, with a certain understandable cynicism towards the strain of Olympias in the mind of Alexander. His contemporary history of Alexander's campaigns had perished; but it was a source to which all the surviving accounts are deeply indebted.

The Museum he set up in Alexandria was in effect the first university in the world. As its name implies, it was dedicated to the service of the Muses, which was also the case with the Peripatetic school at Athens. It was, however, a religious body only in form, in order to meet the legal difficulties of endowment in a world that had never foreseen such a thing as a secular intellectual process. It was essentially a college of learned men engaged chiefly in research and record, but also to a certain extent in teaching. At the outset, and for two or three generations, the Museum at Alexandria presented such a scientific constellation as even Athens at its best could not rival. Particularly sound and good was the mathematical and geographical work. The names of Euclid, familiar to every schoolboy, Eratosthenes, who measured the size of the earth and came within fifty miles of the true diameter, Apollonius who wrote on conic sections, stand out. Hipparchus made the first attempt to catalogue and map the stars with a view to checking any changes that might be occurring in the heavens. Hero devised the first steam-engine. Archimedes came to Alexandria to study, and remained a frequent correspondent of the Museum. The medical school of Alexandria was equally famous. For the first time in the world's history a standard of professional knowledge was set up. Herophilus, the greatest of the Alexandrian anatomists, is said to have conducted vivisections upon condemned criminals. Other teachers, in opposition to Herophilus, condemned the study of anatomy and developed the science of drugs.

But this scientific blaze at Alexandria did not endure altogether for more than a century. The organization of the Museum was not planned to ensure its mental continuity. It was a "royal" college; its professors and fellows (as we may call them) were appointed and paid by Pharaoh. "The republican character," says Mahaffy, "of the private corporations called the schools or academies at Athens was far more stable and independent." Royal patronage was all very well so long as Pharaoh was Ptolemy I, or Ptolemy II, but the strain degenerated, and the long tradition of Egyptian priestcraft presently swallowed up the Ptolemies —and destroyed the Aristotelian mentality of the Museum altogether. The Museum had not existed for a hundred years before its scientific energy was extinct.

Side by side with the Museum, Ptolemy I created a more enduring monument to himself in the great library. This was a combination of state library and state publishing upon a scale hitherto unheard of. It was to be altogether encyclopædic. If any stranger brought an unknown book to Egypt, he had to have it copied for the collection, and a considerable staff of copyists was engaged continually in making duplicates of all the more popular and necessary works. The library, like a university press, had an outward trade. It was a book-selling affair. Under Callimachus, the head of the library during the time of Ptolemy II and III, the arrangement and cataloguing of the accumulations were systematically undertaken.

In those days, it must be remembered, books were not in pages, but rolled like the music-rolls of the modern piano-player, and in order to refer to any particular passage a reader had to roll back or roll forward very tediously, a process which wore out books and readers together. One thinks at once of a simple and obvious little machine by which such a roll could have been quickly wound to and fro for reference, but nothing of the sort seems to have been used. Every time a roll was read it was handled by two perspiring hands. It was to minimize the waste of time and trouble that Callimachus broke up long works, such as the *History of Herodotus*, into "books," or volumes, as we should call them, each upon a separate roll. The library of Alexandria drew a far vaster crowd of students than did the teachers of the Museum. The lodging and catering for these visitors from all parts of the world became a considerable business interest for the Alexandrian population.

It is curious to note how slowly the mechanism of the intellectual life improves. Contrast the ordinary library facilities of a middle-class English home, such as the present writer is now working in, with the inconveniences and deficiencies of the equipment of an Alexandrian writer, and one realizes the enormous waste of time, physical exertion, and attention that went on through all the centuries during which that library flourished. Before the present writer lie half a dozen books, and there are good indices to three of them. He can pick up any one of these six books, refer quickly to a statement, verify a quotation and go on writing. Contrast with that the tedious unfolding of a rolled manuscript. Close at hand are two encyclopædias, a dictionary, an atlas of the world, a biographical dictionary, and other books of reference. They have no marginal indices, it is true; but that, perhaps, is asking for too much at present. There were no such resources in the world in 300 B.C. Alexandria had still to produce the first grammar and the first dictionary. This present book is being written in manuscript; it is then taken by a typist and typewritten very accurately. It can then, with the utmost convenience, be read over, corrected amply, rearranged freely, retyped, and recorrected. The Alexandrian author had to dictate or recopy every word he wrote. Before he

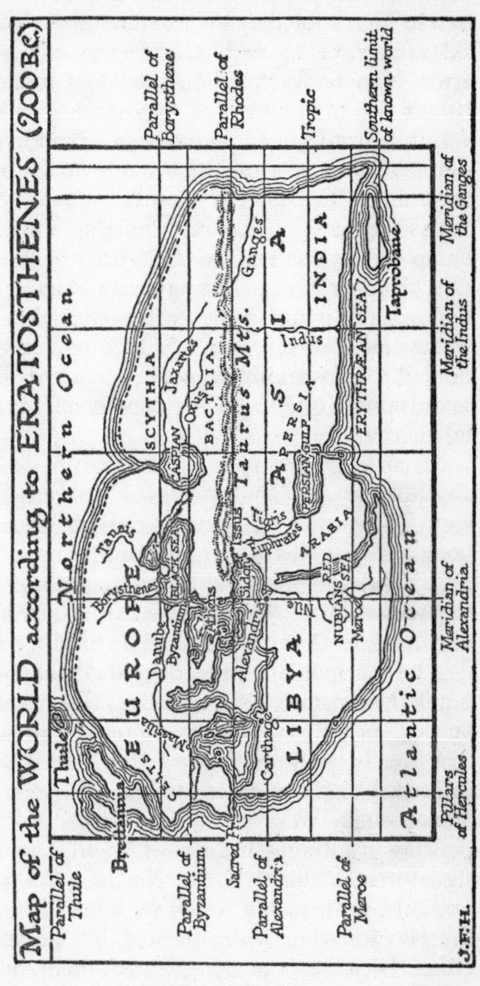

could turn back to what he had written previously, he had to dry his last words by waving them in the air or pouring sand over them; he had not even blotting-paper. Whatever an author wrote had to be recopied again and again before it could reach any considerable circle of readers, and every copyist introduced some new error. New books were dictated to a roomful of copyists, and so issued in a first edition of some hundreds at least. In Rome, Horace and Virgil seem to have been issued in quite considerable editions. Whenever a need for maps or diagrams arose, there were fresh difficulties. Such a science as anatomy, for example, depending as it does upon accurate drawing, must have been enormously hampered by the natural limitations of the copyist. The transmission of geographical fact again must have been almost incredibly tedious. No doubt a day will come when a private library and writing-desk of the year A.D. 1925 will seem quaintly clumsy and difficult; but, measured by the standards of Alexandria, they are astonishingly quick, efficient, and economical of nervous and mental energy.

No attempt seems to have been made at Alexandria to print anything at all. That strikes one at first as a very remarkable fact. The world was crying out for books, and not simply for books. There was an urgent public need for notices, proclamations, and the like. Yet there is nothing in the history of the Western civilizations that one can call printing until the fifteenth century A.D. It is not as though printing was a recondite art or dependent upon any precedent and preliminary discoveries. Printing is the most obvious of dodges. In principle it has always been known. As we have already stated, there is ground, for supposing that the Palæolithic men of the Magdalenian period may have printed designs on their leather garments. The "seals" of ancient Sumer again were printing devices. Coins are print. Illiterate persons in all ages have used wooden or metal stamps for their signatures; William I, the Norman Conqueror of England, for example, used such a stamp with ink to sign documents. In China the classics were being printed by the second century A.D. Yet either because of a complex of small difficulties about ink or papyrus or the form of books, or because of some protective resistance on the part of the owners of the slave copyists, or because the script was too swift and easy to set men thinking how to write it still more easily, as the Chinese character or the Gothic letters did, or because of a gap in the social system between men of thought and knowledge and men of technical skill, printing was not used—not even used for the exact reproduction of illustrations.

The chief reason for this failure to develop printing systematically lies, no doubt, in the fact that there was no abundant supply of printable material of a uniform texture and convenient form.

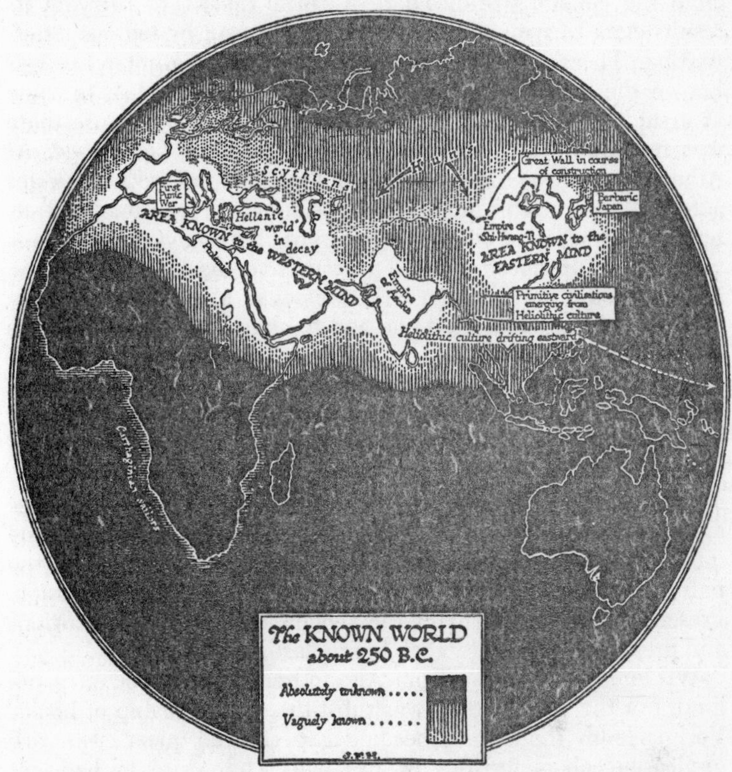

The supply of papyrus was strictly limited, strip had to be fastened to strip, and there was no standard size of sheet. Paper had yet to come from China to release the mind of Europe. Had there been presses, they would have had to stand idle while the papyrus rolls were slowly made. But this explanation does not account for the failure to use block printing in the case of illustrations and diagrams.

These limitations enable us to understand why it was that Alexandria could at once achieve the most extraordinary intellectual triumphs—for such a feat as that of Eratosthenes, for instance, having regard to his poverty of apparatus, is sufficient to put him on a level with Newton or Pasteur—and yet have little or no effect upon the course of politics or the lives and thoughts of people round about her. Her Museum and Library were a centre of light, but it was light in a dark lantern hidden from the general world. There were no means of carrying its results even to sympathetic men abroad except by tedious letter-writing. There was no possibility of communicating what was known there to the general body of men. Students had to come at great cost to themselves to this crowded centre because there was no other way of gathering even scraps of knowledge. At Athens and Alexandria there were bookstalls where manuscript note-books of variable quality could be bought at reasonable prices, but any extension of education to larger classes and other centres would have produced at once a restrictive shortage of papyrus. Education did not reach into the masses at all; to become more than superficially educated one had to abandon the ordinary life of the times and come for long years to live a hovering existence in the neighbourhood of ill-equipped and overworked sages. Learning was not, indeed, so complete a withdrawal from ordinary life as initiation into a priesthood, but it was still something in that nature.

And very speedily that feeling of freedom, that openness and directness of statement which is the vital air of the true intellectual life, faded out of Alexandria. From the first the patronage even of Ptolemy I set a limit to political discussion. Presently the dissensions of the schools let in the superstitions and prejudices of the city mob to scholastic affairs.

Wisdom passed away from Alexandria and left pedantry behind. For the use of books was substituted the worship of books. Very speedily the learned became a specialized queer class with unpleasant characteristics of its own. The Museum had not existed for half a dozen generations before Alexandria was familiar with a new type of human being; shy, eccentric, unpractical, incapable of essentials, strangely fierce upon trivialities of literary detail, as bitterly jealous of the colleague within as of the unlearned without—the Scholarly Man. He was as intolerant as a priest, though he had no altar; as obscurantist as a magician, though he had no cave. For him no method of copying was sufficiently tedious and no rare book sufficiently inaccessible. He was a sort of by-product of the intellectual process of mankind. For many precious generations the new-lit fires of the human intelligence were to be seriously banked down by this by-product.

§ 2

At first the mental activities of Alexandria centred upon the Museum, and were mainly scientific. Philosophy, which in a more vigorous age had been a doctrine of power over self and the material world, without abandoning these pretensions became in reality a doctrine of secret consolation. The stimulant changed into an opiate. The philosopher let the world, as the vulgar say, *rip*, the world of which he was a part, and consoled himself by saying in very beautiful and elaborate forms that the world was illusion and that there was in him something quintessential and sublime, outside and above the world. Athens—politically insignificant, but still a great and crowded mart throughout the fourth century, decaying almost imperceptibly so far as outer seeming went, and treated with a strange respect that was half contempt by all the warring powers and adventurers of the world—was the fitting centre of such philosophical teaching. It was quite a couple of centuries before the schools of Alexandria became as important in philosophical discussion.

§ 3

If Alexandria was late to develop a distinctive philosophy, she was early prominent as a great factory and exchange of religious ideas.

The Museum and Library represented only one of the three sides of the triple city of Alexandria. They represented the Aristotelian, the Hellenic, and Macedonian element. But Ptolemy I had brought together two other factors to this strange centre. First there was a great number of Jews, brought partly from Palestine, but largely also from those settlements in Egypt which had never returned to Jerusalem; these latter were the Jews of the Diaspora or Dispersion, a race of Jews who had not shared the Babylonian Captivity, but who were nevertheless in possession of the Bible and in close correspondence with their co-religionists throughout the world. These Jews populated so great a quarter of Alexandria that the town became the largest Jewish city in the world, with far more Jews in it than there were in Jerusalem. We have already noted that they had found it necessary to translate their scriptures into Greek. And there was a great population of native Egyptians, also for the most part speaking Greek, but with the tradition of forty centuries of temple religion and temple sacrifices at the back of their minds. In Alexandria three types of mind and spirit met, the three main types of the white race; the clear-headed criticism of the Aryan Greek, the moral fervour and monotheism of the Semitic Jew, and the ancient tradition of mysteries and sacrifices that we have already seen at work in the secret cults and occult practices of Greece, ideas which in Hamitic Egypt ruled proudly in great temples in the open light of day.

These three were the permanent elements of the Alexandrian blend. But in the seaport and markets mingled men of every known race, comparing their religious ideas and customs. It is even related that in the third century B.C. Buddhist missionaries came from the court of King Asoka in India, and later on there was certainly a colony of Indian traders in the place. Aristotle remarks in his *Politics* that the religious beliefs of men are apt to borrow their form from political institutions, "men assimilate the lives no less than the bodily forms of the gods to their own," and this age of Greek-speaking great empires under autocratic monarchs was bearing hardly upon those merely local celebrities, the old tribal and city deities. Men were requiring deities with an outlook at least as wide as the empires, and, except where the interests of powerful priesthoods stood in the way, a curious process of assimilation of gods was going on. Men found that though there were many gods, they were all very much alike. Where there had been many gods men came to think there must be really only one god under a diversity of names. He had been everywhere—under an *alias*. The Roman Jupiter, the Greek Zeus, the Babylonian Bel-Marduk, the Egyptian Ammon—Ammon who was the putative father of Alexander and the old antagonist of Amenophis IV—were all sufficiently similar to be identified.

Isis and Horus

"Father of all, in every age,
In every clime adored
By saint, by savage and by sage,
Jehovah, Jove or Lord."

Where there were distinct differences, the difficulty was met by saying that these were different *aspects* of the same god. Bel-Marduk, however, was now a very decadent god indeed, who hardly survived as a pseudonym; Assur, Dagon, and the like, poor old gods of fallen nations, had long since passed out of memory, and did not come into the amalgamation. Osiris, a god popular with the Egyptian commonalty, was already identified with Apis, the sacred bull in the temple of Memphis, and somewhat confused with Ammon. Under the name of Serapis he became the great god of Hellenic Alexandria. He was Jupiter-Serapis. The Egyptian cow goddess, Hathor or Isis, was also represented now in human guise as the wife of Osiris, to whom she bore the infant Horus, who grew up to be Osiris again. These bald statements sound strange, no doubt, to a modern mind, but these identifications and mixing up of one god with another are very illustrative of the struggle the quickening human intelligence was making to cling still to religion and its emotional bonds and fellowship, while making its gods more reasonable and universal.

Serapis

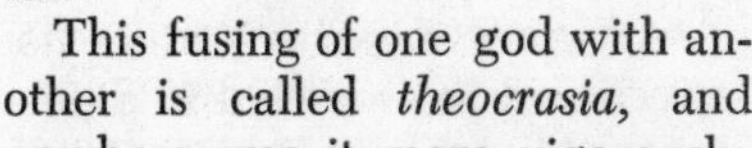

This fusing of one god with another is called *theocrasia,* and nowhere was it more vigorously going on than in Alexandria. Only two peoples resisted it in this period: the Jews, who already had their faith in the One God of Heaven and Earth, Jehovah, and the Persians, who had a monotheistic sun worship.

It was Ptolemy I who set up not only the Museum in Alexandria, but the Serapeum, devoted to the worship of a trinity of gods which represented the result of a process of theocrasia applied more particularly to the gods of Greece and Egypt.

This trinity consisted of the god Serapis (=Osiris+Apis), the goddess Isis (=Hathor, the cow-moon goddess), and the child-god Horus. In one way or another almost every other god was identified with one or other of these three aspects of the one god, even the sun god Mithras of the Persians. And they were each other; they were three, but they were also one. They were worshipped with great fervour, and the jangling of a peculiar instrument, the *sistrum*, a frame set with bells and used rather after the fashion of the tambourine in the proceedings of the modern Salvation Army, was a distinctive accessory to the ceremonies.

And now for the first time we find the idea of immorality becoming the central idea of a religion that extended beyond Egypt. Neither the early Aryans nor the early Semites seem to have troubled very much about immortality, it has affected the Mongolian mind very little, but the continuation of the individual life after death had been from the earliest times an intense preoccupation of the Egyptians. It played now a large part in the worship of Serapis. In the devotional literature of his cult he is spoken of as "the saviour and leader of souls, leading souls to the light and receiving them again." It is stated that "he raises the dead, he shows forth the longed-for light of the sun to those who see, whose holy tombs contain multitudes of sacred books"; and again, "we never can escape him, he will save us, after death we shall still be the care of his providence." The ceremonial burning of candles and the offering of ex-votos—that is to say of small models of parts of the human body in need of succour—was a part of the worship of the Serapeum. Isis attracted many devotees, who vowed their lives to her. Her images stood in the temple, crowned as the Queen of Heaven and bearing the infant Horus in her arms. The candles flared and guttered before her, and the wax ex-votos hung about the shrine. The novice was put through a long and careful preparation, he took vows of celibacy, and when he was initiated his head was shaved and he was clad in a linen garment. . . .

Horus was the only beloved son of Osiris (Serapis). He was also the sun god, and the scarabæus with wings extended was his symbol. In an eclipse, when the solar corona appears, it has a strong resemblance to the extended wings of a scarabæus. Horus was "the sun of righteousness with healing in his wings." Finally he "ascended to the Father" and became one with the Father. In the older Egyptian religion he was the intercessor with the Father for sinners and he is depicted in the Book of the Dead, which was buried with everyone who could afford a copy, pleading for the deceased. Many of the hymns to Horus are singularly like Christian hymns in their spirit and phraseology. That beautiful hymn

"Sun of my soul, thou Saviour dear," was once sung in Egypt to Horus.

In this worship of Serapis, which spread very widely throughout the civilized world in the third and second centuries B.C., we see the most remarkable anticipations of usages and forms of expression that were destined to dominate the European world throughout the Christian era. The essential idea, the living spirit, of Christianity was, as we shall presently show, a new thing in the history of the mind and will of man; but the garments of ritual and symbol and formula that Christianity has worn, and still in many countries wears to this day, were certainly woven in the cult and temples of Jupiter-Serapis, and Isis that spread now from Alexandria throughout the civilized world in the age of theocrasia in the second and first centuries before Christ.

§4

The commercial and intellectual importance of Alexandria continued for many centuries. Anticipating the account we shall presently give of the rise of the Roman power, we may tell here that, under the Empire, Alexandria became the greatest trade centre in the world. The Roman Alexandrian merchants had numerous settlements in South India. At Cranganore on the Malabar coast there was a temple dedicated to Augustus, and the settlement was defended by two Roman cohorts. Embassies were sent from the Emperor to various South Indian potentates. Moreover, Clement, Chrysostom, and other early Christian writers speak about the Indians in Alexandria and their cults.

XXIV

THE RISE AND SPREAD OF BUDDHISM

§ 1. *The Story of Gautama.* § 2. *Teaching and Legend in Conflict.* § 3. *The Gospel of Gautama Buddha.* § 4. *Buddhism and Asoka.* § 5. *Two Great Chinese Teachers.* § 6. *The Corruptions of Buddhism.* § 7. *The Present Range of Buddhism.*

§ 1

IT IS interesting to turn from the mental and moral activities of Athens and Alexandria, and the growth of human ideas in the Mediterranean world, to the almost entirely separate intellectual life of India. Here was a civilization which from the first seems to have grown up upon its own roots and with a character of its own. It was cut off from the civilizations to the west and to the east by vast mountain barriers and desert regions. The Aryan tribes who had come down into the peninsula soon lost touch with their kindred to the west and north, and developed upon lines of their own. This was more particularly the case with those who had passed on into the Ganges country and beyond. They found a civilization already scattered over India, the Dravidian civilization. This had arisen independently, just as the Sumerian, Cretan, and Egyptian civilizations seem to have arisen, out of that widespread development of the Neolithic culture whose characteristics we have already described. They revived and changed this Dravidian civilization much as the Greeks did the Ægean or the Semites the Sumerian.

These Indian Aryans were living under different conditions from those that prevailed to the north-west. They were living in a warmer climate, in which a diet of beef and fermented liquor was destructive; they were forced, therefore, to a generally vegetarian dietary, and the prolific soil, almost unasked, gave them all the food they needed. There was no further reason for them to wander; the crops and seasons were trustworthy. They wanted little clothing or housing. They wanted so little that trade was undeveloped. There was still land for every one who desired to cultivate a patch—and a little patch sufficed. Their political life was simple and comparatively secure; no great conquering powers had arisen as yet in India, and her natural barriers sufficed to stop the early imperialisms to the west of her and to the east. Thousands of comparatively pacific little village republics and chieftainships were spread over the land. There was no sea life, there were no pirate raiders, no strange traders. One might write a history of India coming down to four hundred years ago and hardly mention the sea.

The history of India for many centuries had been happier, less fierce, and more dreamlike than any other history. The noblemen, the rajahs, hunted; life was largely made up of love stories. Here and there a maharajah arose amidst the rajahs and built a city, caught and tamed many elephants, slew many tigers, and left a tradition of his splendour and his wonderful processions.

Yet there was much active thought among the Orientalized Aryans; great epics were composed and handed down by verbal tradition—for there was as yet no writing. There was also much profound philosophical speculation, which has still to be brought into clear relations with the philosophical systems of the west.

It was somewhere between 600 and 500 B.C., when Crœsus was flourishing in Lydia and Cyrus was preparing to snatch Babylon from Nabonidus, that the founder of Buddhism was born in India. He was born in a small republican tribal community in the north of Bengal under the Himalayas, in what is now overgrown jungle country on the borders of Nepal. The little state was ruled by a family, the Sakya clan, of which this man, Siddhattha Gautama, was a member. Siddhattha was his personal name, like Gaius or John; Gautama, or Gôtama, his family name, like Cæsar or Smith; Sakya his clan name, like Julius. The institution of caste was not yet fully established in India, and the Brahmins, though they were privileged and influential, had not yet struggled to the head of the system; but there were already strongly marked class distinctions and a practically impermeable partition between the noble Aryans and the darker common people. Gautama belonged to the former race. His teaching, we may note, was called the Aryan Path, the Aryan Truth.

It is only within the last half-century that the increasing study of the Pali language, in which most of the original sources were written, has given the world a real knowledge of the life and actual thought of Gautama. Previously his story was overlaid by monstrous accumulations of legend, and his teaching violently misconceived. But now we have a very human and understandable account of him.

He was a good-looking, capable young man of fortune, and until he was twenty-nine he lived the ordinary aristocratic life of his time. It was not a very satisfying life intellectually. There was no literature except the oral tradition of the Vedantic epics, and that was chiefly monopolized by the Brahmins; there was even less knowledge. The world was bound by the snowy Himalayas to the north and spread indefinitely to the south. The city of Benares, which had a king, was about a hundred miles away. The chief amusements were hunting and love-making. All the good that life seemed to offer, Gautama enjoyed. He was married at nineteen to a beautiful cousin. For some years they remained childless. He hunted and played and went about in his sunny world of gardens and groves and irrigated rice-fields. And it was amidst this life that a great discontent fell upon him. It was the unhappiness of a fine brain that seeks employment. He lived amidst plenty and beauty, he passed from gratification to gratification, and his soul was not satisfied. It was as if he heard the destinies of the race calling to him. He felt that the existence he was leading was not the reality of life, but a holiday—a holiday that had gone on too long.

While he was in this mood he saw four things that served to point his thoughts. He was driving on some excursion of pleasure, when he came upon a man dreadfully broken down by age. The poor, bent, enfeebled creature struck his imagination. "Such is the way of life," said Channa, his charioteer, and "to that we must all come." While this was yet in his mind he chanced upon a man suffering horribly from some loathsome disease. "Such is the way of life," said Channa. The third vision was of an unburied body, swollen, eyeless, mauled by passing birds and beasts and altogether terrible. "That is the way of life," said Channa.

The sense of disease and mortality, the insecurity and the unsatisfactoriness of all happiness, descended upon the mind of Gautama. And then he and Channa saw one of those wandering ascetics who already existed in great numbers in India. These men lived under severe rules, spending much time in meditation and in religious discussion. For many men before Gautama in that land of uneventful sunshine had found life distressing and mysterious. These ascetics were all supposed to be seeking some deeper reality in life, and a passionate desire to do likewise took possession of Gautama.

He was meditating upon this project, says the story, when the news was brought to him that his wife had been delivered of his first-born son. "This is another tie to break," said Gautama.

He returned to the village amidst the rejoicings of his fellow clansmen. There was a great feast and a Nautch dance to celebrate the birth of this new tie, and in the night Gautama awoke in a great agony of spirit, "like a man who is told that his house is on fire." In the ante-room the dancing girls were lying in strips of darkness and moonlight. He called Channa, and told him to prepare his horse. Then he went softly to the threshold of his wife's chamber, and saw her by the light of a little oil lamp, sleeping sweetly, surrounded by flowers, with his infant son in her arm. He felt a great craving to take up the child in one first and last embrace before he departed, but the fear of waking his wife prevented him, and at last he turned away and went out into the bright Indian moonshine to Channa waiting with the horses, and mounted and rode off into the world.

As he rode through the night with Channa, it seemed to him that Mara, the Tempter of Mankind, filled the sky and disputed with him. "Return," said Mara, "and be a king, and I will make you the greatest of kings. Go on, and you will fail. Never will I cease to dog your footsteps. Lust or malice or anger will betray you at last in some unwary moment; sooner or later you will be mine."

Very far they rode that night, and in the morning he stopped outside the lands of his clan, and dismounted beside a sandy river. There he cut off his flowing locks with his sword, removed all his ornaments, and sent them and his horse and sword back to his house by Channa. Then going on, he presently met a ragged man and exchanged clothes with him, and so having divested himself of all worldly entanglements, he was free to pursue his search after wisdom. He made his way southward to a resort of hermits and teachers in a hilly spur running into Bengal northward from the Vindhya Mountains, close to the town of Rajgir. There a number of wise men lived in a warren of caves, going into the town for their simple supplies and imparting their knowledge by word of mouth to such as cared to come to them.

This instruction must have been very much in the style of the Socratic discussions that were going on in Athens a couple of centuries later. Gautama became versed in all the metaphysics of his age. But his acute intelligence was dissatisfied with the solutions offered him.

The Indian mind has always been disposed to believe that power and knowledge may be obtained by extreme asceticism, by fasting, sleeplessness, and self-torment, and these ideas Gautama now put to the test. He betook himself with five disciple companions to the jungle in a gorge in the Vindhya Mountains, and there he gave himself up to fasting and terrible penances. His fame spread, "like the sound of a great bell hung in the canopy of the skies." But it brought him no sense of truth achieved. One day he was walking up and down, trying to think in spite of his enfeebled state. Suddenly he staggered and fell unconscious. When he recovered, the preposterousness of these semi-magic ways of attempting wisdom was plain to him.

He amazed and horrified his five companions by demanding ordinary food and refusing to continue his self-mortifications. He had realized that whatever truth a man may reach is reached best by a nourished brain in a healthy body. Such a conception was absolutely foreign to the ideas of the land and age. His disciples deserted him, and went off in a melancholy state to Benares. The boom of the great bell ceased. Gautama the wonderful had fallen.

For a time Gautama wandered alone, the loneliest figure in history, battling for light.

When the mind grapples with a great and intricate problem, it makes its advances, it secures its positions step by step, with but little realization of the gains it has made, until suddenly, with an effect of abrupt illumination, it realizes its victory. So, it would seem, it happened to Gautama. He had seated himself under a great tree by the side of the river, to eat, when this sense of clear vision came to him. It seemed to him that he saw life plain. He is said to have sat all day and all night in profound thought, and then he rose up to impart his vision to the world.

§ 2

Such is the plain story of Gautama as we gather it from a comparison of early writings. But common men must have their cheap marvels and wonders.

It is nothing to them that this little planet should at last produce upon its surface a man thinking of the past and the future and the essential nature of existence. And so we must have this sort of thing by some worthy Pali scribe, making the most of it:

"When the conflict began between the Saviour of the World and the Prince of Evil a thousand appalling meteors fell. . . .

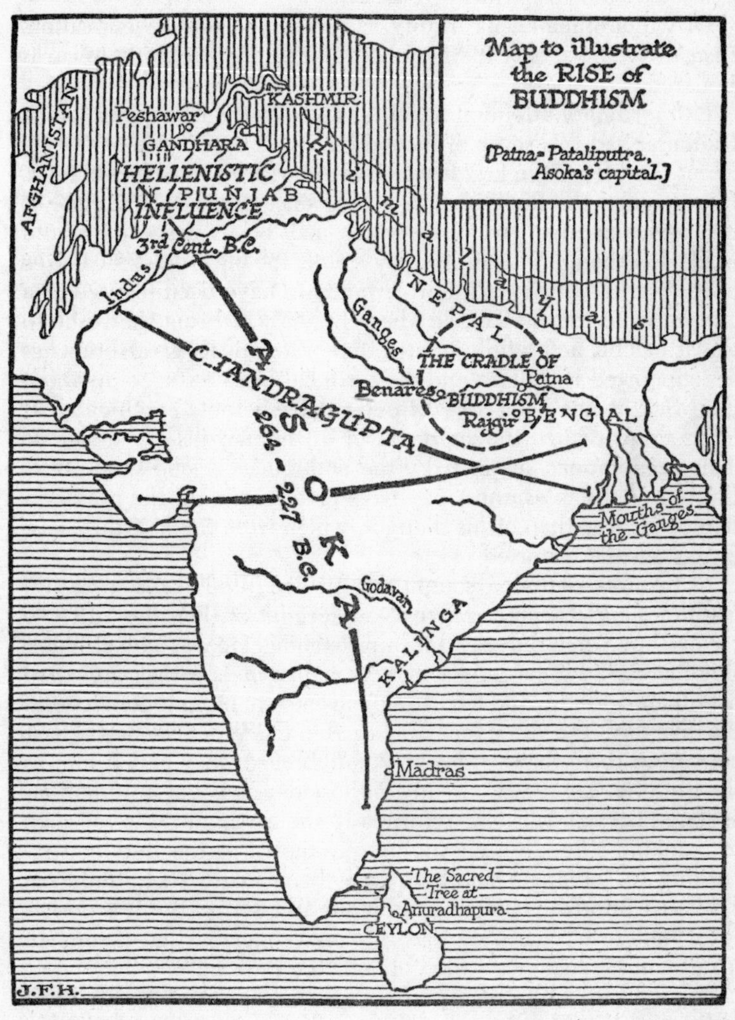

Map to illustrate the RISE of BUDDHISM
[Patna = Pataliputra, Asoka's capital.]
AFGHANISTAN
KASHMIR
Peshawar
GANDHARA
HELLENISTIC INFLUENCE
PUNJAB
3rd Cent. B.C.
Indus
Himalayas
NEPAL
Ganges
THE CRADLE OF BUDDHISM
Patna
Benares
Rajgir
BENGAL
CHANDRAGUPTA
ASOKA
264 - 227 B.C.
Mouths of the Ganges
Godavari
KALINGA
Madras
The Sacred Tree at Anuradhapura
CEYLON
J.F.H.

Rivers flowed back towards their sources; peaks and lofty mountains, where countless trees had grown for ages, rolled crumbling to the earth . . . the sun enveloped itself in awful darkness, and a host of headless spirits filled the air."

Of which phenomena history has preserved no authentication. Instead we have only the figure of a lonely man walking towards Benares.

Extraordinary attention has been given to the tree under which Gautama had this sense of mental clarity. It was a tree of the fig genus, and from the first it was treated with peculiar veneration. It was called the Bo Tree. It has long since perished, but close at hand lives another great tree which may be its descendant, and in Ceylon there grows to this day a tree, the oldest historical tree in the world, which we know certainly to have been planted as a cutting from the Bo Tree in the year 245 B.C. From that time to this it has been carefully tended and watered; its great branches are supported by pillars, and the earth has been terraced up about it so that it has been able to put out fresh roots continually. It helps us to realize the shortness of all human history to see so many generations spanned by the endurance of one single tree. Gautama's disciples unhappily have cared more for the preservation of his tree than of his thought, which from the first they misconceived and distorted.

At Benares Gautama sought out his five pupils, who were still leading the ascetic life. There is an account of their hesitation to receive him when they saw him approaching. He was a blackslider. But there was some power of personality in him that prevailed over their coldness, and he made them listen to his new convictions. For five days the discussion was carried on. When he had at last convinced them that he was now enlightened, they hailed him as the Buddha. There was already in those days a belief in India that at long intervals Wisdom returned to the earth and was revealed to mankind through a chosen person known as the Buddha. According to Indian belief there have been many such Buddhas; Gautama Buddha is only the latest one of a series. But it is doubtful if he himself accepted that title or recognized that theory. In his discourses he never called himself the Buddha.

He and his recovered disciples then formed a sort of Academy in the Deer Park at Benares. They made for themselves huts, and accumulated other followers to the number of threescore or more. In the rainy season they remained in discourse at this settlement, and during the dry weather they dispersed about the country, each giving his version of the new teachings. All their teaching was done, it would seem, by word of mouth. There was probably no writing yet in India at all. We must remember that in the time of the Buddha it is doubtful if even the *Iliad* had been committed to writing. Probably the Mediterranean alphabet, which is the basis of most Indian scripts, had not yet reached India. The master, therefore, worked out and composed pithy and brief verses, aphorisms, and lists of "points," and these were expanded in the discourse of his disciples. It greatly helped them to have these points and aphorisms numbered. The modern mind is apt to be impatient of the tendency of Indian thought to a numerical statement of things, the Eightfold Path, the Four Truths, and so on, but this enumeration was a mnemonic necessity in an undocumented world.

§ 3

The fundamental teaching of Gautama, as it is now being made plain to us by the study of original sources, is clear and simple and in the closest harmony with modern ideas. It is beyond all dispute the achievement of one of the most penetrating intelligences the world has ever known.

We have what are almost certainly the authentic heads of his discourse to the five disciples which embodies his essential doctrine. All the miseries and discontents of life he traces to insatiable selfishness. Suffering, he teaches, is due to the craving individuality, to the torment of greedy desire. Until a man has overcome every sort of personal craving his life is trouble and his end sorrow. There are three principal forms the craving of life takes, and all are evil. The first is the desire to gratify the senses, sensuousness. The second is the desire for personal immortality. The third is the desire for prosperity, worldliness. All these must be overcome—that is to say, a man must no longer be living for himself—before life can become serene. But when they are indeed overcome and no longer rule a man's life, when the first-personal pronoun has vanished from his private thoughts, then he has reached the higher wisdom, Nirvana, serenity of soul. For Nirvana does not mean, as many people wrongly believe, extinction, but the extinction of the futile personal aims that necessarily make life base or pitiful or dreadful.

Now here, surely, we have the completest analysis of the problem of the soul's peace. Every religion that is worth the name, every philosophy, warns us to lose ourselves in something greater than ourselves. "Whosoever would save his life, shall lose it": there is exactly the same lesson.

The teaching of history, as we are unfolding it in this book, is strictly in accordance with this teaching of Buddha. There is, as we are seeing, no social order, no security, no peace or happiness, no righteous leadership or kingship, unless men lose themselves in something greater than themselves. The study of biological progress again reveals exactly the same process—the merger of the narrow globe of the individual experience in a wider being. To forget oneself in greater interests is to escape from a prison.

The self-abnegation must be complete. From the point of view of Gautama, that dread of death, that greed for an endless continuation of his mean little individual life, which drove the Egyptian and those who learnt from him with propitiations and charms into the temples, was as mortal and ugly and evil a thing as lust or avarice or hate. The religion of Gautama is flatly opposite to the "immorality" religions. And his teaching is set like flint against asceticism, as a mere attempt to win personal power by personal pains.

But when we come to the rule of life, the Aryan Path, by which we are to escape from the threefold base cravings that dishonour human life, then the teaching is not so clear. It is not so clear for one very manifest reason: Gautama had no knowledge nor vision of history; he had no clear sense of the vast and many-sided adventure of life opening out in space and time. His mind was confined within the ideas of his age and people, and their minds were shaped into notions of perpetual recurrence, of world following world and of Buddha following Buddha, a stagnant circling of the universe. The idea of mankind as a great Brotherhood pursuing an endless destiny under the God of Righteousness, the idea that was already dawning upon the Semitic consciousness in Babylon at this time, did not exist in his world. Yet his account of the Eightfold Path is, nevertheless, within these limitations, profoundly wise.

Let us briefly recapitulate the eight elements of the Aryan Path. First, Right Views: Gautama placed the stern examination of views and ideas, the insistence upon *truth*, as the first research of his followers. There was to be no clinging to tawdry superstitions. He condemned, for instance, the prevalent belief in the transmigration of souls. In a well-known early Buddhist dialogue there is a destructive analysis of the idea of an enduring individual soul. Next to Right Views came Right Aspirations: because nature abhors a vacuum, and since base cravings are to be expelled, other desires must be encouraged—love for the service of others, desire to do and secure justice, and the like. Primitive and uncorrupted Buddhism aimed not at the destruction of desire, but at the change of desire. Devotion to science and art, or to the betterment of things, manifestly falls into harmony with the Buddhistic Right Aspirations, provided such aims are free from jealousy or the craving for fame. Right Speech, Right Conduct, and Right Livelihood need no expansion here. Sixthly in this list came Right Effort, for Gautama had no toleration for good intentions and slovenly application; the disciple had to keep a keenly critical eye upon his activities. The seventh element of the path, Right Mindfulness, is the constant guard against a lapse into personal feeling or glory for whatever is done or not done. And, finally, comes Right Rapture, which seems to be aimed against the pointless ecstasies of the devout, such witless gloryings, for instance, as those that went to the jingle of the Alexandrian sistrum.

We will not discuss here the Buddhistic doctrine of *Karma,* because it belongs to a world of thought that is passing away. The good or evil of every life was supposed to determine the happiness or misery of some subsequent life, that was in some inexplicable way identified with its predecessor. Nowadays we realize that a life goes on in its consequences for ever, but we find no necessity to suppose that any particular life is resumed. The Indian mind was full of the idea of cyclic recurrence; everything was supposed to come round again. This is a very natural supposition for men to make; so things seem to be until we analyze them. Modern science has made clear to us that there is no such exact recurrence as we are apt to suppose; every day is by an infinitesimal quantity a little longer than the day before; no generation repeats the previous generation precisely; history never repeats itself; change we realize now, is inexhaustible; all things are eternally new. But these differences between our general ideas and those Buddha must have possessed need not in any way prevent us from appreciating the unprecedented wisdom, the goodness, and the greatness of this plan of an emancipated life as Gautama laid it down somewhen in the sixth century before Christ.

And if he failed in theory to gather together all the wills of the converted into the one multifarious activity of our race battling against death and deadness in time and space, he did in practice direct his own life and that of all his immediate disciples into one progressive adventure, which was to preach and spread the doctrine and methods of Nirvana or soul-serenity throughout our fevered world. For them at least his teaching was complete and full. But all men cannot preach or teach; doctrine is but one of many of the functions of life that are fundamentally righteous. To the modern mind it seems at least equally acceptable that a man may, though perhaps against greater difficulties, cultivate the soil, rule a city, make roads, build houses, construct engines, or seek and spread knowledge, in perfect self-forgetfulness and serenity. As much was inherent in Gautama's teaching, but the stress was certainly laid upon the teaching itself, and upon withdrawal from rather than upon the ennoblement of the ordinary affairs of men.

In certain other respects this primitive Buddhism differed from any of the religions we have hitherto considered. It was primarily a religion of conduct, not a religion of observances and sacrifices. It had no temples; and, since it had no sacrifices, it had no sacred order of priests. Nor had it any theology. It neither asserted nor denied the reality of the innumerable and often grotesque gods who were worshipped in India at that time. It passed them by.

§ 4

From the very first this new teaching was misconceived. One corruption was perhaps inherent in its teaching. Because the world of men had as yet no sense of the continuous progressive effort of life, it was very easy to slip from the idea of renouncing self to the idea of renouncing active life. As Gautama's own experiences had shown, it is easier to flee from this world than from self. His early disciples were strenuous thinkers and teachers, but the lapse into mere monastic seclusion was a very easy one, particularly easy in the climate of India, where an extreme simplicity of living is convenient and attractive, and exertion more laborious than anywhere else in the world.

And it was early the fate of Gautama, as it has been the fate of most religious founders since his days, to be made into a wonder by his less intelligent disciples in their efforts to impress the outer world. We have already noted how one devout follower could not but believe that the moment of the master's mental irradiation must necessarily have been marked by an epileptic fit of the elements. This is one small sample of the vast accumulation of vulgar marvels that presently sprang up about the memory of Gautama.

There can be no doubt that for the great multitude of human beings, then as now, the mere idea of an emancipation from self is a very difficult one to grasp. It is probable that even among the teachers Buddha was sending out from Benares there were many who did not grasp it and still less were able to convey it to their hearers. Their teaching quite naturally took on the aspect of salvation, not from oneself—that idea was beyond them – but from misfortunes and sufferings here and hereafter. In the existing superstitions of the people, and especially in the idea of the transmigration of the soul after death, though this idea was contrary to the master's own teaching, they found stuff of fear they could work upon. They urged virtue upon the people lest they should live again in degraded or miserable forms, or fall into some one of the innumerable hells of torment with which the Brahminical teachers had already familiarized their minds. They represented the Buddha as the saviour from almost unlimited torment.

Hariti (painting from Chinese Turkestan, 6th Cent.y A.D.)

[after Foucher]

There seems to be no limit to the lies that honest but stupid disciples will tell for the glory of their master and for what they regard as the success of their propaganda. Men who would scorn to tell a lie in everyday life will become unscrupulous cheats and liars when they have given themselves up to propagandist work; it is one of the perplexing absurdities of our human nature. Such honest souls—for most of them were indubitably honest—were presently telling their hearers of the miracles that attended the Buddha's birth—they no longer called him Gautama, because that was too familiar a name—of his youthful feats of strength, of the marvels of his everyday life, winding up with a sort of illumination of his body at the moment of death.

Of course it was impossible to believe that Buddha was the son of a mortal father. He was miraculously conceived through his mother dreaming of a beautiful white elephant! Previously he had himself been a marvellous elephant possessing six tusks; he had generously given them all to a needy hunter—and even helped him to saw them off. And so on.

Moreover, a theology grew up about the Buddha. He was discovered to be a god. He was one of a series of divine beings, the Buddhas. There was an undying "spirit of all the Buddhas"; there was a great series of Buddhas past and Buddhas (or Buddhisatvas) yet to come. But we cannot go further into these complications of Asiatic theology. "Under the overpowering influence of these sickly imaginations the moral teachings of Gautama have been almost hid from view. The theories grew and flourished; each new step, each new hypothesis, demanded another; until the whole sky was filled with forgeries of the brain, and the nobler and simpler lessons of the founder of the religion were smothered beneath the glittering mass of metaphysical subtleties."

In the third century B.C. Buddhism was gaining wealth and power; and the little groups of simple huts in which the teachers of the Order gathered in the rainy season were giving place to substantial monastic buildings. To this period belong the beginnings of Buddhistic art. Now, if we remember how recent was the adventure of Alexander, that all the Punjab was still under Seleucid rule, that all India abounded with Greek adventurers, and that there was still quite open communication by sea and land with Alexandria, it is no great wonder to find this early Buddhist art strongly Greek in character and the new Alexandrian cult of Serapis and Isis extraordinarily influential in its development.

The kingdom of Gandhara on the north-west frontier near Peshawar, which flourished in the third century B.C., was a typical meeting-place of the Hellenic and Indian worlds. Here are to be found the earliest Buddhist sculptures, and interwoven with them are figures which are recognizably the figures of Serapis and Isis and Horus already worked into the legendary net that gathered about Buddha. No doubt the Greek artists who came to Gandhara were loth to relinquish a familiar theme. But Isis, we are told, is no longer Isis but Hariti, a pestilence goddess whom Buddha converted and made benevolent. Foucher traces Isis from this centre into China, but here other influences were also at work, and the story becomes too complex for us to disentangle in this *Outline*. China had a Taoist deity, the Holy Mother, the Queen of Heaven, who took on the name (originally a male name) of Kuan-yin and who came to resemble the Isis figure very closely. The Isis figure, we feel, must have influenced the treatment of Kuan-yin. Like Isis, she was also Queen of the Seas, Stella Maris. In Japan she was called Kwannon. There seems to have been a constant exchange of the outer forms of religion between east and west. We read in Huc's *Travels* how perplexing he and his fellow-missionary found this possession of a common tradition of worship. "The cross," he says, "the mitre, the dalmatica, the cope, which the Grand Lamas wear on their journeys, or when they are performing some ceremony out of the temple; the service with double choirs, the psalmody, the exorcisms; the censer, suspended from five chains, which you can open or close at pleasure; the benedictions given by the Lamas by extending the right hand over the heads of the faithful; the chaplet, ecclesiastical celibacy, spiritual retirement, the worship of the saints, the fasts, the processions, the litanies, the holy water, all these are analogies between the Buddhists and ourselves."

CHINESE IMAGE OF KUAN-YIN

The cult and doctrine of Gautama, gathering corruptions and variations from Brahminism and Hellenism alike, was spread throughout India by an increasing multitude of teachers in the fourth and third centuries B.C. For some generations at least it retained much of the moral beauty and something of the simplicity of the opening phase. Many people who have no intellectual grasp upon the meaning of self-abnegation and disinterestedness have nevertheless the ability to appreciate a splendour in the reality of these qualities. Early Buddhism was certainly producing noble lives, and it is not only through reason that the latent response to nobility is aroused in our minds. It spread rather in spite of than because of the concessions that it made to vulgar imaginations. It spread because many of the early Buddhists were sweet and gentle, helpful and noble and admirable people, who compelled belief in their sustaining faith.

Quite early in its career Buddhism came into conflict with the growing pretensions of the Brahmins. As we have already noted, this priestly caste was still only struggling to dominate Indian life in the days of Gautama. They had already great advantages. They had the monopoly of tradition and religious sacrifices. But their power was being challenged by the development of kingship, for the men who became clan-leaders and kings were usually not of the Brahminical caste.

Kingship received an impetus from the Persian and Greek invasions of the Punjab. We have already noted the name of King Porus, whom, in spite of his elephants, Alexander defeated and turned into a satrap. There came also to the Greek camp upon the Indus a certain adventurer named Chandragupta Maurya, whom the Greeks called Sandracottus, with a scheme for conquering the Ganges country. The scheme was not welcome to the Macedonians, who were in revolt against marching any further into India, and he had to fly the camp. He wandered among the tribes upon the north-west frontier, secured their support, and after Alexander had departed, overran the Punjab, ousting the Macedonian representatives. He then conquered the Ganges country (321 B.C.), waged a successful war (303 B.C.) against Seleucus I when the latter attempted to recover the Punjab, and consolidated a great empire reaching across all the plain of northern India from the western to the eastern sea. And he came into much the same conflict with the growing power of the Brahmins, into the conflict between crown and priesthood, that we have already noted as happening in Babylonia and Egypt and China. He saw in the spreading doctrine of Buddhism an ally against the growth of priestcraft and caste. He supported and endowed the Buddhistic Order, and encouraged its teachings.

He was succeeded by his son, who was in turn succeeded by Asoka (264 to 227 B.C.), one of the greatest monarchs of history, whose dominions extended from Afghanistan to what is now the province of Madras. He is the only military monarch on record who abandoned warfare after victory. He had invaded Kalinga (225 B.C.), a country along the east coast of Madras, perhaps with some intention of completing the conquest of the tip of the Indian peninsula. The expedition was successful, but he was disgusted by what he saw of the cruelties and horrors of war. He declared, in certain inscriptions that still exist, that he would no longer seek conquest by war, but by religion, and the rest of his life was devoted to the spreading of Buddhism throughout the world.

He seems to have ruled his vast empire in peace and with great ability. He was no mere religious fanatic. But in the year of his one and only war he joined the Buddhist community as a layman, and some years later he became a full member of the Order, and devoted himself to the attainment of Nirvana by the Eightfold Path. How entirely compatible that way of living then was with

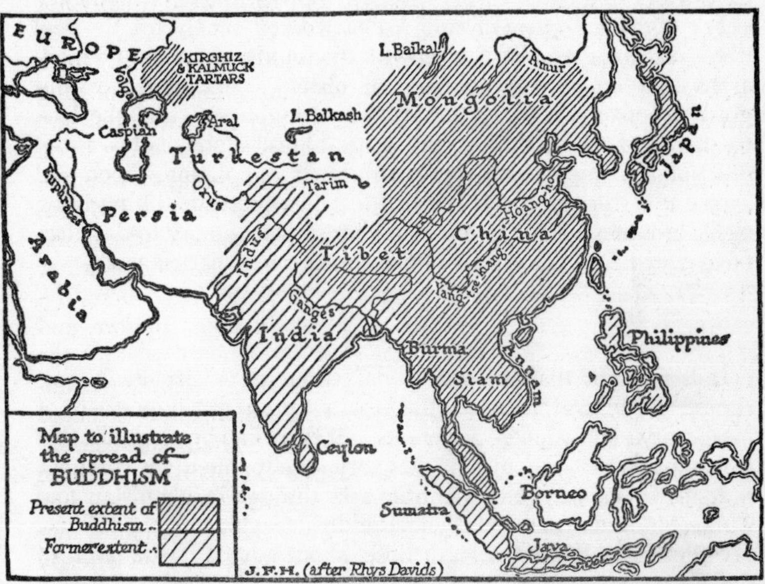

the most useful and beneficent activities of his life shows. Right Aspiration, Right Effort, and Right Livelihood distinguished his career. He organized a great digging of wells in India, and the planting of trees for shade. He appointed officers for the supervision of charitable works. He founded hospitals and public gardens. He had gardens made for the growing of medicinal herbs. Had he had an Aristotle to inspire him, he would no doubt have endowed scientific research upon a great scale. He created a ministry for the care of the aborigines and subject races. He made provision for the education of women. He made—he was the first monarch to make—an attempt to educate his people into a common view of the ends and way of life. He made vast benefactions to the

Buddhist teaching Orders, and tried to stimulate them to a better study of their own literature. All over the land he set up long inscriptions rehearsing the teaching of Gautama, and it is the simple and human teaching and not the preposterous accretions. Thirty-five of his inscriptions survive to this day. Moreover, he sent missionaries to spread the noble and reasonable teaching of his master throughout the world, to Kashmir, to Ceylon, to the Seleucids, and the Ptolemies. It was one of these missions which carried that cutting of the Bo Tree, of which we have already told, to Ceylon.

For eight-and-twenty years Asoka worked sanely for the real needs of men. Amidst the tens of thousands of names of monarchs that crowd the columns of history, their majesties and graciousnesses and serenities and royal highnesses and the like, the name of Asoka shines, and shines almost alone, a star. From the Volga to Japan his name is still honoured. China, Tibet, and even India, though it has left his doctrine, preserve the tradition of his greatness. More living men cherish his memory to-day than have ever heard the names of Constantine or Charlemagne.

§ 5

It is thought that the vast benefactions of Asoka finally corrupted Buddhism by attracting to its Order great numbers of mercenary and insincere adherents, but there can be no doubt that its extension throughout Asia was very largely due to his stimulus.

It made its way into Central Asia through Afghanistan and Turkestan, and so reached China. Buddhist teaching reached China, says Professor Pramatha Nath Bose, about A.D. 64 in the reign of the Emperor Ming-Ti of the Han dynasty. The Pandit Kasyapa was the apostle of China and he was followed by a series of other great teachers. The great days of the Buddhist propaganda in China were the third and fourth centuries A.D. It then underwent grievous persecutions and re-emerged to prominence and the coming of the Tang dynasty.

Buddhism found in China a popular and prevalent religion already established, Taoism, a development of very ancient and primitive magic and occult practices. It was reorganized as a distinctive cult by Chang-Tao-ling in the days of the Han dynasty. Tao means the Way, which corresponds closely with the idea of the Aryan Path. The two religions after an opening struggle spread side by side and underwent similar changes, so that nowadays their outward practice is very similar. Buddhism also encountered Confucianism, which was even less theological and even more a code of personal conduct. And finally it encountered the teachings of Lao Tse, "anarchist, evolutionist, pacifist and moral philosopher," which were not so much a religion as a philosophical rule of life. The teachings of this Lao Tse were later to become incorporated with the Taoist religion by Chen Tuan, the founder of modern Taoism.

Confucius, the founder of Confucianism, like the great southern teacher Lao Tse, and Gautama, lived also in the sixth century B.C. His life has some interesting parallelisms with that of some of the more political of the Greek philosophers of the fifth and fourth. The sixth century B.C. falls into the period assigned by Chinese historians to the Chow dynasty, but in those days the rule of that dynasty had become little more than nominal; the emperor conducted the traditional sacrifices of the Son of Heaven, and received a certain formal respect. Even his nominal empire was not a sixth part of the China of to-day. We have already glanced at the state of affairs in China at this time; practically China was a multitude of warring states open to the northern barbarians. Confucius was a subject in one of those states, Lu; he was of aristocratic birth but poor; and, after occupying various official positions, he set up a sort of Academy in Lu for the discovery and imparting of Wisdom. And we also find Confucius travelling from state to state in China, seeking a prince who would make him his counsellor and become the centre of a reformed world. Plato, two centuries later, in exactly the same spirit, went as adviser to the tyrant Dionysius of Syracuse; and we have already noted the attitudes of Aristotle and Isocrates toward Philip of Macedonia.

The teaching of Confucius centered upon the idea of a noble life which he embodied in a standard or ideal, the Aristocratic Man. This phrase is often translated into English as the Superior Person, but as "superior" and "person," like "respectable" and "genteel," have long become semi-humorous terms of abuse, this rendering is not fair to Confucianism. He did present to his time the ideal of a devoted public man. The public side was very important to him. He was far more of a constructive political thinker than Guatama or Lao Tse. His mind was full of the condition of China, and he sought to call the Aristocratic Man into existence very largely in order to produce the noble state. One of his sayings may be quoted here: "It is impossible to withdraw from the world, and associate with birds and beasts that have no affinity with us.

With whom should I associate but with suffering men? The disorder that prevails is what requires my efforts. If right principles ruled through the kingdom, there would be no necessity for me to change its state."

The political basis of his teachings seems to be characteristic of Chinese moral ideas; there is a much directer reference to the State than is the case with most Indian and European moral and religious doctrine. For a time he was appointed magistrate in Chung-tu, a city of the dukedom of Lu, and here he sought to regulate life to an extraordinary extent, to subdue every relationship and action, indeed, to the rule of an elaborate etiquette. "Ceremonial in every detail, such as we are wont to see only in the courts of rulers and the households of high dignitaries, became obligatory on the people at large, and all matters of daily life were subject to rigid rule. Even the food which the different classes of people might eat was regulated; males and females were kept apart in the streets; even the thickness of coffins and the shape and situation of graves were made the subject of regulations."

This is all, as people say, very Chinese. No other people have ever approached moral order and social stability through the channel of manners. Yet in China, at any rate, the methods of Confucius have had an enormous effect, and no nation in the world to-day has such a universal tradition of decorum and self-restraint.

Later on the influence of Confucius over his duke was undermined, and he withdrew again into private life. His last days were saddened by the deaths of some of his most promising disciples. "No intelligent ruler," he said, "arises to take me as his master, and my time has come to die." . . .

But he died to live. Says Hirth, "There can be no doubt that Confucius has had a greater influence on the development of the Chinese national character than many emperors taken together. He is, therefore, one of the essential figures to be considered in connection with any history of China. That he could influence his nation to such a degree was, it appears to me, due more to the peculiarity of the nation than to that of his own personality. Had he lived in any other part of the world, his name would perhaps be forgotten. As we have seen, he had formed his character and his personal views on man's life from a careful study of documents closely connected with the moral philosophy cultivated by former generations. What he preached to his contemporaries was, therefore, not all new to them; but, having himself, in the study of old records, heard the dim voice of the sages of the past, he be-

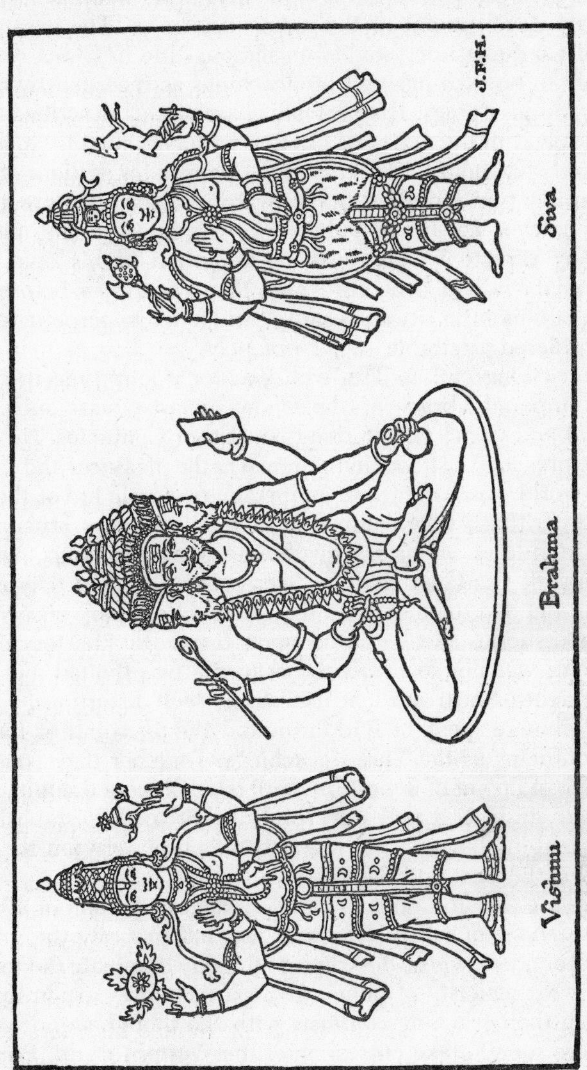
Visnu
Brahma
Siva
J.F.H.

came, as it were, the megaphone phonograph through which were expressed to the nation those views which he had derived from the early development of the nation itself. . . . The great influence of Confucius' personality on national life in China was due not only to his writings and his teachings as recorded by others, but also to his doings. His personal character, as described by his disciples and in the accounts of later writers, some of which may be entirely legendary, has become the pattern for millions of those who are bent on imitating the outward manners of a great man. . . . Whatever he did in public was regulated to the minutest detail by ceremony. This was no invention of his own, since ceremonial life had been cultivated many centuries before Confucius; but his authority and example did much to perpetuate what he considered desirable social practices."

The teaching of Lao Tse, who was for a long time in charge of the imperial library of the Chow dynasty, was much more mystical and vague and elusive than that of Confucius. He seems to have preached a stoical indifference to the pleasures and powers of the world, and a return to an imaginary simple life of the past. He left writings, very contracted in style and very obscure. He wrote in riddles. After his death Lao Tse's teachings, like the teachings of Gautama Buddha, were corrupted and overlaid by legends and had the most complex and extraordinary observances and superstitious ideas grafted upon them. But the teaching of Confucius was not so overlaid, because it was limited and plain and straightforward and lent itself to no such distortions.

The Chinese speak of Buddhism and the doctrines of Lao Tse and Confucius as the Three Teachings. Together they constitute the basis and point of departure of all later Chinese thought. Their thorough study is a necessary preliminary to the establishment of any real intellectual and moral community between the great people of the East and the Western world.

There are certain things to be remarked in common of all these three teachers, of whom Gautama was indisputably the greatest and profoundest, whose doctrines to this day dominate the thought of the great majority of human beings; there are certain features in which their teaching contrasts with the thoughts and feelings that were soon to take possession of the Western world. Primarily they are personal and tolerant doctrines; they are doctrines of a Way, of a Path, of a Nobility; and not doctrines of a church or a general rule. And they offer nothing either for or against the existence and worship of the current gods. The Athenian philoso-

Krishna Kali, as an impersonation of Vengeance Ganesa

phers, it is to be noted, had just the same theological detachment; Socrates was quite willing to bow politely or sacrifice formally to almost any divinity—reserving his private thoughts. This attitude is flatly antagonistic to the state of mind that was growing up in the Jewish communities of Judea, Egypt, and Babylonia, in which the thought of the one God was first and foremost. Neither Gautama nor Lao Tse nor Confucius had any inkling of this idea of a *jealous* God, a God who would have "none other gods," a God of terrible Truth, who would not tolerate any lurking belief in magic, witchcraft, or old customs, or any sacrificing to the god-king or any trifling with the stern unity of things.

§ 6

The intolerance of the Jewish mind did keep its essential faith clear and clean. The theological disregard of the great Eastern teachers, neither assenting or denying, did, on the other hand, permit elaborations of explanation and accumulations of ritual from the very beginning. Except for Gautama's insistence upon Right Views, which was easily disregarded, there was no *self-cleansing* element in either Buddhism, Taoism, or Confucianism. There was no effective prohibition of superstitious practices, spirit-raising, incantations, prostrations, and supplementary worships. At an early stage a process of incrustation began, and continued. The new faiths caught almost every disease of the corrupt religions they sought to replace; they took over the idols and the temples, the altars and the censers.

Tibet to-day is a Buddhistic country, yet Gautama, could he return to earth, might go from end to end of Tibet seeking his own teaching in vain. He would find that most ancient type of human ruler, a god-king, enthroned, the Dalai Lama, the "living Buddha." At Lhasa he would find a huge temple filled with priests, abbotts, and lamas—he whose only buildings were huts and who made no priests—and above a high altar he would behold a huge golden idol, which he would learn was called "Gautama Buddha!" He would hear services intoned before this divinity, and certain precepts, which would be dimly familiar to him, murmured as responses. Bells, incense, prostrations, would play their part in these amazing proceedings. At one point in the service a bell would be rung and a mirror lifted up, while the whole congregation, in an access of reverence, bowed lower. . . .

About this Buddhist countryside he would discover a number

of curious little mechanisms, little wind-wheels and water-wheels spinning, on which brief prayers were inscribed. Every time these things spin, he would learn, it counts as a prayer. "To whom?" he would ask. Moreover, there would be a number of flagstaffs in the land carrying beautiful silk flags, silk flags which bore the perplexing inscription, "*Om Mani padme hum,*" "the jewel is in the lotus." Whenever the flag flaps, he would learn, it was a prayer also, very beneficial to the gentleman who paid for the flag and to the land generally. Gangs of workmen, employed by pious persons, would be going about the country cutting this precious formula on cliff and stone. And this, he would realize at last was what the world had made of his religion! Beneath this gaudy glitter was buried the Aryan Way to serenity of soul.

We have already noted the want of any progressive idea in primitive Buddhism. In that again it contrasted with Judaism. The idea of a Promise gave to Judaism a quality no previous or contemporary religion displayed; it made Judaism historical and dramatic. It justified its fierce intolerance because it pointed to an aim. In spite of the truth and profundity of the psychological side of Gautama's teaching, Buddhism stagnated and corrupted for the lack of that directive idea. Judaism, it must be confessed, in its earlier phases, entered but little into the souls of men; it let them remain lustful, avaricious, worldly or superstitious; but because of its persuasion of a promise and of a divine leadership to serve divine ends, it remained in comparison with Buddhism bright and expectant, like a cared-for sword.

§ 7

For some time Buddhism flourished in India. But Brahminism, with its many gods and its endless variety of cults, always flourished by its side, and the organization of the Brahmins grew more powerful, until at last they were able to turn upon this caste-denying cult and oust it from India altogether. The story of that struggle is not to be told here; there were persecutions and reactions, but by the eleventh century, except for Orissa, Buddhist teaching was extinct in India. Much of its gentleness and charity had, however, become incorporated with Brahminism.

Over great areas of the world it still survives: it is possible that in contact with western science, and inspired by the spirit of history, the original teaching of Gautama, revived and purified, may yet play a large part in the direction of human destiny.

But with the loss of India the Aryan Way ceased to rule the lives of any Aryan peoples. It is curious to note that while the one great Aryan religion is now almost exclusively confined to Mongolian peoples, the Aryans themselves are under the sway of two religions, Christianity and Islam, which are, as we shall see, essentially Semitic. And Buddhism, Taoism, and Christianity alike wear garments of ritual and formula that seem to be derived through Hellenistic channels from that land of temples and priestcraft, Egypt, and from the more primitive and fundamental mentality of the brown Hamitic peoples.

BOOK V

RISE AND COLLAPSE OF THE ROMAN EMPIRE

XXV

THE TWO WESTERN REPUBLICS

§ 1

IT IS now necessary to take up the history of the two great republics of the Western Mediterranean, Rome and Carthage, and to tell how Rome succeeded in maintaining for some centuries an empire even greater than that achieved by the conquests of Alexander. But this new empire was, as we shall try to make clear, a political structure differing very profoundly in its nature from any of the Oriental empires that had preceded it. Great changes in the texture of human society and in the conditions of social inter-relations had been going on for some centuries. The flexibility and transferability of money was becoming a power and, like all powers in inexpert hands, a danger in human affairs. It was altering the relations of rich men to the state and to their poorer fellow-citizens. This new empire, the Roman empire, unlike all the preceding empires, was not the creation of a great conqueror. No Sargon, no Thothmes, no Nebuchadnezzar, no Cyrus nor Alexander nor Chandragupta, was its fountain-head. It was made by a republic. It grew by a kind of necessity through new concentrating and unifying forces that were steadily gathering power in human affairs.

But first it is necessary to give some idea of the state of affairs in Italy in the centuries immediately preceding the appearance of Rome in the world's story.

Before 1,200 B.C., that is to say before the rise of the Assyrian empire, the siege of Troy, and the final destruction of Cnossos, but after the time of Amenophis IV, Italy, like Spain, was probably still inhabited mainly by dark white people of the more fundamental Iberian or Mediterranean race. This aboriginal population was probably a thin and backward one. But already in Italy, as in Greece, the Aryans were coming southward. By 1,000 B.C. immigrants from the north had settled over most of the north and centre of Italy, and, as in Greece, they had intermarried with their darker predecessors and established a group of Aryan languages, the Italian group, more akin to the Keltic (Gaelic) than to any other, of which the most interesting from the historical point of view was that spoken by the Latin tribes in the plains south and east of the river Tiber. Meanwhile the Greeks had been settling down in Greece, and now they were taking to the sea and crossing over to South Italy and Sicily and establishing themselves there. Subsequently they established colonies along the French Riviera and founded Marseilles upon the site of an older Phœnician colony. Another interesting people also had come into Italy by sea. These were a brownish sturdy people, to judge from the pictures they have left of themselves; very probably they were a tribe of those Ægean "dark whites" who were being driven out of Greece and Asia Minor and the islands in between by the Greeks. We have already told the tale of Cnossos and of the settlement of the kindred Philistines in Palestine. These Etruscans, as they were called in Italy, were known even in ancient times to be of Asiatic origin, and it is tempting, but probably unjustifiable to connect this tradition with the *Æneid*, the epic of the Latin poet Virgil, in which Latin civilization is ascribed to Trojan immigrants from Asia Minor. (But the Trojans themselves were probably an Aryan people allied to the Phrygians.) These Etruscan people conquered most of Italy north of the Tiber, from the Aryan tribes who were scattered over that country. Probably the Etruscans ruled over a subjugated Italian population, so reversing the state of affairs in Greece, in which the Aryans were uppermost.

The "Western Mediterranean" map may be taken to represent roughly the state of affairs about 750 B.C.; it also shows the establishments of the Phœnician traders, of which Carthage was the chief, along the shores of Africa and Spain.

Of all the peoples actually in Italy, the Etruscans were by far the most civilized. They built sturdy fortresses of the Mycænean type of architecture; they had a metal industry; they used imported Greek pottery of a very fine type. The Latin tribes on the other side of the Tiber were by comparison barbaric.

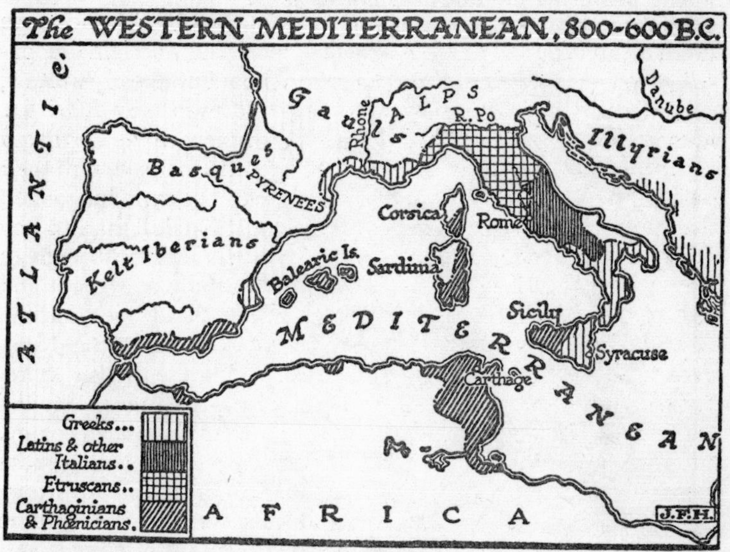

The Latins were still a rude farming people. The centre of their worship was a temple to the tribal god Jupiter, upon the Alban Mount, as shown in map "Early Latium." There they gathered for their chief festivals very much after the fashion of the early tribal gathering we have already imagined at Avebury. This gathering-place was not a town; it was a high place of assembly. There was no population permanently there. There were, however, twelve townships in the Latin league. At one point upon the Tiber there was a ford, and here and there was a trade between Latins and Etruscans. At this ford Rome had its beginnings. Traders assembled there, and refugees from the twelve towns found an asylum and occupation at this trading centre. Upon the seven hills near the ford a number of settlements sprang up, which finally amalgamated into one city.

Most people have heard the story of the two brothers Romulus and Remus, who founded Rome, and the legend of how they were exposed as infants and sheltered and suckled by a wolf.

Little value is now attached to this tale by modern historians. The date 753 B.C. is given for the founding of Rome, but there are Etruscan tombs beneath the Roman Forum of a much earlier date than that, and the so-called tomb of Romulus bears an indecipherable Etruscan inscription.

The peninsula of Italy was not then the smiling land of vineyards and olive orchards it has since become. It was still a rough

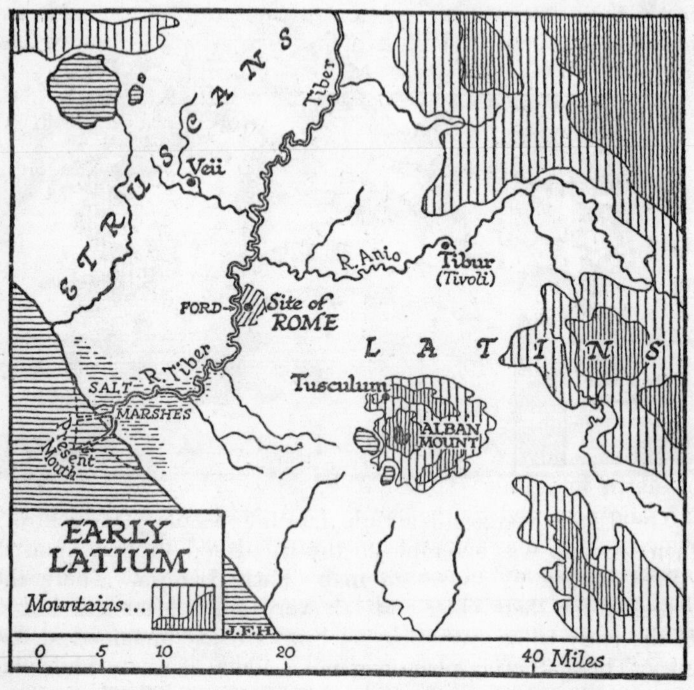

country of marsh and forest, in which the farmers grazed their cattle and made their clearings. Rome, on the boundary between Latin and Etruscan, was not in a very strong position for defence. At first there were, perhaps, Latin kings in Rome; then it would seem the city fell into the hands of Etruscan rulers whose tyrannous conduct led at last to their expulsion, and Rome became a Latin-speaking republic. The Etruscan kings were expelled from Rome in the sixth century B.C., while the successors of Nebuchadnezzar were ruling by the sufferance of the Medes in Babylon, while Confucius was seeking a king to reform the disorders of

China, and while Gautama was teaching the Aryan Way to his disciples at Benares.

Of the struggle between the Romans and the Etruscans we cannot tell in any detail here. The Etruscans were the better armed, the more civilized and the more numerous, and it would probably have gone hard with the Romans if they had had to fight them alone. But two disasters happened to the Etruscans which so weakened them that the Romans were able at last to master them altogether. The first of these was a war with the Greeks of Syracuse in Sicily which destroyed the Etruscan fleet

Etruscan painting of a Ceremonial Burning of the Dead

(474 B.C.), and the second was a great raid of the Gauls from the north into Italy. These latter people swarmed into North Italy and occupied the valley of the Po towards the end of the fifth century B.C., as a couple of centuries later their kindred were to swarm down into Greece and Asia Minor and settle in Galatia. The Etruscans were thus caught between hammer and anvil, and after a long and intermittent war the Romans were able to capture Veii, an Etruscan fortress, a few miles from Rome, which had hitherto been a great threat and annoyance to them.

It is to this period of struggle against the Etruscan monarchs, the Tarquins, that Macaulay's *Lays of Ancient Rome,* familiar to every schoolboy, refers.

But the invasion of the Gauls was one of those convulsions of the nations that leave nothing as it has been before. They carried their raiding right down the Italian peninsula, devastating all Etruria. They took and sacked Rome (390 B.C.). According to Roman legends—on which doubt is thrown—the citadel on the Capitol held out, and this also the Gauls would have taken by surprise at night, if certain geese had not been awakened by their stealthy movements and set up such a cackling as to arouse the garrison. After that the Gauls, who were ill-equipped for siege operations, and perhaps suffering from disease in their camp, were bought off, and departed to the northward again; and, though they made subsequent raids, they never again reached Rome.

The leader of the Gauls who sacked Rome was named Brennus. It is related of him that as the gold of the ransom was being weighed there was some dispute about the justice of the counterpoise, whereupon he flung his sword into the scale, saying, "*Væ victis!*" ("Woe to the vanquished!")—a phrase that has haunted the discussions of all subsequent ransoms and indemnities down to the present time.

For half a century after this experience Rome was engaged in a series of wars to establish herself at the head of the Latin tribes. For the burning of the chief city seems to have stimulated rather than crippled her energies. However much she suffered, most of her neighbours seem to have suffered more. By 290 B.C. Rome was the mistress city of all Central Italy from the Arno to south of Naples. She had conquered the Etruscans altogether, and her boundaries marched with those of the Gauls to the north and with the regions of Italy under Greek dominion (Magna Græcia) to the south. Along the Gaulish boundary she had planted garrisons and colonial cities, and no doubt it was because of that line of defence that the raiding enterprises of the Gauls were deflected eastward into the Balkans.

After what we have already told of the history of Greece and the constitutions of her cities, it will not surprise the reader to learn that the Greeks of Sicily and Italy were divided up into a number of separate city governments, of which Syracuse and Tarentum (the modern Taranto) were the chief, and that they had no common rule of direction or policy. But now, alarmed at the spread of the Roman power, they looked across the Adriatic for help, and found it in the ambitions of Pyrrhus, the king of Epirus. Between the Romans and Pyrrhus these Greeks of Magna Græcia were very much in the same position that Greece proper had been in between the Macedonians and the Persians, half a century before.

The reader will remember that Epirus, the part of Greece that is closest to the heel of Italy, was the native land of Olympias, the mother of Alexander. In the kaleidoscopic changes of the map that followed the death of Alexander, Epirus was sometimes swamped by Macedonia, sometimes independent. This

Pyrrhus was a kinsman of Alexander the Great, and a monarch of ability and enterprise, and he seems to have planned a career of conquest in Italy and Sicily. He commanded an admirable army, against which the comparatively inexpert Roman levies could at first do little. His army included all the established military devices of the time, an infantry phalanx, Thessalian cavalry, and twenty fighting elephants from the East. He routed the Romans at Heraclea (280 B.C.), and, pressing after them, defeated them again at Ausculum (279 B.C.) in their own territory. Then, instead of pursuing the Romans further, he made a truce with them, turned his attention to the subjugation of Sicily, and so brought the sea power of Carthage into alliance against him. For Carthage could not afford to have a strong power established so close to her as Sicily. Rome in those days seemed to the Car-

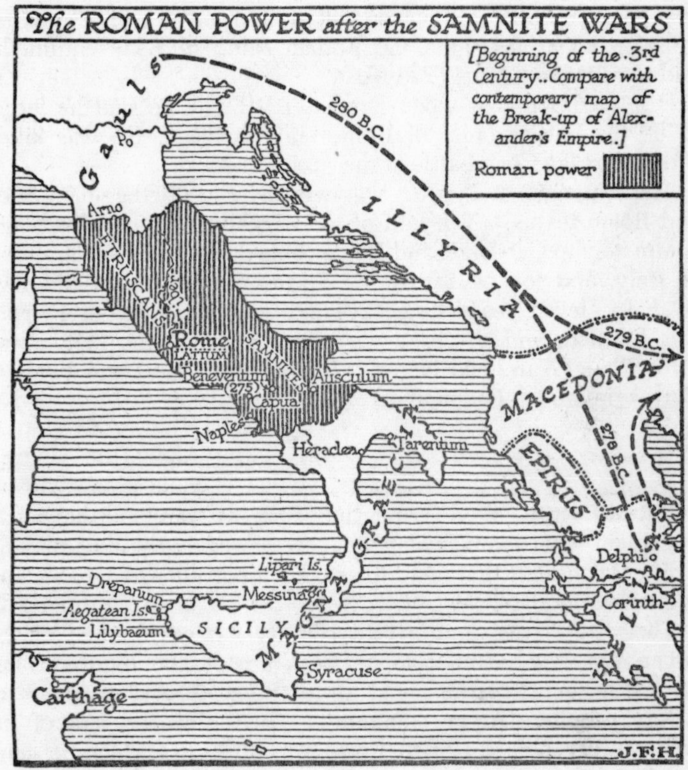

thaginians a far less serious threat than the possibility of another Alexander the Great ruling Sicily. A Carthaginian fleet appeared off the mouth of the Tiber, therefore, to encourage or induce the Romans to renew the struggle—and Rome and Carthage were definitely allied against the invader.

This interposition of Carthage was fatal to Pyrrhus. Without any decisive battle his power wilted, and, after a disastrous repulse in an attack upon the Roman camp of Beneventum, he had to retire to Epirus (275 B.C.).

It is recorded that when Pyrrhus left Sicily he said he left it to be the battleground of Rome and Carthage. He was killed three years later in a battle in the streets of Argos.

The war against Pyrrhus was won by the Carthaginian fleet, and Rome reaped a full half of the harvest of victory. Sicily fell completely to Carthage, and Rome came down to the toe and heel of Italy, and looked across the Straits of Messina at her new rival. In eleven years' time (264 B.C.) the prophecy of Pyrrhus was fulfilled, and the first war with Carthage, the first of the three Punic Wars, had begun. ("Punic" from the Latin *Punicus,* Carthaginian, *i.e.* Phœnician.)

§ 2

But we write "Rome" and the "Romans," and we have still to explain what manner of people these were who were playing a rôle of conquest that had hitherto been played only by able and aggressive monarchs.

Their state was, in the fifth century B.C., a republic of the Aryan type very similar to a Greek aristocratic republic. The earliest accounts of the social life of Rome give us a picture of a very primitive Aryan community. "In the second half of the fifth century before Christ, Rome was still an aristocratic community of free peasants occupying an area of nearly 400 square miles, with a population certainly not exceeding 150,000, almost entirely dispersed over the countryside and divided into seventeen districts or rural tribes. Most of the families had a small holding and a cottage of their own, where father and sons lived and worked together, growing corn for the most part, with here and there a strip of vine or olive. Their few head of cattle were kept at pasture on the neighbouring common land; their clothes and simple implements of husbandry they made for themselves at home. Only at rare intervals and on special occasions would they make their way into the fortified town, which was the centre at once of their religion and their government. Here were the temples of the gods, the houses of the wealthy, and the shops of the artisans and traders, where corn, oil, or wine could be bartered in small quantities for salt or rough tools and weapons of iron."[1]

This community followed the usual traditions of a division into aristocratic and common citizens, who were called in Rome patricians and plebeians. These were the citizens; the slave or outlander had no more part in the state than he had in Greece. But the constitution differed from any Greek constitution in the fact that a great part of the ruling power was gathered into the hands of a body called the Senate, which was neither purely a body of hereditary members nor directly an elected and repre-

[1] Ferrero, *The Greatness and Decline of Rome.*

sentative one. It was a nominated one, and in the earlier period it was nominated solely from among the patricians. It existed before the expulsion of the kings, and in the time of the kings it was the king who nominated the senators. But after the expulsion of the kings (510 B.C.) the supreme government was vested in the hands of two elected rulers, the *consuls;* and it was the consuls who took over the business of appointing senators. In the early days of the Republic only patricians were eligible as consuls or senators, and the share of the plebeians in the government consisted merely in a right to vote for the consuls and other public officials. Even for that purpose their votes did not have the same value as those of their patrician fellow-citizens. But their votes had at any rate sufficient weight to induce many of the patrician candidates to profess a more or less sincere concern for plebeian grievances. In the early phases of the Roman state, moreover, the plebeians were not only excluded from public office, but from intermarriage with the patrician class. The administration was evidently primarily a patrician affair.

The early phase of Roman affairs was therefore an aristocracy of a very pronounced type, and the internal history of Rome for the two centuries and a half between the expulsion of the last Etruscan king, Tarquin the Proud, and the beginning of the first Punic War (264 B.C.), was very largely a struggle for mastery between those two orders, the patricians and the plebeians. It was, in fact, closely parallel with the struggle of aristocracy and democracy in the city states of Greece, and, as in the case of Greece, there were whole classes in the community, slaves, freed slaves, unpropertied free men, outlanders, and the like, who were entirely outside and beneath the struggle. We have already noted the essential difference of Greek democracy and what is called democracy in the world to-day. Another misused word is the Roman term *proletariat,* which in modern jargon means all the unpropertied people in a modern state. In Rome the *proletarii* were a voting division of fully qualified citizens whose property was less than 10,000 copper asses (£275). They were an enrolled class; their value to the state consisted in their raising families of citizens (*proles*=offspring), and from their ranks were drawn the colonists who went to form new Latin cities or to garrison important points. But the proletarii were quite distinct in origin from slaves or freedmen or the miscellaneous driftage of a town slum, and it is a great pity that modern political discussion should be confused by an inaccurate use of a term which has no exact modern equivalent and which expresses nothing real in modern social classification.

The mass of the details of this struggle between patricians and plebeians we can afford to ignore in this *Outline*. It was a struggle which showed the Romans to be a people of a curiously shrewd character, never forcing things to a destructive crisis, but being within the limits of their discretion grasping hard dealers. The patricians made a mean use of their political advantages to grow rich through the national conquests, at the expense not only of the defeated enemy but of the poorer plebeian whose farm had been neglected and who had fallen into debt during his military service. The plebeians were ousted from any share in the conquered lands, which the patricians divided up among themselves. The introduction of money probably increased the facilities of the usurer and the difficulties of the borrowing debtor.

ROMAN COIN STRUCK TO COMMEMORATE THE VICTORY OVER PYRRHUS AND HIS ELEPHANTS

Three sorts of pressure won the plebeians a greater share in the government of the country and the good things that were coming to Rome as she grew powerful. The first of these (1) was the general strike of plebeians. Twice they actually marched right out of Rome threatening to make a new city higher up the Tiber, and twice this threat proved conclusive. The second method of pressure (2) was the threat of a tyranny. Just as in Attica (the little state of which Athens was the capital) Peisistratus raised himself to power on the support of the poorer districts, so there was to be found in most periods of plebeian discontent some ambitious man ready to figure as a leader and wrest power from the senate. For a long time the Roman patricians were clever enough to beat every such potential tyrant by giving in to a certain extent to the plebeians. And finally (3) there were patricians big-minded and far-seeing enough to insist upon the need of reconciliation with the plebeians.

Thus, in 509 B.C., Valerius Poplicola (3), the consul, enacted that whenever the life or rights of any citizen were at stake, there should be an appeal from the magistrates to the general assembly. This Lex Valeria was "the Habeas Corpus of Rome," and it freed the Roman plebeians from the worst dangers of class vindictiveness in the law courts.

In 494 B.C. occurred a strike (1). "After the Latin war the pressure of debt had become excessive, and the plebeians saw with indignation their friends, who had often served the state bravely in the legions, thrown into chains and reduced to slavery at the demand of patrician creditors. War was raging against the Volscians; but the legionaries, on their victorious return, refused any longer to obey the consuls, and marched, though without any disorder, to the Sacred Mount beyond the Anio (up the Tiber). There they prepared to found a new city, since the rights of citizens were denied to them in the old one. The patricians were compelled to give way, and the plebeians, returning to Rome from the 'First Secession,' received the privilege of having officers of their own, tribunes and ædiles."[1]

In 486 B.C. arose Spurius Cassius (2), a consul who carried an Agrarian Law securing public land for the plebeians. But the next year he was accused of aiming at royal power, and condemned to death. His law never came into operation.

There followed a long struggle on the part of the plebeians to have the laws of Rome written down, so that they would no longer have to trust to patrician memories. In 451–450 B.C. the law of the Twelve Tables was published, the basis of all Roman law.

But in order that the Twelve Tables should be formulated, a committee of ten (the *decemvirate*) was appointed in the place of the ordinary magistrates. A second decemvirate, appointed in succession to the first, attempted a sort of aristocratic counter-revolution under Appius Claudius. The plebeians withdrew again, a second time, to the Sacred Mount, and Appius Claudius committed suicide in prison.

In 440 came a famine, and a second attempt to found a popular tyranny upon the popular wrongs, by Spurius Mælius, a wealthy plebeian, which ended in his assassination.

After the sack of Rome by the Gauls (390 B.C.), Marcus Manlius, who had been in command of the Capitol when the geese had saved it, came forward as a popular leader. The plebeians were suffering severely from the after-war usury and profiteering of the patricians, and were incurring heavy debts in rebuilding and restocking their farms. Manlius spent his

[1] J. Wells, *Short History of Rome to the Death of Augustus.*

fortune in releasing debtors. He was accused by the patricians of tyrranous intentions, condemned, and suffered the fate of condemned traitors in Rome, being flung from the Tarpeian Rock, the precipitous edge of that same Capitoline Hill he had defended.

In 376 B.C. Licinius, who was one of the ten tribunes for the people, began a long struggle with the patricians by making certain proposals called the Licinian Rogations, that there should be a limit to the amount of public land taken by any single citizen, so leaving some for everybody, that outstanding debts should be forgiven without interest upon the repayment of the principal, and that henceforth one at least of the two consuls should be a plebeian. This precipitated a ten-year struggle. The plebeian power to stop business by the veto of their representatives, the tribunes, was fully exercised. In cases of national extremity it was the custom to set all other magistrates aside and appoint one leader, the Dictator. Rome had done such a thing during times of military necessity before, but now the patricians set up a Dictator in a time of profound peace, with the idea of crushing Licinius altogether. They appointed Camillus, who had besieged and taken Veii from the Etruscans. But Camillus was a wiser man than his supporters; he brought about a compromise between the two orders in which most of the demands of the plebeians were conceded (367 B.C.), dedicated a temple to Concord, and resigned his power.

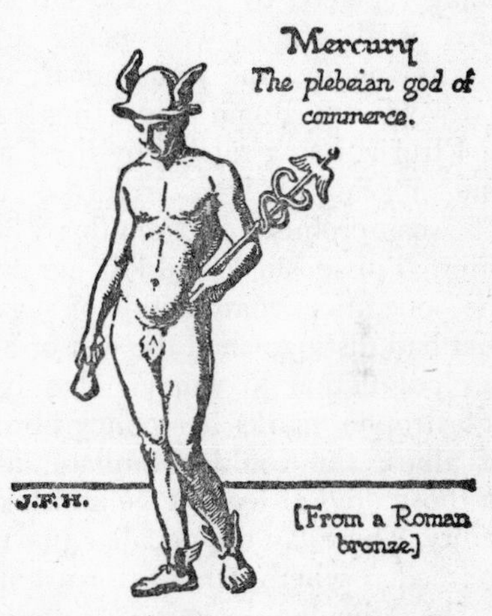

Mercury
The plebeian god of commerce.
[From a Roman bronze.]

Thereafter the struggle between the orders abated. It abated because, among other influences, the social differences between patricians and plebeians were diminishing. Trade was coming to Rome with increasing political power, and many plebeians were growing rich and many patricians becoming relatively poor. Intermarriage had been rendered possible by a change in the law, and social intermixture was going on. While the rich plebeians were becoming, if not aristocratic, at least oligarchic in habits and sympathy, new classes were springing up in Rome with fresh interests and no political standing. Particularly abundant were the freedmen, slaves set free, for the most part artisans, but some of them traders, who were growing wealthy. And the Senate, no longer a purely patrician body—since various official positions were now open to plebeians, and such plebeian officials became senators—was becoming now an assembly of all the wealthy, able, energetic, and influential men in the state. The Roman power was expanding, and as it expanded these old class oppositions of the early Latin community were becoming unmeaning. They were being replaced by new associations and new antagonisms. Rich men of all origins were being drawn together into a common interest against the communistic ideas of the poor.

In 390 B.C. Rome was a miserable little city on the borders of Etruria, being sacked by the Gauls; in 275 B.C. she was ruling and unifying all Italy, from the Arno to the Straits of Messina. The compromise of Camillus (367 B.C.) had put an end to internal dissensions, and left her energies free for expansion. And the same queer combination of sagacity and aggressive selfishness that had distinguished the war of her orders at home and enabled her population to worry out a balance of power without any catastrophe, marks her policy abroad. She understood the value of allies; she could assimilate; abroad as at home she could in those days at least "give and take" with a certain fairness and sanity. There lay the peculiar power of Rome. By that it was she succeeded where Athens, for example, had conspicuously failed.

The Athenian democracy suffered much from that narrowness of "patriotism," which is the ruin of all nations. Athens was disliked and envied by her own empire because she dominated it in a spirit of civic egotism; her disasters were not felt and shared as disasters by her subject-cities. The shrewder, nobler Roman senators of the great years of Rome, before the first Punic War overstrained her moral strength and began her degeneration, were not only willing in the last resort to share their previleges with the mass of their own people, but eager to incorporate their sturdiest antagonists upon terms of equality with themselves. They extended their citizenship cautiously but steadily. Some cities became Roman, with even a voting share in the government. Others had self-government and the right to trade or marry in Rome, without full Roman citizenship. Garrisons of full citizens were set up at strategic points and colonies with variable privileges established amidst the purely conquered peoples. The need to keep communications open in this great and growing mass of citizenship was evident from the first. Printing and paper were not yet available for intercourse, but a system of high roads followed the Latin speech and the Roman rule. The first of these, the Appian Way, ran from Rome ultimately into the heel of Italy. It was begun by the censor Appius Claudis (who must not be confused with the decemvir Appius Claudius of a century earlier) in 312 B.C.

According to a census made in 265 B.C., there were already in the Roman dominions, that is to say in Italy south of the Arno, 300,000 citizens. They all had a common interest in the welfare of the state; they were all touched a little with the diffused kingship of the republic. This was, we have to note, an absolutely new thing in the history of mankind. All considerable states and kingdoms and empires hitherto had been communities by mere obedience to some head, some monarch, upon whose moods and character the public welfare was helplessly dependent. No republic had hitherto succeeded in being anything more than a city state. The so-called Athenian "empire" was simply a city state directing its allies and its subjugated cities. In a few decades the Roman republic was destined to extend its citizenship into the valley of the Po, to assimilate the kindred Gauls, replacing their language by Latin, and to set up a Latin City, Aquileia, at the very head of the Adriatic Sea. In 89 B.C. all free inhabitants of Italy became Roman citizens; in A.D. 212 the citizenship was extended to all free men in the empire.

This extraordinary political growth was manifestly the precursor of all modern states of the western type. It is as interesting to the political student, therefore, as a carboniferous amphibian or an *archæopteryx* to the student of zoological development. It is the primitive type of the now dominant order. Its experiences throw light upon all subsequent political history.

One natural result of this growth of a democracy of hundreds of thousands of citizens scattered over the greater part of Italy was the growth in power of the Senate. There had been in the development of the Roman constitution a variety of forms of the popular assembly, the plebeian assembly, the assembly by tribes, the assembly by centuries, and the like, into which variety we cannot enter here with any fullness; but the idea was established that with the popular assembly lay the power of initiating laws. It is to be noted that there was a sort of parallel government in this system. The assembly by tribes or by centuries was an assembly of the *whole citizen body*, patrician and plebeian together; the assembly of the plebeians was, of course, an assembly only of the plebeian class. Each assembly had its own officials; the former, the consuls, etc., the latter, the tribunes. While Rome was a little state, twenty miles square, it was possible to assemble something like a representative gathering of the people, but it will be manifest that, with the means of communication existing in Italy at that time, it was now impossible for the great bulk of the citizens even to keep themselves informed of what was going on at Rome, much less to take any effective part in political life there. Aristotle, in his *Politics,* had already pointed out the virtual disenfranchisement of voters who lived out of the city and were preoccupied with agriculture pursuits, and this sort of disenfranchisement by mechanical difficulties applied to the vast majority of Roman citizens. With the growth of Rome an unanticipated weakness crept into political life through these causes, and the popular assembly became more and more a gathering of political hacks and the city riffraff, and less and less a representation of the ordinary worthy citizens. The popular assembly came nearest to power and dignity in the fourth century B.C. From that period it steadily declined in influence, and the new Senate, which was no longer a patrician body, with a homogeneous and on the whole a noble tradition, but a body of rich men, ex-magistrates, powerful officials, bold adventurers and the like, pervaded by a strong disposition to return to the idea of hereditary qualification became for three centuries the ruling power in the Roman world.

There are two devices since known to the world which might have enabled the popular government of Rome to go on developing beyond its climax in the days of Appius Claudius the Censor, at the close of the fourth century B.C., but neither of them occurred to the Roman mind. The first of these devices was a proper use of print. In our account of early Alexandria we have already remarked upon the strange fact that printed books did not come into the world in the fourth or third century B.C. This account of Roman affairs forces us to repeat that remark. To the modern mind it is clear that a widespread popular government demands, as a necessary condition for health, a steady supply of correct information upon public affairs to all the citizens and a maintenance of interest. The popular governments in the modern states that have sprung up on either side of the Atlantic during the last two centuries have been possible only through the more or less honest and thorough ventilation of public affairs through the press. But in Italy the only way in which the government at Rome could communicate with any body of its citizens elsewhere was by sending a herald, and with the individual citizen it could hold no communication by any means at all.

The second device, for which the English are chiefly responsible in the history of mankind, which the Romans never used, was the almost equally obvious one of representative government. For the old Popular Assembly (in its threefold form) it would have been possible to have substituted a gathering of delegates. Later on in history, the English did, as the state grew, realize this necessity. Certain men, the Knights of the Shire, were called up to Westminster to speak and vote for local feeling, and were more or less formally elected for that end. The Roman situation seems to a modern mind to have called aloud for such a modification. It was never made.

The method of assembling the *comitia tributa* (one of the three main forms of the Popular Assembly) was by the proclamation of a herald, who was necessarily inaudible to most of Italy, seventeen days before the date of the gathering. The augurs, the priests of divination whom Rome had inherited from the Etruscans, examined the entrails of sacrificial beasts on the night before the actual assembly, and if they thought fit to say that these gory portents were unfavourable, the *comitia tributa* dispersed. But if the augurs reported that the livers were propitious, there was a great blowing of horns from the Capitol and from the walls of the city, and the assembly went on. It was held in the open air, either in the little Forum beneath the Capitol or in a still smaller recess opening out of the Forum, or in the military exercising ground, the Campus Martius, now the most crowded part of modern Rome, but then an open space. Business began at dawn with prayer. There were no seats, and this probably helped to reconcile the citizen to the rule that everything ended at sunset.

After the opening prayer came a discussion of the measures to be considered by the assembly, and the proposals before the meeting were read out. Is it not astonishing that there were no printed copies distributed? If any copies were handed about, they must have been in manuscript, and each copy must have been liable to errors and deliberate falsification. No questions seem to have been allowed, but private individuals might address the gathering with the permission of the presiding magistrate.

The multitude then proceeded to go into enclosures like cattle-pens, according to their tribes, and each tribe voted upon the measure under consideration. The decision was then taken not by the majority of the citizens, but by the majority of tribes, and it was announced by the heralds.

The Popular Assembly by centuries, *comitia centuriata,* was very similar in its character, except that instead of thirty-five tribes there were, in the third century B.C., 373 centuries and there was a sacrifice as well as prayer to begin with. The centuries, originally military (like the "hundreds" of primitive English local government), had long since lost any connection with the number one hundred. Some contained only a few people; some very many. There were eighteen centuries of knights (equites), who were originally men in a position to maintain a horse and serve in the cavalry, though later the Roman knighthood, like knighthood in England, became a vulgar distinction of no military, mental, or moral significance. (These equites became a very important class as Rome traded and grew rich; for a time they were the real moving class in the community. There was as little chivalry left among them at last as there is in the "honours list" knights of England of to-day. The senators from about 200 B.C. were excluded from trade. The equites became, therefore, the great business men, *negotiatores,* and as *publicani* they farmed the taxes.) There were, in addition, eighty (!) centuries of wealthy men (worth over 100,000 asses), twenty-two of men worth over 75,000 asses, and so on. There were two centuries each of mechanics and musicians, and the *proletarii* made up one century. The decision in the *comitia centuriata* was by the majority of centuries.

Is it any wonder that with the growth of the Roman state and the complication of its business, power shifted back from such a Popular Assembly to the Senate, which was a comparatively compact body varying between three hundred as a minimum, and, at the utmost, nine hundred members (to which it was raised by Cæsar), men who had to do with affairs and big business, who knew each other more or less, and had a tradition of government and policy? The power of nominating and calling up the senators vested in the Republic first with the consuls, and when, some time after, "censors" were created, and many of the powers of the consuls had been transferred to them, they were also given this power. Appius Claudius, one of the first of the censors to exercise it, enrolled freedmen in the tribes and called sons of freedmen to the Senate. But this was a shocking arrangement to the conservative instincts of the time; the consuls would not recognize his Senate, and the next censors (304 B.C.) set aside his invitations. His attempt, however, serves to show how far the Senate had progressed from its original condition as a purely patrician body. Like the contemporary British House of Lords, it had become a gathering of big business men, energetic politicians, successful adventurers, great landowners, and the like; its patrician dignity was a picturesque sham; but, unlike the British House of Lords, it was unchecked legally by anything but the inefficient Popular Assembly we have already described and by the tribunes elected by the plebeian assembly. Its legal control over the consuls and proconsuls was not great; it had little executive power; but in its prestige and experience lay its strength and influence. The interests of its members were naturally antagonistic to the interests of the general body of citizens, but for some generations that great mass of ordinary men was impotent to express its dissent from the proceedings of this oligarchy. Direct popular government of a state larger than a city state had already failed therefore in Italy, because as yet there was no public education, no press, and no representative system; it had failed through these mere mechanical difficulties, before the first Punic War. But its appearance is of enormous interest, as the first appearance of a set of problems with which the whole political intelligence of the world wrestles at the present time.

The Senate met usually in a Senate House in the Forum, but on special occasions it would be called to meet in this or that temple; and when it had to deal with foreign ambassadors or its own generals (who were not allowed to enter the city while in command of troops), it assembled in the Campus Martius outside the walls.

§ 3

It has been necessary to deal rather fully with the political structure of the Roman republic because of its immense importance to this day. The constitution of Carthage need not detain us long.

Italy under Rome was a republican country; Carthage was that much older thing, a republican city. She had an "empire," as Athens had an "empire," of tributary states which did not love her, and she had a great and naturally disloyal industrial slave population.

In the city there were two elected "kings," as Aristotle calls them, the *suffetes*, who were really equivalent to the Roman censors; their Semitic name was the same as that used for the Jewish *judges*. There was an impotent public assembly and a senate of leading personages; but two committees of this senate, nominally elected, but elected by easily controlled methods, the Hundred and Four and the Thirty, really constituted a close oligarchy of the richest and most influential men. They told as little as they could to their allies and fellow-citizens, and consulted them as little as possible. They pursued schemes in which the welfare of Carthage was, no doubt, subordinated to the advantage of their own group. They were hostile to new men or novel measures, and confident that a sea ascendancy that had lasted two centuries must be in the very nature of things.

§ 4

It would be interesting, and not altogether idle, to speculate what might have happened to mankind if Rome and Carthage could have settled their differences and made a permanent alliance in the western world. If Alexander the Great had lived, he might have come westward and driven these two powers into such a fusion of interests. But that would not have suited the private schemes and splendours of the Carthaginian oligarchy, and the new Senate of greater Rome was now growing fond of the taste of plunder and casting covetous eyes across the Straits of Messina upon the Carthaginian possessions in Sicily. They were covetous, but they were afraid of the Carthaginian sea-power. Roman popular "patriotism," however, was also jealous and fearful of these Carthaginians, and less inclined to count the cost of a conflict. The alliance Pyrrhus had forced upon Rome and Carthage held good for eleven years, but Rome was ripe for what is called in modern political jargon an "offensive defensive" war. The occasion arose in 264 B.C.

At that time Sicily was not completely in Carthaginian hands. The eastward end was still under the power of the Greek king of Syracuse, Hiero, a successor of that Dionysius to whom Plato had gone as resident court philosopher. A band of mercenaries who had been in the service of Syracuse seized upon Messina (289 B.C.), and raided the trade of Syracuse so that at last Hiero was forced to take measures to suppress them (270 B.C.). Thereupon Carthage, which was also vitally concerned in the suppression of piracy, came to his aid, and put in a Carthaginian garrison at Messina. This was an altogether justifiable proceeding. Now that Tyre had been destroyed, the only capable guardian of sea law in the

Mediterranean was Carthage, and the suppression of piracy was her task by habit as well as by tradition.

The pirates of Messina appealed to Rome, and the accumulating jealousy and fear of Carthage decided the Roman people to help them. An expedition was dispatched to Messina under the consul Appius Claudius (the third Appius Claudius we have had to mention in this history).

So began the first of the most wasteful and disastrous series of wars that has ever darkened the history of mankind. But this is

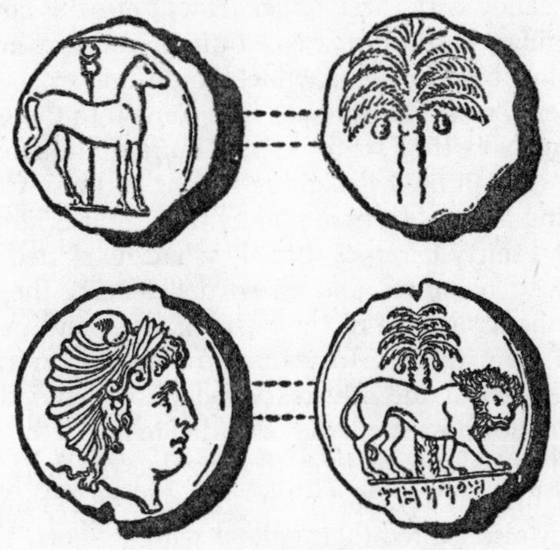

Carthaginian coins.

how one historian, soaked with the fantastic political ideas of our times, is pleased to write of this evil expedition: "The Romans knew they were entering on war with Carthage; but the political instincts of the people were right, for a Carthaginian garrison on the Sicilian Straits would have been a dangerous menace to the peace of Italy." So they protected the peace of Italy from this "menace" by a war that lasted nearly a quarter of a century! They wrecked their own slowly acquired political *moral* in the process.

The Romans captured Messina, and Hiero deserted from the Carthaginians to the Romans. Then for some time the struggle centered upon the town Agrigentum. This the Romans besieged, and a period of trench warfare ensued. Both sides suffered greatly from plague and irregular supplies; the Romans lost 30,000 men; but in the end (262 B.C.) the Carthaginians evacuated the place and retired to their fortified towns on the western coast of the island, of which Lilybæum was the chief. These they could supply easily from the African mainland, and, as long as their sea ascendancy held, they could exhaust any Roman effort against them.

And now a new and very extraordinary phase of the war began. The Romans came out upon the sea, and, to the astonishment of the Carthaginians and themselves, defeated the Carthaginian fleet. Since the days of Salamis there had been a considerable development of naval architecture. Then the ruling type of battleship was a trireme, a galley with three banks (rows) of oars; now the leading Carthaginian battleship was a quinquereme, a much bigger galley with five banks of oars, which could ram or shear the oars of any feebler vessel. The Romans had come into the war with no such shipping. Now they set to work to build quinqueremes, being helped, it is said, in their designing by one of these Carthaginian vessels coming ashore. In two months they built a hundred quinqueremes and thirty triremes. But they had no skilled navigators, no experienced oarsmen, and these deficiencies they remedied partly with the assistance of their Greek allies and partly by the invention of new tactics. Instead of relying upon ramming or breaking the oars of the adversary, which demanded more seamanship than they possessed, they decided to board the enemy, and they constructed a sort of long drawbridge on their ships, held up to a mast by a pulley, and with grappling-hooks and spikes at the end. They also loaded their galleys with soldiers. Then, as the Carthaginian rammed or swept alongside, this *corvus,* as it was called, could be let down and the boarders could swarm aboard him.

Simple as this device was, it proved a complete success. It changed the course of the war and the fate of the world. The small amount of invention needed to counteract the *corvus* was not apparently within the compass of the Carthaginian rulers. At the battle of Mylæ (260 B.C.) the Romans gained their first naval victory and captured or destroyed fifty vessels. At the great battle of Ecnomus (256 B.C.), "probably the greatest naval engagement of antiquity,"[1] in which seven or eight hundred big ships were engaged, the Carthaginians showed that they had learnt nothing from their former disaster. According to rule they out-manœuvred and should have defeated the Romans, but the *corvus* again defeated them. The Romans sank thirty vessels and captured sixty-four.

---

[1] J. Wells, *Short History of Rome to the Death of Augustus.*

Thereafter the war was continued with violent fluctuations of fortune, but with a continuous demonstration of the greater energy, solidarity, and initiative of the Romans. After Ecnomus the Romans invaded Africa by sea, and sent an insufficiently supported army, which after many successes and the capture of Tunis (within ten miles of Carthage) was completely defeated. They lost their sea ascendancy through a storm, and regained it by building a second fleet of two hundred and twenty ships within three months. They captured Palermo, and defeated a great Carthaginian army there (251 B.C.), capturing one hundred and four elephants, and making such a triumphal procession into Rome as that city had never seen before. They made an unsuccessful siege of Lilybæum, the chief surviving Carthaginian stronghold in Sicily. They lost their second fleet in a great naval battle at Drepanum (249 B.C.), losing one hundred and eighty out of two hundred and ten vessels; and a third fleet of one hundred and twenty battleships and eight hundred transports was lost in the same year partly in battle and partly in a storm.

For seven years a sort of war went on between the nearly exhausted combatants, a war of raids and feeble sieges, during which the Carthaginians had the best of it at sea. Then by a last supreme effort Rome launched a fourth fleet of two hundred keels, and defeated the last strength of the Carthaginians at the battle of the Ægation Isles (241 B.C.)—after which Carthage (240 B.C.) sued for peace.

By the terms of this peace, all Sicily, except for the dominions of Hiero of Syracuse, became an "estate" of the Roman people. There was no such process of assimilation as had been practised in Italy; Sicily became a conquered province, paying tribute and yielding profit like the provinces of the older empires. And, in addition, Carthage paid a war indemnity of 3,200 talents (£788,000).

§ 5

For twenty-two years there was peace between Rome and Carthage. It was peace without prosperity. Both combatants were suffering from the want and disorganization that follow naturally and necessarily upon all great wars. The territories of Carthage seethed with violent disorder; the returning soldiers could not get their pay, and mutinied and looted; the land went uncultivated. We read of horrible cruelties in the suppression of these troubles by Hamilcar, the Carthaginian general; of men being crucified by the thousand. Sardinia and Corsica revolted. The "peace of Italy" was scarcely happier. The Gauls rose and marched south; they were defeated, and 40,000 of them killed at Telamon. It is manifest that Italy was incomplete until it reached the Alps. Roman colonies were planted in the valley of the Po, and the great northward artery, the Via Flaminia, was begun. But it shows the moral and intellectual degradation of this post-war period, that, when the Gauls were threatening Rome, human sacrifices were proposed and carried out. The old Carthaginian sea law was broken up—it may have been selfish and monopolistic, but it was at least orderly—the Adriatic swarmed with Illyrian pirates, and, as the result of a quarrel arising out of this state of affairs, Illyria, after two wars, had to be annexed as a second "province." By sending expeditions to annex Sardinia and Corsica, which were Carthaginian provinces in revolt, the Romans prepared the way for the Second Punic War.

The First Punic War had tested and demonstrated the relative strength of Rome, and Carthage. With a little more wisdom on either side, with a little more magnanimity on the part of Rome, there need never have been a renewal of the struggle. But Rome was an ungracious conqueror. She seized Corsica and Sardinia on no just grounds, she increased the indemnity by 1,200 talents, she set a limit, the Ebro, to Carthaginian developments in Spain. There was a strong party in Carthage, led by Hanno, for the propitiation of Rome; but it was natural that many Carthaginians should come to regard their natural adversary with a despairing hatred.

Hatred is one of the passions that can master a life, and there is a type of temperament very prone to it, ready to see life in terms of vindictive melodrama, ready to find stimulus and satisfaction in frightful demonstrations of "justice" and revenge. The fears and jealousies of the squatting-place and the cave still bear their dark blossoms in our lives; we are not four hundred generations yet from the old Stone Age. Great wars, as all Europe knows, give this "hating" temperament the utmost scope, and the greed and pride and cruelty that the First Punic War had released were now producing a rich crop of anti-foreign monomania. The outstanding figure upon the side of Carthage was a great general and administrator, Hamilcar Barca, who now set himself to circumvent and shatter Rome. He was the father-in-law of Hasdrubal and the father of a boy Hannibal, destined to be the most dreaded enemy that ever scared the Roman Senate. The most obvious course before Carthage was the reconstruction of its fleet and naval administration, and the recovery of sea power, but this, it would seem, Hamilcar could not effect. As an alternative he resolved to organize Spain as the base of a land attack upon Italy. He went to Spain as governor in 236 B.C., and Hannibal related afterwards that his father then—he was a boy of eleven—made him vow deathless hostility to the Roman power.

This quasi-insane concentration of the gifts and lives of the Barca family upon revenge is but one instance of the narrowing and embitterment of life that the stresses and universal sense of insecurity of this great struggle produced in the minds of men. A quarter of a century of war had left the whole western world miserable and harsh. While the eleven-year-old Hannibal was taking his vow of undying hatred, there was running about a farmhouse of Tusculum a small but probably very disagreeable child of two, named Marcus Porcius Cato. This boy lived to be eighty-five years old, and his ruling passion seems to have been hatred for any human happiness but his own. He was a good soldier, and had a successful political career. He held a command in Spain, and distinguished himself by his cruelties. He posed as a champion of religion and public morality, and under this convenient cloak carried on a lifelong war against everything that was young, gracious, or pleasant. Whoever roused his jealousy incurred his moral disapproval. He was energetic in the support and administration of all laws against dress, against the personal adornment of women, against entertainments and free discussion. He was so fortunate as to be made censor, which gave him great power over the private lives of public people. He was thus able to ruin public opponents through private scandals. He expelled Manlius from the Senate for giving his wife a kiss in the daytime in the sight of their daughter. He persecuted Greek literature, about which, until late in life, he was totally ignorant. Then he read and admired

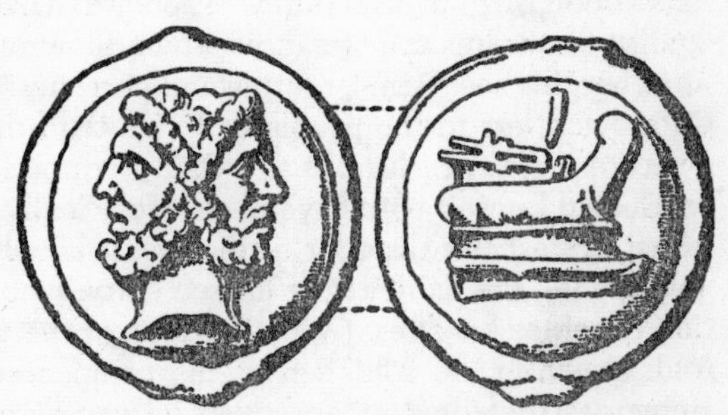

Roman As (bronze, 4th Cent. B.C. Half size)

Demosthenes. He wrote in Latin upon agriculture and the ancient and lost virtues of Rome. From these writings much light is thrown upon his qualities. One of his maxims was that when a slave was not sleeping he should be working. Another was that old oxen and slaves should be sold off. He left the war horse that had carried him through his Spanish campaigns behind him when he returned to Italy, in order to save freight. He hated other people's gardens, and cut off the supply of water for garden use in Rome. After entertaining company when dinner was over he would go out to correct any negligence in the service with a leather thong. He admired his own virtues very greatly, and insisted upon them in his writings. There was a battle at Thermopylæ against Antiochus the Great, of which he wrote, "those who saw him charging the enemy, routing and pursuing them, declared that Cato owed less to the people of Rome than the people of Rome owed to Cato."[1] In his old age Cato became lascivious and misconducted himself with a woman slave. Finally, when his son protested against this disorder of their joint household, he married a young wife, the daughter of his secretary, who was not in a position to refuse his offer. (What became of the woman slave is not told. Probably he sold her.) This compendium of all the old Roman virtues died at an advanced age respected and feared. Almost his last public act was to urge on the Third Punic War and the final destruction of Carthage. He had gone to Carthage as a commissioner to settle certain differences between Carthage and Numidia, and he had been shocked and horrified to find some evidences of prosperity and even of happiness in that country.

From the time of that visit onward Cato concluded every speech he made in the Senate by croaking out, "*Delenda est Carthago*" ("Carthage must be destroyed").

Such was the type of man that rose to prominence in Rome during the Punic struggle, such was the antagonist of Hannibal and the Carthaginian *revanche*, and by him and by Hannibal we may judge the tone and quality of the age.

The two great western powers, and Rome perhaps more than Carthage, were strained mentally and morally by the stresses of the First War. The evil side of life was uppermost. The history of the Second and Third Punic Wars (218 to 201 and 149 to 146 B.C.), it is plain, is not the history of perfectly sane peoples. It is nonsense for historians to write of the "political instincts" of the

---

[1] Plutarch, *Life of Cato.*

Romans or Carthaginians. Quite other instincts were loose. The red eyes of the ancestral ape had come back into the world. It was a time when reasonable men were howled down or murdered; the true spirit of the age is shown in the eager examination for signs and portents of the still quivering livers of those human victims who were sacrificed in Rome during the panic before the battle of Telamon. The western world was indeed black with homicidal monomania. Two great peoples, both very necessary to the world's development, fell foul of one another, and at last Rome succeeded in murdering Carthage.

§ 6

We can only tell very briefly here of the particulars of the Second and Third Punic Wars. We have told how Hamilcar began to organize Spain, and how the Romans forbade him to cross the Ebro. He died in 228 B.C., and was followed by his son-in-law Hasdrubal, who was assassinated in 221 B.C., and succeeded by Hannibal, who was now twenty-six. The actual war was precipitated by the Romans making a breach of their own regulations, and interfering with affairs south of the Ebro. Whereupon Hannibal marched straight through the south of Gaul, and crossed the Alps (218 B.C.) into Italy.

The history of the next fifteen years is the story of the most brilliant and futile raid in history. For fifteen years Hannibal held out in Italy, victorious and unconquered. The Roman generals were no match for the Carthaginian, and whenever they met him they were beaten. But one Roman general, P. Cornelius Scipio, had the strategic sense to take a course that robbed all Hannibal's victories of fruit. At the outbreak of the war he had been sent by sea to Marseilles to intercept Hannibal; he arrived three days late, and instead of pursuing him, he sent on his army into Spain to cut up Hannibal's supplies and reinforcements. Throughout all the subsequent war there remained this Roman army of Spain between Hannibal and his base. He was left "in the air", incapable of conducting sieges or establishing conquests.

Whenever he met the Romans in open fight he beat them. He gained two great victories in North Italy, and won over the Gauls to his side. He pressed south into Etruria, and ambushed, surrounded, and completely destroyed a Roman army at Lake Trasimene. In 216 B.C. he was assailed by a vastly superior Roman force under Varro at Cannæ, and destroyed it utterly. Fifty thousand men are said to have been killed and ten thousand prisoners taken. He was, however, unable to push on and capture Rome because he had no siege equipment.

But Cannæ produced other fruits. A large part of Southern Italy came over to Hannibal, including Capua, the city next in size to Rome, and the Macedonians allied themselves with him. Moreover, Hiero of Syracuse, the faithful ally of Rome, was now dead, and his successor Hieronymus turned over to the Carthaginians. The Romans carried on the war, however, with great toughness and resolution; they refused to treat with Hannibal after Cannæ, they pressed a slow but finally successful blockade and siege of Capua, and a Roman army set itself to reduce Syracuse. The siege of Syracuse is chiefly memorable for the brilliant inventions of the philosopher Archimedes, which long held the Romans at bay. We have already named this Archimedes as one of the pupils and correspondents of the school of the Alexandrian Museum. He was killed in the final storm of the town. Tarentum (209 B.C.), Hannibal's chief port and means of supply from Carthage, at last followed Syracuse (212 B.C.) and Capua (211 B.C.), and his comunications became irregular.

Spain also was wrested bit by bit from the Carthaginian grip. When at last reinforcements for Hannibal under his brother Hasdrubal (not to be confused with his brother-in-law of the same name who was assassinated) struggled through into Italy, they were destroyed at the battle of the Metaurus (207 B.C.), and the first news that came to Hannibal of the disaster was the hacked-off head of his brother thrown into his camp.

Thereafter Hannibal was blockaded into Calabria, the heel of Italy. He had no forces for further operations of any magnitude, and he returned at last to Carthage in time to command the Carthaginians in the last battle of the war.

This last battle, the battle of Zama (202 B.C.), was fought close to Carthage.

It was the first defeat Hannibal experienced; and so it is well to give a little attention to the personality of his conqueror, Scipio Africanus the Elder, who stands out in history as a very fine gentleman indeed, a great soldier and a generous man. We have already mentioned a certain P. Cornelius Scipio who struck at Hannibal's base in Spain; this was his son; until after Zama this son bore the same name of P. Cornelius Scipio, and then the surname of Africanus was given him. (The younger Scipio Africanus, Scipio Africanus Minor, who was later to end the Third Punic War, was the adopted son of the son of this first Scipio

Africanus the Elder.) Scipio Africanus was everything that aroused the distrust, hatred, and opposition of old-fashioned Romans of the school of Cato. He was young, he was happy and able, he spent money freely, he was well versed in Greek literature, and inclined rather to Phrygian novelties in religion than to the sterner divinities of Rome. And he did not believe in the extreme discretion that then ruled Roman strategy.

After the early defeats of the Second Punic War, Roman military operations were dominated by the personality of a general, Fabius, who raised the necessity of avoiding battle with Hannibal into a kind of sacred principle. For ten years "Fabian tactics" prevailed in Italy. The Romans blockaded, cut up convoys, attacked stragglers, and ran away whenever Hannibal appeared. No doubt it was wise for a time after their first defeats to do this sort of thing, but the business of the stronger power, and Rome was the stronger power throughout the Second Punic War, is not to tolerate an interminable war, but to repair losses, discover able generals, train better armies, and destroy the enemy power. Decision is one of the duties of strength.

To such men as young Scipio, the sly, ineffective artfulness of Fabianism, which was causing both Italy and Carthage to bleed slowly to death, was detestable. He clamoured for an attack upon Carthage itself.

"But Fabius, on this occasion, filled the city with alarms, as if the commonwealth was going to be brought into the most extreme danger by a rash and indiscreet young man; in short, he scrupled not to do or say anything he thought likely to dissuade his countrymen from embracing the proposal. With the Senate he carried his point. But the people believed that his opposition to Scipio proceeded either from envy of his success, or from a secret fear that if this young hero should perform some signal exploit, put an end to the war, or even remove it out of Italy, his own slow proceedings through the course of so many years might be imputed to indolence or timidity. . . . He applied to Crassus, the colleague of Scipio, and endeavoured to persuade him not to yield that province to Scipio, but, if he thought it proper to conduct the war in that manner, to go himself against Carthage. Nay, he even hindered the raising of money for that expedition, so that Scipio was obliged to find the supplies as he could. . . . He endeavoured to prevent the young men who offered to go as volunteers from giving in their names, and loudly declared, both in the Senate and Forum, 'That Scipio did not only himself avoid Hannibal, but intended to carry away with him the remaining strength of Italy, persuading the young men to abandon their parents, their wives, and native city, while an unsubdued and potent enemy was still at their doors.' With these assertions he so terrified the people, that they allowed Scipio to take with him only the legions that were in Sicily, and three hundred of those men who had served him with so much fidelity in Spain. . . . After Scipio was gone over into Africa, an account was soon brought to Rome of his glorious and wonderful achievements. This account was followed by rich spoils which confirmed it. A Numidian king was taken prisoner; two camps were burned and destroyed; and in them a vast number of men, arms, and horses; and the Carthaginians sent orders to Hannibal to quit his fruitless hopes in Italy, and return home to defend his own country. Whilst every tongue was applauding these exploits of Scipio, Fabius proposed that his successor should be appointed, without any shadow of reason for it, except what this well-known maxim implies: viz. "That it is dangerous to trust affairs of such importance to the fortune of one man, because it is not likely that he will be always successful.' . . . Nay, even when Hannibal embarked his army and quitted Italy, Fabius ceased not to disturb the general joy and to damp the spirits of Rome, for he took the liberty to affirm, 'That the commonwealth was now come to her last and worst trial; that she had the most reason to dread the efforts of Hannibal when he should arrive in Africa, and attack her sons under the walls of Carthage; that Scipio would have to do with an army yet warm with the blood of so many Roman generals, dictators, and consuls.' The city was alarmed with these declamations, and though the war was removed into Africa, the danger seemed to approach nearer Rome than ever."[1]

Before the battle of Zama there were a brief truce and negotiations, which broke down through the fault of the Carthaginians. As with the battle of Arbela, so the exact day of the battle of Zama can be fixed by an eclipse, which in this case occurred during the fighting. The Romans had been joined by the Numidians, the hinterland people of Carthage, under their king Massinissa, and this gave them—for the first time in any battle against Hannibal—a great superiority of cavalry. Hannibal's cavalry wings were driven off, while at the same time the sounder discipline of Scipio's infantry enabled them to open lanes for the charge of

---

[1] Plutarch's *Lives*.

The EXTENT of the ROMAN POWER & its ALLIANCES about 150 B.C.

the Carthaginian war elephants without being thrown into confusion. Hannibal attempted to extend his infantry line to envelop the Roman infantry mass, but while at Cannæ all the advantage of training and therefore of manœuvring power had been on his side, and he had been able to surround and massacre a crowd of infantry, he now found against him an infantry line better than his own. His own line broke as it extended, the Roman legions charged home, and the day was lost. The Roman cavalry came back from the pursuit of Hannibal's horse to turn what was already a defeat into a disastrous rout.

Carthage submitted without any further struggle. The terms were severe, but they left it possible for her to hope for an honourable future. She had to abandon Spain to Rome, to give up all her war fleet except ten vessels, to pay 10,000 talents (£2,400,000), and, what was the most difficult condition of all, to agree not to wage war without the permission of Rome. Finally a condition was added that Hannibal, as the great enemy of Rome, should be surrendered. But he saved his countrymen from this humiliation by flying to Asia.

These were exorbitant conditions, with which Rome should have been content. But there are nations so cowardly that they dare not merely conquer their enemies; they must *mak' siccar* and destroy them. The generation of Romans that saw greatness and virtue in a man like Cato the Censor, necessarily made their country a mean ally and a cowardly victor.

§ 7

The history of Rome for the fifty-three years that elapsed between the battle of Zama and the last act of the tragedy, the Third Punic War, tells of a hard, ungracious expansion of power abroad and of a slow destruction, by the usury and greed of the rich, of the free agricultural population at home.

The spirit of the nation had become harsh and base; there was no further extension of citizenship, no more generous attempts at the assimilation of congenital foreign populations. Spain was administered badly, and settled slowly and with great difficulty. Complicated interventions led to the reduction of Illyria and Macedonia to the position of tribute-paying provinces; Rome, it was evident, was going to "tax the foreigner" now and release her home population from taxation. After 168 B.C. the old land tax was no longer levied in Italy, and the only revenue derived from

Italy was from the state domains and through a tax on imports from overseas. The revenues from the province of "Asia" defrayed the expenses of the Roman state. At home men of the Cato type were acquiring farms by loans and foreclosure, often the farms of men impoverished by war service; they were driving the free citizens off their land, and running their farms with the pitilessly driven slave labour that was made cheap and abundant. Such men regarded alien populations abroad merely as unimported slaves. Sicily was handed over to the greedy enterprise of tax-farmers. Corn could be grown there by rich men using slaves, and imported very profitably into Rome, and so the home land could be turned over to cattle and sheep feeding. Consequently a drift of the uprooted Italian population to the towns, and particularly to Rome, began.

Of the first conflicts of the spreading power of Rome with the Seleucids, and how she formed an alliance with Egypt, we can tell little here, nor of the tortuous fluctuations of the Greek cities under the shadow of her advance until they fell into actual subjugation. A map must suffice to show the extension of her empire at this time.

The general grim baseness of the age was not without its protesting voices. We have already told how the wasting disease of the Second Punic War—a disease of the state which was producing avaricious rich men exactly as diseases of the body will sometimes produce great pustules, was ended by the vigour of Scipio Africanus. When it had seemed doubtful whether the Senate would let him go as the Roman general, he had threatened an appeal to the people. Thereafter he was a marked man for the senatorial gang, who were steadily changing Italy from a land of free cultivators to a land of slave-worked cattle ranches; they attempted to ruin him before ever he reached Africa; they gave him forces insufficient, as they hoped, for victory; and after the war they barred him strictly from any office. Interest and his natural malice alike prompted Cato to attack him.

Scipio Africanus the Elder seems to have been of a generous and impatient temperament, and indisposed to exploit the popular discontent with current tendencies and his own very great popularity to his own advantage. He went as subordinate to his brother Lucius Scipio, when the latter commanded the first Roman army to pass into Asia. At Magnesia, in Lydia, a great composite army under Antiochus III, the Seleucid monarch, suffered the fate (190 B.C.) of the very similar Persian armies of a hundred and forty years before. This victory drew down upon Lucius Scipio the hostility of the Senate, and he was accused of misappropriating moneys received from Antiochus. This filled Africanus with honest rage. As Lucius stood up in the Senate with his accounts in his hands ready for the badgering of his accusers, Africanus snatched the documents from him, tore them up, and flung the fragments down. His brother, he said, had paid into the treasury 200,000 sestertia (=£2,000,000). Was he now to be pestered and tripped up upon this or that item? When, later on, Lucius was prosecuted and condemned, Africanus rescued him by force. Being impeached, he reminded the people that the day was the anniversary of the battle of Zama, and defied the authorities, amidst the plaudits of the crowd.

The Roman people seem to have liked and supported Scipio Africanus, and, after an interval of two thousand years, men must like him still. He was able to throw torn paper in the face of the Senate, and when Lucius was attacked again one of the tribunes of the people interposed his veto and quashed the proceedings. But Scipio Africanus lacked that harder alloy which makes men great democratic leaders. He was no Cæsar. He had none of the qualities that subdue a man to the base necessities of political life. After these events he retired in disgust from Rome to his estates, and there he died in the year 183 B.C.

In the same year died Hannibal. He poisoned himself in despair. The steadfast fear of the Roman Senate had hunted him from court to court. In spite of the indignant protests of Scipio, Rome in the peace negotiations had demanded his surrender from Carthage, and she continued to make this demand of every power that sheltered him. When peace was made with Antiochus III, this was one of the conditions. He was run to earth at last in Bithynia; the king of Bithynia detained him in order to send him to Rome, but Hannibal had long carried the poison he needed in a ring, and by this he died.

It adds to the honour of the name of Scipio that it was another Scipio, Scipio Nasica, who parodied Cato's "*Delenda est Carthago*" by ending all his speeches in the Senate with "Carthage must stand." He had the wisdom to see that the existence and stimulus of Carthage contributed to the general prosperity of Rome.

Yet it was the second Scipio Africanus, grandson by adoption of Scipio Africanus the Elder, who took and destroyed Carthage. The sole offense of the Carthaginians, which brought about the third and last Punic War, was that they continued to trade and prosper. Their trade was not a trade that competed with that of Rome; when Carthage was destroyed, much of her trade died with her, and North Africa entered upon a phase of economic retrogression; but her prosperity aroused that passion of envy which was evidently more powerful even than avarice in the "old Roman" type. The rich Equestrian order resented any wealth in the world but its own. Rome provoked the war by encouraging the Numidians to encroach upon Carthage until the Carthaginians were goaded to fight in despair. Rome then pounced upon Carthage, and declared she had broken the treaty! She had made war without permission.

The Carthaginians sent the hostages Rome demanded, they surrendered their arms, they prepared to surrender territory. But submission only increased the arrogance of Rome and the pitiless greed of the rich Equestrian order which swayed her counsels. She now demanded that Carthage should be abandoned, and the population removed to a spot at least ten miles from the sea. This demand they made to a population that subsisted almost entirely by overseas trade!

This preposterous order roused the Carthaginians to despair. They called back their exiles and prepared for resistance. The military efficiency of the Romans had been steadily declining through a half-century of narrow-minded and base-spirited government, and the first attacks upon the town in 149 B.C. almost ended in disaster. Young Scipio, during these operations, distinguished himself in a minor capacity. The next year was also a year of failure for the incompetents of the Senate. That august body then passed from a bullying mood to one of extreme panic. The Roman populace was even more seriously scared. Young Scipio, chiefly on account of his name, although he was under the proper age, and in other respects not qualified for the office, was made consul, and bundled off to Africa to save his precious country.

There followed the most obstinate and dreadful of sieges. Scipio built a mole across the harbour, and cut off all supplies by land or sea. The Carthaginians suffered horribly from famine; but they held out until the town was stormed. The street fighting lasted for six days, and when at last the citadel capitulated there were fifty thousand Carthaginians left alive out of an estimated population of half a million. These survivors went into slavery, the whole city was burnt, the ruins were ploughed to express final destruction, and a curse was invoked with great solemnities upon anyone who might attempt to rebuild it.

In the same year (146 B.C.) the Roman Senate and Equestrians also *murdered* another great city that seemed to limit their trade monopolies, Corinth. They had a justification, for Corinth had been in arms against them, but it was an inadequate justification.

§ 8

We must note here, in a brief section, a change in the military system of Rome, after the Second Punic War, that was of enormous importance in her later development. Up to that period the Roman armies had been levies of free citizens. Fighting power and voting power were closely connected; the public assembly by centuries followed the paraphernalia of a military mobilization, and marched, headed by the Equestrian centuries, to the Campus Martius. The system was very like that of the Boers before the last war in South Africa. The ordinary Roman citizen, like the ordinary Boer, was a farmer; at the summons of his country he went "on commando." The Boers fought extraordinarily well, but at the back of their minds was an anxious desire to go back to their farms. For prolonged operations, such as the siege of Veii, the Romans reinforced and relieved their troops in relays; the Boers did much the same at the siege of Ladysmith.

The necessity for subjugating Spain after the Second Punic War involved a need for armies of a different type. Spain was too far off for periodic reliefs, and the war demanded a more thorough training than was possible with these on and off soldiers. Accordingly men were enlisted for longer terms and *paid*. So the paid soldier first appeared in Roman affairs. And booty was added to pay. Cato distributed silver treasure among his command in Spain; and it is also on record that he attacked Scipio Africanus for distributing booty among his troops in Sicily. The introduction of military pay led on to a professional army, and this, a century later, to the disarmament of the ordinary Roman citizen, who was now drifting in an impoverished state into Rome and the larger towns. The great wars had been won, the foundations of the empire had been well and truly laid by the embattled farmers of Rome before 200 B.C. In the process the embattled farmers of Rome had already largely disappeared. The change that began after the Second Punic War was completed towards the close of the century in the reorganization of the army by Marius, as we shall tell in its place. After his time we shall begin to write of "the army," and then of "the legions," and we shall find we are dealing with a new kind of army altogether, no longer held together in the solidarity of a common citizenship. As that tie fails, the legions discover another in *esprit de corps,* in their common difference from and their common interest against the general community. They develop a warmer interest in their leaders, who secure them pay and plunder. Before the Punic Wars it was the tendency of ambitious men in Rome to court the plebeians; after that time they began to court the legions.

§ 9

The history of the Roman Republic thus far is in many respects much more modern in flavour, especially to the American or Western European reader, than anything that has preceded it. For the first time we have something like a self-governing "nation," something larger than a mere city state, seeking to control its own destinies. For the first time we have a wide countryside under one conception of law. We get in the Senate and the popular assembly a conflict of groups and personalities, an argumentative process of control, far more stable and enduring than any autocracy can be, and far more flexible and adaptable than any priesthood. For the first time also we encounter social conflicts comparable to our own. Money has superseded barter, and financial capital has become fluid and free; not perhaps so fluid and free as it is to-day, but much more so than it had ever been before. The Punic Wars were wars of peoples, such as were no other wars we have yet recorded. Indubitably the broad lines of our present world, the main ideas, the chief oppositions, were appearing in those days.

But, as we have already pointed out, certain of the elementary facilities and some of the current political ideas of our time were still wanting in the Rome of the Punic Wars. There were no newspapers, and there was practically no use of elected representatives in the popular assemblies. Julius Cæsar (60 B.C.) caused the proceedings of the Senate to be published by having them written up upon bulletin boards *in albo* (upon the white). It had been the custom to publish the annual edict of the prætor in this fashion. There were professional letter-writers who sent news by special order to rich country correspondents, and these would copy down the stuff upon the *album* (white board). Cicero, while he was governor in Cilicia, got the current news from such a professional correspondent. He complains in one letter that it was not what he wanted; the excerpt was too full of the chariot races and other sporting intelligence, and failed to give any view of the political situation. Obviously this news-letter system was available only for public men in prosperous circumstances.

Another great deficiency of the democratic machinery of the Roman Republic, very understandable to us nowadays, but quite beyond the scope of anyone then, was the absence of any general elementary political education at all. The plebeians of Rome had shown some glimmering of the idea that without knowledge votes cannot make men free, when they had insisted upon the publication of the law of the Twelve Tables; but they had never been able, it was beyond the possibilities of the time, to imagine any further extension of knowledge to the bulk of the people. It is only nowadays that men are beginning to understand fully the political significance of the maxim that "knowledge is power." British Trade Unions, for example, recently set up a Labour College to meet the special needs of able working-men in history, political and social science, and the like. But education in republican Rome was the freak of the individual parent, and the privilege of wealth and leisure. It was mainly in the hands of Greeks, who were in many cases slaves. There was a thin small stream of very fine learning and very fine thinking up to the first century of the monarchy, let Lucretius and Cicero witness, but it did not spread into the mass of the people. The ordinary Roman was not only blankly ignorant of the history of mankind, but also of the conditions of foreign peoples; he had no knowledge of economic laws nor of social possibilities. Even his own interests he did not clearly understand.

Of course, in the little city states of Greece and in that early Roman state of four hundred square miles, men acquired by talk and observation a sufficient knowledge for the ordinary duties of citizenship, but by the beginning of the Punic Wars the business was already too big and complicated for illiterate men. Yet nobody seems to have observed the gap that was opening between the citizen and his state, and so there is no record at all of any attempt to enlarge the citizen by instruction to meet his enlarged duties. From the second century B.C. and onward everyone is remarking upon the ignorance of the common citizen and his lack of political wisdom, everything is suffering from the lack of political solidarity due to this ignorance, but no one goes on to what we should now consider the inevitable corollary, no one proposes to destroy the ignorance complained of. There existed no means whatever for the instruction of the masses of the people in a common political and social ideal. It was only with the development of the great propagandist religions in the Roman world, of which Christianity was the chief and the survivor, that the possibility of such a systematic instruction of great masses of people became apparent in the world. That very great political genius, the Emperor Constantine the Great, six centuries later, was the first to apprehend and to attempt to use this possibility for the preservation and the mental and moral knitting-together of the world community over which he ruled.

But it is not only in these deficiencies of news and of education and of the expedient of representative government that this political system of Rome differed from our own. True, it was far more like a modern civilized state than any other state we have considered hitherto, but in some matters it was strangely primordial and "sub-civilized." Every now and then the reader of Roman history, reading it in terms of debates and measures, policies and campaigns, capital and labour, comes upon something that gives him much the same shock he would feel if he went down to an unknown caller in his house and extended his hand to meet the misshapen hairy paw of *Homo Neanderthalensis* and looked up to see a chinless, bestial face. We have noted the occurrence of human sacrifice in the third century B.C., and much that we learn of the religion of republican Rome carries us far back beyond the days of decent gods, to the age of shamanism and magic. We talk of a legislative gathering, and the mind flies to Westminster; but how should we feel if we went to see the beginning of a session of the House of Lords, and discovered the Lord Chancellor, with bloody fingers, portentously fiddling about among the entrails of a newly killed sheep? The mind would recoil from Westminster to the customs of Benin. And the slavery of Rome was a savage slavery, altogether viler than the slavery of Babylon. We have had a glimpse of the virtuous Cato among his slaves in the second century B.C. Moreover, in the third century B.C., when King Asoka was ruling India in light and gentleness, the Romans were reviving an Etruscan sport, the setting-on of slaves to fight for their lives. One is reminded of West Africa again in the origin of this amusement; it grew out of the prehistoric custom of a massacre of captives at the burial of a chief.

There was a religious touch about this sport; the slaves with hooks, who dragged the dead bodies out of the arena, wore masks to represent the infernal ferryman-god, Charon.

In 264 B.C., the very year in which Asoka began to reign and the First Punic War began, the first recorded gladiatorial combat took place in the forum at Rome, to celebrate the funeral of a member of the old Roman family of Brutus. This was a modest display of three couples, but soon gladiators were fighting by the hundred. The taste for these combats grew rapidly, and the wars supplied an abundance of captives. The old Roman moralists, who were so severe upon kissing and women's ornaments and Greek philosophy, had nothing but good to say for this new development. So long as pain was inflicted, Roman morality, it would seem, was satisfied.

If republican Rome was the first of modern self-governing national communities, she was certainly the "Neanderthal" form of them.

In the course of the next two or three centuries the gladiatorial shows of Rome grew to immense proportions. To begin with, while wars were frequent, the gladiators were prisoners of war. They came with their characteristic national weapons, tatooed Britons, Moors, Scythians, negroes, and the like, and there was perhaps some military value in these exhibitions. Then criminals of the lower classes condemned to death were also used. The ancient world did not understand that a criminal condemned to death still has rights, and at any rate the use of a criminal as a gladiator was not so bad as his use as "material" for the vivisectors of the Museum at Alexandria. But as the profits of this sort of show business grew and the demand for victims increased, ordinary slaves were sold to the trainers of gladiators, and any slave who had aroused his owner's spite might find himself in an establishment for letting out gladiators. And dissipated young men who had squandered their property, and lads of spirit, would go voluntarily into trade for a stated time, trusting to their prowess to survive.

As the business developed, a new use was found for gladiators as armed retainers; rich men would buy a band, and employ it as a bodyguard or hire it out for profit at the shows.

The festivities of a show began with a ceremonial procession (*pompa*) and a sham fight (*prœlusio*). The real fighting was heralded by trumpets. Gladiators who objected to fight for any reason were driven on by whips and hot irons. A wounded man would sometimes call for pity by holding up his forefinger. The spectators would then either wave their handkerchiefs in token of mercy, or condemn him to death by holding out their clenched fists with the thumbs held in some fashion that indicated death. Authorities differ here as to the exact signal. Mayor says thumbs up (to the breast) meant death and thumbs down meant "Lower that sword." The common persuasion is that thumbs down meant death. The slain and nearly dead were dragged out to a particular place, the *spoliarium,* where they were stripped of their arms and possessions, and those who had not already expired were killed.

This organization of murder as a sport and show serves to measure the great gap in moral standards between the Roman community and our own. No doubt cruelties and outrages upon human dignity as monstrous as this still go on in the world, but they do not go on in the name of the law, and without a single dissentient voice. For it is true that until the time of Seneca (first century A.D.) there is no record of any plain protest against this business. The conscience of mankind was weaker and less intelligent then than now. Presently a new power was to come into the human conscience through the spread of Christianity. The spirit of Jesus in Christianity became the great antagonist in the later Roman state of these cruel shows and of slavery, and, as Christianity spread, these two evil things dwindled and disappeared. Professor Gilbert Murray adds that "the Greeks cited gladiatorial shows as a reason for regarding the Romans as *Barbaroi,* and there were riots when some Roman proconsul tried to introduce them in Corinth." The opposition to this ancient cruelty was therefore not purely Christian. "Among Romans the

Gladiators *(from a wall-painting at Pompeii)*

better people evidently disliked them, but a sort of shyness prevented them from frankly denouncing them as cruel. For instance, Cicero, when he had to attend the Circus, took his tablets and his secretary with him, and didn't look. He expresses particular disgust at the killing of an elephant. The games were unhesitatingly condemned by Greek philosophy, and at different times two Cynics and one Christian gave their lives in the arena, protesting against them, before they were abolished."

XXVI

FROM TIBERIUS GRACCHUS TO THE GOD EMPEROR IN ROME

§ 1. *The Science of Thwarting the Common Man.* § 2. *Finance in the Roman State.* § 3. *The Last Years of Republican Politics.* § 4. *The Era of the Adventurer Generals.* § 5. *The End of the Republic.* § 6. *The Coming of the Princeps.* § 7. *Why the Roman Republic Failed.*

§ 1

WE HAVE already twice likened the self-governing community of Rome to a "Neanderthal" variety of the modern "democratic" civilized state, and we shall recur again to this comparison. In form the two things, the first great primitive essay and its later relations, are extraordinarily similar; in spirit they differ very profoundly. Roman political and social life, and particularly Roman political and social life in the century between the fall of Carthage and the rise of Cæsar and Cæsarism, has a very marked general resemblance to the political and social life in such countries as the United States of America or the British Empire to-day. The resemblance is intensified by the common use, with a certain inaccuracy in every case, of such terms as "senate," "democracy," "proletariat," and the like. But everything in the Roman state was earlier, cruder, and clumsier; the injustices were more glaring, the conflicts harsher. There was comparatively little knowledge and few general ideas. Aristotle's scientific works were only beginning to be read in Rome in the first century B.C.; Ferrero,[1] it is true, makes Cæsar familiar with the Politics of Aristotle, and ascribes to him the dream of making a "Periclean Rome," but in doing so Ferrero seems to be indulging in one of those lapses into picturesque romancing which are at once the joy and the snare of all historical writers.

Attention has already been drawn to the profound difference between Roman and modern conditions due to the absence of

[1] *Greatness and Decline of Rome,* bk. i. ch. xi.

a press, of any popular education, or of the representative idea in the popular assembly. Our world to-day is still far from solving the problem of representation and from producing a public assembly which will really summarize, crystallize, and express the thought and will of the community; our elections are still largely an ingenious mockery of the common voter, who finds himself helpless in the face of party organizations which reduce his free choice of a representative to the less unpalatable of two political hacks; but, even so, his vote, in comparison with the vote of an ordinary honest Roman citizen, is an effective instrument. Too many of our histories dealing with this period of Roman history write of "the popular party," and of the votes of the people and so forth, as though such things were as much working realities as they are to-day. But the senators and politicians of Rome saw to it that such things never did exist as clean and wholesome realities. These modern phrases are very misleading unless they are carefully qualified.

We have already described the gatherings of the popular comitia; but that clumsy assembly in sheep-pens does not convey the full extent to which the gerrymandering of popular representation could be carried in Rome. Whenever there was a new enfranchisement of citizens in Italy, there would be the most elaborate trickery and counter-trickery to enroll the new voters into as few or as many of the thirty old "tribes" as possible, or to put them into as few as possible new tribes. Since the vote was taken by tribes, it is obvious that, however great the number of new additions made, if they were all got together into one tribe, their opinion would only count for one tribal vote, and similarly if they were crowded into just a few tribes, old or new.

On the other hand, if they were put into too many tribes, their effect in any particular tribe might be inconsiderate. Here was the sort of work to fascinate every smart knave in politics. The *comitia tributa* could be *worked* at times so as to vote altogether counter to the general feeling of the people. And, as we have already noted, the great mass of voters in Italy were also disenfranchised by distance. About the middle period of the Carthaginian wars there were upwards of 300,000 Roman citizens; about 100 B.C. there were more than 900,000 but in effect the voting of the popular assembly was confined to a few score thousand resident in and near Rome, and mostly men of a base type. And the Roman voters were "organized" to an extent that makes the Tammany machine of New York seem artless and honest.

They belonged to clubs, *collegia sodalicia,* having usually some elegant religious pretensions; and the rising politician, working his way to office, went first to the usurers and then with the borrowed money to these clubs. If the outside voters were moved enough by any question to swarm into the city, it was always possible to put off the voting by declaring the omens unfavourable. If they came in unarmed, they could be intimidated; if they brought in arms, then the cry was raised that there was a plot to overthrow the republic, and a massacre would be organized.

There can be no doubt that all Italy, all the empire, was festering with discomfort, anxiety, and discontent in the century after the destruction of Carthage; a few men were growing very rich, and the majority of people found themselves entangled in an inexplicable net of uncertain prices, jumpy markets, and debts; but yet there was no way at all of stating and clearing up the general dissatisfaction. There is no record of a single attempt to make the popular assembly a straightforward and workable public organ. Beneath the superficial appearances of public affairs struggled a mute giant of public opinion and public will, which sometimes made a great political effort, a rush to vote or suchlike, or broke into actual violence. So long as there was no actual violence, the Senate and the financiers kept on in their own disastrous way. Only when they were badly frightened would governing cliques or parties desist from some nefarious policy and heed the common good.

The real method of popular expression in Italy in those days was not the *comitia tributa,* but the strike and insurrection, the righteous and necessary methods of all cheated or suppressed peoples. We have seen in our own time, in various European states, a decline in the prestige of parliamentary government and a drift towards unconstitutional methods on the part of the masses through exactly the same cause, through the incurable disposition of politicians to gerrymander the electoral machine until the community is driven to explosion.

For insurrectionary purposes a discontented population needs a leader, and the political history of the concluding century of Roman republicanism is a history of insurrectionary leaders and counter-revolutionary leaders. Most of the former are manifestly unscrupulous adventurers who try to utilize the public necessity and unhappiness for their own advancement. Many of the historians of this period betray a disposition to take sides, and are either aristocratic in tone or fiercely democratic; but, indeed, neither side in these complex and intricate disputes has a record of high aims or clean hands. The Senate and the rich Equestrians were vulgar and greedy spirits, hostile and contemptuous towards the poor mob; and the populace was ignorant, unstable, and at least equally greedy. The Scipios in all this record shine by comparison, a group of gentlemen. To the motives of one or the other figures of the time, to Tiberius Gracchus, for example, we may perhaps extend the benefit of the doubt. But for the rest, they do but demonstrate how clever and cunning men may be, how subtle in contention, how brilliant in pretence, and how utterly wanting in wisdom or grace of spirit. "A shambling, hairy, brutish, but probably very cunning creature with a big brain *behind*"; so someone, I think it was Sir Harry Johnston, has described *Homo Neanderthalensis.*

To this day we must still use similar terms to describe the soul of the politician. The statesman has still to oust the politician from his lairs and weapon heaps. History has still to become a record of human dignity.

§ 2

Another respect in which the Roman system was a crude anticipation of our own, and different from any preceding political system we have considered, was that it was a cash- and credit-using system. Money had been in the world as yet for only a few centuries. But its use had been growing; it was providing a fluid medium for trade and enterprise, and changing economic conditions profoundly. In republican Rome, the financier and the "money" interest began to play a part recognizably similar to their rôles to-day.

We have already noted—in our account of Herodotus—that a first effect of money was to give freedom of movement and leisure to a number of people who could not otherwise have enjoyed these privileges. And that is the peculiar value of money to mankind. Instead of a worker or helper being paid in kind and in such a way that he is tied as much in his enjoyment as in his labour, money leaves him free to do as he pleases amidst a wide choice of purchasable aids, eases, and indulgences. He may eat his money or drink it or give it to a temple or spend it in learning something or save it against some foreseen occasion. That is the good of money, the freedom of its universal convertibility. But the freedom money gives the poor man is nothing to the freedom money has given the rich man. With money rich men ceased to be tied to lands, houses, stores, flocks, and herds. They could change the nature and locality of their possessions with an unheard-of freedom. In the third and second century B.C., this release, this untethering of wealth, began to tell upon the general economic life of the Roman and Hellenized world. People began to buy land and the like not for use, but to sell again at a profit; people borrowed to buy, speculation developed. No doubt there were bankers in the Babylon of 1,000 B.C., but they lent in a far more limited and solid way, bars of metal and stocks of goods. That earlier world was a world of barter and payment in kind, and it went slowly—and much more staidly and stably—for that reason. In that state the vast realm of China has remained almost down to the present time.

The big cities before Rome were trading and manufacturing cities. Such were Corinth and Carthage and Syracuse. But Rome never produced a very considerable industrial population, and her warehouses never rivalled those of Alexandria. The little port of Ostia was always big enough for her needs. Rome was a political and financial capital, and in the latter respect, at least, she was a new sort of city. She imported profits and tribute, and very little went out from her in return. The wharves of Ostia were chiefly busy unloading corn from Sicily and Africa and loot from all the world.

After the fall of Carthage the Roman imagination went wild with the hitherto unknown possibilities of finance. Money, like most other inventions, had "happened" to mankind, and men had still to develop—to-day they have still to perfect—the science and morality of money. One sees the thing "catching on" in the recorded life and the writings of Cato the Censor. In his early days he was bitterly virtuous against usury; in his later he was devising ingenious schemes for safe usury.

In this curiously interesting century of Roman history we find man after man asking, "What has happened to Rome?" Various answers are made—a decline in religion, a decline from the virtues of the Roman forefathers, Greek "intellectual poison," and the like. We, who can look at the problem with a large perspective, can see that what had happened to Rome was "money" —the new freedoms and chances and opportunities that money opened out. Money floated the Romans off the firm ground; everyone was getting hold of money, the majority by the simple expedient of running into debt; the eastward expansion of the empire was very largely a hunt for treasure in strong-rooms and temples to keep pace with the hunger of the new need. The Equestrian order, in particular, became the money power. Everyone was developing property. Farmers were giving up corn and cattle, borrowing money, buying slaves, and starting the more intensive cultivation of oil and wine.

Money was young in human experience and wild; nobody had it under control. It fluctuated greatly. It was now abundant and now scarce. Men made sly and crude schemes to corner it, to hoard it, to send up prices by releasing hoarded metals. A small body of very shrewd men was growing immensely rich. Many patricians were growing poor and irritated and unscrupulous. Among the middling sort of people there was much hope, much adventure, and much more disappointment. The growing mass of the expropriated was permeated by that vague, baffled, and hopeless sense of being inexplicably bested, which is the preparatory condition for all great revolutionary movements.

§ 3

The first conspicuous leader to appeal to the gathering revolutionary feeling in Italy was Tiberius Gracchus. He looks more like an honest man than any other figure in this period of history, unless it be Scipio Africanus the Elder. At first Tiberius Gracchus was a moderate reformer of a rather reactionary type. He wished to restore the yeoman class to property, very largely because he believed that class to be the backbone of the army, and his military experience in Spain before and after the destruction of Carthage had impressed upon him the declining efficiency of the legions. He was what we should call nowadays a "Back-to-the-land" man. He did not understand, and few people understand to-day, how much easier it is to shift population from the land into the towns than to return it to the laborious and simple routines of agricultural life. He wanted to revive the Licinian laws, which had been established when Camillus built his Temple of Concord nearly two centuries and a half before (see Chap. xxv, § 2), so far as they broke up great estates and restrained slave labour.

These Licinian laws had repeatedly been revived and repeatedly lapsed to a dead letter again. It was only when the big proprietors in the Senate opposed this proposal that Tiberius Gracchus turned to the people and began a furious agitation for popular government. He created a commission to inquire into the title of all landowners. In the midst of his activities occurred one of the most extraordinary incidents in history. Attalus, the king of the rich country of Pergamum in Asia Minor, died (133 B.C.) and left his kingdom to the Roman people.

It is difficult for us to understand the motives of this bequest. Pergamum was a country allied to Rome, and so moderately secure from aggression; and the natural consequence of such a will was to provoke a violent scramble among the senatorial gangs and a dispute between them and the people for the spoils of the new acquisition. Practically, Attalus handed over his country to be looted. There were, of course, many Italian business people established in the country and a strong party of native rich men in close relations with Rome. To them, no doubt, a coalescence with the Roman system would have been acceptable. Josephus bears witness to such a desire for annexation among the rich men of Syria, a desire running counter to the wishes of both king and people. This Pergamum bequest, astonishing in itself, had the still more astonishing result of producing imitations in other quarters. In 96 B.C. Ptolemy Apion bequeathed Cyrenaica, in North Africa, to the Roman people; in 81 B.C. Alexander II, King of Egypt, followed suit with Egypt, a legacy too big for the courage if not for the appetite of the Senators, and they declined it; in 74 B.C. Nicomedes, King of Bithynia, demised Bithynia. Of these latter testamentary freaks we will say no more here. But it will be manifest how great an opportunity was given Tiberius Gracchus by the bequest of Attalus, of accusing the rich of greed and of proposing to decree the treasures of Attalus to the commonalty. He proposed to use this new wealth to provide seed, stock, and agricultural implements for the resettlement of the land.

His movement was speedily entangled in the complexities of the Roman electoral system—without a simple and straightforward electoral method, all popular movements in all ages necessarily become entangled and maddened in constitutional intricacies, and almost as necessarily lead to bloodshed. It was needed, if his work was to go on, that Tiberius Gracchus should continue to be tribune, and it was illegal for him to be tribune twice in succession. He overstepped the bounds of legality, and stood for the tribuneship a second time. The peasants who came in from the countryside to vote for him came in armed; the cry that he was aiming at a tyranny, the cry that had long ago destroyed Mælius and Manlius, was raised in the Senate, the friends of "law and order" went to the Capitol in state, accompanied by a rabble of dependants armed with staves and bludgeons; there was a conflict, or rather a massacre of the revolutionaries, in which nearly three hundred people were killed, and Tiberius Gracchus was beaten to death with the fragments of a broken bench by two Senators.

Thereupon the Senators attempted a sort of counter-revolution and proscribed many of the followers of Tiberius Gracchus; but the state of public opinion was so sullen and threatening that this movement was dropped, and Scipio Nasica, who was implicated in the death of Tiberius, though he occupied the position of pontifex maximus and should have remained in Rome for the public sacrifices which were the duties of that official, went abroad to avoid trouble.

The uneasiness of Italy next roused Scipio Africanus the Younger to propose the enfranchisement of all Italy. But he died suddenly before he could carry the proposal into effect.

Then followed the ambiguous career of Gaius Gracchus, the brother of Tiberius, who followed some tortuous "policy" that still exercises the minds of historians. He increased the burthens of taxation laid upon the provinces, it is supposed with the idea of setting the modern financiers (the Equites) against the senatorial landowners. He gave the former the newly bequeathed taxes of Asia to farm, and, what is worse, he gave them control of the special courts set up to prevent extortion. He started enormous public works and particularly the construction of new roads, and he is accused of making a political use of the contracts. He revived the proposal to enfranchise Italy. He increased the distribution of subsidized cheap corn to the Roman citizens. . . . Here we cannot attempt to disentangle his schemes, much less to judge him. But that his policy was offensive to the groups that controlled the Senate there can be no doubt whatever. He was massacred by the champions of "law and order," with about three thousand of his followers, in the streets of Rome in 121 B.C. His decapitated head was carried to the Senate on the point of a pike. (A reward of its weight in gold, says Plutarch, had been offered for this trophy; and its captor, acting in the true spirit of a champion of "big business," filled the brain-case with lead on its way to the scales.)

In spite of these prompt, firm measures the Senate was not to enjoy the benefits of peace and the advantages of a control of the imperial resources for long. Within ten years the people were in revolt again.

In 118 B.C. the throne of Numidia, the semi-barbaric kingdom that had arisen in North Africa upon the ruins of the civilized Carthaginian power, was seized by a certain able Jugurtha, who had served with the Roman armies in Spain, and had a knowledge of the Roman character. He provoked the military intervention of Rome. But the Romans found that their military power, under a Senate of financiers and landlords, was very different from what it had been even in the days of the younger Scipio Africanus. "Jugurtha bought over the Commissioners sent out to watch him, the Senators charged with their prosecution, and the generals in command against him."[1] There is a mistaken Roman proverb, "*Pecunia non olet*" (Money does not stink), for the money of Jugurtha stank even in Rome. There was an angry agitation; and a capable soldier of lowly origin, Marius, was carried to the consulship (107 B.C.) on the wave of popular indignation. Marius made no attempt on the model of the Gracchi to restore the backbone of the army by rehabilitating the yeoman class. He was a professional soldier with a high standard of efficiency and a disposition to take short cuts. He simply raised troops from among the poor, whether countrymen or townsmen, paid them well, disciplined them thoroughly, and (106 B.C.) ended the seven years' war with Jugurtha by bringing that chieftain in chains to Rome. It did not occur to anybody that incidentally Marius had also created a professional army with no interest to hold it together but its pay. He then held on to the consulship more or less illegally for several years, and in 102 and 101 B.C. repelled a threatening move of the Germans (who thus appear in our history for the first time), who were raiding through Gaul towards Italy. He gained two victories; one on Italian soil. He was hailed as the saviour of his country, a second Camillus (100 B.C.).

The social tensions of the time mocked that comparison with Camillus. The Senate benefited by the greater energy in foreign affairs and the increased military efficiency that Marius had introduced, but the sullen, shapeless discontent of the mass of the people was still seeking some effective outlet. The rich grew richer and the poor poorer. It was impossible to stifle the consequences of that process for ever by political trickery. The Italian people were still unenfranchised. Two extreme democratic leaders, Saturninus and Glaucia, were assassinated, but that familiar senatorial remedy failed to assuage the populace on this occasion. In

[1] Ferrero.

92 B.C. an aristocratic official, Rutilius Rufus, who had tried to restrain the exactions of the financiers in Asia Minor, was condemned on a charge of corruption so manifestly trumped up that it deceived no one; and in 91 B.C., Livius Drusus, a newly elected tribune of the people, who was making capital out of the trial of Rutilius Rufus, was assassinated. He had proposed a general enfranchisement of the Italians, and he had foreshadowed not only another land law, but a general abolition of debts. Yet for all this vigour on the part of the senatorial usurers, land-grabbers, and forestallers, the hungry and the anxious were still insurgent. The murder of Drusus was the last drop in the popular cup; Italy blazed into a desperate insurrection.

There followed two years of bitter civil war, the Social War. It was a war between the idea of a united Italy and the idea of the rule of the Roman Senate. It was not a "social" war in the modern sense, but a war between Rome and her Italian allies (allies=Socii). "Roman generals, trained in the traditions of colonial warfare, marched ruthlessly up and down Italy, burning farms, sacking towns, and carrying off men, women, and children, to sell them in the open market or work them in gangs upon their estates."[1]

Marius and an aristocratic general, Sulla, who had been with him in Africa and who was his bitter rival, both commanded on the side of Rome. But though the insurgents experienced defeats and looting, neither of these generals brought the war to an end. It was ended in a manner (89 B.C.) by the practical surrender of the Roman Senate to the idea of reform. The spirit was taken out of the insurrection by the concession of their demands "in principle"; and then, as soon as the rebels had dispersed, the usual cheating of the new voters, by such methods as we have explained in § 1 of this chapter, was resumed.

By the next year (88 B.C.) the old round had begun again. It was mixed up with the personal intrigues of Marius and Sulla against each other; but the struggle had taken on another complexion through the army reforms of Marius, which had created a new type of legionary, a landless professional soldier with no interest in life but pay and plunder, and with no feeling of loyalty except to a successful general. A popular tribune, Sulpicius, was bringing forward some new laws affecting debt, and the consuls were dodging the storm by declaring a suspension

---

[1] Ferrero.

of public business. Then came the usual resort to violence, and the followers of Sulpicius drove the consuls from the forum. But here it is that the new forces which the new army had made possible came into play. King Mithridates of Pontus, the Hellenized king of the southern shores of the Black Sea east of Bithynia, was pressing Rome into war. One of the proposed laws of Sulpicius was that Marius should command the armies sent against this Mithridates. Whereupon Sulla marched the army he had commanded throughout the Social War to Rome, Marius and Sulpicius fled, and a new age, an age of military pronunciamentos, began.

Of how Sulla had himself made commander against Mithridates and departed, and of how legions friendly to Marius then seized power, how Marius returned to Italy and enjoyed a thorough massacre of his political opponents and died, sated, of fever, we cannot tell in any detail. But one measure during the Marian reign of terror did much to relieve the social tension, and that was the abolition of three-quarters of all outstanding debts. Nor can we tell here how Sulla made a discreditable peace with Mithridates (who had massacred a hundred thousand Italians in Asia Minor) in order to bring his legions back to Rome, defeat the Marians at the battle of the Colline Gate of Rome, and reverse the arrangements of Marius. Sulla restored law and order by the proscription and execution of over five thousand people. He desolated large parts of Italy, restored the Senate to power, repealed many of the recent laws, though he was unable to restore the cancelled burden of debt, and then, feeling bored by politics and having amassed great riches, he retired with an air of dignity into private life, gave himself up to abominable vices, and so presently died, eaten up with some disgusting disease produced by debauchery.

§ 4

Political life in Italy was not so much tranquillized as stunned by the massacres and confiscations of Marius and Sulla. The scale upon which this history is planned will not permit us to tell here of the great adventurers who, relying more and more on the support of the legions, presently began to scheme and intrigue again for dictatorial power in Rome. In 73 B.C. all Italy was terrified by a rising of the slaves, and particularly of the gladiators, led by a gladiator from Thessaly, Spartacus. He and seventy others had fled out from a gladiatorial "farm" at Capua.

Similar risings had already occurred in Sicily. The forces under Spartacus necessarily became a miscellaneous band drawn from east and west, without any common idea except the idea of dispersing and getting home; nevertheless he held out in southern Italy for two years, using the then apparently extinct crater of Vesuvius for a time as a natural fortress. The Italians, for all their love of gladiatorial display, failed to appreciate this conversion of the whole country into an arena, this bringing of the gladiatorial sword to the door, and when at last Spartacus was overthrown, their terror changed to frantic cruelty, six thousand of his captured followers were crucified—long miles of nailed and drooping victims—along the Appian Way.

Here we cannot deal at any length with Lucullus, who invaded Pontus and fought Mithridates, and brought the cultivated cherry-tree to Europe; nor can we tell how ingeniously Pompey the Great stole the triumph and most of the prestige Lucullus had won in Armenia beyond Pontus. Lucullus, like Sulla, retired into an opulent private life, but with more elegance and with a more gracious end. We cannot relate in any detail how Julius Cæsar accumulated reputation in the west, by conquering Gaul, defeating the German tribes upon the Rhine, and pushing a punitive raid across the Strait of Dover into Britain. More and more important grow the legions; less and less significant are the Senate and the assemblies of Rome. But there is a certain grim humour about the story of Crassus that we cannot altogether neglect.

This Crassus was a great money-lender and forestaller. He was a typical man of the new Equestrian type, the social equivalent of a modern munition profiteer. He first grew rich by buying up the property of those proscribed by Sulla. His earliest exploits in the field were against Spartacus, whom finally he crushed by great payments and exertions after a prolonged and expensive campaign. He then, as the outcome of complicated bargains, secured the command in the east and prepared to emulate the glories of Lucullus, who had pushed east from Pergamum and Bithynia into Pontus, and of Pompey, who had completed the looting of Armenia.

His experiences serve to demonstrate the gross ignorance with which the Romans were conducting their affairs at that time. He crossed the Euphrates, expecting to find in Persia another Hellenized kingdom like Pontus. But, as we have already intimated, the great reservoirs of nomadic peoples that stretched round from the Danube across Russia into Central Asia had been raining back into the lands between the Caspian Sea and the Indus that Alexander had conquered for Hellenism. Crassus found himself against the "Scythian" again; against mobile tribes of horsemen led by a monarch in Median costume. The particular variety of "Scythian" he encountered was called the Parthian. It is possible that in the Parthians a Mongolian (Turanian) element was now mingled with the Aryan strain. But the campaign of Crassus beyond the Euphrates is curiously like the campaign of Darius beyond the Danube; there is the same heavy thrusting of an infantry force against elusive light horsemen; but Crassus was less quick than Darius to realize the need of withdrawal, and the Parthians were better bowmen than the Scythians Darius met. They seem to have had some sort of noisy projectile of unusual strength and force, something that was different from an ordinary arrow. This bow, says Professor J. L. Myres, was probably the composite bow, so-called because it is made of several plates (five or so) of horn, like the springs of a carriage; it discharges a high-speed arrow with a twang. This was the bow the Mongols used. This composite bow (it was not a long bow) was quite old in human experience. It was the bow of Odysseus; the Assyrians had it in a modified form. It went out in Greece, but it survived as the Mongol bow. It was quite short, very stiff to pull, with a flat trajectory, a remarkable range, and a great noise (*cp.* Homer's reference to the twang of the bow). It went out in the Mediterranean because the climate was not good for it, and because there were insufficient animals to supply the horn.

The campaign culminated in that two days' massacre of the hot, thirsty, hungry, and weary Roman legions, which is known as the battle of Carrhæ (53 B.C.). They toiled through the sand, charging an enemy who always evaded their charge and rode round them and shot them to pieces. Twenty thousand of them were killed, and ten thousand marched on eastward as prisoners into slavery in Iran.

What became of Crassus is not clearly known. There is a story, probably invented for our moral benefit and suggested by his usuries, that he fell alive into the hands of the Parthians and was killed by having molten gold poured down his throat.

But this disaster has a very great significance, indeed, to our general history of mankind. It serves to remind us that from the Rhine to the Euphrates, all along to the north of the Alps and Danube and Black Sea, stretched one continuous cloud of nomadic and semi-nomadic peoples, whom the statecraft of imperial Rome was never able to pacify and civilize, nor her military science subdue. We have already called attention to a map showing how the Second Babylonian Empire, the Chaldean Empire, lay like a lamb in the embrace of the Median power. In exactly the same way the Roman Empire lay like a lamb in the embrace of this great crescent of outer barbarians. Not only was Rome never able to thrust back or assimilate that superincumbent crescent, but she was never able to organize the Mediterranean Sea into a secure and orderly system of communication between one part of her empire and another. Quite unknown as yet to Rome, the Mongolian tribes from north-eastern Asia, the Huns, and their kin, walled back and driven out from China by the Tsi and Han dynasties, were drifting and pressing westward, mixing with the Parthians, the Scythians, the Teutons and the like, or driving them before them.

Never at any time did the Romans succeed in pushing their empire beyond Mesopotamia, and upon Mesopotamia their hold was never very secure. Before the close of the republic that power of assimilation which had been the secret of their success was giving way to "patriotic" exclusiveness and "patriotic" greed. Rome plundered and destroyed Asia Minor and Babylonia, which were the necessary basis for an eastward extension to India, just as she had destroyed and looted Carthage and so had no foothold for extension into Africa, and just as she had destroyed Corinth and so cut herself off from an easy way into the heart of Greece. Western European writers, impressed by the fact that later on Rome Romanized and civilized Gaul and South Britain and restored the scene of her earlier devastations in Spain to prosperity, are apt to ignore that over far greater areas to the south and east her influence was to weaken and so restore to barbarism the far wider conquests of Hellenic civilization.

§ 5

But among the politicians of Italy in the first century B.C. there were no maps of Germany and Russia, Africa and Central Asia, and no sufficient intelligence to study them had they existed. Rome never developed the fine curiosities that sent Hanno and the sailors of Pharaoh Necho down the coasts of Africa. When, in the first century B.C., the emissaries of the Han dynasty reached the eastern shores of the Caspian Sea, they found only stories of a civilization that had receded. The memory of Alexander still lived in these lands, but of Rome men only knew that Pompey had come to the western shores of the Caspian and gone away again, and that Crassus had been destroyed. Rome was preoccupied at home. What mental energy remained over in the Roman citizen from the attempt to grow personally rich and keep personally safe was intent upon the stratagems and strokes and counter-strokes of the various adventurers who were now manifestly grappling for the supreme power.

It is the custom of historians to treat these struggles with extreme respect. In particular the figure of Julius Cæsar is set up as if it were a star of culminating brightness and importance in the history of mankind. Yet a dispassionate consideration of the known facts fails altogether to justify this demigod theory of Cæsar. Not even that precipitate wrecker of splendid possibilities, Alexander the Great, has been so magnified and dressed up for the admiration of careless and uncritical readers. There is a type of scholar who, to be plain, sits and, with the merest scraps of justification or with no justification at all, *invents* marvellous world policies for the more conspicuous figures in history.

We are told that Alexander planned the conquest of Carthage and Rome and the complete subjugation of India, and that only his death shattered these schemes. What we know for certain is that he conquered the Persian Empire and never went far beyond its boundaries; and that when he was supposed to be making these vast and noble plans, he was in fact indulging in such monstrous antics as his mourning for his favourite Hephæstion, and as his main occupation he was drinking himself to death. So, too, Julius Cæsar is credited with the intention of doing just that one not impossible thing which would have secured the Roman Empire from its ultimate collapse—namely the systematic conquest and civilization of Europe as far as the Baltic and the Dnieper. He was to have marched upon Germany, says Plutarch, through Parthia and Scythia, round the north of the Caspian and Black Seas.

Yet the fact we have to reconcile with this wise and magnificent project is that at the crest of his power, Cæsar, already a bald, middle-aged man, past the graces and hot impulses of youthful love, spent the better part of a year in Egypt, feasting and entertaining himself in amorous pleasantries with the Egyptian queen Cleopatra. And afterwards he brought her with him to Rome, where her influence over him was bitterly resented. Such complications with a woman mark the elderly sensualist or sentimen-

The ROMAN POWER about 50 B.C.

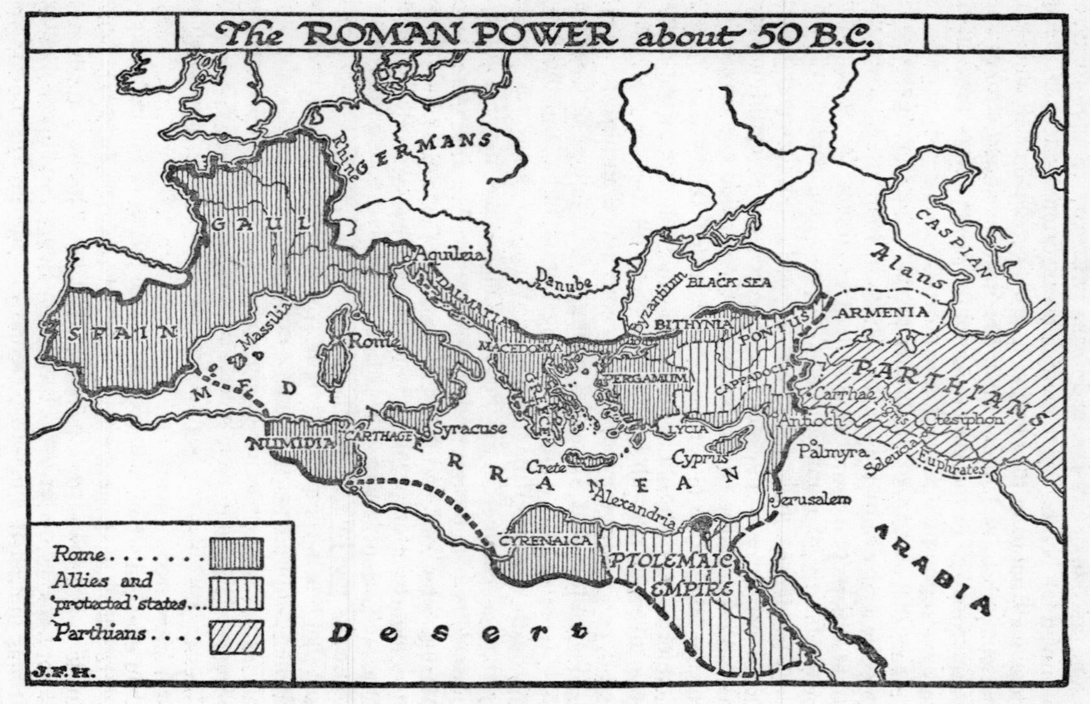

talist—he was fifty-four at the commencement of the *affaire*—rather than the master-ruler of men.

On the side of the superman idea of Cæsar, we have to count a bust in the Naples Museum. It represents a fine and intellectual face, very noble in its expression, and we can couple with that the story that his head, even at birth, was unusually large and finely formed. But there is really no satisfying evidence that this well-known bust does represent Cæsar, and it is hard to reconcile its austere serenity with the reputation for violent impulse and disorderliness that clung to him. Other busts of a quite different man are also, with more probability, ascribed to him.

There can be little doubt that he was a dissolute and extravagant young man—the scandals cluster thick about his sojourn in Bithynia, whither he fled from Sulla; he was the associate of the reprobate Clodius and the conspirator Catiline, and there is nothing in his political career to suggest any aim higher or remoter than his own advancement to power and all the personal glory and indulgence that power makes possible. We will not attempt to tell here of the turns and devices of his career. Although he was of an old patrician family, he came into politics as the brilliant darling of the people. He spent great sums and incurred heavy debts to provide public festivals on the most lavish scale. He opposed the tradition of Sulla, and cherished the memory of Marius, who was his uncle by marriage. For a time he worked in conjunction with Crassus and Pompey, but after the death of Crassus he and Pompey came into conflict.

By 49 B.C. he and Pompey, with their legions, he from the west and Pompey from the east, were fighting openly for predominance in the Roman state. He had broken the law by bringing his legions across the Rubicon, which was the boundary between his command and Italy proper. At the battle of Pharsalos in Thessaly (48 B.C.), Pompey was routed, and, fleeing to Egypt, was murdered, leaving Cæsar more master of the Roman world than ever Sulla had been.

He was then created dictator for ten years in 46 B.C., and early in 45 B.C. he was made dictator for life. This was monarchy; if not hereditary monarchy, it was at least electoral life-monarchy. It was unlimited opportunity to do his best for the world. And by the spirit and quality of his use of this dictatorial power during these four years we are bound to judge him. A certain reorganization of local administration he effected, and he seems to have taken up what was a fairly obvious necessity of the times, a project for the restoration of the two murdered seaports of Corinth and Carthage, whose destruction had wrecked the sea-life of the Mediterranean. But much more evident was the influence of Cleopatra and Egypt upon his mind. Like Alexander before him, his head seems to have been turned by the king-god tradition, assisted no doubt in his case by the adulation of that charming hereditary goddess Cleopatra. We find evidence of exactly that same conflict upon the score of divine pretensions, between him and his personal friends, that we have already recorded in the case of Alexander. So far as the Hellenized east was concerned, the paying of divine honours to rulers was a familiar idea; but it was still repulsive to the lingering Aryanism of Rome.

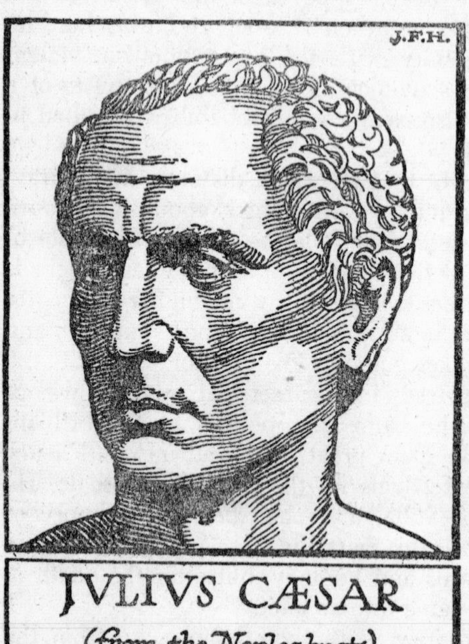

JVLIVS CÆSAR
(from the Naples bust)

Antony, who had been his second in command at Pharsalos, was one of the chief of his flatterers. Plutarch describes a scene at the public games in which Antony tried to force a crown upon Cæsar, which Cæsar, after a little coyness and in face of the manifested displeasure of the crowd, refused. But he had adopted the ivory sceptre and throne, which were the traditional insignia of the ancient kings of Rome. His image was carried amidst those of the gods in the opening *pompa* of the arena, and his statue was set up in a temple with an inscription, "To the Unconquerable God!" Priests even were appointed for his godhead. These things are not the symptoms of great-mindedness, but of a common man's megalomania. Cæsar's record of vulgar scheming for the tawdriest mockeries of personal worship is a silly and shameful record; it is incompatible with the idea that he was a wise and wonderful superman setting the world to rights.

Finally (44 B.C.) he was assassinated by a group of his own friends and supporters, to whom these divine aspirations had become intolerable. He was beset in the Senate, and stabbed in three-and-twenty places, dying at the foot of the statue of his fallen rival Pompey the Great. The scene marks the complete demoralization of the old Roman governing body. Brutus, the ringleader of the murderers, would have addressed the senators, but, confronted by this crisis, they were scuttling off in every direction. For the best part of a day Rome did not know what to make of this event; the murderers marched about with their bloody weapons through an undecided city, with no one gainsaying them and only a few joining them; then public opinion turned against them, some of their houses were attacked, and they had to hide and fly for their lives.

§ 6

But the trend of things was overwhelmingly towards monarchy. For thirteen years more the struggle of personalities went on. One single man is to be noted as inspired by broad ideas and an ambition not entirely egoistic, Cicero. He was a man of modest origin, whose eloquence and literary power had won him a prominent place in the Senate. He was a little tainted by the abusive tradition of Demosthenes, nevertheless he stands out, a noble and pathetically ineffective figure, pleading with the now utterly degenerate, base, and cowardly Senate for the high ideals of the Republic. He was a writer of great care and distinction, and the orations and private letters he has left us make him one of the most real and living figures of this period to the modern reader. He was proscribed and killed in 43 B.C., the year after the murder of Julius Cæsar, and his head and hands were nailed up in the Roman forum. Octavian, who became at last the monarch of Rome, seems to have made an effort to save Cicero; that murder was certainly not his crime.

Here we cannot trace out the tangle of alliances and betrayals that ended in the ascendancy of this Octavian, the adopted heir of Julius Cæsar. The fate of the chief figures is interwoven with that of Cleopatra.

After the death of Cæsar, she set herself to capture the emotions and vanity of Antony, a much younger man than Cæsar, with whom she was probably already acquainted. For a time Octavian and Antony and a third figure, Lepidus, divided the Roman world just as Cæsar and Pompey had divided it before their final conflict. Octavian took the hardier west, and consolidated his power; Antony had the more gorgeous east—and Cleopatra. To Lepidus fell that picked bone, Carthaginian Africa. He seems to have been a good man of good traditions, set upon the restoration of Carthage rather than upon wealth or personal vanities. The mind of Antony succumbed to those same ancient ideas of divine kingship that had already proved too much for the mental equilibrium of Julius Cæsar. In the company of Cleopatra he gave himself up to love, amusements, and a dream of sensuous glory, until Octavian felt that the time was ripe to end these two Egyptian divinities.

In 32 B.C. Octavian induced the Senate to depose Antony from the command of the east, and proceeded to attack him. A great naval battle at Actium (31 B.C.) was decided by the unexpected desertion of Cleopatra with sixty ships in the midst of the fight. It is quite impossible for us to decide now whether this was due to premeditated treachery or to the sudden whim of a charming woman. The departure of these ships threw the fleet of Antony into hopeless confusion, which was increased by the headlong flight of this model lover in pursuit. He went off after her in a swift galley without informing his commanders. He left his followers to fight and die as they thought fit, and for a time they were incredulous that he had gone. The subsequent encounter of the two lovers and their reconciliation is a matter for ironical speculation on the part of Plutarch.

Octavian's net closed slowly round his rival. It is not improbable that there was some sort of understanding between Octavian and Cleopatra, as, perhaps, in the time of Julius Cæsar there may have been between the queen and Antony. Antony gave way to much mournful posturing, varied by love scenes, during this last stage of his little drama. For a time he posed as an imitator of the cynic Timon, as one who had lost all faith in mankind, though one may think that his deserted sailors at Actium had better reason for such an attitude. Finally he found himself and Cleopatra besieged by Octavian in Alexandria. There were some sallies and minor successes, and Antony was loud with challenges to Octavian to decide the matter by personal combat. Being led to believe that Cleopatra had committed suicide, this star of romance stabbed himself, but so ineffectually as to die lingeringly, and he was carried off to expire in her presence (30 B.C.).

Plutarch's account of Antony, which was derived very largely from witnesses who had seen and known him, describes him as of heroic mould. He is compared to the demigod Hercules, from whom, indeed, he claimed descent, and also to the Indian Bacchus. There is a disgusting but illuminating description of a scene in the Senate when he attempted to speak while drunk, and was overtaken by one of the least dignified concomitants of intoxication.

For a little while Cleopatra still clung to life, and, perhaps, to the hope that she might reduce Octavian to the same divine rôle that had already been played by Julius Cæsar and Antony. She had an interview with Octavian, in which she presented herself as beauty in distress and very lightly clad. But when it became manifest that Octavian lacked the god-like spark, and that his care for her comfort and welfare was dictated chiefly by his desire to exhibit her in a triumphal procession through the streets of Rome, she committed suicide. An asp was smuggled to her past the Roman sentries, concealed in a basket of figs, and by its fangs she died.

Octavian seems to have been almost entirely free from the divine aspirations of Julius Cæsar and Antony. He was neither god nor romantic hero; he was a man. He was a man of far greater breadth and capacity than any other player in this last act of the Republican drama in Rome. All things considered, he was perhaps the best thing that could have happened to Rome at that time. He voluntarily resigned the extraordinary powers which he had held since 43, and, to quote his own words, "handed over the republic to the control of the senate and the people of Rome." The old constitutional machinery was once more set in motion; the senate, assembly, and magistrates resumed their functions, and Octavian himself was hailed as the "restorer of the commonwealth and the champion of freedom."

"It was not so easy to determine what relation he himself, the actual master of the Roman world, should occupy towards this revived republic. His abdication, in any real sense of the word, would have simply thrown everything back into confusion. The interests of peace and order required that he should retain at least the substantial part of his authority; and this object was in fact accomplished, and the rule of the emperors founded, in a manner which has no parallel in history. Any revival of the kingly title was out of the question, and Octavian himself expressly refused the dictatorship. Nor was any new office created or any new official title invented for his benefit. But by senate and people he was invested according to the old constitutional forms with certain powers, as many citizens had been before him, and so took his place by the side of the lawfully appointed magistrates of the republic; only, to mark his pre-eminent dignity as the first of them all, the senate decreed that he should take as an additional cognomen that of 'Augustus,' while in common parlance he was henceforth styled Princeps, a simple title of courtesy, familiar to republican usage and conveying no other idea than that of a recognized primacy and precedence over his fellow-citizens.

"The ideal sketched by Cicero in his *De Republica,* of a constitutional president of a free republic, was apparently realized; but it was only in appearance. For in fact the special prerogatives conferred upon Octavian gave him back in substance the autocratic authority he had resigned, and as between the restored republic and its new *princeps* the balance of power was overwhelmingly on the side of the latter."[1]

§ 7

In this manner it was that Roman republicanism ended in a *princeps* or ruling prince, and the first great experiment in a self-governing community on a scale larger than that of a tribe or city collapsed and failed.

The essence of its failure was that it could not sustain unity. In its early stages its citizens, both patrician and plebeian, had a certain tradition of justice and good faith and of the loyalty of all citizens to the law, and of the goodness of the law for all citizens; it clung to this idea of the importance of the law and of law-abidingness nearly into the first century B.C. But the unforeseen invention and development of money, the temptations and disruptions of imperial expansion, the entanglement of electoral methods, weakened and swamped this tradition by presenting old issues in new disguises under which the judgment did not recognize them, and by enabling men to be loyal to the professions of citizenship and disloyal to its spirit. The bond of the Roman people had always been a moral rather than a religious bond; their religion was sacrificial and superstitious; it embodied no such great ideas of a divine leader and of a sacred mission as

[1] H. S. Jones, in *The Encyclopædia Britannica,* article "Rome."

Judaism was developing. As the idea of citizenship failed and faded before the new occasions, there remained no inner, that is to say no real, unity in the system at all. Every man tended more and more to do what was right in his own eyes.

Under such conditions there was no choice between chaos and a return to monarchy, to the acceptance of some chosen individual as the one unifying will in the state. Of course, in that return, there is always hidden the expectation that the monarch will become as it were magic, will cease to be merely a petty human being, and will think and feel as something greater and more noble, as, indeed, a state personage; and, of course, monarchy invariably fails to satisfy that expectation. We shall glance at the extent of this failure in the brief review we are to presently make of the emperors of Rome. We shall find at last one of the more constructive of these emperors, Constantine the Great, conscious of his own inadequacy as a unifying power, turning to the faith, the organization, and teaching network of one of the new religious movements in the empire, to supply just that permeating and correlating factor in men's minds that was so manifestly wanting.

With Cæsar, the civilization of Europe and Western Asia went back to monarchy, and, through monarchy, assisted presently by organized Christianity, it sought to achieve peace, righteousness, happiness, and world order for close upon eighteen centuries. Then almost suddenly it began reverting to republicanism, first in one country and then in another; and, assisted by the new powers of printing and the press and of organized general education, and by the universalist religious ideas in which the world had been soaked for generations, it seems now to have resumed again the effort to create a republican world-state and a world-wide scheme of economic righteousness which the Romans had made so prematurely and in which they had so utterly and disastrously failed.

Certain conditions, we are now beginning to perceive, are absolutely necessary to such a creation; conditions which it is inconceivable that any pre-Christian Roman could have regarded as possible. We may still think the attainment of these conditions a vastly laborious and difficult and uncertain undertaking, but we understand that the attempt must be made because no other prospect before us gives even a promise of happiness or self-respect or preservation of our kind. The first of these conditions is that there should be a common political idea in the minds of all men, an idea of the state thought of as the personal possession of each individual and as the backbone fact of his scheme of duties. In the early days of Rome, when it was a little visible state, twenty miles square, such notions could be and were developed in children in their homes, and by what they saw and heard of the political lives of their fathers; but in a larger country such as Rome had already become before the war with Pyrrhus, there was a need of an organized teaching of the history, of the main laws, and of the general intentions of the state towards everyone if this moral unity was to be maintained. But the need was never realized, and no attempt at any such teaching was ever made. At the time it could not have been made. It is inconceivable that it could have been made. The knowledge was not there, and there existed no class from which the needed teachers could be drawn, and no conception of an organization for any such systematic moral and intellectual training as the teaching organization of Christianity, with its creeds and catechisms and sermons and confirmations, presently supplied.

Moreover, we know nowadays that even a universal education of this sort supplies only the basis for a healthy republican state. Next to education there must come abundant, prompt, and truthful information of what is going on in the state, and frank and free discussion of the issues of the time. Even nowadays these functions are performed only very imperfectly and badly by the press we have and by our publicists and politicians; but badly though it is done, the thing is done, and the fact that it is done at all argues that it may ultimately be done well. In the Roman state it was not even attempted. The Roman citizen got his political facts from rumour and the occasional orator. He stood wedged in the forum, imperfectly hearing a distant speaker. He probably misconceived every issue upon which he voted.

And of the monstrous ineffectiveness of the Roman voting system we have already written.

Unable to surmount or remove these obstacles to a sane and effective popular government the political instincts of the Roman mind turned towards monarchy. But it was not monarchy of the later European type, not hereditary monarchy, which was now installed in Rome. The *princeps* was really like an American wartime president, but he was elected not for four years but for life; he was able to appoint senators instead of being restrained by an elected senate, and with a rabble popular meeting in the place of the house of representatives. He was also *pontifex maximus*,

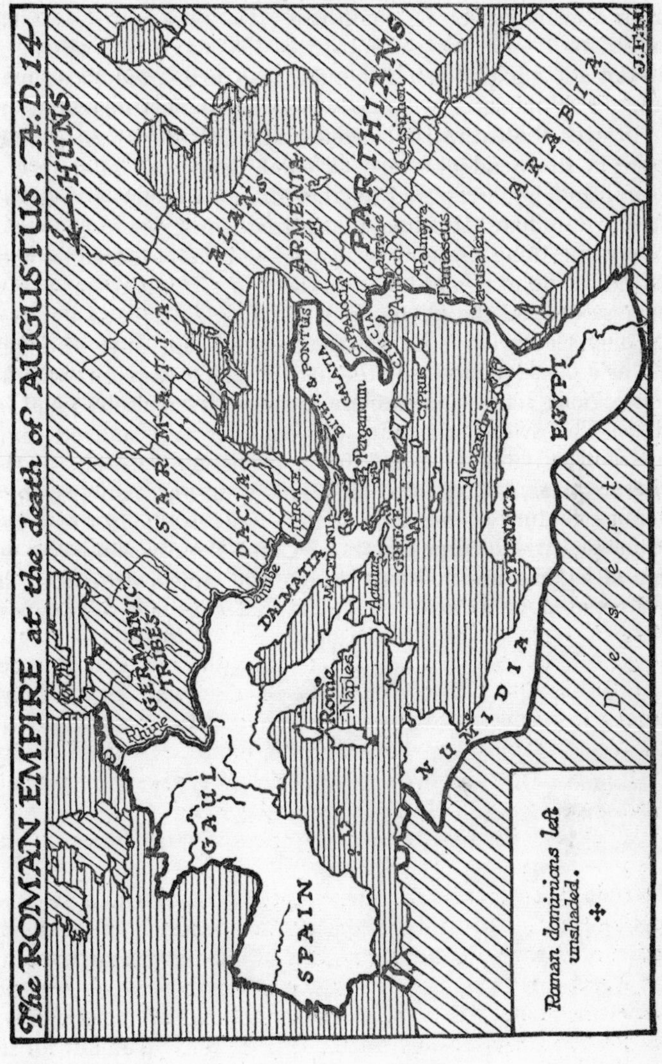
The ROMAN EMPIRE at the death of AUGUSTUS, A.D. 14
HUNS
ALANS
SARMATIA
GERMANIC TRIBES
Rhine
GAUL
SPAIN
DACIA
Danube
DALMATIA
THRACE
MACEDONIA
Actium
GREECE
Rome
Naples
BITHY. & PONTUS
GALATIA
CAPPADOCIA
ARMENIA
CILICIA
Antioch
Carrhae
PARTHIANS
Ctesiphon
Palmyra
Damascus
Jerusalem
Pergamum
CYPRUS
Alexandria
EGYPT
CYRENAICA
NUMIDIA
Desert
ARABIA
Roman dominions left unshaded.
J.F.H.

chief of the sacrificial priests, a function unknown at Washington; and in practice it became usual for him to designate and train his successor and to select for that honour a son or an adopted son or a near relation he could trust. The power of the *princeps* was in itself enormous to entrust to the hands of a single man without any adequate checks, but it was further enhanced by the tradition of monarch-worship which had now spread out from Egypt over the entire Hellenized east, and which was coming to Rome in the head of every Oriental slave and immigrant. By natural and imperceptible degrees the idea of the god-emperor came to dominate the whole Romanized world.

Only one thing presently remained to remind the god-emperor that he was mortal, and that was the army. The god-emperor was never safe upon the Olympus of the Palatine Hill at Rome. He was only secure while he was the beloved captain of his legions. And as a consequence only the hard-working emperors who kept their legions active and in close touch with themselves had long reigns. The sword overhung the emperor and spurred him to incessant activity. If he left things to his generals, one of these generals presently replaced him. This spur was, perhaps, the redeeming feature of the Roman Imperial system. In the greater, compacter, and securer empire of China there was not the same need of legions, and so there was not the same swift end for lazy or dissipated or juvenile monarchs that overtook such types in Rome.

XXVII

THE CÆSARS BETWEEN THE SEA AND THE GREAT PLAINS

§ 1

WESTERN writers are apt, through their patriotic predispositions, to overestimate the organization, civilizing work, and security of the absolute monarchy that established itself in Rome after the accession of Augustus Cæsar. From it we derive the political traditions of Britain, France, Spain, Germany, and Italy, and these countries loom big in the perspectives of European writers. They ignore what Rome destroyed in the East.

By the scale of a world history the Roman Empire ceases to seem so overwhelmingly important. It lasted about four centuries in all before it was completely shattered. The Byzantine Empire was no genuine continuation of it; it was a damaged resumption of the Hellenic Empire of Alexander; it spoke Greek; its monarch had a Roman title, no doubt, but so, for that matter, had the late Tsar of Bulgaria. Mesopotamia developed for the most part upon lines of its own during the Roman period; its recent Hellenic acquisitions were extensively modified by the genius of the Persian and Parthian peoples, and in India and China the influence of Rome was infinitesimal.

During its four centuries of life the empire of Rome had phases of division and complete chaos. Its prosperous years, it they are gathered together and added up, do not amount in all to a couple of centuries. Compared with the quiet steady expansion, the security, and the civilizing task of the contemporary Chinese

Empire, or with Egypt between 4,000 and 1,000 B.C., or with Sumer before the Semitic conquest, this amounts to a mere incident in history. The Persian Empire of Cyrus again, which reached from the Hellespont to the Indus, had as high a standard of civilization; and its homelands remained unconquered and fairly prosperous for over two hundred years. Its predecessor, the Median Empire, had endured for half a century. After a brief submergence by Alexander the Great, it rose again as the Seleucid Empire, which endured for some centuries. The Seleucid dominion shrank at last to the west of the Euphrates, and became a part of the Roman Empire; but Persia, revived by the Parthians as a new Persian Empire, first under the Arsacids and then under the Sassanids, outlived the empire of Rome. It became a refuge for Greek learning from Western suppression, and a hotbed of religious ideas.

The Sassanids repeatedly carried war into the Byzantine Empire, and held the line of the Euphrates steadfastly. In A.D. 616 under Chosroes II they were holding Damascus, Jerusalem, and Egypt, and threatening the Hellespont. But there has been no tradition to keep alive the glories of the Sassanids. The reputation of Rome has flourished through the prosperity of her heirs. The tradition of Rome looms far greater than the reality. A coalescence of the earlier civilizations had occurred, and civilization had spread westward. Semite and Aryan mingled, without combining, in a seething development round the basin of the Mediterranean, and the Roman administration was flung like a net, that broke and was mended again and at last broke altogether, over the whole interplay.

History distinguishes several groups of Roman emperors who were great administrators. The first of these groups began with:—

Augustus Cæsar (27 B.C. to A.D. 14), the Octavian of the previous section, who worked hard at the reorganization of the provincial governments and at financial reform. He established a certain tradition of lawfulness and honesty in the bureaucracy, and he restrained the more monstrous corruptions and tyrannies by giving the provincial citizen the right to appeal to Cæsar. But he fixed the European boundaries of the empire along the Rhine and Danube, so leaving Germany, which is the necessary backbone of a safe and prosperous Europe, to barbarism; and he made a similar limitation in the east at the Euphrates, leaving Armenia independent, to be a constant bone of contention with the Arsacids and Sassanids. It is doubtful whether he considered that he was fixing the final boundaries of the empire along these lines, or whether he thought it desirable to consolidate for some years before any further attempts at expansion.

Tiberius (A.D. 14 to 37) is also described as a capable ruler, but he became intensely unpopular in Rome, and it was alleged that he was addicted to gross and abominable vices. But his indulgence in these and his personal tyrannies and cruelties did not interfere with the general prosperity of the empire. It is difficult to judge him; nearly all our sources of information are manifestly hostile to him.

Caligula (A.D. 37 to 41) was insane, but the empire carried on during four years of his eccentricity at its head. Finally he was murdered in his palace by his servants, and there seems to have been an attempt to restore the senatorial government, an attempt which was promptly suppressed by the household legions.

Claudius (A.D. 41 to 54), the uncle of Caligula, upon whom the choice of the soldiers fell, was personally uncouth, but he seems to have been a hardworking and fairly capable administrator. He advanced the westward boundary of the empire by annexing the southern half of Britain. He was poisoned by Agrippina, the mother of his adopted son Nero, and a woman of great charm and force of character.

Nero (A.D. 54 to 68), like Tiberius, is credited with monstrous vices and cruelties, but the empire had acquired sufficient momentum to carry on through his fourteen years of power. He certainly murdered his devoted but troublesome mother, and his wife—the latter as a mark of devotion to a lady, Poppæa, who then married him. But the domestic infelicities of the Cæsars are no part of our present story. The reader greedy for criminal particulars must go to the classical source, Suetonius. These various Cæsars and their successors and their womenkind were probably no worse essentially than most weak and passionate human beings, but they had no real religion, being themselves gods; they had no wide knowledge on which to build high ambitions, their women were fierce and often illiterate, and they were under no restraints of law or custom. They were surrounded by creatures ready to stimulate their slightest wishes and to translate their vaguest impulses into action. What are mere passing black thoughts and angry impulses with most of us became, therefore, deeds with them. Before a man condemns Nero as a different species of being from himself, he should examine his own secret thoughts very carefully. Nero became intensely unpopular in Rome, and it is interesting to note that he became unpopular not because he murdered and poisoned his intimate relations, but because there was an insurrection in Britain under a certain Queen Boadicea, and the Roman forces suffered a great disaster (A.D. 61), and because there was a destructive earthquake in Southern Italy. The Roman population, true to its Etruscan streak, never religious and always superstitious, did not mind a wicked Cæsar, but it did object strongly to an unpropitious one. The Spanish legions rose in insurrection under an elderly general of seventy-three, Galba, whom they acclaimed emperor. He advanced upon Rome, carried in a litter. Nero, hopeless of support, committed suicide (A.D. 68).

Galba, however, was only one of a group of would-be emperors. The generals in command of the Rhine legions, the Palatine troops, and the eastern armies, each attempted to seize power. Rome saw four emperors in a year, Galba, Otho, Vitellius, and Vespasian; the fourth, Vespasian (A.D. 69–79), from the eastern command, had the firmest grip, and held and kept the prize. But with Nero the line of Cæsars born or adopted ended. Cæsar ceased to be the family name of the Roman emperors, and became a title, Divus Cæsar, the Cæsar god. The monarchy took a step forward towards Orientalism by an increased insistence upon the worship of the ruler. So ended the first group of Cæsars, just ninety-five years of them.

Vespasian (A.D. 69 to 79) and his sons Titus (A.D. 79) and Domitian (A.D. 81) constitute, as it were, a second dynasty, the Flavian; then, after the assassination of Domitian, came a group of emperors related to one another not by blood, but by adoption, the adoptive emperors. Nerva (A.D. 96) was the first of this group, and Trajan (A.D. 98) the second. They were followed by the indefatigable Hadrian (A.D. 117), Antoninus Pius (A.D. 138), and Marcus Aurelius (A.D. 161 to 180). Under both the Flavians and the Antonines the boundaries of the empire crept forward again. North Britain was annexed in A.D. 84, the angle of the Rhine and Danube was filled in, and what is now Transylvania was made into a new province, Dacia. Trajan also invaded Parthia and annexed Armenia, Assyria, and Mesopotamia. Under his rule the empire reached its maximum extent.

Hadrian, his successor, was of a cautious and retractile disposition. He abandoned these new eastern conquests of Trajan and he also abandoned North Britain. He adopted the Chinese idea of the limiting wall against barbarism—an excellent idea so long as the pressure of population on the imperial side of the wall is greater than the pressure from without, but worthless otherwise. He built Hadrian's Wall across Britain, and a palisade between the Rhine and the Danube. The full tide of Roman expansion was past, and in the reign of his successor the North European frontier was already actively on the defensive against the aggression of Teutonic and Slavic tribes.

Marcus Aurelius Antoninus is one of those figures in history about which men differ widely and intensely. To some critics he seems to have been a priggish person; he dabbled in religions, and took a pleasure in conducting priestly ceremonies in priestly garments—a disposition offensive to common men—and they resent his alleged failure to restrain the wickedness of his wife Faustina. The stories of his domestic infelicity, however, rest on no very good foundations, though certainly his son Commodus was a startling person for a good home to produce. On the other hand, he was unquestionably a devoted and industrious emperor, holding social order together through a series of disastrous years of vile weather, great floods, failing harvests and famine, barbaric raids and revolts and at last a terrible universal pestilence. Says F. W. Farrar, quoted in the *Encyclopædia Britannica,* "He regarded himself as being, in fact, the servant of all. The registry of the citizens, the suppression of litigation, the elevation of public morals, the care of minors, the retrenchment of public expenses, the limitation of gladiatorial games and shows, the care of roads, the restoration of senatorial privileges, the appointment of none but worthy magistrates, even the regulation of street traffic, these and numberless other duties so completely absorbed his attention that, in spite of indifferent health, they often kept him at severe labour from early morning till long after midnight. His position, indeed, often necessitated his presence at games and shows; but on these occasions he occupied himself either in reading, or being read to, or in writing notes. He was one of those who held that nothing should be done hastily, and that few crimes were worse than waste of time."

But it is not by these industries that he is now remembered. He was one of the greatest exponents of the Stoical philosophy, and in his *Meditations,* jotted down in camp and court, he has put so much of a human soul on record as to raise up for himself in each generation a fresh series of friends and admirers.

With the death of Marcus Aurelius this phase of unity and

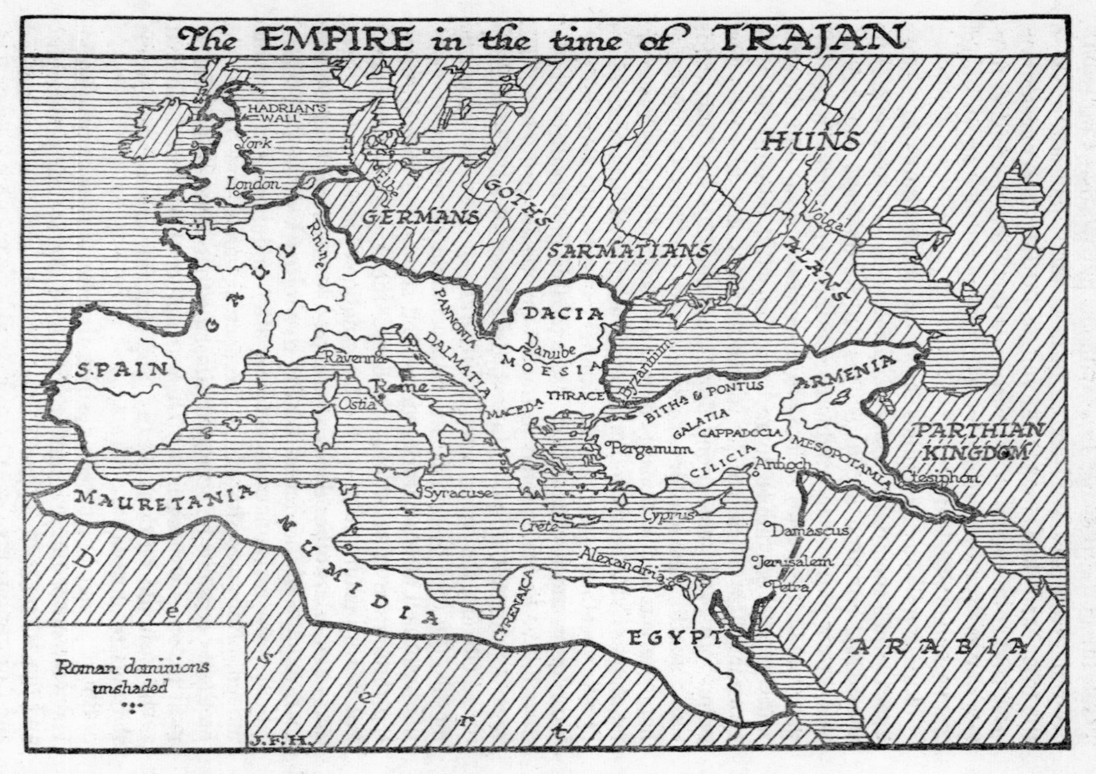

The EMPIRE in the time of TRAJAN

comparatively good government came to an end, and his son Commodus inaugurated an age of disorder. Practically, the empire had been at peace within itself for two hundred years. Now for a hundred years the student of Roman history must master the various criminology of a number of inadequate emperors, while the frontier crumbled and receded under barbarian pressure. One or two only seem to have been able men; such were Septimius Severus, Aurelian, and Probus. Septimius Severus was a Carthaginian, and his sister was never able to master Latin. She conducted her Roman household in the Punic language, which must have made Cato the elder turn in his grave. The rest of the emperors of this period were chiefly adventurers too unimportant to the general scheme of things for us to note. At times there were separate emperors ruling in different parts of the distracted empire. From our present point of view the Emperor Decius, who was defeated and killed during a great raid of the Goths into Thrace in A.D. 251, and the Emperor Valerian, who, together with the great city of Antioch, was captured by the Sassanid Shah of Persia in A.D. 260, are worthy of notice because they mark the insecurity of the whole Roman system, and the character of the outer pressure upon it. So, too, is Claudius, "the Conqueror of the Goths," because he gained a great victory over these people at Nish in Serbia (A.D. 269), and because he died, like Pericles, of the plague.

Through all these centuries intermittent pestilences were playing a part in weakening races and altering social conditions, a part that has still to be properly worked out by historians. There was, for instance, a great plague throughout the empire between the years A.D. 164 and 180 in the reign of the Emperor Marcus Aurelius. It probably did much to disorganize social life and prepare the way for the troubles that followed the accession of Commodus. This same pestilence devastated China, as we shall note in § 5 of this chapter. Considerable fluctuations of climate had also been going on in the first and second centuries, producing stresses and shiftings of population, whose force historians have still to appraise.

But before we go on to tell of the irruptions of the barbarians and the attempts of such later emperors as Diocletian (A.D. 284) and Constantine the Great (A.D. 306) to hold together the heaving and splitting vessel of the state, we must describe something of the conditions of human life in the Roman Empire during its two centuries of prosperity.

§ 2

The impatient reader of history may be disposed to count the two centuries of order between 27 B.C. and A.D. 180 as among the wasted opportunities of mankind. It was an age of spending rather than of creation, an age of architecture and trade in which the rich grew richer and the poor poorer and the soul and spirit of man decayed. Looked at superficially, as a man might have looked at it from an aeroplane a couple of thousand feet in the air, there was a considerable flourish of prosperity. Everywhere, from York to Cyrene and from Lisbon to Antioch, he would have noted large and well-built cities, with temples, theatres, amphitheatres, markets, and the like; thousands of such cities, supplied by great aqueducts and served by splendid high-roads, whose stately remains astonish us to this day. He would have noted an abundant cultivation, and have soared too high to discover that this cultivation was the grudging work of slaves. Upon the Mediterranean and the Red Sea a considerable traffic would be visible; and the sight of two ships alongside each other would not at that altitude reveal the fact that one was a pirate and plundering the other.

And even if the observer came down to closer scrutiny, there would still be much accumulated improvement to note. There had been a softening of manners and a general refinement since the days of Julius Cæsar. With this there had been a real increase of humane feeling. Rome was, in fact, climbing to the level of civilization attained long before by Greece and Babylon and Egypt.

During the period of the Antonines, laws for the protection of slaves from extreme cruelty came into existence, and it was no longer permissible to sell them to the gladiatorial schools. Not only were the cities outwardly more splendidly built, but within the homes of the wealthy there had been great advances in the art of decoration. The gross feasting, animal indulgence, and vulgar display of the earlier days of Roman prosperity were now tempered by a certain refinement. Dress had become richer, finer, and more beautiful. There was a great trade in silk with remote China, for the mulberry tree and the silkworm had not yet begun to move west. By the time silk had ended its long and varied journey to Rome it was worth its weight in gold. Yet it was used abundantly, and there was a steady flow of the precious metals eastward in exchange.

There had been very considerable advances in gastronomy and

the arts of entertainment. Petronius describes a feast given by a wealthy man under the early Cæsars, a remarkable succession of courses, some delicious, some amazing, exceeding anything that even the splendours and the imagination of modern New York could produce; and the festival was varied by music and by displays of tight-rope dancing, juggling, Homeric recitations, and the like.

There was a considerable amount of what we may describe as "rich men's culture" throughout the empire. Books were far more plentiful than they had been before the time of the Cæsars. Men prided themselves upon their libraries, even when the cares and responsibilities of property made them too busy to give their literary treasures much more than a passing examination. The knowledge of Greek spread eastward and of Latin westward, and if the prominent men of this or that British or Gallic city lacked any profound Greek culture themselves, they could always turn to some slave or other, whose learning had been guaranteed of the highest quality by the slave-dealer, to supply the deficiency.

It is quite impossible to deal with either the literature or art of Rome as a thing in itself; both are a continuation and a part of the much greater and more enduring Hellenic culture. Hellenic art and writing threw out a Latin branch. The mother stem existed before the branch grew out, and went on growing after the branch was withered. The native impulse of the Latin mind in literary expression before it was deflected by Greek models was towards a form, if one can call it a form, the *satura,* a form like the modern revue in spirit, a medley of invective, imitation and music. A sort of bard, the *vates,* also sang sarcastic verse, Fescennine verses, to the peasants, and there were orations, dirges, religious litanies. The *satura* developed with writing into a form of prose and verse miscellany, and this again into a more continuous prose narrative. Much of the Latin literature is lost; most of it did not appeal, for some reason or other, to the Christian monks as worthy of preservation, but as reading and book reproduction spread there was probably a very considerable diffusion indeed of prose fiction, of which only a few fragments now remain.

The Roman people of the later Republic and early Empire was certainly a fiction-reading public. The *Satyricon* of Petronius, dating from the time of Nero, is a most illuminating vestige. No one who has ever written fiction can read that brilliant piece of writing and not recognize its high technical quality. Hundreds of such books must have existed and scores of men must have worked at the art before the *Satyricon* became possible. Along another line the poetic satire of Horace and Juvenal owes much to the spirit of the *satura,* and was also a widely diffused type of reading matter. But from the third century B.C. onward the Greek influence imposed the already established forms of the Greek comedy upon the Latin mind, and the Latin comedy is rather a Latinization of that than an indigenous development. Plays by Plautus and Terence are available for the student who wishes to sample their quality.

There was also a distinctive Latin tradition of plain clear prose which Cato the Censor did much to sustain. It is interesting to compare Cæsar's *De Bello Gallico* with Thucydides. In its compact accessibility, if one may shock the earnest scholar by a novel but appropriate image, it is like a fitted dressing-bag beside a toilet-table.

The prestige of Greek learning of an approved and settled type was as high in the Rome of Antoninus Pius as it was in the Oxford and Cambridge of Victorian England. The Greek scholar received the same mixture of unintelligent deference and practical contempt. There was a very considerable amount of Greek scholarship, and of written criticism and commentary. Indeed, there was so great an admiration for Greek letters as almost completely to destroy the Greek spirit; and the recorded observations of Aristotle were valued so highly as to preclude any attempt to imitate his organization of further inquiry. Cicero rivalled Demosthenes and Sallust, the Greek historians. Catullus learnt to reveal his heart from the best Greek models. As Greece had her epics and so forth, the Romans felt they too must have their epics. The age of Augustus was an age of splendid insincerities. Virgil in the *Æneid* set himself modestly but resolutely, and with an elegant successfulness, to parallel the *Odyssey* and *Iliad.* Ovid and Horace challenge comparison with the best elegiac and lyric poets of Greece.

Concurrently with this "Golden Age" of Latin literature the stream of Greek literature continued to flow wide and abundant. Long after the Latin impetus was over, the Hellenic world was still richly productive. It passed without a break into early Christian literature. We have told already of the brilliant intellectual beginnings of Alexandria and of the comparative decline of Athens. If the science of Alexandria presently died away the literary flow continued in fair rivalry with Rome. There was an immense copying of books, without which no rich man's home was complete. History and biography continued. Polybius (*circa*

204–122 B.C.) told of the conquest of Greece by Rome. Plutarch (*circa* A.D. 50–100) made his incomparable studies of great men. A vast variety of dialogues and novels appeared and have now, for the most part, disappeared again. A great and original imaginative writer was Lucian (A.D. ? 120–200), who still commands our interest and admiration. There was a considerable amount of translation between Greek and Latin. The two literatures were almost as close, and as much in the same world of thought, as the American and English to-day.

All this widespread culture of the wealthy householder is to the credit of the early Roman Empire, and Gibbon makes the most of it in the sunny review of the age of the Antonines with which he opens his *Decline and Fall of the Roman Empire.* His design for that great work demanded a prelude of splendour and tranquillity. But he was far too shrewd and subtle not to qualify his apparent approval of the conditions he describes. "Under the Roman Empire," he writes, "the labour of an industrious and ingenious people was variously but incessantly employed in the service of the rich. In their dress, their table, their houses, and their furniture, the favourites of fortune united every refinement of convenience, of elegance and of splendour, whatever could soothe their pride, or gratify their sensuality. Such refinements—under the odious name of luxury, have been severely arraigned by the moralists of every age; and it might perhaps be more conducive to the virtue, as well as happiness, of mankind, if all possessed the necessaries, and none the superfluities of life. But in the present imperfect condition of society, luxury, though it may proceed from vice or folly, seems to be the only means that can correct the unequal distribution of property. The diligent mechanic and the skilful artist, who have obtained no share in the division of the earth, receive a voluntary tax from the possessors of land; and the latter are prompted, by a sense of interest, to improve those estates, with whose produce they may purchase additional pleasure. This operation, the particular effects of which are felt in every society, acted with much more diffuse energy in the Roman world. The provinces would soon have been exhausted of their wealth if the manufacturers and commerce of luxury had not insensibly restored to the industrious subjects the sums which were exacted from them by the arms and authority of Rome." And so on, with a sting of satire in every fold of the florid description.

If we look a little more widely than a hovering aeroplane can do at the movement of races upon the earth, or a little more closely than an inspection of streets, amphitheatres, and banquets goes, into the souls and thoughts of men, we shall find that this impressive display of material prosperity is merely the shining garment of a polity blind to things without and things within, and blind to the future. If, for instance, we compare the two centuries of Roman ascendancy and opportunity, the first and second centuries A.D., with the two centuries of Greek and Hellenic life beginning about 466 B.C. with the supremacy of Pericles in Athens, we are amazed by—we cannot call it an inferiority, it is a complete absence of science. The incuriousness of the Roman rich and the Roman rulers was more massive and monumental even than their architecture.

In one field of knowledge particularly we might have expected the Romans to have been alert and enterprising, and that was geography. Their political interests demanded a steadfast inquiry into the state of affairs beyond their frontiers, and yet that inquiry was never made. There is practically no literature of Roman travel beyond the imperial limits, no such keen and curious accounts as Herodotus gives of the Scythians, the Africans, and the like. There is nothing in Latin to compare with the early descriptions of India and Siberia that are to be found in Chinese. The Roman legions went at one time into Scotland, yet there remains no really intelligent account of Picts or Scots, much less any glance at the seas beyond. Such explorations as those of Hanno or Pharaoh Necho seem to have been altogether beyond the scope of the Roman imagination.

It is probable that after the destruction of Carthage the amount of shipping that went out into the Atlantic through the Strait of Gibraltar fell to inconsiderable proportions. Still more impossible in this world of vulgar wealth, enslaved intelligence, and bureaucratic rule was any further development of the astronomy and physiography of Alexandria. The Romans do not seem even to have inquired what manner of men wove the silk and prepared the spices or collected the amber and the pearls that came into their markets. Yet the channels of inquiry were open and easy; pathways led in every direction to the most convenient "jumping-off places" for explorers it is possible to imagine.

"The most remote countries of the ancient world were ransacked to supply the pomp and delicacy of Rome. The forests of Scythia afforded some valuable furs. Amber was brought overland from the shores of the Baltic to the Danube, and the barbarians were astonished at the price which they received in exchange for so useless a commodity. There was a considerable demand for Babylonian carpets and other manufactures of the East; but the most important branch of foreign trade was carried on with Arabia and India. Every year, about the time of the summer solstice, a fleet of a hundred and twenty vessels sailed from Myoshormos, a port of Egypt on the Red Sea. By the periodical assistance of the monsoons they traversed the ocean in about forty days. The coast of Malabar, or the island of Ceylon, was the usual term of their navigation, and it was in those markets that the merchants from the more remote countries of Asia expected their arrival. The return of the fleet to Egypt was fixed for the months of December or January, and as soon as their rich cargo had been transported, on the backs of camels, from the Red Sea to the Nile, and had descended that river as far as Alexandria, it was poured, without delay, into the capital of the empire."[1]

There were Roman warehouses in South India, and two cohorts were stationed at Cranganore on the Malabar coast, where there was also a temple to Augustus.

Yet Rome was content to feast, exact, grow rich, and watch its gladiatorial shows without the slightest attempt to learn anything of India, China, Persia or Scythia, Buddha or Zoroaster, or about the Huns, the Negroes, the people of Scandinavia, or the secrets of the western sea.

When we realize the uninspiring quality of the social atmosphere which made this indifference possible, we are able to account for the failure of Rome, during its age of opportunity to develop any physical or chemical science, and as a consequence to gain any increased control over matter. Most of the physicians in Rome were Greeks and many of them slaves—for the Roman wealthy did not even understand that a bought mind is a spoilt mind. Yet this was not due to any want of natural genius among the Roman people; it was due entirely to their social and economic conditions.

From the Middle Ages to the present day Italy has produced a great number of brilliant scientific men. And one of the most shrewd and inspired of scientific writers was an Italian, Lucretius, who lived between the time of Marius and Julius Cæsar (about 100 B.C. to about 55 B.C.). This amazing man was of the quality of Leonardo da Vinci (also an Italian) or Newton. He wrote a long Latin poem about the processes of Nature, *De Rerum Natura,*

---

[1] Gibbon.

in which he guessed with astonishing insight about the constitution of matter and about the early history of mankind. Osborn in his *Old Stone Age* quotes with admiration long passages from Lucretius about primitive man, so good and true are they to-day. But this was an individual display, a seed that bore no fruit. Roman science was still-born into a suffocating atmosphere of wealth and military oppression. The true figure to represent the classical Roman attitude to science is not Lucretius, but that Roman soldier who hacked Archimedes to death at the storming of Syracuse.

And if physical and biological science wilted and died on the stony soil of Roman prosperity political and social science never had a chance to germinate. Political discussion would have been treason to the emperor, social or economic inquiry would have threatened the rich. So Rome, until disaster fell upon her, never examined into her own social health, never questioned the ultimate value of her hard officialism. Consequently, there was no one who realized the gravity of her failure to develop any intellectual imagination to hold her empire together, any general education in common ideas that would make men fight and work for the empire as men will fight and work for a dear possession. But the rulers of the Roman Empire did not want their citizens to fight for anything in any spirit at all. The rich had eaten the heart out of their general population, and they were content with the meal they had made. The legions were filled with Germans, Britons, Numidians, and the like; and until the very end the wealthy Romans thought they could go on buying barbarians to defend them against the enemy without and the rebel poor within.

How little was done in education by the Romans is shown by an account of what was done. Says Mr. H. Stuart Jones, "Julius Cæsar bestowed Roman citizenship on 'teachers of the liberal arts; Vespasian endowed professorships of Greek and Latin oratory at Rome; and later emperors, especially Antoninus Pius, extended the same benefits to the provinces. Local enterprise and munificence were also devoted to the cause of education; we learn from the correspondence of the younger Pliny that public schools were founded in the towns of Northern Italy. But though there was a wide diffusion of knowledge under the empire, there was no true intellectual progress. Augustus, it is true, gathered about him the most brilliant writers of his time, and the debut of the new monarchy coincided with the Golden Age of Roman literature; but this was of brief duration, and the beginnings of the Christian era saw the triumph of classicism and the first steps in the decline that awaits all literary movements which look to the past rather than the future."

There is a diagnosis of the intellectual decadence of the age in a treatise upon the sublime by a Greek writer who wrote somewhere in the second, third, or fourth century A.D., and who may possibly have been Longinus Philologus, which states very distinctly one manifest factor in the mental sickness of the Roman world. He is cited by Gibbon: "The sublime Longinus, who, in somewhat a later period and in the court of a Syrian queen (Zenobia), preserved the spirit of ancient Athens, observes and laments the degeneracy of his contemporaries, which debased their sentiments, enervated their courage, and depressed their talents. 'In the same manner,' says he, 'as some children always remain pygmies, whose infant limbs have been too closely confined, thus our tender minds, fettered by the prejudices and habits of a just servitude, are unable to expand themselves or to attain that well-proportioned greatness which we admire in the ancients; who, living under a popular government, wrote with all the same freedom as they acted.'"

But this critic grasped only one aspect of the restraints upon mental activity. The leading-strings that kept the Roman mind in a permanent state of infantilism constituted a double servitude; they were economic as well as political. The account Gibbon gives of the life and activities of a certain Herodes Atticus, who lived in the time of Hadrian, shows just how little was the share of the ordinary citizen in the outward magnificence of the time. This Atticus had an immense fortune, and he amused himself by huge architectural benefactions to various cities. Athens was given a racecourse, and a theatre of cedar, curiously carved, was set up there to the memory of his wife; a theatre was built at Corinth, a racecourse was given to Delphi, baths to Thermopylæ, an aqueduct to Canusium, and so on and so on. One is struck by the spectacle of a world of slaves and common people who were not consulted, and over whose heads, without any participation on their part, this rich man indulged in his displays of "taste." Numerous inscriptions in Greece and Asia still preserve the name of Herodes Atticus, "patron and benefactor," who ranged about the empire as though it was his private garden, commemorating himself by these embellishments. He did not confine himself to splendid buildings. He was also a philosopher, though none of his wisdom has survived. He had a large villa near Athens, and there philosophers were welcome guests so long as they convinced their patron of the soundness of their pretensions, received his discourses with respect, and did not offend him by insolent controversy.

The world, it is evident, was not progressing during these two centuries of Roman prosperity. But was it happy in its stagnation? There are signs of a very unmistakable sort that the great mass of human beings in the empire, a mass numbering something between a hundred and a hundred and fifty millions, was not happy, was probably very acutely miserable, beneath its outward magnificence. True, there were no great wars and conquests within the empire, little of famine or fire or sword to afflict mankind; but, on the other hand, there was a terrible restraint by government, and still more by the property of the rich, upon the free activities of nearly everyone. Life for the great majority who were neither rich nor official, nor the womankind and the parasites of the rich and official, must have been laborious, tedious, and lacking in interest and freedom to a degree that a modern mind can scarcely imagine.

Three things in particular may be cited to sustain the opinion that this period was a period of widespread unhappiness. The first of these is the extraordinary apathy of the population to political events. They saw one upstart pretender to empire succeed another with complete indifference. Such things did not seem to matter to them; hope had gone. When presently the barbarians poured into the empire, there was nothing but the legions to face them. There was no popular uprising against them at all. Everywhere the barbarians must have been outnumbered if only the people had resisted. But the people did not resist. It is manifest that to the bulk of its inhabitants the Roman Empire did not seem to be a thing worth fighting for. To the slaves and common people the barbarian probably seemed to promise more freedom and less indignity than the pompous rule of the imperial official and grinding employment by the rich. The looting and burning of palaces and an occasional massacre did not shock the folk of the Roman underworld as it shocked the wealthy and cultured people to whom we owe such accounts as we have of the breaking down of the imperial system. Great numbers of slaves and common people probably joined the barbarians, who knew little of racial or patriotic prejudices, and were open-handed to any promising recruit. No doubt in many cases the population found that the barbarian was a worse infliction even than the tax-gatherer and the slave-driver. But that discovery came too late for resistance or the restoration of the old order.

And as a second symptom that points to the same conclusion that life was hardly worth living for the poor and the slaves and the majority of people during the age of the Antonines, we must reckon the steady depopulation of the empire. People refused to have children. They did so, we suggest, because their homes were not safe from oppression, because in the case of slaves there was no security that the husband and wife would not be separated, because there was no pride nor reasonable hope in children any more. In modern states the great breeding-ground has always been the agricultural countryside where there is a more or less secure peasantry; but under the Roman Empire the peasant and the small cultivator was either a worried debtor, or he was held in a network of restraints that made him a spiritless serf, or he had been ousted altogether by the gang production of slaves.

A third indication that this outwardly flourishing period was one of deep unhappiness and mental distress for vast multitudes, is to be found in the spread of new religious movements throughout the population. We have seen how in the case of the little country of Judea a whole nation may be infected by the persuasion that life is unsatisfactory and *wrong*, and that something is needed to set it right. The mind of the Jews, as we know, had crystallized about the idea of the Promise of the One True God and the coming of a Saviour or Messiah. Rather different ideas from this were spreading through the Roman Empire. They were but varying answers to one universal question: "What must we do for salvation?" A frequent and natural consequence of disgust with life as it is, is to throw the imagination forward to an afterlife which is to redeem all the miseries and injustices of this one. The belief in such compensation is a great opiate for present miseries. Egyptian religion had long been saturated with anticipations of immortality, and we have seen how central was that idea to the cult of Serapis and Isis at Alexandria. The ancient mysteries of Demeter and Orpheus, the mysteries of the Mediterranean race, revived and made a sort of *theocrasia* with these new cults.

A second great religious movement was Mithraism, a development of Zoroastrianism, a religion of very ancient Aryan origin, traceable back to the Indo-Iranian people before they split into Persians and Hindus. We cannot here examine its mysteries in any detail.[1] Mithras was a god of light, a Sun of Righteousness, and in the shrines of the cult he was always represented as slaying a sacred bull whose blood was the seed of life. Suffice it that, complicated with many added ingredients, this worship of Mithras came into the Roman Empire about the time of Pompey the Great, and began to spread very widely under the Cæsars and Antonines. Like the Isis religion, it promised immortality. Its followers were mainly slaves, soldiers, and distressed people. In its methods of worship, in the burning of candles before the altar and so forth, it has a certain superficial resemblance to the later developments of the ritual of the third great religious movement in the Roman world, Christianity.

Christianity also was a doctrine of immortality and salvation, and it too spread at first chiefly among the lowly and unhappy. Christianity has been denounced by modern writers as a "slave religion." It was. It took the slaves and the downtrodden, and it gave them hope and restored their self-respect so that they stood up for righteousness like men and faced persecution and torment. But of the origins and quality of Christianity we will tell more fully in a later chapter.

§ 3

We have said already that the artistic and literary culture of Rome was merely a branch of the great Hellenic culture which had inherited all that Greece and nearer Asia, Babylon and Egypt, had to bestow. But in certain directions the Roman system gave very definite thrusts of its own, and in none more than in architecture. The Roman Empire marks a new phase of history, a change in scale, which was reflected in the greater boldness and larger size of its buildings. The chief gifts of Rome to architecture were cement and the free use of the arch. Wherever the Roman legions went, went the arch and cement. Cement rendered possible vast domes and vaults, which could be faced with marble. The rich Corinthian column was taken and varied and elaborated and used in conjunction with arches. The arcade is typically Roman. So, too, is the disposition towards rounded buildings and the superposition of arcades in stories. Wherever the Romans went they left amphitheatres, triumphal arches, colonnaded streets, aqueducts and palatial buildings. Also they made roads with

[1] See Legge, *Forerunners and Rivals of Christianity.*

reasonable grades and fine bridges and aqueducts. To this day the Italian is the finest road-maker in the world.

The architecture of Rome had no such orderly development as the Egyptian and Greek. Its earliest efforts followed upon Etruscan lines and were in timber faced with terra-cotta. Gradually stone replaced the timber. But with the coming of the Empire, the Greek architect came to Rome and seized upon the new opportunities and materials that offered themselves to him. Roman architecture did not so much develop as break out. But having broken out it prevailed mightily.

A vigorous sculpture, also Greek in its essentials, went with the Roman eagles. A community of big rich men is almost inevitably productive of portraiture, and the vividly individualized portrait-bust or statue reached its highest developments under the later Republic and the early Cæsars. Painting also continued full of vitality. The fortunate accident of the destruction and preservation of Pompeii and Herculaneum by Vesuvius has enabled the modern world to appreciate the abundance, variety and beauty of pictorial art in the first century A.D. These places were the resorts of rich but by no means pre-eminently rich people, and the wealth of pleasant things they contain gives us the measure of the finer work that is now lost to us.

Another type of work in which the early Roman Empire outshone any preceding phase of civilization was the mosaic. Glasswork was also carried to new levels of beauty, chiefly by Greek and Oriental workmen.

With the misfortunes and disorders that closed in upon the western Roman Empire at the end of the second century A.D., a check came to much of its artistic productivity. Portraiture continued; architecture revived again, but after the third century the fluent naturalism of much of the sculpture stiffened under Oriental influences.

§ 4

We have already shown reason for our statement that the Roman imperial system was a very unsound political growth indeed. It is absurd to write of its statecraft; it had none. At its best it had a bureaucratic administration which kept the peace of the world for a time and failed altogether to secure it.

Let us note here the main factors in its failure.

The clue to all its failure lies in the absence of any free mental activity and any organization for the increase, development, and application of knowledge. It respected wealth and it despised science. It gave government to the rich, and imagined that wise men could be bought and bargained for in the slave markets when they were needed. It was, therefore, a colossally ignorant and unimaginative empire. It foresaw nothing.

It had no strategic foresight, because it was blankly ignorant of geography and ethnology. It knew nothing of the conditions of Russia, Central Asia, and the East. It was content to keep the Rhine and Danube as its boundaries, and to make no effort to Romanize Germany. But we need only look at the map of Europe and Asia showing the Roman Empire to see that a willing and incorporated Germany was absolutely essential to the life and security of Western Europe. Excluded, Germany became a wedge that needed only the impact of the Hunnish hammer to split up the whole system.

Moreover, this neglect to push the boundaries northward to the Baltic left that sea and the North Sea as a region of experiment and training and instruction in seamanship for the Northmen of Scandinavia, Denmark, and the Frisian coast. But Rome went on its way quite stupidly, oblivious to the growth of a newer and more powerful piracy in the north.

The same unimaginative quality made the Romans leave the seaways of the Mediterranean undeveloped. When presently the barbarians pressed down to the warm water, we read of no swift transport of armies from Spain or Africa or Asia to the rescue of Italy and the Adriatic coasts. Instead, we see the Vandals becoming masters of the western Mediterranean without so much as a naval battle.

The Romans had been held at the Euphrates by an array of mounted archers. It was clear that as the legion was organized it was useless in wide open country, and it should have been equally clear that sooner or later the mounted nomads of East Germany, South Russia or Parthia were bound to try conclusions with the empire. But the Romans, two hundred years after Cæsar's time, were still marching about, the same drilled and clanking cohorts they had always been, easily ridden round and shot to pieces. The empire had learnt nothing even from Carrhæ.

The incapacity of the Roman imperialism for novelty in methods of transport again is amazing. It was patent that their power and unity depended upon the swift movement of troops and supplies from one part of the empire to another. The republic made magnificent roads; the empire never improved upon them. Four hundred years before the Antonines, Hero of Alexandria had made the first steam-engine. Beautiful records of such beginnings of science were among the neglected treasures of the rich men's libraries throughout the imperial domains. They were seed lying on stony ground. The armies and couriers of Marcus Aurelius drudged along the roads exactly as the armies of Scipio Africanus had done three centuries before them.

The Roman writers were always lamenting the effeminacy of the age. It was their favourite cant. They recognized that the free men of the forest and steppes and desert were harder and more desperate fighters than their citizens, but the natural corollary of developing the industrial power of their accumulations of population to make a countervailing equipment never entered their heads. Instead, they took the barbarians into their legions, taught them the arts of war, marched them about the empire, and returned them, with their lesson well learnt, to their own people.

In view of these obvious negligences, it is no wonder that the Romans disregard that more subtle thing, the soul of the empire, altogether, and made no effort to teach or train or win its common people into any conscious participation with its life. Such teaching or training would, indeed, have run counter to all the ideas of the rich men and the imperial officials. They had made a tool of religion; science, literature, and education they had entrusted to the care of slaves, who were bred and trained and sold like dogs or horses; ignorant, pompous, and base, the Roman adventurers of finance and property, who created the empire, lorded it with a sense of the utmost security, while their destruction gathered without the empire and within.

By the second and third centuries A.D. the overtaxed and overstrained imperial machine was already staggering towards its downfall.

§ 5

And now it is necessary, if we are to understand clearly the true situation of the Roman Empire, to turn our eyes to the world beyond its northern and eastern borders, the world of the plains, that stretches with scarcely a break from Holland across Germany and Russia to the mountains of Central Asia and Mongolia, and to give a little attention to the parallel empire in China that was now consolidating and developing a far tougher and more enduring moral and intellectual unity than the Romans ever achieved.

"It is the practice," says Mr. E. H. Parker, "even amongst our most highly educated men in Europe, to deliver sonorous sentences, about being 'masters of the world,' 'bringing all nations of the earth under her sway,' and so on, when in reality only some corner of the Mediterranean is involved, or some ephemeral sally into Persia and Gaul. Cyrus and Alexander, Darius and Xerxes, Cæsar and Pompey, all made very interesting excursions, but they were certainly not on a larger scale or charged with greater human interest than the campaigns which were going on at the other end of Asia. Western civilization possessed much in art and science for which China never cared, but, on the other hand, the Chinese developed a historical and critical literature, a courtesy of demeanour, a luxury of clothing, and an administrative system of which Europe might have been proud. In one word, the history of the Far East is quite as interesting as that of the Far West. It only requires to be able to read it. When we brush away contemptuously from our notice the tremendous events which took place on the plains of Tartary, we must not blame the Chinese too much for not interesting themselves in the doings of what to them appear insignificant states dotted round the Mediterranean and Caspian, which, at this time, was practically all the world of which we knew in Europe."[1]

We have already mentioned the name of Shi-Hwang-Ti, who consolidated an empire much smaller, indeed, than the present limits of China, but still very great and populous, spreading from the valleys of the Hwang-ho and the Yang-tse-kiang. He became king of Ts'in in 246 B.C. and emperor in 220 B.C., and he reigned until 210 B.C., and during this third of a century he effected much the same work of consolidation that Augustus Cæsar carried out in Rome two centuries later. At his death there was dynastic trouble for four years, and then (206 B.C.) a fresh dynasty, the Han, established itself and ruled for two hundred and twenty-nine years. The opening quarter century of the Christian era was troubled by a usurper; then what is called the Later Han Dynasty recovered power and ruled for another century and a half until China, in the time of the Antonines, was so devasted by an eleven-year pestilence as to fall into disorder. This same pestilence, we may note, also helped to produce a

[1] E. H. Parker, *A Thousand Years of the Tartars.*

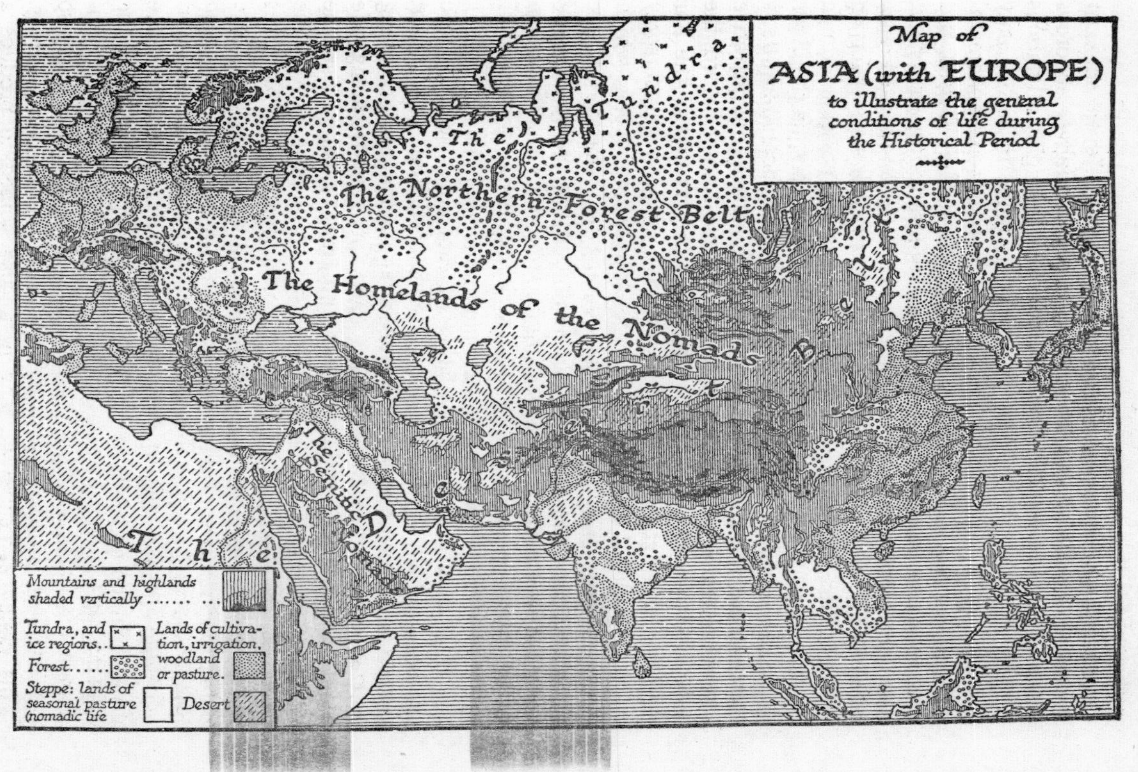
Map of
ASIA (with EUROPE)
to illustrate the general conditions of life during the Historical Period
The Northern Forest Belt
The Homelands of the Nomads
The Semitic Nomads
Mountains and highlands shaded vertically
Tundra, and ice regions
Forest
Steppe: lands of seasonal pasture (nomadic life
Lands of cultivation, irrigation, woodland or pasture.
Desert

century of confusion in the Western world (see § 1). But altogether, until this happened, for more than four hundred years, Central China was generally at peace, and on the whole well governed, a cycle of strength and prosperity unparalleled by anything in the experience of the Western world.

Only the first of the Han monarchs continued the policy of Shi-Hwang-Ti against the *literati.* His successor restored the classics, for the old separatist tradition was broken, and in the uniformity of learning throughout the empire lay, he saw, the cement of Chinese unity. While the Roman world was still blind to the need of any universal mental organization, the Han emperors were setting up a uniform system of education and of literary degrees throughout China that has maintained the intellectual solidarity of that great and always expanding country into modern times. The bureaucrats of Rome were of the most miscellaneous origins and traditions; the bureaucrats of China were, and are still, made in the same mould, all members of one tradition. Since the Han days China has experienced great vicissitudes of political fortune, but they have never changed her fundamental character; she has been divided, but she has always recovered her unity; she has been conquered, and she has always absorbed and assimilated her conquerors.

But from our present point of view, the most important consequences of this consolidation of China under Shi-Hwang-Ti and the Hans was in its reaction upon the unsettled tribes of the northern and western border of China. Throughout the disordered centuries before the time of Shi-Hwang-Ti, the Hiung-nu or Huns had occupied Mongolia and large portions of Northern China, and had raided freely into China and interfered freely in Chinese politics. The new power and organization of the Chinese civilization began to change this state of affairs for good and all.

We have already, in our first account of Chinese beginnings, noted the existence of these Huns. It is necessary now to explain briefly who and what they were. Even in using this word Hun as a general equivalent for the Hiung-nu, we step on to controversial ground. In our accounts of the development of the Western world we have had occasion to name the Scythians, and to explain the difficulty of distinguishing clearly between Cimmerians, Sarmatians, Medes, Persians, Parthians, Goths, and other more or less nomadic, more or less Aryan peoples who drifted to and fro in a great arc between the Danube and Central Asia. While sections of the Aryans were moving south and acquiring and developing civilization, these other Aryan peoples were developing mobility and nomadism; they were learning the life of the tent, the wagon, and the herd. They were learning also to use milk as a food basis, and were probably becoming less agricultural, less disposed to take even snatch crops, than they had been. Their development was being aided by a slow change in climate that was replacing the swamps and forests and parklands of South Russia and Central Asia by steppes, by wide grazing lands that is, which favoured a healthy, unsettled life, and necessitated an annual movement between summer and winter pasture.

These peoples had only the lowest political forms; they split up, they mingled together; the various races had identical social habits: and so it is that the difficulty, the impossibility of sharp distinctions between them arises. Now the case of the Mongolian races to the north and north-west of the Chinese civilization is very parallel. There can be little doubt that the Hiung-nu, the Huns, and the later people called the Mongols, were all very much the same people, and that the Turks and Tartars presently branched off from this same drifting Mongolian population. Kalmucks and Buriats are later developments of the same strain. Here we shall favour the use of the word "Hun" as a sort of general term for these tribes, just as we have been free and wide in our use of "Scythian" in the West.

The consolidation of China was a very serious matter for these Hunnish peoples. Hitherto their overflow of population had gone adventuring southward into the disorders of divided China as water goes into a sponge. Now they found a wall built against them, a firm government, and disciplined armies cutting them off from the grass plains. And though the wall held them back, it did not hold back the Chinese. They were increasing and multiplying through these centuries of peace, and as they increased and multiplied, they spread steadily with house and plough wherever the soil permitted. They spread westward into Tibet and northward and north-westwardly perhaps to the edge of the Gobi desert. They spread into the homes and pasturing and hunting-grounds of the Hunnish nomads, exactly as the white people of the United States spread westward into the hunting-grounds of the Red Indians. And in spite of raid and massacre, they were just as invincible because they had the pressure of numbers and a strong avenging government behind them. Even without the latter support, the cultivating civilization of China has enormous powers of permeation and extension. It has spread slowly and continuously for three thousand years. It is spreading in Manchuria and Siberia to-day. It roots deeply where it spreads.

Partly the Huns were civilized and assimilated by the Chinese. The more northerly Huns were checked and their superabundant energies were turned westward. The southern Huns were merged into the imperial population.

If the reader will examine the map of Central Asia, he will see that very great mountain barriers separate the Southern, Western, and Eastern peoples of Asia. (But he should be wary of forming his ideas from a map upon Mercator's projection, which enormously exaggerates the areas and distances of Northern Asia and Siberia.) He will find that from the central mountain masses three great mountain systems radiate eastward; the Himalayas going south-eastward, south of Tibet, the Kuen Lun eastward, north of Tibet, and the Thien Shan north-eastward to join the Altai mountains. Further to the north is the great plain, still steadily thawing and drying. Between the Thien Shan and the Kuen Lun is an area, the Tarim Basin (= roughly Eastern Turkestan), of rivers that never reach the sea, but end in swamps and intermittent lakes. This basin was much more fertile in the past than it is now. The mountain barrier to the west of this Tarim Basin is high, but not forbidding; there are many practicable routes downward into Western Turkestan, and it is possible to travel either along the northern foothills of the Kuen Lun or by the Tarim valley westward from China to Kashgar (where the roads converge), and so over the mountains to Kokand, Samarkand, and Bokhara. Here then is the natural meeting-place in history of Aryan and Mongolian. Here or round by the sea.

We have already noted how Alexander the Great came to one side of the barrier in 329 B.C. High among the mountains of Turkestan a lake preserves his name. Indeed, so living is the tradition of his great raid, that almost any stone ruin in Central Asia is still ascribed to "Iskander." After this brief glimpse, the light of history upon this region fades again, and when it becomes bright once more it is on the eastern and not upon the western side.

Far away to the east Shi-Hwang-ti had routed the Huns and walled them out of China proper. A portion of these people remained in the north of China, a remnant which was destined to amalgamate with Chinese life under the Hans, but a considerable section had turned westward and (second and first centuries B.C.) driven before them a kindred people called the Yueh-Chi, driving

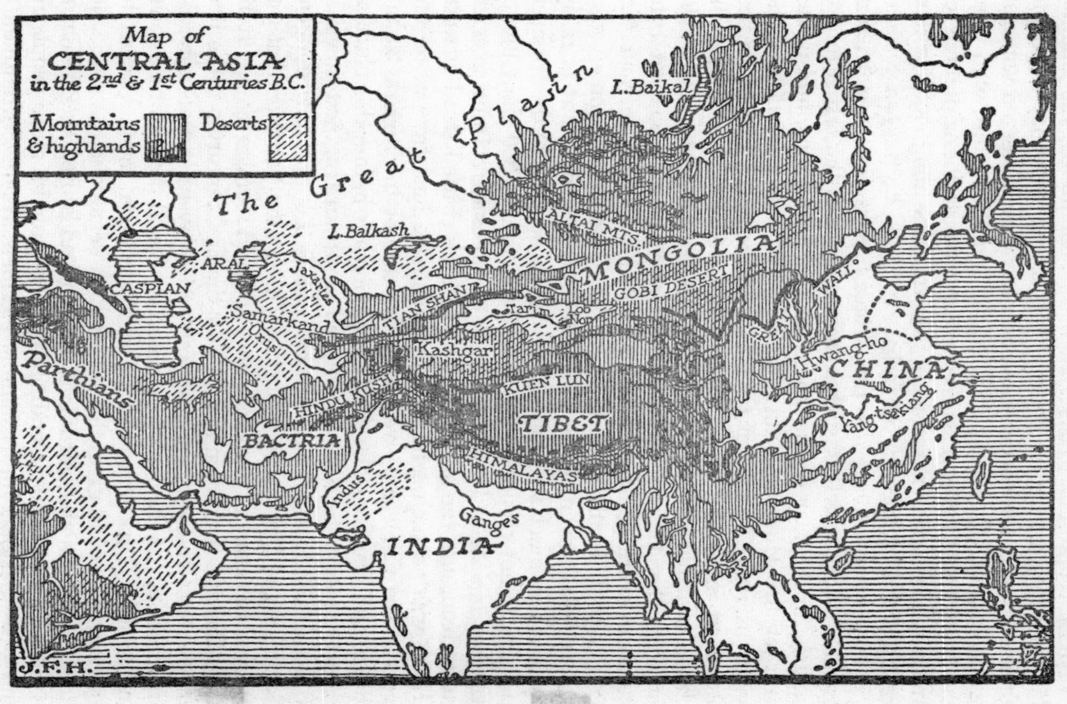

Map of
CENTRAL ASIA
in the 2nd & 1st Centuries B.C.
Mountains & highlands
Deserts
The Great Plain
L. Baikal
ALTAI MTS.
MONGOLIA
GOBI DESERT
GREAT WALL
Hwang-ho
CHINA
Yang-tse-kiang
L. Balkash
TIAN SHAN
Tarim
Lob Nor
Kashgar
KUEN LUN
TIBET
HIMALAYAS
Ganges
INDIA
Indus
HINDU KUSH
BACTRIA
Jaxartes
Samarkand
Oxus
ARAL
CASPIAN
Parthians
J.F.H.

them from the eastern to the western extremity of the Kuen Lun, and at last right over the barrier into the once Aryan region of Western Turkestan. These Yueh-Chi conquered the slightly Hellenized kingdom of Bactria, and mixed with Aryan people there. Later on these Yueh-Chi became, or were merged with Aryan elements, into a people called the Indo-Scythians, who went on down the Khyber Pass and conquered northern portions of India as far as Benares (A.D. 100–150), wiping out the last vestiges of Hellenic rule in India.

This big splash over of the Mongolian races westward was probably not the first of such splashes, but it is the first recorded splash. In the rear of the Yueh-Chi were the Huns, and in the rear of the Huns and turning them now northward was the vigorous Han Dynasty of China. In the reign of the greatest of the Han monarchs, Wu-Ti (140–86 B.C.), the Huns had been driven northward out of the whole of Eastern Turkestan or subjugated, the Tarim Basin swarmed with Chinese settlers, and caravans were going over westward with silk and lacquer and jade to trade for the gold and silver of Armenia and Rome.

The splash over of the Yueh-Chi is recorded, but it is fairly evident that much westward movement of sections of the Hunnish peoples is not recorded. From 200 B.C. to A.D. 200 the Chinese Empire maintained a hard, resolute, advancing front towards nomadism, and the surplus of the nomads drifted steadily west. There was no such settling down behind a final frontier on the part of the Chinese as we see in the case of the Romans at the Rhine and Danube. The drift of the nomads before this Chinese thrust, century by century, turned southward at first towards Bactria. The Parthians of the first century B.C. probably mingled Scythian and Mongolian elements. The "singing arrows" that destroyed the army of Crassus came, it would seem, originally from the Altai and the Thien Shan. After the first century B.C. the line of greater attraction and least resistance lay for a time towards the north of the Caspian. In a century or so all the country known as Western Turkestan was "Mongolized," and so it remains to this day. A second great thrust by China began about A.D. 75, and accelerated the westward drift of the nomads. In 102, Pan Chau, a Chinese general, was sending explorers from his advanced camp upon the Caspian (or as some authorities say, the Persian Gulf) to learn particulars of the Roman power. But their reports decided him not to proceed.

By the first century A.D. nomadic Mongolian peoples were in

evidence upon the eastern boundaries of Europe, already greatly mixed with Nordic nomads and with uprooted Nordic elements from the Caspian-Pamir region. There were Hunnish peoples established between the Caspian Sea and the Urals. West of them were the Alans, probably also a Mongolian people with Nordic elements; they had fought against Pompey the Great when he was in Armenia in 65 B.C. These were as yet the farthest westward peoples of the new Mongolian advance, and they made no further westward push until the fourth century A.D. To the north-west the Finns, a Mongolian people, had long been established as far west as the Baltic.

West of the Huns, beyond the Don, there were purely Nordic tribes, the Goths. These Goths had spread south-eastward from their region of origin in Scandinavia. They were a Teutonic people, and we have already marked them crossing the Baltic in the map we have given of the earlier distribution of the Aryan-speaking people. These Goths continued to move south-eastward across Russia, using the rivers and never forgetting their Baltic water-craft. No doubt they assimilated much Scythian population as they spread down to the Black Sea. In the first century A.D. they were in two main divisions, the Ostrogoths, the east Goths, who were between the Don and the Dnieper, and the Visigoths, or West Goths, west of the Dnieper. During the first century there was quiescence over the great plains, but population was accumulating and the tribes were fermenting. The second and third centuries seem to have been a phase of comparatively moist seasons and abundant grass. Presently, in the fourth and fifth centuries, the weather grew drier and the grass became scanty and the nomads stirred afresh.

But it is interesting to note that in the opening century of the Christian era, the Chinese Empire was strong enough to expel and push off from itself the surplus of this Mongolian nomadism to the north of it, which presently conquered North India and gathered force and mingled with Aryan nomadism, and fell at last like an avalanche upon the weak-backed Roman Empire.

Before we go on to tell of the blows that now began to fall upon the Roman Empire, and of the efforts of one or two great men to arrest the collapse, we may say a few words about the habits and quality of these westward-drifting barbaric Mongolian peoples, who were now spreading from the limits of China towards the Black and Baltic Seas. It is still the European custom to follow the lead of the Roman writers and write of these Huns and their associates as of something incredibly destructive and cruel. But such accounts as we have from the Romans were written in periods of panic, and the Roman could lie about his enemies with a freedom and vigour that must arouse the envy even of the modern propagandist.

He could talk of "Punic faith" as a byword for perfidy while committing the most abominable treacheries against Carthage, and his railing accusations of systematic cruelty against this people or that were usually the prelude and excuse for some frightful massacre or enslavement or robbery on his own part. He had quite a modern passion for self-justification. We must remember that these accounts of the savagery and frightfulness of the Huns came from a people whose chief amusement was gladiatorial shows, and whose chief method of dealing with insurrection and sedition was nailing the offender to a cross to die. From first to last the Roman Empire must have killed hundreds of thousands of men in that way. A large portion of the population of this empire that could complain of the barbarism of its assailants consisted of slaves subject practically to almost any lust or caprice at the hands of their owners. It is well to bear these facts in mind before we mourn the swamping of the Roman Empire by the barbarians as though it was an extinction of all that is fine in life by all that is black and ugly.

The facts seem to be that the Hunnish peoples were the eastern equivalent of the primitive Aryans, and that, in spite of their profound racial and linguistic differences, they mixed with the nomadic and semi-nomadic residuum of the Aryan-speaking races north of the Danube and Persia very easily and successfully. Instead of killing, they enlisted and intermarried with the peoples they invaded. They had that necessary gift for all peoples destined to political predominance—tolerant assimilation. They came rather later in time and their nomadic life was more highly developed than that of the primitive Aryans. The primitive Aryans were a forest and ox-wagon people who took to the horse later. The Hunnish peoples had grown up with the horse. Somewhen about 1,200 or 1,000 years B.C. they began to ride the horse. The bit, the saddle, the stirrup, these are not primitive things, but they are necessary if man and horse are to keep going for long stretches. It is well to bear in mind how modern a thing is riding. Altogether man has not been in the saddle for much more than three thousand years.[1]

---

[1] See Roger Pocock, *Horses*, a very interesting and picturesque little book.

We have already noted the gradual appearance of the war-chariot, the mounted man, and finally of disciplined cavalry in this history. It was from the Mongolian regions of Asia that these things came. To this day men in Central Asia go rather in the saddle than on their proper feet. Says Ratzel,[1] "Strong, long-necked horses are found in enormous numbers on the steppes. For Mongols and Turcomans riding is not a luxury; even the Mongol shepherds tend their flocks on horseback. Children are taught to ride in early youth; and the boy of three years old often takes his first riding-lesson on a safe child's saddle and makes quick progress."

It is impossible to suppose that the Huns and the Alans could have differed very widely in character from the present nomads of the steppe regions, and nearly all observers are agreed in describing these latter as open and pleasant people. They are thoroughly honest and free-spirited. "The character of the herdsmen of Central Asia," says Ratzel,[1] "when unadulterated, is ponderous eloquence, frankness, rough good-nature, pride, but also indolence, irritability, and a tendency to vindictiveness. Their faces show a considerable share of frankness combined with amusing naïveté. . . . Their courage is rather a sudden blaze of pugnacity than cold boldness. Religious fanaticism they have none. Hospitality is universal." This is not an entirely disagreeable picture. Their personal bearing, he says further, is quieter and more dignified than that of the townsmen of Turkestan and Persia. Add to this that the nomadic life prevents any great class inequalities or any extensive development of slavery.

Of course, these peoples out of Asia were totally illiterate and artistically undeveloped. But we must not suppose, on that account, that they were primitive barbarians, and that their state of life was at the level from which the agricultural civilization had long ago arisen. It was not. They, too, had developed, but they had developed along a different line, a line with less intellectual complication, more personal dignity perhaps, and certainly with a more intimate contact with wind and sky.

§ 6

The first serious irruptions of the German tribes into the Roman Empire began in the third century with the decay of the central power. We will not entangle the reader here with the vexed and intricate question of the names, identity, and inter-relationships of

[1] *The History of Mankind*, book v., C.

the various Germanic tribes. Historians find great difficulties in keeping them distinct, and these difficulties are enhanced by the fact that they themselves took little care to keep distinct.

We find in A.D. 236 a people called the Franks breaking bounds upon the Lower Rhine, and another, the Alamanni, pouring into Alsace. A much more serious push southward was that of the Goths. We have already noted the presence of these people in South Russia, and their division by the Dnieper into Western and Eastern Goths. They had become a maritime people again upon the Black Sea—probably their traditional migration from Sweden was along the waterways, for it is still possible to row a boat, with only a few quite practicable portages, from the Baltic right across Russia to either the Black or Caspian Sea—and they had wrested the command of the eastern seas from the control of Rome.

They were presently raiding the shores of Greece. They also crossed the Danube in a great land raid in 247, and defeated and killed the Emperor Decius in what is now Serbia. The province of Dacia vanished from Roman history. In 270 they were defeated at Nish in Serbia by Claudius, and in 276 they were raiding Pontus. It is characteristic of the invertebrate nature of the empire that the legions of Gaul found that the most effective method of dealing with the Franks and the Alamanni at this time was by setting up a separate emperor in Gaul and doing the job by themselves.

Then for a while the barbarians were held, and the Emperor Probus in 276 forced the Franks and the Alamanni back over the Rhine. But it is significant of the general atmosphere of insecurity created by these raids that Aurelian (270–275) fortified Rome, which had been an open and secure city for all the earlier years of the empire.

In A.D. 321 the Goths were again over the Danube, plundering what is now Serbia and Bulgaria. They were driven back by Constantine the Great, of whom we shall have more to tell in the next chapter. About the end of his reign (A.D. 337) the Vandals, a people closely kindred to the Goths, being pressed by them, obtained permission to cross the Danube into Pannonia, which is now that part of Hungary west of the river.

But by the middle of the fourth century the Hunnish people to the east were becoming aggressive again. They had long subjugated the Alani, and now they made the Ostrogoths, the east Goths, tributary. The Visigoths (or west Goths) followed the

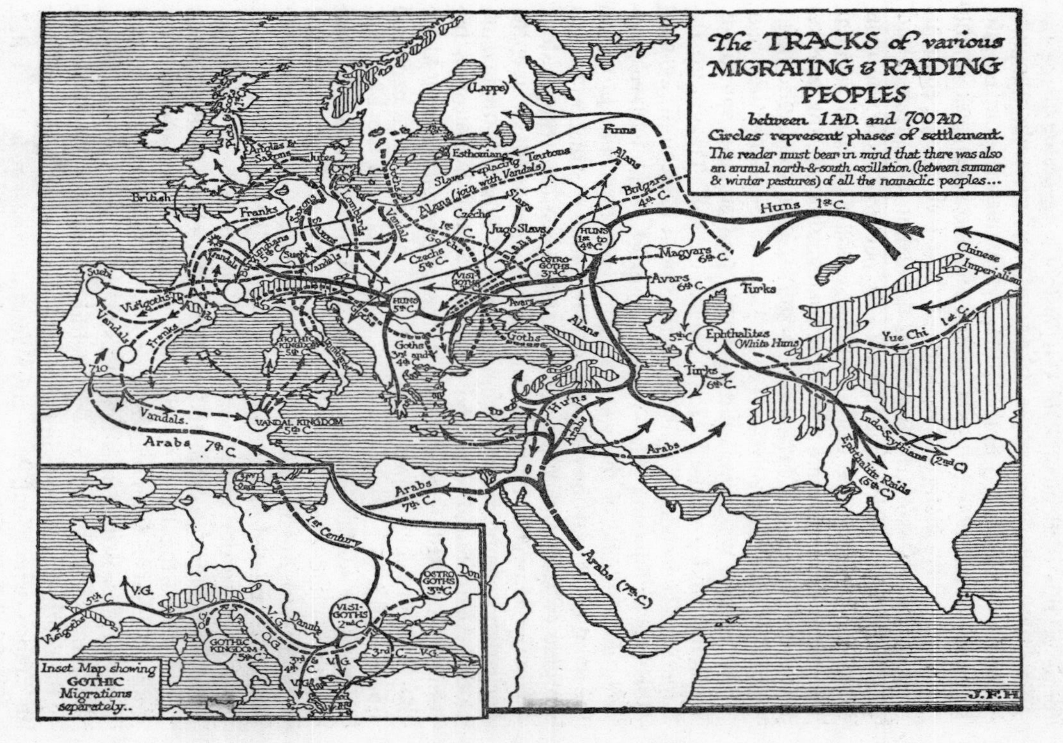
The TRACKS of various MIGRATING & RAIDING PEOPLES
between 1 A.D. and 700 A.D.
Circles represent phases of settlement.
The reader must bear in mind that there was also an annual north-&-south oscillation (between summer & winter pastures) of all the nomadic peoples...
(Lappe)
Finns
Alans
Esthonians
Slavs replacing Teutons
Alans (join with Vandals)
Bulgars 4th C.
Huns 1st C.
British
Franks
Czechs
Jugo Slavs
Czechs 5th C.
Magyars 6th C.
Avars 6th C.
Chinese Imperialism
Turks
Yue Chi 1st C.
Suebi
Visigoths
Vandals
Franks
710
HUNS 5th C.
HUNS 1st to 4th C.
OSTRO GOTHS 3rd C.
Goths
Alans
Ephthalites (White Huns)
5th C.
Turks 6th C.
GOTHIC KINGDOM 5th C.
VANDAL KINGDOM 5th C.
Vandals.
Arabs 7th C.
Huns
Arabs
Indo-Scythians (2nd C.)
Ephthalite Raids (6th C.)
Arabs 7th C.
Arabs (7th C.)
1st Century
OSTRO GOTHS 3rd C.
Don
VISI-GOTHS 2nd C.
Danube
V.G.
O.G.
5th C.
3rd C.
4th C.
Inset Map showing GOTHIC Migrations separately..
J.F.H.

example of the Vandals, and made arrangements to cross the Danube into Roman territory. There was some dispute upon the terms of this settlement, and the Visigoths, growing fierce, assumed the offensive, and at Adrianople defeated the Emperor Valens, who was killed in this battle. They were then allowed to settle in what is now Bulgaria, and their army became nominally a Roman army, though they retained their own chiefs, the foremost of whom was Alaric. It exhibits the complete "barbarization" of the Roman empire that had already occurred, that the chief opponent of Alaric the Goth, Stilicho, was a Pannonian Vandal. The legions in Gaul were under the command of a Frank, and the Emperor Theodosius I (emp. 379–395) was a Spaniard chiefly supported by Gothic auxiliaries.

The empire was now splitting finally into an eastern (Greek-speaking) and a western (Latin-speaking) half. Theodosius the Great was succeeded by his sons Arcadius at Constantinople and Honorius at Ravenna. Alaric made a puppet of the eastern monarch, and Stilicho of the western. Huns now first appear within the empire as auxiliary troops enlisted under Stilicho. In this struggle of East and West, the frontier—if we can still speak of a frontier between the unauthorized barbarian without and the barbarian in employment within—gave way. Fresh Vandals, more Goths, Alans, Suevi, marched freely westward, living upon the country. Amidst this confusion occurred a crowning event. Alaric the Goth marched down Italy, and after a short siege captured Rome (410).

By 425 or so, the Vandals (whom originally we noted in East Germany) and a portion of the Alani (whom we first mentioned in South-east Russia) had traversed Gaul and the Pyrenees, and had amalgamated and settled in the south of Spain. There were Huns in possession of Pannonia, and Goths in Dalmatia. Into Bohemia and Moravia came and settled a Slavic people, the Czechs (451). In Portugal and north of the Vandals in Spain were Visigoths and Suevi. Gaul was divided among Visigoths, Franks, and Burgundians. Britain was being invaded by Low German tribes, the Jutes, Angles and Saxons, before whom the Keltic British of the south-west were flying across the sea to what is now Brittany in France. The usual date given for this invasion is 449 but it was probably earlier. And as the result of intrigues between two imperial politicians, the Vandals of the south of Spain, under their king Genseric, embarked *en masse* for North Africa (429), became masters of Carthage (439) secured the mastery of the sea, raided, captured, and pillaged Rome (455), crossed into Sicily, and set up a kingdom in West Sicily, which endured there for a hundred years (up to 534). At the time of its greatest extent (477) this Vandal kingdom included also Corsica, Sardinia, and the Balearic Isles, as well as much of North Africa.

About this Vandal kingdom facts and figures are given that show very clearly the true nature of these barbarian irruptions. They were not really the conquest and replacement of one people or race by another; what happened was something very different, it was a social revolution started and masked by a superficial foreign conquest. The whole Vandal nation, men, women, and children, that came from Spain to Africa, for example, did not number more than eighty thousand souls. We know this because we have particulars of the transport problem. In their struggle for North Africa, Dr. Schurtz tells us,[1] "there is no trace of any serious resistance offered by the inhabitants; Boniface (the Roman governor of North Africa) had defended Hippo with Gothic mercenaries, while the native population lent no appreciable assistance, and the nomad tribes of the country either adopted a dubious attitude or availed themselves of the difficulties of the Roman governor to make attacks and engage in predatory expeditions. This demoralization resulted from social conditions, which had perhaps developed more unfavourably in Africa than in other parts of the Roman Empire. The free peasants had long ago become the serfs of the great landed proprietors, and were little superior in position to the masses of slaves who were everywhere to be found. And the great landowners had become in their turn easy victims of the policy of extortion followed by unscrupulous governors to an increasingly unprecedented extent in proportion as the dignity of the imperial power sank lower. No man who had anything to lose would now take a place in the senate of the large towns, which had once been the goal of the ambitious, for the senators were required to make up all deficiencies in the revenue, and such deficiencies were now frequent and considerable. . . . Bloody insurrections repeatedly broke out, always traceable ultimately to the pressure of taxation. . . ."

Manifestly the Vandals came in as a positive relief to such a system. They exterminated the great landowners, wiped out all debts to Roman moneylenders, and abolished the last vestiges of military service. The cultivators found themselves better off; the

---

[1] In Helmolt's *History of the World.*

minor officials kept their places; it was not so much a conquest as a liberation from an intolerable deadlock.

It was while the Vandals were still in Africa that a great leader Attila, arose among the Huns. The seat of his government was in the plains east of the Danube. For a time he swayed a considerable empire of Hunnish and Germanic tribes, and his rule stretched from the Rhine into Central Asia. He negotiated on equal terms with the Chinese emperor. He bullied Ravena and Constantinople for ten years. Honoria, the granddaughter of Theodosius II, Emperor of the Eastern empire, one of those passionate young ladies who cause so much trouble in the world, having been put under restraint because of a love affair with a court chamberlain, sent her ring to Attila and called upon him to be her husband and deliverer. He was also urged to attack the Eastern empire by Genseric the Vandal, who was faced by an alliance of the Western and Eastern emperors. He raided southward to the very walls of Constantinople, completely destroying, says Gibbon, seventy cities in his progress, and forcing upon the emperor an onerous peace, which apparently did not involve the liberation of Honoria to her hero.

At this distance of time we are unable to guess at the motives for this omission. Attila continued to speak of her as his affianced bride, and to use the relationship as a pretext for aggressions. In the subsequent negotiations a certain Priscus accompanied an embassy to the camp of the Hunnish monarch, and the fragments that still survive of the narrative he wrote give us a glimpse of the camp and way of living of the great conqueror.

The embassy was itself a curiously constituted body. Its head was Maximin, an honest diplomatist who went in good faith. Quite unknown to him and, at the time, to Priscus, Vigilius, the interpreter of the expedition, had also a secret mission from the court of Theodosius which was to secure by bribery the assassination of Attila. The little expedition went by way of Nish; it crossed the Danube in canoes, dug out of a single tree, and it was fed by contributions from the villages on the route. Differences in dietary soon attracted the attention of the envoys. Priscus mentions mead in the place of wine, millet for corn, and a drink either distilled[1] or brewed from barley. The journey through Hungary will remind the reader in many of its incidents of the

[1] Gibbon.

journeys of travellers in Central Africa during the Victorian period. The travellers were politely offered temporary wives.

Attila's capital was rather a vast camp and village than a town. There was only one building of stone, a bath constructed on the Roman model. The mass of the people were in huts and tents; Attila and his leading men lived in timber palaces in great stockaded enclosures with their numerous wives and ministers about them. There was a vast display of loot, but Attila himself affected

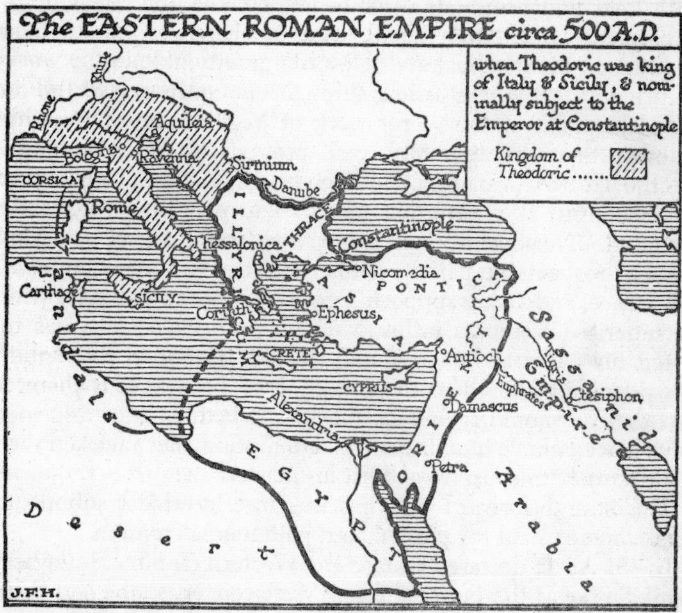

a nomadic simplicity; he was served in wooden cups and platters, and never touched bread. He worked hard, kept open court before the gate of his palace, and was commonly in the saddle. The primitive custom of both Aryans and Mongols of holding great feasts in halls still held good, and there was much hard drinking. Priscus describes how bards chanted before Attila. They "recited the verses which they had composed, to celebrate his valour and his victories. A profound silence prevailed in the hall, and the attention of the guests was captivated by the vocal harmony, which revived and perpetuated the memory of their own exploits; a martial ardour flashed from the eyes of the warriors who were impatient for battle; and the tears of the old men expressed their generous despair, that they could no longer partake of the danger and glory of the field. This entertainment, which might be considered as a school of military virtue, was succeeded by a farce that debased the dignity of human nature. A Moorish and Scythian buffoon successively excited the mirth of the rude spectators by their deformed figures, ridiculous dress, antic gestures, absurd speeches, and the strange, unintelligible confusion of the Latin, the Gothic and the Hunnish languages, and the hall resounded with loud and licentious peals of laughter. In the midst of this intemperate riot, Attila alone, without change of countenance, maintained his steadfast and inflexible gravity."[1]

Although Attila was aware, through the confession of the proposed assassin, of the secret work of Vigilius, he allowed this embassy to return in safety, with presents of numerous horses and the like, to Constantinople. Then he dispatched an ambassador to Theodosius II to give that monarch, as people say, a piece of his mind. "Theodosius," said the envoy, "is the son of an illustrious and respectable parent; Attila, likewise, is descended from a noble race; and *he* has supported, by his actions, the dignity which he inherited from his father Munzuk. But Theodosius has forfeited his parental honours, and, by consenting to pay tribute, has degraded himself to the condition of a slave. It is therefore just that he should reverence the man whom fortune and merit have placed above him; instead of attempting, like a wicked slave, clandestinely to conspire against his master."

This straightforward bullying was met by abject submission. The emperor sued for pardon, and paid a great ransom.

In 451 Attila declared war on the Western empire. He invaded Gaul. So far as the imperial forces were concerned, he had things all his own way, and he sacked most of the towns of France as far south as Orleans. Then the Franks and Visigoths and the imperial forces united against him, and a great and obstinate battle at Troyes (451), in which over 150,000 men were killed on both sides, ended in his repulse and saved Europe from a Mongolian overlord. This disaster by no means exhausted Attila's resources. He turned his attention southward, and overran North Italy. He burnt Aquileia and Padua, and looted Milan, but he made peace at the entreaty of Pope Leo I. He died in 453. . . .

Hereafter the Huns, so far as that name goes in Europe, the Huns of Attila, disappeared out of history. They dissolve into

[1] Gibbon.

the surrounding populations. They were probably already much mixed, and rather Aryan than Mongolian. They did not become, as one might suppose, the inhabitants of Hungary, though they have probably left many descendants there. About a hundred years after came another Hunnish or mixed people, the Avars, out of the east into Hungary, but these were driven out eastward again by Charlemagne in 791–5. The Magyars, the modern Hungarians, came westward later. They were a Turko-Finnish people. The Magyar is a language belonging to the Finno-Ugrian division of the Ural-Altaic tongues. The Magyars were on the Volga about 550. They settled in Hungary about 900. . . . But we are getting too far on in our story, and we must return to Rome.

In 493 Theodoric, a Goth, became King of Rome, but already for seventeen years there had been no Roman emperor. So it was in utter social decay and collapse that the great slave-holding "world-ascendancy" of the god-Cæsars and the rich men of Rome came to an end.

§ 7

But though throughout the whole of Western Europe and North Africa the Roman imperial system had collapsed, though credit had vanished, luxury production had ceased, and money was hidden, though creditors were going unpaid and slaves masterless, the tradition of the Cæsars was still being carried on in Constantinople. We have already had occasion to mention as two outstanding figures among the late Cæsars, Diocletian (284) and Constantine the Great (312), and it was to the latter of these that the world owes the setting up of a fresh imperial centre at Constantinople.

Very early during the imperial period the unsuitability of the position of Rome as a world capital, due to the Roman failure to use the sea, was felt. The destruction of Carthage and Corinth had killed the shipping of the main Mediterranean sea-routes. For a people who did not use the sea properly, having the administrative centre at Rome meant that every legion, every draft of officials, every order, had to travel northward for half the length of Italy before it could turn east or west. Consequently nearly all the more capable emperors set up their headquarters at some subordinate centre in a more convenient position. Sirmium (on the River Save), Milan, Lyons, and Nicomedia (in Bithynia) were among such supplementary capitals. For a time, under Diocletian, Durazzo was the imperial capital. Ravenna, near the head of the Adriatic, was the capital of the last Roman emperors in the time of Alaric and Stilicho.

It was Constantine the Great who determined upon the permanent transfer of the centre of imperial power to the Bosphorus. We have already noted the existence of the city of Byzantium, which Constantine chose to develop into his new capital. It played a part in the story of the intricate Histiæus; it repulsed Philip of Macedon. If the reader will examine its position, he will see that in the hands of a line of capable emperors, and as the centre of a people with some solidarity and spirit and seacraft (neither of which things was vouchsafed to it), it was extraordinarily well placed. Its galleys could have penetrated up the rivers to the heart of Russia and outflanked every barbarian advance. It commanded practicable trade routes to the east, and it was within a reasonable striking distance of Mesopotamia, Egypt, Greece, and all the more prosperous and civilized regions of the world at that period. And even under the rule of a series of inept monarchs and under demoralized social conditions, the remains of the Roman Empire centering at Constantinople held out for nearly a thousand years.

It was the manifest intention of Constantine the Great that Constantinople should be the centre of an undivided empire. But having regard to the methods of travel and transport available at the time, the geographical conditions of Europe and Western Asia do not point to any one necessary centre of government. If Rome faced westward instead of eastward, and so failed to reach out beyond the Euphrates, Constantinople, on the other hand, was hopelessly remote from Gaul. The enfeebled Mediterranean civilization, after a certain struggle for Italy, did in fact let go of the west altogether and concentrated upon what were practically the central vestiges, the stump, of the empire of Alexander. The Greek language resumed its sway, which had never been very seriously undermined by the official use of Latin. This "Eastern" or Byzantine empire is generally spoken of as if it were a continuation of the Roman tradition. It is really far more like a resumption of Alexander's.

The Latin language had not the intellectual vigour behind it, it had not the literature and the science, to make it a necessity to intelligent men and so to maintain an ascendancy over the Greek. For no language, whatever officialdom may do, can impose itself in competition with another that can offer the advantages of a great literature or encyclopædic information. Aggressive languages must bring gifts, and the gifts of Greek were incomparably greater than the gifts of Latin. The Eastern empire was from

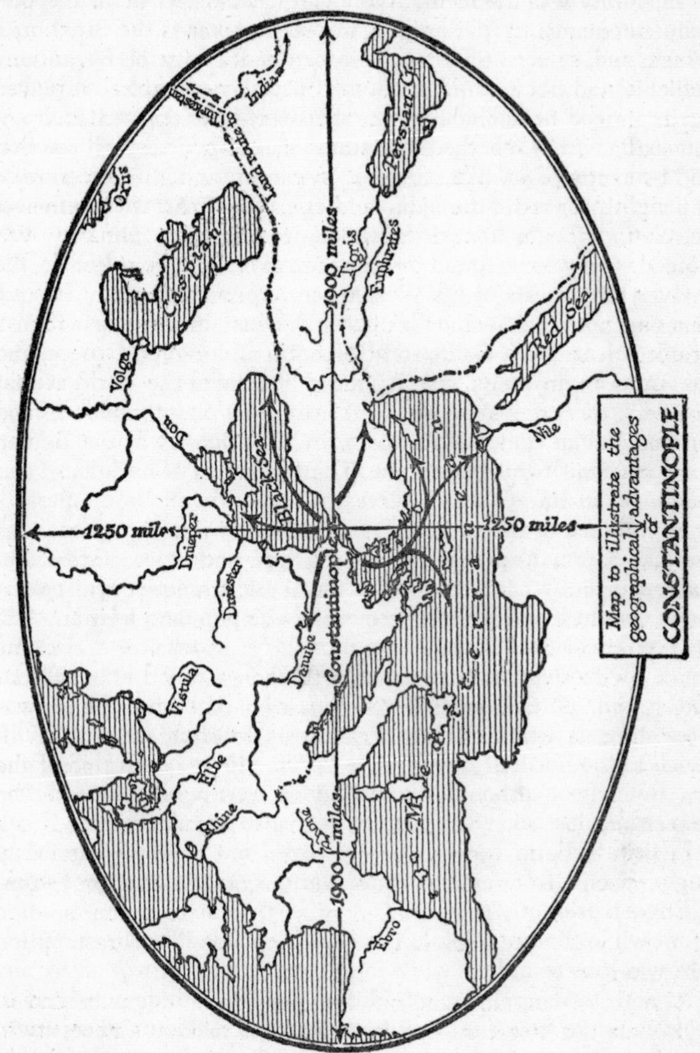

Map to illustrate the geographical advantages of CONSTANTINOPLE

the beginnings of its separation Greek-speaking, and a continuation, though a degenerate continuation, of the Hellenic tradition. Its intellectual centre was no longer in Greece, but Alexandria.

Its mentality was no longer the mentality of free-minded plain-speaking citizens, of the Stagirite Aristotle and the Greek Plato; its mentality was the mentality of the pedants and of men politically impotent; its philosophy was a pompous evasion of real things, and its scientific impulse was dead. Nevertheless, it was Hellenic and not Latin. The Roman had come, and he had gone again. Indeed he had gone very extensively from the west also. By the sixth century A.D. the populations of Europe and North Africa had been stirred up like sediment. When presently in the seventh and eighth centuries the sediment begins to settle down again and populations begin to take on a definite localized character, the Roman is only to be found by name in the region about Rome.

Over large parts of his Western empire we find changed and changing modifications of his Latin speech; in Gaul, where the Frank is learning a Gallic form of Latin and evolving French in the process; in Italy, where, under the influence of Teutonic invaders, the Lombards and Goths, Latin is being modified into various Italian dialects; in Spain and Portugal, where it is becoming Spanish and Portuguese. The fundamental Latinity of the languages in these regions serves to remind us of the numerical unimportance of the various Frankish, Vandal, Avar, Gothic, and the like German-speaking invaders, and serves to justify our statement that what happened to the Western empire was not so much conquest and the replacement of one population by another as a political and social revolution. The district of Valais in South Switzerland also retained a fundamentally Latin speech, and so did the Canton Grisons; and, what is more curious and interesting, is that in Dacia and Mœsia Inferior, large parts of which to the north of the Danube became the modern Roumania (= Romania), although these regions were added late to the empire and lost soon, the Latin speech also remained.

In Britain Latin was practically wiped out by the conquering Anglo-Saxons, from among whose various dialects the root-stock of English presently grew.

But while the smashing of the Roman social and political structure was thus complete, while in the east it was thrown off by the older and stronger Hellenic tradition, and while in the west it was broken up into fragments that began to take on a new and separate life of their own, there was one thing that did not perish, but grew, and that was the tradition of the world empire of Rome and of the supremacy of the Cæsars. When the reality was destroyed the legend had freedom to expand. Removed from the possibility of verification, the idea of a serene and splendid Roman world-supremacy grew up in the imagination of mankind, and still holds it to this day.

Ever since the time of Alexander, human thought has been haunted by the possible political unity of the race. All the sturdy chiefs and leaders and kings of the barbarians, who raided through the prostrate but vast disorder of the decayed empire, were capable of conceiving of some mighty king of kings greater than themselves and giving a real law for all men, and they were ready to believe that elsewhere in space and time, and capable of returning presently to resume his supremacy, Cæsar had been such a king of kings. Far above their own titles, therefore, they esteemed and envied the title of Cæsar. The international history of Europe from this time henceforth is largely the story of kings and adventurers setting up to be Cæsar and Imperator (Emperor). We shall tell of some of them in their places. So universal did this "Cæsaring" become, that the Great War of 1914–18 mowed down no fewer than four Cæsars, the German Kaiser (=Cæsar), the Austrian Kaiser, the Tsar (=Cæsar) of Russia, and that fantastic figure, the Tsar of Bulgaria. The French "Imperator" (Napoleon III) had already fallen in 1871. The last monarch in the world to carry on the Imperial title and the tradition of Divus Cæsar was the British King, who until after the second world war was called the Cæsar of India (a country no real Cæsar ever looked upon), Kaisar-i-Hind. This he inherited from the Great Mogul of whom we shall tell in due course.

BOOK VI

CHRISTIANITY AND ISLAM

XXVIII

THE RISE OF CHRISTIANITY AND THE FALL OF THE WESTERN EMPIRE

§ 1. *Judea at the Christian Era.* § 2. *The Teachings of Jesus of Nazareth.* § 3. *The New Universal Religions.* § 4. *The Crucifixion of Jesus of Nazareth.* § 5. *Doctrines added to the Teachings of Jesus.* § 6. *The Struggles and Persecutions of Christianity.* § 7. *Constantine the Great.* § 8. *The Establishment of Official Christianity.* § 9. *The Map of Europe,* A.D. 500. § 10. *The Salvation of Learning by Christianity.* § 11. *Byzantine Art.*

§ 1

BEFORE we can understand the qualities of Christianity, which must now play a large part in our history, and which opened men's eyes to fresh aspects of the possibility of a unified world, we must go back some centuries and tell of the condition of affairs in Palestine and Syria, in which countries Christianity arose. We have already told the main facts about the origin of the Jewish nation and tradition, about the Diaspora, about the fundamentally scattered nature of Jewry even from the beginning, and the gradual development of the idea of one just God ruling the earth and bound by a special promise to preserve and bring to honour the Jewish people. The Jewish idea was and is a curious combination of theological breadth and an intense racial patriotism. The Jews looked for a special saviour, a Messiah, who was to redeem mankind by the agreeable process of restoring the fabulous glories of David and Solomon, and bringing the whole world at last under the benevolent but firm Jewish heel. As the political power of the Semitic peoples declined, as Carthage followed Tyre into the darkness, and Spain became a Roman province, this dream grew and spread. There can be little doubt that the scattered Phœnicians in Spain and Africa and throughout the Mediterranean, speaking as they did a language closely akin to Hebrew and being deprived of their authentic political rights, became proselytes to Judaism. For phases of vigorous proselytism alternated with phases of exclusive jealousy in Jewish history. On one occasion the Idumeans, being conquered, were all forcibly made Jews.[1] There were Arab tribes who were Jews in the time of Muhammad, and a Turkish people who were mainly Jews in South Russia in the ninth century. Judaism is indeed the reconstructed political ideal of many shattered peoples—mainly Semitic. It is to the Phœnician contingent and to Aramean accessions in Babylon that the financial and commercial tradition of the Jews is to be ascribed. But as a result of these coalescences and assimilations, almost everywhere in the towns throughout the Roman Empire, and far beyond it in the east, Jewish communities traded and flourished, and were kept in touch through the Bible, and through a religious and educational organization. The main part of Jewry never was in Judea and had never come out of Judea.

Manifestly this intercommunicating series of Judaized communities had very great financial and political facilities. They could assemble resources, they could stir up, they could allay. They were neither so abundant nor so civilized as the still more widely diffused Greeks, but they had a tradition of greater solidarity. Greek was hostile to Greek; Jew stood by Jew. Wherever a Jew went, he found men of like mind and like tradition with himself. He could get shelter, food, loans, and legal help. And by reason of this solidarity rulers had everywhere to take account of this people as a help, as a source of loans or as a source of trouble. So it is that the Jews have persisted as a people while Hellenism has become a universal light for mankind.

We cannot tell here in detail the history of that smaller part of Jewry that lived in Judea. These Jews had returned to their old position of danger; again they were seeking peace in, so to speak, the middle of a highway. In the old time they had been between Syria and Assyria to the north and Egypt to the south; now they had the Seleucids to the north and the Ptolemys to the south, and when the Seleucids went, then down came the

---

[1] Josephus.

Roman power upon them. The independence of Judea was always a qualified and precarious thing. The reader must go to the *Antiquities* and the *Wars of the Jews* of Flavius Josephus, a copious, tedious, and maddeningly patriotic writer, to learn of the succession of their rulers, of their high-priest monarchs, and of the Maccabæans, the Herods and the like. These rulers were for the most part of the ordinary eastern type, cunning, treacherous, and blood-stained. Thrice Jerusalem was taken and twice the temple was destroyed. It was the support of the far more powerful Diaspora that prevented the little country from being wiped out altogether, until 70 A.D., when Titus, the adopted son and successor of the emperor Vespasian, after a siege that ranks in bitterness and horror with that of Tyre and Carthage, took Jerusalem and destroyed city and temple together. He did this in an attempt to destroy Jewry, but, indeed, he made Jewry stronger by destroying its one sensitive and vulnerable point.

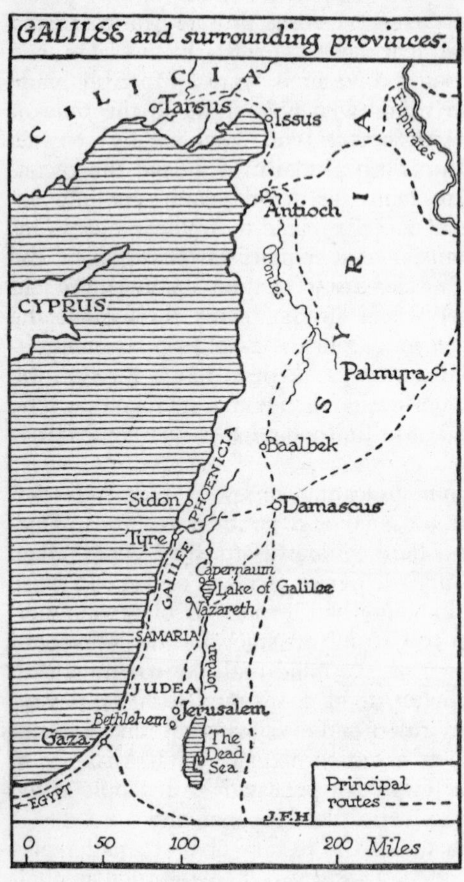

Throughout a history of five centuries of war and civil commotion between the return from captivity and the destruction of Jerusalem, certain constant features of the Jews persisted. He remained obstinately monotheistic; he would have none other gods but the one true God. In Rome, as in Jerusalem, he stood out manfully against the worship of any god-Cæsar. And to the best of his ability he held to his covenants with his God. No graven images could enter Jerusalem; even the Roman standards with their eagles had to stay outside.

Two divergent lines of thought are traceable in Jewish affairs during these five hundred years. On the right, so to speak, are the high and narrow Jews, the Pharisees, very orthodox, very punctilious upon even the minutest details of the law, intensely patriotic and exclusive. Jerusalem on one occasion fell to the Seleucid monarch Antiochus IV because the Jews would not defend it on the Sabbath day, when it is forbidden to work; and it was because the Jews made no effort to destroy his siege train on the Sabbath that Pompey the Great was able to take Jerusalem.

But against these narrow Jews were pitted the broad Jews, the Jews of the left, who were Hellenizers, among whom are to be ranked the Sadducees, who did not believe in immortality. These latter Jews, the broad Jews, were all more or less disposed to mingle with and assimilate themselves to the Greeks and Hellenized peoples about them. They were ready to accept proselytes, and so to share God and his promise with all mankind. But what they gained in generosity they lost in rectitude. They were the worldlings of Judea. We have already noted how the Hellenized Jews of Egypt lost their Hebrew, and had to have their Bible translated into Greek.

In the reign of Tiberius Cæsar a great teacher arose out of Judea who was to liberate the intense realization of the righteousness and unchallengeable oneness of God, and of man's moral obligation to God, which was the strength of orthodox Judaism, from that greedy and exclusive narrowness with which it was so extraordinarily intermingled in the Jewish mind. This was Jesus of Nazareth, the seed rather than the founder of Christianity.

§ 2

The audience to which this book will first be presented will be largely an audience of Christians, with perhaps a sprinkling of Jewish readers, and the former at least will regard Jesus of Nazareth as being much more than a human teacher, and his appearance in the world not as a natural event in history, but as something of a supernatural sort, interrupting and changing that steady development of life towards a common consciousness and a common will, which we have hitherto been tracing in this book. But these persuasions, dominant as they are in Europe and America, are nevertheless not the persuasions of all men or of the great majority of mankind, and we are writing this outline of the story of life with as complete an avoidance of controversial matter as may be. We are trying to write as if this book was to be read as much by Hindus or Moslems or Buddhists as by Americans and Western Europeans. We shall, therefore, hold closely to the apparent facts, and avoid, without any disputation or denial, the theological interpretations that have been imposed upon them.

We shall tell what men have believed about Jesus of Nazareth, but him we shall treat as being what he appeared to be, a man, just as a painter must needs paint him as a man. The documents that testify to his acts and teachings we shall treat as ordinary human documents. If the light of divinity shine through our recital, we will neither help nor hinder it. This is what we have already done in the case of Buddha, and what we shall do later with Muhammad. About Jesus we have to write not theology but history, and our concern is not with the spiritual and theological significance of his life, but with its effects upon the political and everyday life of men.

Almost our only resources of information about the personality of Jesus are derived from the four Gospels, all of which were certainly in existence a few decades after his death, and from allusions to his life in the letters (epistles) of the early Christian propagandists. The first three Gospels, the Gospels of Matthew, Mark, and Luke, many suppose to be derived from some earlier documents; the Gospel of St. John has more idiosyncrasy and is coloured by theology of a strongly Hellenic type. Critics are disposed to regard the Gospel of St. Mark as being the most trustworthy account of the personality and actual words of Jesus. But all four agree in giving us a picture of a very definite personality; they carry the same conviction of reality that the early accounts of Buddha do. In spite of miraculous and incredible additions, one is obliged to say, "Here was a man. This part of the tale could not have been invented."

But just as the personality of Gautama Buddha has been distorted and obscured by the stiff squatting figure, the gilded idol of later Buddhism, so one feels that the lean and strenuous personality of Jesus is much wronged by the unreality and conventionality that a mistaken reverence has imposed upon his figure in modern

Christian art. Jesus was a penniless teacher, who wandered about the dusty sun-bit country of Judea, living upon casual gifts of food; yet he is always represented clean, combed, and sleek, in spotless raiment, erect, and with something motionless about him as though he was gliding through the air. This alone has made him unreal and incredible to many people who cannot distinguish the core of the story from the ornamental and unwise additions of the unintelligently devout.

And it may be that the early parts of the Gospels are accretions of the same nature. The miraculous circumstances of the birth of Jesus, the great star that brought wise men from the east to worship at his manger cradle, the massacre of the male infant children in the region of Bethlehem by Herod as a consequence of these portents, and the flight into Egypt, are all supposed to be such accretionary matter by many authorities. At the best they are events unnecessary to the teaching, and they rob it of much of the strength and power it possesses when we strip it of such accompaniment. So, too, do the discrepant genealogies given by Matthew and Luke, in which there is an endeavour to trace the direct descent of Joseph, his father, from King David, as though it was any honour to Jesus or to anyone to have such a man as an ancestor. The insertion of these genealogies is the more peculiar and unreasonable, because, according to the legend, Jesus was not the son of Joseph at all, but miraculously conceived.

We are left, if we do strip this record of these difficult accessories, with the figure of a being, very human, very earnest and passionate, capable of swift anger, and teaching a new and simple and profound doctrine—namely, the universal, loving Fatherhood of God and the coming of the Kingdom of Heaven. He was clearly a person—to use a common phrase—of intense personal magnetism. He attracted followers and filled them with love and courage. Weak and ailing people were heartened and healed by his presence. Yet he was probably of a delicate physique, because of the swiftness with which he died under the pains of crucifixion. There is a tradition that he fainted when, according to the custom, he was made to bear his cross to the place of execution. When he first appeared as a teacher he was a man of about thirty. He went about the country for three years spreading his doctrine, and then he came to Jerusalem and was accused of trying to set up a strange kingdom in Judea; he was tried upon this charge, and crucified together with two thieves. Long before these two were dead, his sufferings were over.

Now, it is a matter of fact that in the Gospels that body of theological assertion which constitutes doctrinal Christianity finds very qualified support. There is, as the reader may see for himself, no sustained and emphatic assertion in these books of several of the doctrines which Christian teachers of all denominations find generally necessary to salvation. The Gospel support for them is often allusive and indirect. It has to be hunted for and argued about. Except for a few disputed passages it is difficult to get any words actually ascribed to Jesus in which he explained the doctrine of the Atonement or urged any sacrifices or sacraments (that is to say, priestly offices) upon his followers. We shall see presently how, later on, all Christendom was torn by disputes about the Trinity. There is no clear evidence that the apostles of Jesus entertained that doctrine. Nor does he give his claim to be the "Christ" or his participation in the godhead any such prominence as one feels would have been done had he considered it a matter of primary significance. Most astounding is the statement (Matt. xvi. 20), "Then charged he his disciples that they should tell no man that he was Jesus the Christ"! It is difficult to understand this suppression if we suppose he considered this fact was essential to salvation.

The observance of the Jewish Sabbath, again, transferred to the Mithraic Sun-day, is an important feature of many Christian cults; but Jesus deliberately broke the Sabbath, and said that it was made for man, and not man for the Sabbath. He did not say a word about the worship of his mother Mary in the guise of Isis, the Queen of Heaven. Much that is most characteristically Christian in worship and usage, he ignored. Sceptical writers have had the temerity to deny that Jesus can be called a Christian at all. For light upon these extraordinary gaps in his teaching, each reader must go to his own religious guides. Here we are bound to mention these gaps on account of the difficulties and controversies that arose out of them, and we are equally bound not to enlarge upon them.

As remarkable is the enormous prominence given by Jesus to the teaching of what he called the Kingdom of Heaven, and its comparative insignificance in the procedure and teaching of most of the Christian churches.

This doctrine of the Kingdom of Heaven, which was the main teaching of Jesus, and which plays so small a part in the Christian creeds, is certainly one of the most revolutionary doctrines that ever stirred and changed human thought. It is small wonder if the world of that time failed to grasp its full significance, and recoiled in dismay from even a half-apprehension of its tremendous challenges to the established habits and institutions of mankind. It is small wonder if the hesitating convert and disciple presently went back to the old familiar ideas of temple and altar, of fierce deity and propitiatory observance, of consecrated priest and magic blessing, and—these things being attended to—reverted then to the dear old habitual life of hates and profits and competition and pride. For the doctrine of the Kingdom of Heaven, as Jesus seems to have preached it, was no less than a bold and uncompromising demand for a complete change and cleansing of the life of our struggling race, an utter cleansing without and within. To the Gospels the reader must go for all that is preserved of this tremendous teaching; here we are only concerned with the jar of its impact upon established ideas.

The Jews were persuaded that God, the one God of the whole world, was a righteous god, but they also thought of him as a trading god who had made a bargain with their Father Abraham about them, a very good bargain indeed for them, to bring them at last to predominance in the earth. With dismay and anger they heard Jesus sweeping away their dear securities. God, he taught, was no bargainer; there were no chosen people and no favourites in the Kingdom of Heaven. God was the loving father of all life, as incapable of showing favours as the universal sun. And all men were brothers—sinners alike and beloved sons alike—of this divine father. In the parable of the Good Samaritan Jesus cast scorn upon that natural tendency we all obey, to glorify our own people and to minimize the righteousness of other creeds and other races. In the parable of the labourers he thrust aside the obstinate claim of the Jews to have a sort of first mortgage upon God. All whom God takes into the kingdom, he taught, God serves alike; there is no distinction in his treatment, because there is no measure to his bounty. From all, moreover, as the parable of the buried talent witnesses, and as the incident of the widow's mite enforces, he demands the utmost. There are no privileges, no rebates, and no excuses in the Kingdom of Heaven.

But it was not only the intense tribal patriotism of the Jews that Jesus outraged. They were a people of intense family loyalty, and he would have swept away all the narrow and restrictive family affections in the great flood of the love of God. The whole Kingdom of Heaven was to be the family of his followers. We are told that, "While he yet talked to the people, behold, his mother and his brethren stood without, desiring to speak with him. Then one said unto him, Behold, thy mother and thy brethren stand without, desiring to speak with thee. But he answered and said unto him that told him, who is my mother? and who are my brethren? And he stretched forth his hand towards his disciples, and said, Behold my mother and my brethren! For whosoever shall do the will of my Father which is in heaven, the same is my brother, and sister, and mother."[1]

And not only did Jesus strike at patriotism and the bonds of family loyalty in the name of God's universal fatherhood and the brotherhood of all mankind, but it is clear that his teaching condemned all the gradations of the economic system, all private wealth and personal advantages. All men belonged to the kingdom; all their possessions belonged to the kingdom; the righteous life for all men, the only righteous life, was the service of God's will with all that we had, with all that we were. Again and again he denounced private riches and the reservation of any private life.

"And when he was gone forth into the way, there came one running, and kneeled to him, and asked him, Good master, what shall I do that I may inherit eternal life? And Jesus said unto him, Why callest thou me good? there is none good but one, that is, God. Thou knowest the commandments, Do not commit adultery, Do not kill, Do not steal, Do not bear false witness, Defraud not, Honour thy father and mother. And he answered and said unto him, Master, all these things have I observed from my youth. Then Jesus beholding him loved him, and said unto him, One thing thou lackest: go thy way, sell whatsoever thou hast, and give to the poor, and thou shalt have treasure in heaven: and come take up the cross, and follow me. And he was sad at that saying, and went away grieved: for he had great possessions.

"And Jesus looked round about, and saith unto his disciples, How hardly shall they that have riches enter into the kingdom of God! And the disciples were astonished at his words. But Jesus answered again, and saith unto them, Children, how hard is it for them that trust in riches to enter into the kingdom of God! It is easier for a camel to go through the eye of a needle, than for a rich man to enter into the kingdom of God."[2]

Moreover, in his tremendous prophecy of this kingdom which

---

1 Matt. xii. 46–50.

2 Mark x. 17–25.

was to make all men one together in God, Jesus had small patience for the bargaining righteousness of formal religion. Another large part of his recorded utterances is aimed against the meticulous observance of the rules of the pious career. "Then came together unto him the Pharisees, and certain of the scribes, which came from Jerusalem. And when they saw some of his disciples eat bread with defiled, that is to say, with unwashen, hands, they found fault. For the Pharisees, and all the Jews, except they wash their hands oft, eat not, holding the tradition of the elders. And when they come from the market, except they wash, they eat not. And many other things there be, which they have received to hold, as the washing of cups, and pots, brazen vessels, and of tables. Then the Pharisees and scribes asked him, Why walk not thy disciples according to the tradition of the elders, but eat bread with unwashen hands? He answered and said unto them, Well hath Isaiah prophesied of you hypocrites, as it is written,

"This people honoureth me with their lips,
"But their heart is far from me.
"Howbeit, in vain do they worship me,
"Teaching for doctrines the commandments of men.

"For laying aside the commandment of God, ye hold the tradition of men, as the washing of pots and cups: and many other such things ye do. And he said unto them, Full well ye reject the commandment of God, that ye may keep your own tradition."[1]

So, too, we may note a score of places in which he flouted that darling virtue of the formalist, the observance of the Sabbath.

It was not merely a moral and social revolution that Jesus proclaimed; it is clear from a score of indications that his teaching had a political bent of the plainest sort. It is true that he said his kingdom was not of this world, that it was in the hearts of men and not upon the throne; but it is equally clear that wherever and in what measure his kingdom was set up in the hearts of men, the outer world would be in that measure revolutionized and made new.

Whatever else the deafness and blindness of his hearers may have missed in his utterances, it is plain that they did not miss his resolve to revolutionize the world. Some of the questions that were brought to Jesus and the answers he gave enable us to guess at the drift of much of his unrecorded teaching. The directness of

---

[1] Mark vii. 1–9.

his political attack is manifest by such an incident as that of the coin—

"And they send unto him certain of the Pharisees and of the Herodians, to catch him in his words. And when they were come, they say unto him, Master, we know that thou art true, and carest for no man: for thou regardest not the person of men, but teachest the way of God in truth: Is it lawful to give tribute to Cæsar, or not? Shall we give, or shall we not give? But he, knowing their hypocrisy, said unto them, Why tempt ye me? Bring me a penny, that I may see it. And they brought it. And he saith unto them, Whose is this image and superinscription? And they said unto him, Cæsar's. And Jesus answering said unto them, Render to Cæsar the things that are Cæsar's, and to God the things that are God's"[1] —which, in view of all else that he had taught, left very little of a man or his possessions for Cæsar.

The whole tenor of the opposition to him and the circumstances of his trial and execution show clearly that to his contemporaries he seemed to propose plainly, and did propose plainly, to change and fuse and enlarge all human life. But even his disciples did not grasp the profound and comprehensive significance of that proposal. They were ridden by the old Jewish dream of a king, a Messiah to overthrow the Hellenized Herods and the Roman overlord, and restore the fabled glories of David. They disregarded the substance of his teaching, plain and direct though it was: evidently they thought it was merely his mysterious and singular way of setting about the adventure that would at last put him on the throne of Jerusalem. They thought he was just another king among the endless succession of kings, but of a quasi-magic kind, and making quasi-magic professions of an impossible virtue.

"And James and John, the sons of Zebedee, come unto him, saying Master, we would that thou shouldest do for us whatsoever we shall desire. And he said unto them, What would ye that I should do for you? They said unto him, Grant unto us that we may sit, one on thy right hand, and the other on thy left hand, in thy glory. But Jesus said unto them, Ye know not what ye ask: can ye drink of the cup that I drink of? and be baptized with the baptism that I am baptized with? And they said unto him, We can. And Jesus said unto them, Ye shall indeed drink of the cup that I drink of; and with the baptism that I am baptized withal shall ye be baptized: but to sit on my right hand and on my

---

[1] Mark xii. 13–17.

left hand is not mine to give; but it shall be given to them for whom it is prepared. And when the ten heard it, they began to be much displeased with James and John. But Jesus called them to him, and saith unto them, Ye know that they which are accounted to rule over the Gentiles exercise lordship over them; and their great ones exercise authority upon them. But so shall it not be among you: but whosoever will be great among you, shall be your minister: and whosoever of you will be the chiefest, shall be servant of all. For even the Son of man came not be ministered unto, but to minister, and to give his life a ransom for many."[1]

This was cold comfort for those who looked for a due reward for their services and hardships in his train. They could not believe this hard doctrine of a kingdom of service which was its own exceeding great reward. Even after his death upon the cross, they could still, after their first dismay, revert to the belief that he was nevertheless in the vein of the ancient world of pomps and privileges; that presently by some amazing miracle he would become undead again and return, and set up his throne with much splendour and graciousness in Jerusalem. They thought his life was a stratagem and his death a trick.

He was too great for his disciples. And in view of what he plainly said, is it any wonder that all who were rich and prosperous felt a horror of strange things, a swimming of their world at his teaching? Perhaps the priests and the rulers and the rich men understood him better than his followers. He was dragging out all the little private reservations they had made from social service into the light of a universal religious life. He was like some terrible moral huntsman digging mankind out of the snug burrows in which they had lived hitherto. In the white blaze of this kingdom of his there was to be no property, no privilege, no pride and precedence; no motive indeed and no reward but love. Is it any wonder that men were dazzled and blinded and cried out against him? Even his disciples cried out when he would not spare them the light. Is it any wonder that the priests realized that between this man and themselves there was no choice but that he or priestcraft should perish? Is it any wonder that the Roman soldiers, confronted and amazed by something soaring over their comprehension and threatening all their disciplines, should take refuge in wild laughter, and crown him with thorns and robe him in purple and make a mock Cæsar of

[1] Mark x. 35–45.

him? For to take him seriously was to enter upon a strange and alarming life, to abandon habits, to control instincts and impulses, to essay an incredible happiness. . . .

Is it any wonder that to this day this Galilean is too much for our small hearts?

§ 3

Yet be it noted that while there was much in the real teachings of Jesus that a rich man or a priest or a trader or an imperial official or any ordinary respectable citizen could not accept without the most revolutionary changes in his way of living, yet there was nothing that a follower of the actual teaching of Gautama Sakya might not receive very readily, nothing to prevent a primitive Buddhist from being also a Nazarene, and nothing to prevent a personal disciple of Jesus from accepting all the recorded teachings of Buddha.

Again, consider the tone of this extract from the writings of a Chinaman, Mo Ti, who lived somewhen in the fourth century B.C., when the doctrines of Confucius and of Lao Tse prevailed in China, before the advent of Buddhism to that country, and note how "Nazarene" it is.

"The mutual attacks of state on state; the mutual usurpations of family on family; the mutual robberies of man on man; the want of kindness on the part of the sovereign and of loyalty on the part of the minister; the want of tenderness and filial duty between father and son—these, and such as these, are the things injurious to the empire. All this has arisen from want of mutual love. If but that one virtue could be made universal, the princes loving one another would have no battle-fields; the chiefs of families would attempt no usurpations; men would commit no robberies; rulers and ministers would be gracious and loyal; fathers and sons would be kind and filial; brothers would be harmonious and easily reconciled. Men in general loving one another, the strong would not make prey of the weak; the many would not plunder the few, the rich would not insult the poor, the noble would not be insolent to the mean; and the deceitful would not impose upon the simple."[1]

This is extraordinarily like the teaching of Jesus of Nazareth cast into political terms. The thoughts of Mo Ti came close to the Kingdom of Heaven.

---

[1] Hirth, *The Ancient History of China*, chap. viii.

This essential identity is the most important historical aspect of these great world religions. They were in their beginnings quite unlike the priest, altar and temple cults, those cults for the worship of definite finite gods that played so great and so essential a part in the earlier stages of man's development between 15,000 B.C. and 600 B.C. These new world religions, from 600 B.C. onward, were essentially religions of the heart and of the universal sky. They swept away all those various and limited gods that had served the turn of human needs since the first communities were welded together by fear and hope. And presently when we come to Islam we shall find that for a third time the same fundamental new doctrine of the need of a universal devotion of all men to one Will reappears. Warned by the experiences of Christianity, Muhammad was very emphatic in insisting that he himself was merely a man, and so saved his teaching from much corruption and misrepresentation.

We speak of these great religions of mankind which arose between the Persian conquest of Babylon and the break-up of the Roman Empire as rivals; but it is their defects, their accumulations and excrescences, their differences of language and phrase, that cause the rivalry; and it is not to one overcoming the other or to any new variant replacing them that we must look, but to the white truth in each being burnt free from its dross, and becoming manifestly the same truth—namely, that the hearts of men, and therewith all the lives and institutions of men, must be subdued to one common Will ruling them all. "St. Paul," says Dean Inge in one of his *Outspoken Essays*, "understood what most Christians never realize, namely, that the Gospel of Christ is not *a* religion, but religion itself in its most universal and deepest significance."

And though much has been written foolishly about the antagonism of science and religion, there is, indeed, no such antagonism. What all these world religions declare by inspiration and insight, history as it grows clearer, and science as its range extends, display, as a reasonable and demonstrable fact, that men form one universal brotherhood, that they spring from one common origin, that their individual lives, their nations and races, interbreed and blend and go on to merge again at last in one common human destiny upon this little planet amidst the stars. And the psychologist can now stand beside the preacher and assure us that there is no reasoned peace of heart, no balance and no safety in the soul, until a man in losing his life has found it, and has schooled and disciplined his instincts, and narrow affections. The history of our race and personal religious experience run so closely parallel as to seem to a modern observer almost the same thing; both tell of a being at first scattered and blind and utterly confused, feeling its way slowly to the serenity and salvation of an ordered and coherent purpose. That, in the simplest, is the outline of history; whether one have a religious purpose or disavow a religious purpose altogether, the lines of the outline remain the same.

§ 4

In the year A.D. 30, while Tiberius, the second emperor, was Emperor of Rome and Pontius Pilate was procurator of Judea, a little while before the Feast of the Passover, Jesus of Nazareth came into Jerusalem. Probably he came then for the first time. Hitherto he had been preaching chiefly in Galilee, and for the most part round and about the town of Capernaum. In Capernaum he had preached in the synagogue.

His entry into Jerusalem was a pacific triumph. He had gathered a great following in Galilee—he had sometimes to preach from a boat upon the Lake of Galilee, because of the pressure of the crowd upon the shore—and his fame had spread before him to the capital. Great crowds came out to greet him. It is clear they did not understand the drift of his teaching, and that they shared the general persuasion that by some magic of righteousness he was going to overthrow the established order. He rode into the city upon the foal of an ass that had been borrowed by his disciples. The crowd accompanied him with cries of triumph and shouts of "Hosanna," a word of rejoicing.

He went to the temple. Its outer courts were cumbered with the tables of money-changers and with the stalls of those who sold doves to be liberated by pious visitors to the temple. These traders upon religion he and his followers cast out, overturning the tables. It was almost his only act of positive rule.

Then for a week he taught in Jerusalem, surrounded by a crowd of followers who made his arrest by the authorities difficult. Then officialdom gathered itself together against this astonishing intruder. One of his disciples, Judas, dismayed and disappointed at the apparent ineffectiveness of this capture of Jerusalem, went to the Jewish priests to give them his advice and help in the arrest of Jesus. For this service he was rewarded with thirty pieces of silver. The high priest and the Jews generally had many reasons for dismay at this gentle insurrection that was filling the streets with excited crowds; for example, the Romans might misunderstand it or use it as an occasion to do some mischief to the whole Jewish people. Accordingly the high priest Caiaphas, in his anxiety to show his loyalty to the Roman overlord, was the leader in the proceedings against this unarmed Messiah, and the priests and the orthodox mob of Jerusalem were the chief accusers of Jesus.

How he was arrested in the garden of Gethsemane, how he was tried and sentenced by Pontius Pilate, the Roman procurator, how he was scourged and mocked by the Roman soldiers, and crucified upon the hill called Golgotha, is told with unsurpassable dignity in the Gospels.

The revolution collapsed utterly. The disciples of Jesus with one accord deserted him, and Peter, being taxed as one of them, said, "I know not the man." This was not the end they had anticipated in their great coming to Jerusalem. His last hours of aching pain and thirst upon the cross were watched only by a few women and near friends. Towards the end of the long day of suffering this abandoned leader roused himself to one supreme effort, cried out with a loud voice, "My God! my God! why hast thou forsaken me?" and—leaving these words to echo down the ages, a perpetual riddle to the faithful—died.

It was inevitable that simple believers should have tried to enhance the stark terrors of this tragedy by foolish stories of physical disturbances similar to those which had been invented to emphasize the conversion of Gautama. We are told that a great darkness fell upon the earth, and that the veil of the temple was rent in twain; but if, indeed, these things occurred, they produced not the slightest effect upon the minds of people in Jerusalem at that time. It is difficult to believe nowadays that the order of nature indulged in any such meaningless comments. Far more tremendous is it to suppose a world apparently indifferent to those three crosses in the red evening twilight, and to the little group of perplexed and desolated watchers. The darkness closed upon the hill; the distant city set about its preparations for the Passover; scarcely anyone but that knot of mourners on the way to their homes troubled whether Jesus of Nazareth was still dying or already dead. . . .

The souls of the disciples were plunged for a time into utter darkness. Then presently came a whisper among them and stories, rather discrepant stories, that the body of Jesus was not in the tomb in which it had been placed, and that first one and then another had seen him alive. Soon they were consoling themselves with the conviction that he had risen from the dead, that he had shown himself to many, and had ascended visibly into heaven. Witnesses were found to declare that they had positively seen him go up, visibly in his body. He had gone through the blue—to God. Soon they had convinced themselves that he would presently come again, in power and glory, to judge all mankind. In a little while, they said, he would come back to them; and in these bright revivals of their old-time dream of an assertive and temporal splendour they forgot the greater measure, the giant measure, he had given them of the Kingdom of God.

§ 5

The story of the early beginnings of Christianity is the story of the struggle between the real teachings and spirit of Jesus of Nazareth and the limitations, amplifications, and misunderstandings of the very inferior men who had loved and followed him from Galilee, and who were now the bearers and custodians of his message to mankind. The Gospels and the Acts of the Apostles present a patched and uneven record, but there can be little question that on the whole it is a quite honest record of those early days.

The early Nazarenes, as the followers of Jesus were called, present from the first a spectacle of a great confusion between these two strands, his teaching, on the one hand, and the glosses and interpretations of the disciples on the other. They continued for a time his disciplines of the complete subjugation of self; they had their goods in common, they had no bond but love. Nevertheless, they built their faith upon the stories that were told of his resurrection and magical ascension, and the promised return. Few of them understood that the renunciation of self is its own reward, that it is itself the Kingdom of Heaven; they regarded it as a sacrifice that entitled them to the compensation of power and dominion when presently the second coming occurred. They had now all identified Jesus with the promised Christ, the Messiah so long expected by the Jewish people. They found out prophecies of the crucifixion in the prophets—the Gospel of Matthew is particularly insistent upon these prophecies. Revived by these hopes, enforced by the sweet and pure lives of many of the believers, the Nazarene doctrine began to spread very rapidly in Judea and Syria.

And presently there arose a second great teacher, whom many modern authorities regard as the real founder of Christianity —Saul of Tarsus, or Paul. Saul, apparently, was his Jewish and Paul his Roman name; he was a Roman citizen, and a man of much wider education and a much narrower intellectuality than Jesus seems to have been. By birth he was probably a Jew, though some Jewish writers deny this; he had certainly studied under Jewish teachers. But he was well versed in the Hellenic theologies of Alexandria, and his language was Greek. Some classical scholars profess to find his Greek unsatisfactory; he did not use the Greek of Athens, but the Greek of Alexandria, but he used it with power and freedom. Professor Gilbert Murray calls it "very good." "He is affected by the philosophical jargon of the Hellenistic schools and by that of Stoicism. But his mastery of sublime language is amazing." He was a religious theorist and teacher long before he heard of Jesus of Nazareth, and he appears in the New Testament narrative, at first, as the bitter critic, antagonist, and active persecutor of the Nazarenes.

The present writer has been unable to find any discussion of the religious ideas of Paul before he became a follower of Jesus. They must have been a basis, if only a basis of departure, for his new views, and their phraseology certainly supplied the colour of his new doctrines. We are almost equally in the dark as to the teachings of Gamaliel, who is named as the Jewish teacher at whose feet he sat. Nor do we know what Gentile teachings had reached him. It is highly probable that he had been influenced by Mithraism. He uses phrases curiously like Mithraistic phrases. What will be clear to anyone who reads his various Epistles, side by side with the Gospels, is that his mind was saturated by an idea which does not appear at all prominently in the reported sayings and teaching of Jesus, the idea of a sacrificial person who is offered up to God as an atonement for sin. What Jesus preached was a new birth of the human soul; what Paul preached was the ancient religion of priests and altar and the propitiatory bloodshed. Jesus was to him the Easter lamb, that traditional human victim without spot or blemish who haunts all the religions of the dark white peoples. Paul came to the Nazarenes with overwhelming force because he came to them with this completely satisfactory explanation of the disaster of the crucifixion. It was a brilliant elucidation of what had been utterly perplexing.

Paul had never seen Jesus. His knowledge of Jesus and his teaching must have been derived from the hearsay of the original disciples. It is clear that he apprehended much of the spirit of Jesus and his doctrine of a new birth, but he built this into a theological system, a very subtle and ingenious system, whose appeal to this day is chiefly intellectual. And it is clear that the faith of the Nazarenes, which he found as a doctrine of motive and a way of living, he made into a doctrine of *belief*. He found the Nazarenes with a spirit and hope, and he left them Christians with the beginning of a creed.

But we must refer the reader to the Acts of the Apostles and the Pauline Epistles for an account of Paul's mission and teaching. He was a man of enormous energy, and he taught at Jerusalem, Antioch, Athens, Corinth, Ephesus, and Rome.

Possibly he went into Spain. The manner of his death is not certainly known, but it is said that he was killed in Rome during the reign of Nero. A great fire had burnt a large part of Rome, and the new sect was accused of causing this. The rapid spread of Christian teaching certainly owes more to Paul than to any other single man. Within two decades of the crucifixion this new religion was already attracting the attention of the Roman rulers in several provinces. If it had acquired a theology in the hand of Saint Paul, it still retained much of the revolutionary and elementary quality of the teachings of Jesus. It had become somewhat more tolerant of private property; it would accept wealthy adherents without insisting upon the communization of their riches, and Saint Paul has condoned the institution of slavery ("Slaves, be obedient to your masters"), but it still sets its face like flint against certain fundamental institutions of the Roman world. It would not tolerate the godhead of Cæsar; not even by a mute gesture at the altar would the Christians consent to worship the emperor, though their lives were at stake in the matter. It denounced the gladiatorial shows. Unarmed, but possessing enormous powers of passive resistance, Christianity thus appeared at the outset plainly as rebellion, striking at the political if not at the economic essentials of the imperial system. The first evidences of Christianity in non-Christian literature we find when perplexed Roman officials began to write to one another and exchange views upon the strange problem presented by this infectious rebellion of otherwise harmless people.

Much of the history of the Christians in the first two centuries of the Christian era is very obscure. They spread far and wide throughout the world, but we know very little of their ideas or their ceremonies and methods during that time. As yet they had no settled creeds, and there can be little doubt that there were wide local variations in their beliefs and disciplines during this formless period. But whatever their local differences, everywhere they seem to have carried much of the spirit of Jesus; and though everywhere they aroused bitter enmity and active counter-propaganda, the very charges made against them witness to the general goodness of their lives.

During this indefinite time a considerable amount of a sort of theocrasia seems to have gone on between the Christian cult and the almost equally popular and widely diffused Mithraic cult, and the cult of Serapis-Isis-Horus. From the former it would seem the Christians adopted Sun-day as their chief day of worship instead of the Jewish Sabbath, the abundant use of candles in religious ceremonies, the legend of the adoration by the shepherds, and probably, also, those ideas and phrases, so distinctive of certain sects to this day, about being "washed in the blood" of Christ, and of Christ being a blood sacrifice. For we have to remember that a death by crucifixion is hardly a more bloody death than hanging; to speak of Jesus shedding his blood for mankind is really a most inaccurate expression. Even when we remember that he was scourged, that he wore a crown of thorns, and that his side was pierced by a spear, we are still far from a "fountain filled with blood." But Mithraism centred upon some now forgotten mysteries about Mithras sacrificing a sacred and benevolent bull; all the Mithraic shrines seem to have contained a figure of Mithras killing this bull, which bleeds copiously from a wound in its side, and from this blood a new life sprang. The Mithraist votary actually bathed in the blood of the sacrificial bull, and was "born again" thereby. At his initiation he went beneath a scaffolding on which the bull was killed, and the blood ran down on him. Here we seem to be dealing with a survival of the primitive blood sacrifice at seed-time, which was perhaps the primary religious idea of the earliest temple civilizations.

The contributions of the Alexandrine cult to Christian thought and practices were even more considerable. In the personality of Horus, who was at once the son of Serapis and identical with Serapis, it was natural for the Christians to find an illuminating analogue in their struggles with the Pauline mysteries. From that to the identification of Mary with Isis, and her elevation to a rank quasi-divine—in spite of the saying of Jesus about his mother and his brothers that we have already quoted—was also a very natural step. Natural, too, was it for Christianity to adopt, almost insensibly, the practical methods of popular religions of the time. Its priests took on the head-shaving and the characteristic garments of the Egyptian priests, because that sort of thing seemed to be the right way of distinguishing a priest. One accretion followed another. Almost insensibly the originally revolutionary teaching was buried under these customary acquisitions. We have already tried to imagine Gautama Buddha returning to Tibet, and his amazement at the worship of his own image in Lhassa. We will but suggest the parallel amazement of some earnest Nazarene who had known and followed his dusty and travel-worn Master through the dry sunlight of Galilee, restored suddenly to this world and visiting, let us say, a mass in St. Peter's at Rome, at learning that the consecrated wafer upon the altar was none other than his crucified teacher.

Religion in a world community is not many things but one thing, and it was inevitable that all the living religious faiths in the world at the time, and all the philosophy and religious thought that came into contact with Christianity, should come to an account with Christianity and exchanged phrases and ideas. The hopes of the early Nazarenes had identified Jesus with the Christ; the brilliant mind of Paul had surrounded his career with mystical significance. Jesus had called men and women to a giant undertaking, to the renunciation of self, to the new birth into the kingdom of love. The line of least resistance for the flagging convert was to intellectualize himself away from this plain doctrine, this stark proposition, into complicated theories and ceremonies, that would leave his essential self alone. How much easier is it to sprinkle oneself with blood than to purge oneself from malice and competition; to eat bread and drink wine and pretend one had absorbed divinity; to give candles rather than the heart; to shave the head and retain the scheming privacy of the brain inside it! The world was full of such evasive philosophy and theological stuff in the opening centuries of the Christian era. It is not for us here to enlarge upon the distinctive features of Neoplatonism, Gnosticism, Philonism, and the like teachings which abounded in the Alexandrian world. But it was all one world with that in which the early Christians were living. The writings of such men as Origen, Plotinus, and Augustine witness to the inevitable give and take of the time.

Jesus called himself the Son of God and also the Son of Man; but he laid little stress on who he was or what he was, and much upon the teachings of the Kingdom. In declaring that he was more than a man and divine, Paul and his other followers, whether they were right or wrong, opened up a vast field of argument. Was Jesus God? Or had God created him? Was he identical with God or separate from God? It is not the function of the historian to answer such questions, but he is bound to note them, and to note how unavoidable they were, because of the immense influence they have had upon the whole subsequent life of western mankind. By the fourth century of the Christian Era we find all the Christian communities so agitated and exasperated by tortuous and elusive arguments about the nature of God as to be largely negligent of the simpler teachings of charity, service, and brotherhood that Jesus had inculcated.

The chief views that the historian notices are those of the Arians, the Sabellians, and the Trinitarians. The Arians followed Arius, who taught that Christ was less than God; the Sabellians taught that he was a mode or aspect of God—God was Creator, Saviour, and Comforter, just as one man may be father, trustee, and guest; the Trinitarians, of whom Athanasius was the great leader, taught that the Father, the Son, and the Holy Ghost were three distinct Persons, but one God. The reader is referred to the Athanasian Creed for the exact expression of the latter mystery, and for the alarming consequences to him of any failure to grasp and believe it. To Gibbon he must go for a derisive statement of these controversies. The present writer can deal with them neither with awe nor derision; they seem to him, he must confess, a disastrous ebullition of the human mind entirely inconsistent with the plain account of Jesus preserved for us in the Gospels. Orthodoxy became a test not only for Christian office, but for Christian trade and help. A small point of doctrine might mean affluence or beggary to a man. It is difficult to read the surviving literature of the time without a strong sense of the dogmatism, the spites, rivalries, and pedantries of the men who tore Christianity to pieces for the sake of these theological refinements. Most of the Trinitarian disputants—for it is chiefly Trinitarian documents that survive—accuse their antagonists, probably with truth, of mean and secondary motives, but they do so in a manner that betrays their own base spirit very clearly.

Arius, for example, is accused of adopting heretical opinions because he was not appointed Bishop of Alexandria. Riots and excommunications and banishments punctuated these controversies, and finally came official persecutions. These fine differences about the constitution of the Deity interwove with politics and international disputes. Men who quarrelled over business affairs, wives who wished to annoy their husbands, developed antagonistic views upon this exalted theme. Most of the barbarian invaders of the empire were Arians; probably because their simple minds found the Trinitarian position incomprehensible.

It is easy for the sceptic to mock at these disputes. But even if we think that these attempts to say exactly how God was related to himself were presumptuous and intellectually monstrous—nevertheless we are bound to recognize that beneath these preposterous refinements of impossible dogmas there lay often a real passion for truth—even if it was truth ill conceived. Both sides produced genuine martyrs. And the zeal of these controversies, though it is a base and often malicious zeal, did at any rate make the Christian sects very energetically propagandist and educational. Moreover, because the history of the Christian body in the fourth and fifth centuries is largely a record of these unhappy disputes, that must not blind us to the fact that the spirit of Jesus did live and ennoble many lives among the Christians. The text of the Gospels, though it was probably tampered with during this period, was not destroyed, and Jesus of Nazareth, in his own manifest inimitable greatness, still taught through that text. Nor did these unhappy quarrels prevent Christianity from maintaining a united front against gladiatorial shows and against the degrading worship of idols and of the god-Cæsar.

§ 6

So far as it challenged the divinity of Cæsar and the characteristic institutions of the empire, Christianity is to be regarded as a rebellious and disintegrating movement, and so it was regarded by most of the emperors before Constantine the Great. It encountered considerable hostility, and at last systematic attempts to suppress it. Decius was the first emperor to organize an official persecution, and the great era of the martyrs was in the time of Diocletian (303 and following years). The persecution of Diocletian was, indeed, the crowning struggle of the old idea of the god-emperor against the already great and powerful organization that denied his divinity. Diocletian had reorganized the monarchy upon lines of extreme absolutism; he had abolished the last vestiges of republican institutions; he was the first emperor to surround himself completely with the awe-inspiring etiquette of an eastern monarch. He was forced by the logic of his assumptions to attempt the complete eradication of a system that flatly denied them. The tests in the persecution was that the Christian was required to offer sacrifice to the emperor.

"Though Diocletian, still averse to the effusion of blood, had moderated the fury of Galerius, who proposed that everyone refusing to offer sacrifice should immediately be burnt alive, the penalties inflicted on the obstinacy of the Christians might be deemed sufficiently rigorous and effectual. It was enacted that their churches, in all the provinces of the empire, should be demolished to their foundations; and the punishment of death was denounced against all who should presume to hold any secret assemblies for the purpose of religious worship. The philosophers, who now assumed the unworthy office of directing the blind zeal of persecution, had diligently studied the nature and genius of the Christian religion; and as they were not ignorant that the speculative doctrines of the faith were supposed to be contained in the writings of the prophets, of the evangelists, and of the apostles, they most probably suggested the order that the bishops and presbyters should deliver all their sacred books into the hands of the magistrates, who were commanded, under the severest penalties, to burn them in a public and solemn manner. By the same edict, the property of the church was at once confiscated; and the several parts of which it might consist were either sold to the highest bidder, united to the imperial domain, bestowed on the cities or corporations, or granted to the solicitations of rapacious courtiers. After taking such effectual measures to abolish the worship, and to dissolve the government of the Christians, it was thought necessary to subject to the most intolerable hardships the condition of those perverse individuals who should still reject the religion of nature, of Rome and of their ancestors. Persons of liberal birth were declared incapable of holding any honours or employments; slaves were for ever deprived of the hopes of freedom; and the whole body of the Christians were put out of the protection of the law. The judges were authorized to hear and to determine every action that was brought against a Christian; but the Christians were not permitted to complain of any injury which they themselves had suffered; and those unfortunate sectaries were exposed to the severity, while they were excluded from the benefits, of public justice. . . . This edict was scarcely exhibited to the public view, in the most conspicuous place in Nicomedia, before it was torn down by the hands of a Christian, who expressed at the same time, by the bitterest of invectives, his contempt as well as abhorrence for such impious and tyrannical governors. His offence, according to the mildest laws, amounted to treason and deserved death, and if it be true that he was a person of rank and education, those circumstances could serve only to aggravate his guilt. He was burnt, or rather roasted, by a slow fire; and his executioners, zealous to revenge the personal insult which had been offered to the emperors, exhausted every refinement of cruelty without being able to subdue his patience, or to alter the steady and insulting smile which in his dying agonies he still preserved in his countenance."[1]

So with the death of this unnamed martyr the great persecution opened. But, as Gibbon points out, our information as to its severity is of very doubtful value. He estimates the total of victims as about two thousand, and contrasts this with the known multitudes of Christians martyred by their fellow-Christians during the period of the Reformation. Gibbon was strongly prejudiced against Christianity, and here he seems disposed to minimize the fortitude and sufferings of the Christians. In many provinces, no doubt, there must have been a great reluctance to enforce the edict. But there was a hunt for the copies of Holy Writ, and in many places a systematic destruction of Christian churches. There were tortures and executions, as well as a great crowding of the gaols with Christian presbyters and bishops. We have to remember that the Christian community was now a very considerable element of the population, and that an influential proportion of the officials charged with the execution of the edict were themselves of the proscribed faith. Galerius, who was in control of the eastern provinces, was among the most vigorous of the persecutors, but in the end, on his death-bed (311), he realized the futility of his attacks upon this huge community, and granted toleration in an edict the gist of which Gibbon translates as follows:—

"Among the important cares which have occupied our mind for the utility and preservation of the empire, it was our intention

[1] Gibbon. *The Decline and Fall of the Roman Empire*, chap. xvi.

to correct and re-establish all things according to the ancient laws and public discipline of the Romans. We were particularly desirous of reclaiming into the way of reason and nature the deluded Christians who had renounced the religion and ceremonies instituted by their fathers; and presumptuously despising the practice of antiquity, had invented extravagant laws and opinions according to the dictates of their fancy, and had collected a various society from the different provinces of our empire. The edicts which we have published to enforce the worship of the gods having exposed many of the Christians to danger and distress, many having suffered death, and many more who still persist in their impious folly being left destitute of any public exercise of religion, we are disposed to extend to those unhappy men the effects of our wonted clemency. We permit them, therefore, freely to profess their private opinions and to assemble in their conventicles without fear or molestation, provided always that they preserve a due respect to the established laws and government. By another rescript we shall signify our intentions to the judges and magistrates; and we hope that our indulgence will engage the Christians to offer up their prayers to the deity whom they adore, for our safety and prosperity, for their own, and for that of the republic."

In a few years Constantine the Great was reigning, first as associated emperor (312) and then as the sole ruler (324), and the severer trials of Christianity were over. If Christianity was a rebellious and destructive force towards a pagan Rome, it was a unifying and organizing force within its own communion. This fact the genius of Constantine grasped. The spirit of Jesus, for all the doctrinal dissensions that prevailed, made a great freemasonry throughout and even beyond the limits of the empire. The faith was spreading among the barbarians beyond the border; it had extended into Persia and Central Asia. It provided the only hope of moral solidarity he could discern in the great welter of narrow views and self-seeking over which he had to rule. It, and it alone, had the facilities for organizing *will*, for the need of which the empire was falling to pieces like a piece of rotten cloth. In 312 Constantine had to fight for Rome and his position against Maxentius. He put the Christian monogram upon the shields and banners of his troops, and claimed that the God of the Christians had fought for him in his complete victory at the battle of the Milvian Bridge, just outside Rome. By this act he renounced all those pretensions to divinity that the vanity of Alexander the Great had first brought into the western world, and with the applause and enthusiastic support of the Christians he established himself as a monarch more absolute even than Diocletian.

In a few years' time Christianity had become the official religion of the empire, and in A.D. 337 Constantine upon his deathbed was baptized a Christian.

§ 7

The figure of Constantine the Great is at least as cardinal in history as that of Alexander the Great or Augustus Cæsar. We know very little of his personality or his private life; no Plutarch, no Suetonius, has preserved any intimate and living details about him. Abuse we have of him from his enemies, and much obviously fulsome panegyric to set against it; but none of these writers give us a living character of him, he is a party symbol for them, a partisan flag. It is stated by the hostile Zosimus that, like Sargon I, he was of illegitimate birth; his father was a distinguished general and his mother, Helena, an innkeeper's daughter of Nish in Serbia. Gibbon, however, is of opinion that there was a valid marriage. In any case it was a lowly marriage, and the personal genius of Constantine prevailed against serious disadvantages. He was comparatively illiterate, he knew little or no Greek. It appears to be true that he banished his eldest son Crispus, and caused him to be executed at the instigation of the young man's stepmother, Fausta; and it is also recorded that he was afterwards convinced of the innocence of Crispus, and caused Fausta to be executed—according to one account by being boiled to death in her bath, and according to another by being exposed naked to wild beasts on a desolate mountain—while there is also very satisfactory documentary evidence that she survived him. If she was executed, the fact remains that her three sons, together with two nephews, became the appointed heirs of Constantine. Clearly there is nothing solid to be got from this libellous tangle, and such *soufflé* as is possible with these scanty materials is to be found admirably done by Gibbon (chap. xviii). Gibbon, because of his anti-Christian animus, is hostile to Constantine; but he admits that he was temperate and chaste. He accuses him of prodigality because of his great public buildings, and of being vain and dissolute (!) because in his old age he wore a wig—Gibbon wore his own hair tied with a becoming black bow —and a diadem and magnificent robes. But all the later emperors after Diocletian wore diadems and magnificent robes.

Yet if the personality of Constantine the Great remains phantom-like, if the particulars of his domestic life reveal nothing but a vague tragedy, we can still guess at much that was in his mind. It must, in the closing years of his life, have been a very lonely mind. He was more of an autocrat than any previous emperor had been—that is to say, he had less counsel and help. No class of public-spirited and trustworthy men remained; no senate nor council shared and developed his schemes. How much he apprehended the geographical weakness of the empire, how far he saw the complete disaster that was now so near, we can only guess. He made his real capital at Nicomedia in Bithynia; Constantinople across the Bosphorus was still being built when he died. Like Diocletian, he seems to have realized the broken-backed outline of his dominions, and to have concentrated his attention on foreign affairs, and more particularly on the affairs of Hungary, South Russia, and the Black Sea. He reorganized all the official machinery of the empire; he gave it a new constitution and sought to establish a dynasty. He was a restless remaker of things; the social confusion he tried to fix by assisting in the development of a caste system. This was following up the work of his great predecessor Diocletian. He tried to make a caste of the peasants and small cultivators, and to restrict them from moving from their holdings. In fact, he sought to make them serfs. The supply of slave labour had fallen off because the empire was no longer an invading but an invaded power; he turned to serfdom as the remedy. His creative efforts necessitated unprecedentedly heavy taxation. All these things point to a lonely and forcible mind. It is in his manifest understanding of the need of some unifying moral force if the empire was to hold together that his claim to originality lies.

It was only after he had turned to Christianity that he seems to have realized the fierce dissensions of the theologians. He made a great effort to reconcile these differences in order to have one uniform and harmonious teaching in the community, and at his initiative a general council of the Church was held at Nicæa, a town near Nicomedia and over against Constantinople, in 325. Eusebius gives a curious account of this strange gathering, over which the emperor, although he was not yet a baptized

Christian, presided. It was not his first council of the Church, for he had already (in 314) presided over a council at Arles. He sat in the middle of the council of Nicæa upon a golden throne, and, as he had little Greek, we must suppose he was reduced to watching the countenances and gestures of the debaters, and listening to their intonations. The council was a stormy one. When old Arius rose to speak, one, Nicholas of Myra, struck him in the face, and afterwards many ran out, thrusting their fingers into their ears in affected horror at the old man's heresies. One is tempted to imagine the great emperor, deeply anxious for the soul of his empire, firmly resolved to end these divisions, bending towards his interpreters to ask them the meaning of the uproar.

The views that prevailed at Nicæa are embodied in the Nicene Creed, a strictly Trinitarian statement, and the emperor sustained the Trinitarian position. But afterwards, when Athanasius bore too hardly upon the Arians, he had him banished from Alexandria; and when the Church at Alexandria would have excommunicated Arius, he obliged it to readmit him to communion.

§ 8

This date, A.D. 325, is a very convenient date in our history. It is the date of the first complete general ("œcumenical") council of the entire Christian world. (That at Arles we have mentioned had been a gathering of only the western half.) It marks the definite entry upon the stage of human affairs of the Christian Church and of Christianity as it is generally understood in the world to-day. It marks the exact definition of Christian teaching by the Nicene Creed.

It is necessary that we should recall the reader's attention to the profound differences between this fully developed Christianity of Nicæa and the teaching of Jesus of Nazareth. All Christians hold that the latter is completely contained in the former, but that is a question outside our province. What is clearly apparent is that the teaching of Jesus of Nazareth was a *prophetic teaching* of the new type that began with the Hebrew prophets. It was not priestly, it had no consecrated temple, and no altar. It had no rites and ceremonies. Its sacrifice was "a broken and a contrite heart." Its only organization was an organization of preachers, and its chief function was the sermon. But the fully fledged Christianity of the fourth century, though it preserved as its nucleus the teachings of Jesus in the Gospels, was mainly a *priestly religion*, of a type already familiar to the world for thousands of years. The centre of its elaborate ritual was an altar, and the essential act of worship the sacrifice, by a consecrated priest, of the Mass. And it had a rapidly developing organization of deacons, priests, and bishops.

But if Christianity had taken on an extraordinary outward resemblance to the cults of Serapis, Ammon, or Bel-Marduk, we must remember that even its priestcraft had certain novel features. Nowhere did it possess any quasi-divine image of God. There was no head temple containing the god, because God was everywhere. There was no holy of holies. Its widespread altars were all addressed to the unseen universal Trinity. Even in its most archaic aspects there was in Christianity something new.

A very important thing for us to note is the rôle played by the emperor in the fixation of Christianity. Not only was the council of Nicæa assembled by Constantine the Great, but all the great councils, the two at Constantinople (381 and 553), Ephesus (431), and Chalcedon (451), were called together by the imperial power. And it is very manifest that in much of the history of Christianity at this time the spirit of Constantine the Great is as evident as, or more evident than, the spirit of Jesus. He was, we have said, a pure autocrat. The last vestiges of Roman republicanism had vanished in the days of Aurelian and Diocletian. To the best of his lights he was trying to remake the crazy empire while there was yet time, and he worked without any councillors, any public opinion, or any sense of the need of such aids and checks. The idea of stamping out all controversy and division, stamping out all thought, by imposing one dogmatic creed upon all believers, is an altogether autocratic idea, it is the idea of the single-handed man who feels that to work at all he must be free from opposition and criticism. The history of the Church under his influence now becomes, therefore, a history of the violent struggles that were bound to follow upon his sudden and rough summons to unanimity. From him the Church acquired the disposition to be authoritative and unquestioned, to develop a centralized organization and run parallel to the empire.

A second great autocrat who presently contributed to the stamping upon Catholic Christianity of a distinctly authoritative character was Theodosius I, Theodosius the Great (379–395). He forbade the unorthodox to hold meetings, handed over all churches to the Trinitarians, and overthrew the heathen temples throughout the empire, and in 390 he caused the great statue of Serapis at Alexandria to be destroyed. There was to be no rivalry, no qualification to the rigid unity of the Church.

Here we cannot tell of the vast internal troubles of the Church, its indigestions of heresy; of Arians and Paulicians, of Gnostics and Manichæans. Had it been less authoritative and more tolerant of intellectual variety, it might perhaps have been a still more powerful body than it became. But, in spite of all these disorders, it did for some time maintain a conception of human unity more intimate and far wider than was ever achieved before. By the fifth century Christendom was already becoming greater, sturdier, and more enduring than any empire had ever been, because it was something not merely imposed upon men, but interwoven with the texture of their minds. It reached out far beyond the utmost limits of the empire, into Armenia, Persia, Abyssinia, Ireland, Germany, India, and Turkestan. "Though made up of widely scattered congregations, it was thought of as one body of Christ, one people of God. This ideal unity found expression in many ways. Intercommunication between the various Christian communities was very active. Christians upon a journey were always sure of a warm welcome and hospitable entertainment from their fellow-disciples. Messengers and letters were sent freely from one church to another. Missionaries and evangelists went continually from place to place. Documents of various kinds, including gospels and apostolic epistles, circulated widely. Thus in various ways the feeling of unity found expression, and the development of widely separated parts of Christendom conformed more or less closely to a common type."[1]

Christendom retained at least the formal tradition of this general unity of spirit until 1054, when the Latin-speaking Western church and the main and original Greek-speaking church, the "Orthodox" church, severed themselves from one another, ostensibly upon the question of adding two words to the creed. The older creed had declared that the "Holy Ghost proceeded from the Father." The Latins wanted to add, and they did add "*Filioque*" (= and from the son), and placed the Greeks out of their communion because they would not follow this lead. But already, as early as the fifth century, the Christians in Eastern Syria, Persia, Central Asia—there were churches at Merv, Herat, and Samarkand—and India had detached themselves on a similar

---

[1] *Encyclopædia Britannica*, art. "Church History," p. 336.

score. These extremely interesting Asiatic Christians are known in history as the Nestorian Church, and their influence extended into China. The Egyptian and Abyssinian churches also detached themselves very early upon similarly inexplicable points. Long before this formal separation of the Latin and Greek-speaking halves of the main Church, however, there was a practical separation following upon the breaking up of the empire. Their conditions diverged from the first. While the Greek-speaking Eastern Empire held together and the emperor at Constantinople remained dominant in the Church, the Latin half of the empire, as we have already told, collapsed, and left the Western church free of any such imperial control.

Moreover, while ecclesiastical authority in the empire of Constantinople was divided between the high-bishops, or patriarchs, of Constantinople, Antioch, Alexandria, and Jerusalem, authority in the West was concentrated in the Patriarch, or Pope, of Rome. The Bishop of Rome had always been recognized as first among the patriarchs, and all these things conspired to justify exceptional pretensions upon his part to the quasi-imperial authority. With the final fall of the Western Empire, he took over the ancient title of *pontifex maximus* which the emperors had held, and so became the supreme sacrificial priest of the Roman tradition. Over the Christians of the West his supremacy was fully recognized, but from the beginning it had to be urged with discretion within the dominions of the Eastern emperor and the jurisdictions of the other four patriarchs.

Ideas of worldly rule by the Church were already prevalent in the fourth century. Saint Augustine, a citizen of Hippo in North Africa, who wrote between 354 and 430, gave expression to the developing political ideas of the Church in his book *The City of God*. *The City of God* leads the mind very directly towards the possibility of making the world into a theological and organized Kingdom of Heaven. The city, as Augustine puts it, is "a spiritual society of the predestined faithful," but the step from that to a political application was not a very wide one. The Church was to be the ruler of the world over all nations, the divinely-led ruling power over a great league of terrestrial states. In later years these ideas developed into a definite political theory and policy. As the barbarian races settled and became Christian, the Pope began to claim an overlordship of their kings. In a few centuries the Pope had become in theory, and to a certain extent in practice, the high priest, censor, judge, and divine monarch of Christendom; his influence extended in the west far beyond the utmost range of the old empire, to Ireland, Norway and Sweden, and over all Germany. For more than a thousand years this idea of the unity of Christendom, of Christendom as a sort of vast Amphictyony, whose members even in wartime were restrained from many extremities by the idea of a common brotherhood and a common loyalty to the Church, dominated Europe. The history of Europe from the fifth century onward to the fifteenth is very largely the history of the failure of this great idea of a divine world government to realize itself in practice.

§ 9

We have already given an account in the previous chapter of the chief irruptions of the barbarian races. We may now, with the help of a map, make a brief review of the political divisions of Europe at the close of the fifth century. No vestige of the Western Empire, the original Roman Empire, remained as a distinct and separate political division. Politically it was completely broken up. Over many parts of Europe a sort of legendary overlordship of the Hellenic Eastern Empire as *the* Empire held its place in men's minds. The emperor at Constantinople was, in theory at least, still emperor.

In Britain, the quite barbaric Teutonic Angles, Saxons and Jutes had conquered the eastern half of England; in the west of the island the Britons still held out, but were gradually being forced back into Wales and Cornwall. The Anglo-Saxons seem to have been among the most ruthless and effective of the barbarian conquerors, for, wherever they prevailed, their language replaced the Keltic or Latin speech—it is not certain which—used by the British. These Anglo-Saxons were as yet not Christianized.

Most of Gaul, Holland, and the Rhineland was under the fairly vigorous, Christianized, and much more civilized kingdom of the Franks. But the Rhone valley was under the separate kingdom of the Burgundians. Spain and some of the south of France were under the rule of the Visigoths, but the Suevi were in possession of the north-west corner of the peninsula.

Of the Vandal kingdom in Africa we have already written; and Italy, still in its population and habits Roman, came under the rule of the Ostrogoths. There was no emperor left in Rome; Theodoric I ruled there as the first of a line of Gothic kings, and his rule extended across the Alps into Pannonia and down the Adriatic to Dalmatia and Serbia.

To the east of the Gothic kingdom the emperors of Constantinople ruled definitely. The Bulgars were still at this time a Mongolian tribe of horse-riding nomads in the region of the Volga; the Aryan Serbs had recently come southward to the

shores of the Black Sea into the original home of the Visigoths; the Turko-Finnish Magyars were not yet in Europe. The Lombards were as yet north of the Danube.

The sixth century was marked by a phase of vigour on the part of the Eastern Empire under the Emperor Justinian (527–565). The Vandal kingdom was recovered in 534; the Goths were expelled from Italy in 553. So soon as Justinian was dead (565), the Lombards descended into Italy and settled in Lombardy, but they left Ravenna, Rome, Southern Italy, and North Africa under the rule of the Eastern Empire.

Such was the political condition of the world in which the idea of Christendom developed. The daily life of that time was going on at a very low level indeed, physically, intellectually, and morally. It is frequently said that Europe in the sixth and seventh centuries relapsed into barbarism, but that does not express the reality of the case. It is far more correct to say that the civilization of the Roman Empire had passed into a phase of extreme demoralization. Barbarism is a social order of an elementary type, orderly within its limits; but the state of Europe beneath its political fragmentation was a social disorder. Its *morale* was not that of a kraal, but that of a slum. In a savage kraal a savage knows that he belongs to a community, and lives and acts accordingly; in a slum, the individual neither knows of nor acts in relation to any greater being.

Only very slowly and weakly did Christianity restore that lost sense of community and teach men to rally about the idea of Christendom. The social and economic structure of the Roman Empire was in ruins. That civilization had been a civilization of wealth and political power sustained by the limitation and slavery of the great mass of mankind. It had presented a spectacle of outward splendour and luxurious refinement, but beneath that brave outward show were cruelty, stupidity, and stagnation. It had to break down, it had to be removed before anything better could replace it.

We have already called attention to its intellectual deadness. For three centuries it had produced neither science nor literature of any importance. It is only where men are to be found neither too rich and powerful to be tempted into extravagant indulgences nor too poor and limited to care for anything beyond the daily need that those disinterested curiosities and serene impulses can have play that give sane philosophy and science and great art to the world, and the plutocracy of Rome had made such a class impossible. When men and women are unlimited and unrestrained, the evidence of history shows clearly that they are all liable to become monsters of self-indulgence; when, on the other hand, they are driven and unhappy, then their impulse is towards immoderate tragical resorts, towards wild revolts or towards the austerities and intensities of religion.

It is not, perhaps, true to say that the world became miserable in these "dark ages" to which we have now come; much nearer the truth is it to say that the violent and vulgar fraud of Roman imperialism, that world of politicians, adventurers, landowners and financiers, collapsed into a sea of misery that was already there. Our histories of these times are very imperfect; there were few places where men could write, and little encouragement to write at all; no one was sure even of the safety of his manuscript or the possibility of its being read. But we know enough to tell that this age was an age not merely of war and robbery, but of famine and pestilence. No effective sanitary organization had yet come into the world, and the migrations of the time must have destroyed whatever hygienic balance had been established. Attila's ravages in North Italy were checked by an outbreak of fever in 452. There was a great epidemic of bubonic plague towards the end of the reign of Justinian (565), which did much to weaken the defence of Italy against the Lombards. In 543 ten thousand people had died in one day in Constantinople (Gibbon says "each day"). Plague was raging in Rome in 590. The seventh century was also a plague-stricken century. The Englishman Bede, one of the few writers of the time, records pestilences in England in 664, 672, 678, and 683, no fewer than four in twenty years! Gibbon couples the Justinian epidemic with the great comet of 531, and with the very frequent and serious earthquakes of that reign. "Many cities of the east were left vacant, and in several districts of Italy the harvest and the vintage withered on the ground." He alleges "a visible decrease of the human species, which has never been made good, in some of the fairest countries of the globe." To many in those dark days it seemed that all learning and all that made life seemly and desirable was perishing.

How far the common lot was unhappier under these conditions of squalor and insecurity than it had been under the grinding order of the imperial system it is impossible to say. There was possibly much local variation, the rule of violent bullies here and a good-tempered freedom there, famine this year and plenty the next. If robbers abounded, tax-gatherers and creditors had disappeared. Such kings as those of the Frankish and Gothic kingdoms were really phantom rulers to most of their so-called subjects; the life of each district went on at a low level, with little trade or travel. Greater or lesser areas of country-side would be dominated by some able person, claiming with more or less justice the title of lord or count or duke from the tradition of the later empire or from the king. Such local nobles would assemble bands of retainers and build themselves strongholds. Often they adapted pre-existing buildings. The Colosseum at Rome, for example, the arena of many great gladiatorial shows, was converted into a fortress, and so was the amphitheatre at Arles. So also was the great tomb of Hadrian at Rome.

In the decaying and now insanitary towns and cities, shrunken bodies of artisans would hold together and serve the needs of the cultivating villages about them by their industry, placing themselves under the protection of some adjacent noble.

§ 10

A very important share in the social recrystallization that went on in the sixth and seventh centuries after the breakdown and fusion of the fourth and fifth was taken by the Christian monastic orders that were now arising in the Western world.

Monasteries had existed in the world before Christianity. During the period of social unhappiness among the Jews before the time of Jesus of Nazareth, there was a sect of Essenes who lived apart in communities vowed to austere lives of solitude, purity, and self-denial. Buddhism, too, had developed its communities of men who withdrew from the general effort and commerce of the world to lead lives of austerity and contemplation. Indeed, the story of Buddha, as we have told it, shows that such ideas must have prevailed in India long before his time, and that at last he repudiated them. Quite early in the history of Christianity there arose a similar movement away from the competition and heat and stress of the daily life of men. In Egypt, particularly, great numbers of men and women went out into the desert and there lived solitary lives of prayer and contemplation, living in absolute poverty in caves or under rocks, and subsisting on the chance alms of those whom their holiness impressed. Such lives would signify little to the historian—they are, indeed, of their very nature lives withdrawn from history—were it not for the turn this monastic tendency presently took among the more energetic and practical Europeans.

One of the central figures in the story of the development of monasticism in Europe is Saint Benedict, who lived between 480 and 544. He was born at Spoleto in Italy, and he was a young man of good family and ability. The shadow of the times fell upon him, and, like Buddha, he took to the religious life and at first set no limit to his austerities. Fifty miles from Rome is Subiaco, and there at the end of a gorge of the Anio, beneath a jungle growth of weeds and bushes, rose a deserted palace built by the Emperor Nero, overlooking an artificial lake that had been made in those days of departed prosperity by damming back the waters of the river. Here, with a hair shirt as his chief possession, Benedict took up his quarters in a cave in the high southward-looking cliff that overhangs the stream, in so inaccessible a position that his food had to be lowered to him on a cord by a faithful admirer. Three years he lived here, and his fame spread as Buddha's did about a thousand years before under similar circumstances.

As in the case of Buddha, the story of Benedict has been overlaid by foolish and credulous disciples with a mass of silly stories of miracles and manifestations. But presently we find him no longer engaged in self-torment, but controlling a group of twelve monasteries, the resort of a great number of people. Youths are brought to him to be educated, and the whole character of his life has changed.

From Subiaco he removed farther southward to Monte Cassino, half-way between Rome and Naples, a lonely and beautiful mountain in the midst of a great circle of majestic heights. Here, it is interesting to note that in the sixth century A.D. he found a temple of Apollo and a sacred grove, and the country-side still worshipping at this shrine. His first labours had to be missionary labours, and it was with difficulty that he persuaded the simple pagans to demolish their temple and cut down their grove. The establishment upon Monte Cassino became a famous and powerful centre within the lifetime of its founder. Mixed up with the imbecile inventions of marvel-loving monks about demons exorcised, disciples walking on the water, and dead children restored to life, we can still detect something of the real spirit of Benedict. Particularly significant are the stories that represent him as discouraging extreme mortification. He sent a damping message to a solitary who had invented a new degree in saintliness by chaining himself to a rock in a narrow cave. "Break thy chain," said Benedict, "for the true servant of God is chained not to rocks by iron, but to righteousness by Christ."

And next to the discouragement of solitary self-torture it is Benedict's distinction that he insisted upon hard work. Through the legends shines the clear indication of the trouble made by his patrician students and disciples who found themselves obliged to toil instead of leading lives of leisurely austerity under the ministrations of the lower-class brethren. A third remarkable thing about Benedict was his political influence. He set himself to reconcile Goths and Italians, and it is clear that Totila, his Gothic king, came to him for counsel and was greatly influenced by him. When Totila retook Naples from the Greeks, the Goths protected the women from insult and treated even the captured soldiers with humanity. When Belisarius, Justinian's general, had taken the same place ten years previously, he had celebrated his triumph by a general massacre.

Now the monastic organization of Benedict was a very great beginning in the Western world. One of his prominent followers was Pope Gregory the Great (540–604), the first monk to become pope (590); he was one of the most capable and energetic of the popes, sending successful missions to the unconverted, and particularly to the Anglo-Saxons. He ruled in Rome like an independent king, organizing armies, making treaties. To his influence is due the imposition of the Benedictine rule upon nearly the whole of Latin monasticism.

Closely associated with these two names in the development of a civilizing monasticism out of the merely egotistic mortifications of the early recluses is that of Cassiodorus (490–585). He was evidently much senior to Pope Gregory, and younger by ten years than Benedict, and, like these two, he belonged to a patrician family, a Syrian family settled in Italy. He had a considerable official career under the Gothic kings; and when, between 545 and 553, the overthrow of those kings and the great pestilence paved the way for the new barbaric rule of the Lombards, he took refuge in a monastic career. He founded a monastery upon his private estates, and set the monks he gathered to work in quite the Benedictine fashion, though whether his monks actually followed the Benedictine rule that was being formulated about the same time from Monte Cassino we do not know. But there can be no question of his influence upon the development of this great working, teaching, and studying order. It is evident that he was profoundly impressed by the universal decay of education and the possible loss of all learning and of the ancient literature by the world; and from the first he directed his brethren to the task of preserving and restoring these things. He collected ancient MSS. and caused them to be copied. He made sun-dials, water-clocks, and similar apparatus, a little last gleam of experimental science in the gathering darkness. He wrote a history of the Gothic kings, and, what is more significant of his sense of the needs of the time, he produced a series of school books on the liberal arts and a grammar. Probably his influence was even greater than that of Saint Benedict in making monasticism into a powerful instrument for the restoration of social order in the Western world.

The spread of monasteries of the Benedictine order or type in the seventh and eighth centuries was very considerable. Everywhere we find them as centres of light, restoring, maintaining, and raising the standard of cultivation, preserving some sort of elementary education, spreading useful arts, multiplying and storing books, and keeping before the eyes of the world the spectacle and example of a social backbone. For eight centuries thenceforth the European monastic system remained a system of patches and fibres of enlightenment in what might otherwise have been a wholly chaotic world. Closely associated with the Benedictine monasteries were the schools that grew presently into the medieval universities. The schools of the Roman world had been altogether swept away in the general social breakdown. There was a time when very few priests in Britain or Gaul could read the Gospel or their service books. Only gradually was teaching restored to the world. But when it was restored, it came back not as the duty work of a learned slave, but as the religious service of a special class of devoted men.

In the East, also, there was a breach of educational continuity, but there the cause was not so much social disorder as religious intolerance, and the break was by no means so complete. Justinian closed and dispersed the shrunken and intellectually degenerate schools of Athens (529), but he did this very largely in order to destroy a rival to the new school he was setting up in Constantinople, which was more directly under imperial control.

Since the new Latin learning of the developing western universities had no text-books and literature of its own, it had, in spite of its strong theological bias to the contrary, to depend very largely upon the Latin classes and the Latin translations of the Greek literature. It was obliged to preserve far more of that splendid literature than it had a mind to do.

§ 11

From the transfer of the seat of Empire to Byzantium onward a new type of architecture and a new artistic spirit appears in the world, the Byzantine. It reached a high development under the Emperor Justinian (527–565), of whom we shall tell in the next chapter; it declined and rose to a fresh culmination in the eleventh century. It is still a living artistic tradition in Eastern Europe. It expresses the restraints and impulses of the new official Christianity. Oriental qualities and particularly Egyptian and Persian tendencies are imposed upon the classical tradition. Splendour takes the place of frankness and grace.

One characteristic of its decoration is a peculiar rigidity; all the flexibility of Greek and Roman painting and sculpture has gone, and in its place we have mosaics showing flat, symmetrical, erect figures in full face. Hardly ever is there a profile or any stir of foreshortening. It is as if that natural body which the Greeks idolized had become reprehensible, a thing of fear. So a great and solemn dignity is attained. The huge mosaic figures of God the Creator, the Virgin and Child, the mighty Saints, seem to brood over the spectators from the great domes upon which they are put. Painting and the illumination of books displayed the same glowing stiffness. Sculpture, on the other hand, decayed, and highly coloured lattices of carved ornament displaced modelled forms. Gold, silver, and enamelled work were done with an unprecedented brilliance. Textile fabrics brought from the east were often frankly Persian in design. Presently Islamic influence was to come in, with a still completer suppression of bodily form.

Music also became massive and important. The music of the early Christian centuries was devout and enthusiastic rather than elaborate, and it derived from Semitic rather than from Hellenic sources. Secular music was flatly prohibited. "A Christian maiden," said St. Jerome, "ought not to know what a lyre or a flute is." Psalm-singing and instrumentation were taken over by the Christians from the Jewish services, and restricted more or less entirely to organized choirs. Antiphonal singing was common. The congregation sang hymns—in unison, of course, for as yet part-singing had not been devised. It was a great outlet for suppressed emotions. There appeared a profusion of hymns in Greek and Latin; some are said to survive in existing hymns. St. Gregory, Gregory the Great, that mighty church organizer of whom we shall have more to tell in a subsequent chapter, established the liturgical music of the church in the sixth century.

XXIX

THE HISTORY OF ASIA DURING THE DECAY OF THE WESTERN AND BYZANTINE EMPIRES

§ 1. *Justinian the Great.* § 2. *The Sassanid Empire in Persia.* § 3. *The Decay of Syria under the Sassanids.* § 4. *The First Message from Islam.* § 5. *Zoroaster and Mani.* § 6. *Hunnish Peoples in Central Asia and India.* § 7. *The Dynasties of Han and Tang in China.* § 8. *Intellectual Fetters of China.* § 9. *Early Chinese Art.* §10. *The Travels of Yuan Chwang.*

§ 1

IN THE preceding two chapters we have concentrated our attention chiefly on the collapse, in the comparatively short space of four centuries, of the political and social order of the western part of the great Roman Empire of Cæsar and Trajan. We have dwelt upon the completeness of that collapse. To any intelligent and public-spirited mind living in the time and under the circumstances of St. Benedict or Cassiodorus, it must have seemed, indeed, as if the light of civilization was waning and near extinction. But with the longer views a study of universal history gives us, we can view those centuries of shadow as a phase, and probably a necessary phase, in the onward march of social and political ideas and understandings. And if, during that time, a dark sense of calamity rested upon Western Europe, we must remember that over large portions of the world there was no retrogression.

With their Western prepossessions, European writers are much too prone to underrate the tenacity of the Eastern Empire that centred upon Constantinople. This empire embodied a tradition much more ancient than that of Rome. If the reader will look at the map we have given of its extent in the sixth century, and if he will reflect that its official language had then become Greek, he will realize that what we are dealing with here is only nominally a branch of the Roman Empire; it is really the Hellenic Empire of which Herodotus dreamt and which Alexander the Great founded. True it called itself Roman and its people "Romans," and to this day modern Greek is called "Romaic." True also that Constantine the Great knew no Greek and that Justinian's accent was bad. These superficialities of name and form cannot alter the fact that the empire was in reality Hellenic, with a past of six centuries at the time of Constantine the Great, and that while the real Roman Empire crumpled up completely in four centuries, this Hellenic "Roman Empire" held out for more than eleven—from 312, the beginning of the reign of Constantine the Great, to 1453, when Constantinople fell to the Ottoman Turks.

And while we have had to tell of something like a complete social collapse in the west, there were no such equivalent breakdowns in the east. Towns and cities flourished, the countryside was well cultivated, trade went on. For many centuries Constantinople was the greatest and richest city in the world. We will not trouble ourselves here with the names and follies, the crimes and intrigues, of its tale of emperors. As with most monarchs of great states, they did not guide their empire; they were carried by it. We have already dealt at some length with Constantine the Great (312–337), we have mentioned Theodosius the Great (379–395), who for a little while reunited the empire, and Justinian I (527–565). Presently we shall tell something of Heraclius (610–641).

Justinian, like Constantine, may have had Slav blood in his veins. He was a man of great ambition and great organizing power, and he had the good fortune to be married to a woman of equal or greater ability, the Empress Theodora, who had in her youth been an actress of doubtful reputation. But his ambitious attempts to restore the ancient greatness of the empire probably overtaxed its resources. As we have told, he reconquered the African province from the Vandals and most of Italy from the Goths. He also recovered the south of Spain. He built the great and beautiful Church of Sancta Sophia in Constantinople, founded a university, and codified the law. But against this we must set his closing of the schools of Athens. Meanwhile a great plague swept the world, and at his death this renewed and expanded empire of his collapsed like a pricked bladder. The greater part of his Italian conquests was lost to the Lombards. Italy was, indeed, at that time almost a desert; the Lombard historians assert they came into an empty country. The Avars and Slavs struck down from the Danube country toward the Adriatic, Slav populations establishing themselves in what is now Serbia, Croatia, and Dalmatia, to become the Yugo-Slavs of to-day. Moreover, a great and exhausting struggle began with the Sassanid Empire in Persia.

But before we say anything of this struggle, in which the Persians thrice came near to taking Constantinople, and which was decided by a great Persian defeat at Nineveh (627), it is necessary to sketch very briefly the history of Persia from the Parthian days.

§ 2

We have already drawn a comparison between the brief four centuries of Roman imperialism and the obstinate vitality of the imperialism of the Euphrates-Tigris country. We have glanced very transitorily at the Hellenized Bactrian and Seleucid monarchies that flourished in the eastern half of Alexander's area of conquest for three centuries, and told how the Parthians came down into Mesopotamia in the last century B.C. We have described the battle of Carrhæ and the end of Crassus. Thereafter for two centuries and a half the Parthian dynasty of the Arsacids ruled in the east and the Roman in the west, with Armenia and Syria between them, and the boundaries shifted east and west as either side grew stronger. We have marked the utmost eastward extension of the Roman Empire, under Trajan (see map to chap. 27, § 1), and we have noted that about the same time the Indo-Scythians (chap. 27, § 5) poured down into India.

In 226 occurred a revolution, and the Arsacid dynasty gave way to a more vigorous line, the Sassanid, a national Persian line, under Ardashir I. In one respect the empire of Ardashir I presented a curious parallelism with that of Constantine the Great, a hundred years later. Ardashir attempted to consolidate it by insisting upon religious unity, and adopted as the state religion the old Persian faith of Zoroaster, of which we shall have more to say later.

This new Sassanid Empire immediately became aggressive, and under Sapor I, the son and successor of Ardashir, took Antioch. We have already noted how the Emperor Valerian was defeated (260) and taken prisoner. But as Sapor was retiring from a victorious march into Asia Minor he was fallen upon and defeated by Odenathus, the Arab king of a great desert trading centre, Palmyra.

For a brief time under Odenathus, and then under his widow Zenobia, Palmyra was a considerable state, wedged between the two empires. Then it fell to the Emperor Aurelian, who carried off Zenobia in chains to grace his triumph at Rome (272).

We will not attempt to trace the fluctuating fortunes of the Sassanids during the next three centuries. Throughout that time war between Persia and the empire of Constantinople wasted Asia Minor like a fever. Christianity spread widely and was persecuted, for after the Christianization of Rome the Persian monarch remained the only god-monarch on earth, and he saw in Christianity merely the propaganda of his Byzantine rival. Constantinople became the protector of the Christians and Persia of the Zoroastrians; in a treaty of 422 the one empire agreed to tolerate Zoroastrianism and the other Christianity. In 483 the Christians of the east split off from the Orthodox church and became the Nestorian church; which, as we have already noted, spread its missionaries far and wide through Central and Eastern Asia. This separation from Europe, since it freed the Christian bishops of the east from the rule of the Byzantine patriarchs, and so lifted from the Nestorian church the suspicion of political disloyalty, led to a complete toleration of Christianity in Persia.

With Chosroes I (531–579) came a last period of Sassanid vigour. He was the contemporary and parallel of Justinian. He reformed taxation, restored the orthodox Zoroastrianism, extended his power into Southern Arabia (Yemen), which he rescued from the rule of Abyssinian Christians, pushed his northern frontier into Western Turkestan, and carried on a series of wars with Justinian. His reputation as an enlightened ruler stood so high that, when Justinian closed the schools of Athens, the last Greek philosophers betook themselves to his Court. They sought in him the philosopher king—that mirage which, as we have noted, Confucius and Plato had sought in their day. The philosophers found the atmosphere of orthodox Zoroastrianism even less to their taste than orthodox Christianity, and in 549 Chosroes had the kindness to insert a clause in an armistice with Justinian permitting their return to Greece, and ensuring that they should not be molested for their pagan philosophy or their transitory pro-Persian behaviour.

It is in connection with Chosroes that we hear of a new Hunnish people in Central Asia, the Turks, who are, we learn, first in alliance with him and then with Constantinople.

Chosroes II (590–628), the grandson of Chosroes I, experienced extraordinary fluctuations of fortune. At the outset of his career he achieved astonishing successes against the empire of Constantinople. Three times (in 608, 615, and 626) his armies reached Chalcedon, which is over against Constantinople; he took Antioch, Damascus, and Jerusalem (614), and from Jerusalem he carried off a cross, said to be the true cross on which Jesus was crucified, to his capital, Ctesiphon. (But some of this or some other true cross had already got to Rome. It had been brought from Jerusalem, it was said, by the "Empress Helena," the idealized and canonized mother of Constantine—a story for which Gibbon displayed small respect.[1]) In 619 Chosroes II conquered that facile country, Egypt. This career of conquest was at last arrested by the Emperor Heraclius (610), who set about restoring the ruined military power of Constantinople. For some time Heraclius avoided a great battle while he gathered his forces. He took the field in good earnest in 623. The Persians experienced a series of defeats, culminating in the battle of Nineveh (627); but neither side had the strength for the complete defeat of the other. At the end of the struggle there was still an undefeated Persian army upon the Bosphorus, although there were victorious Byzantine forces in Mesopotamia.

In 628 Chosroes II was deposed and murdered by his son. An indecisive peace was concluded between the two exhausted empires a year or so later, restoring their old boundaries; and the true cross was sent back to Heraclius, who replaced it in Jerusalem with much pomp and ceremony.

§ 3

So we give briefly the leading events in the history of the Persian as of the Byzantine Empire. What are more interesting for us and less easy to give are the changes that went on in the lives of the general population of those great empires during that time. The present writer can find little of a definite character about the great pestilence that we know swept the world in the second and sixth centuries of this era. Certainly they depleted population, and probably they disorganized social order in those regions just as much as we know they did in the Roman and Chinese empires.

The late Sir Mark Sykes—whose untimely death in Paris during the influenza epidemic of 1919 was an irreparable loss to Great Britain—wrote in *The Caliph's Last Heritage* a vivid review of

[1] *The Decline and Fall of the Roman Empire*, chap. xxiii.

the general life of Nearer Asia during the period we are considering. In the opening centuries of the present era, he says: "The direction of military administration and imperial finance became entirely divorced in men's minds from practical government; and notwithstanding the vilest tyranny of sots, drunkards, tyrants, lunatics, savages, and abandoned women, who from time to time held the reins of government, Mesopotamia, Babylonia, and Syria contained enormous populations, huge canals and dykes were kept in repair, and commerce and architecture flourished in spite of a perpetual procession of hostile armies and a continual changing of the nationality of the governor. Each peasant's interest was centred in his ruling town; each citizen's interest was in the progress and prosperity of his city; and the advent of an enemy's army may have sometimes been looked on even with satisfaction, if his victory was assured and the payment of his contracts a matter of certainty.

"A raid from the north,[1] on the other hand, must have been a matter for dread. Then the villagers had need to take refuge behind the walls of the cities, from whence they could decry the smoke which told of the wreck and damage caused by the nomads. So long, however, as the canals were not destroyed (and indeed, they were built with such solidity and caution that their safety was assured), no irreparable damage could be effected. . . .

In Armenia and Pontus the condition of life was quite otherwise. These were mountain districts, containing fierce tribes headed by powerful native nobility under recognized ruling kings, while in the valleys and plains the peaceful cultivator provided the necessary economic resources. . . . Cilicia and Cappadocia were now thoroughly subject to Greek influence, and contained numerous wealthy and highly civilized towns, besides possessing a considerable merchant marine. Passing from Cilicia to the Hellespont, the whole Mediterranean coast was crowded with wealthy cities and Greek colonies, entirely cosmopolitan in thought and speech, with those municipal and local ambitions which seem natural to the Grecian character. The Grecian Zone extended from Caria to the Bosphorus, and followed the coast as far as Sinope on the Black Sea, where it gradually faded away.

"Syria was broken up into a curious quilt-like pattern of principalities and municipal kingdoms; beginning with the almost barbarous states of Commagene and Edessa (Urfa) in the north.

---

[1] Turanians from Turkestan or Avars from the Caucasus.

South of these stood Bambyce, with its huge temples and priestly governors. Towards the coast a dense population in villages and towns clustered around the independent cities of Antioch, Apamea, and Emesa (Homs); while out in the wilderness the great Semitic merchant city of Palmyra was gaining wealth and greatness as the neutral trading-ground between Parthia and Rome. Between the Lebanon and Anti-Lebanon we find, at the height of its glory, Heliopolis (Baalbek), the battered fragments of which

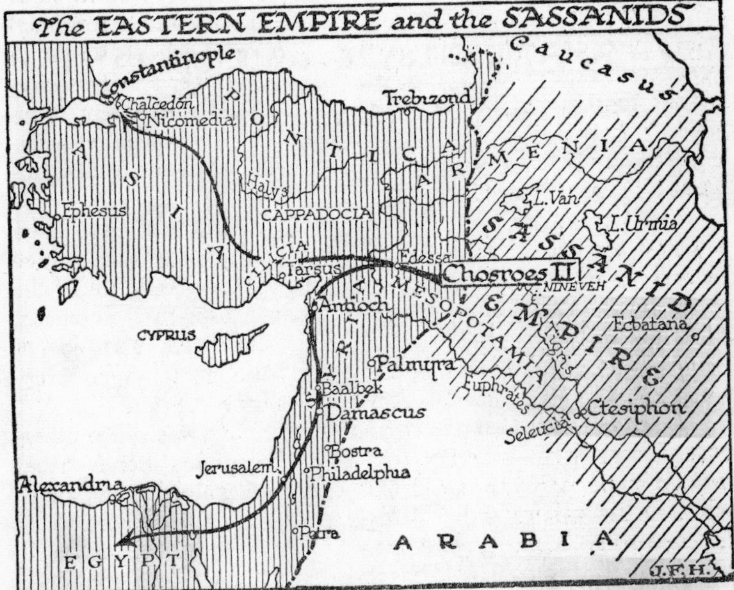

even now command our admiration. . . . Bending in towards Galilee we find the wondrous cities of Gerasa and Philadelphia (Amman), connected by solid roads of masonry and furnished with gigantic aqueducts. . . . Syria is still so rich in ruins and remains of the period that it is not difficult to picture to oneself the nature of its civilization. The arts of Greece, imported long before, had been developed into magnificence that bordered on vulgarity. The richness of ornamentation, the lavish expense, the flaunting wealth, all tell that the tastes of the voluptuous and artistic Semites were then as now. I have stood in the colonnades of Palmyra and I have dined in the Hotel Cecil, and, save that the latter is built of iron, daubed with sham wood, sham stucco, sham gold, sham velvet, and sham stone, the effect is identical. In Syria there were slaves in sufficient quantity to make real buildings, but the artistic spirit is as debased as anything made by machinery. Over against the cities the village folk must have dwelt pretty much as they do now, in houses of mud and dry stone wall; while out in the distant pastures the Bedouin tended their flocks in freedom under the rule of the Nabatean kings of their own race, or performed the office of guardians and agents of the great trading caravans.

"Beyond the herdsmen lay the parching deserts, which acted as the impenetrable barrier and defence of the Parthian Empire behind the Euphrates, where stood the great cities of Ctesiphon, Seleucia, Hatra, Nisibin, Harran, and hundreds more whose very names are forgotten. These great townships subsisted on the enormous cereal wealth of Mesopotamia, watered as it then was by canals, whose makers' names were even then already lost in the mists of antiquity. Babylon and Nineveh had passed away; the successors of Persia and Macedon had given place to Parthia; but the people and the cultivation were the same as when Cyrus the Conqueror had first subdued the land. The language of many of the towns was Greek, and the cultured citizens of Seleucia might criticize the philosophies and tragedies of Athens; but the millions of the agricultural population knew, possibly, no more of these things than many an Essex peasant of to-day knows of what passes in the metropolis."

Compare with this the state of affairs at the end of the seventh century.

"Syria was now an impoverished and stricken land, and her great cities, though still populated, must have been encumbered with ruins which the public funds were not sufficient to remove. Damascus and Jerusalem themselves had not recovered from the effects of long and terrible sieges; Amman and Gerasa had declined into wretched villages under the sway and lordship of the Bedouin. The Hauran, perhaps, still showed signs of the prosperity for which it had been noted in the days of Trajan; but the wretched buildings and rude inscriptions of this date all point to a sad and depressing decline. Out in the desert, Palmyra stood empty and desolate save for a garrison in the castle. On the coasts and in the Lebanon a shadow of the former business and wealth was still to be seen; but in the north, ruin, desolation, and abandonment must have been the common state of the country, which had been raided with unfailing regularity for one hundred years and had been held by an enemy for fifteen. Agriculture must have declined, and the population notably decreased through the plagues and distresses from which it had suffered.

"Cappadocia had insensibly sunk into barbarism; and the great basilicas and cities, which the rude countrymen could neither repair nor restore, had been levelled with the ground. The Anatolian peninsula had been ploughed and harrowed by the Persian armies; the great cities had been plundered and sacked."

§ 4

It was while Heraclius was engaged in restoring order in this already desolated Syria after the death of Chosroes II and before the final peace with Persia that a strange message was brought to him. The bearer had brought it to an imperial outpost in the wilderness south of Damascus. The letter was in Arabic, the obscure Semitic language of the nomadic peoples of the southern desert;

and probably only an interpretation reached him—presumably with deprecatory notes by the interpreter.

It was an odd, florid challenge from someone who called himself "Muhammad the Prophet of God." This Muhammad, it appeared, called upon Heraclius to acknowledge the one true God and to serve Him. Nothing else was definite in the document.

There is no record of the reception of this missive, and presumably it went unanswered. The emperor probably shrugged his shoulders, and was faintly amused at the incident.

But at Ctesiphon they knew more about this Muhammad. He was said to be a tiresome false prophet, who had incited Yemen, the rich province of Southern Arabia, to rebel against the King of Kings. Kavadh was much occupied with affairs. He had deposed and murdered his father Chosroes II, and he was attempting to reorganize the Persian military forces. To him also came a message identical with that sent to Heraclius. The thing angered him. He tore up the letter, flung the fragments at the envoy—and bade him begone.

When this was told to the sender, far away in the squalid little town of Medina, he was very angry. "Even so, O Lord!" he cried; "rend Thou his kingdom from him." (A.D. 628.)

§ 5

But before we go on to tell of the rise of Islam in the world, it will be well to complete our survey of the condition of Asia in the dawn of the seventh century. And a word or so is due to religious developments in the Persian community during the Sassanid period.

From the days of Cyrus onward Zoroastrianism had prevailed over the ancient gods of Nineveh and Babylon. Zoroaster (the Greek spelling of the Iranian "Zarathustra"), like Buddha, was an Aryan. We know nothing of the age in which he lived—some authorities make him as early as 1,000 B.C., others make him contemporary with Buddha or Confucius; and as little do we know of his place of birth or his exact nationality. His teachings are preserved to us in the Zend Avesta; but here, since they no longer play any great part in the world's affairs, we cannot deal with them in any detail. The opposition of a good god, Ormuzd, the god of light, truth, frankness, and the sun, and a bad god, Ahriman, god of secrecy, cunning, diplomacy, darkness, and night, formed a very central part of his religion. As we find it in history, it is already surrounded by a ceremonial and sacerdotal system; it has no images, but it has priests, temples, and altars on which burn a sacred fire and at which sacrificial ceremonies are performed. Among other distinctive features is its prohibition of either the burning or the burial of the dead. The Parsees of India, the last surviving Zoroastrians, still lay their dead out within certain open towers, the Towers of Silence, to which the vultures come.

Under the Sassanid kings from Ardashir onward (A.D. 227), this religion was the official religion: its head was the second person in the state next to the king, and the king in quite the ancient fashion was supposed to be divine or semi-divine and upon terms of peculiar intimacy with Ormuzd.

But the religious fermentation of the world did not leave the supremacy of Zoroastrianism undisputed in the Persian Empire. Not only was there a great eastward diffusion of Christianity, to which we have already given notice, but new sects arose in Persia, incorporating the novel ideas of the time. One early variant or branch of Zoroastrianism, Mithraism, we have already named. It had spread into Europe by the first century B.C., after the eastern campaigns of Pompey the Great. It became enormously popular with the soldiers and common people, and, until the time of Constantine the Great, continued to be a serious rival to Christianity. Mithras was a god of light, "proceeding" from Ormuzd and miraculously born, in much the same way that the third person in the Christian Trinity proceeds from the first. Of this branch of the Zoroastrian stem we need say no more. In the third century A.D., however, another religion, Manichæism, arose, which deserves some notice now.

Mani, the founder of Manichæism, was born the son of a good family of Ecbatana, the old Median capital (A.D. 216). He was educated at Ctesiphon. His father was some sort of religious sectary, and he was brought up in an atmosphere of religious discussion. There came to him that persuasion that he at last had the complete light, which is the moving power of all religious initiators. He was impelled to proclaim his doctrine. In A.D. 242, at the accession of Sapor I, the second Sassanid monarch, he began his teaching.

It is characteristic of the way in which men's minds were moving in those days, that his teaching included a sort of theocrasia. He was not, he declared, proclaiming anything new. The great religious founders before him had all been right: Moses, Zoroaster, Buddha, Jesus Christ—all had been true prophets, but to him it was appointed to clarify and crown their imperfect and confused teaching. This he did in Zoroastrian language. He explains the perplexities and contradictions of life as a conflict of light and darkness. Ormuzd was God and Ahriman Satan. But how man was created, how he fell from light into darkness, how he is being disentangled and redeemed from the darkness, and of the part played by Jesus in this strange mixture of religions, we cannot explain here even if we would. Our interest with the system is historical and not theological.

But of the utmost historical interest is the fact that Mani not only went about Iran preaching these new and, to him, these finally satisfying ideas of his, but into Turkestan, into India, and over the passes into China. This freedom of travel is to be noted. It is interesting, also, because it brings before us the fact that Turkestan was no longer a country of dangerous nomads, but a country in which cities were flourishing and men had the education and leisure for theological argument.

The ideas of Mani spread eastward and westward with great rapidity, and they were a most fruitful rootstock of heresies throughout the entire Christian world for nearly a thousand years.

Somewhen about A.D. 270 Mani came back to Ctesiphon and made many converts. This brought him into conflict with the official religion and the priesthood. In 277 the reigning monarch had him crucified and his body, for some unknown reason, flayed, and there began a fierce persecution of his adherents. Nevertheless, Manichæism held its own in Persia with Nestorian Christianity and orthodox Zoroastrianism (Mazdaism) for some centuries.

§ 6

It becomes fairly evident that in the fifth and sixth centuries A.D. not merely Persia, but the regions that are now Turkestan and Afghanistan were far more advanced in civilization than were the French and English of that time. The obscurity of the history of these regions has been lifted in the last two decades, and a very considerable literature, written not only in languages of the Turkish group, but in Sogdian and another Aryan language, has been discovered. These extant manuscripts date from the seventh century onward. The alphabet is an adaptation of the Aramaic, introduced by Manichæan missionaries, and many of the MSS. discovered—parchments have been found in windows in the place of glass—are as beautifully written as any Benedictine production. Mixed up with a very extensive Manichæan literature are translations of the Christian scriptures and Buddhistic writings. Much of this material still awaits examination.

This central Asiatic country, Sir Denison Ross declares, was still largely Aryan in speech and culture, its art was still largely Indian and Persian in its affinities. Everything points to the conclusion that those centuries which were centuries of disaster and retrogression in Europe, were comparatively an age of progress in Middle Asia eastward into China. Some day we shall have a connected history written of the things that happened in this region during the dark centuries of European disorder. Through some favourable climate change, its civilization had a phase of exceptional elaboration. In Berlin one may see a collection of wall paintings from Turkestan of this period which anticipate the costumes and equipment of thirteenth-century France and Germany (six centuries later), in a quite extraordinary way. All the familiar figures and symbols of the Kings, Queens and Knaves of a pack of cards, for example, are to be seen depicted in these brilliant pictures. There was a life there as rich and fine as that of European medievalism at its brightest, and wonderfully like it. Dark and fair people mingle in these scenes and red-haired men, usually a result of racial admixture, abound.

A steady westward drift to the north of the Caspian of Hunnish peoples, who were now called Tartars and Turks, was still going on in the sixth century, but it must be thought of as an overflow rather than as a migration of whole peoples. The world from the Danube to the Chinese frontiers was still largely a nomadic world, with towns and cities growing up upon the chief trade routes. We need not tell in any detail here of the constant clash of the Turkish peoples of Western Turkestan with the Persians to the south of them, the age-long bickering of Turanian and Iranian. We hear nothing of any great northward marches of the Persians, but there were great and memorable raids to the south, both by the Turanians to the east and the Alans to the west of the Caspian, before the big series of movements of the third and fourth century westward that carried the Alans and Huns into the heart of Europe. There was a nomadic drift to the east of Persia and southward through Afghanistan towards India, as well as this drift to the north-west. These streams of nomads flowed by Persia on either side. We have already mentioned the Yueh-Chi, who finally descended into India as the Indo-Scythians in the second century. A backward, still nomadic section of these Yueh-Chi remained in Central Asia, and became numerous upon the steppes of Turkestan, as the Ephthalites or White Huns. After being a nuisance and a danger to the Persians for three centuries, they finally began raiding into India in the footsteps of their kinsmen about the year 470, less than a quarter of a century after the death of Attila. They did not migrate into India; they went to and fro, looting in India and returning with their loot to their own country, just as later the Huns established themselves in the great Danube plain and raided all Europe.

The history of India during these seven centuries we are now reviewing is punctuated by these two invasions of the Yueh-Chi, the Indo-Scythians, who, as we have said, wiped out the last traces of Hellenic rule, and the Ephthalites. Before the former of these, the Indo-Scythians, a wave of uprooted populations, the Sakas, had been pushed; so that altogether India experienced three waves of barbaric invasion, about A.D. 100, about A.D. 120, and about A.D. 470. But only the second of these invasions was a permanent conquest and settlement. The Indo-Sythians made their headquarters on the North-west Frontier and set up a dynasty, the Kushan dynasty, which ruled most of North India as far east as Benares.

The chief among these Kushan monarchs was Kanishka (date unknown), who added to North India Kashgar, Yarkand, and Khotan. Like Asoka, he was a great and vigorous promoter of Buddhism, and these conquests, this great empire of the North-west Frontier, must have brought India into close and frequent relations with China and Tibet.

The subsequent divisions and coalescences of power in India are difficult to deal with in the limited space at our command. Sometimes all India was a patchwork-quilt of states; sometimes such empires as that of the Guptas prevailed over great areas. The Gupta Empire flourished throughout the fourth, fifth and sixth centuries, and under its patronage modern Hinduism arose and there was a period of great literary activity. These things made little difference in the ordinary way of life of the Indian peoples. Brahminism held its own against Buddhism, and the two religions prospered side by side. The mass of the population was living then very much as it lives to-day; dressing, cultivating, and building its houses in much the same fashion.

The irruption of the Ephthalites is memorable not so much because of its permanent effects as because of the atrocities perpetrated by the invaders. These Ephthalites very closely resembled the Huns of Attila in their barbarism; they merely raided, they produced no such dynasty as the Kushan monarchy; and their chiefs retained their headquarters in Western Turkestan. Mihiragula, their most capable leader, has been called the Attila of India. One of his favourite amusements, we are told, was the expensive one of rolling elephants down precipitous places in order to watch their sufferings. His abominations roused his Indian tributary princes to revolt, and he was overthrown (528). But the final ending of the Ephthalite raids into India was effected not by Indians, but by the destruction of the central establishment of the Ephthalites on the Oxus (565) by the growing power of the Turks working in alliance with the Persians. After this break-up, the Ephthalites dissolved very rapidly and completely into the surrounding populations, much as the European Huns did after the death of Attila a hundred years earlier. Nomads without central grazing-lands must disperse; nothing else is possible. Some of the chief Rajput clans of to-day in Rajputana in North India are descended, it is said, from these White Huns.

An Ephthalite Coin.....

Very regretfully we must refrain here from any account of the development of chivalry among these little Rajput states, curiously analogous to the contemporary knightly developments in Europe.

Nor can we trace here, because no student has yet prepared the way for us, even in broad outline, the development of Indian art between the days of Alexander and the coming of Islam. The Hellenic influence upon Indian sculpture and architecture was profound, and there was probably a constant coming and going of artists, and particularly of painters, between Persia and Central Asia and India. Buddhistic art is strongly Hellenic, and when in the second and subsequent centuries A.D. Buddhism, as we have already told, spread into China, it carried a certain Hellenic grace and quality into the Chinese representations of Buddha, and into Chinese religious art generally. But India had a deadly climate for abandoned works of art; dynasties that are almost completely forgotten lived beautiful and luxurious lives, and left little that has survived of all their beauty.

One fascinating monument of this time is to be seen in the painted Caves of Ajanta which are just rotting into invisibility. Happily, copies have been made of them and are accessible through the India Society. Ajanta is in Hyderabad in the Ajanta Hills. Between the second and seventh centuries A.D. there was a Buddhist monastery there, with great halls and galleries hollowed out of the rock, and during this period and mainly in the fifth and sixth centuries these caves were adorned with paintings, at the cost of various monarchs and rich men, by a number of accomplished artists. To-day we see these vestiges with amazement, so eloquent are they of an opulent, brilliant and sensuous Court life, that has otherwise passed altogether out of the memory of man. The subjects of the paintings are still in many cases a matter for speculation; some are scenes from the life of Buddha and legends about him; some seem to concern the god Indra, some are just everyday Court life; one scene is supposed to represent the reception of an embassy from Chosroes II. These caves and paintings were visited in the days of Muhammad by Yuan Chwang, a Chinese traveller, about whom we shall have much to tell a little later.

§ 7

These seven centuries which saw the beginning and the end of the emperors in Rome, and the complete breakdown and recasting of the social, economic, political and religious life of Western Europe, saw also very profound changes in the Chinese world. It is too commonly assumed by both Chinese, Japanese, and European historians, that the Han dynasty, under which we find China at the beginning of this period, and the Tang dynasty, with which it closed, were analogous ascendancies controlling a practically similar empire, and that the four centuries of division that elapsed between the end of the Han dynasty (220) and the beginning of the Tang period (618) were centuries of disturbance rather than essential change. The divisions of China are supposed to be merely political and territorial, and, deceived by the fact that, at the close as at the commencement of these four centuries, China occupied much the same position in Asia, and was still recognizably China, still with a common culture, a common script, and a common body of ideas, they ignore the very fundamental breaking down and reconstruction that went on, and the many parallelisms to the European experience that China displayed.

It is true that the social collapse was never so complete in the Chinese as in the European world. There remained throughout the whole period considerable areas in which the elaboration of the arts of life could go on. There was no such complete deterioration in cleanliness, decoration, artistic and literary production as we have to record in the West, and no such abandonment of any search for grace and pleasure We note, for instance, that "tea" appeared in the world and its use spread throughout China. China began to drink tea in the sixth century A.D. And there were Chinese poets to write delightfully about the effects of the first cup and the second cup and the third cup, and so on. China continued to produce beautiful paintings long after the fall of the Han rule. In the second, third and fourth centuries some of the most lovely landscapes were painted that have ever been done by men. A considerable production of beautiful vases and carvings also continued. Fine building and decoration went on. Printing from wood blocks began about the same time as tea-drinking, and with the seventh century came a remarkable revival of poetry.

Certain differences between the great empires of the East and West were all in favour of the stability of the former. China had no general coinage. The cash and credit system of the Western world, at once efficient and dangerous, had not strained her economic life. Not that the monetary idea was unknown. For small transactions the various provinces were using perforated zinc and brass "cash," but for larger there was nothing but stamped ingots of silver. This great empire was still carrying on most of its business on a basis of barter like that which prevailed in Babylon in the days of the Aramean merchants. And so it continued to do to the dawn of the twentieth century.

We have seen how under the Roman Republic economic and social order was destroyed by the too great fluidity of property that money brought about. Money became abstract, and lost touch with the real values it was supposed to represent. Individuals and communities got preposterously into debt, and the world was saddled by a class of rich men who were creditors, men who did not handle and administer any real wealth, but who had the power to call up money. No such development of "finance" occurred in China. Wealth in China remained real and visible. And China had no need for any Licinian law, nor for a Tiberius Gracchus. The idea of property in China did not extend far beyond tangible things. There was no "labour" slavery, no gang servitude. There were girl slaves who did domestic work and women who were bought and sold, but that was only a slight extension of the ordinary domestic subjection of women. The occupier and user of the land was in most instances practically the owner of it, paying only a land tax. There was certain amount of small-scale landlordism, but no great estates. Landless men worked for wages paid mostly in kind—as they were in ancient Babylon.

These things made for stability, and the geographical form of China for unity; nevertheless, the vigour of the Han dynasty declined, enervated perhaps by luxury, and when at last at the close of the second century A.D. the world catastrophe of the great pestilence struck the system, the same pestilence that inaugurated a century of confusion in the Roman Empire, the dynasty fell like a rotten tree before a gale. And the same tendency to break up into a number of warring states and the same eruption of barbaric rulers were displayed in East and West alike.

Mr. Fu ascribes much of the political nervelessness of China in this period to Epicureanism, arising, he thinks, out of the sceptical individualism of Lao-Tse. This phase of division is known as the "Three Kingdom Period." The fourth century saw a dynasty of more or less civilized Huns established as rulers in the province of Shen-si. This Hunnish kingdom included not merely the north of China, but great areas of Siberia; its dynasty absorbed the Chinese civilization, and its influence carried Chinese trade and knowledge to the Arctic circle. Mr. Fu compares this Siberian monarchy to the empire of Charlemagne in Europe, which we shall presently describe; it was the barbarian becoming "Chinized," as Charlemagne was a barbarian becoming Romanized.

Out of a fusion of these Siberian with native North Chinese elements arose the Suy dynasty, which conquered the south. This Suy dynasty marks the beginning of a renascence of China. Under a Suy monarch the Lu-chu isles were annexed to China, and there was a phase of great literary activity. The number of volumes at this time in the imperial library was increased, we are told, to 54,000. The dawn of the seventh century saw the beginning of the great Tang dynasty which was to endure for three centuries.

The renascence of China that began with Suy and culminated in Tang was, Mr. Fu insists, a real new birth. "The spirit," he writes, "was a new one; it marked the Tang civilization with entirely distinctive features. Four main factors had been brought together and fused: (1) Chinese liberal culture; (2) Chinese classicism; (3) Indian Buddhism; and (4) Northern bravery.

"A new China had come into being. The provincial system, the central administration and the military organization of the Tang dynasty were quite different from those of their predecessors. The arts had been much influenced and revivified by Indian and Central Asiatic influences. The literature was no mere continuation of the old; it was a new production. The religious and philosophical

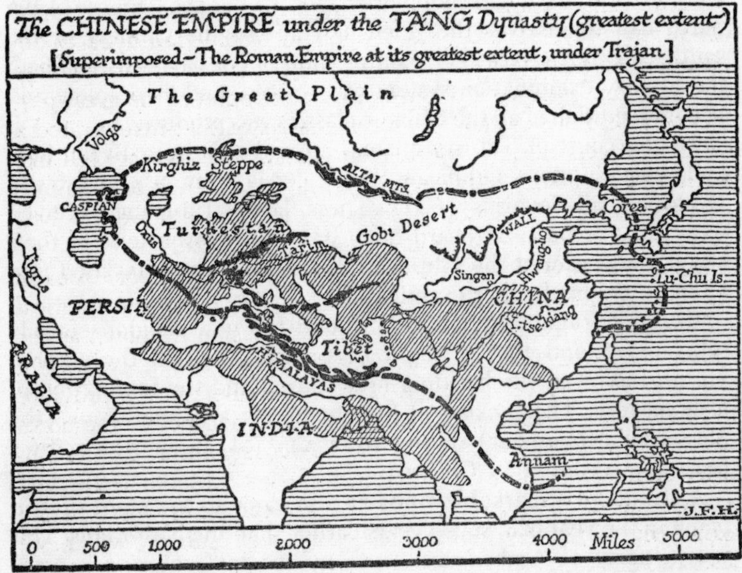

schools of Buddhism were fresh features. It was a period of substantial change.

"It may be interesting to compare this making of China with the fate of the Roman Empire in her later days. As the Roman world was divided into the eastern and western halves, so was the Chinese world into the southern and the northern. The barbarians in the case of Rome and in the case of China made similar invasions. They established dominions of a similar sort. Charlemagne's empire corresponded to that of the Siberian dynasty (Later Wei); the temporary recovery of the Western empire by Justinian corresponded to the temporary recovery of the north by Liu Yu. The Byzantine line corresponded to the southern dynasties. But from this point the two worlds diverged. China recovered her unity; Europe has still to do so."

The dominions of the Emperor Tai-tsung (627), the second Tang monarch, extended southward into Annam and westward to the Caspian Sea. His southern frontier in that direction marched with that of Persia. His northern ran along the Altai from the Kirghis steppe, north of the desert of Gobi. But it did not include Korea, which was conquered and made tributary by his son. This Tang dynasty civilized and incorporated into the Chinese race the whole of the southward population, and just as the Chinese of the north call themselves the "men of Han" so the Chinese of the south call themselves the "men of Tang." The law was codified, the literary examination system was revised, and a complete and accurate edition of all the Chinese classics was produced.

To the court of Tai-tsung came an embassy from Byzantium, and, what is more significant, from Persia came a company of Nestorian missionaries (635). These latter Tai-tsung received with great respect; he heard them state the chief articles of their creed, and ordered the Christian scriptures to be translated into Chinese for his further examination.

In 638 he announced that he found the new religion entirely satisfactory, and that it might be preached within the empire. He also allowed the building of a church and the foundation of a monastery. There exists at Sian-fu to-day a carved stone (the Nestorian Monument) dating from A.D. 781, upon which these facts are recorded in Chinese.

A still more remarkable embassy also came to the court of Tai-tsung in the year 628, seven years earlier than the Nestorians. This was a party of Arabs, who came by sea to Canton in a trading vessel from Yanbu, the port of Medina in Arabia. (Incidentally it is interesting to know that there were such vessels engaged in an east and west trade at this time.) These Arabs had been sent by that Muhammad we have already mentioned, who styled himself "The Prophet of God," and the message they brought to Tai-tsung was probably identical with the summons which was sent in the same year to the Byzantine emperor Heraclius and to Kavadh in Ctesiphon.

But the Chinese monarch neither neglected the message as Heraclius did, nor insulted the envoys after the fashion of the parricide Kavadh. He received them well, expressed great interest in their theological views, and assisted them, it is said, to build a mosque for the Arab traders in Canton—a mosque which survives to this day. It is one of the oldest mosques in the world.

§ 8

The urbanity, the culture, and the power of China under the early Tang rulers are in so vivid a contrast with the decay, disorder, and divisions of the Western world, as at once to raise some of the most interesting questions in the history of civilization. Why did not China keep this great lead she had won by her rapid return to unity and order? Why does she not to this day dominate the world culturally and politically?

For a long time she certainly did keep ahead. It is only a thousand years later, in the sixteenth and seventeenth centuries, with the discovery of America, the spread of printed books and education in the West, and the dawn of modern scientific discovery, that we can say with confidence that the Western world began to pull ahead of China again. Under the Tang rule, her greatest period, and then again under the artistic but rather decadent Sung dynasty (960–1279), and again during the period of the cultured Mings (1368–1644), China presented a spectacle of prosperity, happiness, and artistic activity far in front of any contemporary state. And seeing that she achieved so much, why did she not achieve more? Chinese shipping was upon the seas, and there was a considerable overseas trade during that time. Why did the Chinese never discover America or Australia?

There are old Bushmen rock paintings which may show that isolated Chinese ships reached South Africa at some unknown date, and there are said to be traces of Chinese visitors in Mexico, but if so, neither of these casual explorations seems to have been followed up any more than the circumnavigation of Africa by the Carthaginians or the early visits of the Northmen to America were followed up. There are also, says Mr. Vogan, Chinese rock carvings in New Zealand and New California. It needs something more than individual genius and unsupported enterprise for a discovery to be secured for the community and to fructify into established and usable knowledge. The community itself must be ready.

There was, indeed, as much isolated observation, ingenuity, and invention in China as in any part of the world. The Chinese knew of gunpowder in the sixth century, they used coal and gas heating locally centuries before these things were used in Europe; their bridge-building, their hydraulic engineering were admirable;

the knowledge of materials shown in their enamel and lacquer ware is very great. Why did they never organize the system of record and co-operation in inquiry that has given the world modern science? And why, in spite of their general training in good manners and self-restraint, did intellectual education never soak down into the general mass of the population? Why are the masses of China to-day, and why have they always been, in spite of an exceptionally high level of natural intelligence, illiterate?

It is customary to meet such questions with rather platitudinous answers. We are told that the Chinaman is the most conservative of human beings, that, in contrast with the European races, his mind is twisted round towards the past, that he is the willing slave of etiquette and precedent to a degree inconceivable to Western minds. He is represented as having a mentality so distinct that one might almost expect to find a difference in brain structure to explain it. The appeals of Confucius to the wisdom of the ancients are always quoted to clinch this suggestion.

If, however, we examine this generalization more closely, it dissolves into thin air. The superior intellectual initiative, the liberal enterprise, the experimental disposition that is supposed to characterize the Western mind, is manifest in the history of that mind only during certain phases and under exceptional circumstances. For the rest, the Western world displays itself as traditional and conservative as China. And, on the other hand, the Chinese mind has, under conditions of stimulus, shown itself quite as inventive and versatile as the European, and the very kindred Japanese mind even more so. For, take the case of the Greeks, the whole swing of their mental vigour falls into the period between the sixth century B.C. and the decay of the Alexandrian Museum under the late Ptolemies in the second century B.C. There were Greeks before that time and Greeks since, but a history of a thousand years of the Byzantine Empire showed the Hellenic world at least as intellectually stagnant as China. Then we have already drawn attention to the comparative sterility of the Italian mind during the Roman period, and its abundant fertility since the Renaissance of learning. The English mind again had a phase of brightness in the seventh and eighth centuries, and it did not shine again until the fifteenth. Again, the mind of the Arabs, as we shall presently tell, blazed out like a star for half a dozen generations after the appearance of Islam, having never achieved anything of importance before or since. On the other hand, there was always a great deal of scattered inventiveness in China, and the progress of Chinese art witnesses to new movements and vigorous innovations. We exaggerate the reverence of the Chinese for their fathers; parricide was a far commoner crime among the Chinese emperors than it was even among the rulers of Persia. Moreover, there have been several liberalizing movements in China, several recorded struggles against the "ancient ways."

It has already been suggested that phases of real intellectual progress in any community seem to be connected with the existence of a detached class of men, sufficiently free not to be obliged to toil or worry exhaustively about mundane needs, and not rich and powerful enough to be tempted into extravagances of lust, display, or cruelty. They must have a sense of security, but not a conceit of superiority. This class, we have further insinuated, must be able to talk freely and communicate easily. It must not be watched for heresy or persecuted for any ideas it may express. Such a happy state of affairs certainly prevailed in Greece during its best days. A class of intelligent, free gentlefolk is, indeed, evident in history whenever there is a record of bold philosophy or effective scientific advances.

In the days of Tang and Sung and Ming there must have been an abundance of pleasantly circumstanced people in China of just the class that supplied most of the young men of the Academy at Athens, or the bright intelligence of Renaissance Italy, or the members of the London Royal Society, that mother-society of modern science; and yet China did not produce in these periods of opportunity any such large beginnings of recorded and analyzed fact.

If we reject the idea that there is some profound racial difference between China and the West which makes the Chinese by nature conservative and the West by nature progressive, then we are forced to look for the operating cause of this difference in progressiveness in some other direction. Many people are disposed to find that operating cause, which has, in spite of her original advantages, retarded China so greatly during the last four or five centuries, in the imprisonment of the Chinese mind in a script and in an idiom of thought so elaborate and so difficult that the mental energy of the country has been largely consumed in acquiring it. This view deserves examination.

We have already given an account of the peculiarities of Chinese writing and of the Chinese language. The Japanese writing is derived from the Chinese, and consists of a more rapidly written system of forms. A great number of these forms are ideograms taken over from the Chinese and used exactly as the Chinese ideograms are used, but also a number of signs are used to express syllables; there is a Japanese syllabary after the fashion of the Sumerian syllabary we have described in an earlier chapter. The Japanese writing remains a clumsy system, as clumsy as cuneiform, though not so clumsy as Chinese; and there has been a movement in Japan to adopt a Western alphabet. Korea long ago went a step farther and developed a true alphabet from the same Chinese origins.

With these exceptions all the great writing systems now in use in the world are based on the Mediterranean alphabets, and are beyond comparison more easily learnt and mastered than the Chinese. This means that while other peoples learn merely a comparatively simple, straightforward method of setting down the language with which they are familiar, the Chinaman has to master a great multitude of complex word-signs and word-groups. He must not simply learn the signs, but the established grouping of those signs, to present various meanings. He must familiarize himself, therefore, with a number of exemplary classical works. Consequently, in China, while you will find great numbers of people who know the significance of certain frequent and familiar characters, you discover only a few whose knowledge is sufficiently extensive to grasp the meaning of a newspaper paragraph, and still fewer who can read any subtlety of intention or fine shades of meaning. In a lesser degree this is true also of Japan. No doubt European readers, especially of such word-rich unsystematic languages as English or Russian, vary greatly among themselves in regard to the extent of books they can understand and how far they understand them; their power varies according to their vocabularies; but the corresponding levels of understanding among the Chinese represent a far greater expenditure of time and labour upon their attainment. A mandarin's education in China is, mainly, learning to read.

And it may be that the consequent preoccupation of the educated class during its most susceptible years upon the Chinese classics gave it a bias in favour of this traditional learning upon which it had spent so much time and energy. Few men who have toiled to build up any system of knowledge in their minds will willingly scrap it in favour of something strange and new. This disposition is as characteristic of the West as of the East, it is shown as markedly by the scholars of the British and American universities as by any Chinese mandarins; and the British at the present time, in spite of the great and manifest advantages in popular education and national propaganda the change would give them, refuse to make any move from their present barbaric orthography towards a phonetic alphabet and spelling. The peculiarities of the Chinese script, and the educational system arising out of that script, must have acted age after age as an invincible filter that favoured the plastic and scholarly mind as against the restive and originating type, and kept the latter out of positions of influence and authority. There is much that is plausible in this explanation.

It was not, however, until the comparatively recent Ming dynasty that the classical examination system was established in its full severity. The Ming dynasty (1368–1644) was a patriotic and conservative dynasty, resuming possession of China after the rule of the Mongols. The first of the Ming emperors, says Mr. L. Y. Chen, when he reorganized the examination system upon more exacting lines, said: "This will bring all the intellectuals of the world into my trap." The "Five Classics and the Four Books" have imprisoned the mind of China. By the time a man has toiled through these his system of values is as rigid and incurable as that of a classical scholar at Oxford.

There have been several attempts to simplify the Chinese writing and to adopt an alphabetical system. In the early days of Buddhism in China, when there was a considerable amount of translation from Sanscrit, Indian influences came near to achieving this end; two Chinese alphabets were, indeed, invented, and each had some little use. But what hindered the general adoption of these, and what stands in the way of any phonetic system of Chinese writing to-day, is this, that while the literary script and phraseology is the same from one end of China to the other, the spoken language of the common people, both in pronunciation and in its familiar idioms, varies so widely that men from one province may be incomprehensible to men from another. There is, however, a "standard Chinese," a rather bookish spoken idiom, which is generally understood by educated people; and it is upon the possibility of applying an alphabetical system of writing to this standard Chinese that the hopes of many modern educational reformers in China are based at the present time. A Chinese alphabet has been formed; it is taught in the common schools, and newspapers and pamphlets are issued in it. And the rigid examination system that killed all intellectual initiatives has been destroyed.

There has also been a considerable simplification in the direction of introducing spoken idioms into written Chinese. This makes for ease and lucidity; even in the old characters, such Chinese is more easily read and written, and it is far better adapted than classical Chinese to the needs of modern literary expression.

But there may be other causes, also, that kept China from pushing forward to the definite leadership of mankind. The very success and early prosperity and general contentment of China in the past must have worked to justify in that land all the natural self-complacency and conservatism of our species. No animal need change when its conditions are "good enough" for present survival. And in this matter man is still an animal. Until the nineteenth century, for more than two thousand years, there was little in the history of China that could cause any serious doubts in the mind of a Chinaman of the general superiority of his own civilization to that of the rest of the world, and there was no reason apparent, therefore, for any alteration. China produced a profusion of beautiful art, some delightful poetry, astonishing cookery, and thousands of millions of glowingly pleasant lives generation after generation. It was and is a country of small properties; all hands are wanted, and can be absorbed in old ancestral agricultural jobs. Moreover, there are outlets for expansive forces. To the north and west there is still great room for settlement. Nothing has occurred, therefore, no intense internal tension, to break up the patriarchal Chinese family clan which marries its sons at an early age and retains them at home before they achieve economic independence. So that China went on age by age, and still goes on, without any such general boredom, servitude, indignity, and misery as underlay the rule of the rich in the Roman Empire, and led at last to its collapse. There was much poverty, much discontent, but it was not massed uprooted poverty, it was not a necessary popular discontent. After every convulsion, after every disaster, population recovered; the wounds healed. For a thousand years the Chinese system though it creaked and swayed at times, seemed proof against decay. Dynastic changes there were, rebellions, phases of disorder, famines, pestilences; two great invasions that set foreign dynasties upon the throne of the Son of Heaven; but no such shock as to revolutionize the order of the daily round. The emperors and dynasties might come and go; the mandarins, the examinations, the classics, and the traditions and habitual life remained. From the days of the Tang dynasty onward, though Chinese civilization spread slowly and steadily into Annam, into Cambodia, into Siam, into Tibet, into Nepal, Korea, Mongolia and Manchuria, there is little more than geographical progress to record. The Chinese of the seventh century A.D. were in all essentials as civilized a people as they were a thousand years later.

§ 9

Here we may, perhaps, make a remark or so about the art and architecture of China during this period of the Han and Tang

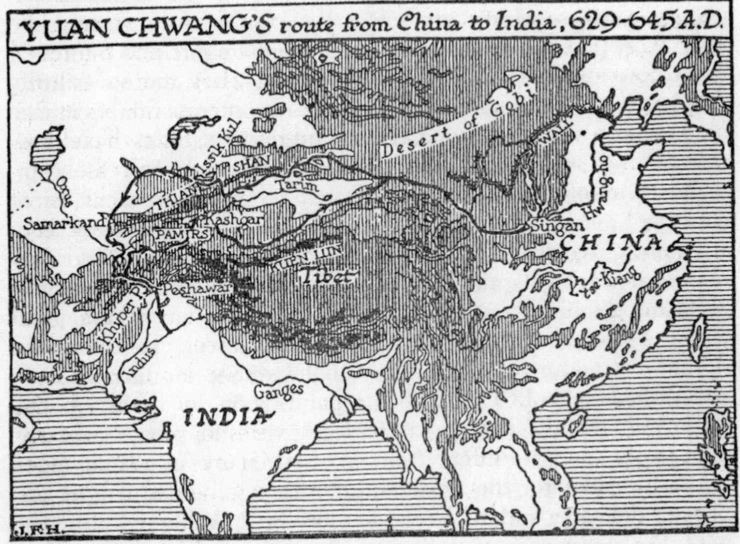

and the intervening dynasties. For reasons that we are quite unable to analyze the Chinese have always preferred the use of timber and brick to that of stone in building. Yet there is plentiful good building-stone to be found in China. Hardly any ruins, and no buildings apart from the Great Wall, earlier than the eleventh century A.D. are known to history. But pictures and records testify to a long tradition going back to the Ts'in dynasty or earlier.

The earliest forms of building derived directly from the Mongol tent. The main feature is the great roof, which may be double or triple and with carved and lacquered woodwork. The roof itself may be covered with glazed and brilliantly coloured tiles. Generally, buildings are of one story, spreading horizontally. A frequent feature in Chinese design is the honorific archway. Bridges of stone abound, and some are very beautiful. The heaven-pointing pagoda is a third type of erection, and these and terraces and balustradings complete the general scheme of Chinese buildings. This was the architectural landscape of China at the beginning of the Christian era, and so it remains to this day. The pagoda is said, perhaps incorrectly, to be due to Indian Buddhist initiatives, and to be the Chinese equivalent of the Indian monumental *stupa*.

The same indifference to enduring materials affects our knowledge of Chinese plastic art before the Han dynasty. Almost the only exception is bronze. We know of bronze jars and figures of the Chow and even the Shang dynasties. They are so skilfully and beautifully done that they imply the contemporary existence of a whole world of sympathetic productions that have now perished. It is only with the Han dynasty and after the commencement of the Christian era that we come to a phase of Chinese life that has left many vestiges in any other material.

Painting, we are told, was the essential art of China, and very beautiful work was already being done in the Han period. Ku-Kai-Chih (fourth century A.D.) is named as one of the great Chinese masters of the brush. Some of his work survives, and it shows a maturity and mastery that indicate an already well-established school. The Chinese painting is invariably watercolour; in the place of great frescoes we find pictures on silk and paper, and it differs from Western work in displaying a positive dislike for the representation of relief. It is flat, atmospheric, delicate, and it deals far more with landscape and less with the close representation of the human body. The Tang dynasty marks what many critics consider to be the supreme period of Chinese painting.

Chinese sculpture by no means kept pace with Chinese pictorial art, and is hardly to be mentioned beside European work, but on the other hand Chinese pottery is pre-eminent. The Chinese fired their pottery at much higher temperatures than the Western world, and produced porcelain and unequalled glazes by the end of the Tang period. The Han pottery was already very hard and fine. Great numbers of glazed earthenware figures of attendants, horses, camels and so forth, dating from the Tang period, are now in European homes and collections. They came out of graves, and they were put into these graves in lieu of the butchered slaves and animals of a more barbaric past. These graveside massacres, to provide the departed Mongol chieftain with service and beasts of burden in the land of shades, went on in China until the seventh or sixth century B.C. Then images were substituted. The Huns in the time of Attila still observed the ancient custom of a real slaughter, but it had been extinct in Egypt before the earliest dynasties and had already given place there to the funeral images.

§ 10

In 629, the year after the arrival of Muhammad's envoys at Canton and thirty odd years after the landing of Pope Gregory's missionaries in England, a certain learned and devout Buddhist named Yuan Chwang, or as some authorities prefer to spell it, Hiuen-Tsiang, started out from Sian-fu (Signan), Tai-tsung's capital, upon a great journey to India. He was away sixteen years; he returned in 645, and he wrote an account of his travels which is treasured as a Chinese classic. One or two points about his experience are to be noted here because they contribute to our general review of the state of the world in the seventh century A.D.

Yuan Chwang was as eager for marvels and as credulous as Herodotus, and without the latter writer's fine sense of history; he could never pass a monument or ruin without learning some fabulous story about it. Chinese ideas of the dignity of literature perhaps prevented him from telling us much detail of how he travelled, who were his attendants, how he was lodged, or what he ate and how he paid his expenses—details precious to the historian; nevertheless, he gives us a series of illuminating flashes upon China, Central Asia, and India in the period now under consideration.

His journey was an enormous one. He went and came back by way of the Pamirs. He went by the northern route, crossing the Desert of Gobi, passing along the southern slopes of the Thien Shan, skirting the great deep blue lake of Issik Kul, and so to Tashkend and Samarkand, and then more or less in the footsteps of Alexander the Great southward to the Khyber Pass and Peshawar. He returned by the southern route, crossing the Pamirs from Afghanistan to Kashgar, and so along the line of retreat the Yueh-Chi had followed in the reverse direction seven centuries before, and by Yarkand, along the slopes of the Kuen Lun, to rejoin his former route near the desert end of the

Great Wall. Each route involved some hard mountaineering. His journeyings in India are untraceable; he was there fourteen years, and he went all over the peninsula from Nepal to Ceylon.

At that time there was an imperial edict forbidding foreign travel, so that Yuan Chwang started from Sian-fu like an escaping criminal. There was a pursuit to prevent him carrying out his project. How he bought from a strange greybeard a lean red-coloured horse that knew the desert paths, how he dodged a frontier guard-house with the help of a "foreign person" who made him a bridge of brushwood lower down the river, how he crossed the desert guided by the bones of men and cattle, how he saw a mirage, and how twice he narrowly escaped being shot by arrows when he was getting water near the watch-towers on the desert track, the reader will find in the *Life*. He lost his way in the Desert of Gobi, and for four nights and five days he had no water; when he was in the mountains among the glaciers, twelve of his party were frozen to death. All this is in the *Life;* he tells little of it in his own account of his travels.

He shows us the Turks, this new development of the Hun tradition, in possession not only of what is now Turkestan, but all along the northern route. He mentions many cities and considerable cultivation. He is entertained by various rulers, allies of more or less nominally tributaries to China, and among others by the Khan of the Turks, a magnificent person in green satin, with his long hair tied with silk.

"The gold embroidery of this grand tent shone with a dazzling splendour; the ministers of the presence in attendance sat on mats in long rows on either side, all dressed in magnificent brocade robes, while the rest of the retinue on duty stood behind. You saw that although it was a case of a frontier ruler, yet there was an air of distinction and elegance. The Khan came out from his tent about thirty paces to meet Yuan Chwang, who, after a courteous greeting, entered the tent. . . . After a short interval envoys from China and Kao-chang were admitted and presented their despatches and credentials, which the Khan perused. He was much elated, and caused the envoys to be seated; then he ordered wine and music for himself and them and grape-syrup for the pilgrim. Hereupon all pledged each other, and the filling and draining of the winecups made a din and bustle, while the mingled music of various instruments rose loud: although the airs were the popular strains of foreigners, yet they pleased the senses and exhilarated the mental faculties.

After a little, piles of roasted beef and mutton were served for the others, and lawful food, such as cakes, milk, candy, honey, and grapes, for the pilgrim. After the entertainment, grape-syrup was again served, and the Khan invited Yuan Chwang to improve the occasion, whereupon the pilgrim expounded the doctrines of the 'ten virtues,' compassion for animal life, and the paramitas and emancipation. The Khan, raising his hands, bowed, and gladly believed and accepted the teaching."

Yuan Chwang's account of Samarkand is of a large and prosperous city, "a great commercial entrepôt, the country about it very fertile, abounding in trees and flowers and yielding many fine horses. Its inhabitants were skilful craftsmen, smart and energetic." At that time, we must remember, there was hardly such a thing as a town in Anglo-Saxon England.

As his narrative approached his experiences in India, however, the pious and learned pilgrim in Yuan Chwang got the better of the traveller, and the book becomes congested with monstrous stories of incredible miracles. Nevertheless, we get an impression of houses, clothing and the like, closely resembling those of the India of to-day. Then, as now, the kaleidoscopic variety of an Indian crowd contrasted with the blue uniformity of the multitude in China. In the time of Buddha it is doubtful if there were reading and writing in India; now reading and writing were quite common accomplishments. Yuan Chwang gives an interesting account of a great Buddhist university of Nalanda, where ruins have quite recently been discovered and excavated. Nalanda and Taxilla seem to have been considerable educational centres as early as the opening of the schools of Athens. He also visited the caves at Ajanta of which we have told. The caste system Yuan Chwang found fully established in spite of Buddha, and the Brahmins were now altogether in the ascendant. He names the four main castes we have mentioned, but his account of their functions is rather different. The Sudras, he says, were the tillers of the soil. Indian writers say that their function was to wait upon the "twice-born" castes above them.

But, as we have already intimated, Yuan Chwang's account of Indian realities is swamped by his accumulation of legends and pious inventions. For these he had come, and in these he rejoiced. The rest, as we shall see, was a task that had been set him. The faith of Buddha, which in the days of Asoka, and even so late as Kanishka, was still pure enough to be a noble inspiration, we now discover absolutely lost in a wilderness of preposterous rubbish, a philosophy of endless Buddhas, tales of manifestations and marvels like a Christmas pantomime, miraculous conceptions by six-tusked elephants, charitable princes giving themselves up to be eaten by starving tigresses, temples built over a sacred nail-paring, and the like. We cannot give such stories here; if the reader like that sort of thing, he must go to the publications of the Royal Asiatic Society or the India Society, where he will find a delirium of such imaginations. And in competition with this Buddhism, intellectually undermined as it now was and smothered in gilded decoration, Brahminism was everywhere gaining ground again, as Yuan Chwang notes with regret.

Side by side with these evidences of a vast intellectual decay in India, we may note the repeated appearance in Yuan Chwang's narrative of ruined and deserted cities. Much of the country was still suffering from the ravages of the Ephthalites and the consequent disorders. Again and again we find such passages as this: "He went north-east through a great forest, the road being a narrow, dangerous path, with wild buffalo and wild elephants, and robbers and hunters always in wait to kill travellers, and emerging from the forest he reached the country of Kou-shih-na-ka-lo (Kúsinagara). The city walls were in ruins, and the towns and villages were deserted. The brick foundations of the 'old city' (that is, the city which had been the capital) were above ten *li* in circuit; there were very few inhabitants, the interior of the city being a wild waste." This ruin was, however, by no means universal; there is at least as much mention of crowded cities and villages and busy cultivations.

The *Life* tells of many hardships upon the return journey: he fell among robbers; the great elephant that was carrying the bulk of his possessions was drowned; he had much difficulty in getting fresh transport. Here we cannot deal with these adventures.

The return of Yuan Chwang to Sian-fu, the Chinese capital, was, we gather, a triumph. Advance couriers must have told of his coming. There was a public holiday; the streets were decorated by gay banners and made glad with music. He was escorted into the city with great pomp and ceremony. Twenty horses were needed to carry the spoils of his travels; he had brought with him hundreds of Buddhist books written in Sanscrit, and made of trimmed leaves of palm and birch bark strung together in layers; he had many images great and small of Buddha, in gold, silver, crystal, and sandal-wood; he had holy pictures, and no fewer than one hundred and fifty well-authenticated true relics of Buddha. Yuan Chwang was presented to the emperor, who treated him as a personal friend, took him into the palace, and questioned him day by day about the wonders of these strange lands in which he had stayed so long. But while the emperor asked about India, the pilgrim was disposed only to talk about Buddhism.

The subsequent history of Yuan Chwang contains two incidents that throw light upon the mental workings of this great monarch, Tai-tsung, who was probably quite as much a Moslem as he was a Christian or a Buddhist. The trouble about all religious specialists is that they know too much about their own religion and how it differs from others; the advantage, or disadvantage, of such creative statesmen as Tai-tsung and Constantine the Great is that they know comparatively little of such matters. Evidently the fundamental good of all these religions seemed to Tai-tsung to be much the same fundamental good. So it was natural to him to propose that Yuan Chwang should now give up the religious life and come into his foreign office, a proposal that Yuan Chwang would not entertain for a moment. The emperor then insisted at least upon a written account of the travels, and so got this classic we treasure. And finally Tai-tsung proposed to this highly saturated Buddhist that he should now use his knowledge of Sanscrit in translating the works of the great Chinese teacher, Lao Tse, so as to make them available for Indian readers.

It seemed, no doubt, to the emperor a fair return and a useful service to the fundamental good that lies beneath all religions. On the whole, he thought Lao Tse might very well rank with or even a little above Buddha, and, therefore, that if his work was put before the Brahmins, they would receive it gladly. In much the same spirit Constantine the Great had done his utmost to make Arius and Athanasius settle down amicably together. But naturally enough this suggestion was repulsed by Yuan Chwang. He retired to a monastery, and spent the rest of his years translating as much as he could of the Buddhist literature he had brought with him into elegant Chinese writing.

XXX
MUHAMMAD AND ISLAM

§ 1. *Arabia before Muhammad.* § 2. *Life of Muhammad to the Hegira.* § 3. *Muhammad becomes a Fighting Prophet.* § 4. *The Teachings of Islam.* § 5. *The Caliphs Abu Bekr and Omar.* § 6. *The Great Days of the Omayyads.* § 7. *The Decay of Islam under the Abbasids.* § 8. *Arabic Culture.* § 9. *Arabic Art.*

§ 1

WE HAVE already described how in A.D. 628 the courts of Heraclius, of Kavadh, and of Tai-tsung were visited by Arab envoys sent from a certain Muhammad, "The Prophet of God," at the small trading town of Medina in Arabia. We must tell now who this prophet was who had arisen among the nomads and traders of the Arabian desert.

From time immemorial Arabia, except for the fertile strip of the Yemen to the south, had been a land of nomads, the headquarters and land of origin of the Semitic peoples. From Arabia at various times waves of these nomads had drifted north, east, and west into the early civilizations of Egypt, the Mediterranean coast and Mesopotamia. We have noted in this history how the Sumerians were swamped and overcome by such Semitic waves, how the Semitic Phœnicians and Canaanites established themselves along the eastern shores of the Mediterranean, how Semitic peoples had adopted a settled life in Babylonia and Assyria, how the Hyksos conquered Egypt, how the Arameans established themselves in Syria with Damascus as their capital, and how the Hebrews partially conquered their "Promised Land." At some unknown date the Chaldeans drifted in from Eastern Arabia and settled in the old Southern Sumerian lands. With each invasion first this and then that section of the Semitic peoples comes into history. But each of such swarmings still leaves a tribal nucleus behind to supply fresh invasions in the future.

The history of the more highly organized empires of the horse and iron period, the empires of roads and writing, shows

Arabia thrust like a wedge between Egypt, Palestine, and the Euphrates-Tigris country, and still a reservoir of nomadic tribes who raid and trade and exact tribute for the immunity and protection of caravans. There are temporary and flimsy subjugations. Egypt, Persia, Macedonia, Rome, Syria, Constantinople, and again Persia, claim some unreal suzerainty in turn over Arabia, profess some unsubstantial protection. Under Trajan there was a Roman province of "Arabia," which included the then fertile region of the Hauran and extended as far as Petra. Now and then some Arab chief and his trading city rises to temporary splendour. Such was that Odenathus of Palmyra, whose brief career we have noted; and another such transitory desert city whose ruins still astonish the traveller was Baalbek.

After the destruction of Palmyra, the desert Arabs began to be spoken of in the Roman and Persian records as Saracens.

In the time of Chosroes II, Persia claimed a certain ascendancy over Arabia, and maintained officials and tax collectors in the Yemen. Before that time the Yemen had been under the rule of the Abyssinian Christians for some years, and before that for seven centuries it had had native princes professing, be it noted, the Jewish faith.

Until the opening of the seventh century A.D. there were no signs of any unwonted or dangerous energy in the Arabian deserts. The life of the country was going on as it had gone on for long generations. Wherever there were fertile patches—where-ever, that is, there was a spring or a well—a scanty agricultural population subsisted, living in walled towns, walled because of the Bedouin who wandered with their sheep, cattle and horses over the desert. Upon the main caravan routes the chief towns rose to a certain second-rate prosperity, and foremost among them were Medina and Mecca. In the beginning of the seventh century Medina was a town of about 15,000 inhabitants all told; Mecca may have had 20,000 or 25,000. Medina was a comparatively well-watered town, with abundant date groves; its inhabitants were Yemenites, from the fertile land to the south. Mecca was a town of a different character, built about a spring of water with a bitter taste, and inhabited by recently settled Bedouin.

Mecca was not merely nor primarily a trading centre; it was a place of pilgrimage. Among the Arab tribes there had long existed a sort of Amphictyony centring upon Mecca and certain other sanctuaries; there were months of truce to war and blood feuds, and customs of protection and hospitality for the pilgrim.

In addition there had grown up an Olympic element in these gatherings; the Arabs were discovering possibilities of beauty in their language, and there were recitations of war poetry and love songs. The sheiks of the tribes, under a "king of the poets," sat in judgment and awarded prizes; the prize songs were sung through all Arabia.

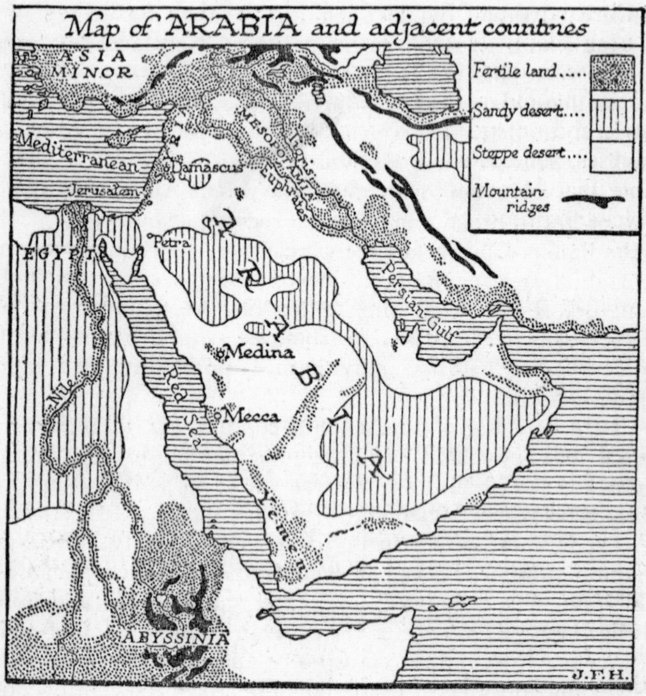

The Kaaba, the sanctuary at Mecca, was of very ancient date. It was a small square temple of black stones which had for its corner-stone a meteorite. This meteorite was regarded as a god, and all the little tribal gods of Arabia were under his protection. The permanent inhabitants of Mecca were a tribe of Bedouin who had seized this temple and constituted themselves its guardians. To them there came in the months of truce a great concourse of people, who marched about the Kaaba ceremonially, bowed themselves, and kissed the stone, and also engaged in trade and poetical recitations. The Meccans profited much from these visitors.

All of this is very reminiscent of the religious and political state of affairs in Greece fourteen centuries earlier. But the paganism of these more primitive Arabs was already being assailed from several directions. There had been a great proselytizing of Arabs during the period of the Maccabeans and Herods in Judea; and, as we have already noted, the Yemen had been in succession under the rule of Jews (Arab proselytes to Judaism, *i.e.*), Christians, and Zoroastrians. It is evident that there must have been plenty of religious discussion during the pilgrimage fairs at Mecca and the like centres. Naturally enough, Mecca was a stronghold of the old pagan cult which gave it its importance and prosperity; Medina, on the other hand, had Jewish proclivities, and there were Jewish settlements near by. It was inevitable that Mecca and Medina should be in a state of rivalry and bickering feud.

§ 2

It was in Mecca about the year A.D. 570 that Muhammad, the founder of Islam, was born. He was born in considerable poverty and even by the standards of the desert he was uneducated; it is doubtful if he ever learnt to write. He was for some years a shepherd's boy; then he became the servant of a certain Kadija the widow of a rich merchant. Probably he had to look after her camels or help in her trading operations; and he is said to have travelled with caravans to the Yemen and to Syria. He does not seem to have been a very useful trader, but he had the good fortune to find favour in the lady's eyes, and she married him, to the great annoyance of her family. He was then only twenty-five years old. It is uncertain if his wife was much older, though tradition declares she was forty. After the marriage he probably made no more long journeys. There were several children, one of whom was named Abd Manif—that is to say, the servant of the Meccan god Manif, which demonstrates that at that time Muhammad had made no religious discoveries.

Until he was forty he did, indeed, live a particularly undistinguished life in Mecca, as the husband of a prosperous wife. There may be some ground for the supposition that he became partner in a business in agricultural produce. To anyone visiting Mecca about A.D. 600 he would probably have seemed something of a loafer, a rather shy, good-looking individual, sitting about and listening to talk, a poor poet, and an altogether second-rate man.

About his internal life we can only speculate. Imaginative writers have supposed that he had great spiritual struggles, that he went out into the desert in agonies of doubt and divine desire. "In the silence of the desert night, in the bright heat of noontide desert day, he, as do all men, had known and felt himself alone yet not in solitude, for the desert is of God, and in the desert no man may deny Him."[1] Maybe that was so, but there is no evidence of any such desert trips. Yet he was certainly thinking deeply of the things about him. Possibly he had seen Christian churches in Syria; almost certainly he knew much of the Jews and their religion, and he heard their scorn for this black stone of the Kaaba that ruled over the three hundred odd tribal gods of Arabia. He saw the pilgrimage crowds, and noted the threads of insincerity and superstition in the paganism of the town. It oppressed his mind. The Jews had, perhaps, converted him to a belief in the One True God, without his knowing what had happened to him.

At last he could keep these feelings to himself no longer. When he was forty he began to talk about the reality of God, at first apparently only to his wife and a few intimates. He produced certain verses, which he declared had been revealed to him by an angel. They involved an assertion of the unity of God and some acceptable generalizations about righteousness. He also insisted upon a future life, the fear of hell for the negligent and evil, and the reservation of paradise for the believer in the One God. Except for his claim to be a new prophet, there does not seem to have been anything very new about these doctrines at the time, but this was seditious teaching for Mecca, which partly subsisted upon its polytheistic cult, and which was therefore holding on to idols when all the rest of the world was giving them up. Like Mani, Muhammad claimed that the prophets before him, and especially Jesus and Abraham, had been divine teachers, but that he crowned and completed their teaching. Buddhism, however, he did not name, probably because he had never heard of Buddha. Desert Arabia was in a theological backwater.

For some years the new religion was the secret of a small group of simple people, Kadija, the Prophet's wife, Ali, an adopted son, Zeid, a slave, and Abu Bekr, a friend and admirer. For some years it was an obscure sect in a few households of Mecca, a mere scowl and muttering at idolatry, so obscure and unim-

---

[1] Sir Mark Sykes.

portant that the leading men of the town did not trouble about it in the least. Then it gathered strength. Muhammad began to preach more openly, to teach the doctrine of a future life, and to threaten idolaters and unbelievers with hell fire. He seems to have preached with considerable effect. It appeared to many that he was aiming at a sort of dictatorship in Mecca, and drawing many susceptible and discontented people to his side; and an attempt was made to discourage and suppress the new movement.

Mecca was a place of pilgrimage and a sanctuary; no blood could be shed within its walls; nevertheless, things were made extremely disagreeable for the followers of the new teacher. Boycott and confiscation were used against them. Some were driven to take refuge in Christian Abyssinia. But the Prophet himself went unscathed because he was well connected, and his opponents did not want to begin a blood feud. We cannot follow the fluctuations of the struggle here, but it is necessary to note one perplexing incident in the new Prophet's career, which, says Sir Mark Sykes, "proves him to have been an Arab of the Arabs." After all his insistence upon the oneness of God, he wavered. He came into the courtyard of the Kaaba and declared that the gods and goddesses of Mecca might, after all, be real, might be a species of saints with a power of intercession.

His recantation was received with enthusiasm, but he had no sooner made it than he repented, and his repentance shows that he had indeed the fear of God in him. His lapse from honesty proves him honest. He did all he could to repair the evil he had done. He said that the devil had possessed his tongue, and he denounced idolatry again with renewed vigour. The struggle against the antiquated deities, after a brief interval of peace, was renewed again more grimly, and with no further hope of reconciliation.

For a time the old interests had the upper hand. At the end of ten years of prophesying, Muhammad found himself a man of fifty, and altogether unsuccessful in Mecca. Kadija, his first wife, was dead, and several of his chief supporters had also recently died. He sought a refuge at the neighbouring town of Tayf, but Tayf drove him out with stones and abuse. Then, when the world looked darkest to him, opportunity opened before him. He found he had been weighed and approved in an unexpected quarter. The city of Medina was much torn by internal dissension, and many of its people, during the time of pilgrimage to Mecca, had been attracted by Muhammad's teaching. Probably the numerous Jews in Medina had shaken the ancient idolatry of the people. An invitation was sent to him to come and rule in the name of his God in Medina.

He did not go at once. He parleyed for two years, sending a disciple to preach in Medina and destroy the idols there. Then he began sending such followers as he had in Mecca to Medina to await his coming there; he did not want to trust himself to unknown adherents in a strange city. This exodus of the faithful continued, until at last only he and Abu Bekr remained.

In spite of the character of Mecca as a sanctuary, he was very nearly murdered there. The elders of the town evidently knew of what was going on in Medina, and they realized the danger to them if this seditious prophet presently found himself master of a town on their main caravan route to Syria. Custom must bow to imperative necessity, they thought; and they decided that, blood feud or no blood feud, Muhammad must die. They arranged that he should be murdered in his bed; and in order to share the guilt of this breach of sanctuary they appointed a committee to do this, representing every family in the city except Muhammad's own. But Muhammad had already prepared his flight; and when in the night they rushed into his room, they found Ali, his adopted son, sleeping, or feigning sleep, on his bed.

The flight (the Hegira) was an adventurous one, the pursuit being pressed hard. Expert desert trackers sought for the spoor to the north of the town, but Muhammad and Abu Bekr had gone south to certain caves where camels and provisions were hidden, and thence he made a great detour to Medina. There he and his faithful companion arrived, and were received with great enthusiasm on September 20, 622. It was the end of his probation and the beginning of his power.

§ 3

Until the Hegira, until he was fifty-one, the character of the founder of Islam is a matter of speculation and dispute. Thereafter he is in the light. We discover a man of great imaginative power, but tortuous in the Arab fashion, and with most of the virtues and defects of the Bedouin.

The opening of his reign was "very Bedouin." The rule of the One God of all the earth, as it was interpreted by Muhammad, began with a series of raids—which for more than a year were invariably unsuccessful—upon the caravans of Mecca. Then came a grave scandal, the breaking of the ancient customary truce of the Arab Amphictyony in the sacred month of Rahab. A party of Moslems, in this season of profound peace, treacherously attacked a small caravan and killed a man. It was their only success, and they did it by the order of the Prophet.

Presently came a battle. A force of seven hundred men had come out from Mecca to convoy home another caravan, and they encountered a large raiding party of three hundred. There was a fight, the battle of Badr, and the Meccans got the worst of it. They lost about fifty or sixty killed and as many wounded. Muhammad returned in triumph to Medina, and was inspired by Allah and this success to order the assassination of a number of his opponents among the Jews in the town who had treated his prophetic claims with a disagreeable levity.

But Mecca resolved to avenge Badr, and at the battle of Uhud, near Medina, inflicted an indecisive defeat upon the Prophet's followers. Muhammad was knocked down and nearly killed, and there was much running away among his followers. The Meccans, however, did not push their advantage and enter Medina.

For some time all the energies of the Prophet were concentrated upon rallying his followers, who were evidently much dispirited. The Koran records the chastened feelings of those days. "The *suras* of the Koran," says Sir Mark Sykes, "which are attributed to this period, excel nearly all the others in their majesty and sublime confidence." Here, for the judgment of the reader, is an example of these majestic utterances, from the recent orthodox translation by the Maulvi Muhammad Ali.[1]

"Oh, you who believe! If you obey those who disbelieve, they will turn you back upon your heels, so you will turn back losers.

"Nay! Allah is your Patron, and He is the best of the helpers.

"We will cast terror into the hearts of those who disbelieve, because they set up with Allah that for which He has sent down no authority, and their abode is the fire; and evil is the abode of the unjust.

"And certainly Allah made good to you His promise, when you slew them by His permission, until when you became weak-hearted and disputed about the affair and disobeyed after He had shown you that which you loved; of you were some who desired this world, and of you were some who desired the hereafter; then He turned you away from them that He might try

[1] Published by the *Islamic Review*.

you; and He has certainly pardoned you, and Allah is Gracious to the believers.

"When you ran off precipitately, and did not wait for anyone, and the Apostle was calling you from your rear, so He gave you another sorrow instead of your sorrow, so that you might not grieve at what had escaped you, nor at what befell you; and Allah is aware of what you do.

"Then after sorrow He sent down security upon you, a calm coming upon a party of you, and there was another party whom their own souls had rendered anxious; they entertained about Allah thoughts of ignorance quite unjustly, saying: We have no hand in this affair. Say: surely the affair is wholly in the hands of Allah. They conceal within their souls what they would not reveal to you. They say: Had we any hand in the affair, we would not have been slain here. Say: had you remained in your houses, those for whom slaughter was ordained would certainly have gone forth to the places where they would be slain, and that Allah might test what was in our breasts and that He might purge what was in your hearts; and Allah knows what is in the breasts.

"As for those of you who turned back on the day when the two armies met, only the devil sought to cause them to make a slip on account of some deeds they had done, and certainly Allah has pardoned them; surely Allah is Forgiving, Forbearing."

Inconclusive hostilities continued for some years, and at last Mecca made a crowning effort to stamp out for good and all the growing power of Medina. A mixed force of no fewer than 10,000 men was scraped together, an enormous force for the time and country. It was, of course, an entirely undisciplined force of footmen, horsemen, and camel riders, and it was prepared for nothing but the usual desert scrimmage. Bows, spears, and swords were its only weapons. When at last it arrived amid a vast cloud of dust in sight of the hovels and houses of Medina, instead of a smaller force of the same kind drawn up for battle, as it had expected, it found a new and entirely disconcerting phenomenon, a trench and a wall. Assisted by a Persian convert, Muhammad had entrenched himself in Medina!

This trench struck the Bedouin miscellany as one of the most unsportsmanlike things that had ever been known in the history of the world. They rode about the place. They shouted their opinion of the whole business to the besieged. They discharged a few arrows, and at last encamped to argue about this amazing outrage. They could arrive at no decision. Muhammad would not come out; the rains began to fall, the tents of the allies got wet and the cooking difficult, views became divergent and tempers gave way, and at last this great host dwindled again into its constituent parts without ever having given battle (627). The bands dispersed north, east, and south, became clouds of dust, and ceased to matter. Near Medina was a castle of Jews, against whom Muhammad was already incensed because of their disrespect for his theology. They had shown a disposition to side with the probable victor in this last struggle, and Muhammad now fell upon them, slew all the men, nine hundred of them, and enslaved the women and children. Possibly many of their late allies were among the bidders for these slaves. Never again after this quaint failure did Mecca make an effective rally against Muhammad, and one by one its leading men came over to his side.

We need not follow the windings of the truce and the treaty that finally extended the rule of the Prophet to Mecca. The gist of the agreement was that the faithful should turn towards Mecca when they prayed instead of turning towards Jerusalem, as they had hitherto done, and that Mecca should be the pilgrimage centre of the new faith. So long as the pilgrimage continued, the men of Mecca, it would seem, did not care very much whether the crowd assembled in the name of one god or many. Muhammad was getting more and more hopeless of any extensive conversion of the Jews and Christians, and he was ceasing to press his idea that all these faiths really worshipped the same One God. Allah was becoming more and more his own special God, tethered now by this treaty to the meteoric stone of the Kaaba, and less and less God the Father of all Mankind. Already the Prophet had betrayed a disposition to make a deal with Mecca and at last it was effected. The lordship of Mecca, was well worth the concession. Of comings and goings and a final conflict we need not tell. In 629 Muhammad came to the town as its master. The image of Manif, the god after whom he had once named his son, was smashed under his feet as he entered the Kaaba.

Thereafter his power extended, there were battles, treacheries, massacres; but on the whole he prevailed, until he was master of all Arabia; and when he was master of all Arabia in 632, at the age of sixty-two, he died.

Throughout the concluding eleven years of his life, after the Hegira, there is little to distinguish the general conduct of Muhammad from that of any other welder of peoples into a monarchy. The chief difference is his use of a religion of his own creation as his cement. He was diplomatic, treacherous, ruthless, or compromising as the occasion required, and as any other Arab king might have been in his place; and there was singularly little spirituality in his kingship. Nor was his domestic life during the time of power and freedom one of exceptional edification. Until the death of Kadija, when he was fifty, he seems to have been the honest husband of one wife, but then, as many men do in their declining years, he developed a disagreeably strong interest in women.

He married two wives after the death of Kadija, one being the young Ayesha, who became and remained his favourite and most influential partner; and subsequently a number of other women, wives and concubines, were added to his establishment. This led to much trouble and confusion, and, in spite of many special and very helpful revelations on the part of Allah, these complications still require much explanation and argument from the faithful.

There was, for example, a scandal about Ayesha; she was left behind on one occasion when the howdah and the camel went on, while she was looking for her necklace among the bushes; and so Allah had to intervene with some heat and denounce her slanderers. Allah also had to speak very plainly about the general craving among this household of women for "this world's life and its ornature" and for "finery." Then there was much discussion because the Prophet first married his young cousin Zanib to his adopted son Zaid, and afterwards, "when Zaid had accomplished his want of her," the Prophet took her and married her—but, as the inspired book makes clear, only in order to show the difference between an adopted and a real son. "We gave her to you as a wife, so that there should be no difficulty for the believers in respect of the wives of their adopted sons, when they have accomplished their want of them, and Allah's command shall be performed." Yet surely a simple statement in the Koran should have sufficed without this excessively practical demonstration. There was, moreover, a mutiny in the harem on account of the undue favours shown by the Prophet to an Egyptian concubine who had borne him a boy—a boy for whom he had a great affection, since none of Kadija's sons had survived. These domestic troubles mingle inextricably with our impression of the Prophet's personality. One of his wives was a Jewess, Safiyya, whom he had married on the evening of the battle in which her husband had been captured and executed. He viewed the captured women at the end of the day, and she found favour in his eyes and was taken to his tent.

These are salient facts in these last eleven years of Muhammad's career. Because he, too, founded a great religion, there are those who write of this evidently lustful and rather shifty leader as though he were a man to put beside Jesus of Nazareth or Gautama, or Mani. But it is surely manifest that he was a being of commoner clay; he was vain, egotistical, tyrannous, and a self-deceiver; and it would throw all our history out of proportion if, out of an insincere deference to the possible Moslem reader, we were to present him in any other light.

Yet, unless we balance it, this insistence upon his vanity, egotism, self-deception, and hot desire does not complete the justice of the case. We must not swing across from the repudiation of the extravagant pretentions of the faithful to an equally extravagant condemnation. Can a man who has no good qualities hold a friend? Because those who knew Muhammad best believed in him most. Kadija for all her days believed in him—but she may have been a fond woman. Abu Bekr is a better witness, and he never wavered in his devotion. Abu Bekr believed in the Prophet, and it is very hard for anyone who reads the history of these times not to believe in Abu Bekr. Ali, again, risked his life for the Prophet in his darkest days. Muhammad was no impostor, at any rate, though at times his vanity made him behave as though Allah was at his beck and call, and as if his thoughts were necessarily God's thoughts.

And if his blood-stained passion with Safiyya amazes and disgusts our modern minds, his love for little Ibrahim, the son of Mary the Egyptian, and his passionate grief when the child died, reinstate him in the fellowship of all those who have known love and loss.

He smoothed the earth over the little grave with his own hands. "This eases the afflicted heart," he said. "Though it neither profits nor injures the dead, yet it is a comfort to the living."

§ 4

But the personal quality of Muhammad is one thing and the quality of Islam, the religion he founded, is quite another. Muhammad was not pitted against Jesus or Mani, and his relative stature is only a very secondary question for us; it is Islam which was pitted against the corrupted Christianity of the seventh century and against the decaying tradition of the Zoroastrian Magi with which the historian has the greater concern. And whether it was though its Prophet or whether it was in spite of its Prophet and through certain accidents in its origin and certain qualities of the desert from which it sprang, there can be no denying that Islam possesses many fine and noble attributes. It is not always through sublime persons that great things come into human life. It is the folly of the simple disciple which demands miraculous frippery on the majesty of truth and immaculate conceptions for righteousness.

A year before his death, at the end of the tenth year of the Hegira, Muhammad made his last pilgrimage from Medina to Mecca. He made then a great sermon to his people of which the tradition is as follows. There are, of course, disputes as to the authenticity of the words, but there can be no dispute that the world of Islam, a world still of three hundred million people, receives them to this day as its rule of life, and to a great extent observes it. The reader will note that the first paragraph sweeps away all plunder and blood feuds among the followers of Islam. The last makes the believing Negro the equal of the Caliph. They may not be sublime words, as certain utterances of Jesus of Nazareth are sublime, but they established in the world a great tradition of dignified fair dealing, they breathe a spirit of generosity, and they are human and workable. They created a society more free from widespread cruelty and social oppression than any society had ever been in the world before.

"Ye people: Hearken to my words; for I know not whether, after this year, I shall ever be amongst you here again. Your lives and property are sacred and inviolable amongst one another until the end of time.

"The Lord hath ordained to every man the share of his inheritance; a testament is not lawful to the prejudice of heirs.

"The child belongeth to the parent; and the violator of wedlock shall be stoned.

"Whoever claimeth falsely another for his father, or another for his master, the curse of God and the angels and of all mankind shall rest upon him.

"Ye people! Ye have rights demandable of your wives, and they have rights demandable of you. Upon them it is incumbent not to violate their conjugal faith nor commit any act of open impropriety; which things if they do, ye have authority to shut them up in separate apartments and to beat them with stripes, yet not severely. But if they refrain therefrom, clothe them and feed them suitably. And treat your women well, for they are with you as captives and prisoners; they have not power over anything as regards themselves. And ye have verily taken them on the security of God, and have made their persons lawful unto you by the words of God.

"And your slaves, see that ye feed them with such food as ye eat yourselves, and clothe them with the stuff ye wear. And if they commit a fault which ye are not inclined to forgive, then sell them, for they are the servants of the Lord, and are not to be tormented.

"Ye people! hearken to my speech and comprehend the same. Know that every Moslem is the brother of every other Moslem. All of you are on the same equality."

This insistence upon kindliness and consideration in the daily life is one of the main virtues of Islam, but it is not the only one. Equally important is the uncompromising monotheism, void of any Jewish exclusiveness, which is sustained by the Koran. Islam from the outset was fairly proof against the theological elaborations that have perplexed and divided Christianity and smothered the spirit of Jesus. And its third source of strength has been in the meticulous prescription of methods of prayer and worship, and its clear statement of the limited and conventional significance of the importance ascribed to Mecca. All sacrifice was barred to the faithful; no loophole was left for the sacrificial priest of the old dispensation to come back into the new faith. It was not simply a new faith, a purely prophetic religion, as the religion of Jesus was in the time of Jesus, or the religion of Guatama in the lifetime of Guatama, but it was so stated as to remain so. Islam to this day has learned doctors, teachers, and preachers; but it has no priests.

It was full of the spirit of kindliness, generosity and brotherhood; it was a simple and understandable religion; it was instinct with the chivalrous sentiment of the desert; and it made its appeal straight to the commonest instincts in the composition of ordinary men. Against it were pitted Judaism, which had made a racial hoard of God; Christianity, talking and preaching endlessly now of trinities, doctrines, and heresies no ordinary man could make head or tail of; and Mazdaism, the cult of the Zoroastrian Magi, who had inspired the crucifixion of Mani. The bulk of the people to whom the challenge of Islam came did not trouble very much whether Muhammad was lustful or not, or whether he had done some shifty and questionable things; what appealed to them was that this God, Allah, he preached, was by the test of the conscience in their hearts a God of righteousness, and that the honest acceptance of his doctrine and method opened the door wide, in a world of uncertainty, treachery, and intolerable divisions, to a great and increasing brotherhood of trustworthy men on earth, and to a paradise not of perpetual exercises in praise and worship, in which saints, priests, and anointed kings were still to have the upper places, but of equal fellowship and simple and understandable delights such as their souls craved for. Without any ambiguous symbolism, without any darkening of altars or chanting of priests, Muhammad had brought home those attractive doctrines to the hearts of mankind.

§ 5

The true embodiment of the spirit of Islam was not Muhammad but his close friend and supporter Abu Bekr. There can be little doubt that if Muhammad was the mind and imagination of primitive Islam, Abu Bekr was its conscience and its will. Throughout their life together it was Muhammad who said the thing, but it was Abu Bekr who believed the thing. When Muhammad wavered, Abu Bekr sustained him. Abu Bekr was a man without doubts, his beliefs cut down to acts cleanly as a sharp knife cuts. We may feel sure that Abu Bekr would never have temporized about the minor gods of Mecca, or needed inspirations from Allah to explain his private life. When, in the eleventh year of the Hegira (632), the Prophet sickened of a fever and died, it was Abu Bekr who succeeded him as Caliph and leader of the people (Kalifa=successor), and it was the unflinching confidence of Abu Bekr in the righteousness of Allah which prevented a split between Medina and Mecca, which stamped down a widespread insurrection of the Bedouin against taxation for the common cause, and carried out a great plundering raid into Syria that the dead Prophet had projected. And then Abu Bekr, with that faith which moves mountains, set himself simply and sanely to organize the subjugation of the whole world to Allah—with little armies of 3,000 or 4,000 Arabs—according to those letters the Prophet had written from Medina in 628 to all the monarchs of the world.

And the attempt came near to succeeding. Had there been in Islam a score of men, younger men, to carry on his work, of Abu

Bekr's quality, it would certainly have succeeded. It came near to succeeding because Arabia was now a centre of faith and will, and because nowhere else in the world until China was reached, unless it was upon the steppes of Russia or Turkestan, was there another

The BEGINNINGS of the MOSLEM POWER

community of free-spirited men with any power of belief in their rulers and leaders. The head of the Byzantine Empire, Heraclius, the conqueror of Chosroes II, was past his prime and suffering from dropsy, and his empire was exhausted by the long Persian war. The motley of people under his rule knew little of him and cared less. Persia was at the lowest depths of monarchist degradation; the parricide Kavadh II had died after a reign of a few months, and a series of dynastic intrigues and romantic murders enlivened the palace but weakened the country. The war between

Persia and the Byzantine Empire was only formally concluded about the time of the beginning of Abu Bekr's rule. Both sides had made great use of Arab auxiliaries; over Syria a number of towns and settlements of Christianized Arabs were scattered who professed a baseless loyalty to Constantinople; the Persian marches between Mesopotamia and the desert were under the control of an Arab tributary prince, whose capital was at Hira. Arab influence was strong in such cities as Damascus, where Christian Arab gentlemen would read and recite the latest poetry from the desert competitors. There was thus a great amount of easily assimilable material ready at hand for Islam.

And the military campaigns that now began were among the most brilliant in the world's history. Arabia had suddenly become a garden of fine men. The name of Khalid stands out as the brightest star in a constellation of able and devoted Moslem generals. Whenever he commanded he was victorious, and when the jealousy of the second Caliph, Omar, degraded him unjustly and inexcusably,[1] he made no ado, but served Allah cheerfully and well as a subordinate to those over whom he had ruled. We cannot trace the story of this warfare here; the Arab armies struck simultaneously at Byzantine Syria and the Persian frontier city of Hira, and everywhere they offered a choice of three alternatives; either pay tribute, or confess the true God and join us, or die. They encountered armies, large and disciplined but spiritless armies, and defeated them. And nowhere was there such a thing as a popular resistance. The people of the populous irrigation lands of Mesopotamia cared not a jot whether they paid taxes to Byzantium or Persepolis or to Medina; and of the two, Arabs or Persian court, the Arabs, the Arabs of the great years, were manifestly the cleaner people, more just and more merciful. The Christian Arabs joined the invaders very readily, and so did many Jews. Just as in the west, so now in the east, an invasion became a social revolution. But here it was also a religious revolution with a new and distinctive mental vitality.

It was Khalid who fought the decisive battle (636) with the army of Heraclius upon the banks of the Yarmuk, a tributary of the Jordan. The legions, as ever, were without proper cavalry; for seven centuries the ghost of old Crassus had haunted the east in vain; the imperial armies relied for cavalry purposes upon

---

[1] But Schurtz, in Helmolt's *History of the World,* says that the private life of the gallant Khalid was a scandal to the faithful. He committed adultery, a serious offence in a world of polygamy.

Christian Arab auxiliaries, and these deserted to the Moslems as the armies joined issue. A great parade of priests, sacred banners, pictures, and holy relics was made by the Byzantine host, and it was further sustained by the chanting of monks. But there was no magic in the relics and little conviction about the chanting. On the Arab side the Emirs and sheiks harangued the troops, and, after the ancient Arab fashion, the shrill voices of women in the rear encouraged their men. The Moslem ranks were full of believers before whom shone victory or paradise. The battle was never in doubt after the defection of the irregular cavalry. An attempt to retreat dissolved into a rout and became a massacre. The Byzantine army had fought with its back to the river, which was presently choked with its dead.

Thereafter Heraclius slowly relinquished all Syria, which he had so lately won back from the Persians, to his new antagonists. Damascus soon fell, and a year later the Moslems entered Antioch. For a time they had to abandon it again to a last effort from Constantinople, but they re-entered it for good under Khalid.

Meanwhile, on the eastern front, after a swift initial success which gave them Hira, the Persian resistance stiffened. The dynastic struggle had ended at last in the coming of a king of kings, and a general of ability had been found in Rustam. He gave battle at Kadessia (637). His army was just such another composite host as Darius had led into Thrace or Alexander defeated at Issus; it was a medley of levies. He had thirty-three war elephants, and he sat on a golden throne upon a raised platform behind the Persian ranks, surveying the battle, which throne will remind the reader of Herodotus, the Hellespont, and Salamis more than a thousand years before. The battle lasted three days; each day the Arabs attacked and the Persian host held its ground until nightfall called a truce. On the third day the Arabs received reinforcements, and towards the evening the Persians attempted to bring the struggle to an end by a charge of elephants. At first the huge beasts carried all before them, then one was wounded painfully and became uncontrollable rushing up and down between the armies. Its panic affected the others; for a time both armies remained dumbfounded in the red light of sunset, watching the frantic efforts of these grey, squealing monsters to escape from the tormenting masses of armed men that hemmed them in. It was by the merest chance that at last they broke through the Persian and not through the Arab array, and that it was the Arabs who were able to charge home upon the resulting confusion.

The twilight darkened to night, but this time the armies did not separate. All through the night the Arabs smote in the name of Allah, and pressed upon the shattered and retreating Persians. Dawn broke upon the vestiges of Rustam's army in flight far beyond the litter of the battlefield. Its path was marked by scattered weapons and war material, abandoned transport, and the dead and dying. The platform and the golden throne were broken down, and Rustam lay dead among a heap of dead men. . . .

Already in 634 Abu Bekr had died and given place to Omar, the Prophet's brother-in-law, as Caliph; and it was under Omar (634–644) that the main conquests of the Moslems occurred. The Byzantine Empire was pushed out of Syria altogether. But at the Taurus Mountains the Moslem thrust was held. Armenia was overrun, all Mesopotamia was conquered, and Persia beyond the rivers. Egypt[1] passed almost passively from Greek to Arab; in a few years the Semitic race, in the name of God and His Prophet, had recovered nearly all the dominions it had lost to the Aryan Persians a thousand years before. Jerusalem fell early, making a treaty without standing siege, and so the True Cross, which had been carried off by the Persians a dozen years before, and elaborately restored by Heraclius, passed once more out of the rule of Christians. But it was still in Christian hands; the Christians were to be tolerated, paying only a poll tax; and all the churches and all the relics were left in their possession.

Jerusalem made a peculiar condition for its surrender. The city would give itself only to the Caliph Omar in person. Hitherto he had been in Medina organizing armies and controlling the general campaign. He came to Jerusalem (638), and the manner of his coming shows how swiftly the vigour and simplicity of the first Moslem onset was being sapped by success. He came the six-hundred-mile journey with only one attendant; he was mounted on a camel, and a bag of barley, another of dates, a water-skin and a wooden platter were his provision for the journey. He was met outside the city by his chief captains, robed splendidly in silks and with richly caparisoned horses. At this amaz-

[1] The conquest of Egypt by the Arabs cut off Abyssinia from the rest of Christendom, and we hear no more of this remote country for a thousand years. It remained Christian, and in the middle of the fifteenth century a mission from Abyssinia turned up in Rome to enquire about certain doctrinal points. There had long been a legend in Christendom of a great Christian land in the east, the land of Prester John, which seems to have been based upon confused tales of Abyssinia mixed up with other tales of Mongol chiefs Christianized by the Nestorians.

ing sight the old man was overcome with rage. He slipped down from his saddle, scrabbled up dirt and stones with his hands, and pelted these fine gentlemen, shouting abuse. What was this insult? What did this finery mean? Where were his warriors? Where were the desert men? He would not let these popinjays escort him. He went on with his attendant, and the smart emirs rode afar off —well out of range of his stones. He met the Patriarch of Jerusalem, who had apparently taken over the city from its Byzantine rulers, alone. With the Patriarch he got on very well. They went round the Holy Places together, and Omar, now a little appeased, made sly jokes at the expense of his too magnificent followers.

Equally indicative of the tendencies of the time is Omar's letter ordering one of his governors who had built himself a palace at Kufa, to demolish it again.

"They tell me," he wrote, "you would imitate the palace of Chosroes,[1] and that you would even use the gates that once were his. Will you also have guards and porters at those gates, as Chosroes had? Will you keep the faithful afar off and deny audience to the poor? Would you depart from the custom of our Prophet, and be as magnificent as those Persian emperors, and descend to hell even as they have done?"[2]

§ 6

Abu Bekr and Omar I are the two master figures in the history of Islam. It is not within our scope here to describe the wars by which in a hundred and twenty-five years Islam spread itself from the Indus to the Atlantic and Spain, and from Kashgar, on the borders of China, to Upper Egypt. Two maps must suffice to show the limits to which the vigorous impulse of the new faith carried the Arab idea and the Arabic scriptures, before worldliness, the old trading and plundering spirit, and the glamour of the silk robe had completely recovered their paralyzing sway over the Arab intelligence and will. The reader will note how the great tide swept over the footsteps of Yuan Chwang, and how easily in Africa the easy conquests of the Vandals were repeated in the reverse direction. And if the reader entertains any delusions about a fine civilization, either Persian, Roman, Hellenic, or Egyptian, being submerged by this flood, the sooner he dismisses

---

[1] At Ctesiphon.

[2] Paraphrased from Schurtz in Helmolt's *History of the World.*

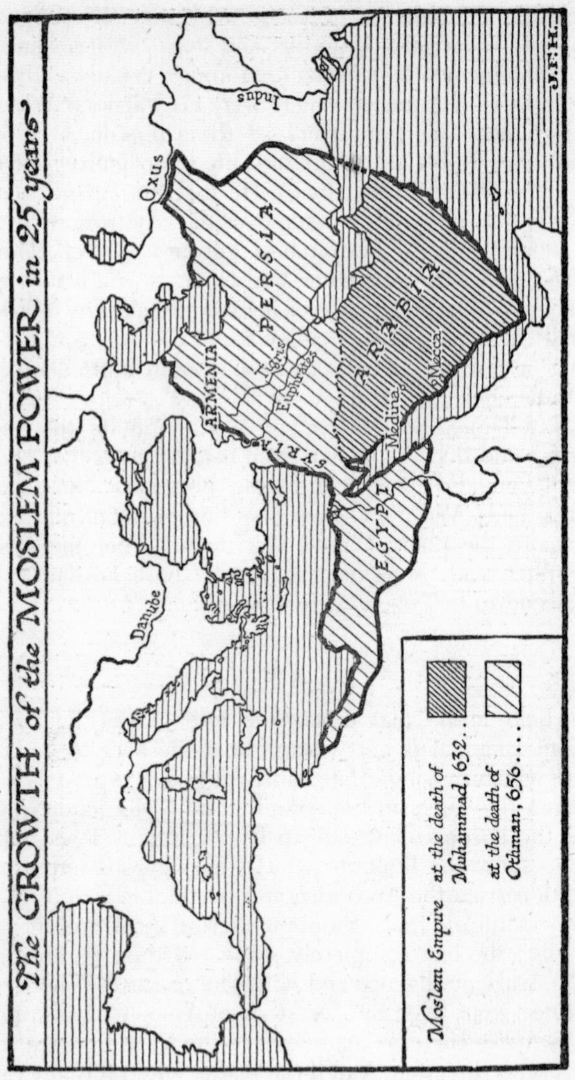

such ideas the better. Islam prevailed because it was the best social and political order the times could offer. It prevailed because everywhere it found politically apathetic peoples robbed, oppressed, bullied, uneducated, and unorganized, and it found selfish and unsound governments out of touch with any people at all. It was

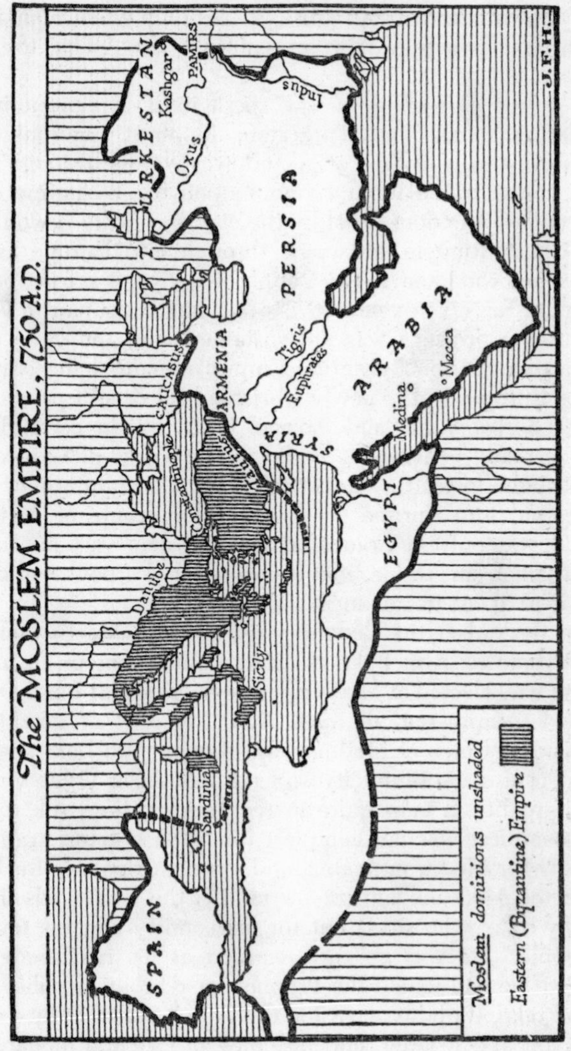

the broadest, freshest, and cleanest political idea that had yet come into actual activity in the world, and it offered better terms than any other to the mass of mankind. The capitalistic and slave-holding system of the Roman Empire and the literature and culture and social tradition of Europe had altogether decayed and broken down before Islam arose; it was only when mankind lost faith in the sincerity of its representatives that Islam, too, began to decay.

The larger part of its energy spent itself in conquering and assimilating Persia and Turkestan; its most vigorous thrusts were northwardly from Persia and westwardly through Egypt. Had it concentrated its first vigour upon the Byzantine Empire there can be little doubt that by the eighth century it would have taken Constantinople and come through into Europe as easily as it reached the Pamirs. The Caliph Moawiya, it is true, besieged the capital for seven years (672–678), and Suleiman in 717 and 718; but the pressure was not sustained, and for three or four centuries longer the Byzantine Empire remained the crazy bulwark of Europe. In the newly Christianized or still pagan Avars, Bulgars, Serbs, Slavs, and Saxons, Islam would certainly have found as ready converts as it did in the Turks of Central Asia. And though, instead of insisting upon Constantinople, it first came round into Europe by the circuitous route of Africa and Spain, it was only in France, at the end of a vast line of communications from Arabia, that it encountered a power sufficiently vigorous to arrest its advance.

From the outset the Bedouin aristocrats of Mecca dominated the new empire. Abu Bekr, the first Caliph, was in an informal shouting way elected at Medina, and so were Omar I and Othman, the third Caliph, but all three were Meccans of good family. They were not men of Medina. And though Abu Bekr and Omar were men of stark simplicity and righteousness, Othman was of a baser quality, a man quite in the vein of those silk robes, to whom conquest was not conquest for Allah but for Arabia, and especially for Mecca in Arabia, and more particularly for himself and for the Meccans and for his family, the Omayyads. He was a worthy man, who stood out for his country and his town and his "people." He was no early convert as his two predecessors had been; he had joined the Prophet for reasons of policy in fair give and take. With his accession the Caliph ceases to be a strange man of fire and wonder, and becomes an Oriental monarch, like many Oriental monarchs before and since, a fairly good monarch by Eastern standards as yet but nothing more.

The rule and death of Othman brought out the consequences of Muhammad's weaknesses as clearly as the lives of Abu Bekr and Omar had witnessed to the divine fire in his teaching. Muhammad had been politic at times when Abu Bekr would have been firm, and the new element of aristocratic greediness that came in with Othman was one fruit of those politic movements. And the legacy of that carelessly compiled harem of the Prophet, the family complications and jealousies which had lurked in the background of Moslem affairs during the rule of the first two Caliphs, was now coming out into the light of day. Ali, who was the nephew, the adopted son, and the son-in-law of the Prophet —he was the husband of the Prophet's daughter Fatima—had considered himself the rightful Caliph. His claims formed an undertow to the resentment of Medina and of the rival families of Mecca against the advancement of the Omayyads. But Ayesha, the favourite wife of the Prophet, had always been jealous of Fatima and hostile to Ali. She supported Othman. . . . The splendid opening of the story of Islam collapses suddenly into this squalid dispute and bickering of heirs and widows.

In 656 Othman, an old man of eighty, was stoned in the streets of Medina by a mob, chased to his house, and murdered; and Ali became at last Caliph, only to be murdered in his turn (661). In one of the battles in this civil war, Ayesha, now a gallant mischievous old lady, distinguished herself by leading a charge, mounted on a camel. She was taken prisoner and treated well.

While the armies of Islam were advancing triumphantly to the conquest of the world, this sickness of civil war smote at its head. What was the rule of Allah in the world to Ayesha when she could score off the detested Fatima, and what heed were the Omayyads and the partisans of Ali likely to take of the unity of mankind when they had a good hot feud of this sort to entertain them, with the caliphate as a prize? The world of Islam was rent in twain by the spites, greeds, and partisan silliness of a handful of men and women in Medina. That quarrel still lives. To this day one main division of the Moslems, the Shiites, maintain the hereditary right of Ali to be Caliph *as an article of faith!* They prevail in Persia and India.

But an equally important section, the Sunnites, with whom it is difficult for a disinterested observer not to agree, deny this peculiar addendum to Muhammad's simple creed. So far as we can gather at this length of time, Ali was an entirely commonplace individual.

To watch this schism creeping across the brave beginnings of Islam is like watching a case of softening of the brain. To the copious literature of the subject we must refer the reader who wishes to learn how Hasan, the son of Ali, was poisoned by his wife, and how Husein, his brother, was killed. We do but name them here, because they still afford a large section of mankind scope for sentimental partisanship and mutual annoyance. They are the two chief Shiite martyrs. Amidst the coming and going of their conflicts the old Kaaba at Mecca was burnt down, and naturally there began endless disputation whether it should be rebuilt in exactly its ancient form or on a much larger scale.

In this and the preceding sections we have seen once more the inevitable struggle of this newest and latest unifying impulse in the world's affairs against the everyday worldliness of mankind, and we have seen also how from the first the complicated household of Muhammad was like an evil legacy to the new faith. But as this history now degenerates into the normal crimes and intrigues of an Oriental dynasty, the student of history will realize a third fundamental weakness in the world-reforms of Muhammad. He was an illiterate Arab, ignorant of history, totally ignorant of all the political experiences of Rome and Greece, and almost as ignorant of the real history of Judea; and he left his followers with no scheme for a stable government embodying and concentrating the general will of the faithful, and no effective form to express the very real spirit of democracy (using the word in its modern sense) that pervades the essential teaching of Islam. His own rule was unlimited autocracy, and autocratic Islam has remained. Politically, Islam was not an advance, but a retrogression from the traditional freedoms and customary laws of the desert. The breach of the pilgrims' truce that led to the battle of Badr is the blackest mark against early Islam. Nominally, Allah is its chief ruler—but, practically, its master has always been whatever man was vigorous and unscrupulous enough to snatch and hold the Caliphate—and, subject to revolts and assassinations, its final law has been that man's will.

For a time, after the death of Ali, the Omayyad family was in the ascendant, and for nearly a century they gave rulers to Islam.

The Arab historians are so occupied with the dynastic squabbles and crimes of the time, that it is difficult to trace the external history of the period. We find Moslem shipping upon the seas defeating the Byzantine fleet in a great sea-fight off the coast of Lycia (A.D. 655), but how the Moslems acquired this victorious fleet thus early we do not clearly know. It was probably chiefly Egyptian. For some years Islam certainly controlled the Eastern Mediterranean, and in 669 and again in 674, during the reign of Muawiya (661–680), the first great Omayyad Caliph made two sea attacks upon Constantinople. They had to be sea attacks because Islam, so long as it was under Arab rule, never surmounted the barrier of the Taurus Mountains. During the same period the Moslems were also pressing their conquests further and further into Central Asia. While Islam was already decaying at its centre, it was yet making great hosts of new adherents and awakening a new spirit among the hitherto divided and aimless Turkish peoples. Medina was no longer a possible centre for its vast enterprises in Asia, Africa, and the Mediterranean, and so Damascus became the usual capital of the Omayyad Caliphs.

Chief among these, as for a time the clouds of dynastic intrigue clear, are Abdal Malik (685–705) and Walid I (705–714), under whom the Omayyad line rose to the climax of its successes. The western boundary was carried to the Pyrenees, while to the east the domains of the Caliph marched with China. The son of Walid, Suleiman (715), carried out a second series of Moslem attacks upon Constantinople which his father had planned and proposed. As with the Caliph Muawiya half a century before, the approach was by sea—for Asia Minor, as we have just noted, was still unconquered—and the shipping was drawn chiefly from Egypt. The emperor, a usurper, Leo the Isaurian, displayed extraordinary skill and obstinacy in the defence; he burnt most of the Moslem shipping in a brilliant sortie, cut up the troops they had landed upon the Asiatic side of the Bosphorus, and after a campaign in Europe of two years (716–717), a winter of unexampled severity completed their defeat.

From this point onward the glory of the Omayyad line decays. The first tremendous impulse of Islam was now spent. There was no further expansion and a manifest decline in religious zeal. Islam had made millions of converts, and had digested those millions very imperfectly. Cities, nations, whole sects and races, Arab pagans, Jews, Christians, Manichæans, Zoroastrians, Turanian pagans had been swallowed up into this new vast empire of Muhammad's successors. It has hitherto been the common characteristic of all the great unifying religious initiators of the world, the common oversight, that they have accepted the moral and theological ideals to which the first appeal was made, as though they were universal ideals. Muhammad's appeal, for example, was to the traditional chivalry and underlying monotheistic feelings of the intelligent Arabs of his time. These things were latent in the mind and conscience of Mecca and Medina; he did but call them forth.

Then, as the new teaching spread and stereotyped itself, it had to work on a continually more uncongenial basis, it had to grow in soil that distorted and perverted it. Its sole textbook was the Koran. To minds untuned to the melodies of Arabic, this book seemed to be, as it seems to many European minds to-day, a mixture of fine-spirited rhetoric with—to put it plainly —formless and unintelligent gabble. Countless converts missed the real thing in it altogether. To that we must ascribe the readiness of the Persian and Indian sections of the faith to join the Shiite schism upon a quarrel that they could at least understand and feel. And to the same attempt to square the new stuff with old prepossessions was due such extravagant theology as presently disputed whether the Koran was and always had been co-existent with God.[1] We should be stupefied by the preposterousness of this idea if we did not recognize in it at once the well-meaning attempt of some learned Christian convert to Islamize his belief that "In the beginning was the Word, and the Word was with God, and the Word was God."[2]

None of the great unifying religious initiators of the world hitherto seems to have been accompanied by any understanding of the vast educational task, the vast work of lucid and varied exposition and intellectual organization involved in its propositions. They all present the same history of a rapid spreading like a little water poured over a great area, and then of superficiality and corruption.

In a little while we hear stories of an Omayyad Caliph, Walid II (743–744), who mocked at the Koran, ate pork, drank wine, and did not pray. Those stories may have been true or they may have been circulated for political reasons. There began a puritan reaction in Mecca and Medina against the levity and luxury of Damascus. Another great Arab family, the Abbas family, the Abbasids, had long been scheming for power, and was making capital out of the general discontent. The feud of the Omayyads and the Abbasids was older than Islam; it had been going on before Muhammad was born. These Abbasids took up the tradition of the Shiite "martyrs," Ali and his sons Hasan and Husein, and identified themselves with it. The banner of the Omayyads was white; the Abbasids adopted a black banner, black in mourn-

---

[1] Sir Mark Sykes.

[2] St. John's Gospel, chap. i, 1.

ing for Hasan and Husein, black because black is more impressive than any colour; moreover, the Abbasids declared that all the Caliphs after Ali were usurpers. In 749 they accomplished a carefully prepared revolution, and the last of the Omayyad Caliphs was hunted down and slain in Egypt. Abul Abbas was the first of the Abbasid Caliphs, and he began his reign by collecting into one prison every living male of the Omayyad line upon whom he could lay hands and causing them all to be massacred. Their bodies, it is said, were heaped together, a leathern carpet was spread over them, and on this gruesome table Abul Abbas and his councillors feasted. Moreover, the tombs of the Omayyad Caliphs were rifled, and their bones burnt and scattered to the four winds of heaven. So the grievances of Ali were avenged at last, and the Omayyad line passed out of history.

There was, it is interesting to note, a rising on behalf of the Omayyads in Khorasan which was assisted by the Chinese emperor.

§ 7

But the descendants of Ali were not destined to share in this triumph for long. The Abbasids were adventurers and rulers of an older school than Islam. Now that the tradition of Ali had served its purpose, the next proceeding of the new Caliph was to hunt down and slaughter the surviving members of his family, the descendants of Ali and Fatima.

Clearly the old traditions of Sassanid Persia and of Persia before the Greeks were returning to the world. With the accession of the Abbasids the control of the sea departed from the Caliph, and with it went Spain and North Africa, in which, under an Omayyad survivor in the former case, independent Moslem states now arose.

The centre of gravity of Islam shifted across the desert from Damascus to Mesopotamia. Mansur, the successor of Abul Abbas, built himself a new capital at Bagdad near the ruins of Ctesiphon, the former Sassanid capital. Turks and Persians as well as Arabs became Emirs, and the army was reorganized upon Sassanid lines. Medina and Mecca were now only of importance as pilgrimage centres, to which the faithful turned to pray. But because it was a fine language, and because it was the language of the Koran, Arabic continued to spread until presently it had replaced Greek and become the language of educated men throughout the whole Moslem world.

Of the Abbasid monarchs after Abul Abbas we need tell little here. A bickering war went on year by year in Asia Minor, in which neither Byzantium nor Bagdad made any permanent gains, though once or twice the Moslems raided as far as the Bosphorus. A false prophet, Mokanna, who said he was God, had a brief but troublesome career. There were plots, there were insurrections; they lie flat and colourless now in the histories, like dead flowers in an old book. One other Abbasid Caliph only need be named, and that quite as much for his legendary as for his real importance, Haroun-al-Raschid (786–809). He was not only the Caliph of an outwardly prosperous empire in the world of reality, but he was also the Caliph of an undying empire in the deathless world of fiction, he was the Haroun-al-Raschid of the *Arabian Nights*.

Sir Mark Sykes[1] gives an account of the reality of his empire from which we will quote certain passages. He says: "The Imperial Court was polished, luxurious, and unlimitedly wealthy; the capital, Bagdad, a gigantic mercantile city surrounding a huge administrative fortress, wherein every department of state had a properly regulated and well-ordered public office; where schools and colleges abounded; whither philosophers, students, doctors, poets, and theologians flocked from all parts of the civilized globe. . . . The provincial capitals were embellished with vast public buildings, and linked together by an effective and rapid service of posts and caravans; the frontiers were secure and well garrisoned, the army loyal, efficient, and brave; the governors and ministers honest and forbearing. The empire stretched with equal strength and unimpaired control from the Cilician gates to Aden, and from Egypt to Central Asia. Christians, Pagans, Jews, as well as Moslems, were employed in the government service. Usurpers, rebellious generals, and false prophets seemed to have vanished from the Moslem dominions. Traffic and wealth had taken the place of revolution and famine. . . . Pestilence and disease were met by Imperial hospitals and government physicians. . . . In government business the rough-and-ready methods of Arabian administration had given place to a complicated system of Divans, initiated partly from the Roman, but chiefly taken from the Persian system of government. Posts, Finance, Privy Seal, Crown Lands, Justice, and Military Affairs were each administered by separate bureaux in the hands of ministers and officials; an army of clerks, scribes, writers and accountants swarmed into these offices and

[1] *The Caliph's Last Heritage.*

gradually swept the whole power of the government into their own hands by separating the Commander of the Faithful from any direct intercourse with his subjects. The Imperial Palace and the entourage were equally based on Roman and Persian precedents. Eunuchs, closely veiled 'harems' of women, guards, spies, go-betweens, jesters, poets, and dwarfs clustered around the person of the Commander of the Faithful, each, in his degree, endeavouring to gain the royal favour and indirectly distracting the royal mind from affairs of business and state. Meanwhile the mercantile trade of the East poured gold into Bagdad, and supplemented the other enormous stream of money derived from the contributions of plunder and loot despatched to the capital by the commanders of the victorious raiding forces which harried Asia Minor, India, and Turkestan. The seemingly unending supply of Turkish slaves and Byzantine specie added to the richness of the revenues of Irak and, combined with the vast commercial traffic of which Bagdad was the centre, produced a large and powerful moneyed class, composed of the sons of generals, officials, landed proprietors, royal favourites, merchants, and the like, who encouraged the arts, literature, philosophy, and poetry as the mood took them, building palaces for themselves, vying with each other in the luxury of their entertainments, suborning poets to sound their praises, dabbling in philosophy, supporting various schools of thought, endowing charities, and, in fact, behaving as the wealthy have always behaved in all ages.

"I have said that the Abbasid Empire in the days of Haroun-al-Raschid was weak and feeble to a degree, and perhaps the reader will consider this a foolish proposition when he takes into consideration that I have described the Empire as orderly, the administration definite and settled, the army efficient, and wealth abundant. The reason I make the suggestion is that the Abbasid Empire had lost touch with everything original and vital in Islam, and was constructed entirely by the reunion of the fragments of the empires Islam had destroyed. There was nothing in the empire which appealed to the higher instinct of the leaders of the people; the holy war had degenerated into a systematic acquisition of plunder. The Caliph had become a luxurious Emperor or King of Kings; the administration had changed from a patriarchal system to a bureaucracy. The wealthier classes were rapidly losing all faith in the religion of the state; speculative philosophy and high living were taking the place of Koramic orthodoxy and Arabian simplicity. The solitary bond which could have held the empire together, the sternness and plainness of the Moslem faith, was completely neglected by both the Caliph and his advisers. . . . Haroun-al Raschid himself was a wine-bibber, and his palace was decorated with graven images of birds and beasts and men. . . .

"For a moment we stand amazed at the greatness of the Abbasid dominion; then suddenly we realize that it is but as a fair husk enclosing the dust and ashes of dead civilizations."

Haroun-al-Raschid died in 809. At his death his great empire fell immediately into civil war and confusion, and the next great event of unusual importance in this region of the world comes two hundred years later when the Turks, under the chiefs of the great family of the Seljuks, poured southward out of Turkestan, and not only conquered the empire of Bagdad, but Asia Minor also. Coming from the north-east as they did, they were able to outflank the great barrier of the Taurus Mountains, which had hitherto held back the Moslems. They were still much the same people as those of whom Yuan Chwang gave us a glimpse four hundred years earlier, but now they were Moslems, and Moslems of the primitive type, men whom Abu Bekr would have welcomed to Islam. They caused a great revival of vigour in Islam, and they turned the minds of the Moslem world once more in the direction of a religious war against Christendom. For there had been a sort of truce between these two great religions after the cessation of the Moslem advance and the decline of the Omayyads. Such warfare as had gone on between Christianity and Islam had been rather border-bickering than sustained war. It became only a bitter fanatical struggle again in the eleventh century.

§ 8

But before we go on to tell of the Turks and the Crusaders, the great wars that began between Christendom and Islam, and which have left a quite insane intolerance between these great systems right down to the present time, it is necessary to give a little more attention to the intellectual life of the Arabic-speaking world which was now spreading more and more widely over the regions which Hellenism had once dominated. For some generations before Muhammad, the Arab mind had been, as it were, smouldering, it had been producing poetry and much religious discussion; under the stimulus of the national and racial successes, it presently blazed out with a brilliance second only to that of the Greeks during their best period. It revived the human pursuit of science. If the Greek was the father, then the Arab was the foster-father of the scientific method. Through the Arabs it was, and not by the Latin route, that the modern world received that gift of light and power.

But when we write Arab here, we must write it with a certain reservation. The Arabic culture of Islam has something of the same relation to the original Arab as the Hellenic culture after the days of Alexander had to the original European Greek. It was no longer racially pure. It had incorporated with it a group of pre-existing cultures, the Persian of the Arsacid dynasty, and the Coptic of Hellenized Egypt. Persia and Egypt learnt to talk Arabic with great promptitude, but they remained in quality Persia and Egypt.

The early conquests of the Arabs had brought the Arabic culture into close contact with the Greek literary tradition—not, it is true, in the original Greek, but through the Syrian translations of the Greek writers. The Nestorian Christians, the Christians to the east of orthodoxy, seem to have been much more intelligent and active-minded than the court theologians of Byzantium, and at a much higher level of general education than the Latin-speaking Christians of the west. They had been tolerated during the latter days of the Sassanids, and they were tolerated by Islam until the ascendancy of the Turks in the eleventh century. They were the intellectual backbone of the Persian world. They had preserved much of the Hellenic medical science, and had even added to it. In the Omayyad times most of the physicians in the Caliph's dominions were Nestorians, and no doubt many learned Nestorians professed Islam without any serious compunction or any great change in their work and thoughts. They had preserved much of Aristotle both in Greek and in Syrian translations. They had a considerable mathematical literature. Their equipment makes the contemporary resources of Saint Benedict or Cassiodorus seem very pitiful. To these Nestorian teachers came the fresh Arab mind out of the desert, keen and curious, and learnt much and improved upon its teaching. It learnt much and acquired much. Persia had been for many centuries a country of intense and subtle theological and speculative activity. These activities now clothed themselves in Arabic phrases and became a process of heresy and schism in the Moslem Church. The Shiite schism was essentially Persian.

But the Persians with the Hellenic learning were not the only teachers available for the Arabs. Throughout all the rich cities of the East the kindred Jews were scattered with their own distinctive literature and tradition, and the Arab and the Jewish mind reacted upon one another to a common benefit. The Arab was informed and the Jew sharpened to a keener edge. The Jews have never been pedants in the manner of their language; we have already noted that a thousand years before Islam they spoke Greek in Hellenized Alexandria, and now all over this new Moslem world they were speaking and writing Arabic. Some of the greatest of Jewish literature was written in Arabic, the religious writings of Maimonides, for example. Indeed, it is difficult to say, in the case of this Arabic culture, where the Jew ends and the Arab begins, so important and essential were its Jewish factors.

Moreover, there was a third source of inspiration, more particularly in mathematical science, to which at present it is difficult to do justice—India. There can be little doubt that the Arab mind during its period of splendour was in close and effective contact with Sanskrit literature and with Indo-Persian physical science.

The distinctive activities of the Arab mind were already manifest under the Omayyads, although it was during the Abbasid time that it made its best display. History is the beginning and core of all sound philosophy and all great literature, and the first Arab writers of distinction were historians, biographers, and quasi-historical poets. Romantic fiction and the short story followed as a reading public developed, willing to be amused. And as reading ceased to be a special accomplishment, and became necessary to every man of affairs and to every youth of breeding, came the systematic growth of an educational system and an educational literature. By the ninth and tenth centuries there are not only grammars but great lexicons, and a mass of philological learning in Islam.

And a century or so in advance of the West, there grew up in the Moslem world at a number of centres, at Basra, at Kufa, at Bagdad and Cairo, and at Cordoba, out of what were at first religious schools dependent upon mosques, a series of great universities. The light of these universities shone far beyond the Moslem world, and drew students to them from east and west. At Cordoba in particular there were great numbers of Christian students, and the influence of Arab philosophy coming by way of Spain upon the universities of Paris, Oxford, and North Italy, and upon Western European thought generally, was very considerable indeed. The name of Averroes (Ibnrushd) of Cordoba (1126–1198) stands out as that of the culminating influence of Arab philosophy upon European thought. He developed the teachings of Aristotle upon lines that made a sharp division between religious and scientific truth, and so prepared the way for the liberation of scientific research from the theological dogmatism that restrained it both under Christianity and under Islam. Another great name is that of Avicenna (Ibnsina), the Prince of Physicians (980–1037), who was born at the other end of the Arabic world at Bokhara, and who travelled in Khorasan. . . . The book-copying industry flourished at Alexandria, Damascus, Cairo, and Bagdad, and about the year 970 there were twenty-seven free schools open in Cordoba for the education of the poor.

"In mathematics," say Thatcher and Schwill,[1] "the Arabs built on the foundations of the Greek mathematicians. The origin of the so-called Arabic numerals is obscure. Under Theodoric the Great, Boëthius made use of certain signs which were in part very like the nine digits which we now use." One of the pupils of Gerbert also used signs which were still more like ours; but the zero, it is stated, was unknown until the ninth century, when it was invented by a Moslem mathematician named Muhammad-Ibn-Musa, who also was the first to use the decimal notation, and who gave the digits the value of position. This, however, is disputed by many Indians, who claim the zero and the decimal system as a distinctly Indian contribution.

"In geometry the Arabs did not add much to Euclid, but algebra is practically their creation; also, they developed spherical trigonometry, inventing the sine, tangent, and cotangent. In physics they invented the pendulum, and produced works on optics. They made progress in the science of astronomy. They built several observatories, and constructed many astronomical instruments which are still in use. They calculated the angle of the ecliptic and the precession of the equinoxes. Their knowledge of astronomy was undoubtedly considerable.

"In medicine they made great advances over the work of the Greeks. They studied physiology and hygiene, and their *materia medica* was practically the same as ours to-day. Many of their methods of treatment are still in use among us. Their surgeons understood the use of anæsthetics, and performed some of the most difficult operations known. At the time when in Europe the practice of medicine was forbidden by the Church, which expected cures to be effected by religious rites performed by the clergy, the Arabs had a real science of medicine.

---

[1] *A General History of Europe.*

"In chemistry they made a good beginning. They discovered many new substances, such as potash, nitrate of silver, corrosive sublimate, and nitric and sulphuric acid." The word "alcohol" is Arabic, though the substance was known under the name of "spirits of wine" to Pliny (A.D. 100). ". . . In manufactures they outdid the world in variety and beauty of design and perfection of workmanship. They worked in all the metals—gold, silver, copper, bronze, iron and steel. In textile fabrics they have never been surpassed. They made glass and pottery of the finest quality. They knew the secrets of dyeing, and they manufactured paper. They had many processes of dressing leather, and their work was famous throughout Europe. They made tinctures, essences and syrups. They made sugar from the cane, and grew many fine kinds of wine. They practised farming in a scientific way, and had good systems of irrigation. They knew the value of fertilizers, and adapted their crops to the quality of the ground. They excelled in horticulture, knowing how to graft and how to produce new varieties of fruit and flowers. They introduced into the West many trees and plants from the East, and wrote scientific treatises on farming."

One item in this account must be underlined here because of its importance in the intellectual life of mankind, the manufacture of paper. This the Arabs seemed to have learnt from the Chinese by way of Central Asia. The Europeans acquired it from the Arabs. Until that time books had to be written upon parchment or papyrus, and after the Arab conquest of Egypt Europe was cut off from the papyrus supply. Until paper became abundant, the art of printing was of little use, and newspapers and popular education by means of books was impossible. This was probably a much more important factor in the relative backwardness of Europe during the dark ages than historians seem disposed to admit. . . .

And all this mental life went on in the Moslem world in spite of a very considerable amount of political disorder. From first to last the Arabs never grappled with the problem, the still unsolved problem, of the stable progressive state; everywhere their form of government was absolutist and subject to the convulsions, changes, intrigues, and murders that have always characterized the extremer forms of monarchy. But for some centuries, beneath the crimes and rivalries of courts and camps, the spirit of Islam did preserve a certain general decency and restraint in life; the Byzantine Empire was impotent to shatter this civilization, and the Turkish danger in the north-east gathered strength only very slowly. Until the Turk fell upon it, the intellectual life of Islam continued. Perhaps it secretly flattered itself that it would always be able to go on, in spite of the threat of violence and unreason in its political direction. Hitherto, in all countries, that has been the characteristic attitude of science and literature. The intellectual man has been loth to come to grips with the forcible man. He has generally been something of a courtier and time-server. Possibly he has never yet been quite sure of himself. Hitherto men of reason and knowledge have never had the assurance and courage of the religious fanatic. But there can be little doubt that they have accumulated settled convictions and gathered confidence during the last few centuries; they have slowly found a means to power through the development of popular education and popular literature, and to-day they are far more disposed to say things plainly and to claim a dominating voice in the organization of human affairs than they have ever been before in the world's history.

§ 9

The Moslem conquests are associated with new types of architecture, called variously Saracenic, Mohammedan and Arabic. But the true Arab, says Gayet, was never an artist. He built, because he had to build, mosques, palaces, tombs, cities, but he found his workmen and architects among the Egyptians, Syrians, and Persians he had conquered. Arabic art in Persia was a mere continuation of Persian art, but in Egypt and Syria there was a real adaptation to new conditions and a new type and character of building and decoration appeared. This was "Arab" art strictly speaking. To the west in North Africa and Spain was developed a special variation characterized by the horseshoe arch. Syria and Egypt, long before the coming of the Arabs, had diverged from Byzantine forms by replacing the round arch by the pointed arch, and had gone far beyond Byzantine art in the disuse of modelled forms. For Hellenic realism they were substituting patterning, and the Arab temperament, contemplative and ecstatic, was all for enhancing this process. "Not to obey a religious precept," says Gayet—for there are many early Arab representative paintings—"but through an instinct." In the common matters of life, and apart from any culture, the Arab displays an extreme disinclination to strip his body or look upon a body. Gradually in the evolution of Arab art the decoration passes from conventionalized animal and vegetable forms to geometrical interlacings, "arabesques." Roofs and vaults become more and more deeply encrusted, pierced screens multiply, and even the outward form becomes polyhedral. The vaults are covered with circular and polygonal studs which descend at last like stalactites. A new mysterious beauty is produced by these suppressions and sublimations, like the beauty of crystals and ripples and the subtle and obscure rhythms of inanimate things, a beauty diametrically opposed to the unrestricted freedoms, the glorious vulgarities, the exuberant vitality, of Hellenic art.

Associated in our minds with these structural developments as characteristically Arabic are the minaret and the bulbous cupola, and a brilliant use of glazed and often richly ornamented tiles. An enormous use is made in decoration of texts and phrases from the Koran in the beautiful sweeping Arabic writing.

XXXI

CHRISTENDOM AND THE CRUSADES

§ 1

LET us turn again now from this intellectual renascence in the cradle of the ancient civilizations to the affairs of the Western world.

We have described the complete economic, social, and political break-up of the Roman imperial system in the West, the confusion and darkness that followed in the sixth and seventh centuries, and the struggles of such men as Cassiodorus to keep alight the flame of human learning amidst these windy confusions. For a time it would be idle to write of states and rulers. Smaller or greater adventurers seized a castle or a countryside and ruled an uncertain area. The British Islands, for instance, were split up amidst a multitude of rulers; and numerous Keltic chiefs in Ireland and Scotland and Wales and Cornwall fought and prevailed over and succumbed to each other: the English invaders were also divided into a number of fluctuating "kingdoms," Kent, Wessex, Essex, Sussex, Mercia, Northumbria and East Anglia, which were constantly at war with one another.

So it was over most of the Western world. Here a bishop would be the monarch, as Gregory the Great was in Rome; here a town or a group of towns would be under the rule of the duke or prince of this or that. Amidst the vast ruins of the city of Rome, half-independent families of quasi-noble adventurers and their retainers maintained themselves. The Pope kept a sort of general predominance there, but he was sometimes more than balanced by a "Duke of Rome." The great arena of the Colosseum had been made into a privately-owned castle, and so, too, had the vast circular tomb of the Emperor Hadrian; and the adventurers who had possession of these strongholds and their partisans waylaid each other and fought and bickered in the ruinous streets of the once imperial city. The Tomb of Hadrian was known after the days of Gregory the Great as the Castle of St. Angelo, the Castle of the Holy Angel, because, when he was crossing the bridge over the Tiber, on his way to St. Peter's to pray against the great pestilence which was devastating the city, he had had a vision of a great angel standing over the dark mass of the mausoleum and sheathing a sword, and he had known then that his prayers would be answered. This Castle of St. Angelo played a very important part in Roman affairs during this age of disorder.

Spain was in much the same state of political fragmentation as Italy or France or Britain; and in Spain the old feud of Carthaginian and Roman was still continued in the bitter hostility of their descendants and heirs, the Jew and the Christian. So that when the power of the Caliph had swept along the North African coast to the Straits of Gibraltar, it found in the Spanish Jews ready helpers in its invasion of Europe. A Moslem army of Arabs and of Berbers, the nomadic Hamitic people of the African desert and mountain hinterland who had been converted to Islam, crossed and defeated the West Goths in a great battle in 711. In a few years the whole country was in their possession.

In 720 Islam had reached the Pyrenees, and had pushed round their eastern end into France; and for a time it seemed that the faith was likely to subjugate Gaul as easily as it had subjugated the Spanish peninsula. But presently it struck against something hard, a new kingdom of the Franks, which had been consolidating itself for some two centuries in the Rhineland and North France.

Of this Frankish kingdom, the precursor of France and Germany, which formed the western bulwark of Europe against the faith of Muhammad, as the Byzantine Empire behind the Taurus Mountains formed the eastern, we shall now have much to tell; but first we must give some account of the new system of social groupings out of which it arose.

§ 2

It is necessary that the reader should have a definite idea of the social condition of Western Europe in the eighth century. It was not a barbarism. Eastern Europe was still barbaric and savage; things had progressed but little beyond the state of affairs described by Gibbon in his account of the mission of Priscus to Attila (see ch. 27, § 6). But Western Europe was a shattered civilization without law, without administration, with roads destroyed and education disorganized, but still with great numbers of people with civilized ideas and habits and traditions.

It was a time of confusion, of brigandage, of crimes unpunished and universal insecurity. It is very interesting to trace how, out of the universal mêlée, the beginnings of a new order appeared. In a modern breakdown there would probably be the formation of local vigilance societies, which would combine and restore a police administration and a roughly democratic rule. But in the broken-down Western Empire of the sixth, seventh, and eighth centuries, men's ideas turned rather to leaders than to committees, and the centres about which affairs crystallized were here barbaric chiefs, here a vigorous bishop or some surviving claimant to a Roman official position, here a long-recognized landowner or man of ancient family, and here again some vigorous usurper of power. No solitary man was safe.

So men were forced to link themselves with others, preferably people stronger than themselves. The lonely man chose the most powerful and active person in his district and became *his* man. The freeman or the weak lordling of a petty territory linked himself to some more powerful lord. The protection of that lord (or the danger of his hostility) became more considerable with every such accession. So very rapidly they went on a process of political crystallization in the confused and lawless sea into which the Western Empire had liquefied. These natural associations and alliances of protector and subordinates grew very rapidly into a sort of system, *the feudal system,* traces of which are still to be found in the social structure of every European community west of Russia. It varied enormously in its manifestations.

This process speedily took on technical forms and laws of its own. In such a country as Gaul it was already well in progress in the days of insecurity *before* the barbarian tribes broke into the empire as conquerors. The Franks when they came into Gaul brought with them an institution, which we have already noted in the case of the Macedonians, and which was probably of very wide distribution among the Nordic people, the gathering about the chief or war king of a body of young men of good family, the companions or *comitatus*, his counts or captains. It was natural in the case of invading peoples that the relations of a weak lord to a strong lord should take on the relations of a count to his king, and that a conquering chief should divide seized and confiscated estates among his companions. From the side of the decaying empire there came to feudalism the idea of the grouping for mutual protection of men and estates; from the Teutonic side came the notions of knightly association, devotion, and personal service. The former was the economic side of the institution, the latter the chivalrous.

The analogy of the aggregation of feudal groupings with crystallization is a very close one. As the historian watches the whirling and eddying confusion of the fourth and fifth centuries in Western Europe, he begins to perceive the appearance of these pyramidal growths of heads and subordinates and sub-subordinates, which jostle against one another, branch, dissolve again, or coalesce. "We use the term 'feudal system' for convenience' sake, but with a degree of impropriety if it conveys the meaning 'systematic.' Feudalism in its most flourishing age was anything but systematic. It was confusion roughly organized. Great diversity prevailed everywhere, and we should not be surprised to find some different fact or custom in every lordship. Anglo-Norman feudalism attained in the eleventh and twelfth centuries a logical completeness and a uniformity of practice which, in the feudal age proper, can hardly be found elsewhere through so large a territory. . . .

"The foundation of the feudal relationship proper was the *fief*, which was usually land, but might be any desirable thing, as an office, a revenue in money or kind, the right to collect a toll, or operate a mill. In return for the fief, the man became the *vassal* of his lord; he knelt before him, and, with his hands between his lord's hands, promised him fealty and service. . . . The faithful performance of all the duties he had assumed in homage constituted the vassal's right and title to his fief. So long as they were fulfilled, he, and his heir after him, held the fief as his property, practically and in relation to all under tenants as if he were the owner. In the ceremony of homage and investiture, which is the creative contract of feudalism, the obligations assumed by the two parties were, as a rule, not specified in exact terms. They were determined by local custom. . . . In many points of detail the vassal's services differed widely in different parts of the feudal world. We may say, however, that they fall into two classes, general and specific. The general included all that might come under the idea of loyalty, seeking the lord's interests, keeping his secrets,

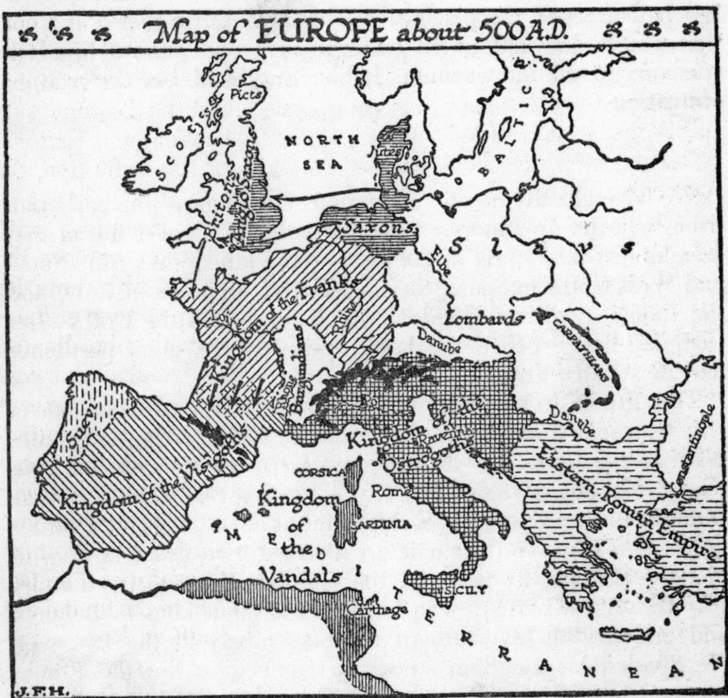

betraying the plans of his enemies, protecting his family, etc. The specific services are capable of more definite statement, and they usually received exact definition in custom and sometimes in written documents. The most characteristic of these was the military service, which included appearance in the field on summons with a certain force, often armed in a specified way, and remaining a specified length of time. It often included, also, the duty of guarding the lord's castle, and of holding one's own castle subject to the plans of the lord for the defence of his fief. . . . Theoretically regarded, feudalism covered Europe with a network of these fiefs, rising in graded ranks one above the other from the smallest, the knight's fee, at the bottom, to the king at the top, who was the supreme landowner, or who held the kingdom from God. . . ."[1]

But this was the theory that was superimposed upon the established facts. The reality of feudalism was its voluntary cooperation.

"The feudal state was one in which, it has been said, private law had usurped the place of public law." But rather is it truer that public law had failed and vanished and private law had come in to fill the vacuum. Public duty had become private obligation.

§ 3

We have already mentioned various kingdoms of the barbarian tribes who set up a more or less flimsy dominion over this or that area amidst the debris of the empire, the kingdoms of the Suevi and West Goths in Spain, the East-Gothic kingdom in Italy, and the Italian Lombard kingdom which succeeded the Goths after Justinian had expelled the latter and after the great pestilence had devastated Italy.

The Frankish kingdom was another such barbarian power which arose first in what is now Belgium, and which spread southward to the Loire, but it developed far more strength and solidarity than any of the others. It was the first real state to emerge from the universal wreckage. It became at last a wide and vigorous political reality, and from it are derived two great powers of modern Europe, France and the German Empire. Its founder was Clovis (481–511), who began as a small king in Belgium and ended with his southern frontiers nearly at the Pyrenees. He divided his kingdom among his four sons, but the Franks retained a tradition of unity in spite of this division, and for a time fraternal wars for a single control united rather than divided them. A more serious split arose, however, through the Latinization of the Western Franks, who occupied Romanized Gaul and who learnt to speak the corrupt Latin of the subject population, while the Franks of the Rhineland retained their Low German speech. At a low level of civilization, differences in language cause very powerful political strains. For a hundred and fifty years the Frankish world was split in two, Neustria, the nucleus of France, speaking a Latinish speech, which became at

---

[1] *Encyclopædia Britannica* Twelfth Edition, article "Feudalism," by Professor G. B. Adams.

last the French language we know, and Austrasia, the Rhineland, which remained German. The Franks differed from the Swabians and South Germans, and came much nearer the Anglo-Saxons in that they spoke a "Low German" and not a "High German" dialect. Their language resembled Plattdeutsch and Anglo-Saxon,

and was the direct parent of Dutch and Flemish. In fact, the Franks where they were not Latinized became Flemings and "Dutchmen" of South Holland (North Holland is still Friesisch—*i.e.*, Anglo-Saxon). The "French" which the Latinized Franks and Burgundians spoke in the seventh to the tenth centuries was remarkably like the Rumansch language of Switzerland, judging from the vestiges that remain in old documents.

We will not tell here of the decay of the dynasty, the Merovingian dynasty, founded by Clovis; nor how in Austrasia a certain court official, the Mayor of the Palace, gradually became the king *de facto* and used the real king as a puppet. The position of Mayor of the Palace also became hereditary in the seventh century, and in 687 a certain Pepin of Heristhal, the Austrasian Mayor of the Palace, had conquered Neustria and reunited all the Franks. He was followed in 721 by his son, Charles Martel, who also bore no higher title than Mayor of the Palace. (His poor little Merovingian kings do not matter in the slightest degree to us here.) It was this Charles Martel who stopped the Moslems. They had pushed as far as Tours when he met them, and in a great battle between that place and Poitiers (732) utterly defeated them and broke their spirit. Thereafter the Pyrenees remained their utmost boundary; they came no further into Western Europe.

Charles Martel divided his power between two sons, but one resigned and went into a monastery, leaving his brother Pepin sole ruler. This Pepin it was who finally extinguished the descendants of Clovis. He sent to the Pope to ask who was the true king of the Franks, the man who held the power or the man who wore the crown; and the Pope, who was in need of a supporter, decided in favour of the Mayor of the Palace. So Pepin was chosen king at a gathering of the Frankish nobles in the Merovingian capital, Soissons, and anointed and crowned. That was in 751. The Franco-Germany he united was consolidated by his son Charlemagne. It held together until the death of his grandson Louis (840), and then France and Germany broke away again —to the great injury of mankind. It was not a difference of race or temperament, it was a difference of language and tradition that split these Frankish peoples asunder.

That old separation of Neustria and Austrasia still works out in bitter consequences. In 1916 the ancient conflict of Neustria and Austrasia had broken out into war once more. In the August of that year the present writer visited Soissons, and crossed the temporary wooden bridge that had been built by the English after the battle of the Aisne from the main part of the town to the suburb of Saint Médard. Canvas screens protected passengers upon the bridge from the observation of the German sharpshooters who were sniping from their trenches down the curve of the river. He went with his guides across a field and along by the wall of an orchard in which a German shell exploded as he passed. So he reached the battered buildings that stand upon the site of the ancient Abbey of St. Médard, in which the last Merovingian was deposed and Pepin the Short was crowned in his stead. Beneath these ancient buildings there were great crypts, very useful as dug-outs—for the German advanced lines were not more than a couple of hundred yards away. The sturdy French soldier lads were cooking and resting in these shelters, and lying down to sleep among the stone coffins that had held the bones of their Merovingian kings.

§ 4

The populations over which Charles Martel and King Pepin ruled were at very different levels of civilization in different districts. To the west and south the bulk of the people consisted of Latinized and Christian Kelts; in the central regions these rulers had to deal with such more or less Christianized Germans as the Franks and Burgundians and Alemanni; to the north-east were still pagan Frisians and Saxons; to the east were the Bavarians, recently Christianized through the activities of St. Boniface, and to the east of them again pagan Slavs and Avars. The "paganism" of the Germans and Slavs was very similar to the primitive religion of the Greeks; it was a manly religion in which temple, priest, and sacrifices played a small part, and its gods were like men, a kind of 'school prefects" of more powerful beings who interfered impulsively and irregularly in human affairs. The Germans had a Jupiter in Odin, a Mars in Thor, a Venus in Freya, and so on. Throughout the seventh and eighth centuries a steady process of conversion to Christianity went on amidst these German and Slavonic tribes.

It will be interesting to English-speaking readers to note that the most zealous and successful missionaries among the Saxons and Frisians came from England. Christianity was twice planted in the British Isles. It was already there while Britain was a part of the Roman Empire; a martyr, St. Alban, gave his name to the town of St. Albans, and nearly every visitor to Canterbury has also visited little old St. Martin's Church which was used during the Roman times. From Britain, as we have already said, Christianity spread beyond the imperial boundaries into Ireland—the chief missionary was St. Patrick—and there was a vigorous monastic movement with which are connected the names of St. Columba and the religious settlements of Iona. Then in the fifth and sixth centuries came the fierce and pagan English, and they cut off the early Church of Ireland from the main body of Christianity. In the seventh century Christian missionaries were converting the English, both in the north from Ireland and in the south from Rome. The Rome mission was sent by Pope Gregory the Great just at the close of the sixth century. The story goes that he saw English boys for sale in the Roman slave market, though it is a little difficult to understand how they got there. They were very fair and good-looking. In answer to his inquiries, he was told that they were Angles. "Not Angles, but Angels," said he, "had they but the gospel."

The mission worked through the seventh century. Before that century was over, most of the English were Christians; though Mercia, the central English kingdom, held out stoutly against the priests and for the ancient faith and ways. And there was a swift progress in learning upon the part of these new converts. The monasteries of the kingdom of Northumbria in the north of England became a centre of light and learning. Theodore of Tarsus was one of the earliest archbishops of Canterbury (668–690). "While Greek was utterly unknown in the west of Europe, it was mastered by some of the pupils of Theodore. The monasteries contained many monks who were excellent scholars. Most famous of all was Bede, known as the Venerable Bede (673–735), a monk of Jarrow (on Tyne). He had for his pupils the six hundred monks of that monastery, besides the many strangers who came to hear him. He gradually mastered all the learning of his day, and left at his death forty-five volumes of his writings, the most important of which are 'The Ecclesiastical History of the English' and his translation of the Gospel of John into English. His writings were widely known and used throughout Europe. He reckoned all dates from the birth of Christ, and through his works the use of Christian chronology became common in Europe. Owing to the large number of monasteries and monks in Northumbria that part of England was for a time far in advance of the south in civilization."[1]

In the seventh and eighth centuries we find the English missionaries active upon the eastern frontiers of the Frankish kingdom. Chief among these was St. Boniface (680–755), who was born at Crediton, in Devonshire, who converted the Frisians, Thuringians, and Hessians, and who was martyred in Holland.

Both in England and on the Continent the ascendant rulers seized upon Christianity as a unifying force to cement their conquests. Christianity became a banner for aggressive chiefs—as it did in Uganda in Africa in the bloody days before that country was annexed to the British Empire.

After Pepin, who died in 768, came two sons, Charles and

---

[1] *A General History of Europe*, Thatcher and Schwill.

another, who divided his kingdom; but the brother of Charles died in 771, and Charles then became sole king (771–814) of the growing realm of the Franks. This Charles is known in history

as Charles the Great, or Charlemagne. As in the case of Alexander the Great and Julius Cæsar, posterity has enormously exaggerated his memory. He made his wars of aggression definitely religious wars. All the world of North-western Europe which is now Great Britain, France, Germany, Denmark, and

Norway and Sweden, was in the ninth century an arena of bitter conflict between the old faith and the new. Whole nations were converted to Christianity by the sword, just as Islam in Arabia, Central Asia, and Africa had converted whole nations a century or so before.

With fire and sword Charlemagne preached the Gospel of the Cross to the Saxons, Bohemians, and as far as the Danube into what is now Hungary; he carried the same teaching down the Adriatic coast, through what is now Dalmatia, and drove the Moslems back from the Pyrenees as far as Barcelona.

Moreover, he it was who sheltered Egbert, an exile from Wessex, in England, and assisted him presently to establish himself as king in Wessex (802). Egbert subdued the Britons in Cornwall, as Charlemagne conquered the Britons of Brittany, and, by a series of wars, which he continued after the death of his Frankish patron, made himself at last the first King of all England (828).

But the attacks of Charlemagne upon the last strongholds of paganism provoked a vigorous reaction on the part of the unconverted. The Christianized English had retained very little of the seamanship that had brought them from the mainland, and the Franks had not yet become seamen. As the Christian propaganda of Charlemagne swept towards the shores of the North and Baltic Seas, the pagans were driven to the sea. They retaliated for the Christian persecutions with plundering raids and expeditions against the northern coasts of France and against Christian England.

These pagan Saxons and English of the mainland and their kindred from Denmark and Norway are the Danes and Northmen of our national histories. They were also called Vikings,[1] which means "inletmen," because they came from the deep inlets of the Scandinavian coast. They came in long black galleys, making little use of sails. Most of our information about these wars and invasions of the pagan Vikings is derived from Christian sources, and so we have abundant information of the massacres and atrocities of their raids and very little about the cruelties inflicted upon their pagan brethren, the Saxons, at the hands of Charlemagne. Their animus against the Cross and against monks and nuns was extreme. They delighted in the burning of monasteries and nunneries and the slaughter of their inmates.

---

[1] N. B.—Vik-ings, not Vi-kings: Vik = a fiord or inlet.

Throughout the period between the fifth and the ninth centuries these Vikings or Northmen were learning seamanship, becoming bolder, and ranging further. They braved the northern seas until the icy shores of Greenland were a familiar haunt, and

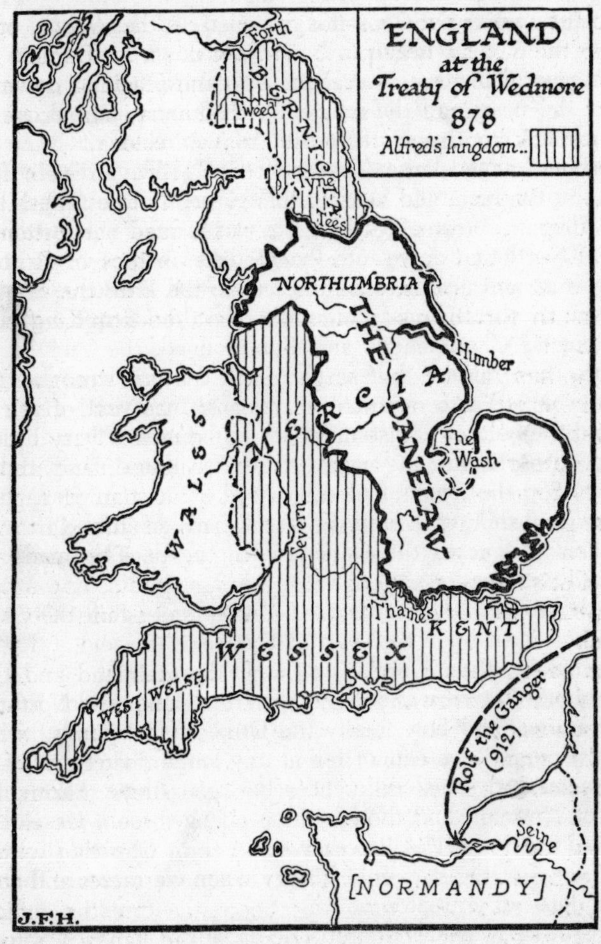

by the ninth century they had settlements (of which Europe in general knew nothing) in America. The Northmen had no permanent settlement in America. Somewhere about 1,000 there was an attempt to settle in some part of America called "Vinland," but the land was held only for two years. A skin canoe appeared one day full of painted Indians, who struck the Northmen as very ugly customers. There seems to have been a silent, mutual inspection, but no trade nor conflict. The new world stared at the old. Later there was trouble, and the Northmen, outnumbered and far from home, packed up and re-embarked. No other Northmen settlement upon American soil is recorded. In the twelfth century many of their sagas began to be written down in Iceland. They saw the world in terms of valiant adventure. They assailed the walrus, the bear, and the whale. In their imaginations, a great and rich city to the south, a sort of confusion of Rome and Byzantium, loomed large. They called it "Miklagard" (the great city—compare Icelandic Miklabaer "the great farm") or Micklegarth. The magnetism of Micklegarth was to draw the descendants of these Northmen down into the Mediterranean by two routes, by the west and also across Russia from the Baltic, as we shall tell later. By the Russian route went also the kindred Swedes.

So long as Charlemagne and Egbert lived, the Vikings were no more than raiders; but as the ninth century wore on, these raids developed into organized invasions. In several districts of England the hold of Christianity was by no means firm as yet. In Mercia, in particular, the pagan Northmen found sympathy and help. By 886 the Danes had conquered a fair part of England, and the English king, Alfred the Great, had recognized their rule over their conquests, the Dane-law, in the pact he made with Guthrum their leader.

A little later, in 911, another expedition under Rolf the Ganger established itself upon the coast of France in the region that was known henceforth as Normandy (=Northman-dy).

But of how there was presently a fresh conquest of England by the Danes, and how finally the Duke of Normandy became King of England, we cannot tell at any length. There were very small racial and social differences between Angle, Saxon, Jute, Dane, or Norman; and though these changes loom large in the imaginations of the English, they are seen to be very slight rufflings indeed of the stream of history when we measure them by the standards of a greater world.

The issue between Christianity and paganism vanished presently from the struggle. By the Treaty of Wedmore the Danes agreed to be baptized if they were assured of their conquests; and the descendants of Rolf in Normandy were not merely Christianized, but they learnt to speak French from the more civilized people about them, forgetting their own Norse tongue. Of much greater significance in the history of mankind are the relations of Charlemagne with his neighbours to the south and east, and to the imperial tradition.

§ 5

Through Charlemagne the tradition of the Roman Cæsar was revived in Europe. The Roman Empire was dead and decaying; the Byzantine Empire was far gone in decline; but the education and mentality of Europe had sunken to a level at which new creative political ideas were probably impossible. In all Europe there survived not a tithe of the speculative vigour that we find in the Athenian literature of the fifth century B.C. There was no power to postulate a new occasion or to conceive and organize a novel political method.

Official Christianity had long overlaid and accustomed itself to ignore those strange teachings of Jesus of Nazareth from which it had arisen. The Roman Church, clinging tenaciously to its possession of the title of *pontifex maximus*, had long since abandoned its appointed task of achieving the Kingdom of Heaven. It was preoccupied with the revival of Roman ascendancy on earth, which it conceived of as its inheritance. It had become a political body, using the faith and needs of simple men to forward its schemes. It clung to the tradition of the Roman Empire and to the idea that it was the natural method of European unity. Europe, in a series of attempts to restore it, drifted towards a dreary imitation and revival of the misconceived failures of the past.

For eleven centuries, from Charlemagne onwards, "Emperors" and "Cæsars" of this line and that come and go in the history of Europe like fancies in a disordered mind. We shall have to tell of a great process of mental growth in Europe, of enlarged horizons and accumulating power, but it was a process that went on independently of, and in spite of, the political forms of the time, until at last it shattered those forms altogether. Europe, during those eleven centuries of the imitation Cæsars which began with Charlemagne, and which closed only in the monstrous bloodshed of 1914-1918, has been like a busy factory owned by a somnambulist, who is sometimes quite unimportant and sometimes disastrously in the way. Or, rather than a somnambulist, let us say by a corpse that magically simulates a kind of life. The Roman Empire staggers, sprawls, is thrust off the stage, and reappears, and—if we may carry the image one step further—it is the Church of Rome which plays the part of the magician and keeps this corpse alive.

And throughout the whole period there is always a struggle going on for the control of the corpse between the spiritual and various temporal powers. We have already noted the spirit of St. Augustine's *City of God.* It was a book which we know Charlemagne read, or had read to him—for his literary accomplishments are rather questionable. He conceived of this Christian Empire as being ruled and maintained in its orthodoxy by some such great Cæsar as himself. He was to rule even the Pope.

But at Rome the view taken of the revived empire differed a little from that. There the view taken was that the Christian Cæsar must be anointed and guided by the Pope—who would even have the power to excommunicate and depose him. Even in the time of Charlemagne this divergence of view was apparent. In the following centuries it became acute.

The idea of the revived Empire dawned only very gradually upon the mind of Charlemagne. At first he was simply the ruler of his father's kingdom of the Franks, and his powers were fully occupied in struggles with the Saxons and Bavarians, and with the Slavs to the east of them, with the Moslem in Spain, and with various insurrections in his own dominions. And as the result of a quarrel with the King of Lombardy, his father-in-law, he conquered Lombardy and North Italy. We have noted the establishment of the Lombards in North Italy about 570 after the great pestilence, and after the overthrow of the East Gothic kings by Justinian. These Lombards had always been a danger and a fear to the Popes, and there had been an alliance between Pope and Frankish King against them in the time of Pepin. Now Charlemagne completely subjugated Lombardy (774), sent his father-in-law to a monastery, and carried his conquests beyond the present north-eastern boundaries of Italy into Dalmatia in 776. In 781 he caused one of his sons, Pepin, who did not outlive him, to be crowned King of Italy in Rome.

There was a new Pope, Leo III, in 795, who seems from the first to have resolved to make Charlemagne emperor. Hitherto the Court at Byzantium had possessed a certain indefinite authority over the Pope. Strong emperors like Justinian had bullied the Popes and obliged them to come to Constantinople; weak emperors had annoyed them ineffectively. The idea of a breach, both secular and religious, with Constantinople had long been entertained at the Lateran,[1] and in the Frankish power there seemed

[1] The Lateran was the earlier palace of the Popes in Rome. Later they occupied the Vatican.

to be just the support that was necessary if Constantinople was to be defied.

So at his accession Leo III sent the keys of the tomb of St. Peter and a banner to Charlemagne as the symbols of his sovereignty in Rome as King of Italy. Very soon the Pope had to appeal to the protection he had chosen. He was unpopular in Rome; he was attacked and ill-treated in the streets during a procession, and obliged to fly to Germany (799). Eginhard says

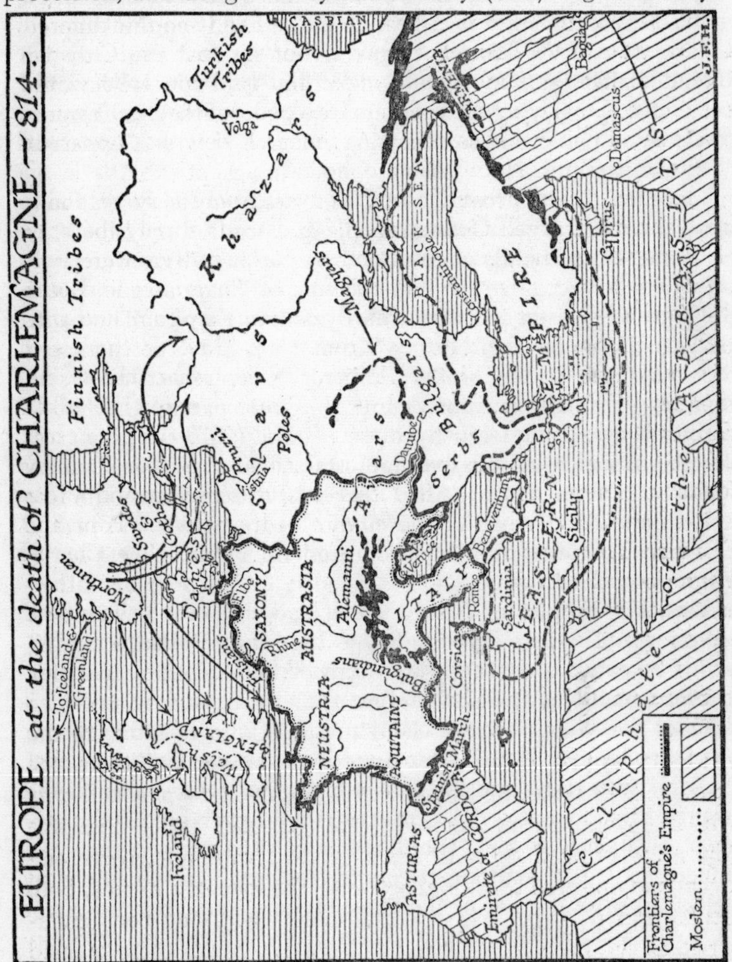

his eyes were gouged out and his tongue cut off; he seems, however, to have had both eyes and tongue again a year later. Charlemagne brought him back and reinstated him (800).

Then occurred a very important scene. On Christmas Day in the year 800, as Charles was rising from prayer in the Church of St. Peter, the Pope, who had everything in readiness, clapped a crown upon his head and hailed him Cæsar and Augustus. There was great popular applause. But Eginhard, the friend and biographer of Charlemagne, says that the new emperor was by no means pleased by this coup of Pope Leo's. If he had known this was to happen, he said, "he would not have entered the church, great festival though it was." No doubt he had been thinking and talking of making himself emperor, but he had evidently not intended that the Pope should make him emperor. He had had some idea of marrying the Empress Irene, who at that time reigned in Constantinople, and so becoming monarch of both Eastern and Western Empires. He was now obliged to accept the title in the manner that Leo III had adopted, as a gift from the Pope, and in a way that estranged Constantinople and secured the separation of Rome from the Byzantine Church. At first Byzantium was unwilling to recognize the imperial title of Charlemagne. But in 811 a great disaster fell upon the Byzantine Empire. The pagan Bulgarians, under their Prince Krum (802–815), defeated and destroyed the armies of the Emperor Nicephorus, whose skull became a drinking-cup for Krum. The great part of the Balkan peninsula was conquered by these people. (The Bulgarian and the English nations thus became established as political unities almost simultaneously.) After this misfortune Byzantium did not dispute this revival of the empire in the West, and in 812 Charlemagne was formally recognized by Byzantine envoys as Emperor and Augustus.

Thus the Empire of Rome, which had died at the hands of Odoacer in 476, rose again in 800 as the "Holy Roman Empire." While its physical strength lay north of the Alps, the centre of its idea was Rome. It was, therefore, from the beginning a divided thing of uncertain power, a claim and an argument rather than a necessary reality. The German sword was always clattering over the Alps into Italy, and missions and legates toiling over in the reverse direction. But the Germans could never hold Italy permanently, because they could not stand the malaria that the ruined, neglected, undrained country fostered. And in Rome, as well as in several other of the cities of Italy, there smouldered a more ancient tradition, the tradition of the aristocratic republic, hostile to both Emperor and Pope.